Archimedes in the Middle Ages

VOLUME THREE

Memoirs of the
AMERICAN PHILOSOPHICAL SOCIETY
held at Philadelphia
for Promoting Useful Knowledge
Volume 125   Part A

ARCHIMEDES

in the Middle Ages

VOLUME THREE

THE FATE OF THE MEDIEVAL ARCHIMEDES
1300 to 1565

PART I: The Moerbeke Translations of
Archimedes at Paris in the
Fourteenth Century

PART II: The Arabo-Latin and Handbook
Traditions of Archimedes in the
Fourteenth and Early Fifteenth
Centuries

MARSHALL CLAGETT

THE AMERICAN PHILOSOPHICAL SOCIETY
Independence Square
Philadelphia
1978

Library of Congress Catalog Card Number 76-9435
International Standard Book Number 0-87169-125-6
US ISSN 0065-9738

PREFACE

With this volume, I conclude my direct investigation of Archimedean traditions in the Middle Ages. As will be evident to the reader, special effort has also been made to disentangle the medieval elements still working in the Renaissance. Indeed the major part of this volume is so directed. My objective here, as always, has been to present as fully as possible the textual material on which the investigation is based. Many texts or parts of texts have been edited for the first time from manuscripts and some have been re-edited from earlier editions. I have appended English translations to each of these texts except for the case of the extracts from Giorgio Valla's *De expetendis et fugiendis rebus opus* (added to Part III, Chapter 2, Section V) since the material included there is presented more fully, though in somewhat different form, in the *Praeparatio ad Archimedis opera* of Francesco Maurolico that is given as Text A in Part III, Chapter 5 and accompanied by a complete English translation. All of the translations are my own except for that given as Text B of Part III, Chapter 4, Section III, which is an English translation attributed to Thomas Salusbury of Federigo Commandino's *De iis quae vehuntur in aqua* (and of Tartaglia's Italian translation of Book I of Archimedes' *De insidentibus aquae*, the latter produced from the Latin translation of William of Moerbeke, and presented by me in Section II of the same chapter). In addition to these more or less complete texts, I have also presented in the footnotes countless extracts drawn from manuscript and printed sources. In the discursive chapters and sections preceding the texts, or in the chapters without texts, I have attempted to analyse the understanding of Archimedean texts displayed by Latin authors. The hurried reader will no doubt go immediately to the last chapter (Part III, Chapter 7) for a retrospective summary of the medieval Archimedean material. But I hope that such a reader will be led back to the texts themselves and their more detailed treatment in the earlier chapters. One infelicity of the machine composition used for this volume ought to be observed by the reader. The dot of multiplication, which is positioned properly for magnitudes represented by capital letters, is often too high for minuscules, thus leaving a rather strange appearance to some of the formulas. However, this does not, I believe, produce any mathematical ambiguity.

As in Volume Two, I have gathered the diagrams together in a separately bound fascicle that also includes Appendixes, a Bibliography of works cited in both Volumes Two and Three, and Indexes. I do not cite the textual page numbers in the subheads on the pages of diagrams (as I did in Volume Two) since the diagrams often do double and even triple duty in the discussions, the Latin texts, and the English translations, and this would accordingly produce a rather confusing set of numbers in each subhead. But the diagrams are all numbered in an easily identifiable order, with the Roman numeral standing for the Part and the succeeding Arabic numerals for the Chapter, the Section and the ordinal position of the diagram within the given section. For the preparation of the Indexes I owe special thanks to my former assistant, Dr. Charles Zuckerman. I must also thank once more my secretary, Mrs. Ann Tobias, for preparing and mounting the finished diagrams, as well as for typing and retyping this long and complex volume. I have already acknowledged the manifold help I have received from others in the preface to Volume Two. To these, I should add the names of two recent assistants, Glenn Sterr and Peter Marshall, who helped in reading the proofs of Volume Three. I should also acknowledge the persistent help and friendship of my colleague Herman Goldstine, whose wide knowledge of mathematics and its history was always at my beck and call. Finally, I must again thank the Director and staff of the Institute for Advanced Study—my academic home—and the American Philosophical Society (and particularly, its editorial staff) for their help—financial, and of other kinds—in publishing this volume.

M.C.

Contents

Part IV: Appendixes, Bibliography, Diagrams, and Indexes

Appendixes

PART I

The Moerbeke Translations of Archimedes at Paris in the Fourteenth Century

CHAPTER 1

The *Quadripartitum numerorum*
of Johannes de Muris

In Volume One of this work, I mentioned briefly the flurry of activity
concerned with William of Moerbeke's translations of Archimedes' works
at Paris in the fourteenth century.[1] The schoolman who seems to have
played the central role in the early consideration of the "Greek" Archimedes was Johannes de Muris, an eminent mathematician and astronomer
whose tenure at the University of Paris (in the College of Sorbonne)
can be traced from at least 1317 to some time after 1345.[2] We know
from the conclusion of one work that he composed a series of tracts
in 1321, one of which was a treatise on the quadrature of the circle.[3]
Since that treatise does not appear to be extant, we cannot be sure whether
it was based on one of the earlier quadrature tracts that developed out
of the version of the *De mensura circuli* translated by Gerard of Cremona
from the Arabic (and which I published in Volume One), or whether it
was based on a reading of the Moerbeke translation of that tract from
the Greek. However, I shall have more to say about Johannes' concern
with the quadrature problem later.

The first sure evidence of Johannes' knowledge of the Moerbeke translations occurs in his *Quadripartitum numerorum*, completed in 1343.[4] The
pertinent section appears in Book IV, Tract 1, *De moventibus et motis*,
Chapter 31. This chapter I have edited and translated below.

Several points are worthy of special note in connection with this section of the *Quadripartitum numerorum*. The first is that Johannes apparently was acquainted with *On Spiral Lines* of Archimedes in the

[1] Vol. 1, pp. 11–12.

[2] See L. Thorndike, *A History of Magic and Experimental Science*, Vol. 3 (New York,
1934), pp. 294–324; P. Duhem, *Le Système du monde*, Vol. 4 (2nd printing, Paris, 1954),
pp. 34–38, 51–60. The best account of the life and works of Johannes de Muris is
the article on him by E. Poulle in the *Dictionary of Scientific Biography*, Vol. 7
(New York, 1973), pp. 128–33. Cf. also L. Gushee, "New Sources for the Biography of
John de Muris," *Journal of the American Musicological Society*, Vol. 22 (1969), pp. 3–26.

[3] Thorndike, *A History of Magic*, Vol. 3, pp. 298, 299 n. 24.

[4] Paris, BN lat. 7190, 100v. Cf. Duhem, *Le Système*, Vol. 4, p. 34. I have published
the second tract of Book IV of the *Quadripartitum numerorum* in my *The Science of
Mechanics in the Middle Ages* (Madison, Wisc., 1959), pp. 126–35.

Moerbeke translation, either directly or in the form of an abridgment entitled *Circuli quadratura*, a hybrid tract composed in 1340 from thirteen
of the first eighteen propositions of *On Spiral Lines* and the first proposition of *On the Measurement of the Circle* (both in the Moerbeke translation). The fact that in this chapter Johannes puts the spiral in the
context of the quadrature problem seems to indicate that he was acquainted with the content of the hybrid tract, and indeed, as I shall
show in Chapter 5, below, it was probably Johannes who composed the
hybrid tract (and certainly it was he who later inserted it in Chapter 8
of his *De arte mensurandi*). If Johannes was the author, then it is clear that
in 1343 (and in fact in 1340) he had direct access to the Moerbeke translations, or at least to those of *On Spiral Lines* and *On the Measurement of the Circle*. Even if Johannes did not compose the hybrid tract
and its commentary, his direct access to the Moerbeke translations might
also be supposed from the fact that he associated the spiral with
Archimedes by name, while the hybrid tract in all of its manuscripts carries
no indication of Archimedes' ultimate authorship. Such direct familiarity
with the Moerbeke translation is further supported by the fact that when
he quotes from *On Spiral Lines* in Chapter 31 of the *Quadripartitum
numerorum*, Johannes preserves readings that are found in the full
Moerbeke translation rather than in the hybrid tract. For example, in line
7, he preserves *affigatur*, which is found in the Moerbeke text, rather
than the *assignatur*, present in all manuscripts of the hybrid tract. Furthermore, in lines 13–14, he repeats the definition of the origin of the spiral
as found in the Moerbeke translation rather than the modified definition in
the hybrid tract.[5] The source of his alternate Latin term for a spiral,
namely *volutio* (line 28), appears in the preface to *On Spiral Lines* but is
absent in the hybrid tract, which omits the preface to *On Spiral Lines*.
Of course, he might have drawn that alternate name from another medieval
source describing spiral lines, but I have been unable to find that
term used for a spiral in any place except the Moerbeke translation (see
the Commentary, lines 27–29). Finally, one can suppose that Johannes
was acquainted with more than the hybrid tract from the fact that he seems
to allude in lines 5–6 to the unfaithful character of those translations
when he says, "Oh, would that we had his books faithfully translated!"
although I admit that this sentence might be interpreted as an expression
of hope for a translation since he knows of none. However, such an interpretation seems unlikely when we consider the fact that in his edition of

---

[5] See Commentary, lines 7–11. There are, however, two instances when the quoted passages agree with the hybrid tract against the Moerbeke translation. In line 11, after
elicam (actually *elicem* in the Moerbeke translation), Johannes as well as the author of the
hybrid tract omits *i.e. revolutionem*, which is found in the Moerbeke translation. In the second
case, Moerbeke has *rectum* after *circulationis* in line 15. This is omitted both by Johannes
and the compositor of the hybrid tract. But this case is of no great significance, since Johannes
is making no effort in this quotation to quote the definition precisely, and indeed the appearance of *rectum* in this position is an error on Moerbeke's part (see below, Chapter 5
of Part I, Commentary, *Definitions*, lines 9, 10–12).

the *De arte mensurandi*, apparently written shortly after the *Quadripartitum numerorum*, he knew and cited the Moerbeke translations of *On the Sphere and the Cylinder* and *On Conoids and Spheroids* (see Chapter 6), and also the commentary of Eutocius on the first of those works (see Chapter 3). Hence, it seems probable that Johannes already knew the Moerbeke translations in their full form.[6]

It will be clear also, from the chapter here edited, that Johannes expected to take up elsewhere in a geometrical context the questions of the determination of the ratio of a straight line to a curve and the quadrature of the circle. It seems that he kept his promise in regard to these questions by inserting the above-mentioned hybrid tract on quadrature in the *De arte mensurandi* (see Chapter 5 below). At least, it seems abundantly clear that his reference to a future discussion of these questions in a geometrical context is indeed a reference to his intention to compose the *De arte mensurandi*. One can well suppose that he meant for these two works, the *Quadripartitum numerorum* and the *De arte mensurandi*, to constitute a full treatment of mathematics as known and used in his age.

In my text below, I have placed within quotation marks Johannes' citations from *On Spiral Lines*. As in the case of all of the texts of these three volumes, I have been free with capitalization and punctuation. The text is based primarily on the first of the three manuscripts noted below, and the marginal folio numbers are to that manuscript. The references to *O* in the variant readings are to *On Spiral Lines* in the Moerbeke translation as given in Vol. Two, 13rS–T.

Sigla

Pa = Paris, BN lat. 7190, 80′ r–v (this sheet is unnumbered but lies between folios 79 and 80; hence, my use of 80′), 14c.

Fb = Vienna, Nationalbibl. 4770, 316v–17v, 15c.

Fc = Vienna, Nationalbibl. 10954, 126v–27v, 16c.

---

[6] It is tempting to suppose that Johannes de Muris had visited Avignon earlier in his career. We know that he was summoned to Avignon by a papal letter of 1344, "to treat or correct certain difficulties in the calendar" (Thorndike, *A History of Magic*, Vol. 3, p. 268; cf. the report of Guy Beaujouan, *École Practique des Hautes Études. IVe Section, Sciences historiques et philologiques. Annuaire 1964/1965* [Paris, 1965], p. 259). This summons could have arisen from the fact that he was already known at Avignon. If he did visit Avignon earlier, he may well have seen the Moerbeke holograph, Vat. Ottob. lat. 1850, and perhaps had a copy made of it which he brought back to Paris where he could have studied it at leisure and where it would have been available to other scholars. I hasten to add that this is entirely speculative, since there is no direct evidence of an earlier visit or even that Vat. Ottob. lat. 1850 was at Avignon. Be that as it may, he obviously had read a copy of it somewhere, as the texts I am here editing plainly reveal. It could be that he had seen the fourteenth-century copy of *On Spiral Lines* in manuscript *R* (Vat. Reg. lat. 1253, 14r–33r). But, of course, that manuscript contained no other Archimedean texts and hence could not have provided the knowledge of the Moerbeke translations of other Archimedean works exhibited by Johannes de Muris later in the *De arte mensurandi*.

Johannis de Muris

Quadripartitum numerorum, Lib. IV, Tract. 1, Cap. 31

80′r /31ª de motu elyco qui valet ad quadraturam circuli [Fig. I.1.1].

Post motum qui fit secundum lineam rectam et secundum lineam circularem est et alius motus neuter qui fit per lineam elicam que nec est circularis neque portio circuli neque recta, quem motum, ut puto, primus
5 Archimenides geometrorum excellentissimus adinvenit. O utinam eius libros translatos fideliter haberemus!

De elica autem sermo brevis. "Si recta affigatur linea in plano manente altero termino ipsius eque velociter circumducta quotiens[cunque] restituitur iterum unde incepit moveri, simul autem cum linea circumducta
10 feratur aliquod signum eque velociter ipsum sibi ipsi per rectam incipiens a manente termino, signum elicam describet in plano." Exemplariter elica est tortuosa revolutio nullum centrum habens ad modum testudinis vermis cornuti quem limacem nominamus. Et vocatur "terminus recte manens ipsius circumducte principium elicis vel revolutionis," positio linee unde
15 incipit motus "principium circulationis," sicut patet in hac figura. *AB* linea, *B* terminus linee immobilis; giretur *AB* super *B*. Describit circulum *AEH*. In hac autem circulatione moveatur signum *B* per lineam *BA* equaliter et in tempore equali girationis. Describet ergo *B* revolu-
19 tionem tortuosam *BLMNOPQA* quam elicem appellamus. Si autem non
80′v / peragrasset *B* lineam *BA* totam sed mediam in tempore unius circulationis aucta fuisset elix et circulatio geminata. Est autem proportio totius periferie ad partes eius sicut et linearum (*!* linee?) ad partes earum (*!* eius), quam modo ostendere non tempus est. Sed indubitanter scio quod per

1 de . . . circuli *Pa om. FbFc*
5 Geometra *Fc*
8 quotienscunque *O* quotiens *PaFbFc*
9 unde *FbFcO* unum *Pa* / incepit *FbFcO* incipit *Pa*
10 velociter *PaO* velocitatis *FbFc*
11 manente *FbFc* movente *Pa* / Exemplariter *Pa* Exemplaris *FbFc*
13 limacon *Fb*
14 vel *PaO* idem *FbFc* / positio *PaO* punctus *FbFc*
16 gyret *Fc*
17 *post* B *add. Pa* repende *sed om. FbFc*
18 B *om. Fc*
19 —PQA *FbFc*—PA A *Pa*
20 BA *Pa* AB *FbFc*
21 elix *Pa* elica *FbFc*
23 quam modo *PaFb* quem modum *Fc* / tempus est *Pa. tr. FbFc*

elicas lineas proportio recti ad curvum demonstratur et circuli quadratura,
25 sicut per Dei gratiam alias explanabimus loco suo cuilibet theoreumata
geometrica concedenti.

Et opinor satis probabiliter quod per talem lineam elicam, nominatam
forte alio nomine laulabus, latine volutionem, possent apparentia salvari
de motibus planetarum tollendo ecentricos et epiciclos. Sed ad hec non
30 vacavit tempus cogitandi. Non enim ab initio operis nisi circa numeros
intendere volebamus. Ad tollendum ergo ignorantiam negationis sufficiat
hec audisse.

Johannes de Muris

On Numbers, in Four Parts, Book IV, Tract 1, Chapter 31

The 31st on spiral motion which is valuable for the quadrature of a circle.

Following motion which takes place along a straight line and that which
occurs along a circular line, there is a third which is neither. It takes
place along a spiral line, which line is neither circular nor an arc of a
circle nor straight. This motion, I think, Archimedes, the most excellent
of geometers, first discovered. Oh, would that we had his books faithfully translated!

Here is a brief statement on the spiral:[1] "If a straight line drawn in
a plane revolves at uniform speed about one extremity which remains
fixed and it returns to the position from which it started, and if, in
the same time as the line revolves, some point moves with uniform speed
along the straight line beginning from the extremity which remains fixed,
the point will describe a spiral in the plane." For example, the spiral is
a twisting revolution having no center, in the manner of the hornlike shell
of the worm which we call a snail. And "the fixed extremity of the
straight line which revolves is called the origin of the spiral or of the
revolution."[2] The position of the line from which the motion begins [is
called] "the origin of circulation" [i.e., "the initial line"], as is evident
in the figure [Fig. I .1.1]. Let there be line AB, with B its fixed extremity;
let AB be revolved about B. It describes circle AEH. Moreover, in this
revolution let point B be moved along line BA uniformly in a time
equal to that of the revolution. Therefore, B will describe the twisting

24 elicas lineas *Pa tr. FbFc*
28 laulabus *Pa om. FbFc* / volutionem *om. FbFc, corr. ex* volavionem *(?) in Pa*;
   cf. Moerbeke in De figuris elicis, Vol. 2, 11vP
29 Sed *Pa* si *FbFc* / ad hec *FbFc* adhuc *Pa*
29–30 non vacavit *Pa* vacabit *FbFc*
31 ergo *Pa* igitur *FbFc* / ignorantiam *Pa* ignorantionem *Fb* ignorationem *Fc*

[1] See Commentary, lines 7–11.
[2] *Ibid.*, lines 13–15.

revolution *BLMNOPQA* which we call a spiral.[3] But if *B* does not move through the whole line *BA* but only through half of it in the time of one revolution, the spiral will be increased and the revolution doubled. Further, the ratio of the whole circumference to its parts is that of the lines (line?) to their (its?) parts,[4] which proposition there is no time now to demonstrate. But without doubt I know that the ratio of a straight line to a curve, as well as the quadrature of a circle, is demonstrated by means of spiral lines, as, by the Grace of God, we shall explain elsewhere in its place to anyone conceding geometric theorems.[5]

And I believe it probable enough that by means of the spiral line— perhaps named by another name as the *laulab* (in Latin, the *volutio*)— the phenomena of the motions of the planets could be saved, leaving aside eccentrics and epicycles.[6] But there has been no time free for thinking about these things. For, from the beginning of [this] work, we have wished to take up nothing but numbers. Therefore, for removing ignorance in this matter, it has to suffice that these things have been heard.

Commentary

7–11 "Si . . . plano." This is a quotation from *On Spiral Lines* of Archimedes in the Moerbeke translation. As I noted in the Introduction to this text, the presence of *affigatur* seems to indicate that it was taken directly from Moerbeke's translation rather than indirectly through the hybrid tract (cf. the text of the Moerbeke translation in Vol. 2, 13rS–T and that of the hybrid tract, Chapter 5 of this part, *Descriptiones*, lines 2–6).

13–15 "Et . . . circulationis." These are approximate quotations from *On Spiral Lines*. As I said earlier, the passage is much closer to the Moerbeke translation than to the hybrid tract (for these passages, see the lines immediately following those cited in the previous comment). The Moerbeke text (Vol. 2, 13rT) has: "Vocetur igitur terminus quidem recte manens ipsius circumducte principium elicis vel revolutionis" while the hybrid tract reads: "Terminus quidem recte manens initium revolutionis vocetur." Thus the words *circumducte* and *principium elicis* in Johannes' quotation were almost certainly taken from the Moerbeke translation directly since they are absent in the hybrid tract.

15–19 "AB . . . appellamus." This example appears to be Johannes' own. At least there is no spiral in *On Spiral Lines* of Archimedes with the same lettering.

[3] *Ibid.*, lines 15–19.
[4] *Ibid.*, lines 21–23.
[5] See the Introduction to this text and that of the text in Chapter 5 for the implications of this statement.
[6] See Commentary, lines 27–29.

21–23 "Est . . . est." This seems to be a somewhat imprecise reference to Proposition 14 of *On Spiral Lines*, which also appeared in the hybrid tract as Proposition 10.

27–29 "Et . . . epiciclos." This reference is probably to the *De motibus celorum* of al-Biṭrūjī, as translated by Michael Scot, where the Arabic word *laulab* is introduced for a spiral in the course of an explanation of celestial motions that abandons eccentrics and epicycles (see the edition of F. Carmody, Berkeley, Los Angeles, 1952, pp. 98–99), or it may be to some summary of this system, such as that of Bacon (*ibid.*, p. 36) or of Albertus Magnus (*ibid.*, p. 37). Albertus gives *gyros* and *torculatus* as synonyms for *laulab*. (I have found no tract that gives *volutio* except the Moerbeke translation of *On Spiral Lines*.) Incidentally, the term *laulab* is not here the Archimedean spiral in a plane (as Johannes seems to imply by introducing this term in conjunction with the Archimedean definition) but rather is like a coiled spring, the markings on a barber pole or the threads of a screw (and indeed the Arabic term also means "screw"). In short, it is what the schoolmen of the fourteenth century called the "gyrative line" (see P. Duhem, *La Système du monde*, [Vol. 7, Paris, 1956], pp. 143–46). This latter term was used for a spiral staircase, i.e. *scala girativa* (Johannes de Fontana, *Bellicorum instrumentorum liber*, Munich, Staatsbibl. Icon. 242, 25v: "Scala girativa apud sapientes ingeniosos esse dicitur et a paucis fabricata. . . . Linea girati[v]a dicitur quia in girum fabricatur, et proprie intra tur[r]es, cuius decla[ra]tio tibi satis. Ostendi Padue tibi consimiles in ecclexia Sancti Antonii." The same work, 48r, once more relates a serpentine tower to a gyrative line: "Serpentina turris tot habet utilitates quot et linea girativa que ad colunam aplicatur ut in libello de aque ductibus intitulato ostenditur"). The so-called Michael Scot translation from the Arabic of Aristotle's *Physics* (*Aristotelis opera*, Vol. 4 [Venice, 1562], 234rC) has "motus gyrativus aut motus tortuosus" (cf. MS Paris, BN lat. 16141, 120r, text No. 44) to translate κεκλασμένης κίνησις ἢ ἡ τῆς ἕλικος (Bk. V, 228b, 24). The use of *spira* to translate the Arabic rendering of ἕλιξ is found in Michael Scot's translation of Aristotle's *De anima* (ed. of F. S. Crawford, *Averrois . . . Commentarium magnum in Aristotelis de anima libros* [Cambridge, Mass. 1953], p. 257 (see 420a, 13)), but I am not sure when the expression *linea spiralis* was first applied to a spiral line. It was made popular when adopted by Jacobus Cremonensis in his translation of *On Spiral Lines* in about 1450 (see below, Part III, Chap. 6, Sect. I).

CHAPTER 2

The *De arte mensurandi* attributed to Johannes de Muris

In Chapter 1 above, I discussed the use of *On Spiral Lines* of Archimedes in the *Quadripartitum numerorum* of Johannes de Muris. The next five chapters will be concerned with the further usage of the Moerbeke translations of Archimedes and Eutocius in the *De arte mensurandi* usually assigned to Johannes de Muris. In a preliminary treatment of this text many years ago,[1] I came to the conclusion that this long and sprawling work consisted of two principal parts: the first including the initial eight chapters as composed by Johannes de Muris and the second comprising the last four chapters as added by an unknown Continuator. After a more detailed consideration of the *De arte mensurandi* I can no longer hold to my former opinion, although we must still conclude, I believe, that there are two chief parts, each by a different author. But it now appears that the original author composed only the first four chapters and almost all of the first part of the fifth chapter. A Continuator then stepped in and completed much of the rest of the work. At least, it is quite certain that he finished the second and third parts of the fifth chapter as well as the final four chapters (Chapters 9–12) and it is highly probable that he also composed Chapters 6–8. Furthermore, it now appears that the original author was not Johannes de Muris but rather an unknown geometer of the late thirteenth or early fourteenth century, while the Continuator was none other than Johannes de Muris. This re-interpretation of the problem of the authorship of the *De arte mensurandi* must now be argued in detail before we can consider, in the succeeding sections, the various parts of the text which employ the Moerbeke translations.

Our first consideration must be of the evidence indicating the dual authorship of the *De arte mensurandi*. In the proemium of the work, the original author outlines its scope and objectives:[2]

---

[1] "The Use of the Moerbeke Translations of Archimedes in the Works of Johannes de Muris," *Isis*, Vol. 43 (1952), pp. 236–42.

[2] Paris, BN lat. 7380, 1r–v: "Quamvis plures de arte mensurandi inveniantur tractatus quia tamen quidam sunt prolixi, quidam nimis difficiles, nec eorum aliquis ad omnium mensuras se extendat, ideo ego, cupiens de mensuris omnium facere unum tractatum, presens

11

Many tracts on the art of measuring exist. But since certain [of them] are prolix and certain ones exceedingly difficult and none of them covers the measures of all things, therefore I, desiring to produce a tract on the measures of all things, have in a compendious way composed the present work by drawing from the many [other] tracts. And accordingly any one at all will be able with ease to measure the things to be measured if he considers only the method of proceeding and omits the demonstrations given in the same place, [for it is] in the demonstrations that difficulty lies. I have thought it worth while to include the demonstrations as well, lest anyone might say that we have spoken without reason and in order that more credence be given to our words by those who see that their proof is at hand. I have also added in this tract certain things, the knowledge of which is expeditious for the art of measuring and without which it is not easy to measure. The division of the present tract into chapters follows:

In the first chapter [sexagesimal] fractions are treated. By their multiplication, division, and the extraction of [their] roots, lines of the sort necessary for measurement are found. We give a demonstrative treatment of this kind of procedure that is not [found] demonstrated elsewhere.

In the second [chapter] the finding of chords of any arcs of a circle is treated. The doctrine of this procedure is quite conducive to the art of measuring and to the composition of astronomical tables.

In the third chapter the knowledge of the lines of a triangle is taught. The triangle is the primary rectilinear figure and all other [rectilinear] figures are resolvable into it by a knowledge of its angles, and contrariwise.

In the fourth [chapter] the art of linear measurement is treated, that is, measurement according to length, breadth and depth.

opus ex pluribus tractatibus collectum composui satis breve. Et ex quo de facili poterit unusquisque mensurare mensuranda si solum modum operandi consideraverit omissis demonstrationibus ibidem contentis in quibus difficultas consistit, quas etiam demostrationes (!) apponere dignum duxi (*corr. ex* duci) ne aliquis diceret nos aliqua sine ratione dixisse, et ut fides dictis nostris adhiberetur pocior considerantibus eorum probationem prom⟨p⟩tam esse. Adiciendo (? or Adiciente?) etiam in hoc tractatu quedam, quorum cognitio expedit ad artem mensurandi et sine quibus non est facile mensurare. Ac presentem tractatum per capitula distinguens: In primo capitulo tractatur de minuciebus per quarum multiplicationem, divisionem et radicum extractionem inveniuntur linee ex quibus oportet mensurare cuiusmodi tractatum demostravimus alias non demostratum. In secundo tractatur de inventione cordarum quorumlibet arcuum circuli: cuiusmodi doctrina multum confert ad artem mensurandi et ad compositionem tabularum astronomie. In tertio capitulo docetur cognitio linearum trianguli, qui est figura prima rectilinea et in quam omnes alie resolvuntur ex cognitione angulorum eiusdem et econverso. In quarto traditur ars mensurandi secundum lineam, videlicet altitudinem (! latitudinem?), longitudinem et profunditatem. In quinto tractatur de mensuris superficierum rectilinearum que crescere possunt in infinitum per additionem unius lateris. In sexto traditur quedam distinctio corporum et de numero corporum rectilineorum omnino regularium, quot sunt et quare plura esse non possunt. In septimo de mensura regularium corporum huiusmodi. In octavo traditur de comparatione diametri ad circumferentiam circuli et qualiter ex circumferentia nota elicitur diameter et econverso, et de inventione centri circuli transeuntis per tria puncta data cuius ars /lv/ ad compositionem astrolabii invenitur esse necessaria. In nono de mensura superficiei circularis et ostensione huius quod sit omnium figurarum capacissima. In decimo de mensura sperici corporis et eius superficiei. In undecimo et ultimo capitulo traditur ars mensurandi corpora omnino irregularia.''

In the fifth [chapter] the measurement of rectilinear surfaces is treated. These are surfaces which can be infinitely increased [as to number of sides] by adding one side [successively].

In the sixth [chapter] a certain distinction with respect to bodies is treated. In addition, we treat of a number of rectilinear bodies that are completely regular—[discussing] how many they are and why there cannot be more.

In the seventh [chapter] we treat of the measure of regular bodies of this sort.

In the eighth [chapter] the comparison of the diameter to the circumference of a circle is treated, as well as how to find the center of a circle which passes through three given points. The art of this last [technique] is found to be necessary for the construction of an astrolabe.

In the ninth [chapter] circular surface [is treated], as well as the demonstration that it [the circle] is the most capacious of all [isoperimetric] figures.

In the tenth [chapter] we treat of the measure of a spherical body and its surface.

In the eleventh and final chapter, the art of measuring bodies that are completely irregular is treated.

It is clear from this proemium that the original author intended not only to present the metric formulas found in so many of the practical handbooks of mensuration but also the demonstrations or proofs of the geometric validity of these formulas. It is also apparent that he intended to complete his work in eleven chapters. The first four chapters and the first part of the fifth are clearly the work of the original author as he moves to carry out his stated objectives. But then abruptly toward the end of the first part a different author appears. This is heralded in the basic manuscript BN lat. 7380—the direct or indirect source of all the extant copies—by a change of scribal hand and by a change from parchment to paper. On the bottom of folio 21v (on parchment) we read an incomplete sentence:[3] "But if it [i.e. a surface] is inaccessible, i.e. such a one that cannot be easily measured, like a wood or a lake [. . . .]" Then on the paper folio which follows (22r) we read:

And in this lake the quaternion is submerged, because we have found nothing more of this work. But I propose (with God's help) to complete what is absent, in as brief a fashion as I can, by following the series of titles announced beforehand in the prologue, [that is, those] which the author has named in the beginning. Therefore, I continue the exposition at the point where it says "like a wood or a lake." If, therefore, that inaccessible surface. . . .

---

[3] BN lat. 7380, 21v: "Si vero fuerit inaccessibilis, hoc est, talis quod non possit de facili metiri, ut nemus vel stannum [=stagnum]." Then on 22r: "Et in hoc stanno submersus est quaternus, quia nil plus apud nos de hoc opere repertum est. Sed propono [*add. mg.* cum opere divino] quod deest perficere, modo quo potero breviori, iuxta seriem predictorum in prologo titulorum, quos actor iste in principio nominavit. Continuo ergo sic dicta dicendis: 'ut nemus aut stannum.' Si ergo illa superficies inaccessibilis. . . ." Mr. Stephen Victor was the first to point out these passages and to realize their crucial nature for the distinction of the two authors involved in the composition of the *De arte mensurandi*. See his "Johannes de Muris' Autograph of the *De arte Mensurandi*," *Isis*, Vol. 61 (1970), pp. 389–95 (and see particularly, notes 10 and 11).

Hence it is abundantly clear that the Continuator, who proposes to complete the work according to the list of chapters given in the beginning of the work, is now on the scene. One ought reasonably to conclude, in view of the change of hand and writing materials and of the remarks about the end of the quaternion and the Continuator's inability to find any more of this work, that it is the new scribe himself who is composing the remainder of the work, or at least that the new scribe is writing the continuation at the immediate direction of the Continuator. On the verso of the next folio, at the very end of the first part of Chapter 5, the Continuator speaks in greater detail of his own role and that of his predecessor:[4]

This author, whose name I do not know but who was a subtle geometer, certainly covered the art of the measurement of figures in a general way. He also briefly [treated of the measurement] of the area of a rectangular surface figure (also called a rectangular parallelogram) from a knowledge of its sides. Furthermore from the knowledge of the perpendicular in a triangular figure [he was able] to reduce every polygonal figure [to triangles] unless that figure is originally a triangle, even though the polygon is increased [in the number of sides] in the manner of [whole] numbers, namely by adding one side [at a time] [if we start] at a triangle. However, in order that a more special investigation of measurement may be had, I wish to discourse upon plane figures individually: in the first place on those which are rectilinear and then upon those which are curvilinear. Among the rectilinear figures, we shall first speak of the square. After [treating] the rectangle, we shall then treat certain quadrilateral figures whose names we do not have but which anyone calls by any name that pleases him. In the second place, [we shall speak] of triangles, then pentagons, hexagons and other polylateral figures, as the context demands. And when this has been done, I think the author's promise for the fifth chapter of this work will have been carried out sufficiently. And in order that this matter may be clearly demonstrated, I propose, following the style of the author, certain geometrical elements as suppositions that are already conceded. If anyone has any hesitation about these geometrical elements, let him consult the book of Euclid to set his mind at ease.

It is clear from an examination of the two additonal parts of Chapter 5 that the new author has followed his proposed program closely and

---

[4] *Ibid.*, 23v: "Quamvis autem actor iste cuius nomen ignoro subtilis tamen geometer pro constanti de mensura figurarum rectilinearum sufficienter in generali artem tetigerit et in brevi per cognitionem laterum figure superficialis rectangule, que parallelogrammum rectangulum aliter nominatur, et per notitiam perpendicularis in figura triangula reducendo omnem figuram poligonam licet crescat in infinitum per additionem unius lateris ad instar numerorum ad triangulum nisi ipsa triangulus preexistat, verumptamen ut circa mensuras specialius exercitium habeatur volo circa figuras planas discurrere sigillatim, et primo inter omnes de rectilineis, secundo de curvilineis erit sermo. Inter vero rectilineas ante dicemus de quadrato; post de altera parte longiori sequentur de quibusdam figuris quadrilateris quarum nomina non habemus, sed quilibet suo libito vocat eas, et secundo de triangulis et inde de pentagonis, hexagonis et ceteris multilateris prout exiget ille locus. Et in hoc estimo satis fecisse capitulo quinto huius libri secundum quod promiserat iste actor. Et ut negotium clarius ostendatur sequendo stilum actoris proponam aliqua geometrica elementa pro dignitatibus iam concessis de quibus siquis hesitet videat librum Euclidis et patificet mentem suam."

all of the various specific figures which he mentions in the list above are treated in some detail. However, it will also be noted that he proposes to speak of curvilinear as well as rectilinear figures. This promise is not carried out in Chapter 5. But when we turn to Chapter 6, we see that much attention has been given to circles, segments of circles and various lunes, although no such treatment was promised by the original author for Chapter 6. And indeed the treatment of solids promised by the original author is delayed until Proposition 35 and only extends through Proposition 39. Thus it is evident that Chapter 6 was also the work of the new author rather than that of the original author and that he had not found any other copy of the original tract. In fact, at the beginning of Proposition 35 in MS BN lat. 7380, the Continuator refers to the following note at the bottom of the page: "Hic melius inciperes 7^m sed hoc actor iste quem perficimus in suis titulis non premisit." In short, the Continuator feels obligated to follow the original author's wishes even though Propositions 35–39 do not fit in with the treatment of circles and lunes that the Continuator has made the focus of Chapter 6. His authorship of Chapter 6 seems to be confirmed by the proemium of Chapter 9, which was penned by the Continuator:[5]

In regard to the ninth chapter our author promised to complete the measurement of a circular surface. [This intention was expressed] in his [list of] titles, which, sorry to say, I believe he was prevented by death from completing. For if he had been able to finish it, I believe that, based on the things he premised in this work, he would have explained [some] marvelous things concerning the geometric art. But as this [i.e., his promised subject for Chapter 9] would be a continuation of the measure of curvilinear surfaces with respect to rectilinear which I have already completed in the sixth chapter along with certain other things, there now remains [of his originally intended subject] for this chapter [9] only to demonstrate that a circle is the most capacious of figures.

Thus it seems evident that it was the Continuator who composed the section (which is indeed the major part) of Chapter 6 dealing with the measure of curvilinear surfaces. Now if this is so, then Proposition 1 of Chapter 6 supplies evidence for the Continuator's composition of Chapter 8, for the author of that proposition declares his intention to establish the ratio of circumference to diameter "later" (and a marginal note adds: "in the beginning of the eighth chapter").[6] That proposition also declares the author's intention to explain Archimedes' demonstration of the ratio of a straight line to a curve by means of spirals. Since the determination of

---

[5] *Ibid.*, 66v: "In hoc 9° capitulo actor noster in suis titulis, quos morte preventus ut puto unde prothdolor non complevit, cum per ea que premisit in hoc opere res mirabiles circa artem geometricam ipsum estimo declarasse si perficere valuisset, promisit de mensura circularis superficiei terminare. Sed ut esset continuatio mensure superficierum curvilinearum ad rectilineas iam illum titulum in 6° capitulo una cum quibusdam aliis expedivi, nunc autem secundum ipsum restat tantum in hoc capitulo demonstrare circulum esse omnium capacissimam figurarum."

[6] See Chapter 4 below, note 1.

π occupies the major part of Chapter 8 and a hybrid tract on quadrature excerpted from the *On Spiral Lines* is inserted in Chapter 8 to constitute the second major part of Chapter 8, it certainly appears that it was the author of Proposition 1 of Chapter 6 who composed or put together Chapter 8. And in our discussion above, we have shown the probability that it was the Continuator who composed Proposition 1 of Chapter 6. Hence, it would appear that he was also the author of Chapter 8. One must suspect that, if he was the author of the two long additions to Chapter 5, as well as the major parts of Chapter 6 and Chapter 8, he was also the author of Chapter 7. Other evidence to support the Continuator's authorship of Chapter 7, in addition to his original and almost conclusive statement on folio 22r that he had found no more of the original work, is that Chapter 7 contains much more than was promised by the original author, as for example, the treatment of the problem of finding two proportional means (see my Chapter 3 below). Since this last mentioned problem was drawn from Moerbeke's translation of Eutocius, as we shall see, and similarly much of Chapters 8 and 10 depends on the Archimedean translations, it would seem to corroborate our suggestion that a single man with an interest in and access to the Moerbeke translations composed all of the above-mentioned sections. In view of the further fact that the Continuator expressly tells us that he is the author of the remaining chapters,[7] it seems likely that the Continuator had found no more of the original work than that included in the first 21 folios of Paris, BN lat. 7380.

We are now prepared to take up the question of the identities of the two authors. None of the seven manuscripts bears any clear indication of authorship. But MS Paris, BN lat. 7380 has the following statement in a later hand (that of Oronce Finé, the sixteenth-century mathematician) on the first folio: "Credo authorem huius fuisse Ioannem de Muris cum

---

[7] Just following the passage quoted above in note 5, the Continuator makes it even clearer that nothing remained from the original author to complete the demonstration in Chapter 9 (BN lat. 7380, 66v): "Non autem recipio ipsum actorem hanc conclusionem proponentem sic putasse. . . . Sed intelligo proponentem. . . ." (That is, the Continuator finds it necessary to speculate on what the original author meant by this conclusion, thus showing that he had nothing on this conclusion from the original author. Incidentally, this brief discussion by the Continuator is perhaps the poorest section of the material added by him. That the Continuator composed the remaining Chapters 10–12, is demonstrated by his remarks in the beginning of the tenth chapter (see below, Part I, Chapter 6) and also by the following remark at the end of Chapter 11, *ibid.*, 72v: "Multa quidem corpora varia subtilis considerator poterit anime fabricare que non est utile neque artis singulariter enarrare. Sed quoniam horum doctrina sub regulis precedentibus est inclusa, ideo in hoc cum laude dei qui stillum nostrum ad finem attulit preoptant 11^m capitulum et per consequens actoris ignoti promissio iuxta id quod potuit nostri paucitas ingenii finiatur. Nunc autem restat solum ex additione nostra 12^m capitulum breviter adimplere in quo primo artem de binomiis antepromissam tam figuris quam numeris exponemus ut fiant aliqua de precedentibus promptiora, deinde ad proportiones diversorum corporum intendemus ut demus occasionem posteris interius perscrutandi ad quod adiuvare dignetur qui dat sapientiam petentibus affluenter." Incidentally, some later manuscripts label the second part of Chapter 12 as Chapter 13 (Magl. XI, 2; Schweinfurt H.67).

faciat mentionem infra de suo quadripartito numerorum." And indeed Finé's statement is quite correct. The *Quadripartitum numerorum* is twice cited in the first person. The first citation occurs in Proposition 17 of Part 2 of Chapter 5:[8] ". . . by the art which I have explained elsewhere in the *Quadripartitum numerorum*." The second appears in Proposition 2 of Chapter 10 (see my Chapter 6 below): "And this art I have set in order elsewhere in the *Quadripartitum numerorum*." It seems clear, then, that it was Johannes de Muris who made these statements. But both statements appear in sections of the *De arte mensurandi* indisputedly composed by the Continuator. Hence, on the ground of internal evidence alone, we are led to the conclusion that Johannes de Muris was the Continuator. When we add to this internal evidence the paleographical similarities between the hand of the scribe producing the continuation and that of Johannes de Muris pointed out by Mr. Stephen Victor, we reach the further conclusion that not only was Johannes the author of the continuation but that he was also the scribe.[9] In reaching the conclusion that Johannes de Muris was the Continuator, we are in agreement, at least for Chapter 8 of the *De arte mensurandi*, with the scribe or editor who put together the various quadrature tracts contained in MS Glasgow, Univ. Libr. Gen. 1115, dated 4 Dec., 1480, which includes Proposition 1 from Chapter 8 of the *De arte mensurandi* (see below, Part II, Chapter 1) and introduces it with the following title (213r): "Extractum a commento Johannis de Muris, capitulo octavo, ut facilius intelligantur que dicta sunt supra textum Archimenidis."

Turning away from the Continuator, now identified as Johannes de Muris, to the original author, I must immediately confess that I have

[8] *Ibid.*, 27r: ". . . per artem quam in quadripartito numerorum alias explanavi." It may be objected that this appears only in the margin, but it has a mark indicating the exact point of insertion and is like all of the other insertions that surely were a part of the Continuator's text. Furthermore, the second citation, appearing in Proposition 2 of Chapter 10, is unambiguously in the body of the text and not in the margin.

[9] Mr. Victor's convincing case for Johannes de Muris' role as the scribal continuator is contained in his previously cited article "Johannes de Muris' Autograph," pp. 394–95. It is based on a complex of codicological, textual, and paleographical evidence. Having neatly identified scribe B of folios 22–58, 66–83 as the actual author of the continuation, he then points to the close similarity between B's hand and that of MS Escorial 0.II.10 identified with near certainty by Prof. Guy Beaujouan as the hand of Johannes de Muris. Furthermore, Johannes de Muris seems not only to have written out the folios indicated above (no doubt much of it as a first draft although some of it as a revision of a first draft), but he also contributed the major share of the marginalia in those parts not written by him: folios 1–21 (the beginning of the tract written by scribe A) and folios 59–65 (the hybrid quadrature tract written down by scribe C but added by Johannes de Muris to the codex). Incidentally, one of Johannes de Muris' most interesting marginal comments on the original tract occurs where the original author has given a proof of the following proposition (14v): "8. Si fuerint 2 anguli alicuius trianguli noti, erit omnium laterum proportio adinvicem nota, et altero secundum quamvis mensuram noto fient reliqua nota, eruntque perpendicularis et anguli eius noti." Perhaps because the author has based his proof in part on a table of chords, Johannes says (15r): "Reductio istius proportionis sufficeret ptholomeo, non autem archimenidi." This shows, on Johannes' part, an acute awareness of the difference between a formal geometric proof and the use of approximations.

found no evidence to assist in his identification. The predilection of that author in the first five chapters for trigonometric considerations makes it seem probable that he was interested in astronomy.

If we are correct in identifying Johannes de Muris as the Continuator and also in assigning to the Continuator Chapters 6–8 as well as the second and third parts of Chapter 5 and Chapters 9–12, then it is apparent that Johannes de Muris is responsible for all of the sections using Archimedes in the *De arte mensurandi* edited in the succeeding chapters. A possible exception may be the hybrid tract on quadrature appearing in parchment on folios 59r-65r of Paris BN lat. 7380 where it was inserted by Johannes de Muris in Chapter 8 of the *De arte mensurandi*. It was, however, written down by a different scribe. Still, even though Johannes de Muris did not write out this tract, there are some indications that he was its author, as I shall point out in Chapter 5 below.

Our conclusions concerning Johannes de Muris' role in the preparation of our extant version of the *De arte mensurandi* also tend to solve or rather eliminate a puzzle that originally arose when I considered Johannes de Muris to be the original author. If, as I had supposed earlier, Johannes was the original author and if he occupied himself with this task after 1343 (i.e. after the composition of the *Quadripartitum numerorum*), which is most probable, as I indicated in Chapter 1 above, then the Continuator, who twice confesses ignorance of the name of the original author (see notes 4 and 7), would have had to have been writing shortly after him but without knowing so celebrated a scholar as Johannes de Muris. I had assumed that the Continuator would have had to write within the next few years after 1343, since there is strong evidence that manuscript BN lat. 7380 was once owned by Nicole Oresme and Oresme's mathematical activities almost certainly were confined to the late 1340's and early 1350's. But if Johannes de Muris is accepted as the Continuator rather than as the original author, the puzzle vanishes. Furthermore, this would mean that Johannes' edited version of the whole work was completed after 1343 and probably before 1345.[10]

---

[10] I have already noted in Chapter 1 that Johannes de Muris in his *Quadripartitum numerorum*, completed in 1343, spoke of his intention of treating the quadrature problem by reference to spiral lines later in a geometrical context. I have taken this to be a reference to his intention to take up the problem in his edited version of the *De arte mensurandi* (cf. also the remarks in Chapters 4 and 5 below). I have said that the *De arte mensurandi* was probably completed before 1345 because in that year he turned to the calendric problem and no later date for his mathematical activity has been established. It is also worth noting that an insert, apparently in Johannes de Muris' hand, and designated as folio 38 of BN lat. 7380, carries on its verso the following statement: "Anno domini 1344 [=1345, n.s.] in februario iuxta finem erit coniunctio triplex 3 planetarum superiorum. . . ." We do not know, however, when he made this insert and indeed he might well have used the piece to make his insertion later than the writing on the reverse side. I should also add that Johannes de Muris was the author of a tract predicting the great conjunction of 1345 (see L. Thorndike, *A History of Magic and Experimental Science*, Vol. 3 [New York, 1934], pp. 305–06).

CHAPTER 3

The Problem of Proportional
Means in Chapter 7 of the
De arte mensurandi

Some years ago, I published an account of the knowledge of Moerbeke's translations of Archimedes present in the works of Johannes de Muris.[1] I failed at that time to discuss the source of the treatment of the problem of finding two proportional means between two given quantities that appears in the *De arte mensurandi*, Chapter 7, Proposition 16 (which is in one of those sections of the *De arte mensurandi* added by Johannes de Muris). Since the solutions presented in the *De arte mensurandi* all seem to have had their origin in Moerbeke's translation of Eutocius' *Commentary on the Sphere and the Cylinder*, Book II, Prop. 1, it would appear that the Moerbeke translations were more widely known by Johannes than I realized earlier. Although the text published below, when compared with Volume Two, 38rG, 36vC–M, R–T, reveals that the Moerbeke translation is the probable source of the discussion, it is worth noticing that Johannes has not slavishly copied the account given in the Moerbeke translation. It will be seen that Johannes has taken the account of the origin of the problem from the so-called Letter of Eratosthenes to King Ptolemy given by Eutocius, although he has simplified and altered the account. Similarly, he has much changed the account of the "Platonic" solution of the problem without, however, changing its essential nature. The second solution is that associated with the name of Hero by Eutocius and the brief third solution is an allusion to the method presented as that of Philo of Byzantium by Eutocius, although in the latter case the medieval author has only drawn from Eutocius the reduction of the Philonian solution to that of Hero.

One may well ask whether Johannes could have taken his discussion of the solution of Plato from its presentation in the *Verba filiorum* of the Banū Mūsā, translated by Gerard of Cremona in the twelfth century (and borrowed from the *Verba filiorum* by Leonardo Fibonacci in his

---

[1] "The Use of the Moerbeke Translations of Archimedes in the Works of Johannes de Muris," *Isis*, Vol. 43 (1952), pp. 236–42.

Practica geometrie) and his discussion of the Philonian solution from its presentation by Leonardo or by Jordanus de Nemore in his *Liber de triangulis*.[2] The answer to both parts of this question is, I am sure, a negative one. I conclude this mainly from the fact that none of the earlier medieval discussions of mean proportionals mentions the precise origin of the problem in the duplicating of a cubical altar in the manner of Eutocius.[3] Furthermore, there is no known medieval account of Hero's solution other than that in the Moerbeke translation of Eutocius. Finally, a comparison of the texts of Moerbeke and that of Johannes de Muris reveals enough verbal identities to indicate that Johannes drew freely from the Moerbeke texts. Assuming that this is so, it is further evidence of the use in Paris of some manuscript of the Moerbeke translation of Archimedes (and probably of the only known complete manuscript, Vat. Ottob. lat. 1850).[4] Incidentally, Johannes de Muris made extensive use of the mean-proportionals theorem in the succeeding propositions of Chapter 7.[5]

I have listed below in the *Sigla* the five manuscripts of the *De arte mensurandi* which I have employed in preparing the texts of this and the succeeding chapters. Other manuscripts which I have examined but not collated include: Paris, BN lat. 7216 and 14736, both 15c; Florence, Bibl. Naz. Magl. XI.2, 1r–89r, after 1450, Magl. XI.44, 2r–26v, 16c incomplete (this breaks off toward the end of Prop. 8 of the first part of Chapter 5); Glasgow, Univ. Libr. Gen. 1115, 213r–14v, 1480 (frag. Chap. 8); Schweinfurt, Stadtbibl. H.67, 16c, including enunciations only (see below, Part III, Chap. 2, Sect. II, n. 12), and the two extracts mentioned in notes 7 and 8 of this chapter.

As I have said earlier (see above, Chapter 2, n. 9), Mr. Stephen Victor

---

[2] M. Clagett, *Archimedes in the Middle Ages*, Vol. 1: *The Arabo-Latin Tradition* (Madison, Wisc., 1964), pp. 340–45, 366, 658–65.

[3] All other accounts limit the origin of the problem of duplicating a cube to a response of the Delian oracle and thus none mentions the story of Minos' ordering the cubical altar except the Pseudo-Eratosthenes letter given by Eutocius. The other accounts appearing in various works of Plutarch, Theon, and John Philoponus are all cited and translated into German by E. P. Wolfer, *Eratosthenes von Kyrene als Mathematiker und Philosoph* (Groningen, 1954), pp. 4–12. Cf. Vitruvius, *De architectura*, IX, 217, 5 (i.e., Preface to Book IX, Sect. 13), which could have been read in the fourteenth century; it does not give the story about King Minos but only the Delian version.

[4] Clagett, *Archimedes*, Vol. 1, pp. 11–12, 720 (Addendum to page 12).

[5] I shall make no attempt to include the full text of these additional propositions which reduce a number of problems to Proposition 16, but I can illustrate them by giving the full text of Proposition 17 and the enunciations of the succeeding propositions [except Prop. 23 which makes no use of Prop. 16] (Paris, BN lat. 7380, 54v–56r): "17ᵃ. Cubum datum duplicare. Lineam unius basis cubi dati dupla et inter has duas lineas duas alias medias proportionales per precedentem studeas invenire. Eam vero lineam que locum minoris medie proportionalis optinet cubica, volo dicere, super eam cubum describe per primam huius. Et iste cubus erit duplus cubi dati, quod est propositum. Linee quoque que locum maioris medie proportionalis possidet cubus duplus est precedentis et bis duplus, i.e., quadruplus, cubi dati. Cubus autem linee maioris, scilicet duple ad primam, que locum maioris extremi vendicat, duplus est precedentis et bis duplus anteprecedentis ac bis bis duplus, i.e., octuplus, dati cubi. Hec autem natura numerorum te non permitteret ignorare. Sicut inter 2 et 4, qui pro duabus lineis assumantur, sunt duo media proportionalia licet surda,

has made a convincing case for Johannes de Muris' scribal role in the continuation of *Pd* (although certain problems concerning the marginal notes and lacunae in the text demand fuller explanation).[6] Thus *Pd*, as the

scilicet radix [cubica] de 16 et radix [cubica] de 32. Sicut enim duo ad radicem [cubicam] de 16 ita et ipsa ad radicem [cubicam] de 32 et hec ad 16 (*!* 4). Cum mediorum productum equale sit producto extremorum, vides ergo quod cubus radicis de 16 duplus est ad cubum duorum. Est enim cubus duorum 8. Sed cubus radicis cubice de 16 est ipsemet 16; quare duplus; ita in aliis consequenter. 18ª Datum solidum rectangulum geminare. . . . 19ª Propositum cubum cubice triplicare. . . . Additio. Eodem mode si quadruplare quintuplare volueris cubum datum. . . . 20ª Si inter unitatem et quemlibet numerum duo media proportionalia continue statuantur, minus mediorum radicem cubicam eiusdem numeri esse necesse est. . . . 21ª Cuiuslibet numeri latus cubicum geometrice signare. . . . 22ª Datum solidum rectangulum cubicare. . . . 24ª Datam speram duplare. . . .''

[6] Most of the lacunae that appear in the parts of the codex written by Johannes de Muris (Victor's scribe B) involve the omission of a proposition number or a proposition and book or chapter number for a citation from Euclid's *Elements* or from the *De arte mensurandi* itself. These lacunae usually follow the word *per*. I have observed some 14 of these lacunae (29v, line 18; 32r, 16; 33v, 15; 35r, 22; 36r, 2; 36v, 20; 38r, 3; 39v, 28; 43v, 5; 66v, 22; 68v, 20; 73r, 6; 77r, 22, 24), and there are no doubt others in this long and complex work. One could explain the omission of the proposition numbers of citations from the *De arte mensurandi* by the suggestion that the numbers of the propositions were added later, and there is some evidence that, from the sixth chapter onward, the numbers were added later, that is after the completion of the treatise. But against this argument is the fact that many citations to propositions from the *De arte mensurandi* occurring after Chapter 6 are given in the body of the text. For example, in X.13, Johannes cites VIII.14 and VI.22; in X.14 he cites VII.22; in X.15 he cites VIII.16, and so on. All of these references can be readily found in my text of Chapter 10 given below in Part I, Chapter 6. They all occur in the body of the text. It is possible, I suppose, that he may have left lacunae which he later filled in with the proper numbers. (This may be the case in his citation of VII.22 in X.14.) But many of the citations seem to be in the same ink and are spaced as if they are continuous with the rest of the text. The conclusion of all this is, I believe, that whether or not he added the now visible numbers of the propositions after he completed the text, he must have had some temporary numbers assigned to the propositions. Victor suggests that the omission of the propositions from Euclid might have been mere forgetfulness on the part of Johannes de Muris and that he intended to fill them in later. This could well be, but it is astonishing how many times he does include the correct citation to the *Elements*, in fact so often as to suggest that he had a copy of the *Elements* always at hand as he composed his work. I suppose one could say that occasionally, as he was developing the proof, he did not want to interrupt his concentration by finding the appropriate proposition number. One lacuna (35v, line 3) does not demand a proposition number but rather a large number of seven figures that was later added in the margin. I am not sure of Johannes' reason for omitting this number. Incidentally, some of the marginalia indicate that for at least some of the chapters Johannes had an earlier draft from which he was copying. For example, in the third part of Chapter 5 (34v), Johannes gives the enunciation of Proposition 2, followed immediately by the proof of Proposition 3. He rectifies this by giving the proof of Proposition 2 and the enunciation of Proposition 3 in the margin below, with the proper signs to indicate where this marginal material is to be added. One can only explain this by suggesting that at this point he was indeed copying from another draft. Also puzzling is the fact that in Chapter 10 (69r), Proposition 17 precedes Propositions 15 and 16. This could again mean that he was copying from an original draft. Or perhaps, he decided to change the order of the propositions when he was in the process of adding the numbers. It is of interest that this rearrangement of numbers occurs at just the point where he apparently decided to extend his original plans for Chapter 10 by adding an additional eight propositions (see below, Part I, Chapter 6).

author's copy, is almost certainly the direct or indirect source of all of the extant manuscripts. It is not surprising, therefore, that in the various texts which I have edited from the *De arte mensurandi, Pd* is again and again the only manuscript to have the full reading. *Pe* is a quite faithful copy of *Pd* and generally repeats even its slips, lacunae and errors. *Xb* is an intelligent copy with beautifully drawn figures, and on occasion it suggests readings for the lacunae left in *Pd* (this is particularly true of the text given below in Chap. 5 of this Part). On the whole it is fairly accurate, although in the case of the text presented in the next chapter it has an unusually large number of careless omissions of whole phrases and sentences. *Ua* is also an intelligent copy, which freely corrects or shortens the text. It is marked by a tendency to replace the names of numbers with Indo-Arabic numerals. Finally, it should be observed that the latest manuscript, *Xn*, is quite complete but often misreads the letters designating geometrical quantities. Naturally, in view of its seminal role, I have almost exclusively followed manuscript *Pd*, giving preference to its readings except where they are carelessly wrong, at which points I have corrected it on the basis of the other manuscripts or on my own, always of course including the original reading among the variants. All references to marginal readings in *Pd* are to Johannes de Muris' additions. They are incorporated in the text without brackets since these are the author's additions. Manuscript *Pe* is the only manuscript without diagrams. The marginal folio references are to manuscript *Pd*.

It should be remarked finally that the proposition of the *De arte mensurandi* edited in this chapter circulated independently and anonymously in at least two manuscripts. One is MS Bern, Bürgerbibl. A. 50, 176v–77r, 15c, where the text differs radically from Johannes de Muris' pristine version. Indeed this extract is quite incomplete and somewhat erroneous (it alters the introduction slightly, leaves out the construction and use of the instrument in connection with the "Platonic" solution, and it omits the third method entirely). It was published by H. Suter without identification of the author.[7] The second manuscript including this proposition is Paris,

---

[7] "Die Quaestio 'De proportione dyametri quadrati ad costam eiusdem' des Albertus de Saxonia," *Zeitschrift für Mathematik und Physik*, Hist.-lit. Abth., Vol. 32 (1887), pp. 52–54. For the sake of comparison with my text of the excerpt from Johannes de Muris' *De arte mensurandi*, I repeat here Suter's text of this anonymous piece. His references to Figures 13 and 14 can be located in my Figures I.3.1 and I.3.3. Suter's text follows:

"Datis duabus lineis inequalibus, inter eas duas medias proportionales invenire.

Istud theorema fuit antiquitus sic introductum: quidam rex juvenis ludo talario deditus jussit sibi edificari capellam et in ea altare cubicum construi; quo facto considerans altare respectu capellae nimis parvum, jussit altare duplicari, et cum artifices latomi (latonii) artem duplicandi cubum non haberent, ad jussum regis congregati fuerunt geometrae, cumque multo tempore studuissent super duplicationem cubi, dixit tandem unus eorum, hoc nullo modo posse fieri, nisi primo inter duas lineas datas quarum una ad aliam dupla sit, inventae fuerint duae aliae mediae proportionales, eo quod cubus lineae duplae ad cubum lineae dimidiae seu subduplae octuplus esse probatur. Et cum inter unum et ejus octuplum sint duae proportiones vel media proportionalia, scil. 2 et 4, quorum primum duplum est simpliciter (?), et tales ideo lineas eandem proportionem habentes quaerere necesse est; et hoc problema inter eos cubi duplicatio (duplus) vocabatur. — Ad praedictum autem theorema

Arsenal 763, 292r–93v, 15c.[8] In contrast to the first extract, this one follows the text of the *De arte mensurandi* rather closely. I have not

concludendum tali modo venire nitebantur: sint *.a.b.* et *.b.c.* (Fig. 13) [see Fig. I.3.1] duae lineae rectae inequales ad libitum datae, ad angulum rectum extremitatibus earum junctis, et utraque eorum quantumlibet in continuum et directum pertractis, et sint illae *.a.b.d.* et *.c.b.e.* (*d*) quatuor angulos rectos super *.b.* statuentes; deinde duos triangulos orthogonos constitue, scil. *.c.d.e.* et sit angulus *.d.* rectus, et *.d.e.a.* triangulus angulo recto *.e.,* qui qualiter habeant figurari et stabiliri inferius docebo; palam itaque est, quod cum ab angulo recto *.d.* perpendicularis super basim insistat in triangulo *.c.d.e.,* per 8^{am} sexti Euclidis *.b.d.* erit media proportionalis inter duas portiones basis, quae sunt *.c.b.* et *.b.e.* Similiter et per eandem in triangulo *.d.e.a.* *.b.e.* erit media proportionalis inter *.b.d.* et *.a.b.*; est ergo ut *.c.b.* ad *.b.d.* sic *.b.d.* ad *.b.e.* quod erat demonstrandum. Sed quia per istum modum difficile imo forte impossibile est, tales duas lineas invenire in omnibus nisi tantum in rationalibus, non tamen in omnibus rationalibus, in irrationalibus autem non (?), ideo ponitur alius modus generalis et communis tam in rationalibus quam irrationalibus qui talis est: sint *.a.b.* et *.b.g.* (Fig. 14) [see Fig. I.3.3] duae lineae rectae datae inequales ad angulum rectum jacentes super *.b.* Perfecto autem parallelogrammo *.b.d.a.g.,* dyameter protrahatur per medium secta in *.e.,* educanturque latera *.d.g.* et *.d.a.* in directum usque in *.z.* et *.h.,* appositaque regula super punctum *.b.* contingente, totiensque moveatur ipsa regula, quod resecet *.d.h.z.* tali nempe pacto, quod et ipsa *.b.* contingente *.e.h.* et *.e.z.* sint equales, de quo circinus praebeat fiduciam; ducque perpendicularem super *.d.g.* quam ipsa dividet per medium per 30. primi addita 10. ejusdem. Quia igitur *.d.g.* per duo equalia divisa est in *.c.* et ei in longum additur *.g.z.,* palam est quod illud, quod fit ex *.d.z.* in *.g.z.* cum quadrato *.g c.* equum est quadrato lineae *.c.z.* per 6^{am} 2^{i} Euclidis. Igitur eodem quadrato quadrato lineae *.e.c.* addito utrobique, erit quod fit ex *.d.z.* in *.g.z.* cum quadratis linearum *.g.c.* et *.e.c.,* et inde quadrato lineae *.e.g.* per penultimam primi Euclidis, equale quadratis linearum *.c.z.* et *.c.e.,* hoc est quadrato *.z.e.* per eandem; quod ergo fit ex *.d.z.* in *.g.z.* cum quadrato lineae *.e.g.* equum est quadrato lineae *.e.z.* Similiter demonstrabitur, quod idem quod fit ex *.d.h.* in *.a.h.* cum quadrato *.e.a.* est equale quadrato lineae *.e.h.,* intellecta perpendiculari ab *.e.* super latus *.d.a.* Et quia quadratum lineae *.e.h.* equum est quadrato lineae *.e.z.,* cum *.e.h.* et *.e.z.* positae sint equales, ergo quod fit ex eis id est earum quadrata est equale ei quod fit ex mediis, id est duo quadrata duarum linearum equalium *.e.z.* et *.e.h.* sunt equalia duabus superficiebus quae fiunt ex mediis, scil. ex lineis *.d.z.* et *.g.z.* cum quadrato lineae *.e.g.* et *.d.h.* et *.a.h.* cum quadrato lineae *.e.a.* Demptis autem duobus quadratis equalibus duarum linearum equalium *.e.g.* et *.e.a.* a duabus praedictis superficiebus relinquitur, quod hae duae superficies quae fiunt ex *.d.z.* in *.g.z.* et ex *.d.h.* in *.a.h.* sint equales, quia si ab equalibus equalia demas etc. Tunc sequitur demonstrative hae duae superficies sunt equales, ergo quatuor earum latera sunt proportionalia per 15 (13) sexti, et haec quatuor latera sunt hae quatuor lineae, scil. *.d.z.,* *.g.z.* et *.d.h.* et *.a.h.* Sequitur ergo: sicut *.d.z.* ad *.d.h.* sic *.a.h.* ad *.g.z.,* et similiter sicut *.d.h.* ad *.d.z.* ita *.g.z.* ad *.a.h.* per eandem 15 sexti; sed etiam sicut *.d.z.* ad *.d.h.* sic *.a.b.* ad *.a.h.* et *.g.z.* ad *.g.b.* (*.g.b.* ad *.g.z.*) per 4^{am} sexti Euclidis. Ex his ergo concluditur principale propositum, quia, sicut *.d.z.* ad *.d.h.* sic *.a.b.* ad *.a.h.* per 4^{am} sexti, et *.a.b.* ad *.a.h.* sic *.a.h.* ad *.g.z.,* cum eadem sit proportio *.a.b.* ad *.a.h.* sicut *.d.z.* ad *.d.h.,* ut praedictum est, et eodem modo sicut *.d.h.* ad *.d.z.* sic *.g.z.* ad *.a.h.* per 4^{am} sexti; sicut ergo sequitur, sicut *.a.b.* ad *.a.h.* sic *.a.h.* ad *.g.z.,* ita sequitur, sicut *.g.b.* ad *.g.z.* ita *.g.z.* ad *.a.h.,* ergo per conversam proportionalitatem: sicut *.a.h.* ad *.g.z.* sic *.g.z.* ad *.g.b.,* et ergo sicut *.a.b.* ad *.a.h.* sic *.a.h.* ad *.g.z.* ita *.g.z.* ad *.g.b.* Inventae sunt igitur duae lineae mediae proportionales inter duas lineas datas, quae sunt *.a.h.* et *.g.z.,* haec omnia patent in figura."

[8] I must thank Mr. Stephen Victor for alerting me to Arsenal 763. He notes that, like Paris, BN lat. 14736 (which I mentioned earlier), the Arsenal manuscript is from the library of St. Victor in Paris. He also informed me that MS Florence, Bibl. Naz. Magl. XI.2, which I have noted above as one of the later copies of the *De arte mensurandi*, has two glued-in folios (58bis and 58ter) that contain, in a sixteenth-century hand, three more solutions of the problem of the mean proportionals: "Philonis bizantii inventum," "Inventum per compendium excerptum," "Architae inventum." These do not seem to be in any of the conventional translations, i.e. Moerbeke's, Cremonensis', or Valla's.

reported its variant readings. Finally, the reader should note that this proposition of Johannes de Muris was translated into German by Dürer and published in his *Unterweysung der Messung* (Nuremberg, 1525). I have given the text of this translation below in Part III, Chapter 6, Section III, note 4, passages [3] and [4].

As usual, I have capitalized the enunciations to indicate the use of a larger hand in the manuscripts. Furthermore, I have capitalized geometrical quantities, although the scribes did not. The references to Euclid are to the Campanus version, and in a number of instances, I have added case endings where only numbers have been given, e.g., *per 8ᵃᵐ 6ⁱ* for *per 8.6ⁱ*. When the numbers of the propositions in the Campanus version of the *Elements* differ from those in the Greek text, I have given the latter in parentheses in the English translation, e.g., VI.15 (=Gr.VI.16).

Sigla

Pd = Paris, BN lat. 7380, 53v–54r, middle of 14c.
Pe = Paris, BN lat. 7381, 111r–12v, 15c.
Xb = Vatican, Vat. lat. 9410, 49r–50r, 15c.
Ua = Utrecht, Bibl. Univ. 725, 69r–v, 15c.
Xn = Vatican, Ottob. lat. 1423, 64r–65r, late 15c or early 16c.

Johannis de Muris De arte mensurandi
Chapter 7, Proposition 16

Johannis de Muris

De arte mensurandi, Cap. 7ᵐ, Propositio 16ᵃ

53v /DATIS DUABUS LINEIS INEQUALIBUS QUIBUSCUNQUE INTER EAS DUAS PROPORTIONALES MEDIAS INVENIRE.
Istud theoreuma fuit antiquitus introductum, quia unus imperator altare cubicum iusserat fabricari; quo viso eius despiciens parvitatem iussit altare
5   duplicari. Et cum artifices artem duplicandi cubum non haberent, ad iussum imperatoris fuerunt geometre tunc temporis pariter congregati. Cum autem multo tempore studuissent ad cubi duplicationem, dixit unus inter eos hoc non posse fieri nisi primo inter duas datas lineas quarum una ad aliam dupla fuerit invente sint due medie proportionales, eo quod
10   cubus linee duple ad cubum linee dimidie octuplus esse probatur; et cum inter unum et eius octuplum sint duo media proportionalia, scilicet duo

7 dixit: tandem dixit *Ua*
8 lineas *tr. Ua ante* duas
9–13 eo . . . est *mg. Pd*
10 probabitur *Xn*

et quatuor, quorum primum duplum est simpli extremi, inde in lineis eandem proportionem querere necesse est. Et hoc probleuma apud eos cubi duplatio vocatum est.

15 Ad predictum autem theoreuma concludendum "Datis duabus lineis etc." variis mediis nitebantur. Primus modus [Fig. I.3.1.]: Sint *EB, BG* due date ad libitum linee recte inequales, inter quas etc. Iunge eas ad rectos, educta utraque quantumlibet in continuum et directum et sint *EBC, GBD,* quatuour angulos rectos super *B* statuentes. Deinde duos triangulos
20 orthogonos constitue, scilicet *GCD,* et sit angulus *C* rectus, et *CDE* stante angulo *D* recto, qui quomodo valeant figurari inferius declarabo. Palam utique est, quod cum ab angulo recto *C* perpendicularis supra basim insistat in triangulo *GDC,* per 8[am] sexti *CB* est media proportionalis inter duas sectiones basis que sunt *GB, BD.* Similiter etiam per eandem,
25 in triangulo *CDE, DB* est media proportionalis inter *CB, BE.* Est ergo ut *GB* ad *BC* ita *BC* ad *BD* et *BD* ad *BE,* quod fuit propositum demonstrare.

Restat duos triangulos orthogonos statuere supradictos gnomone cupreo parato *QPR* angulo *P* recto per 45[am] (?) primi [Fig. I.3.2]; lateri *QP*
30 concavato infige regulam *TS* orthogonaliter, angulo *TSP* recto existente. Moveatur autem regula ad libitum sursum et deorsum, nunc versus *Q,* modo versus *P,* equidistanter tamen lateri gnomonis *PR,* cum opus fuerit. Hoc autem instrumento fabricato, apta latus gnomonis *PR* ut contingat punctum *G* linee prius date angulo *P* recto posito super lineam *EC*
35 ubilibet pro nunc donec fixus manere cogatur. Altero autem latere gnomonis *QP* iacente super lineam *BD,* move igitur regulam *TS* usquequo angulus *TSP* rectus super lineam *BD* coaptetur contingente cum regula punctum *E* alterius linee date. Hac autem positione stante, erit latus gnomonis *PR* sicut latus trianguli *GC,* et aliud latus gnomonis *PQ*
40 sicut latus trianguli *CD,* et regula sicut latus *DE.* Et cum duo anguli

12 simpli *PdPeUa ad minus ras. Xb* simplici *Xn* / extremitati *Xn* / inde *PdPe* ideo *XbUaXn*
15 *mg. Magl. XI.2:* "Primus hic modus fuit Platonis inventum"
17 linee *tr. Ua ante* date / rectos *PdPeXn* rectos angulos *Xb* rectum B *Ua*
18 *mg Pd:* 1[us] modus
20 C: E *Pe*
21 valeant: habeant *Ua* / figurari *tr. Ua post* declarabo
22 utique: itaque *Ua*
23 media *PeXbXn* medie *PdUa*
25 media: medie *Ua* / CB, BE *corr. ex* DB, BE *in PdPeXbXn et* duas sectiones basis CB, BE *in Ua*
28 Restat: Restat iam *Ua*
31 regula *mg. Pd* / Q: P *Ua*
32 P: Q *Ua*
32–33 cum . . . PR *om. Xn*
36 usquoque *?Pd*
37 cum: tamen *Ua*
39 trianguli GC *PdXbXn* trianguli GT *Pe* GC trianguli GCD *Ua*
40 trianguli *om. Ua*

gnomonis *RPS, PST* sint ambo recti, manifestum est illos duos triangulos orthogonos esse statutos, quod fuit propositum. Constat ergo totum propositum fore notum.

Secundus modus: Alius modus [Fig. I.3.3]. Sint *AB, BG* due recte
45 date inequales ad angulum rectum iacentes super *B*. Perfecto autem parallelogrammo rectangulo *BD*, dyameter *AG* protrahatur, per medium secta in *E* educanturque latera *DG, DA* in directum usque *Z* et *H*. Appositaque regula super punctum *B* contingenter tociens moveatur ipsa, quod resecet *DH, DZ*, tali nempe pacto quod et ipsa *B* contingente *EH, EZ*
50 sint equales, de quo circinus prebebit fiduciam. Ducque *ET* perpendicularem super *DG*, quam ipsa dividet per medium, per 26^{am} primi, addita 10^a eiusdem. Quia ergo *DG* per duo equalia divisa est in *T* et ei in longum additur *GZ*, palam est quod id quod fit ex *DZ* in *GZ* cum quadrato *GT* equum est quadrato linee *TZ*, per 6^{am} 2^i. Ergo eodem, scilicet
55 quadrato linee *ET* addito utrobique, erit quod fit ex *DZ* in *GZ* cum quadratis linearum *GT, ET* et inde quadrato *EG*, per penultimam primi, equale quadratis linearum *TZ, TE*, hoc est quadrato *ZE* per eandem. Quod ergo fit ex *DZ* in *GZ* cum quadrato *GE* equum est quadrato linee *EZ*. Similiter demonstrabitur, quod id quod fit ex *DH* in *HA* cum
60 quadrato *EA* est equale quadrato linee *EH*, intellecta perpendiculari ab *E* super latus *DA*. Et quia quadratum linee *EH* equale est quadrato linee *EZ*, cum *EH, EZ* posite sint equales, igitur per conceptionem demptis equalibus quadratis linearum equalium *GE, EA*, sequitur quod [id quod] fit
64 ex *DZ* in *GZ* equum est ei quod fit ex *DH* in *HA*. Cum igitur id quod
54r fit ex extremis ei quod ex mediis equale sit, /sequitur eas quatuor esse proportionales per 15^{am} 6^i. Sicut igitur *DZ* ad *DH* ita *HA* ad *GZ*. Sed et sicut *DZ* ad *DH* ita et *GZ* ad *GB* per 4^{am} 6^i, et *BA* ad *HA* per eandem. Ergo sicut *BA* ad *HA* ita *HA* ad *GZ* et *GZ* ad *GB*. Invente ergo sunt due medie proportionales inter duas datas, quod fuit
70 propositum demostrare.

42 statutos *XbUaXn* statuto eo *PdPe*
47 usque: usque ad *Ua*
49 resecet: referet ?*Pe* / DH: DÇ DF *Pe*
53 additur: addita *Ua*
57 TE:DE *Pe*
57–59 hoc. . . . EZ *om. Xb*
58 GE: ergo *Pe*
59 quod^1 *om. Pe*
60 linee *om. Ua* / E *om. Pe*
61 *post* DA *add. Ua* que perpendicularis sit EX / equale est: equatur *Ua*
62 cum . . . EZ *om. Xb* / conceptionem: communem conceptionem *Ua*
62–63 demptis . . . sequitur *mg. Pd*
63 id quod *Ua, om. PdPeXbXn*
64 DZ . . . ex^2 *mg. Pd*
66 *post* 6^i *add. Ua* videlicet sicut extremum primum ad medium primum ita et medium secundum ad extremum secundum / DH: DZ *Pe*
67 et^1 *om. Ua*
69 proportionales . . . duas: linee proportionales continue scilicet HA GZ inter 2 lineas AB BG *Ua* / fuit: fuerit *Pe*

Tertius modus sequitur et alia figura [Fig. I.3.4] eadem cum precedente [Fig. I.3.3], differens tamen in hoc, quod *HZ* regula movetur circa *B* donec *BH, CZ* fiant equales. Et tunc necessario *EH, EZ* fiunt equales. Et ex similitudine triangulorum orthogonorum, totalis scilicet et duorum 75 partialium, scilicet *DHZ* et *ABH, BGZ*, argue quod sicut *BA* ad *HA*, ita *HA* ad *GZ*, et *GZ* ad *GB* per eadem media que prius deducendo (?).

Johannes de Muris

On the Art of Measuring, Chapter 7, Proposition 16.

WITH ANY TWO UNEQUAL LINES GIVEN, TO FIND TWO MEAN PROPORTIONALS BETWEEN THEM.

This theorem was introduced in Antiquity, for one emperor ordered that a cubical altar be fabricated. After having seen it, and disliking its smallness, he ordered that the altar be doubled. And since the builders did not have [any knowledge of] the art of doubling a cube, the geometers of the time were brought together at the order of the emperor. When they had studied the duplication of the cube for a long time, one of them said that it could be done only by first finding two mean proportionals between two given lines of which one was double the other, because it is proved that the cube of the doubled line is eight times the cube of its half. And since between one and eight there are two proportional means, namely 2 and 4, of which the first is double the lesser extreme, hence it is necessary to seek the same ratio in lines. And this problem has been called in their circle "duplication of a cube."[1]

They were accustomed to advance the solution of this problem "With any two unequal lines, etc.," by various means. The first method [follows; see Fig. I.3.1]:[2] Let *EB* and *BG* be the two unequal lines selected at will and between which, etc. Join them in right angles, projecting each continually and directly as far as you like. Let these [continued] lines be *EBC* and *GBD*, producing four right angles at *B*. Then construct two right triangles, namely, *GCD* (with angle *C* its right angle) and *CDE* (with *D* its right angle); and how they are to be so constructed I shall declare below. Thus it is clear that, since a perpendicular from right angle *C*

---

72 HZ regula *tr. Ua*
73 CZ: EZ *Ua*
75 BGZ *om. Pe* / argue: arguo *Pe*
76 prius: plus *Ua* / deducende *?Pd*

---

[1] See Commentary, lines 3–14.
[2] *Ibid.*, lines 16–42.

stands on the base in triangle GDC, by the [corollary to the] eighth proposition of [Book] VI [of the *Elements*][3] CB is the mean proportional between the two segments of the base, which are GB and BD. In this same way, and by the same [proposition], in triangle CDE, DB is the mean proportional between CB and BE. Therefore, $GB/BC = BC/BD = BD/BE$. Q.E.D.   .

It remains to construct the two above-mentioned right triangles by means of copper gnomon QPR [see Fig. I.3.2], constructed with angle P a right angle by I.45 (? I.11?) [of the *Elements* of Euclid].[4] To the inner side QP afix the rule TS perpendicularly so that TSP is a right angle. Let the rule be moved up and down freely, now towards Q and now towards P, but [always remaining] parallel to side PR of the gnomon, since this is necessary. With this instrument constructed,[5] apply side PR of the gnomon so that it touches point G of the previously given line and right angle P is placed on line EC, anywhere for the moment until it is compelled to remain fixed. With the other side QP of the gnomon cutting line BD, move the rule TS until right angle TSP is applied to line BD and the rule meets point E of the other given line. With this position assumed, side PR of the gnomon will be as side GC of triangle $[GCD]$ and the other side PQ of the gnomon will be as side CD of triangle $[CDE]$, while the rule $[TS]$ will be as side DE. And since the two angles RPS and PST of the gnomon are both right angles, it is evident that the two right triangles have been constructed as was proposed. It is clear, therefore, that the whole proposed [problem] will be known.

A second method follows, [see Fig. I.3.3]. Another method [of finding the means]:[6] Let AB, BG be the two given unequal straight lines meeting at B in a right angle. With the rectangle BD completed, let the diagonal AG be drawn, and the latter is bisected at E. And let sides DG and DA be continued directly to Z and H. And with the rule placed in contact with point B, let it (remaining in contact with B) be moved to cut DH and DZ in such a way that EH and EZ become equal, of which situation a compass will provide assurance. And draw ET perpendicular to DG, which it will bisect, by I.26 (and in addition I.10) [of the *Elements*].[7] Since DG has been bisected in T and line GZ is added to it, it is clear that (1) $DZ \cdot GZ + GT^2 = TZ^2$, by II.6 [of the *Elements*].[8] Then (2) $DZ \cdot GZ + GT^2 + ET^2 = TZ^2 + TE^2$, and (3) $DZ \cdot GZ + GE^2 = EZ^2$, by the penultimate proposition of Bk. I [of the *Elements*].[9] Similarly, (4) $DH \cdot HA + EA^2 = EH^2$, if a perpendicular is thought of as drawn from E to line DA. Since $EH^2 = EZ^2$, EH and EZ being posited as equal, hence by the axiom ["equals subtracted from equals leave equals"], if

[3] *Ibid.*, line 23.

[4] *Ibid.*, line 29.

[5] *Ibid.*, line 33.

[6] *Ibid.*, lines 44–70.

[7] *Ibid.*, lines 51–52.

[8] *Ibid.*, line 54.

[9] For I.46 (=Gr. I.47) of the *Elementa*, see Clagett, *Archimedes*, Vol. 1, p. 78. Cf. the Campanus version of the *Elementa* (Basel, 1546), pp. 37–38.

GE^2 and EA^2 are subtracted [from equations (3) and (4), which are equal], it follows that (5) $DZ \cdot GZ = DH \cdot HA$. Since the product of the extremes is equal to the product of the means, it follows that these four terms are proportionals, by VI.15 (=Gr. VI.16) [of the *Elements*].[10] Hence, (6) $DZ/DH = HA/GZ$. But (7) $DZ/DH = GZ/GB$, by VI.4 [of the *Elements*], and (8) $DZ/DH = BA/HA$. Therefore, [by (6), (7), and (8) together], (9) $BA/HA = HA/GZ = GZ/GB$. Hence the two mean proportionals between the two given lines have been found. Q.E.D.

A third method follows,[11] with another figure [see Fig. I.3.4] the same as the preceding one [see Fig. I.3.3], differing however in this, that the rule HZ is moved about B until BH and CZ become equal. And then necessarily EH and EZ become equal. And from the similitude of right triangles, i.e., the whole and the two partial triangles: DHZ and ABH, BGZ, argue, by the same deductions produced before [in the second method], that $BA/HA = HA/GZ = GZ/GB$.

Commentary

3–14 "Istud. . . . est." In general, this passage reflects the introductory lines of the so-called Letter of Eratosthenes to King Ptolemy, as given in the Moerbeke translation of Eutocius' commentary on Book II, Prop. 1, of Archimedes' *On the Sphere and the Cylinder* (see Vol. 2, 38rG), although apparently Johannes deliberately omitted the proper names of Minus and Glaucus. As in the account of Eutocius, he states that, if the side of the first cube is doubled, a cube eight times that of the first cube is produced. But he then adds, on his own, that between 1 and 8 there are two mean proportionals, namely 2 and 4, and so if we consider all of these numbers as cubes and seek to find a cube that is not eight times the original cube but only twice, we must take the linear cube roots of these numbers, and thus we would have $\sqrt[3]{8}/\sqrt[3]{4} = \sqrt[3]{4}/\sqrt[3]{2} = \sqrt[3]{2}/1$, or, at least, this seems to me to be his reasoning.

16–42 "Sint. . . . propositum[1]." This is an elaborated paraphrase of the "Platonic" method given by Eutocius (see Vol. 2, 36vC–G). Notice that the author has first given the figure as constructed. It is only afterwards that he shows its construction by means of the instrument. But in Eutocius' text, the construction is first performed, from which it follows that the problem is solved. I think we can be certain that John felt his presentation to be clearer than that of the Moerbeke text.

23 "8[am] sexti" Actually, it is the corollary to VI.8 that is intended here. It runs in the Campanus version of the *Elementa* (Basel, 1546), p. 145: "Unde etiam manifestum est, quia in omni triangulo rectangulo, si ab eius angulo recto ad basin perpendicularis

[10] See Commentary, line 66.
[11] *Ibid.*, lines 71–76.

ducatur, erit ipsa perpendicularis inter duas sectiones ipsius basis proportionalis: itemque utrumque latus inter totam basin atque sibi coterminalem basis portionem.''

29 "45^{am} (?) primi" The reference to I.45 (=Gr. I.46) of the *Elementa* seems to be an error since it involves the construction of a square (*Elementa*, Basel, 1546, p. 47). I would suppose that I.11 is the proper citation (*ibid.*, p. 14): "Data linea recta a puncto in ea signato perpendicularem extrahere. . . .''

33 "Hoc . . . fabricato," Notice that John's instrument differs slightly from that described in the Moerbeke text, as it has only one grooved arm instead of two. Without a second arm with a groove (*TL* in the Moerbeke figure: Fig. Es. 20), John's instrument would seem to be unsatisfactory for keeping *ST* parallel to *PR* while still being free to move up and down in the single grooved arm *QP* (see Fig. I.3.2).

44-70 "Sint. . . . demostrare." This is a free paraphrase of the solution assigned to Hero by Eutocius (see Vol. 2, 36vG-M).

51-52 "per^2 . . . eiusdem." For I.10, see the *Elementa* (Basel, 1546), p. 14: "Proposita recta linea, eam per aequalia dividere." (The proof is based on the construction of an equilateral triangle on a given line but will hold also for an isosceles triangle.) In citing I.26, John is concluding that by dropping the perpendicular *ET*, $\triangle DET$ is made congruent to $\triangle ETG$, and hence that $DT = TG$. For I.26, see *ibid.*, pp. 22-23: "Omnium duorum triangulorum, quorum duo anguli unius duobus angulis alterius et uterque se respicienti aequales fuerint, latus quoque unius lateri alterius aequale, fueritque latus illud aut inter duos angulos aequales, aut uni eorum oppositum, erunt quoque duo unius reliqua latera duobus reliquis alterius trianguli lateribus, unumquodque se respicienti aequalia, angulusque reliquus unius angulo reliquo alterius aequalis.''

54 "per . . . 2^i" For II.6, see the *Elementa* (Basel, 1546), p. 44: "Si recta linea in duo aequalia dividatur, alia vero ei linea in longum addatur, quod ex ductu totius iam compositae, in eam quae iam adiecta est, cum eo quod ex ductu dimidiae in seipsam, aequum est ei quadrato quod ab ea quae constat ex adiecta et dimidia in seipsam ducta describitur.''

66 "per 15^{am} 6^i" This is a reference to the second half of VI.15 (=Gr. VI.16), which runs in the Campanus version of the *Elementa* (Basel, 1546), pp. 149-50: ". . . . Si vero quod sub prima et ultima continetur aequum fuerit ei quod duabus reliquis continetur rectangulum, quatuor lineas proportionales esse convenit.''

71-76 "Tertius. . . . deducendo (?)." These few lines were suggested by the third paragraph of the solution assigned by Eutocius to Philo of Byzantium (see Vol. 2, 36vR-T), where Eutocius relates Philo's solution to that of Hero.

CHAPTER 4

Johannes de Muris' Version of Proposition III of Archimedes' *On the Measurement of the Circle*

In Chapter 6 of the *De arte mensurandi*, Johannes de Muris begins a group of problems on the measurement of the circle with the following statement:[1]

To measure the area of a given circle, following a previous estimation of the ratio of the diameter of a circle to its circumference.

This ratio perhaps no one yet has truly reduced to number, although Archimedes, the most fervent searcher among the geometers, thought he had demonstrated the ratio of a straight line to a curve by means of spirals. I propose to explain his intention in this regard and concerning the quadrature of the circle in the eighth chapter of this work. Be content [for now] with the [approximate] concord between the prior [terms], which is that three times the diameter of the circle

[1] Paris, BN lat. 7380, 42r: "1ª. Circuli dati planiciem mensurare, iuxta dudum estimatum dyametri ad periferiam circuli proportionem, quam adhuc forte nemo veraciter numeravit, licet Archimenides geometrarum ferventissimus* perscrutator recti ad curvum proportionem per elicas putaverit demonstrasse, cuius intentionem de hoc et circuli quadratura in 8° capitulo huius operis explicare propono. In priorum concordantia** sis contentus, que est quod dyameter circuli triplata cum sui parte 7ª periferie coequatur; a periferiaque dempta 22ª parte sui 3ª remanentis ad equalitatem dyametri reducta est. Cuius concordantie** in sequentibus (*mg. add.* in principio 8ⁱ capituli) modum dicam, supposito etiam quod quis forte contentaretur, si circulus super planum continue et regulariter moveretur usquequo circuli revolutio compleretur, linea in plano descripta, si qua fuerit, equalis est linee circulari. Hiis autem positis usquequo equalitatem curvi ad rectum plenius demonstremus, facile est circulum mensurare. Communis modus est iste: Semidyametrum, duc in semiperiferiam; aut dyametrum in semicircumferentiam, medietate producti retenta; aut dyametrum in semi-periferiam aut periferiam in semidyametrum, producto mediato; aut totam dyametrum in totam periferiam, assumpta quarta producti; aut quadratum dyametri sume 11ᵉˢ, et producti sumpta 14ª; aut a quadrato dyametri deme eius 7ᵃᵐ et 7ᵐᵉ mediatatem; quod omnibus hiis modis provenit aream circuli demonstrabit. Hii autem modi non nisi per magisterium numerorum differunt, quibus progenitores hactenus contenti sunt. Et hec deductiones supponunt quod ex ductu semidyametri in semiperiferiam quoddam parallelogrammum rectangulum generetur equalitatem circuli complectens, de quo videbitur in sequenti." [*BN lat. 7381, 89r, has *fluentissimus*. **BN lat. 7380 has *experientia* (*experientie* in the second usage) in the text and *concordantia* (*concordantie* in the second usage) in the margin; all of the other manuscripts have *concordantia* (and *concordantie*). There were no other helpful variant readings for this passage in the other manuscripts: Vat. lat. 9410, 38v; Vat. Ottob. lat. 1423, 52r–v; Utrecht, Bibl. Univ. 725, 58v.]

31

with the addition of a seventh part of it is equal to the circumference [i.e., $d \cdot 3\frac{1}{7} = c$], and that, if from the circumference $\frac{1}{22}$ part is taken, one-third of its remainder is equal to the diameter (i.e., $[c - (c/22)] \cdot \frac{1}{3} = d$). I shall speak on the method of [determining] this concord in the following (i.e., in the beginning of the eighth chapter), it having been supposed that perhaps one ought to be satisfied that, if a circle were continuously and regularly moved on a plane until it completes a revolution, the line described in the plane (if there is such a line) is equal to a circular line. Then with these things assumed (until we demonstrate more fully the equality of a curve to a straight line), it is easy to measure the circle. The common method is this: Multiply (1) the radius by the semicircumference, or (2) the diameter by the semicircumference, keeping half of the product, or (3) either the diameter by the semiperiphery or the circumference by the radius with half the product [retained], or (4) the whole diameter by the whole circumference, with one-fourth of the product taken; or (5) take 11 times the square of the diameter and then assume $\frac{1}{14}$ of the product, or (6) subtract one-seventh of the square of the diameter from the square of the diameter and [then subtract] one-half of the one-seventh [i.e., $d^2 - (d^2/7) - (d^2/14) = A$]. The result produced by all of these methods will demonstrate the area of the circle. These methods, with which our ancestors have until now been satisfied, differ only in the dominion of numbers. And these deductions assume that from the product of a radius and a semicircumference a rectangle is generated which is equal to the circle. This will be evident in what follows.

This passage seems to serve as an advance announcement of Johannes' intention to treat the ratio of the circumference to the diameter in Chapter 8 and certainly of his plan to include the hybrid tract *On the Quadrature of the Circle* (or its substance) at that point. The hybrid tract will be treated in the next chapter, where it will be shown that John did indeed insert the tract in Chapter 8. The objective of this present chapter is to present Johannes' version of Archimedes' determination of the bounds between which π falls. All of the propositions regarding circular measurement in the remainder of Chapter 6 (i.e., prior to the determination of the bounds of the ratio as found in Chapter 8) will simply assume the equality of $d \cdot 3\frac{1}{7} = c$, or, as we would say in modern parlance, that $\pi = 3\frac{1}{7}$. They also assume that it is possible to have a straight line equal to a circular line. For temporary justification until he later can prove the equality of a straight line to a circular line, Johannes cites the case of a circle rolling on a plane through one rotation and thereby tracing on the plane a straight line equal to the circumference of the circle. This is similar to the justification found among the postulates of the Corpus Christi Version of the *De mensura circuli* published in Volume 1 of my study (pages 166–67, 170–71). Furthermore, Johannes also points out in this introductory passage that all of his formulations for the measure of the circle assume that a rectangle is formed from the radius and the semicircumference of a circle and that rectangle equals the area of the circle, which is of course not proved until Chapter 8 where the hybrid tract on quadrature is inserted.

Now let us pass on to Johannes' first proposition in Chapter 8 of the

De arte mensurandi. It will be immediately evident from the text of this proposition given below that it is but a close paraphrase of Proposition III of Archimedes' *On the Measurement of the Circle*, although Archimedes' name is not mentioned in connection with this proposition. The first question that comes to mind on examining this proposition is that of whether it was constructed on the basis of Gerard of Cremona's translation from the Arabic, which was very popular and was the object of several paraphrases (see Vol. 1, Chaps. 2, 3, 5), or on the basis of the translation of William of Moerbeke from the Greek (see Vol. 2, 22vO–23rI). There is no conclusive evidence for the determination of this question, but I am inclined to believe that both translations served for Johannes' version. In support of his dependence on the Moerbeke translation, we can note that in the various bisections of the angles involved in the proof of the proposition, Johannes uses the phrase: "Secetur . . . in duo equa" (see lines 18, 28, 37, 44 etc.) which is also used in the Moerbeke translation (Vol. 2, 22vQ), while Gerard's translation and the versions based on it use the expression: "Dividam . . . in duo media" (Volume 1, page 48, lines 90, 97, 100–101 etc.; page 112, lines 13–14; page 116, line 72; etc.). (Similarly, the incomplete translation of Plato of Tivoli from the Arabic uses the phrase: "angulum . . . in duo equa . . . dividemus" or a like phrase [*ibid.*, page 24, lines 82–83; page 26, lines 90–91; etc.], and the translation of the pertinent proposition from the *Verba filiorum* of the Banū Mūsā from the Arabic uses: "dividam angulum . . . in duo media." [*ibid.*, page 266, lines 31, 32–33, etc.].) Also, Johannes uses the phrase *multo magis* to render the idea "by an [even] greater amount." He does this in the course of completing the following argument: since the circumference is less or more than the circumscribed or inscribed polygon of 96 sides, its ratio to the diameter is "by an [even] greater amount" less or more than the ratio of the perimeter of the circumscribed or inscribed polygon to the diameter (see below, lines 69, 133). This phrase *multo magis* Moerbeke also uses (see Vol. 2, 23rD), while the phrase is missing from the Gerard translation, appearing only in the somewhat later Florentine Version (see Volume 1, page 122, line 165; page 132, lines 350–51). Further, the omission of the number 265 from the beginning of the proof in the Gerard translation while it is present in the texts of both Moerbeke (see Vol. 2, 22vP) and Johannes (see below, line 17) may be adduced as further evidence of the use of Moerbeke's text. However, I have recently found the additional phrase including that number in a copy of the Gerard text (Vat. lat. 4275, 82v, c. 2; cf. Appendix I, Sect. 2), although to be sure this is a quite late copy produced after the time of Johannes de Muris. These various points, then, are mere hints that Johannes de Muris had his eye on the Moerbeke translation of *On the Measurement of the Circle*. This would not be surprising in view of the use he made of Moerbeke's translations in other parts of his work. But Johannes probably also made use of one or another version of *On the Measurement of the Circle* from the Arabic, since the numbers

598⅛, 3013½ ¼, 5924½ ¼, 1838⁹/₁₁, 66, 1009⅙, 6336, and 2017¼ appear in Gerard's translation correctly as they do in Johannes' paraphrase, but they appeared in an incorrect form in Moerbeke's translation before being corrected by Coner in the sixteenth century (see Vol. 2, 22vQ*var*, 23rG*var*, 23rH*var*, and 23rI*var*).

The next point of interest in regard to the proposition being considered is that Johannes altered its enunciation while keeping the same Archimedean proof. John specifies the bounds within which the ratio of circumference to diameter falls as 3⅐ and 3⅛. In short, he substitutes 3⅛ for 3¹⁰/₇₁ as the lower bound. He does this perhaps because his primary interest is mensuration and he might have conceived of it being easier to lay off with a ruler a measure falling between 3⅐ and 3⅛ times the diameter than a measure falling between 3⅐ and 3¹⁰/₇₁. Or he might simply have wanted to achieve the same order of fractions for the two bounds. At the conclusion of that point Johannes shows his skill as a computer, for, in showing that 3¹⁰/₇₁ is greater than 3⅛, he notes the equality of ¹⁰/₇₁ with the fractional sum: ⅛ + ¹/₆₄ + ¹/₇₁ · ¹/₆₄. And indeed if one makes decimal computations of these, he finds ¹⁰/₇₁ = 0.140845 and ⅛ + ¹/₆₄ + ¹/₇₁ · ¹/₆₄ = 0.140845. In concluding his proof, Johannes remarks that one may make other numerical determinations by, for example, making further bisections of the angle, but that whatever values would be found for these bounds, those new values would themselves be included between the values 3⅐ and 3⅛.[2] These values of 3⅐ and 3⅛ were also given as the bounds of π by Giovanni Fontana (see below, Part II, Chap. 4, Sect. II, note 7), Jacobus Cremonensis in his translation of *On the Measurement of the Circle* (see Appendix IV, Sect. 1), Piero della Francesca (see below, Part III, Chap. 2, Sect. 3, note 33), Luca Pacioli (see below, Part III, Chap. 2, Sect. IV, note 42), and Oronce Finé (see below, Part III, Chap. 6, Sect. IV, note 52). The last of these probably took these bounds from Johannes de Muris, since he owned Johannes de Muris' autograph copy of the *De arte mensurandi*.[3] We should also note that Johannes de Muris, in his autograph copy, at the bottom of 58r, adds the following: "3¹⁴¹/₉₉₄. Ista est media inter extrema per equid[istantiam]. [3 et] ⅛ · ⅛ · ¹/₁₃ · ¹/₅₀ etc. simplices, hoc est, 3 gradus, 8 minutie, 30 secunde, 6 tertie, 39 quarte, ita ponitur in almagesto." Now 3¹⁴¹/₉₉₄ equals approximately 3.1418511 (and indeed this is not too far from the arithmetic mean between 3⅐

[2] Following this first proposition with its determination of the bounds of the ratio of the circumference to the diameter, the author includes three other propositions, two of which involve the calculation determined in the first proposition. Since these are calculation exercises and do not give us any further knowledge of the spread of the Moerbeke translations, I shall content myself here with merely noting the enunciations (Paris, BN lat. 7380, 66r): "2. Data circuli dyametro circumferentiam perscrutari. . . . 3. Data circuli circumferentia dyametrum rimaii."

[3] On the last folio of BN lat. 7380, 83v, is the indication of Finé's ownership: "Nunc Orontii finei Delphinatis ex permutatione alterius libri cum Ioanne de castro doctore et theologo bursario collegii magistri gervasii christiani." This indicates he got this book by an exchange with Joannes de Castro.

≈ 3.1428571 and $3^{10}/_{71}$ = 3.1408500).[4] Then using a curious medieval system of representing fractions, Johannes restates the fraction in terms of the sum of simple fractions (i.e. fractions with numerator 1). We can rewrite his sum in the following, unambiguous way: $^1/_8 + (^1/_8 \cdot ^1/_8) + (^1/_{64} \cdot ^1/_{13})$ $+ (^1/_{832} \cdot ^1/_{50})$. If we reduce this sum to decimal fractions, the value of the mean becomes approximately 3.1418509, which is equivalent in the first six decimal places to the value of $3^{141}/_{994}$ expressed in decimal numbers above. It is also evident that Johannes in this note gives a value in sexagesimal numbers, which he claims is found in the *Almagest*: 3; 8, 30, 6, 39 (≈3.141697). But Ptolemy in the *Almagest* (VI, 7) gives only 3; 8, 30, which he says is close to the mean between the Archimedean bounds (see below, Part III, Chap. 2, Sect. II, note 39). Ptolemy's value reduces to 3.14166 . . . , in decimal form. Hence, Johannes' sexagesimal value is apparently his own extension of Ptolemy's value. I hardly need remind the reader that Archimedes' determination of the bounds between which π must lie gives no justification for using the arithmetic mean between the bounds as the value of π. This practice of using the arithmetic mean seems to have arisen among medieval authors from Ptolemy's remark and from the procedure used by Leonardo Fibonacci (see Appendix I, Sect. 3 B[3]).

My text is based on the same manuscripts given in the previous chapter and thus primarily on *Pd* (and its faithful copy *Pe*). And so I have omitted in my variant readings many of the faulty readings of *Xb, Ua,* and *Xn* where they diverge erroneously from *PdPe*. As I have noted previously, the usually good manuscript *Xb* is quite careless in its omissions of phrases and sentences in this section. Note the curious error in all manuscripts where the number 4673½ is written as 4763½. This seems to have been a slip committed by Johannes de Muris when he composed his version with an eye on the Archimedean text. In the first part of the proof the letter *M* is used to specify two different points. For its first use I have altered it to *M'*. In my translation, I have made one move for economy's sake: after rendering the phrase *per penultimam primi* the first time it appears as "by the penultimate [proposition] of [Book] I [i.e., I.46 (=Gr. I.47) of the *Elements*]," I have shortened the translation merely to "by I.46 (=Gr. I.47)." Again I have included Johannes de Muris' marginal additions in *Pd* in the text without brackets, although I have of course indicated which additions these are in the variant readings.

Sigla

Pd = Paris, BN lat. 7380, 56v–58r, middle of 14c.
Pe = Paris, BN lat. 7381, 116r–119v, 15c.
Xb = Vatican, Vat. lat. 9410, 52v–54r, 15c.
Ua = Utrecht, Bibl. Univ. 725, 71v–72v, 15c.
Xn = Vatican, Ottob. lat. 1423, 67v–69v, late 15c or early 16c.

[4] It is quite clear how Johannes arrived at the figure $3^{141}/_{994}$. If we convert $3^1/_7$ and $3^{10}/_{71}$ to improper fractions of the same denomination we get $^{1562}/_{497}$ and $^{1561}/_{497}$; their mean is thus $^{3123}/_{994}$ or $3^{141}/_{994}$. Cf. below, Part III, Chap. 2, Sect. II, n. 15.

Johannis de Muris De arte mensurandi
Chapter 8, Proposition 1

Johannis de Muris
De arte mensurandi, Cap. 8^m, Propositio 1^a

/1^a. PROPORTIONEM CIRCUMFERENTIE CIRCULI AD DYA-METRUM MINOREM ESSE TRIPLA SESQUISEPTIMA ET MAI-OREM TRIPLA SESQUIOCTAVA CONVENIT DEMONSTRARE.

Describatur circulus super centrum *E*, cuius semidyameter *EG*,
5 circulum contingens *ZG* [Fig. I.4.1]. Arcus autem lateris hexagoni equianguli circulo inscripti per medium dividatur, et per punctum divisionis transeat *EZ*. Erit ergo angulus *E* trianguli *ZEG* tertia recti per 1^{am} 2^i huius. Educatur ergo *ZG* usque *M'*. Sitque *GM'* equalis *ZG*. Dico quod *ZE* dupla est *ZG*. Angulus enim *GEM'* est tertia recti quia equalis
10 angulo *ZEG* per 4^{am} primi. Ergo cum angulus *EGM'* sit rectus per 15^{am} 3^{ii}, erit angulus *M'* due tertie recti. Similiterque angulus *Z* due tertie recti per idem medium, angulus et *E* totalis due tertie recti. Igitur cum 3 anguli *Z, E, M'* sint equales, latera erunt equalia. Quare triangulus *ZEM'* est equilaterus. Et quoniam *ZM'* divisa est per medium in *G* ex yposthesi, *EZ*
15 dupla est ad *ZG*, quod fuit probandum. Si ergo sponte ponamus *EZ* 306, erit necessario *ZG* 153. Et cum triangulus *EGZ* sit orthogonus, erit per penultimam primi latus *EG* 265 et pars modica.

Prima sectio [anguli.] Secetur igitur angulus *E* trianguli *ZEG* in duo equa per 9^{am} primi per lineam *EH*. Erit eadem proportio *ZE* ad *EG* que est *ZH*
20 ad *HG* per 3^{am} 6^i. Ergo et coniunctim que est proportio *ZE, EG* simul ad *EG* ea est *ZG* ad *HG*. Igitur et permutatim que est proportio *ZE, EG* simul ad *ZG* ea est *EG* ad *HG*. Nunc autem *ZE, EG* simul sunt plus quam 571, quia *ZE* posita est 306 et *EG* inventa est 265 et plus modico. Sed *ZG* est 153. Ergo proportio *ZE, EG* simul ad *ZG* est ea que est 571 ad 153 et adhuc
25 maior licet modico per 8^{am} 5^i. Ergo et similiter proportio *EG* ad *HG* est maior quam 571 ad 153. Quare posita *EG* 571 et *HG* 153 erit per penultimam primi latus *EH* 591 et ⅛ et pars modica.

---

1 1^a *Pd* Capitulum 8 prima principalis propositio huius 8^i *Pe* Octavi capituli propositio
prima *Ua*
5 contingens: continens *PeXn*
8 Educatur. . . . Dico *om. Xb*
11–12 Similiterque . . . recti *om. Xb*
13 triangulus: angulus *Pe*
15–16 quod. . . . *ZG om. Xb*
18 anguli *Pe om. PdXb, et UaXn om.* Prima . . . anguli
21–22 Igitur . . . *HG om. XbXn*
21 *ZE: ZG Pe*
24–26 et. . . . 153^1 *om. Ua*
26 posito *Pe*

Secunda sectio anguli. Secetur iterum angulus *GEH* in duo equa sicut prius per lineam *ET*. Erit eadem proportio *HE* ad *EG* que est *HT* ad *TG*
30 per eandem 6[i]. Ergo et coniunctim eadem est *HE, EG* ad *EG* que est *HG* ad *TG*. Igitur et permutatim eadem est *HE, EG* ad *HG* que est *EG* ad *TG*. Nunc autem *HE, EG* sunt plus quam 1162⅛ quia *EG* posita est 571 et *HE* inventa est 591⅛ et plus modico. Sed *HG* est 153. Ergo proportio *HE, EG* ad *HG* est maior ea que est 1162⅛ ad 153. Ergo et similiter proportio *EG* ad
35 *TG* est maior ea que est 1162⅛ ad 153. Quare posita *EG* 1162⅛ et *TG* 153, erit per penultimam primi latus *ET* 1172 et ⅛ et pars modica.

Tertia sectio anguli. Secetur rursum angulus *GET* in duo equa sicut prius per *EK*. Erit eadem proportio *ET* ad *EG* que est *TK* ad *KG* per eandem 6[i]. Ergo et coniunctim et permutatim eadem est *ET, EG* ad *TG* que est *EG* ad
40 *KG*. Nunc autem *ET, EG* sunt plus quam 2334 et ¼ et *TG* posita 153. Ergo proportio *ET, EG* ad *EG* est maior quam 2334¼ ad 153. Ergo et similiter *EG* ad *KG* maior est quam 2334¼ ad 153. Quare posita *EG* 2334 et ¼ et *KG* 153, per penultimam primi erit latus *EK* 2339¼ et pars modica.

Quarta sectio anguli. Secetur denuo angulus *KEG* in duo equa per *EL*.
45 Erit *KE* ad *EG* sicut *KL* ad *LG*. Ergo coniunctim et permutatim eadem est proportio *KE, EG* ad *KG* que est *EG* ad *LG*. Nunc autem *KE, EG* sunt plus quam 4763½ (*!* 4673½) et *KG* est 153. Ergo proportio *KE, EG* ad *KG* maior est quam 4763½ (*!* 4673½) ad 153. Ergo et similiter *EG* ad *LG* maior est quam 4763½ (*!* 4673½) ad 153. Volo dicere tanta est et amplius. Cum
50 igitur dudum angulus *ZEG* positus fuit tertia recti, erit ipse 12[a] pars 4 rectorum. Eius ergo medietas, que est angulus *HEG*, est 24[a] pars; medietasque huius, que est *TEG*, est 48[a]; ac eius dimidium, quod est *KEG*,
57r est 96[a] pars, / eius medietas, que est angulus *LEG*, 192[a] pars 4 rectorum. Sit ergo *GM* modo equalis *LG* in directum; erit angulus *GEM* equalis angulo
55 *GEL* per 4[am] primi. Ergo angulus totalis *LEM* est 96[a] pars 4 rectorum. Quare et linea *LM* est latus poligonii equilateri circulo circumscripti habentis 96 latera. Quoniam igitur demonstratum est quod proportio *EG* ad *LG* est maior ea que est 4763 (*!* 4673) et ½ ad 153, et ipsius *EG* dupla est *AG* quia est dyameter, ipsiusque *LG* dupla est *LM*, item eadem proportio,
60 scilicet proportio *AG* ad *LM*, est maior quam 4763½ (*!* 4673½) ad 153. Igitur e converso proportio *LM* ad *AG* est minor quam 153 ad 4763½ (*!* 4673½). Ergo si numerus *LM*, qui est 153, 96[es] sumatur, exibit quantitas perimetri totius poligonii, que erit 14688. Igitur proportio perimetri poligonii ad *AG* dyametrum minor est proportione quam habet 14688 ad
65 4763½ (*!* 4673½). Continet autem maior numerus minorem tribus vicibus

30 EG[2]: HG *Pe*
32 1162⅛: 2162⅛ *Xb hic et ubique*
35 153[2]: 152 *Pe*
36 ET: EG *Pe*
43 153 *mg. Pd*
46 KG *corr. ex* LG
51 HEG *Ua* HET *PdPeXbXn*
56 conscripti *Pe*
61,62 152 *Pe*

insuper et 667½, que sunt minora 7ᵃ parte minoris. Igitur perimeter poligonii continet dyametrum circuli tribus vicibus et insuper aliquas partes dyametri que sunt minores 7ᵃ parte eiusdem. Et quoniam periferia circuli minor est perimetro poligonii circumscripti, multo magis proportio
70 periferie ad suam dyametrum est minor proportione tripla sesquiseptima, quod fuit propositum in prima parte theoreumatis introducti.

57v   /Describatur ergo circulus *ABG* supra centrum *E* [Fig. I.4.2.], sitque *GB* latus hexagoni quod est equale semidyametro. Iungatur autem *AB* et intelligatur *EB* iuncta. Erit triangulus *EBG* equilaterus. Ergo quilibet
75 angulorum eius est due tertie recti per 32ᵃᵐ primi. Igitur cum angulus *GEB* sit extrinsecus, erunt duo anguli *BAE*, *ABE* intrinseci due tertie recti. Sed cum illi sint equales per 5ᵃᵐ primi, erit angulus *A* tertia recti. Angulus autem *ABG* super arcum in semicirculo consistens rectus est per 30ᵃᵐ 3ⁱⁱ. Ergo angulus reliquus *AGB* est due tertie recti. Si autem intelligatur *GB* ducta in
80 directum usque *D*, sitque *BD* equalis *BG*, iuncta quoque *AD*, erit formatus triangulus *ADG* equilaterus. Erit ergo *AG* dupla *BG*. Aut aliter: quia *AG* est dyameter et *BG* latus hexagoni, erit necessario *AG* dupla ipsius *BG*. Ergo si sponte ponamus *AG* 1560, erit *BG* 780. Quare per penultimam primi, cum triangulus *ABG* sit orthogonus, erit latus *AB* 1531 (*!* 1351) fere
85 quia deest pars modica.

Prima sectio anguli. Secetur igitur angulus *BAG* in duo equa per 9ᵃᵐ primi, ducta linea *AH*, iunctaque *HG*. Statuti sunt duo trianguli *AHG* et *HZG* equianguli; quod patet, angulus enim *HGZ* equalis est angulo *BAH* per 20ᵃᵐ 3ⁱⁱ et per consequens angulo *HAG*, cum divisus sit per medium
90 angulus *BAG*; angulus autem *AHG*, qui rectus est, communis est utrique [tri]angulo, ergo et tertius equalis tertio; sunt ergo equianguli. Que igitur est proportio *AH* ad *HG* ea est *GH* ad *HZ* et *AG* ad *GZ* per 4ᵃᵐ 6ⁱ. Et quia angulus *BAG* sectus est per medium erit per 3ᵃᵐ 6ⁱ eadem proportio *BA* ad *AG* que est *BZ* ad *ZG*. Ergo coniunctim eadem est *BA*, *AG* ad *AG* que est
95 *BG* ad *ZG*. Igitur et permutatim eadem est *BA*, *AG* ad *BG* que est *AG* ad *ZG*. Nunc autem *BA*, *AG* simul iuncte sunt minus quam 2911, quia *BA* minus est quam 1351 ex modico et *AG* posita est 1560. Sed *BG* est 780. Ergo minor est proportio *BA*, *AG* ad *BG* quam 2911 ad 780. Ergo et similiter minor est proportio *AG* ad *GZ* quam 2911 ad 780. Sed proportio
100 *AG* ad *ZG* est ea que est *AH* ad *HG*, ut visum est nuper. Ergo et proportio *AH* ad *HG* minor est quam 2911 ad 780. Quare posita *AH* 2911, *HG* vero 780, erit per penultimam primi latus *AG* 3013 et ¾ minus parte modica.

66 minoris *corr. Pd ex* dyametri
71 *post* introducti *add. Pe* In hac pagina debet figurari circulus magnus *et tunc magnam lacunam habet*
78 est *om. Pe*
80 erit *PdXbUa* esset *PeXn*
91 triangulo *Ua* angulo *PdPeXbXn*
98–99 Ergo . . . 780 *om. Xb*
98,99,101 2911: 2921 *Xb*
101 AH²: AG *Pe*

Secunda sectio anguli. Secetur iterum angulus HAG in duo equa per AT. Statuti sunt duo trianguli equianguli sicut prius. Ergo coniunctim et
105 permutatim erit eadem proportio deducta sicut ante. Sunt autem AH, HG simul minus quam 5924 et ¾, HG vero est 780. Igitur minor est proportio AH, AG ad HG quam habeant numeri supradicti, et per consequens minor est proportio AT ad TG quam inter numeros antedictos. Quare posita AT 5924¾, TG vero 780, erit per penultimam primi AG inquirenda sicut prius.
110 Sed quia numeri exeuntes non sunt in sua proportione primi, igitur sume primos per 34^{am} 7^{mi}, qui sunt 1823 pro linea AT et 240 pro TG, et pro AG per penultimam primi 1838^9/$_{11}$ minus parte modica.

Tertia sectio anguli. Secetur rursum angulus TAG in duo equa per AK. Et facta deductione sicut prius erit proportio AK ad KG minor quam
115 3661^9/$_{11}$ ad 240. Quare posita AK 3661^9/$_{11}$ et KG 240, erit linea AG inquirenda sicut prius. Sed numeri non erunt primi eiusdem proportionis. Igitur sume primos, qui sunt 1007 et 66, per 34^{am} 7^{mi}. Quare posita AK 1007 et KG 66, erit per penultimam primi AG 1009^1/$_6$ minus parte modica.

Quarta sectio anguli. Secetur denuo angulus KAG in duo equa per AL et
120 eadem deductione facta velud ante erit inventa proportio KA, AG simul ad KG minor quam 2016^1/$_6$ ad 66. Ergo et proportio AL ad LG minor est quam inter numeros supradictos. Quare posita AL 2016^1/$_6$ et LG 66, erit per penultimam primi AG 2017¼ minus parte modica. Est ergo proportio AG ad GL minor quam 2017¼ ad 66. Igitur e converso per 2^{am} partem 8^e 5^i
125 maior est proportio GL ad AG quam 66 ad 2017¼. Et quoniam GB periferia
58r / est 6^a pars circumferentie circuli divisa quater per medium, erit periferia LG 96^a pars circumferentie. Igitur LG recta est latus poligonii equilateri circulo inscripti 96 latera continentis. Quare sumpta LG 96^{es}, que est 66, exibit perimeter totius poligonii 6336, dyameter autem AG est 2017¼
130 minus parte modica. Ergo proportio perimetri poligonii ad dyametrum circuli est maior quam 6336 ad 2017¼ per 8^{am} 5^i. Continet autem maior numerus minorem tribus vicibus et insuper 284 et ¼, que sunt minora ^{10}/$_{71}$^{mis} minoris. Multo magis ergo et periferia circuli, cum sit maior perimetro poligonii sicut circumscriptum suo inscripto, continet dyametrum tribus
135 vicibus et insuper plus quam ^{10}/$_{71}$ eiusdem. Sunt autem ^{10}/$_{71}$ in simplicibus ⅛ et 8^e 8^a et huius ^{1}/$_{71}$. Quare proportio circumferentie ad suam dyametrum est maior tripla sesquioctava, quod fuit propositum in secunda parte theoreumatis preassumpti. Sic ergo patet totum propositum.

Nec ignores quod et sub aliis numeris minoribus aut extensis ac sub alia
140 divisione vel sectionibus anguli in circulo assumpti posset eadem proportio circumferentie ad dyametrum investigari. Tamen qualitercunque operetur illa proportio inter 7^{am} et 8^{am} triplata dyametro necessario inclusa est.

103 anguli *om. Pe*
107–108 AH . . . proportio *om. Xn*
112 1838 *om. Xb*
113,119 anguli *om. Pe*
117–18 per. . . . 66: pro AK et KG *Ua*
124 per . . . 5^i *mg. PdPe om. XbUaXn*
142 *post* est *add. Pe* Hic debet figurari magnus semiciruclus

Johannes de Muris

On The Art of Measuring, Chapter 8, Proposition 1

I. IT IS NECESSARY TO DEMONSTRATE THAT THE RATIO OF
THE CIRCUMFERENCE OF A CIRCLE TO ITS DIAMETER IS LESS
THAN 3$\frac{1}{7}$ AND GREATER THAN 3$\frac{1}{8}$.

Let a circle be described about center *E*, with radius *EG* and *ZG* tangent
to the circle (see Fig. I.4.1). Let the arc of a side of a regular hexagon
inscribed in the circle be bisected. Let *EZ* pass through the point of division. Therefore, ∠*E* of △*ZEG* is ⅓ of a right angle, by II.1 of this [work, the
De arte mensurandi].[1] Therefore, let *ZG* be extended to *M'*, with *GM'*
equal to *ZG*. I say that *ZE* = 2 *ZG*. For ∠*GEM'* is ⅓ of a right angle
because it is equal to ∠*ZEG*, by I.4 [of the *Elements*][2]; therefore, since
∠*EGM'* is a right angle by III.15 (=Gr. III.16),[3] ∠*M'* is ⅔ of a right angle.
Similarly, ∠*Z* is ⅔ of a right angle by the same means, and the total angle at
E is ⅔ of a right angle. Therefore, since the three angles *Z*, *E*, *M'* are equal,
the sides are equal and hence △*ZEM'* is equilateral. And since *ZM'* is
bisected in *G* by hypothesis, *EZ* = 2 *ZG*, which was to be proved. If,
therefore, we freely place *EZ* to be 306, *ZG* will necessarily be 153. And
since △*EGZ* is a right triangle, side *EG* will necessarily be 265 plus a small
part, by the penultimate [proposition] of [Book] I [i.e., by I.46 (=Gr. I.47)
of the *Elements*].[4]

The First Division of the Angle: Therefore, let ∠*E* of △*ZEG* be bisected
by line *EH*, by means of I.9.[5] Therefore, *ZE/EG* = *ZH/HG*, by VI.3.[6]
Therefore, by composition, (*ZE* + *EG*)/*EG* = *ZG/HG*. Hence, alternately, (*ZE* + *EG*)/*ZG* = *EG/HG*. Now *ZE* + *GE* > 571, because *ZE*
has been posited as 306 and *EG* as 265 plus a small amount. But *ZG* = 153.
Therefore, (*ZE* + *EG*)/*ZG* > 571/153, by V.8.[7] Therefore, similarly,
EG/HG > 571/153. Therefore, with *EG* posited as 571 and *HG* as 153,
side *EH* will be 591⅛ plus a small part, by I.46 (=Gr. I.47).[8]

The Second Division of the Angle: Let ∠*GEH* be bisected as before by line
ET. Then *HE/EG* = *HT/TG*, by VI.3.[9] Therefore, by composition,
(*HE* + *EG*)/*EG* = *HG/TG*. Therefore, alternately, (*HE* + *EG*)/*HG*

---

[1] See Commentary, lines 7–8.

[2] See *Archimedes in the Middle Ages*, Vol. 1, p. 90, comment 36. Cf. *Elementa* (Basel,
1546), p. 9.

[3] *Archimedes in the Middle Ages*, Vol. 1, p. 164, comment 149–50. Cf. *Elementa* (Basel,
1546), p. 66.

[4] *Archimedes in the Middle Ages*, Vol. 1, p. 78, comment 25. Cf. *Elementa* (Basel, 1546), p.
47.

[5] *Elementa* (Basel, 1546), p. 13: "Datum angulum, per aequalia secare."

[6] *Archimedes in the Middle Ages*, Vol. 1, p. 139, comment 15. Cf. *Elementa* (Basel, 1546, p.
140).

[7] See Commentary, line 25.

[8] See note 4.

[9] See note 6.

= *EG/TG*. Now *HE* + *EG* > 1162⅛, because *EG* has been posited as 571 and *HE* has been found to be 591⅛ plus a small amount. But *HG* = 153. Therefore, (*HE* + *EG*)/*HG* > 1162⅛/153. Therefore, similarly, *EG/TG* > 1162⅛/153. Hence, with *EG* posited as 1162⅛ and *TG* = 153, side *ET* will be 1172½ plus a small part, by I.46 (=Gr. I.47).[10]

The Third Division of the Angle: Again, let ∠*GET* be bisected as before by line *EK*. Then *ET/EG* = *TK/KG*, by VI.3. Therefore, by composition and alternation, (*ET* + *EG*)/*TG* = *EG/KG*. Now *ET* + *EG* > 2334¼, and with *TG* posited as 153. Therefore, (*ET* + *EG*)/*TG* > 2334¼/153. Therefore, similarly, *EG/KG* > 2334¼/153. Hence, with *EG* posited as 2334¼ and *KG* as 153, side *EK* will be 2339¼ plus a small part, by I.46 (=Gr. I.47).[11]

The Fourth Division of the Angle: Once more, let ∠*KEG* be bisected by line *EL*. Then *KE/EG* = *KL/LG*. Therefore, by composition and alternation, (*KE* + *EG*)/*KG* = *EG/LG*. Now *KE* + *EG* > 4673½ and *KG* = 153. Therefore, (*KE* + *EG*)/*KG* > 4673½/153. Therefore, similarly, *EG/LG* > 4673½/153. I wish to say it is so much and more. Since ∠*ZEG* was earlier posited as ⅓ of a right angle, hence it would be 1/12 of 4 right angles. Therefore, its half, which is ∠*HEG*, is 1/24 part; and the half of that, which is ∠*TEG*, is 1/48 part; and the half of that, which is ∠*KEG*, is 1/96 part; and the half of that, which is ∠*LEG*, is 1/192 part of 4 right angles. Therefore, let *GM* now be equal in extension to *LG*. Hence, ∠*GEM* = ∠*GEL*, by I.4.[12] Therefore, the whole ∠*LEM* is 1/96 part of 4 right angles. Hence, line *LM* is the side of a regular polygon circumscribed about the circle and having 96 sides. Therefore, since it has been demonstrated that *EG/LG* > 4673½/153, and *EG* = 2 *AG* (because it is the diameter) and *LG* = 2 *LM*, so the equivalent ratio *AG/LM* > 4673½/153. Therefore, by inversion, *LM/AG* < 153/4673½. Therefore, if the number of *LM*, which is 153, is taken 96 times, it will produce the magnitude of the perimeter of the whole polygon, which will be 14688. Therefore, (perimeter of polygon/diameter *AG*) < 14688/4673½. Now the larger number contains the smaller number three times plus 667½, and 667½/4673½ < ⅐. Therefore, the perimeter of the polygon contains the diameter of the circle 3 times plus some parts which are less than ⅐ part of it (the diameter). And since the circumference of the circle is less than the perimeter of the circumscribed polygon, the ratio of the circumference to its diameter is less than 3⅐ by an [even] greater amount, which was posed in the first part of the theorem which was introduced.

Therefore, let circle *ABG* be described about center *E* [see Fig. I.4.2] and let *GB* be the side of an [inscribed, regular] hexagon, which side is equal to the radius. Let *AB* be joined and understand *EB* as joined. Therefore, △*EBG* will be equilateral. Therefore, any angle of it is ⅔ of a

---

[10] See note 4.
[11] See note 4.
[12] See note 2.

right angle, by I.32. Therefore, since $\angle GEB$ is an exterior angle, the two interior angles BAE and ABE [together] equal ⅔ of a right angle. But since these angles are equal, by I.5, $\angle A$ will be ⅓ of a right angle.[13] Further, $\angle ABC$, being in a semicircle, is a right angle, by III.30 (=Gr. III.31).[14] Therefore, the remaining angle AGB is ⅔ of a right angle. Moreover, if GB is understood to be extended to D, and $BD = BG$, with AD joined, an equilateral $\triangle ADG$ will be formed. Therefore, $AG = 2\,BG$. Or in another way: since AG is the diameter and BG is the side of an [inscribed] hexagon, AG will necessarily be double BG. Therefore, if we freely place $AG = 1560$, then $BG = 780$. Hence, by I.46 (=Gr. I.47),[15] since $\triangle ABG$ is a right triangle, side AB will be almost 1351, as it falls short by a small part.

The First Division of the Angle: Hence, let $\angle BAG$ be bisected by I.9,[16] with lines AH and HG both drawn. Two equiangular triangles AHG and HZG have been formed. This is evident, for $\angle HGZ = \angle BAH$, by III.20 (=Gr. III.21),[17] and consequently $\angle HGZ = \angle HAG$, since $\angle BAG$ was bisected; while $\angle AHG$, which is a right angle, is common to each triangle; hence the third angle is equal to the third angle; and so they are equiangular. Therefore, $AH = GH = AG$, by VI.4. And because $\angle BAG$ has been bisected, $BA/AG = BZ/ZG$. Therefore, by composition $(BA + AG)/AG = BG/ZG$. Therefore, alternately, $(BA + AG)/BG = AG/ZG$. Now $BA + AG < 2911$, because BA is less than 1351 by a small amount and AG has been posited as 1560. But $BG = 780$. Therefore, $(BA + AG)/BG < 2911/780$. Hence, similarly, $AG/GZ < 2911/780$. But $AG/ZG = AH/HG$, as was seen above. Therefore, $AH/HG < 2911/780$. With AH posited as 2911 and HG as 780, side AG will be 3013¾ less a small part, by I.46 (=Gr. I.47).[18]

The Second Division of the Angle: Again, let $\angle HAG$ be bisected by line AT. Two equiangular triangles are formed as before. Therefore, by composition and alternation, the same ratio is deduced as before. But $AH + HG < 5924¾$, while HG is 780. Therefore, $(AH + HG)/HG < 5924¾/780$, and consequently $AT/TG < 5924¾/780$. Hence, with AT posited as 5924¾ while $TG = 780$, AG ought to be sought as before by I.46 (=Gr. I.47).[19] But since the numbers are not prime in their ratio, therefore take the primes by VII.34 (=Gr. VII.33),[20] these primes being 1823 for line AT and 240 for TG, and 1838⁹⁄₁₁ (less a small part) for AG, by I.46 (=Gr. I.47).[21]

[13] *Archimedes in the Middle Ages*, Vol. 1, pp. 90–91, comment 63. Cf. *Elementa* (Basel, 1546), p. 10.

[14] *Archimedes in the Middle Ages*, Vol. 1, p. 220, comment 56. Cf. *Elementa* (Basel, 1546), p. 77.

[15] See note 4.

[16] See note 5.

[17] See Commentary, line 89.

[18] See note 4.

[19] See note 4.

[20] See Commentary, line 111.

[21] See note 4.

The Third Division of the Angle: Again, let $\angle TAG$ be bisected by AK, and with the deduction made as before, $AK/KG < 3661\frac{9}{11}/240$. Hence, with AK posited as $3661\frac{9}{11}$ and KG as 240, line AL ought to be sought as before. But the numbers are not prime in their ratio. Therefore, by VII.34 (=Gr. VII.33),[22] take the primes, which are 1007 and 66. Hence, with AK posited as 1007 and KG as 66, AG will be $1009\frac{1}{6}$ less a small part, by I.46 (=Gr. I.47).[23]

The Fourth Division of the Angle: Once more, let $\angle KAG$ be bisected by AL, and with the deduction made as before: $(KA + AG)/KG < 2016\frac{1}{6}/66$. Therefore, $AL/LG < 2016\frac{1}{6}/66$. Hence, with AL posited as $2016\frac{1}{6}$ and LG as 66, AG will be $2017\frac{1}{4}$ less a small part, by I.46 (=Gr. I.47).[24] Therefore, $AG/GL < 2017\frac{1}{4}/66$. Therefore, by inverting the ratios by means of the second part of V.8,[25] $GL/AG > 66/2071\frac{1}{4}$. And since the arc GB, which has been bisected 4 times, is $\frac{1}{6}$ part of the circumference, the arc LG will be $\frac{1}{96}$ part of the circumference. Therefore, straight line LG is the side of a regular polygon inscribed in the circle and having 96 sides. Hence, with LG, equal to 66, taken 96 times, the resulting perimeter of the whole polygon will be 6336, while the diameter is $2017\frac{1}{4}$ less a small amount. Therefore, (perimeter of polygon/diameter of circle) $> 6336/2017\frac{1}{4}$, by V.8.[26] Moreover, the higher number contains the smaller 3 times and $284\frac{1}{4}$, and $284\frac{1}{4}/2017\frac{1}{4} < 10/71$. Therefore, since the circumference of the circle is greater than the perimeter of the polygon as something circumscribed is greater than that inscribed in it, the circumference contains the diameter 3 times and in addition more than $\frac{10}{71}$ of the diameter. Now $\frac{10}{71}$ [approximately] equals in simple [fractions]: $\frac{1}{8} + \frac{1}{64} + \frac{1}{71} \cdot \frac{1}{64}$. Hence the ratio of the circumference to the diameter is greater than $3\frac{1}{8}$, which was proposed in the second part of the previously assumed theorem. Thus the whole proposition follows.

Nor will you be ignorant of the fact that the same ratio of circumference to diameter could be investigated by means of other smaller or larger numbers and by means of further division or bisections of the angle assumed in the circle. Still, in whatever way it is determined, this ratio is necessarily included between $3\frac{1}{7}$ and $3\frac{1}{8}$.

Commentary

7–8 "per . . . huius" See *De arte mensurandi*, Chap. 2, Prop. 1, MS BN lat. 7380, 5r: "1ª. Cuiuslibet portionis circuli ad totam circumferentiam que est anguli dicte portioni correspondentis ad quatuor rectos eandem proportionem esse conveniet."

[22] See note 20.
[23] See note 4.
[24] See note 4.
[25] See note 7.
[26] See note 7.

25 "per . . . 5^i" For Prop. V.8, see the Campanus version of the *Elementa* (Basel, 1546), p. 119; "8. Si duae quantitates inaequales ad unam quantitatem proportionentur, maior quidem maiorem, minor vero minorem obtinebit proportionem, illius autem ad illas, ad minorem quidem proportio maior, ad maiorem vero minor erit."

89 "per . . . 3^{ii}" For Prop. III.20 (=Gr. III.21), see the Campanus version of the *Elementa* (Basel, 1546), p. 70: "20. Si in una circuli portione, anguli super arcum consistant, angulos quoslibet aequales esse necesse est."

111 "per . . . 7^{mi}" For Prop. VII.34 (=Gr. VII.33), see the Campanus version of the *Elementa* (Basel, 1546), p. 193: "34. Numeros secundum proportionem numerorum assignatorum minimos invenire."

CHAPTER 5

The Hybrid *Circuli quadratura*
of 1340

In the preceding chapters, I have several times mentioned a quadrature tract interposed by Johannes de Muris in the eighth chapter of the *De arte mensurandi*. We can be sure that it was inserted by Johannes de Muris in MS BN lat. 7380, for on folio 58r (58v is blank) a note in Johannes' hand says: "Vade ad circuli quadraturam in pergameno sequenti: 'Circulo dato etc.' Verte folium." Hence Johannes is instructing us (or perhaps a future scribe) to proceed to the tract *Circuli quadratura*, which follows on the parchment leaves (59r–65r). Now I shall argue here that it is also possible that Johannes de Muris was the author of this tract even though the copy inserted in *Pd* is not in his hand, that is, it is possible that he put together this tract from the Moerbeke translations of *On Spiral Lines* and *On the Measurement of the Circle*, adding frequent comments. Before discussing its authorship, however, let us first examine the nature and scope of the work. It consists, one might say, of two unequal parts, each with its own colophon. The first comprises thirteen propositions and seven definitions, all drawn in substance from Moerbeke's translation of *On Spiral Lines*: Propositions 1–3 = *On Spiral Lines* 3–5; Propositions 4–5 = *On Spiral Lines* 7–8; Propositions 6–7 = *On Spiral Lines* 1–2; Definitions 1–7 = *On Spiral Lines*, Definitions 1–4, 6 (since Definitions 4–5 = *On Spiral Lines*, Definition 4 and Definitions 6–7 = *On Spiral Lines* Definition 6); Propositions 8–12 = *On Spiral Lines* 12–16; Proposition 13 = *On Spiral Lines* 18. The second part consists of one proposition, the fourteenth, which is taken from Proposition 1 of the Moerbeke translation of *On the Measurement of the Circle*. The colophon at the end of the first part, i.e., at the end of Proposition 13 reads (see text and translation below): "Here ends the demonstration of the equality of a straight line to the circumference of a circle, and consequently the ratio of something straight to something curved, which many people have denied. In the year 1340." That of the second part, i.e., at the end of Proposition 14, reads simply, "Here ends the Quadrature of the Circle." Hence, the objective of the first part was to include just those propositions from *On Spiral Lines* that would lead to the demonstration of the equality of a straight line to the circum-

45

ference of a circle, while that of the second was to demonstrate that a right triangle, one of whose sides including the right angle was just such a straight line equal to a circumference (with the other side including the right angle equal to the radius of the circle), is equal to the circle. As will be shown below, it is evident that the author, although taking his propositions substantially (and a good part of the time verbatim) from the Moerbeke translation, added original touches, sometimes in the form of a paraphrase of the Moerbeke text and sometimes in the form of added commentary. In consequence, his work must be considered as the first Latin exposition of and commentary on the *On Spiral Lines*, albeit a partial one.

At first glance, it may seem puzzling that two separate colophons have been included. I would suppose that the reason for this is simply that the work was completed in two steps. Let us imagine that the Moerbeke manuscript Vat. Ottob. lat. 1850 (or some unknown copy of it) fell into the author's hands in 1340, or sometime earlier, and on reading the first work therein (which is *On Spiral Lines*), he suddenly realized that here was a way to solve the very old problem of the rectification of a curved line, and so he deftly extracted the appropriate propositions leading to this rectification, adding what he thought to be necessary in the way of commentary. Needless to say, he was undoubtedly aware of the well-known proposition of Archimedes on the quadrature of the circle that had circulated so widely since the end of the twelfth century, and I would imagine further that he might well have decided to add that proposition as he ran across it later in the Moerbeke manuscript, again with the decision to include a commentary. It seems to me probable that this addition was made shortly after the completion of the extracts from *On Spiral Lines* in 1340. At any rate, I am convinced that this addition was made prior to 1343, for, as we shall see immediately below when we discuss the probability that Johannes de Muris was the author of the hybrid tract, the juxtaposition of the two parts seems already known to Johannes in 1343 when he completed his *Quadripartitum numerorum*, and indeed a knowledge of this juxtaposition was further (and even more clearly) indicated in Chapter 6 of the *De arte mensurandi*, written after the *Quadripartitum*.

We are now in the position to look at the various strands that link the hybrid tract with the French astronomer. It seems reasonable from the earlier passage of the *Quadripartitum numerorum*, edited above in the first chapter, that Johannes de Muris expected to include the tract or its content in a later geometric work, for he says: "But without doubt I know that the ratio of a straight line to a curve, as well as the quadrature of a circle, is demonstrated by means of spiral lines, as, by the Grace of God, we shall explain elsewhere in its place to anyone conceding geometric theorems." The first part of this statement with its distinction between determining the ratio of a straight line to a curve and the quadrature of a circle fits well the actually existing two-part division of the hybrid tract. The second part appears to announce his intention to explain these subjects in a geometrical context, i.e., in the *De arte mensurandi* soon to be edited. Further, it is of some significance to our interpretation of this passage that just prior to it Johannes links the spiral with Archimedes and expresses the lament: "Oh, would that we had his books faithfully translated!" This seems to be a clear indication that Johannes knew of the Moerbeke translations directly and not just through the hybrid tract, which in its various copies carries no indication of Archimedes' ultimate authorship. In confirmation of this conclusion, may I also call attention to the evidence cited above in Chapter 1 indicating a direct knowledge on Johannes' part of the Moerbeke text of *On Spiral Lines* (and not merely of the hybrid tract) at the time when Johannes composed the *Quadripartitum numerorum*. From such evidence, it seems a reasonable conclusion that in 1343 Johannes knew both the hybrid tract of 1340 and the original Moerbeke translation. But we have not yet, to this point, established that Johannes knew of them both because he was indeed the compositor of the hybrid tract.

Our next piece of evidence is the statement of Chapter 6 of the *De arte mensurandi*, quoted above in the beginning of Chapter 4. When talking about the ratio of the diameter of a circle to its circumference, Johannes says: "This ratio perhaps no one has yet truly reduced to number, although Archimedes . . . thought that he had demonstrated the ratio of a straight line to a curve by means of spirals. I propose to explain his intention in this regard and concerning the quadrature of the circle in the eighth chapter of this work." The first part of this statement is clear evidence that Johannes had a knowledge of *On Spiral Lines*, and in all probability of the hybrid tract as well, since he singles out the basic objective of the first part of the hybrid tract. This is further supported by the fact that in the second part of the statement this objective is coupled with the quadrature of the circle, as indeed it was in the hybrid tract. Hence, the second part of the statement is an indication that Johannes expects to explain Archimedes' intention concerning the two objectives of the hybrid tract. Both parts of the statement, in connecting these objectives with Archimedes himself, show that it cannot merely be the hybrid tract alone with which Johannes is familiar, for, as I said earlier, none of the manuscripts of the hybrid tract indicate Archimedes' authorship. All of this seems to bolster my previous conclusions concerning the earlier passage in the *Quadripartitum*.

In addition, one might further see, in the passage from Chapter 6 of the *De arte mensurandi* under consideration, a tenuous indication that it was Johannes who composed the hybrid tract, for he says that he is going "to explain his [Archimedes'] intention" regarding the ratio of a straight line to a curve and the quadrature of a circle. And indeed one can look on the paraphrasing and added commentary that appear in the hybrid tract as an effort to explain Archimedes. It seems to me that this conclusion is substantially confirmed by an examination of the commentary itself. Its style is very much like that displayed in Johannes' sections of the

De arte mensurandi itself. Particularly persuasive is the tendency on the part of the commentator to illustrate geometrical arguments by the use of numbers, a favorite device of Johannes de Muris. Already in the *Quadripartitum* he had declared that a certain theorem could be explained by letters of the alphabet, "but to me numbers are clearer."[1] Furthermore, in a number of places in the *De arte mensurandi*, he has illustrated the geometry by an appeal to numbers. For example, in Chapter 7, Proposition 17, where he treats the duplication of the cube, he introduces a numerical illustration by saying, "this the nature of numbers would not permit you to ignore. . . ."[2] This sounds like the remark of the commentator at hand when he says in his commentary to Proposition 13 of the hybrid tract (line 128), "Numbers will teach you this." (Cf. also Prop. 5, lines 29–30; Prop. 6, lines 12–13 and Prop. 14, lines 28–31.)

There is a marginal addition made by Johannes on the bottom of 59v of *Pd* that may bear on the question of authorship of the hybrid tract; and even if it does not, it is worth singling out as evidence of Johannes' cleverness as a mathematician. This note occurs in the course of the proof of Proposition 4 (=*On Spiral Lines*, Prop. 7). Both the original text of the hybrid tract and *On Spiral Lines* merely say that one can perform the required *neusis* fundamental to the proof (see the text below, Prop. 4, line 24). Johannes' note specifies that it can be done "per instrumentum co⟨n⟩choydeale," i.e. by means of a conchoidal instrument. He could have only learned about such an instrument by reading Eutocius' *Commentary on the Sphere and the Cylinder* in the translation of William of Moerbeke. Such an instrument is described in Eutocius' presentation of Nicomedes' solution to the problem of finding two proportional means (see Vol. 2, 38vF-Q). We know that by the time he composed Chapter 7 of the *De arte mensurandi*, Johannes de Muris had read the *Commentary* of Eutocius, since as we have seen he extracted three solutions to the mean-proportionals problem from it (see above, Chapter 3). I think it possible that as early as 1340, when the *Circuli quadratura* was composed, he had not yet read this part of the Moerbeke translation, or at least he had not yet realized that such an instrument could also be used to solve the *neusis* at hand in *On Spiral Lines*. Then I would suppose that, as he prepared to add the *Circuli quadratura* to his *De arte mensurandi*, the notion occurred to him that Nicomedes' instrument could be used for the solution of this *neusis*. Hence, his note. It was a most perceptive move on his part,[3] for the section on the instrument in Moerbeke's translation is by no means lucid. Yet he must have understood the instrument well enough to see that it could be applied to the quite different problem arising in *On Spiral Lines* (see below, my commentary to Prop. 4, lines 24–25). Now this added note,

---

[1] M. Clagett, *The Science of Mechanics in the Middle Ages* (Madison, 1959), p. 129.

[2] See above, Chapter 3 of this part, note 5.

[3] Compare the remarks of T. L. Heath, *The Works of Archimedes* (Cambridge, 1897), pp. cv–cvii.

in a sense, complements a comment concerning the *neusis* of the third proposition (=*On Spiral Lines*, Prop. 5). This comment is an elaboration beyond Archimedes' text. It tries to explain why a solution to the *neusis* of that proposition is possible (see my commentary to Prop. 3, lines 14–17). The next step would seem to be to indicate a method of solution. Although Johannes does not take that step for the *neusis* of Proposition 3 (perhaps because it does not demand any special instrument or higher curve), the added note to Proposition 4 reveals him taking precisely that step in suggesting the use of the conchoidal instrument. Hence, one might conclude from considering the comment of Proposition 3 in juxtaposition with the note of Proposition 4, that the latter was an outgrowth of Johannes' earlier interest in the *neusis* manifested by the former. I readily admit that this is an exceedingly tenuous argument. I make it only because it is compatible with the evidence of style already noted.

In point of actual fact, the major part of the commentary that is strung through Propositions 1–12 and added in separate sections of Proposition 13 and 14 gives no clues to the authorship, other than those discussed above. It consists largely of an appeal to the appropriate theorems of Euclid's *Elements* necessary to support Archimedes' arguments. However, the commentator also adds references to the theorems already proved in the work at hand, as an examination of the text below readily reveals. The interesting point about these internal references is that in all but one case the numbers of the propositions cited are those of *On Spiral Lines* itself rather than those adopted for the hybrid tract (see the text below, Prop. 12, line 16; Prop. 13, lines 32, 59–60, 64, 77, 112, 121). The most probable conclusion (in spite of the one exception) is that when the original author prepared this hybrid tract, he apparently did not have a successive numbering that differed from the numbers used in *On Spiral Lines*, for even in the one exception there is evidence that the number was altered from its original number in *On Spiral Lines* (see the variant reading to Prop. 12, line 23). One can imagine that when Johannes de Muris took the copy of the *Circuli quadratura*, editing and correcting it preparatory to its inclusion in the *De arte mensurandi*, he then added the successive numbers that now appear in *Pd*. (Incidentally, someone later added in the right-hand margins of *Pd* the Archimedean numbers for the first three propositions, i.e., opposite the first proposition he has added "3 Arch.," opposite the second "4" and the third "5".) As a matter of fact, it is surprising that when Johannes added the successive numbering now present in *Pd*, in only the one case mentioned above does he seem to have changed the original numbers from *On Spiral Lines* (Prop. 12, line 23). Furthermore, in one marginal addition (Prop. 5, line 20), Johannes also retained the original number from *On Spiral Lines*. This seems rather careless on Johannes' part, particularly when we realize that the reader would have been unable to know that these propositions were extracted from *On Spiral Lines*, there being no indication in the tract that Archimedes was the author nor *On Spiral Lines* the title. This is somewhat similar to Johannes de Muris' omission in Proposition 1 of Chapter 8 of the *De arte mensurandi* of the fact that this determination of π had its origin in Proposition 3 of *On the Measurement of the Circle* of Archimedes (see above, Chap. 4). Also careless was Johannes' omission of the important diagrams from Fig. I.5.4 through Fig. I.5.11b. This left the inexperienced reader stranded. Incidentally, one other interesting omission by the original author of the hybrid tract as he prepared it from *On Spiral Lines* was of the so-called Lemma of Archimedes stated in the preface of *On Spiral Lines*. Still the author demonstrates in his commentary that he understood it and assumed it to be so (see my commentary to Proposition 2, lines 5–13).

The hybrid tract appears in all five manuscripts of the *De arte mensurandi* which I have used for the various texts edited in this volume (and in Magliabecchi XI.2, which I have not collated), although it is missing in two further fourteenth-century manuscripts (Paris, BN lat. 7216 and 14376). In *Pd* it is, as I have said, written on parchment in a hand that is not Johannes de Muris' and placed between Propositions 1 and 2 of Chapter 8. We have already noted that it was Johannes de Muris who so inserted it there. Furthermore, Johannes added in his hand on the bottom of 64v (and thus before the conclusion of Proposition 14 on the inserted folio 65r) a fifteenth proposition that was clearly not a part of the original text. It is the converse of Proposition 14 and runs: "Dato quadrato equum circulum figurare." It has the colophon: "Explicit quadrati circulatura." I have omitted it from my text of the hybrid tract below in this chapter, since it was not a part of the original tract and makes no use of the translations of William of Moerbeke. However, I have given it in full below in Part III, Chapter 1, Sect. I, note 9.

One should also note that the scribe of the original hybrid tract did not give a single title to the tract. It was rather Johannes, at the time of writing out manuscript *Pd*, who placed at the top of the first page of the tract (59r): "Incipit circuli quadratura," to which he added the further comment: "Interposita huic capitulo." Hence, all that the original scribe of the inserted tract has given us in the way of titles is found in the colophons of Propositions 13 and 14, cited above. Three of the four remaining copies which I have used follow Johannes by giving the added title (see below, Variant Readings, Proposition 1, lines 1–2), with only the fifteenth-century manuscript *Xb* omitting the added title. For the sake of convenience I too have followed Johannes in referring to the whole tract by the title *Circuli quadratura*. Again, it should be noted that the later manuscripts *Xb* and *Ua* have on occasion attempted to correct or add to the readings of *Pd*, at least where the mathematical demands of the text are clear. Note that in my text I occasionally refer to the readings of the original Moerbeke manuscript, Vat. Ottob. lat. 1850, which I abbreviate as *O*, and which of course has been edited in Volume 2 above. Once more, as in the previous texts of this chapter, I have closely followed the reading of manuscript *Pd*, noting those divergencies in the other manuscripts that appear critical and helpful. Johannes de Muris' additions have been indicated in the variant readings by reference to *m.B* in MS *Pd*.

Concerning the diagrams for the hybrid tract, we should note first that no diagrams appear in manuscripts *Pe* and *Xn* (nor in Magl. XI.2), some are missing or inaccurately drawn in *Ua*, and many are missing in the basic manuscript *Pd*. Virtually all of them, however, are present in manuscript *Xb*. Indeed, since many of the important diagrams in the later propositions of the hybrid tract were not added by the original scribe in *Pd* or by Johannes de Muris but most of them do appear in *Xb* in a form similar to their appearance in manuscript *O*, it raises the possibility that the scribe of *Xb* had seen *O*. One might answer that the scribe of *Xb* constructed them on the basis of the text and mathematical sense. But this would not explain why in Fig. I.5.6 as given by *Xb* the letter *Z* appears on the diagram while in the text *T* is used instead of the *Z* which was in manuscript *O*. The letter *Z* was also used in manuscript *R* (Vat. Reg. lat. 1253, 22r), which included *On Spiral Lines* in the Moerbeke translation. So it could be that the scribe of *Xb* saw either manuscript *O* or manuscript *R*. Confirmation of this seems to lie in the fairly large number of textual readings where *Xb* agrees with *O* (and *R*) against the remaining manuscripts of the hybrid tract: Prop. 8, line 10*var*; Prop. 9, line 7*var* "HAG"; Prop. 12, line 22*var* (this is a particularly significant one); Prop. 13, line 12*var*; Prop. 13, line 88*var*; Prop. 13, line 98*var*; Prop. 14, line 7*var*. I do not see how all of these identical or similar readings of *Xb* and *O* could have been mere accidental coincidences. Incidentally, the last of these references is to a reading in Proposition 14 and thus to Proposition 1 of *On the Measurement of the Circle*. If *Xb* got this one from the Moerbeke translation directly, then it must have been from manuscript *O* rather than from manuscript *R* since *R* does not contain *On the Measurement of the Circle*. And so if one of these readings was taken from *O*, then presumably all of them were taken from that manuscript. All of these evidences of a close relationship between *Xb* and *O* might also be explained by the possibility that the scribe of *Xb* possessed, in addition to a manuscript of the tradition of *Pd*, a copy of the hybrid tract that was more accurate than the one that Johannes de Muris inserted in the *De arte mensurandi*. This argument would require that this better copy of the hybrid tract contained a complete set of diagrams and some readings from *O* that had been altered in the copy included in *Pd*. One further possibility remains for the source of *Xb*'s diagrams (if not for his textual readings). This is raised by the same figure noted above, Fig. I.5.6. This figure not only included the letter *Z* on the spiral but beyond that also the letters *H* and *Q*. I do not know where the *Q* came from, but the letter *H* was apparently included on the diagram in Greek manuscript A even though it was not mentioned in the text of the proposition (and hence was not included by William of Moerbeke on the diagram in manuscript *O*). Thus it is not impossible that the scribe of

Xb had seen Greek manuscript A as well as manuscript *O*. Note that I have rearranged the comments on the fourteenth proposition that appear in an incorrect order on folios 64r–v of *Pd*, presenting them in the order appropriate to the text. I have added the bracketed numbers relating the comments to the text. The reader will be able to determine the location of the comments in the manuscript by consulting the marginal references.

The marginal references in my text below are, as usual, to manuscript *Pd*.

Sigla

Pd = Paris, BN lat. 7380, 59r–65r (Note: folio 65 is an inserted strip with the conclusion of the text), middle of 14c.
Pe = Paris, BN lat. 7381, 121r–32r, 15c.
Xb = Vatican, Vat. lat. 9410, 54r–59r, 15c.
Ua = Utrecht, Bibl. Univ. 725, 72v–76v, 15c.
Xn = Vatican, Ottob. lat. 1423, 70v–76v, late 15c or early 16c.

The *Circuli quadratura* of 1340

59r

/[Incipit circuli quadratura
(Interposita huic capitulo)]

1ª. (=Arch. SL 3) CIRCULO DATO POSSIBILE EST ACCIPERE RECTAM MAIOREM PERIFERIA ET ETIAM CIRCULIS DATIS
5 QUOTCUNQUE MULTITUDINE POSSIBILE EST UNAM RECTAM SUMERE MAIOREM OMNIBUS PERIFERIIS.

Circumscripto enim poligonio ad circulum manifestum est quod linea composita ex omnibus lateribus poligonii maior est periferia circuli, quoniam omne comprehendens alterum maius est eo. Latera autem
10 poligonii circumscripti periferiam circuli comprehendunt.

Similiter si cuilibet circulo poligonium circumscribatur, recta linea composita ex omnibus lateribus poligoniorum maior est omnibus periferiis circulorum eadem ratione que dicta est.

Hec autem ex communi scientia constant.

Prop. 1

1–2 Incipit . . . capitulo *Pd (in m. B) om. Xb* Incipit circuli quadratura huic operi interposita ("incipit . . . interposita" *bis*) quadratura *Pe* De circuli quadratura huic capitulo interposita *Ua* Nota quod huic capitulo inserta erat in exemplari et superaddita circuli quadratura immediate post primum capitulum [*!* primam propositionem?] et ita inseritur hic in isto volumine. Post quam quadratura⟨m⟩ circuli nonum capitulum sequitur huius artis *Xn*
    3 *mg. m. rec. (?) vel m. B (?):* 3 Archi
    11 pologonium *Pd*
    12 pologoniorum *Pd*

2ª. (=Arch. SL 4) DUABUS LINEIS DATIS INEQUALIBUS, RECTA SCILICET ET CIRCULI PERIFERIA, POSSIBILE EST AC-CIPERE RECTAM MAIORE DATARUM LINEARUM MINOREM, MINORE AUTEM MAIOREM.

5   Sic ponatur linea *AB* maior periferia circuli *F* et sit excessus *CB*, qui quidem non est sicut punctus; dividatur in duo per *D* [Fig. I.5.1.]. Aufferatur autem ex linea *AB* linea *DB*. Manifestum est quod linea *AD* minor erit *AB*, quia pars minor toto, et erit maior periferia *F*, quia ipsa maior linea *AC*, que ponebatur equalis periferie circuli *F*. Sed sit circuli

10 periferia maior linea *AC* et excessus sit *CB*, qui divisus sit in duo per *D*; additaque *CD* super *AC* exit linea *AD* maior recta *AC* et minor periferia circuli, quoniam est ipsa minor suo equali, scilicet *AB*, per ypothesim. Igitur propositum est conclusum.

3ª. (=Arch. SL 5) CIRCULO DATO ET RECTA CIRCULUM CON-TINGENTE POSSIBILE EST A CENTRO CIRCULI RECTAM DUCERE AD CONTINGENTEM, ITA UT RECTA INTERMEDIA CONTINGENTIS ET PERIFERIE CIRCULI AD EAM QUE EX

5   CENTRO AD PERIFERIAM MINOREM PROPORTIONEM HABEAT QUAM PERIFERIA CIRCULI INTERMEDIA CONTACTUS CON-TINGENTIS ET PROTRACTE AD DATAM QUAMCUNQUE CIRCULI PERIFERIAM.

Detur circulus *ABG*, cuius centrum *K*, contingens circulum *DZ* in

10 puncto *B* [Fig. I.5.2]; data sit et periferia circuli quantacunque; pos-sibile autem est data periferia sumere rectam maiorem et sit *E* extra circulum recta maior data periferia. Ducatur a *K* centro equidistans [ipsi] *DZ*, que sit *KH*, et ponatur *HT* equalis ipsi *E*, que sit continuata usque *B*. Hoc autem possibile est. Nam contingit ducere *BT* ita parvam

15 rectam et continuare eam usque ad equidistantem dictam, ut sit una linea *BTH*; tunc *TH* recta erit necessario maior quantacunque circuli periferia data; immo etiam tota circuli periferia, per precedentem.

59v   Dico [itaque] quod minor est / proportio *ZT* ad *TK* quam periferie *BT* ad datam prius periferiam. A *K* [itaque] centro copulata ducatur *TK*

20 usque *Z*. Eandem igitur proportionem habet *ZT* ad *TK* quam habet *BT* recta ad *TH*, quia trianguli *BTZ*, *KTH* sunt equianguli, quoniam angulus *KTH* equalis angulo *BTZ*, quia contra se positi, per 15ᵃᵐ [primi] Euclidis. Similiter angulus *THK* equalis angulo *ZBT*, quia coalterni, per 29ᵃᵐ [primi] Euclidis, et per eandem angulus *THK* (*! TKH*) angulo *BZT*. Ergo

Prop. 2
    1 *mg. m. rec. (?) vel m. B (?):* 4 [Archi]

Prop. 3
    1 *mg. m. rec. (?) vel m. B (?) Pd*: 5 [Archi] / *mg. Pd (m. C?) Xb, om. Ua Xn:*
    Pᵃ soror / *mg. Pe:* Soror prima
    13 ipsi¹ *mg. Pd (m. B) PeUaXbXn*
    19 itaque *mg. Pd (m. B) PeXbXn, om. Ua*
    22 BTZ *Ua* BTH *PdPeXbXn* / primi *add. m. rec. Pd, Ua, om. PdXbXn*
    24 primi *add. m. rec. Pd., UaXB, om. PdXn*

25   per 4^{am} 6^i Euclidis latera equos angulos respicientia sunt proportionalia.
Sed *BT* curva maior est *BT* recta sicut arcus est maior sua corda et *TH*
maior data periferia quia equalis *E* que fuit posita maior data periferia.
Ergo per 8^{am} 5^i Euclidis minor erit proportio *ZT* [ad *TK*] quam *BT* periferie
ad datam periferiam, quod est propositum.

   4^a. (=Arch. SL 7) CIRCULO DATO ET IN EO LINEA MINORE
DYAMETRO QUANTUMLIBET EXTRADUCTA POSSIBILE EST A
CENTRO CIRCULI RECTAM ADNECTERE AD EDUCTAM UT
INTERMEDIA PERIFERIE ET EDUCTE AD CONIUNCTAM AB
5   ULTIMO INTERCEPTE AD ULTIMUM EXTRADUCTE STATUTAM
HABEAT PROPORTIONEM ET SI DATA PROPORTIO MAIOR SIT
EA QUAM HABET MEDIETAS IN CIRCULO DATE AD EAM QUE A
CENTRO AD IPSAM DUCTAM CATHETUM.

   Sit datus circulus *AGI* super semidyametrum *KG* et *AG* linea minor
10   dyametro extraducta usque ad *E* [Fig. I.5.3]; recta adnexa ad eductam
a centro circuli sit *KE*, intermedia periferie et educte sit *IE*, coniuncta
ab ultimo intercepte ad ultimum extraducte sit *IG*, statuta autem proportio *Z* [ad] *H*. Dico quod eadem est proportio *EI* ad *IG* que est *Z* ad
H. Si proportio statuta *Z* ad *H* sit maior ea que est *GT* ad *TK*, fiat *KL*
15   equidistans *AE*, et erigatur super punctum *G* ad rectos *GL* et cathetus
KT super *AG*. Erunt ergo trianguli *KTG*, *KGL* equianguli, quia angulus
KGT equalis est angulo *GKL*, quia coalterni per 29^{am} [primi] Euclidis,
et sunt ambo ortogoni. Ergo per 4^{am} 6^i Euclidis, ut *GT* ad *TK* ita *GK* ad
GL. Sed proportio *Z* ad *H* ex ypothesi maior est proportione *GT* ad *TK*,
20   ergo et ipsa proportio *Z* ad *H* maior est proportione *GK* ad *GL*.
Quam autem proportionem habet *Z* ad *H* eam habeat *GK* ad minorem
GL, quia possibile est hoc [per conceptionem, quanta est prima magnitudo
ad secundam tanta est tertia ad aliquam quartam, in commento 2^e 12^{mi}
Euclidis]. Et sit ad *IN* que transeat ad *G* quia fieri potest [per instrumentum
25   co⟨n⟩choydeale]. Et ideo sequitur sicut *Z* ad *H* ita *KG*, hoc est *KI*, quia
ambe a centro, ad *IN*. Modo sicut *KI* ad *IN* ita *EI* ad *IG*, per 4^{am} 6^i
Euclidis. Nam trianguli *KIN*, *EIG* sunt equianguli, propter angulos
coalternos et contra se positos et per 33^{am} (! 32^{am}) primi Euclidis. Ergo
sicut *Z* ad *H*, que est proportio statuta, ita *EI* ad *IG*, quod est propositum.

      28 ad TK *mg. Pd (m. B)*, *UaXbPeXn*

Prop. 4
         1 *mg. Pd (m. C?)*, *PeXb*, *om. UaXn*: 2^a *soror*
        10 adnexa *bis Pd*
        13 ad^1 *addidi*
        14 GT *in ras m. B in Pd et in mg. Pd*
        17 primi *add. m. rec. Pd, Pe*
        19 TK *UaXn, m. rec. Pd* TH *PdPeXnXb*
        20 et ipsa *mg. m. C in Pd*
     22–24 per . . . Euclidis *mg. Pd (m. B)*, *XbXn*, *om. Ua*, *tr. Pe post* ergo *in lin. 20*
     24–25 per . . . co⟨n⟩choydeale *mg. Pd (m. B)*, *om. Ua* / co⟨n⟩choydeale (*forte*
           rochoydeale?) *mg. Pd* Rothoydeale *PeXb* rethcoydeale *Xn*

60r

/5ª. (=Arch. SL 8) CIRCULO DATO ET IN EO LINEA MINORE DYAMETRO ET ALIA CIRCULUM CONTINGENTE APUD TER-MINUM IN CIRCULO DATE POSSIBILE EST A CENTRO CIRCULI ADNECTERE QUANDAM RECTAM AD CONTINGENTEM, UT
5 ACCEPTA AB IPSA MEDIA INTER PERIFERIAM CIRCULI ET DATAM IN CIRCULO LINEAM AD ACCEPTAM A CONTINGENTE STATUTAM PROPORTIONEM HABEAT, ET SI DATA PROPORTIO MINOR SIT EA QUAM HABET MEDIETAS IN CIRCULO DATE AD EAM QUE A CENTRO CIRCULI CATHETUM AD IPSAM
10 DUCTAM.

Sit datus circulus $ABGD$ super centrum K et in eo recta minor dyametro GA, contingat autem circulum XL in puncto G, et proportio statuta quam habet Z ad H sit minor ea quam habet GT ad KT cathetum super GA [Fig. I.5.4]. Erit itaque et ipsa proportio statuta minor ea quam habet
15 GK ad GL, si equidistans sit KL ad TG, quoniam trianguli GTK, KGL sunt equianguli, quare per 4^{am} 6^i Euclidis et cetera sicut in precedente. Habeat autem KG ad GX eam proportionem quam habet Z ad H. Hoc autem possibile est per 8^{am} 5^i Euclidis, posita GX maior GL. Describatur igitur circuli periferia super tria puncta K, X, L. Secundum doctrinam
20 [5^i huius,] quoniam igitur maior est GX quam GL et ad rectos angulos sunt KG, XL, possibile est ei que est MG per continuationem KG usque ad periferiam circuli KXL equalem ponere eam que est IN tendentem ad K centrum. Nam si tendatur IN prope GM, erit IN maior GM. Si autem prope X, erit minor. Ergo inter X et M necessario est IN equalis ei que est
25 GM. Dico ergo quod EB ad IG habet proportionem statutam. [Dico itaque quod EB ad IG proportionem habet statutam.] Quod itaque continetur ab XI in IL ad id quod fit ex KE in IL eandem habet proportionem quam XI ad KE. Nam si una quantitas per duas inequales multiplicatur, pro-portioni multiplicantium equalis erit proportio productorum, quod in
30 numeris clare patet per [19^{am} 7^i] Euclidis. Quod autem fit ex KI in IN equale est producto ab XI in IL et quod fit ex KI in GL equale est pro-ducto ex KE in IL. Ergo IN ad GL est sicut XI ad KE. Unde sillogismus talis est: sicut XI in IL, scilicet [IN] in KI, ad KE in IL, scilicet KI in GL, ita XI ad KE; sed sicut XI in IL, scilicet IN in IK, ad KE in IL,
35 scilicet KI in GL, ita IN ad GL; ergo sicut IN ad GL ita XI ad KE et econverso sicut XI ad KE ita IN ad GL. Prima patet per 21^{am} 7^i Euclidis,

---

Prop. 5

1 *mg. Pd (m. C), PeXb, om. UaXn:* 3ª soror
11 eo *XbUaXn* ea *PdPe*
12 contingat *OUa* continguat *Xb* continguunt *PdPeXn*
15 equidistans *XbUa* equidem *PdPe*
20 5^i huius *mg. Pd (m. B), PeUaXbXn*
24 *post* necessario *del. Pd* maior
25–26 Dico . . . statutam *mg. Pd (m. B), PeXn, om. UaXb, delendum est*
30 per . . . Euclidis *Ua, om. Xb* per (+*lac.*) Euclidis *mg. Pd (m. B) PeXn*
32 *post* IL *omnes MSS lacunam habent / ante* XI *del. m. C in Pd* ea
33 IN *Xb om. PdPeUaXn*
36 21^{am} *PdXbPeXn* 20^{am} *Ua*

et hac scilicet per 34^{am} 3ⁱⁱ eiusdem assumpta per easdem. Est ergo *IN* ad *GL* sicut *XI* ad *KE*. Sed *IN* ad (*!* et) *GM* posite sunt equales. Quare sicut *IN* ad *GL* ita *GM* ad *GL* et inde *GM* ad *GL* sicut *XI* ad *KE*. Nunc

40 autem sicut *GM* ad *GL* ita *XG* ad *GK* per 34^{am} [3ⁱ] Euclidis, quoniam quod fit ex *GM* in *KG* equum est ei quod fit ex *XG* in *GL*, hoc est productum

60v mediorum est equale producto / extremorum; igitur sunt proportionales; habet igitur se *GM* ad *GL* sicut *XG* ad *KG*, hoc est *KB*, que ambe a centro. Ergo *XG* ad *BK* sicut *XI* ad *KE*. Quare et ita reliqua relique,

45 scilicet *IG* ad *BE*, sicut *XI* ad *KE*, per 5^{am} 5ⁱ vel 7^{am} 7ⁱ Euclidis. Nam *XG* tota ad *KB* totam est sicut *XI* ad *KE*, hoc est sicut pars prime ad partem secunde, ergo et ita *IG* pars reliqua prime ad *BE* partem reliquam secunde. Modo *XG* ad *KB* fuit posita sicut *H* ad *Z*. Ergo *IG* ad *BE* sicut *H* ad *Z* et econverso *BE* ad *IG* sicut *Z* ad *H*, que est proportio statuta, quod fuit

50 propositum demonstrare.

6^a. (=Arch. SL 1) SI PER ALIQUAM LINEAM ALIQUOD SIGNUM EQUE VELOCITER MOTUM FERATUR, ET IN IPSA DUE LINEE ACCIPIANTUR, ACCEPTE EANDEM PROPORTIONEM AD IN-VICEM HABEBUNT QUAM TEMPORA IN QUIBUS SIGNUM

5 LINEAS AMBULAVIT.

Feratur ergo aliquod signum per lineam *AB* eque velociter motum et sumantur due linee in ea *CD*, *DE* [Fig. I.5.5]. Sit autem tempus *ZH* in quo signum lineam *CD* perambulat, in quo autem lineam *DE* sit tempus *HT*. Et dico quod *CD* linea ad lineam *DE* eandem habet proportionem quam

10 habet tempus *ZH* ad tempus *HT*. Componantur autem ex lineis *CD*, *DE* linee *AD*, *DB* secundum talem compositionem, ut excedat linea *AD* lineam *DB*. Hoc autem possibile est ut si ponatur *AC* 8, *CD* 4, erit *AD* 12; et ponatur *EB* 6, *DE* 2, et *DB* 8. Sic ergo erit *AD* maior linea *DB*. Et quociens continetur linea *CD* in linea *AD*, tociens contineatur tempus *ZH* in tempore

15 *LH*. Quociens etiam continetur *DE* in linea *DB* tociens contineatur *HT* tempus in tempore *KH*. Hiis suppositis, quoniam signum eque velociter per lineam *AB* delatum est, palam est quod in quanto tempore fertur per lineam *CD*, in tanto tempore fertur per unamquamque lineam equalem ei que est *CD*. Igitur et per lineam compositam *AD* in tanto tempore delatum

20 est quantum est tempus *LH*, quoniam tociens linea *CD* componitur in linea *AD* quociens tempus *ZH* in tempore *LH*. Itaque per lineam *BD* in tanto tempore motum est signum quantum est tempus *KH*. Quoniam igitur maior fuit posita *AD* linea quam *DB*, manifestum est quod in pluri tempore signum per lineam *DA* motum est quam per *BD*. Quare tempus *LH* est

---

Prop. 6

3 accepte *corr. mg. Pd (m. C?) ex* accipe
8 HT *PeO om. Xb* HC *PdPe*
9 quem *Pd*
14,17 tempore *UaXbO* tempus *PdPeXn*
18 tempore *UaXb* tempus *PdPeXn*
21 BD *UaO* CD *PdPeXbXn*

25 maius tempore *KH*. Similiter autem ostendetur, si ex temporibus *ZH*, *HT* componantur tempora secundum quamvis compositionem, ut excedat unum tempus alterum, proportio linearum. Et est conversa precedentis deductionis; quare propositum.

7ª. (=Arch. SL 2) SI DUOBUS SIGNIS UTROQUE PER ALIQUAM LINEAM MOTO NON EANDEM TAMEN EQUE VELOCITER
61r IPSUM SIBI IPSI ACCIPIUNTURQUE DUE LINEE / IN UTRAQUE LINEARUM QUE IN TEMPORIBUS EQUALIBUS A SIGNIS
5 PERMEENTUR, EANDEM PROPORTIONEM HABEBUNT AC-CEPTE UNIUS LINEE QUAM ACCEPTE ALTERIUS SIBI IPSIS.

Sit per lineam *AB* motum aliquod signum equevelociter per totum et aliquod per lineam *KL*, accipianturque in linea *AB* due: *CD*, *DE*, et in linea *KL*: *ZH*, *HT* [Fig. I.5.5]. In equali autem tempore moveantur signa sibi
10 ipsis. Dico quod eandem proportionem habet *CD* ad *DE* quam habet *ZH* ad *HT*; quod clare patet per immediatam, nam equalitas mobilium hoc convincit. Et post hec due conclusiones sicut petitiones vel suppositiones appellari.

[Descriptiones]

Prima descriptio. Si recta linea assignatur in plano manente altero termino illius eque velociter circumducta quocienscunque restituitur iterum unde incepit, simul autem cum linea circumducta feratur aliquod
5 signum eque velociter ipsum sibi ipsi per rectam incipiens a manente termino, signum elicam describet in plano.

Secunda. Terminus quidem recte manens initium revolutionis vocetur.

Tertia. Positio autem linee a qua incepit recta circumferri principium circulationis.
10 Quarta. Si quidem in prima circulatione lineam signum perambulet, prima vocetur.

Quinta. Si autem in secunda circulatione, secunda circulatio dicatur.

Sexta. Si a signo quod est principium elicis ducatur aliqua recta et recte huius ad eandem circulatio fiat, precedens vocetur.
15 Septima. Que autem ad alteram partem, sequens.

Prop. 7
> 8 linea² *O om. Ua* BA *PdPeXb*
> 10 quam: quem *Pd*
> 11 immediatam *UaXbXn* immediatum *PdPe*
> 12 petitiones *?Pd, XbXn* positiones *PeUa*

Descriptiones
> 1 [Descriptiones] *addidi*
> 2 assignatur: affigatur *O*
> 6 elicam *PdUaXbXn* elicam *PeO*; cf. *Quadripart., IV, 31, 1, lin. 11*

8ª. (=Arch. SL 12) SI AD ELICEM UNA CIRCULATIONE DESCRIPTAM A PRINCIPIO ELICIS RECTE INCIDANT QUOT-CUNQUE EQUALES ANGULOS ADINVICEM FACIENTES, EQUALI INVICEM SE EXCEDUNT.

5 Sit elix, AB, AG, AD, AE, AT (! AZ) equales angulos super principium elicis describentes [Fig. I.5.6]. Dico quod equali excedit AG eam que AB et AD eam que AG, et sic deinceps. In quo enim tempore linea que circumducitur ab AB ad AG pertingit, etiam (! in) hoc tempore signum quod per rectam fertur excessum perambulat quo excedit AG eam que AB.

10 In quo autem tempore ab AG ad AD, in hoc perambulat excessum quo excedit AD eam que AG, et equaliter movetur, quia anguli sunt equales. Ergo in tempore equali illos excessus perambulat. Equali ergo linee invicem se excedunt. Et inde manifestum est quod quelibet linea precedenti et sequenti circumposita per equidistantiam dici potest.

9ª. (=Arch. SL 13) SI RECTA LINEA ELICEM CONTINGAT, SECUNDUM UNUM SOLUM PUNCTUM CONTINGERE NE-CESSE EST.

Sit elix in qua A, B, G, D, principium eius A, initium circulationis AD,
5 contingit autem elicem recta ZE [Fig. I.5.7]. Dico quod secundum solum punctum contingit. Si enim possibile est, contingat secundum duo
61v puncta, que sunt G, H et / iungantur AG, AH, et angulus HAG in duo equalia dividatur per 9ᵃᵐ primi Euclidis usque ad elicem et sic per lineam AC (! AT). Equali ergo excedit AH eam que AT et AT eam que AG per
10 immediate dictam. Quare circumposite sunt AH, AG ei que est AT. Igitur duple sunt AH, AG simul iuncte ad eam que est AT. Sed eius que est AO in duo equa scindentis angulum in trigono AGH maiores sunt AH, AG simul iuncte quam duple. Quia AO brevior est quam AT et quia GH transit per O, ergo secat ZE revolutionem, scilicet elicem, quod est contra
15 ypothesim. Quare propositum.

10ª. (=Arch. SL 14) SI AD ELICEM IN PRIMA CIRCULATIONE DESCRIPTAM INCIDANT DUE RECTE A PUNCTO QUOD EST PRINCIPIUM REVOLUTIONIS, ET AD PRIMI CIRCULI PERI-FERIAM EDUCANTUR, EANDEM PROPORTIONEM ADINVICEM
5 HABEBUNT QUE AD ELICEM INCIDUNT, QUAM PERIFERIE CIRCULI AB INITIO SUI LINEARUM ULTIMIS RESPONDENTES.

Sit elix $ABGDET$ in prima circulatione descripta [Fig. I.5.8];

Prop. 8

5 AT (! AZ): AZ *O et in figura Xb*
8 AG *Xo* AD *PdPeXbUaXn* / etiam *PdPeUaXn* et *Xn* in *O*
10 in² *Xb O* et *PdPeUa*

Prop. 9

7 HAG *Xb* qui continetur ab AH, AG *O* AHG *PdPeUaXn*
8 9ᵃᵐ *Xm, lac. in aliis MSS*
13 AT *Xb* AC *PdPeUaXn*

Prop. 10

7 -T *O* -C *PdPe (hic et alibi sed non ubique)*

principium revolutionis, scilicet elicis, sit *A*, initium circulationis *TA*, circulus primus *TKH*. Educantur autem ab *A* ad elicem *AE*, *AD* transeuntes
10 usque ad circuli periferiam in *Z*, *H*, ut sit una linea *AEZ* et una similiter *ADH*. Dico quod eandem proportionem habebit *AE* ad *AD* quam *TKZ* periferia ad *TKH* periferiam, posita equalitate motus *T* per periferiam et *A* per rectam. In quo enim tempore *T* periferiam *TKZ* describit, in eo similiter *A* per lineam *AE* fertur. Rursum et in quo tempore *T* periferiam
15 *TKH* ambulat, in eo etiam *A* lineam *AD*. Igitur eadem est proportio *AE* ad *AD* que est periferie *TKZ* respondentis *AZ* ad periferiam *TKH* ad *AD* lineam respondentem. Et item accidit si ad terminum revolutionis incidat altera eductarum, aliasque proportiones poteris invenire, si fuerit tibi cura.

11ª. (=Arch. SL 15) SI AD DESCRIPTAM IN SECUNDA CIRCULA-TIONE REVOLUTIONEM A PRINCIPIO EIUSDEM RECTE LINEE PRODUCANTUR, EANDEM ADINVICEM PROPORTIONEM HABE-BUNT QUAM DICTE PERIFERIE CUM TOTA CIRCULI PERIFERIA
5 EDUCTARUM ULTIMIS TERMINATE.

Sit revolutio, scilicet elix, *ABGDT* in prima circulatione descripta, *TLEM* in secunda; producantur recte *AE*, *AL* ad revolutionem in secunda circulatione descriptam [Fig. I.5.9]. Dico quod eadem est proportio *AL* ad *AE* que est *TKZ* periferie cum tota eiusdem circuli periferia ad *TKH*
10 periferiam cum tota circuli periferia supradicta. In equali enim tempore [*A*] per rectam delatum *AL* perambulat et *T* periferiam *TKZ* cum tota circuli periferia. Et iterum *A*, *AE* et *T*, totam circuli periferiam et adhuc *TKH* periferiam, utroque moto equaliter sibi ipsi. Igitur propositum per
62r 17ᵃᵐ 3ⁱⁱ (! 11ᵃᵐ 5ⁱ) Euclidis. Eodem modo / potest ostendi, in tertia revolu-
15 tione proportio linearum ad periferiarum proportionem cum tota periferia bis accepta, et sic deinceps tociens accepta periferia quotus est numerus circulationum minus uno. Et si ad terminum elicis recta cadat, idem ac-cidet suo modo, ut *AT* a principio elicis ad eius terminum in prima circula-tione et *AQ* in secunda. Eadem namque proportio *AQ* ad *AT* que est totius
20 periferie primi circuli et adhuc periferie a *S* ad ultimum linee *AB* respond-entis (! *GDT*?) ad totam eiusdem circuli periferiam semel sumptam.

12ª. (=Arch. SL 16) SI REVOLUTIONEM IN PRIMA CIRCULA-TIONE DESCRIPTAM RECTA LINEA CONTINGAT, ET A CON-TACTU AD SIGNUM QUOD EST REVOLUTIONIS PRINCIPIUM RECTA LINEA COMPLERETUR, ANGULI QUOS FACIT CON-
5 TINGENS AD COPULATAM INEQUALES ERUNT.

Sit elix ut supra, *ZE* contingens in *D*, *A* vero centrum sive principium

14 AE: AC (?)Pd
16 respondentis PdXb, suprascr. Ua reductis PeUaXn

Prop. 11
6 -T O -C PdPe (hic et alibi sed non ubique)
11 [A] O om. MSS
20 a S corr. ex AS

Prop. 12
6 ZE corr. ex ZR in MSS, cf. O et lin. 12 infra

elicis [Fig. I.5.10]. Dico angulum *ZDA* obtusum, *ADE* acutum. Secundum longitudinem *AD*, posito *A* centro, fiat circulus *DNC*. Manifestum est quod periferia ⟨*CND*⟩ cadit extra elicem, *CRD* intra. Angulus igitur

10   *ZDA* non est acutus quia maior maxima acutorum, scilicet angulo ex dyametro et circumferentia *RDA*, per 15^am 3^ii Euclidis. Neque rectus, quoniam si sic *EDZ* contingeret circulum *DCN* per 17^am 3^ii; itaque possibile est ab *A* ducere rectam ad contingentem, ut recta intermedia contingentis et periferie circuli ad eam que ex centro minorem propor-

15   tionem habeat ea quam habet curva intermedia contactus et concidentis periferiam ad datam periferiam per 5^am huius. Concidatur ergo *AI*, scindens elicem in *L*, periferiam autem *DCN* in *R*. Et habeat *IR* ad *AR* minorem proportionem quam *DR* periferia ad *DNC* periferiam. Ergo et tota, scilicet coniunctim, *AI* ad *AR* minorem habebit proportionem quam

20   *RDNC* periferia ad *DNC* periferiam, hoc est quam habet *SHKT* periferia ad *HKT* periferiam, quia illi duo circuli sunt concentrici et divisi proportionaliter. Nunc autem *SHKT* [periferia ad *HKT*] periferiam hanc habet proportionem quam *AL* ad *AD* per 10^am huius. Ergo minorem habet proportionem *AI* ad *AR* quam *AL* ad *AD*, quod est impossibile per 8^am

25   5^ii Euclidis. Non ergo rectus est angulus *ADZ*, neque acutus, [ut visum]; est ergo obtusus; quare et reliquus est acutus. Idem erit si apud terminum suum elicis [sit] contingens.

13^a. (=Arch. SL 18) SI REVOLUTIONEM IN PRIMA CIRCULA-
TIONE DESCRIPTAM RECTA LINEA CONTINGAT APUD TER-
MINUM REVOLUTIONIS, A SIGNO AUTEM QUOD EST PRIN-
CIPIUM REVOLUTIONIS AD RECTOS ANGULOS PRINCIPIO

5   CIRCULATIONIS DUCATUR ALIQUA RECTA, CONCIDET CUM
62v   CONTINGENTE ET / RECTA INTERMEDIA CONTINGENTIS ET
PRINCIPIUM REVOLUTIONIS EQUALIS ERIT PERIFERIE CIR-
CULI PRIMI.

Sit revolutio que *ABGDT* [Fig. I.5.11a]. Sit autem *A* signum principium

10   revolutionis. Que autem *TA* linea principium circulationis, porro autem *TKH* circulus primus. Contingat autem aliqua revolutionem apud *T*, que *TZ*, et ab *A* ducatur ad rectos angulos ipsi *TA* que *AZ*. Concidet itaque ad eam que *TZ*, quoniam que *ZT*, *TA* angulum acutum continent. Concidant autem apud *Z*. Ostendendum igitur quod *ZA* equalis est

15   periferie circuli *TKH*. Si enim non, aut maior est aut minor.

7 ADE *corr. ex* ADR *in MSS, cf. O et lin. 11 infra ubi RDA est alius angulus*
9 ⟨CND⟩ *addidi*
15 quam *XbUa* que *PdPeXn*
21 HKT: KT *O, sed cf. Heiberg*
22 periferia ad HKT *Xb O, om. PdPeUaXn*
23 10^am *corr. Pd (m. B) ex* 14^am (?)
25 ut visum *Xb, om. UaXn, lac. PdPe*
27 sit *Xb, om. UaXn, lac. PdPe*

Prop. 13
12 Concidet *XbO, om. Ua, lac. PdPeXn*

[Prima pars probationis]

Sit prius si possibile est maior. Accipiam itaque aliquam rectam *LA*,
ea quidem que est *ZA* recta minorem, periferia autem circuli *TKH*
maiorem. Est itaque circulus quidem qui *TKH* et in circulo linea minor
20 dyametro que *TH*. Erit proportio quam habet que *TA* ad *AL* maior ea
quam habet medietas ipsius *HT* ad eam que ad *A* cathetum ad ipsam
ductam, propterea quod et ipsa quam que *TA* ad *AZ*. Possibile igitur est
ab *A* producere ad eductam eam que *AN*, ut intermedia periferie et extraducte, que est *NR*, ad *TR* eandem habeat proportionem quam habet que
25 *TA* ad *AL*. Habebit igitur que *NR* ad *TA* proportionem quam habet que
TR recta ad *AL*. Que autem *TR* ad *AL* minorem habet proportionem
quam que *TR* periferie ad periferiam circuli *TKH*. Qui quidem enim *TR*
recta minor est *TR* periferia, que autem *AL* recta periferia circuli *TKH*
maior. Minorem ergo proportionem habebit et que *NR* ad *TA* quam que
30 *TR* periferia ad periferiam circuli *THK*. Quam autem proportionem *TR*
periferia cum tota periferia circuli *THK* habet ad periferiam circuli *THK*,
hanc habet que *QA* ad *AT*; ostensum est hoc per 15ᵃᵐ huius conversam.
Concidet itaque per 5ᵃᵐ huius (*!* 18ᵃᵐ 5ⁱ?). Minorem ergo proportionem
habet que *NA* ad *AR* quam que *QA* ad *AT*, quod est impossibile. Que
35 quidem enim *NA* maior est ea que *AQ*, que autem *AR* equalis est ipsi *TA*.
Non ergo maior est que *ZA* periferia circuli *THK*.

[Commentarius super primam partem probationis]

"Accipiam itaque—" Sit assumpta aliqua linea recta que sit *AL* et sic
per 4ᵃᵐ huius minor *AZ* et maior periferia circuli *THK*. Quod autem hoc
40 possibile sit fuit ostensum in 4ᵃ huius.
"Est itaque circulus quidem—" Circulus est *TKH* et in eo circulo linea
TH que est minor dyametro; et super eam cathetus, scilicet perpendicularis *AO*. Quare ipsa *TH* divisa est per medium in *O* per 3ᵃᵐ 3ⁱⁱ Euclidis.
63r Sic ergo constituti sunt / duo trianguli *ATO*, *ATZ*, qui sunt equianguli.
45 Nam angulus *A* trianguli *TAZ* rectus per ypothesim, similiter et angulus
O trianguli *TOA*. Item angulus *Z* trianguli *TZA* equalis est angulo *A* trianguli *TAO*, patetque reliquus. Nam angulus *ATO* et *ATZ* communis est
utroque triangulo. Ergo reliquus equalis est reliquo. Sunt ergo equianguli.
Igitur per 4ᵃᵐ 6ⁱ Euclidis latera equos angulos respicientia sunt pro-
50 portionalia. Ergo sicut *TO* ad *AO* ita *TA* ad *AZ*, hoc est dictu, ille proportiones sunt equales sicut equalis est proportio 4 ad 2 proportioni 40
ad 20 quia utrobique dupla et una dupla non est maior neque
minor alia.
"Erit proportio quam habet que *TA* ad *AL* maior ea proportione quam

16 [Prima . . . probationis] *addidi*
25 TA²: RA *O (sed RA = TA)*
36 *Post* THK *add.* PdPe *principium secunde partis probationis*: Sit itaque rursum
si est possibile que ZA [minor] periferia circuli THK *sed iter. infra, cf. lin. 87,
et sic hic delevi*
49–50 proportionalia *UaXb* equalia *PdPeXn*

55 habet medietas ipsius *HT*," que est *TO*, ad *AO*, que est cathetus super
TH, quod patet. Nam linea *AL* minor est linea *AZ*; quare per 8^am 5^i
Euclidis maior erit proportio *TA* ad *AL* quam *TA* ad *AZ* et quia *TA* ad
AZ est equalis proportioni *TO* ad *AO*, maior erit proportio *TA* ad *AL* quam
TO ad *AO*. Sic ergo accedit ad 7^am huius: "Circulo dato in eoque linea
60 minori dyametro etc."

"Possibile est igitur ab *A*" centro ad lineam minorem dyametro
eductam in continuum et directum, que est *HN*, productum *AN* sic ut
NR ad *RT* eandem habeat proportionem quam *TA* ad *AL*, que sit sicut
proportio statuta, iuxta 7^am huius. Ergo permutatim sicut *NR* ad *TA* ita
65 *RT* ad *AL*. Sed *TR* ad *AL* minorem habet proportionem quam *TR* periferia
ad periferiam circuli *TKH* per 8^am 5^i Euclidis, quia *TR* recta minor est *TR*
curva sicut corda minor arcu suo et *AL* maior est per ypothesim periferia
circuli *TKH*. Ergo et *NR* ad *TA*, hoc est *RA* quia *TA*, *RA* equales cum *A*
centro, minorem habet proportionem quam *TR* periferia ad periferiam
70 circuli *TKH*. Igitur et coniunctim tota *NA* ad *RA* minorem habet proportionem quam tota periferia *TKH* cum periferia *TR* ad periferiam
circuli *TKH*; volo dicere, quod minor est proportio *NR* ad *RA* quam *RT*
curve ad totam periferiam, ergo minor est proportio primi et secundi ad
secundum, scilicet *NR* ad (*!* et) *RA* simul, que est *NA*, ad *RA* quam *TR*
75 curve et totius periferie simul ad ipsam totam periferiam. Sed proportio
TR curve cum tota periferia ad ipsam totam periferiam circuli *TKH* est
equalis proportioni *QA* ad *AT*, per 15^am [huius], hoc est *AR*. Ergo minor
est proportio *NA* ad *RA* quam *QA* ad *RA*, quod est impossibile. Manifestum et contra 8^am 5^i Euclidis. Nam cum due quantitates inequales
80 comparuntur ad tertiam, maioris ad tertiam est maior proportio quam
minoris ad ipsam tertiam quantitatem. Nunc autem *NA* est maior quam
QA, ut totum sua parte. Ergo *NA* ad *RA* est maior proportio quam *QA* ad
63v *RA*. Ergo impossibile conclusum / est notum. Ergo id ex quo sequitur est
impossibile. Hoc autem fuit ex positione quod *AZ* recta esset maior
85 periferia circuli *TKH*. Non ergo maior.

[Secunda pars probationis]

Sit itaque rursus si possibile est minor que *ZA* periferia circuli *THK*
[Fig. I.5.11b]. Accipiam itaque quandam rectam eam que *AL*, ea quidem
que *AZ* maiorem, periferia autem circuli *THK* minorem. Et ducam a *T*
90 *TM* equidistantem ipsi *AZ*. Rursum igitur circulus est qui *THK*, et in ipso
linea minor dyametro, que est *TH*, et alia contingens circulum apud *T*.
Et proportio quam habet que *AT* ad *AL* minor ea quam habet medietas
ipsius *HT* ad cathetum ab *A* ad ipsam ductam, quoniam et ipsa quam habet
que *TA* ad *AZ* ⟨minor est⟩. Possibile ergo est ab *A* producere eam que

---

77 [huius] *addidi*
86 [Secunda. . . . probationis] *addidi*
88 rectam *XbO* numerum *PdPeUaXn*
94 ⟨minor est⟩ *O, om. omnes MSS*

95 *AP* ad contingentem, ut *RN* intermedia eius que in circulo recte et
periferie ad eam que *TP* acceptam a contingente, hanc habeat proportionem quam habet que *TA* ad *AL*. Secat itaque que *AP* circulum apud
R, revolutionem autem apud *Q*. Et habebit permutatim eandem proportionem que *NR* ad *TA* quam habet que *TP* ad *AL*. Que autem *TP* ad
100 *AL* maiorem habet proportionem quam que *TR* periferia ad periferiam
circuli *THK*. Que quidem enim *TP* recta maior est periferia *TR*. Que
autem *AL* minor periferia circuli *THK*. Maiorem ergo proportionem
habet *NR* ad *AR* quam que *TR* periferia ad periferiam circuli *THKT*.
Quare et ea que *RA* ad *AN* maiorem proportionem habet quam periferia
105 circuli *THKT* ad periferiam *TKR*. Quam autem proportionem habet
periferia circuli *THKT* ad periferiam *TKR*, scilicet tota, hanc habet que
TA recta ad *AQ*; ostensum enim est hoc. Maiorem ergo proportionem
habet que *RA* ad *AN* quam que *TA* ad *AQ*, quod quidem impossibile.
Non ergo maior est neque minor que *ZA* periferia circuli *THK*. Equalis
110 ergo.

[Commentarius super secundam partem probationis]

"Accipiam itaque—" Per 4[am] huius possibile est quod *AL* sit minor
circuli periferia et maior qua *AZ*.

"Et ducam" per 31[am] primi Euclidis. Et in ipso linea *TH* minor dyametro
115 quia omnis linea ducta per circulum non per centrum minor est dyametro
per 7[am] 3[ii] Euclidis.

"Et alia contingens" quia ex ypothesi a *T* extrahitur *TM* equidistans
ipsi *AZ*. Et angulus *TAZ* rectus. Sequitur quod angulus *MTA* est rectus
per 29[am] primi Euclidis. Ergo *MT* contingens est circulum in *T* per 15[am]
120 3[ii] Euclidis.

"Possibile est ergo—" Per 8[am] huius, quam habet que *TA* ad *AL*, que
sit sicut proportio statuta, habeat ergo et sit sicut *RN* ad *TP* sic *TA* ad *AL*.
Ergo et permutatim sicut *RN* ad *TA* ita *TP* ad *AL*.

"Quare et ea que *RA*—" Patet ex proportione quatuor quantitatum:
125 Si fuerit proportio primi ad secundum maior proportione tertii ad quartum
fueritque secundum maior primo et quartum tertio, erit necessario
proportio secundi ad differentiam eius super primum maior proportione
quarti ad differentiam eius super tertium. Quod numeri te docebunt:

64r / sicut quatuor quantitates 1[m] 3, 2[m] 9, 3[m] 4, 4[m] 16. Est ergo proportio primi ad
130 secundum maior, quia subtripla, proportione tertii ad quartum, quia sub-
quadrupla, estque secundum maius primo et quartum tertio. Dico quod
proportio secundi [scilicet 9,] ad differentiam eius super primum, scilicet

98 R *XbO* T *PdPeUaXn*
99 NR *corr. ex* NT (*cf. lin. 123 infra*) / TA: RA *O (sed TA = RA)*
103, 105, 106 THKT:THK *O*
106 hunc *Pd*
111 [Commentarius . . . probationis] *addidi*
113 qua *XbUa* que *PdPeXn*
123 permutatim *XbUaXn* permutatem *PdPe*
132 scilicet 9 *Ua, om. alii MSS*

ad 6, maior, quia [sesquialtera,] proportione quarti [,scilicet 16,] ad differentiam eius super tertium, scilicet ad 12, quia [sesquitertia]. Sed sic est
135   in proposito. Nam *RN* est primum, *TA* secundum, *TR* periferia tertium,
circulus totus quartum. Sed iam visum est quod proportio primi ad
secundum est maior proportione tertii ad quartum estque secundum maior
primo et quartum tertio. Ergo proportio secundi, scilicet *TA* vel *RA* sibi
equalis, ad differentiam eius super *RN*, que differentia est *AN*, maior est
140   proportione quarti, scilicet circuli, ad differentiam eius super periferiam
TR, que differentia est periferia *TKR*. Et sic patet propositum illud quod
non erat in commento positum.

Explicit demonstratio equalitatis linee recte ad circumferentiam circuli,
et per consequens proportio recti ad curvum, quam plurimi negaverunt.
145   Anno 1340°.

14ᵃ. (=Arch. MC 1) OMNIS CIRCULUS EST EQUALIS TRIGONO
RECTANGULO, CUIUS QUE QUIDEM EX CENTRO EST EQUALIS
UNI EARUM QUE CIRCA RECTUM ANGULUM, PERIMETER
AUTEM BASI.

5   Habitudinetur circulus *ABGD* trigono *E*, ut dictum est [Fig. I.5.12].
Dico quod sunt equales. Si enim est possibile, sit maior circulus et
inscribatur tetragonum *AG*. Et secentur periferie in duo equa et sint
portiones iam minores excessu quo excedit circulus trigonum [1].
Rectilineum ergo adhuc est maius trigono [2]. Accipiatur centrum *N* et
10   cathetum que *NX* [3]. Minor ergo que *NX* latere trigoni quod ex centro.
Est autem perimeter rectilinei minor reliquo latere, quoniam et perimetro
circuli. Est ergo rectilineum minus trigono *E* [4], quod quidem est inconveniens [5].

Sit autem, si possibile est, circulus minor trigono *E* et circumscribatur
15   tetragonum et secentur periferie in duo equa. Et ducantur contingentes
per signa. Rectus ergo qui ab *OAR* per 17ᵃᵐ 3ⁱⁱ Euclidis. Linea ergo
OR est maior linea *MR*, que enim *MR* est equalis *RA* [6]. Et trigonum
ergo *ROP* est maius quam dimidium figure *OZAM* [7]. Accipiantur
sectores similes ipsi *PZA* minores excessu quo excedit trigonus *E* circulum
20   *ABGD*. Adhuc ergo circumscriptum rectilineum est minus trigono *E*,
quod quidem est inconveniens, est enim maius, quia que *NA* est equalis
catheto trigoni, perimeter autem maior base trigoni [8]. Equalis ergo est
circulus ille trigono supradicto. Sed trigonum quadrare contingit, ergo et
circulum.

133 sesquialtera *Xb, lac. PdPeXn* 1½ *Ua* / *ante* proportione *del. (?) Pd* quam /
proportione *?Pd (cf. lin. 127, 130, 137, 140)* quam proportioni *Xn* quam proportio
PeXbUa / scilicet 16 *Ua, om. alii MSS*
134 sesquitertia *Xb, lac. PdPeXn,* 1⅓ *Ua*
138–39 sibi equalis *Xb* sunt equales *PdPeXn*
145 Anno 1340° *PdPeXb, om. UaXn*

Prop. 14
7 inscribatur *XbO* scribatur *PdPeUaXn*
10 quod *Xb* quare *PdPeUaXn*

25   [Commentarius]

64r mg   [1] Quoniam possibile est tociens dividere portiones ut remaneant sectores minores excessu illo.

     [2] Quando aliqua data quantitas ad duas inequales comparatur, illa maior est que minus exceditur a data, ut si 10 comparetur ad 8 et 6, minus

30 exceditur 8 a 10, quia in duobus, quam 6, quia in 4. Igitur 8 maior est quam 6. Sed circulus comparatur ad rectilineum inscriptum et ad trigonum *E*. Et per ypothesim minus exceditur rectilineum quam trigonum (*!*), quia portiones rectilinei supponuntur minores quam id quo

34 exceditur trigonus a circulo. Ergo rectilineum maius est trigono *E*.

64r mg   [3] *NX* cathetus super latus rectilinei, scilicet super latus *AZ*.

64v   [4] Probatio: quia si minus latus trigoni quod est equale semidyametro circuli ducatur in latus sibi coterminale ad angulum rectum, scilicet in lineam equalem circumferentie circuli, producti medietas est area trianguli. Similiter si *NX*, que est perpendicularis super latus rec-

40 tilinei, ducatur in perimetrum, scilicet in omnes lineas rectilinei simul iunctas vel in unam equalem omnibus lateribus simul iunctis, producti medietas est area rectilinei, quod patet per triangulos in quibus resolvitur rectilineum. Constat autem quod area rectilinei minor est area trianguli, quia ex minoribus lineis producitur, quia *NX* minor *NA* et perimeter

45 rectilinei minor latere trianguli equali circumferentie circuli. Quare rectilineum minus est trigono *E*.

64r mg   [5] Quia contra predicta, nam dictum est rectilineum est maius.

64v   [6] *MR* est equalis *RA*, quia latera rectilinei circumscripti sunt equalia propter tetragonum circumscriptum et portiones divisas in duo equalia ad

50 que trahuntur contingentes. Et *OR* maior est *AR* per 18^{am} primi Euclidis.

     [7] Et trigonum *ROP* maius est dimidio figure *OZAM* [sub] *OZ* recta, *OM* recta, *ZAM* periferia. Patet quia triangulus *OAR* maior est triangulo *ARM*; ergo et maior est minori quam *ARM*, cuiusmodi est figura *ARM*, *AM* existente curvo sive periferia. Quod autem triangulus *OAR* maior sit

55 triangulo *ARM* patet per 38^{am} primi Euclidis. Nam basis *OR* trianguli *OAR* non est equalis sed maior basi [*RM*] trianguli *ARM*, ut visum est. Ergo triangulus *OAR* non est equalis triangulo *ARM* sed maior, quia ex minoribus lineis producitur minor quantitas sicut ex maioribus maior. Sed triangulus *OAP* est equalis triangulo *OAR* et figura *PAZ* figure *ARM*.

60 Ergo totus triangulus *OPR* maior est quam dimidium figure *OZAM*.

     [8] Quando aliqua quantitas data duabus inequalibus comparatur, minor est illa que minus excedit datam quantitatem. Sed rectilineum circumscriptum minus excedit circulum quam trigonum *E*, ut positum est. Ergo

---

30 a: ad *Pd*

39 perpendicularis *XbUa* a perpendiculari *Xn* a perpen (+ *lac.*) *PdPe*

40 perimetrum *XbUa* perimetro *PdPeXn*

51 dimidio *Ua* dimidie *PdPeXbXn* / OZ *XbUa* OR *PdPeXn*

56 RM *Xb*, *lac. PdPeUaXn*

61 data *corr. mg. Pd ex* ducta

62 datam *corr. mg. Pd ex* ductam

rectilineum minus est trigono E, quod est impossibile, quia est neces-
65 sario maius trigono E. Patet quia NA cathetus super latus rectilinei est
equalis catheto trigoni, quia semidyametro circuli. Sed perimeter rectilinei
65r maior est perimetro / circuli, scilicet circumferentia circuli, et per consequens maior linea recta trianguli que est equalis circumferentie circuli.
Ergo rectilineum maius est trigono E.
70 Explicit circuli quadratura.

[Here Begins the Quadrature of the Circle
(Interposed in this chapter)]

1. WITH A CIRCLE GIVEN, IT IS POSSIBLE TO FIND A
STRAIGHT LINE GREATER THAN THE CIRCUMFERENCE; AND
ALSO WITH ANY NUMBER OF CIRCLES GIVEN, IT IS POSSIBLE
TO HAVE A STRAIGHT LINE GREATER THAN [THE SUM OF]
ALL THE CIRCUMFERENCES.[1]

For with a polygon circumscribed about the circle, it is manifest that
the line composed of all of the sides of the polygon is greater than the
circumference of the circle, since everything including another is greater
than it. But the sides of the circumscribed polygon include the circumference of the circle.

Similarly, if a polygon is circumscribed about any [i.e., each] circle
[of several circles], the line composed of all of the sides of [all of] the
polygons is greater than [the sum of] all of the circumferences, by the
same reasoning as that stated.

But these things are evident by common knowledge [i.e., by axiom].[2]

2. WITH TWO UNEQUAL LINES GIVEN, ONE A STRAIGHT
LINE AND THE OTHER A CIRCUMFERENCE OF A CIRCLE, IT
IS POSSIBLE TO HAVE A STRAIGHT LINE LESS THAN THE
GREATER OF THE GIVEN LINES AND GREATER THAN THE
LESSER.[1]

Thus let line AB be posited as greater than the circumference of
circle F [by Prop. I], and let the excess be CB, which indeed is not as a
point [see Fig. I.5.1].[2] Let that excess be bisected at D. Let line DB be
subtracted from line AB. It is evident that line AD will be less than AB
because a part is less than the whole, and it will be greater than the
circumference of F because it is greater than line AC which was posited
as equal to the circumference of circle F.

68 linea recta Ua linee recte $PdPeXbXn$

Prop. 1
[1] See Commentary, Prop. 1, lines 3–4, 4–6.
[2] *Ibid.*, lines 7–13.

Prop. 2
[1] See Commentary, Prop. 2, lines 1–4.
[2] *Ibid.*, lines 5–13.

Now let the circumference of the circle be greater than line AC and let [its] excess be CB, which we let be bisected at D. And with CD added to AC there results a line AD greater than the straight line AC and less than the circumference of the circle, since it is less than a line equal to it, namely AB, by hypothesis. Therefore, the proposition has been concluded.

3. WITH A CIRCLE AND A STRAIGHT LINE TANGENT TO THE CIRCLE GIVEN, IT IS POSSIBLE TO DRAW FROM THE CENTER OF THE CIRCLE TO THE TANGENT A STRAIGHT LINE SUCH THAT [THE SEGMENT OF] THE STRAIGHT LINE INTERCEPTED BETWEEN THE TANGENT AND THE CIRCUMFERENCE OF THE CIRCLE HAS A LESSER RATIO TO THE RADIUS THAN THE ARC OF THE CIRCLE INTERCEPTED BETWEEN THE POINT OF TANGENCY AND THE PROTRACTED STRAIGHT LINE TO ANY GIVEN ARC OF THE CIRCLE.[1]

Let ABG be the given circle, its center K, and let DZ be the tangent to the circle in point B[2] [see Fig. I.5.2]. Also let any arc at all of the circle be given. Now it is possible to take a straight line greater than the given arc [by Prop. 1] and let E [drawn] outside of the circle[3] be the straight line greater than the given arc. Then from center K let KH be drawn parallel to DZ and let HT be placed equal to E and continued to B.[4] This is possible, for one can draw BT as a small straight line [i.e., as small as we like with TH being as large as we like], and continue it [i.e., increase it] until the required equidistance [of TH and E is obtained] so that BTH will be a single line.[5] Then straight line TH will necessarily be greater than any given arc of the circle, in fact, even than the whole circumference of the circle, by the preceding [proposition, Prop. 2].

I say that $ZT/TK <$ arc BT/given arc.[6] And so from center K let TK be drawn and joined to Z. Hence, $ZT/TK = BT/TH$, for triangles BTZ and KTH are equiangular[7] since $\angle KTH = \angle BTZ$ by I.15 of Euclid —these angles being vertical angles, and similarly $\angle THK = \angle ZBT$ by I.29 of Euclid—these angles being alternate angles, and by the same proposition $\angle TKH = \angle BZT$. Therefore, by VI.4 of Euclid, the sides opposite the equal angles are proportional. But curve BT is greater than straight line BT as an arc is greater than its chord, and TH is greater than the given arc since it is equal to E which was posited as greater than the given arc. Therefore, by VI.8 of Euclid,[8] $ZT/TK <$ arc BT/given arc, which was proposed.

Prop. 3
[1] See Commentary, Prop. 3, lines 1–8.
[2] *Ibid.*, lines 9–10.
[3] *Ibid.*, lines 11–12.
[4] *Ibid.*, lines 13–14.
[5] *Ibid.*, lines 14–17.
[6] *Ibid.*, lines 18–19.
[7] *Ibid.*, lines 21–25.
[8] *Ibid.*, line 28.

4. WITH A CIRCLE GIVEN, AND IN IT A LINE LESS THAN THE DIAMETER, WHICH LINE HAS BEEN EXTENDED AS MUCH AS WE LIKE,[1] IT IS POSSIBLE TO PROJECT FROM THE CENTER OF THE CIRCLE TO THE EXTENDED LINE A STRAIGHT LINE[2] SUCH THAT THE [SEGMENT OF THE] STRAIGHT LINE INTERCEPTED BETWEEN THE CIRCUM-FERENCE AND THE EXTENDED LINE HAS A GIVEN RATIO TO THE LINE CONNECTING THE EXTREMITY [AT THE CIRCUMFERENCE] OF THE INTERCEPTED LINE WITH THE EXTREMITY [AT THE CIRCUMFERENCE] OF THE EXTENDED LINE, IT BEING ASSUMED THAT THE GIVEN RATIO IS GREATER THAN THAT WHICH HALF THE LINE GIVEN IN THE CIRCLE HAS TO THE PERPENDICULAR DRAWN FROM THE CENTER TO THE GIVEN LINE.

Let the given circle be AGI with radius KG and AG the line less than the diameter and extended to E [see Fig. I.5.3]. Let the line pro-jected from the center of the circle to the extended line be KE, the inter-cepted segment between the circumference and the extended line be IE, the line conjoined between the extremity of the intercept [at the circum-ference] to the extremity of the extended line [at the circumference] be IG, the given ratio be Z/H. I say that $EI/IG = Z/H$.

If the given ratio $Z/H > GT/TK$, let KL be drawn parallel to AE, and let GL be drawn at right angles [to GE] at point G and let KT be drawn perpendicular to AG. Therefore, triangles KTG and KGL are equi-angular since $\angle KGT = \angle GKL$ by I.29 of Euclid,[3] these angles being alter-nate and both [triangles] are right [triangles]. Therefore, by VI.4 of Euclid,[4] $GT/TK = GK/GL$. But $Z/H > GT/TK$ by hypothesis. Therefore, $Z/H > GK/GL$. So Z has to H the same ratio as GK to [some magnitude] less than GL. For this is possible by the axiom: Just as a first magnitude is to a second, so a third magnitude is to some fourth, [as given] in the comment of XII.2 of Euclid.[5] Let it be to IN, which verges toward G, for this can be done [by the Conchoidal Instrument].[6] And, therefore, it follows that $Z/H = KG/IN = KI/IN$ (KG and KI both being radii). Now $KI/IN = EI/IG$, by VI.4 of Euclid.[4] For triangles KIN and EIG are equiangular because of the alternate and vertical angles and because of I.32 of Euclid.[7] Therefore, the given ratio $Z/H = EI/IG$, which was proposed.[8]

Prop. 4
    [1] See Commentary, Prop. 4, lines 1–2.
    [2] *Ibid.*, line 3.
    [3] See Commentary, Prop. 3, lines 21–25.
    [4] *Ibid.*
    [5] See Commentary, Prop. 4, lines 22–24.
    [6] *Ibid.*, lines 24–25.
    [7] *Ibid.*, line 28.
    [8] *Ibid.*, lines 9–29.

5. WITH A CIRCLE GIVEN, AND IN IT A [STRAIGHT] LINE LESS THAN THE DIAMETER AND ANOTHER [LINE] TANGENT TO THE CIRCLE AT THE EXTREMITY OF THE LINE GIVEN IN THE CIRCLE, IT IS POSSIBLE TO DRAW A CERTAIN STRAIGHT LINE FROM THE CENTER OF THE CIRCLE TO THE TANGENT[1] SUCH THAT ITS SEGMENT INTERCEPTED BETWEEN THE CIRCUMFERENCE OF THE CIRCLE AND THE [LINE] GIVEN IN THE CIRCLE HAS A GIVEN RATIO TO THE SEGMENT OF THE TANGENT [BETWEEN THE POINT OF TANGENCY AND THE INTERSECTION OF THE TANGENT WITH THE LINE PROJECTED FROM THE CENTER], ASSUMING THAT THE GIVEN RATIO IS LESS THAN THAT WHICH HALF THE LINE GIVEN IN THE CIRCLE HAS TO THE PERPENDICULAR DRAWN TO THIS GIVEN LINE.

Let the given circle be *ABGD* with center *K*, and in it straight line *GA* less than the diameter, and let *XL* be tangent to the circle in point *G* [see Fig. I.5.4]. And let the given ratio $Z/H < GT/KT$, *TK* being perpendicular to *GA*. And so the given ratio $[Z]/[H] < GK/GL$, if *KL* is parallel to *TG* and since triangles *GTK* and *KGL* are equiangular; hence by VI.4 of Euclid[2] etc., as in the preceding [proposition]. Further, let $KG/GX = Z/H$. This is possible by V.8 of Euclid,[3] *GX* having been placed greater than *GL*. Therefore, let the circumference of a circle be described through the three points *K, X,* and *L*. Then, since $GX > GL$ and *XL* is perpendicular to *KG*, it is possible by the [fifth proposition of this work] [i.e., the *On Spiral Lines*] to place a [line] *IN* equal to *MG* (produced by continuing *KG* to the circumference of circle *KXL*) and verging toward the center *K*.[4] For if *IN* verged near *GM*, *IN* will be greater than *GM*, but if near *X* it will be smaller. Hence, between *X* and *M* there will necessarily be an *IN* equal to *GM*. I say, therefore, that $EB/IG = Z/H$.

[Proof:] $(XI \cdot IL)/(KE \cdot IL) = XI/KE$, for if a quantity is multiplied by two unequal quantities, the ratio of the products will be equal to the ratio of the multipliers, which in numbers is clearly evident by VII.19 of Euclid.[5] Now $KI \cdot IN = XI \cdot IL$ and $KI \cdot GL = KE \cdot IL$. Hence, $IN/GL = XI/KE$. Therefore, a syllogism follows:

$$(1) \quad (XI \cdot IL)/(KE \cdot IL) = (IN \cdot KI)/(KI \cdot GL) = XI/KE.$$

But

$$(2) \quad (XI \cdot IL)/(KE \cdot IL) = (IN \cdot IK)/(KI \cdot GL) = IN/GL.$$

Prop. 5

[1] The author repeats Moerbeke's error of translation from the Greek. It should be *lineam* rather than *contingentem*. In fact, it makes little difference in the enunciation, since the protracted line is extended to the tangent, as is evident in the proof.

[2] See Commentary, Prop. 3, lines 21–25.

[3] *Ibid.*, line 28.

[4] See Commentary, Prop. 5, lines 19–25.

[5] *Ibid.*, line 30.

Therefore (3) $IN/GL = XI/KE$, and, conversely, $XI/KE = IN/GL$. The first [premise] is evident by VII.21 of Euclid[6] together with the assumption of the identity $[KI \cdot IN = XI \cdot IL]$ by III.34 (=Gr. III.35) of the same work.[7] [The second premise also is evident by VII.21 with the assumption of the identity: $KI \cdot GL = KE \cdot IL$, by VI.2 of Euclid.[8]] Therefore, $IN/GL = XI/KE$. But IN and GM have been posited as equal. Hence, $IN/GL = GM/GL$, and thus $GM/GL = XI/KE$. But $GM/GL = XG/GK$ by III.34 of Euclid, since $GM \cdot KG = XG \cdot GL$, i.e., the product of the means is equal to the products of the extremes, and hence the terms are proportionals, therefore $GM/GL = XG/KG = XG/KB$, KG and KB both being radii. Therefore, $XG/BK = XI/KE$. Hence, as the remainder is to the remainder, i.e., $IG/BE = XI/KE$,[9] by V.5 or VII.7 of Euclid,[10] for the whole XG is to the whole KB as XI is to KE, i.e., as the part of the first is to the part of the second, hence as part IG remaining from the first to part BE remaining from the second. Now $XG/KB = H/Z$ by supposition. Therefore $IG/BE = H/Z$ and, inverting the ratios, $BE/IG = Z/H$, the latter being the given ratio, which conclusion is that we proposed to demonstrate.

6. IF SOME POINT IS TRANSPORTED WITH UNIFORM MOVEMENT ALONG SOME LINE, AND IF IN THIS [LINE] TWO LINES ARE TAKEN, THESE LINES WILL HAVE THE SAME RATIO BETWEEN THEM AS THE TIMES IN WHICH THE POINT HAS TRAVERSED THESE LINES.

For let some point be transported with uniform movement along line AB, in which are taken two lines CD and DE [see Fig. I.5.5]. Further, let ZH be the time in which the point traverses line CD and HT the time in which the point traverses line DE. I say that line CD/line DE = time ZH/time HT. For let lines AD and DB be composed out of lines CD, DE in such a way that line AD exceeds line DB. This is possible, for if AC is posited as 8, CD as 4, AD will be 12; and if EB is posited as 6, DE as 2, DB will be 8. Thus AD will be greater than line DB.[1] And let time ZH be contained in time LH as many times as line CD is contained in line AD. Also, let time HT be contained in time KH as many

---

[6] *Ibid.*, line 36.

[7] *Ibid.*

[8] I have added the reference to VI.2, which reads in the Campanus version of the *Elementa* (Basel, 1546), p. 139: "Si linea recta duo trianguli latera secans, reliquo fuerit aequidistans, eam duo illa latera proportionaliter secare."

[9] For $\dfrac{XG}{XI} = \dfrac{BK}{KE}$, and, *dividendo,* $\dfrac{XG - XI}{XI} = \dfrac{BK - KE}{KE}$; or $\dfrac{IG}{XI} = \dfrac{BE}{KE}$, and alternately, $\dfrac{IG}{BE} = \dfrac{XI}{KE}$.

[10] See Commentary, Prop. 5, line 45, where the propositions are given and their inappropriateness for the proof is suggested.

Prop. 6

[1] See Commentary, Prop. 6, lines 12–13.

times as [line] *DE* is contained in line *DB*. Then, with these things supposed, since the point has been transported with a uniform movement along line *AB*, it is clear that it traverses any line equal to *CD* in the same time in which it traverses *CD*. Therefore, it has been transported through the composite line *AD* in a time equal to *LH*, because time *ZH* is contained in time *LH* as many times as line *CD* is contained in line *AD*. And so the point is moved through line *BD* in a time equal to *KH*. Hence, since line *AD* was posited as greater than line *DB*, it is manifest that the point is moved through line *DA* in a greater time than through line *BD*. Consequently, time *LH* is greater than time *KH*. The ratio of lines may be similarly demonstrated if times are composed out of times *ZH* and *HT* in such fashion that one time exceeds the other, and this is the converse of the preceding argument.[2] Hence the proposition.

7. IF TWO POINTS ARE DISPLACED WITH UNIFORM [BUT UNEQUAL] MOVEMENTS, EACH ALONG A DIFFERENT LINE, AND IF IN EACH OF THESE LINES ARE TAKEN TWO LINES SUCH THAT THE FIRST LINE SEGMENT IN THE ONE LINE IS TRAVERSED BY ITS POINT IN THE SAME TIME AS THE FIRST LINE SEGMENT IN THE SECOND LINE IS TRAVERSED BY THE OTHER POINT, AND SIMILARLY THE SECOND LINE SEGMENTS IN THE TWO LINES ARE TRAVERSED IN EQUAL TIMES, THEN THE LINE SEGMENTS IN THE ONE LINE WILL HAVE THE SAME RATIO AS THE LINE SEGMENTS IN THE SECOND LINE.[1]

Let there be a point moved uniformly throughout line *AB* and another point along line *KL* [see previous Fig. I.5.5]. And let two lines *CD* and *DE* be taken in line *AB* and [two] lines *ZH* and *HT* in line *KL*. Further, the points are moved through the respective lines in equal times.[2] I say that *CD*/*DE* = *ZH*/*HT*. This is clearly evident by the preceding [proposition], for the equality [i.e., uniformity] of the [motions of the] mobiles leads to this conviction. And afterwards these two conclusions [can] be called postulates or suppositions.

[Definitions][1]

Definition 1. If a straight line assigned[2] in a plane revolves at uniform speed about one extremity of it which remains fixed and it returns to the position from which it started, and if, in the same time as the line revolves, some point moves with uniform speed along the straight line

---

[2] *Ibid.*, lines 25–28.

Prop. 7
  [1] See Commentary, Prop. 7, lines 1–6.
  [2] *Ibid.*, lines 11–12.

Defs.
  [1] See Commentary, *Def.*, line 1.
  [2] *Ibid.*, line 2.

beginning from the extremity which remains fixed, the point will describe a "spiral" in the plane.

2. Let the fixed extremity of the straight line[3] be called the "origin of the spiral."[4]

3. Let the position of the line from which the line begins to revolve [be called] the "origin of revolution"[5] [i.e., the "initial line"].

4. If the point traverses a line in the first revolution, let it be called the "first."[6]

5. If in the second revolution, let it be called the "second revolution."[7]

6. If from the origin of the spiral some straight line is drawn, let that which is in the direction in which the revolution of this line is made be called "forward."[8]

7. [Let] that which is in the opposite direction [be called] "backward."

[Propositions Continued]

8. IF ANY NUMBER OF STRAIGHT LINES ARE DRAWN FROM THE ORIGIN OF THE SPIRAL TO MEET A SPIRAL DESCRIBED IN A SINGLE[1] REVOLUTION AND PRODUCE ANGLES EQUAL TO EACH OTHER, THESE LINES WILL EXCEED ONE ANOTHER EQUALLY.

Let there be a spiral in which AB, AG, AD, AE and AT describe equal angles on the origin of the spiral [see Fig. I.5.6]. I say that $AG - AB = AD - AG = \ldots$ (and so on). For in the time in which the line revolves from AB to AG the point carried along the straight line traverses the excess of AG over AB. Further, in the time in which the line revolves from AG to AD, the point traverses the excess of AD over AG. And it moves equally [in both cases] because the angles are equal. Therefore, it traverses those excesses in the same time and hence the lines exceed each other by an equal amount. And thence it is manifest that any line can be said to be "circumlocated" with respect to the line "forward" and to the line "backward" by an equal distance.[2]

9. IF A STRAIGHT LINE IS TANGENT TO A SPIRAL, IT IS NECESSARY THAT IT IS TANGENT IN ONE POINT ONLY.

Let there be a spiral on which [points] A, B, G and D [lie] with A its

---

[3] The Moerbeke translation has *recte . . . circumducte;* the latter term is missing here.

[4] The author has substituted *initium revolutionis* for Moerbeke's *principium elicis vel revolutionis.*

[5] See Commentary, *Def.*, line 9.

[6] *Ibid.*, lines 10–12.

[7] *Ibid.*

[8] Notice that the author has omitted the definitions which are numbered (5) and (7) in the Moerbeke translation.

Prop. 8

[1] The author alters Moerbeke's reading of *qualicunque* to *una.*

[2] See Commentary, Prop. 8, lines 12–14.

origin, *AD* its initial line, and *ZE* the straight line tangent to the spiral [see Fig. I.5.7]. I say that it is tangent in one point only. For, if it is possible, let it be tangent in two points, which are *G* and *H*. Let *AG* and *AH* be drawn and, by I.9 of Euclid,[1] let ∠*HAG* be bisected [by a line extending] up to the spiral and thus be line *AT*. Therefore, *AH* exceeds *AT* by the same amount that *AT* exceeds *AG*, by the [preceding proposition] just stated [i.e., Prop. 8 = *On Spiral Lines* 12]. Therefore, *AH* and *AG* are "circumlocated" [by an equal amount] in relationship to *AT*. Therefore, *AH* + *AG* = 2 *AT*. But *AH* + *AG* > 2 *AO*,[2] *AO* bisecting the angle in △*AGH*. Since *AO* < *AT* and *GH* passes through *O*, therefore *ZE* cuts the spiral,[3] which is contrary to the hypothesis. Hence the proposition.

10. IF TWO LINES ARE DRAWN FROM THE POINT WHICH IS THE ORIGIN OF THE SPIRAL TO A SPIRAL DESCRIBED IN THE FIRST REVOLUTION AND [THE LINES] ARE EXTENDED TO THE CIRCUMFERENCE OF THE FIRST CIRCLE,[1] THE LINES MEETING THE SPIRAL WILL HAVE THE SAME RATIO TO ONE ANOTHER AS THE ARCS OF THE CIRCLE SITUATED BETWEEN THE [EXTREMITY OF THE] INITIAL LINE OF THE SPIRAL AND THE EXTREMITIES OF THE [TWO] LINES [DRAWN TO THE SPIRAL AND EXTENDED TO THE CIRCUMFERENCE OF THE FIRST CIRCLE].

Let *ABGDET* be a spiral described in the first revolution [see Fig. I.5.8]. Let the origin of the spiral[2] be *A*, the initial line *TA*, the first circle *TKH*. From *A* let lines *AE* and *AD* be drawn to the spiral, being extended to the circumference of the circle at *Z* and *H*, so that one line is *AEZ* and the other similarly is *ADH*. I say that *AE*/*AD* = arc *TKZ*/ arc *TKH*, the uniformity of motion of *T* along the circumference and that of *A* along the straight line having been posited. For in the time that *T* describes the arc *TKZ*, *A* is similarly carried through line *AE*. Further, in the time that *T* traverses arc *TKH*, *A* also [traverses] line *AD*. Therefore, the ratio of *AE* to *AD* is as that of arc *TKZ* (corresponding to line *AZ*) to arc *TKH* (corresponding to line *AD*). And it is also true if one of the extended lines is drawn to the end of the spiral, and you will be able to find other ratios, if you care to.[3]

Prop. 9
   [1] For I.9, see the Campanus version of the *Elementa* (Basel, 1546), p. 13: "Datum angulum, per aequalia secare."
   [2] See Commentary, Prop. 9, lines 11–13.
   [3] *Ibid.*, line 14.

Prop. 10
   [1] "First circle" and "second circle" were defined in the seventh definition of the Archimedean text, but this definition was omitted by the author, perhaps because he understood his own definitions 4 and 5 to be defining these terms. See Commentary, *Def.*, lines 10–12.
   [2] See Commentary, Prop. 9, line 14.
   [3] See Commentary, Prop. 10, line 18.

11. IF STRAIGHT LINES ARE DRAWN FROM THE ORIGIN OF
THE SPIRAL TO A SPIRAL DESCRIBED IN THE SECOND REVO-
LUTION, THESE LINES WILL HAVE THE SAME RATIO TO ONE
ANOTHER AS THE SAID ARCS TERMINATED AT THE EXTREMI-
TIES OF THE EXTENDED LINES,[1] WITH THE WHOLE CIRCUM-
FERENCE OF THE CIRCLE [ADDED TO EACH ARC SITUATED
BETWEEN THE EXTREMITY OF THE INITIAL LINE AND THE
EXTREMITY OF ITS EXTENDED LINE].

Let *ABGDT* be the spiral[2] described in the first revolution, *TLEM*
that described in the second revolution [see Fig. I.5.9]. Let lines *AE* and
AL be extended to the spiral described in the second revolution. I say that

$$\frac{AL}{AE} = \frac{(\text{arc } TKZ + \text{circum. of circle})}{(\text{arc } TKH + \text{circum. of circle})}.$$

For in the same time that *A* is carried through straight line *AL*, *T* traverses
the circumference of the whole circle and also arc *TKZ*. And also in
the same time that *A* traverses *AE*, *T* traverses the whole circumference
plus arc *TKH*, each being moved uniformly. Therefore, the proposition
follows by V.11 of Euclid.[3] In the same way it can be demonstrated
that in the third revolution the ratio of the lines [is equal] to the ratio of
the arcs with the whole circumference added twice [to each arc]; and
in successive [revolutions] the circumference is taken as many times as
there are revolutions minus one. And if [one] line falls on the extremity
of the spiral, the same will follow in its own way, as [for example] *AT*
drawn from the origin of the spiral to its end in the first revolution, and
AQ in the second revolution. For the ratio of *AQ* to *AT* is the same as
that of (1) the sum of the whole circumference of the first circle plus
the arc from *S* to the end of the [spiral] line *AB*[*GDT* in the first revolu-
tion] to (2) the whole circumference of the same [first] circle taken once.[4]

12. IF A STRAIGHT LINE BE TANGENT TO A SPIRAL DE-
SCRIBED IN THE FIRST REVOLUTION AND FROM THE [POINT
OF] CONTACT TO THE POINT WHICH IS THE ORIGIN OF THE
SPIRAL A STRAIGHT LINE WERE JOINED, THE ANGLES WHICH
THE TANGENT MAKES WITH THE JOINED LINE WILL BE
UNEQUAL.[1]

Let there be a spiral as above, with *ZE* tangent [to it] at *D* and *A*
the center or origin of the spiral [see Fig. I.5.10]. I say that $\angle ZDA$ is
obtuse and $\angle ADE$ acute. Let circle *DNC* be drawn with center *A* and

Prop. 11

[1] See Commentary, Prop. 11, line 5.
[2] See Commentary, Prop. 9, line 14.
[3] See Commentary, Prop. 11, lines 13–14.
[4] *Ibid.*, lines 19–21.

Prop. 12

[1] See Commentary, Prop. 12, lines 1–5.

radius *AD*. It is manifest that arc *CND* falls outside the spiral and *CRD* inside of it. Hence ∠*ZDA* is not acute because it is greater than the largest of the acute angles, namely the angle *RDA* [composed] of the diameter and the circumference, by III.15 (=Gr. III.16) of Euclid.[2] Nor is it a right angle. For, if so, *EDZ* would be tangent to circle *DCN*, by III.17 (=Gr. III.18).[3] And so it is possible to draw a straight line from *A* to the tangent such that the segment between the tangent and the circumference of the circle has a lesser ratio to the radius than the arc intercepted between the point of tangency and the line intersecting the circumference has to a given arc, by the fifth [proposition] of this work [*On Spiral Lines*] Therefore, let *AI*, cutting the spiral in *L*, intersect the circumference *DCN* in *R*. And let *IR/AR* < arc *DR*/arc *DCN*. Therefore, *componendo*, the whole *AI/AR* < arc *RDNC*/arc *DCN*, or *AI/AR* < arc *SHKT*/arc *HKT* since the two circles are concentric and divided proportionally. Now arc *SHKT*/arc *HKT* = *AL/AD*, by the tenth [proposition] of this work [*On Spiral Lines*]. Hence *AI/AR* < *AL/AD*, which is impossible by V.8 of Euclid.[4] Therefore, ∠*ADZ* is not a right angle, nor is it acute, as was seen. Therefore, it is obtuse, and the remaining angle [*ADE*] is acute. And the same will be so if the tangent is at the end of the spiral.[5]

13. IF A STRAIGHT LINE IS TANGENT TO A SPIRAL DE-SCRIBED IN THE FIRST REVOLUTION AT THE END OF THE SPIRAL AND A STRAIGHT LINE IS DRAWN FROM THE ORIGIN OF THE SPIRAL AT RIGHT ANGLES TO THE INITIAL LINE, IT [THE SECOND STRAIGHT LINE] WILL INTERSECT THE TANGENT, AND THE STRAIGHT LINE SEGMENT INTERCEPTED BETWEEN THE TANGENT AND THE ORIGIN OF THE SPIRAL WILL BE EQUAL TO THE CIRCUMFERENCE OF THE FIRST CIRCLE.

Let there be a spiral *ABGDT* [see Fig. I.5.11a]. Let *A* be the origin of the spiral, line *TA* its initial line, *TKH* the first circle. Further, let *TZ* be tangent to the spiral at *T*, and from *A* let *AZ* be drawn perpendicular to *TA*. And so *TZ* will intersect it, since *ZT* and *TA* contain an acute angle [by the preceding proposition]. Moreover, let these lines meet at *Z*. Therefore, it must be shown that *ZA* is equal to the circumference of circle *TKH*. For, if not, it is either greater or less than it.

[The First Part of the Proof]

First, let it be greater, if that is possible. And so I shall take some line

---

[2] For III.15 (=Gr. III.16), see Clagett, *Archimedes*, Vol. 1, pp. 430–31.

[3] For III.17 (=Gr. III.18), see *ibid.*, Vol. 1, p. 90, c. 61. Cf. *Elementa* (Basel, 1546), p. 69.

[4] For V.8, see Commentary, Prop. 3, line 28.

[5] This is added because it is the tangent at the end of the spiral that is expressed in Prop. 13 (=*On Spiral Lines* 18).

LA less than straight line *ZA* but greater than the circumference of circle *TKH*. And so there is a circle *TKH* and in this circle a line *TH* less than the diameter. The ratio which *TA* has to *AL* will be greater than that which ½ *HT* has to the perpendicular drawn from *A* to *HT*, since it [*TA/AL*] is greater than *TA/AZ*. It is then possible to draw *AN* from *A* to the [tangent] line extended, such that the intercept *NR* between the circumference and the extended line has to *TR* the same ratio as *TA* to *AL*. Therefore,

$$\frac{NR}{TA^1} = \frac{\text{straight line } TR}{\text{straight line } AL} .$$

But

$$\frac{TR}{AL} < \frac{\text{arc } TR}{\text{circum. of circle } TKH} ,$$

for straight line *TR* is less than arc *TR*, while straight line *AL* is greater than the circumference of circle *TKH*. Therefore,

$$[1] \quad \frac{NR}{TA^1} < \frac{\text{arc } TR}{\text{circum. of circle } THK} .$$

But

$$[2] \quad \frac{(\text{arc } TR + \text{circum. cir. } THK)}{(\text{circum. cir. } THK)} = \frac{QA}{AT} .$$

This has been demonstrated by the converse of the fifteenth [proposition] of this work [*On Spiral Lines*]. And so [1] joins with [2] by V.18 [of Euclid][2]. Therefore, *NA/AR* < *QA/AT*, which is impossible, for *NA* > *AR* and *AR* = *TA*. Therefore, *ZA* is not greater than the circumference of circle *THK*.

[Commentary to the First Part of the Proof]

"And so I shall take—" Let there be assumed some straight line *AL*, and so by the fourth [proposition] of this work [*On Spiral Lines*] it is less than *AZ* and greater than the circumference of circle *THK*. But that this is possible has been demonstrated in the fourth [proposition] of this work.

"And so there is a circle—" The circle is *TKH* and in the circle [there is] a line *TH* which is less than the diameter. And on the line there is a perpendicular, namely *AO*. Hence this *TH* has been bisected in *O*, by III.3 of Euclid.[3] Thus two triangles, *ATO* and *ATZ*, have been formed. These are equiangular, for ∠*A* of △*TAZ* is a right angle by hypothesis,

---

Prop. 13

[1] The Moerbeke translation and the Greek text of *On Spiral Lines*, Prop. 18, have *RA*, but *RA* = *TA*.

[2] See Commentary, Prop. 13, line 33.

[3] See Clagett, *Archimedes*, Vol. 1, p. 78, c. 40.

and so too is $\angle O$ of $\triangle TAO$. Also $\angle Z$ of $\triangle TZA$ is equal to $\angle A$ of $\triangle TAO$; and [the equality of] the remaining [angles] is evident, for $\angle ATO$ and $\angle ATZ$ constitute a common angle to both triangles. Hence the remaining angle is equal to the remaining angle. Hence the triangles are equiangular. Therefore, by VI.4 of Euclid,[4] the sides opposite these angles are proportional. Hence, $TO/AO = TA/AZ$, which is to say that these ratios are equal, just as $4/2 = 40/20$ since each is a double ratio and one double is not greater than or less than another double.[5]

"The ratio which TA has to AL will be greater than that which ½ TH," which is TO, has to AO, which is the perpendicular on TH. This is evident, for line $AL <$ line AZ. Hence, by V.8 of Euclid,[6] $TA/AL > TA/AZ$. And because $TA/AZ = TO/AO$, hence $TA/AL > TO/AO$. So this leads up to the seventh [proposition] of this work [*On Spiral Lines*]: "With a circle given and in it a line less than the diameter, etc."[7]

"It is then possible to draw from A," the center, to the line HN (which line HN has been produced by extending the line less than the diameter continually and directly) a line AN produced so that $NR/RT = TA/AL$. This latter ratio is the given ratio, according to the seventh [proposition] of this work [*On Spiral Lines*]. Therefore, alternately, $NR/TA = RT/AL$. But, by V.8 of Euclid,[6]

$$\frac{TR}{AL} < \frac{\text{arc } TR}{\text{circum. cir. } TKH},$$

since straight line TR is less than curve TR, as a chord is less than its arc, and AL, by hypothesis, is greater than the circumference of circle TKH. Therefore, the ratio of NR to TA (i.e., to RA since $TA = RA$, both being radii from center A) is less than the ratio of arc TR to the circumference of circle TKH. Therefore, *componendo*, the whole

$$\frac{NA}{RA} < \frac{(\text{whole circum. } TKH + \text{arc } TR)}{\text{circum. cir. } TKH}.$$

In other words, because

$$\frac{NR}{RA} < \frac{\text{arc } RT}{\text{whole circum.}},$$

therefore the ratio of the first term plus the second to the second (i.e., $NR + RA$, which is NA, to RA) is less than the sum of arc TR plus the whole circumference to this whole circumference. But

---

[4] See Commentary, Prop. 3, lines 21–25.

[5] Again notice the preoccupation with numerical illustrations of the geometrical argument.

[6] See Commentary, Prop. 3, line 28.

[7] Note that the wording of the enunciation has been altered: *et* has been omitted while *-que* has been added to *eo*; and *minore* has been altered to *minori*. See Commentary, Prop. 4, lines 1–2.

$$\frac{(TR + \text{whole circum.})}{\text{whole circum. of cir. } TKH} = \frac{QA}{AT} = \frac{QA}{RA},$$

by the fifteenth [proposition of this work: *On Spiral Lines*]. Therefore $NA/RA < QA/RA$, which is impossible. This is manifest and is against V.8 of Euclid.[6] For when two unequal magnitudes are compared to a third, the ratio of the greater to the third is greater than that of the lesser to this third magnitude. But $NA > QA$, as the whole than its part. Therefore, $NA/RA > QA/RA$. Therefore, the conclusion is known to be impossible. Hence that from which it follows is impossible. But the conclusion was drawn from the assumption that straight line AZ would be greater than the circumference of circle TKH. Hence it is not greater.

[Second Part of the Proof]

And so again, if it is possible, let ZA be less than the circumference of circle THK [see Fig. I.5.11b]. And so I shall take a certain line AL greater than AZ but less than the circumference of circle THK. And from T I shall draw TM parallel to TZ. Again, therefore, the circle is THK and in it the line TH less than the diameter, and another line tangent to the circle at T. And the ratio of AT to AL is less than that of $\frac{1}{2} HT$ to the perpendicular drawn to it from A, since it is also less than that of TA to AZ. Therefore, it is possible from A to draw line AP to the tangent, such that RN, the intercept between the straight line in the circle and the circumference, has the same ratio to TP (taken from the tangent) as TA has to AL. And so let AP cut the circle at R and the spiral at Q. And so, alternately, $NR/TA = TP/AL$.

But

$$\frac{TP}{AL} > \frac{\text{arc } TP}{\text{circum. cir. } THK},$$

straight line TP being greater than arc TR and AL being less than the circumference of circle THK. Therefore,

$$\frac{NR}{AR} > \frac{\text{arc } TR}{\text{circum. cir. } THKT}.$$

Hence,

$$\frac{RA}{AN} > \frac{\text{circum. cir. } THKT}{\text{arc } TKR}.$$

But the ratio which the circumference of circle $THKT$ has to arc TKR is the same as that of straight line TA to AQ, for this has been demonstrated. Therefore, $RA/AN > TA/AQ$, which indeed is impossible. Therefore, ZA is neither greater nor less than the circumference of circle THK. Therefore, it is equal to it.

[Commentary to the Second Part of the Proof]

"And so I shall take—" By the fourth [proposition] of this work [*On Spiral Lines*], it is possible for *AL* to be less than the circumference of the circle and greater than *AZ*.

"And I shall draw" by I.31 of Euclid.[8] And in this [circle] line *TH* is less than the diameter because every line drawn in a circle but not through the center is less than the diameter, by III.7 of Euclid.[9]

"And another line tangent" for by hypothesis *TH* is drawn from *T* parallel to *AZ* and ∠*TAZ* is a right angle. It follows that ∠*MTA* is a right angle by I.29 of Euclid.[10] Therefore, *MT* is tangent to the circle in *T*, by III.15 (=Gr. III.16).[11]

"Therefore, it is possible—" By the eighth [proposition] of this work [*On Spiral Lines*], *TA/AL* is as a given ratio. Therefore, *RN/TP* = *TA/AL*. Hence, alternately, *RN/TA* = *TP/AL*.

"Hence *RA/AN*—" This is evident from the ratios of four quantities. If the ratio of the first to the second is greater than the ratio of the third to the fourth and if the second is greater than the first and the fourth than the third, then necessarily the ratio of the second to the difference between it and the first is greater than the ratio of the fourth to the difference between it and the third. Numbers will teach you this,[12] as when there are four quantities: the first 3, the second 9, the third 4, and the fourth 16. Hence, the ratio of the first to the second, since it is ⅓, is greater than the ratio of the third to the fourth since that is ¼, and also the second is greater than the first and the fourth than the third. I say that the ratio of the second [i.e., 9] to the difference between it and the first, i.e., 6, since it is 3/2, is greater than the ratio of the fourth, [i.e., 16] to the difference between it and the third, i.e., 12, since that is 4/3. But it is thus in the proposed [statement]. For *RN* is the first, *TA* the second, arc *TR* the third, the whole circle the fourth. But it has already been seen that the ratio of the first to the second is greater than the ratio of the third to the fourth and that the second is greater than the first and the fourth than the third. Therefore, the ratio of the second, namely *TA* or its equal *RA*, to the difference *RA* − *RN*, which difference is *AN*, is greater than the ratio of the fourth, namely, the circle, to the difference between the circle and arc *TR*, which difference is the arc *TKR*. And thus is evident that which was proposed [in the commentary] but not in the proof.[13]

---

[8] See Commentary, Prop. 13, line 114.

[9] *Ibid.*, line 116.

[10] See Commentary, Prop. 3, lines 21–25.

[11] The pertinent part of III.15 (=Gr. III.16) in the Campanus version of the *Elementa* (Basel, 1546), p. 66, runs: "Unde etiam manifestum est, omnem lineam rectam a termino diametri cuiuslibet circuli orthogonaliter ductam, circulum ipsum contingere."

[12] See note 5 above.

[13] In the context of medieval Euclidian mathematics, the word *commentum* usually meant the "proof" or anything that explained or proved the enunciation. See M. Clagett, "The Medieval Latin Translations from the Arabic of the *Elements* of Euclid," *Isis*, Vol. 44 (1953), p. 19.

Here ends the demonstration of the equality of a straight line to the circumference of a circle, and consequently the ratio of something straight to something curved, which many people have denied. In the year 1340.

14. EVERY CIRCLE IS EQUAL TO A RIGHT TRIANGLE, THE RADIUS OF WHICH CIRCLE IS EQUAL TO ONE OF THE SIDES INCLUDING THE RIGHT ANGLE, THE CIRCUMFERENCE TO THE BASE.

Let circle $ABGD$ be related to $\triangle E$ in the manner stated [see Fig. I.5.12]. I say that they are equal. For, if it is possible, let the circle be greater and let square AG be inscribed. And let the arcs be bisected, and let the segments [so formed] already be less than the excess by which the circle exceeds the triangle [1]. Therefore, the polygon is even greater than the triangle [2]. Let the center N be taken and the perpendicular NX [3]. Therefore, NX is less than the side of the triangle which is the radius. But the perimeter of the polygon is less than the other side [of the triangle] since it is less than the circumference of the circle. Therefore, the polygon is less than $\triangle E$ [4], which is contradictory [5].

Now, if it is possible, let the circle be less than $\triangle E$, and let a square be circumscribed and let the arcs be bisected, and let tangents be drawn through the points [of bisection]. Therefore, by III.17 (=Gr. III.18) of Euclid,[1] $\angle OAR$ is a right angle. Therefore, line OR is greater than line MR, for line MR is equal to RA [6]. And $\triangle ROP$ is greater than half the figure $OZAM$ [7]. Let the [sum of the] sectors [i.e., figures] similar to PZA be less than the excess by which $\triangle E$ exceeds circle $ABGD$. Therefore, the circumscribed polygon is even less than $\triangle E$, which is indeed contradictory, for it is greater since NA is equal to the altitude of the triangle and the perimeter is greater than the base of the triangle [8]. Therefore, that circle is equal to the above-mentioned triangle. But the triangle can be squared, therefore also the circle.

[Commentary]

[1] Since it is possible to divide the arcs any number of times until the segments remain less than that excess.

[2] When some given magnitude is compared to two unequal magnitudes, the greater is that which is exceeded less by the given magnitude. For example, if 10 is compared to 8 and 6, 8 is less exceeded by 10 (it being exceeded in the amount of 2) than is 6 (it being exceeded in the amount of 4). Therefore 8 > 6. But the circle is compared to the inscribed polygon and to $\triangle E$. And by hypothesis the polygon is less exceeded than is the triangle, for the segments [bounded by the circumference and the sides] of the polygon are [in sum] less than the amount in which the

Prop. 14
   [1] See Commentary, Prop. 14, line 16.

triangle is exceeded by the circle. Therefore, the polygon is greater than $\triangle E$.

[3] NX is a perpendicular to a side of the polygon, namely to side AZ.

[4] Proof: For if the lesser side of the triangle, which is equal to the radius of the circle, is multiplied into the side co-terminal with it at the right angle, namely, into the line equal to the circumference of the circle, half of the product is the area of the triangle. Similarly, if NX, which is perpendicular to a side of the polygon, is multiplied into the perimeter, i.e., into all of the sides of the polygon joined together, or into a line equal to all of the sides joined together, half the product is the area of the polygon, which is evident by the triangles into which the polygon is resolved. But it is clear that the area of the polygon is less than the area of the triangle, for it is produced from lesser lines, since NX is less than NA and the perimeter of the polygon is less than the side of the triangle equal to the circumference of the circle. Therefore, the polygon is less than $\triangle E$.

[5] For it is against what has been said before, it having been said that the polygon is greater.

[6] MR is equal to RA, since the sides of the circumscribed polygon are equal as the result of the circumscribed square and the bisected arcs to which the tangents are drawn. And $OR > AR$, by I.18 of Euclid.[2]

[7] And $\triangle ROP$ is greater than half the figure $OZAM$ included by straight line OZ, straight line OM and arc ZAM. This is evident because $\triangle OAR > \triangle ARM$; therefore, it is greater than that which is less than $\triangle ARM$, namely, the figure ARM, AM being a curve or an arc. That $\triangle OAR > \triangle ARM$ is evident by I.38 of Euclid.[3] For the base OR of $\triangle OAR$ is not equal to, but is greater than, the base RM of $\triangle ARM$, as has been seen. Therefore, $\triangle OAR$ is not equal to, but is greater than, $\triangle ARM$, for from lesser lines is produced a lesser quantity just as from greater a greater. But $\triangle OAP = \triangle OAR$ and figure PAZ = figure ARM. Therefore, the whole triangle OPR is greater than half the figure $OZAM$.

[8] When some given magnitude is compared to two unequal magnitudes, the lesser is that which exceeds the given magnitude by a lesser amount. But the circumscribed polygon exceeds the circle by a lesser amount than does $\triangle E$, as has been posited. Therefore, the polygon is less than $\triangle E$, which is impossible, for it is necessarily greater than $\triangle E$. This is obvious because NA, the perpendicular to a side of the polygon, is equal to the altitude of the triangle, since it is equal to the radius of the circle, but the perimeter of the polygon is greater than the perimeter of the circle, that is, than the circumference of the circle, and consequently greater than the straight line of the triangle equal to the circumference of the circle. Therefore, the polygon is greater than $\triangle E$.

Here ends the Quadrature of the Circle.

---

[2] *Ibid.*, line 50.

[3] That is, by not fulfilling the conditions of equality specified in Prop. I.38 of the *Elementa* (Basel, 1546), p. 31: "Si duo trianguli super bases aequales atque inter duas lineas aequidistantes ceciderint, aequales eos esse necesse est."

Commentary

Proposition 1

   3–4 "Circulo . . . periferia" The author has added this to *On Spiral Lines*, Prop. 3, apparently feeling that it would be necessary to establish the proposition for a single circle before extending it to any number of circles. He was undoubtedly conscious of the fact that in his Proposition 3 (=*On Spiral Lines*, Prop. 5), the proposition is applied to a single circle, or at least to a given arc.

   4–6 "et . . . periferiis" This is taken from the Moerbeke translation with slight verbal changes.

   7–13 "Circumscripto. . . . est." This proof is longer and verbally quite different from the comparable proof of *On Spiral Lines*, Prop. 3. It is specifically based on the assumption that "everything including another is greater than it." This is probably the "common knowledge" or axiom referred to in the last line of the proof. Notice that a similar postulate was included in the Cambridge Version of the *De mensura circuli* (see Clagett, *Archimedes*, Vol. 1, p. 68, Petitio 3; cf. discussion, pp. 63–64).

Proposition 2

   1–4 "Duabus . . . maiorem." The enunciation is accurately repeated from the Moerbeke translation of *On Spiral Lines*, Prop. 4, except that a *quidem* has been omitted after *maiore*.

   5–13 "Sic. . . . conclusum." The proof is quite different from that found in *On Spiral Lines*, Prop. 4. The author does not, as Archimedes did, specifically use the so-called Lemma of Archimedes, although he does advance the same basic idea, when he adds that the excess of line AB over the circumference of a circle is not as a point but as a line CB. This is in agreement with the interpretation of Postulate 5 of *On the Sphere and the Cylinder* as holding that the difference between quantities of the same kind is itself a quantity of that same kind or in the cases of lines that the difference is a line and not a point (see E. J. Dijksterhuis, *Archimedes* [Copenhagen, 1956], p. 148).

Proposition 3

   1–8 "Circulo . . . periferiam." This was drawn verbatim from the Moerbeke translation of *On Spiral Lines*, Prop. 5, except that the author has properly added *rectam* in line 2 and *contingentis* in lines 6–7. The word order has been altered slightly by the author.

   9–10 "in puncto B" This replaces *penes B* in the Moerbeke translation.

  11–12 "extra circulum" This is missing in the Moerbeke translation and merely refers to E as drawn separately rather than on the circle.

13–14 "et . . . *B*" This states the *neusis* and might be better rendered as "let *HT* be placed equal to *E* while verging toward *B*." Notice this author has replaced Moerbeke's *extensa* with *continuata*. The better translation would have been *inclinans* or *tendens*.

14–17 "Hoc. . . . precedentem." This passage is missing in the Moerbeke translation and probably reflects a mechanical solution of the *neusis* posed in lines 13–14. Actually all that the author intends here is that, since *BT* can be as small as we like, *HT* can accordingly be as large as we like, and hence it is possible on altering the size of *BT*, by shifting it around, to find some *HT* equal to line *E* while *BTH* remains a straight line beginning from *B*. It seems to me that it is quite perceptive of the author to recognize that Archimedes is merely posing the possibility or existence of a solution. Cf. the remarks of T. L. Heath, *Archimedes*, p. civ.

18–19 "Dico . . . periferiam." This formal *diorismos* of the proposition is missing in the Moerbeke translation.

21–25 "quia. . . . proportionalia" This represents commentary on the author's part and is missing in the Moerbeke translation. I.15 runs in the Campanus version of the *Elementa* (Basel, 1546), p. 17: "Omnium duarum linearum seinvicem secantium, omnes anguli contra se positi sunt aequales." For I.29, see *ibid.*, p. 25: "Si duabus lineis aequidistantibus linea supervenerit, duo anguli coalterni aequales sunt." For VI.4, see *ibid.*, p. 141: "Omnium duorum triangulorum, quorum anguli unius angulis alterius sunt aequales, latera aequos angulos continentia* sunt proportionalia." (*The excellent Campanus MS of the 13c, New York, Columbia Univ. Libr. Plimpton 156, 50r, has *respicientia*.)

28 "8^{am} 5^i Euclidis" For V.8, see *Elementa* (Basel, 1546), p. 119: "Si duae quantitates inaequales ad unam quantitatem proportionentur, maior quidem maiorem, minor vero minorem obtinebit proportionem. Illius autem ad illas, ad minorem quidem proportio maior, ad maiorem vero minor erit."

Proposition 4

1–2 "Circulo . . . extraducta" This is an expansion of the Moerbeke wording made necessary by the omission of Prop. 6 of *On Spiral Lines*, not needed by the author for the ultimate proof of his Proposition 13 (=*On Spiral Lines*, Prop. 18). He has also added the term *quantumlibet* ("as much as we like").

3 "rectam" The addition of *rectam* to Moerbeke's wording makes the meaning clearer. The remainder of the enunciation is in Moerbeke's words except for substitution in line 5 of *extraducte* for *educte*.

9–29 "Sit. . . . propositum." This proof is very much expanded beyond the few lines in the Moerbeke text, for all the geometric steps are here included. Notice also that the author has advanced a formal proof, with construction and *diorismos* carefully detailed.

22–24 "quia . . . Euclidis" The crucial part of the comment on XII.2 in the Campanus version of the *Elementa* (Basel, 1546), p. 389, runs: "Manifestum est ex hoc communi scientia, scilicet quanta est quaelibet magnitudo ad aliquam secundam, tantam necesse est esse quamlibet tertiam ad aliquam quartam. . . ." This in fact is one of the additional axioms added to the first book (*ibid.*, p. 3).

24–25 "per . . . co⟨n⟩choydeale" This phrase was added in the margin by Johannes de Muris to the rather laconic statement in the text. I have already remarked in the introduction to this tract that the assertion that this construction is possible by the conchoidal instrument apparently demonstrates a knowledge on the part of Johannes de Muris of the section in Eutocius' commentary *On the Sphere and the Cylinder* as translated by Moerbeke where Nicomedes' conchoidal instrument is described in the solution of the problem of finding two proportional means. The fact that Johannes apparently made this transfer to the problem at hand shows considerable ingenuity for a medieval mathematician. Cf. Heath, *Archimedes*, pp. cv–cvii, for a discussion of the mechanical solution of the *neuseis* involved in these propositions of *On Spiral Lines*.

28 "33^{am} (! 32^{am}) primi Euclidis" Although all manuscripts have I.33, I am reasonably certain that the author must have meant to refer to the second part of I.32 in the Campanus version (Basel, 1546), p. 27: "Omnes autem tres angulos eius [i.e., omnis trianguli] duobus rectis angulis aequos esse necesse est." The argument clearly is that if two angles of one triangle are respectively equal to two angles of another, the third angles must be equal, since the angles of each triangle must equal two right angles.

Proposition 5

19–25 "Secundum. . . . *GM*." The author relates this *neusis* to the "doctrine" of *On Spiral Lines*, Prop. 5 (his own Prop. 3). In fact, all that he is doing here as in that earlier proposition is to call attention to the *possibility* or *existence* of the construction, i.e., since it is possible to have *IN* greater than *GM* in the neighborhood of *M* and smaller than *GM* in the neighborhood of *X*, it is therefore possible between *X* and *M* to have *IN* equal to *GM*. Presumably, as in Prop. 7 (his own Prop. 4), he realized that he could use the *instrumentum conchoideale* to effect the solution.

30 "19^{am} 7^i Euclidis" For VII.19, see the *Elementa* (Basel, 1546), p. 183: "Si duo numeri unum multiplicant, erit proportio duorum inde productorum tanquam duorum multiplicantium."

36 "21^{am} 7^i Euclidis" For VII.21 (=Gr. VII.20), see *Elementa* (Basel, 1546), p. 185: "Numeri secundum quamlibet proportionem minimi numerant quoslibet in eadem proportione, minor minorem et maior maiorem aequaliter." For III.34, *ibid.*, p. 81: "Si intra circulum duae rectae lineae sese invicem secent, quod sub duabus partibus unius earum procedit, aequum est ei rectangulo quod sub duabus alterius lineae partibus continetur."

45 "5^{am} 5^i vel 7^{am} 7^i Euclidis" For V.5, see *Elementa* (Basel, 1546), p. 117: "Si fuerint duae quantitates quarum una sit pars alterius, minuaturque ab utraque ipsarum ipsa pars, erit reliquum reliquo atque totum toti aeque multiplex. Vel sic, minuaturque ab utraque ipsarum ipsa pars aliquota, erit reliquum reliqui tota pars, quota totum totius." For VII.7, see *ibid.*, p. 176: "Si fuerint duo numeri quorum unus alterius pars, detrahaturque ab ambobus ipsa pars, erit reliquus tota pars reliqui, quota totus totius." These propositions are, I believe, not appropriate for the proof, since the magnitudes here involved are not shown to be parts and multiples in the Greek and medieval sense of these terms. Rather the proof calls for the technique of *dividendo* or the subtraction of ratios as given in Euclid V.17; *ibid.*, p. 126: "Si fuerint quantitates coniunctim proportionales, easdem disiunctim quoque proportionales esse."

Proposition 6

12–13 "Hoc. . . . *DB*." Again the author resorts to numbers not present in the Moerbeke translation of Prop. 1 of *On Spiral Lines*. Otherwise, the author has followed the Moerbeke translation closely.

25–28 "Similiter. . . . deductionis" Notice that the detailed second part of the comparable sentence in the Moerbeke text has been replaced by the phrase "proportio linearum." However, the proof is still clear. Notice further that the author has felt it necessary to indicate that the argument that starts with times and ends with lines is the reverse of the preceding argument.

Proposition 7

1–6 "Si . . . ipsis." The author has changed Moerbeke's wording somewhat, without however altering the basic meaning of the enunciation.

11–12 "quod . . . convincit" Notice that the author has reduced the specific argument of the Moerbeke translation of *On Spiral Lines*, Prop. 2 (which involved reference to the ratios of specific times) to the general statement that the uniformity of velocities guarantees the proof.

Definitions

1 "[Descriptiones]" The definitions originally given in the Moerbeke text are pared down to those which the author felt necessary for the propositions leading to the proof of Prop. 13 (=*On Spiral Lines*, Prop. 18).

2 "assignatur" This word is substituted for "affigatur" in the Moerbeke translation, which is a literal rendering of the Greek: ἐπιζευχθῇ.

9 "circulationis" After this word, Moerbeke added *rectum*. This, however, should have been *recta* and joined with the next definition. Hence, the author made an intelligent decision in leaving out the *rectum* here, but unfortunately he was committed to Moerbeke's incorrect rendering of εὐθεῖα, ἄν by *rectum*. *Si* and so he had to do the best he could with the next definition (see the succeeding comment).

10–12 "Si. . . . dicatur." It is clear that in trying to make sense out of Moerbeke's rendering of the fourth definition (which the author breaks into two definitions), he was misled as to what was being defined here, apparently thinking that they were "first" and "second revolutions" (perhaps in the sense of "first circle" and "second circle"). Moerbeke's translation of ἄν as if it were ἄν and the coupling of *rectum* (itself a mistranslation of εὐθεῖα) with the preceding definition were the principal reasons for the author's misunderstanding. Heath's translation reveals the actual intent of Archimedes' definition (*Archimedes*, p. 166): "4. Let the length which the point that moves along the straight line describes in one revolution be called the *first distance*, that which the same point describes in the second revolution the *second distance*, and similarly let the distances described in further revolutions be called after the number of the particular revolution." At any rate, as I have suggested, the author may have thought of this fourth definition (embraced by his fourth and fifth definitions) as defining "first circle" and "second circle," which were in fact defined in the last definition of Archimedes omitted by this author.

Proposition 8

12–14 "Ergo. . . . potest." These lines are original with the author and replace the conclusion of the proof given in the Moerbeke translation of *On Spiral Lines*, Prop. 12.

Proposition 9

11–13 "Sed . . . duple." Notice that the point O is specified by the author and included on the diagram, although such is not the case in the Moerbeke translation of *On Spiral Lines*, Prop. 13. The statement, $AH + AG > 2\ AO$, is easily proved: see the translation of P. Ver Eecke, *Les Oeuvres complètes d'Archimède*, Vol. 1, (Paris, 1960), p. 263, note 4.

14 "revolutionem, scilicet elicem" I have simply translated this phrase as "spiral" here and elsewhere. A similar phrase is in the Moerbeke translation. But the author himself on other occasions (e.g., see Prop. 10, line 8) reminds the reader that *revolutio* means "spiral," probably because he fears some confusion with *circulatio*.

Proposition 10

18 "aliasque . . . cura" This further generalization is added by the author and is thus missing in the Moerbeke translation of *On Spiral Lines*, Prop. 14.

Proposition 11

5 "eductarum ultimis terminate" This phrase is not in the Moerbeke translation of *On Spiral Lines*, Prop. 15, since the text of Archimedes means to refer back to the preceding proposition by the expression *dicte periferie*. The phrase added here is merely an effort to make the proposition independently clear.

13–14 "Igitur . . . 17^{am} 3^{ii} (*!* 11^{am} 5^i)" The argument runs: The ratio of the total arcs traversed is as the ratio of the times. But the ratios of the straight lines traversed is also as this same ratio of times. Hence the ratio of the arcs is as the ratio of the straight lines. The citation of III.17 of Euclid (present in all of the manuscripts) makes absolutely no sense in the argument, since it refers to a tangent to a circle. I am sure that the proposition originally intended by the author was Prop. V.11 (ed. of Basel, 1546), p. 121: "Si fuerint quantitatum proportiones alicui uni aequales, ipsas quoque proportiones sibi invicem aequales esse necesse est."

19–21 "Eadem . . . sumptam." The author has added this sentence beyond the Moerbeke translation of *On Spiral Lines*, Prop. 15. While it is somewhat confused in the existing manuscripts, its intention is made clear in my translation.

Proposition 12

1–5 "Si . . . erunt." This enunciation omits the added phrase in the Moerbeke translation of *On Spiral Lines*, Prop. 16, to the effect that the angle in the forward direction is obtuse, that in the backward direction acute. But, in fact, this emerges clearly enough in the proof.

Proposition 13

33 "Concidet . . . huius (*!* 18 5^i?)." The manuscripts have *per 5^{am} huius*, but I fail to see that Prop. 5 of *On Spiral Lines* applies at this point. Rather, the point worth noting, as is evident in the author's commentary below, is that the statement

[1] $\dfrac{NR}{TA} < \dfrac{\text{arc } TR}{\text{circum. cir. } THK}$ can be transformed by *compo-*

nendo into the statement $\dfrac{NA}{AR} < \dfrac{(\text{arc. } TR + \text{circum. cir. } THK)}{\text{circum. cir. } THK}$,

and this altered statement then allows for it to be "joined with" statement [2], and thus to produce the conclusion that $\dfrac{NA}{AR} < \dfrac{QA}{AT}$. Hence the reference to 5^{am} *huius* ought rather to be a reference to the procedure of *componendo*. But this procedure is justified by V.18 of the *Elementa* (Basel, 1546), p. 127: "Si fuerint quantitates disiunctim proportionales, coniunctim quoque proportionales erunt." Hence, my correction to "V.18" in the translation.

114 "31^{am} primi Euclidis" For I.31, see the *Elementa* (Basel, 1546), p. 26: "A puncto extra lineam dato, lineae propositae aequidistantem ducere."

116 "7^{am} 3^{ii} Euclidis" While the author cites III.7, III.14 (=Gr. III.15) seems more immediately pertinent. III.7 in the Campanus version of the *Elementa* (Basel, 1546), p. 58, runs: "Si in diametro circuli punctus praeter centrum signetur et ab eo ad circumferentiam lineae plurimae ducantur, quae super centrum transierit, omnium erit longissima. Quae vero diametrum perficiet, omnium erit brevissima. . . ." For III.14 see *ibid.*, p. 65: "Si intra circulum plurimae rectae lineae ceciderint, diametrum eius omnium longissimam . . . esse necesse est."

Proposition 14

16 "17^{am} 3^{ii} Euclidis" For III.17 (=Gr. III.18), see the *Elementa* (Basel, 1546), p. 69: "Si circulum linea recta contingat, a contactu vero ad centrum linea recta ducatur, necesse est eam super lineam contingentem esse perpendicularem."

50 "18^{am} primi Euclidis" For I.18, see *Elementa* (Basel, 1546), p. 18: "Omnis trianguli longius latus, maiori angulo oppositum est."

CHAPTER 6

The Use of the Moerbeke Translations of Archimedes in Chapter 10 of the *De arte mensurandi*

To this point we have considered the use of Moerbeke's translations of *On Spiral Lines, On the Measurement of the Circle* and Eutocius' *Commentary on the Sphere and the Cylinder* in various chapters of the *De arte mensurandi* and the *Quadripartitum numerorum*. This list can now be extended by the addition of the Moerbeke translations of *On the Sphere and the Cylinder* and *On Conoids and Spheroids*, both of which are cited in Chapter 10 of the *De arte mensurandi*. It must be recalled initially that Chapter 10 is one of those chapters composed by the Continuator. We have already argued in Chapter 2 for the identification of the Continuator with Johannes de Muris. It is evident from the text given below that the citations from *On the Sphere and the Cylinder* are extensive and accurate. On the other hand, those from *On Conoids and Spheroids*, while literally accurate, are completely misused, thus producing erroneous conclusions in Propositions 22–24. For Johannes has attempted to apply propositions framed by Archimedes for ellipsoids to solids generated by the rotation of circular segments about their chords (see below, notes to Propositions 22–24).

In reviewing briefly the content of Chapter 10 of the *De arte mensurandi*, we should first remark that the Continuator states in the first paragraph of his Proemium to Chapter 10 that the work of the original author was not completed; or, if it was, no copy has fallen into his hands. Hence, he asserts, he does not know how the original author would have treated the topics specified for the tenth and eleventh chapters, namely, the measure of a spherical body and that of bodies that are irregular. But, the Continuator adds, he will do the best he can. In fact, he considerably expanded the original proposal for Chapter 10 beyond the measurement of a sphere to include theorems concerning pyramids, cones, prisms, cylinders, rhomboidal bodies and the segments of these various figures. He further remarks in his Proemium on the importance and uniqueness of Archimedes' *On the Sphere and the Cylinder* and his *On Conoids and*

89

Spheroids for the demonstrations that follow in Chapter 10. However, it looks as if the citations of *On Conoids and Spheroids* here and at the end of the Proemium are something of an afterthought. At least it is curious that the two references in the Proemium to *On Conoids and Spheroids* are both found in the margin of Johannes' copy, i.e. *Pd*, rather than in the body of the text. It is also strange that, while most of the enunciations of the propositions from *On the Sphere and the Cylinder* used in the Continuator's demonstrations are given in the Proemium, none of the propositions later used from *On Conoids and Spheroids* is stated in the Proemium. Finally, in this connection it can be noted that just before giving his list of Archimedean propositions in the Proemium, Johannes tells the reader that he has to have for consultation this "book" rather than these "books," thus apparently confirming the idea that the references to *On Conoids and Spheroids* were added later.

The probable explanation of these facts is that Johannes decided only later to add the last eight propositions (i.e., Propositions 18–25) after completing the propositions that demanded the use of *On the Sphere and the Cylinder* and had as their object the surface and volume of a sphere. Having decided to add propositions concerning the figure which he called "the arcuate rhombus" (and certain others), he then realized that he wanted to cite Archimedes' *On Conoids and Spheroids*. But since he had not given the appropriate enunciations in the Proemium, he perhaps felt compelled to give their substance in Propositions 22–24. He may then have thought it proper to add to the Proemium of Chapter 10 the two statements concerning *On Conoids and Spheroids* which we have noted below. This reasoning receives apparent confirmation from a note added by Johannes de Muris to the bottom of folio 69r in *Pd* (i.e., after Proposition 17): "Hic proprie finis 10^{mi} capituli. Resume (?) 8 propositiones; in papiro sunt." This seems to mean that Johannes has added the last eight propositions beyond the subject suggested by the original author for Chapter 10. Indeed Proposition 17 does complete the subject of the sphere. The reader is then advised to continue on to the last eight propositions that are contained on the succeeding sheets of paper. A further bit of evidence that Johannes expanded Chapter 10 beyond his original intention is found in the fact that in Proposition 25 a further theorem from *On the Sphere and the Cylinder* (Prop. I.19) is cited together with its enunciation given in full. But this theorem was not given in the corpus of enunciations from *On the Sphere and the Cylinder* found in the Proemium of Chapter 10. There are many other examples of additions made by Johannes de Muris to other chapters of the *De arte mensurandi*.[1]

Returning to the discussion of Archimedes in the Proemium to Chapter

---

[1] For example, see the three unnumbered propositions added after Proposition 16 of Chapter 6 of the *De arte mensurandi*. They are given on the bottom margin of folio 43v in MS *Pd* and are labeled in *Pe* (94r) as "addita," "alia addita" and again "alia addita." No demonstrations are given. There is also an unnumbered proposition prior to Proposition 22 in the same chapter. Its enunciation is given in *Pd* in the upper margin of folio 46r

10, we should note that Johannes de Muris tells us that Archimedes composed *On the Sphere and the Cylinder* for Dositheus after the death of Conon, which of course he got from the Proemium of Archimedes' work (see Vol. 2, 23vA, F-G). As we look beyond the Proemium to the actual geometry of Chapter 10, it will be immediately apparent that there is very little geometrical originality in the treatment of the various propositions. As the author himself points out, to give demonstrations of the key propositions on which his demonstrations are based would be no more than recounting the work of Archimedes. In fact, the main purposes of the chapter are [1] to derive simple metrical formulas from propositions already proved by Euclid and Archimedes, and, on occasion, [2] to give numerical examples of the use of the metrical formulas so derived (see Propositions 1–4, 10, 12, 17 and 24). It is in the course of giving a numerical example involving surds in Proposition 2 that the Continuator cites his own *Quadripartitum numerorum*, thus allowing us to conclude that Johannes de Muris was the Continuator (see my Chapter 2 above) and hence the author of Chapter 10.

In my treatment of the use of the Moerbeke translations in the *De arte mensurandi*, I shall make no effort to add the occasional references to the Propositions of Chapter 10 found in the second part of Chapter 12, for they are mostly redundant and give no new information on our proposed topic. However, it can be remarked that in Proposition 24 of the second part of Chapter 12, the Continuator directly cites Proposition I.32 (=Gr. I.34) and I.33 (=Gr. I.35) of *On the Sphere and the Cylinder*.[2]

---

with the designation of "addita." The proof is given on a strip inserted here in the manuscript (cf. *Pe*, 96v, where the enunciation and proof are simply added to the body of the text but without number). See also the additions (so labeled) to Propositions 19 (*Pd*, 54v), 22 (*ibid.*), and 23 (*Pd*, 56r).

[2] See MS Paris, BN lat. 7380, 80v: "24ᵃ. Datam speram per aliam secundum proportionem statutam sectam reddere. Sit *A* spera data et proportio statuta *H* ad *Z*. Quoniam omnis chilindrus basem habens maximum circulum eorum qui in spera, altitudinem autem equalem dyametro spere est hemiolus spere, igitur cum chilindrus sit sectus secundum proportionem statutam *H* ad *Z* per 21ᵃᵐ huius de spera non poterit amplius dubitari. Sit ergo chilindrus predictus spere circumscriptus *C*, qui secetur per alium qui sit *D* secundum proportionem *H* ad *Z* per 21ᵃᵐ huius, et in eo inscribatur spera *B*. Dico igitur speram *A* per sperulam *B* secari secundum proportionem *H* ad *Z*. Nam sicut chilindrus *C* ad speram *A* ita chilindrus *D* ad speram *B*. Est enim utrobique proportio hemiola per 33ᵃᵐ Archimenidis in de spera et chilindro. Ergo permutatim sicut chilindrus ad chilindrum ita spera *A* ad speram *B*. Sed chilindrorum est proportio *H* ad *Z* per ypothesim, ergo et sperarum; quare propositum. Item aliter inscribatur conus spere date sic ut habeat basem maximum circulum eorum qui in spera, altitudinem autem equalem semidyametro spere et illum conum seca per alium conum secundum proportionem statutam per 22ᵃᵐ huius quem conum inscribe uni spere, hoc est, eidem cono speram circumscribe per modum dictum et argue ex proportione conorum proportionem sperarum sicut dictum est de chilindro nuper et habebis propositum. Nam omnis spera quadrupla est coni habentis basem equalem maximo circulo eorum qui in spera, altitudinem autem equalem semidyametro spere per 32ᵃᵐ Archimenidis ubi supra. Igitur cum conus sit sectus in proportione statuta per 22ᵃᵐ huius, igitur etiam spera." (Note: I have added case endings to all numbers indicating propositions cited from Chapter 12 of the *De arte mensurandi* and from *On the Sphere and the Cylinder*; they are missing in the manuscript.)

In my text of Chapter 10 of the *De arte mensurandi*, I have, as in the preceding sections, depended primarily on *Pd*. Again, I have added case endings for the numbers referring to propositions drawn from the *Elements* and the various chapters of the *De arte mensurandi* (for example, giving "per 9ᵃᵐ" instead of "per 9"). Note that *Pd* changes from the spelling *dyameter* used throughout the manuscript to *diameter* in the latter part of Chapter 10. However, I have retained *dyameter* throughout. The diagrams are taken from *Pd*. The author has attempted only occasionally (see Figs. I.6.1 and I.6.2) to give the solid figures in perspective. His figures, which are simply plane sections (a triangle for a cone, a circle for a sphere and so on), are ordinarily understandable when correlated with the text (an exception is Figure I.6.7, which had to be reconstructed for immediate understanding). As before, I have added Johannes' marginal additions to the text without brackets. The marginal folio references in my text are to MS *Pd*.

Sigla

Pd = Paris, BN lat. 7380, 67r–70v, middle of 14c.
Pe = Paris, BN lat. 7381, 134r–43r, 15c.
Xb = Vatican, Vat. lat. 9410, 60v–64v, 15c.
Ua = Utrecht, Bibl. Univ. 725, 80r–87r, 15c.
Xn = Vatican, Ottob. lat. 1423, 77v–84r, late 15c or 16c.

Johannis de Muris De arte mensurandi
Chapter 10

_{67r}

/Incipit 10ᵐ capitulum

In hiis autem duobus ultimis capitulis proposuit actor ab initio sui operis, quod nobis reliquit incompletum aut ad manus nostras saltem completio non pervenit, determinare de mensura corporis sperici et corporum 5 aliorum omnino irregularium. Quid autem intendebat et per que media fuisset processurus non valeo cogitare. Sed iuxta propositum sui tituli generalis intendo prosequi prout mihi poterit occurrere nutu Dei mensuras tam in corporibus spericis et portionibus eorundem quam piramidibus lateratis et rotundis, prismatibus et chilindro atque rombo et 10 diversis sectionibus eorundem ac de vasorum capacitate et eorum compositione et de monstruosis corporibus et gilbosis, una cum aliis que

2 initio: principio *Xb*
5–6 media fuisset *PeXb, tr. PdUaXn*
7 nutu *PdUaXn* nuptu *PeXb*
9 prismatibus *mg. Pd, om. Xb* / pro rombo hab. *Xb lacunam*

tunc temporis apparebunt. Et in hoc cum Dei laude finis operi debitus imponetur.

Ad demonstrationem autem eorum que secuntur Euclidis elementa non
15 sufficiunt, ut in eis que anterius precesserunt, liber enim ille ad talia non pervenit, nec aliqua doctrina quam viderim nisi solus liber Archimenidis in de spera et chilindro quem ad suum amicum Dositheum post mortem Cononis flebilem prostillavit ac liber eiusdem de conoydalibus et speroydalibus nuncupatus, fuerunt enim hii tres philosophi contemporanei veri-
20 tatis geometrice firmi dilectores adinvicem mutuo rescribentes. Hos autem a longe Archimenides superavit. Nullus autem antiquorum ad multas conclusiones solemnes quesitas potuit attingere nisi solus Archimenides temporibus retroactis. Que tamen restant altiora intellectus peritissimus investiget, cum in hiis nec in aliis inquisitionis terminus non ponatur.
25 Etsi nobis appareat pars scitorum maior utique pars remanet ignotorum.

Propositiones ergo Archimenidis ubi supra sunt iste quas nobis loco dignitatum petimus quo ad presens, eas enim resolvere a compositione aut recitatione libri Archimenidis non differet. Igitur librum habeas atque stude.

30 13ª primi. Omnis chilindri recti superficies preter bases equalis est circulo cuius que ex centro habeat proportionem mediam lateris chilindri et dyametri basis chilindri.

14ª primi. Omnis coni equicrurii preter basem superficies est equalis circulo cuius que ex centro habet mediam proportionem lateris coni et
35 eius que ex centro circuli qui est basis coni.

18ª primi. Omni rombo ex conis equicruriis composito est equalis conus qui basem habet equalem superficiei alterius coni continentium rumbum, altitudinem autem equalem catheto a vertice alterius coni ducto ad unum latus alterius coni.

40 31ª primi. Omnis spere superficies est quadrupla maximi circuli eorum qui per ipsam.

32ª primi. Omnis spera est quadrupla coni habentis basem equalem maximo circulo eorum qui in spera, altitudinem autem eam que ex centro spere.

45 33ª primi. Omnis chilindrus basem habens maximum circulum eorum qui in spera, altitudinem autem equalem dyametro spere, est hemiolus spere et superficies ipsius cum basibus hemiola superficiei spere.

40ª primi. Omnis portionis spere minoris hemisperio superficies est

12 finis: terminus *Xb*
18 Cononis *corr. ex* Cenonis *PdPeXbXn et* Zenonis *Ua*
18–19 ac . . . nuncupatus *mg. Pd*
18 gonoydalibus *Pe*
20 firmi *PdPeXb* fervidi *UaXn*
22 sollemnes *Pd om. Xb* solmnes *PeUa* solemnas *Xn* / quesitas: que sicut *Xb*
27 petimus *?Pd, PeXb, om. UaXn*
28 differet *Pd, lac. Xn* differt *?Pe* differe *Ua* diffinitionem *Xb*
36 rombo *PdPeXb* rumbo *UaXnXo*

equalis circulo cuius que ex centro est equalis producte a vertice por-
50   tionis ad periferiam circuli qui est basis portionis spere.

42ª primi. Omni sectori spere est equalis conus qui basem habet equalem
superficiei portionis spere que secundum sectorem, altitudinem autem
equalem ei que ex centro.

2ª secundi. Omni portioni spere est equalis conus basem habens
55   eandem portioni, altitudinem autem rectam que ad altitudinem portionis
habet proportionem eandem quam simul ambo, scilicet que ex centro
spere et altitudo relique portionis, ad altitudinem alterius portionis.

Omnes istas conclusiones in libro de spera et chilindro Archimenides
demonstravit. Qui liber sic incipit: "Archimenides Dositheo gaudere.
60   Prius quidem misi tibi ex hiis que a nobis speculanda sunt, etc." Et
liber de conoydalibus et speroydalibus sic incipit: "Archimenides
Dositheo bene agere."

67v   /1.ª PRISMATIS QUANTITATEM MENSURARE.

Prisma est corpus columpnare lateratum cuius basis est superficies
rectilinea plurilatera, ut trigona, tetragona, pentagona, hexagona, et sic
quamdiu libuerit augmentare, sive equilatera sive inequilatera. De-
5   scribatur. Cuius quantitas sic habetur. Aree basis quantitatem inventam
per 9ᵃᵐ prime partis 5ⁱ huius duc in eius altitudinem, quod autem exit
est numerus prismatis quem tu queris.

Exemplum: Sit prisma cuius basis triangula *ABC* inequilatera, sicut 3,
4, 5 [Fig. I.6.1]. Erit ergo area basis 6. Sitque altitudo eius *BD* 10.
10   Igitur erit eius quantitas 60, a diffinitione corporis. Nam dum in superficiem ducitur altitudo corpus dicimus provenire. Eodem modo corpus serratile mensuratur, quia una species prismatis est cuius due bases sunt
triangule et tres [altere superficies] parallelogramme. Ymo sub hac mensura
cadit omne corpus rectilineum cuius bases opposite sunt equales sive
15   sit eque distantium laterum quia parium sive equidistantium linearum,
quod si eius superficies omnes volueris mensurare huius artem in precedentibus habuisti. Et vide quod interdum numerus mensure superficiei
corporis excedit numerum quantitatis corporalis, ut si cubus assit cuius
basis latus sit duo pedes, erit quantitas cubi 8 pedes; sed quantitas super-
20   ficierum eius 24 pedes, nam quelibet superficies eius continet 4 pedes
et quia 6 sunt superficies. Igitur propositum. Item cum in eodem cubo
sint 8 pedes, quorum quilibet cubus exeat, et in quolibet sunt 6 superficies, palam est quod in eo sunt 48 pedes quadrati; ita in aliis suo modo.

60–62 Et . . . agere *mg. Pd*
62 *post* agere *add. Pe* et cetera

Prop. 1
2 columpnare *PdPe* columnare *XbUaXn*
7 tu queris *PdXbXn, om. Ua* queris *Pe*
11–15 Eodem. . . . linearum *mg. Pd*
16 huius: huiusmodi *Ua*
22 sunt *PdPeUaXn* sint *Xb*

2.ª PIRAMIDIS LATERATE MENSURAM PROPALARE.

Quoniam omnis piramis laterata est subtripla sue columpne per 3ᵃᵐ additarum post 8ᵃᵐ 12ᵐⁱ et, per immediate [precedentem,] mensuram columpne sive prismatis habuisti, habes propositum tibi notum. Vis
5   huius exemplum [Fig. I.6.2a]. Sit piramis cuius basis triangulus in-equilaterus sicut in precedente *ABC*, ut 3, 4, 5, eius autem altitudo sive axis 10, erit quantitas prismatis 60 per antedictam. Eiusque tertia pars 20, que est quantitas quam inquiris.

Accidit et quandoque latera basis esse surda, quare et basis. Igitur
10 oportet te scire artem surdorum, tam in multiplicatione quam divisione, et radicum extractione, in quibus ex arismetica te supponimus esse doctum. Et hanc artem in quadripartito numerorum alias ordinavi.

Exemplum: Sit piramis laterata cuius basis triangulus equilaterus et eius unumquodque latus 10 [Fig. I.6.2b]. Erit superficies surda per 5ᵃᵐ 3ᵉ
15 partis 5ⁱ huius et nominatur radix: 5 radices de 75. Sit autem altitudo quanta vis. Sit ergo 10. Duc igitur 10 in 5 radices de 75. Exit 50 radices de 75, que sunt una radix de 187500, per 2ᵃᵐ 3ᵉ partis 5ⁱ huius, cuius tertia pars est radix de 20833 ⅓, que est quantitas piramidis antedicte. Sic ergo hec piramis erit surda. Et esset in vulgo per numeros
20 fere 144 et parvum plus et mecanico sufficit ita loqui. In lineis ergo et superficiebus atque corporibus surditatem cadere necesse est.

3.ª CHILINDRI QUANTITATEM SUPERFICIALEM METIRI.

Est autem chilindrus columpna rotunda, cuius bases duo circuli equi-distantes et equales. Sit ergo chilindrus cuius basis circulus *A* eiusque circuli dyameter *GD* [Fig. I.6.3]. Latus autem sive altitudo chilindri
5   *EZ*. Inventa ergo sit *H*, per 10ᵃᵐ 6ⁱ, media inter *GD, EZ*. Et facta *H* semidyametro super eam circulum describe, qui sit *B*. Erit autem iste circulus *B* equalis superficiei chilindri preter bases, per 13ᵃᵐ primi Archi-menidis in de spera et chilindro. Igitur cum scias circulum mensurare ex prima sexti huius, nonquam quantitatem superficiei chilindri poteris
10 amplius ignorare.

Exemplum: Sit chilindrus cuius basis circulus habens dyametrum *GD* 7, latus eius *EZ* 28, media *H* erit 14; super quam si circulus describatur, erit eius area 616, equalis quantitati superficiali chilindri preter bases.

Aliter ad idem: Periferiam circuli qui est basis chilindri, que est 22 ex

Prop. 2

      2 columpne *PdPeXb* columne *UaXn*
      3 precedentem *UaXn, om. PdPeXb*
      8 quam inquiris *PdXbXn* quam tu queris *Pe* scilicet pyramidis *Ua*
      10 *post* quam *add. Xb* in
      15 5 radices *mg. Pd*
      20 mecanico *PeXn* mechanico *Ua* mecanice *?Pd, Xb*

Prop. 3

      9 nonquam *PdXb* nunquam *PeXn* nota tibi erit *Ua* / quantitatem *mg. Pd*
      12 quam *PeXbUa* quem *PdXn*
      13 superficiali: superficiei *Xn*

15 ypothesi, duc in eius chilindri altitudinem, que est 28 per positum. Exit
616, eadem quantitas que et ante, cui si addas quantitatem duarum
basium chilindri, qui sunt duo circuli equales, exibit 693, tota superficialis quantitas chilindralis; quod est propositum.

68r /4.ª CHILINDRI CORPOREAM INQUIRERE QUANTITATEM.

Aream unius basis, qui est circulus, inventam per primam 6ⁱ huius,
duc in altitudinem chilindri et exibit a diffinitione quantitas que fuerat
inquirenda.

5 Esto exemplum: Sit alicuius chilindri basis circulus cuius dyameter 7
[Fig. I.6.4]. Erit area basis 38½, per primam 6ⁱ huius. Sitque
eius altitudo 10. Area ergo sumpta 10ᵉˢ dat 385, chilindri scilicet quantitatem. Si autem tibi linearum surditas occurrerit, age sicut in precedentibus est ostensum.

5.ª CONI EQUICRURII SUPERFICIEM INVENIRE.

Conus equicrurius est piramis rotunda cuius basis est circulus, vertex
autem punctus a quo omnes linee ducte ad periferiam circuli sunt equales.
Cuius superficies taliter mensuratur: Sit conus equicrurius cuius basis
5 circulus A [Fig. I.6.5], semidyameter autem G, latus vero coni sit D.
Invenias ergo inter G et D lineam mediam per 10ᵃᵐ 6ⁱ, que sit E. Facta
autem E semidyametro secundum eius longitudinem circulum describe, qui
sit B. Erit autem ille circulus B equalis superficiei conice preter basem,
per 14ᵃᵐ Archimenidis ubi supra. Ergo circulo B mensurato per primam
10 6ⁱ huius, quantitas superficialis preter basem coni equicrurii nota stabit,
quam basem, quia circulus est, adde predicte quantitati, et propositum
erit notum. Et nota quod eadem est proportio superficiei coni ad suam
basem que est lateris coni ad semidyametrum basis per 15ᵃᵐ Archimenidis
ubi supra, ex qua posses ipsius superficiem mensurare.

6.ª CONI EQUICRURII MAGNITUDINEM PERSCRUTARI.

Quoniam omnis conus equicrurius [Fig. I.6.6] subtriplex est sui
chilindri, scilicet sue columpne rotunde per 9ᵃᵐ 12ᵐⁱ, in qua sic omnis
columpna rotunda sue piramidi triplex esse probatur, et quoniam chilindri
5 quantitas nota est per 4ᵃᵐ huius, igitur et eius 3ª pars nota erit, que est
conus. Altitudo autem coni huius sive axis nota est per notitiam lateris
coni et semidyametri circuli qui est basis, per penultimam primi; nam a
quadrato lateris deme quadratum semidyametri, remanet quadratum axis

17 693 *mg. Pd*
17–18 superficialis *mg. Pd*

Prop. 5
    6 Invenias: invenies *Xn*
    6–7 Facta autem E *om. Xb*
    7 E: A *Pe*
    14 qua *?Pd* quo *PeXbUaXn*

Prop. 6
    8 remanet quadratum: res quadrata *Xb*

coni, quod est propositum. Et ita inquiritur etiam axis piramidis
10   laterate si de illo fuerit dubitatum.

7.ª SPERAM DATAM IN DUO EQUA DIVIDERE.

In spera data circulum ad libitum describe super centrum *B* [Fig. I.6.7]
ipsumque circulum in duo equa partire, scilicet periferiam eius sicut fit de
linea recta quia in hoc nihil differt per 10ᵃᵐ primi, cum a cuspide in
5   cuspidem sit recta. Aut circino non mutato ipsum circulum descriptum
in 6 equa divide cum semidyameter sit equalis lateri hexagoni per 15ᵃᵐ
4ⁱ et 2ᵃᵐ 2ⁱ huius. Et necessario circulus in duo equa divisus est. Nam si
in 6 equa, ergo et in duo. Et in punctis divisionum sicut *A*, *C* fac ergo
circulum transire per illa 3 puncta *A*, *B*, *C* et illum circulum esse maximum
10   in spera eamque per equalia dividi necesse est cum ille circulus sit communis basis utriusque hemisperii semidyametrique sint equales; quare
propositum.

8.ª SPERICAM SUPERFICIEM MENSURARE.

Quoniam superficies cuiuslibet spere quadrupla est maximi circuli
eorum qui in spera per 31ᵃᵐ Archimenidis ubi supra, igitur maximum
circulum, i.e. speram per equalia dividentem, per precedentem inventum
5   studeas mensurare per primam 6ⁱ huius. Et eius aream sume quater; quod
exit est equale superficiei spere dicte.

Aliter: ex 33ª eiusdem [Archimenidis]: superficies chilindri cum basibus
basem habentis circulum maximum qui in spera, altitudinem autem
dyametrum spere, est hemiola superficiei spere. Nunc autem iam scivisti
10   chilindri superficiem invenire per 3ᵃᵐ huius. Ergo ab ea superficie chilindri
3ª parte dempta, remanet superficies spere nostre.

9.ª SPERICE PORTIONIS SUPERFICIALIS QUANTITATEM CON-CLUDERE.

Sit primo illa portio superficialis minor superficie hemisperii. Ex 40ª
primi Archimenidis ubi sepe, circulus habens semidyametrum equalem
5   linee producte a vertice portionis ad periferiam circuli existentis basis
portionis est equalis superficiei portionis quam tu queris.

Exemplum: Sit illa portio minor superficie hemisperii in spera cuius
maximus circulus *ABG* [Fig. I.6.8] et basis portionis *AG* ad rectos maximo
68v   circulo, / vertex autem sit *B*, recta descendens a vertice portionis super
10   periferiam circuli qui est basis *BA*. Facta autem *BA* semidyametro
circuloque girato qui sit *D*, erit ipse equalis superficiei portionis antedicte.
Igitur circulo *D* mensurato per primam 6ⁱ huius, erit et portio mensurata,

Prop. 7
     10 dividi *corr. ex* dividere

Prop. 8
     11 nostre: nota *Ua*

Prop. 9
     4 sepe *PdXbXn* supra *Pe* supra sepe *Ua*
     12 erit: esset *Pe*

quod est propositum. Sed sit illa portio maior hemisperio, ut est ACG, cuius basis circulis qui circa dyametrum AG ad rectos maximo circulo, recta autem a vertice portionis ad periferiam basis CA. Qua facta semi-dyametro circuli Z, erit ipse circulus equalis superficiei portionis hemis-perium excedentis, quod demonstratur ubi dictum est. Sic habetur propositum.

10.ᵃ SPERICI CORPORIS CONTINENTIAM PATEFACERE.

Quia omnis spera quadrupla est coni habentis basem equalem maximo circulo eorum qui in spera, altitudinem autem equalem semidyametro spere per 32ᵃᵐ Archimenidis ubi ante, et coni huius mensuram habuisti in 6ᵃ huius, igitur mensura spere nullatenus te latebit.

Exemplum placet adducere [Fig. I.6.9]: Sit spera cuius dyameter 7; erit quantitas chilindri hemisperii 134¾ per 4ᵃᵐ huius, cuius 3ᵃ pars 44¹¹/₁₂ est coni quantitas, per 6ᵃᵐ huius, quam sume quater, exit 179⅔ totius spere quantitas quam querebas, quod est propositum.

Aliter: ex 33ᵃ eiusdem chilindrus habens basem maximum circulum eorum qui in spera, altitudinem autem dyametrum spere, est hemiolus spere. Igitur cum chilindrus dicte spere sit 269½, per 4ᵃᵐ huius, dempta 3ᵃ parte remanet 179⅔ spere quantitas antedicta.

Aliter: per cubum, quia cubus speram circumscribens ad chilindrum eiusdem spere est in proportione supertripartiente undecima per [2ᵃᵐ Archimenidis de mensura circuli et primam et 4ᵃᵐ huius]. Igitur a quanti-tate cubi, que est 343 per ypothesim quantitis dyametri, demptis ³/₁₄, que sunt 73½, remanet 269½, quantitas scilicet chilindralis, a qua dempta tertia parte sicut prius remanet quantitas sperica supradicta. Aut sic: quia proportio cubi ad chilindrum circa eandem speram nota est et chilindri ad speram, ergo per 7ᵃᵐ 6ⁱ huius et proportio cubi ad speram et est super-decipartiens undecima. Igitur a cubo qui est 343 ex ypothesi deme ¹⁰/₂₁ que sunt 163⅓, remanet 179⅔, que magnitudinem spericam comprehendunt; quod est propositum.

11.ᵃ SECTORIS SPERE MAGNITUDINEM COMPREHENDERE.

Sit spera in qua maximus circulus ABG super centrum D [Fig. I.6.10] sitque conus basem habens circulum equalem superficiei spere que est secundum periferiam ABG per ea que in 9ᵃ huius, altitudinem autem equalem semidyametro BD. Erit sector spere $ABGD$ equalis dicto cono per 42ᵃᵐ Archimenidis ubi prius. Et quoniam mensura coni habita est per 6ᵃᵐ huius, igitur et sectoris; quod est propositum.

Prop. 10

    15 supertripartiente *corr. ex* supertripartiens
    15–16 [2ᵃᵐ . . . huius] *addidi, lac. in MSS*
    21–22 superdecipartiens: super10partiens *in MSS*

Prop. 11

    4 ea que in *mg. Pd*

12.ª SPERICE PORTIONIS CORPULENTIAM OSTENDERE.

Sit in spera maximus circulus, cuius dyameter *AG*, centrum *T* [Fig. I.6.11]. Et secetur spera plano *BZ* ad rectos ipsi *AG* super punctum *E*. Et fiat sicut *TA*, *AE* simul ambe ad *EA*, ita *DE* ad *GE*, quod erit si *TAE*
5 ducatur in *GE* et productum dividatur per *AE*, exibit *DE*. Et rursum fiat sicut *TG*, *GE* simul ad *GE*, ita *RE* ad *EA*, quod fiet sicut nuper, describanturque coni a circulo qui circa dyametrum *BZ* habentes vertices puncta *D*, *R*. Dico quod conus *BZD* equalis est portioni spere ex parte *G*, conus autem *BZR* portioni ex parte *A* per 2ᵃᵐ 2ⁱ Archimenidis ubi olim.
10 Et quoniam cuiuslibet coni mensura prescripta est in 6ª huius, igitur et dictarum portionum cognita est mensura; quod est propositum.

Exemplum: Sit semidyameter spere *TA* 14, et *TE* 7; erit *GE* 7; queritur *DE*. Sicut *TA*, *AE* simul, hoc est 35, ad *AE*, hoc est 21, ita *DE* ad *GE* que est 7. Duc ergo 35 in 7 et productum divide per 21, exit 11⅔ pro linea *DE*,
15 que ponatur altitudo coni cuius basis super dyametrum *BZ*. Et ille conus erit equalis portioni sperice, que est *BGZ*; ita in alia portione.

13.ª SPERICAM SUPERFICIEM QUADRARE.

Quoniam superficies spere quadrupla est maximi circuli eorum qui in spera per 31ᵃᵐ Archimenidis ubi nuper circulique quadratura conclusa est in 14ª 8ⁱ huius, ergo et superficiei sperice quadratura. Aut sic: maximus
5 circulus eiusdem spere quadretur per 14ᵃᵐ 8ⁱ huius. Et illud quadratum quadrupletur per ea que in 22ª huius 6ⁱ et erit illud quadratum equale superficiei spere; quod est propositum.

69r ### /14.ª SPERAM CUBICARE.

Hoc autem nichil aliud est quam spere date equum cubum describere, quod sic sit. Quia cubus spere circumscriptus est in proportione nota ad

Prop. 12

4 TAE *mg. Pd*

6 RE *Pd, mg. Ua* TE *PeXbXn*

9 *post* Archimenidis *add Ua mg.* nota quod secunda secundi dicit: Quod omni portioni sphere equatur conus habens basim eandem portioni, altitudinem autem rectam habentem ad altitudinem portionis proportionem eandem quam simul ambo, scilicet semidiameter sphere et altitudo (*?*) relique portionis, habent ad altitudinem alterius portionis. Exempli gratia, sit portio sphere maior ABZ [Fig. I.6.11a] cuius basis circularis existat dyameter ZEB similiter et portionis minoris ZGB. Desideramus primo quantitatem minoris portionis. Describes conum BDZ cuius basis est circulus habens dyametrum ZEB, axis vero DGE___ (*lac.*) ita se habens ad___(*lac.*) est GF sicut semidiameter et sagitta (*?*) EA ad ipsam (*?*) sagittam (*?*) maioris portionis circuli sphere maioris. Eritque conus BDZ equalis portioni minori BGZ.

12–16 Sit. . . . portione *mg. Pd*

12 semidyameter: dyameter *Pe*

Prop. 14

2 spere date *corr. ex* sphere date *Ua et* spera data *PdPeXbXn*

3 nota *mg. Pd*

speram que est superdecipartiens 11^a per ea que in 10^a huius, igitur a
5   cubo illo demptis 10^{mis}/21 remanet solidum rectangulum, ut probabitur,
equale spere. Sed illud solidum potest cubicari per 22^{am} 7^{mi} huius, ergo
et spera; quod est propositum.

Ostenditur probandum: Cubus antedictus in 21 partes equas dividatur
per divisionem basis et lateris eius per 5^{am} 4^i huius et amotis 10 ex illis
10   partibus restant 11 tales que faciunt solidum rectangulum per 25^{am} 11^{mi};
quare propositum.

Aliter sic [Fig. I.6.12]: Sit circulus maximus A spere date equalis
quadrato B per 14^{am} 8^i huius. Ducatur autem area utriusque in dyametrum
spere. Exibit chilindrus C equalis solido rectangulo per conceptionem:
15   si equalia equaliter augeantur equalia sunt producta, vel per 21^{am} 7^{mi} et ex
diffinitione. Sed chilindrus C est hemiolus date spere ex 33^a Archimenidis
ubi dudum, ergo et solidum D est hemiolum eiusdem spere. Ab eo igitur
solido dempta tertia parte sui, solidum rectangulum remanens, quod sit
E, est equale spere date. Hoc autem solidum antedictum E potest cubicari
20   in F per 22^{am} 7^{mi} huius. Ergo spera data equalis cubo F necessario conclusa
est; quod est propositum.

15.^{a} DATO CONO VEL CHILINDRO EQUAM SPERAM FIGU-
RARE.

Sit conus A, cui voluimus equam speram invenire [Fig. I.6.13]. Sit
ipsius A coni hemiolus chilindrus E, cuius basis circulus qui circa dyame-
5   trum GD, axis autem EZ. Sumantur itaque per 16^{am} 7^{mi} huius ipsarum
GD, EZ due medie proportionales que sint HT, MN, ita ut GD ad HT
ita HT ad MN et MN ad EZ. Intelligatur quoque chilindrus, cuius basis
circulus qui circa dyametrum HT, axis vero RL equalis HT. Qua posita
diametro spera B describatur. Dico igitur conum A equalem esse spere B.
10   Constat namque chilindrum E equalem esse chilindro R. Quoniam ut est
GD ad HT ita HT ad MN et MN ad EZ, ergo permutatim ut GD ad MN et
reliqua. Sed equalis est HT ipsi RL per ypothesim. Ergo sicut GD ad MN,
hoc est, sicut quadratum GD ad quadratum HT, ita circulus E ad circulum
R, per 2^{am} 12^{mi}. Quare sicut circulus E ad circulum R ita RL ad EZ.
15   Chilindrorum ergo E, R bases et altitudines, id est, axes, sunt proportionales. Igiter per 12^{am} 12^{mi} dicti chilindri sunt equales. Chilindrus autem
R hemiolus est spere que circa dyametrum HT per 9^{am} 12^{mi}; quare et
chilindrus E eiusdem spere hemiolus concedetur. Et quia pridem idem
chilindrus E coni A hemiolus ponebatur, ergo spera cuius dyameter HT et
20   conus A necessario sunt equales per 9^{am} 5^i; quod est propositum. Vice

4 superdecimpartiens: super10partiens *in MSS*
10 *post* 11^{mi} *add.* Xb huius
14 rectangulo *mg.* Pd
14–15 conceptionem . . . 7^{mi} *mg.* Pd, *om.* Xb
17 hemiolum *corr. ex* hemiolus

Prop. 15
1 vel chilindro *mg.* Pd
5 huius *mg.* Pd

autem coni *A* posito chilindro, ipsum esse equalem spere eadem deductione tenendum est.

16.ª DATO CUBO EQUAM SPERAM STATUERE.

Sit cubus cuius basis sit equalis circulo *A* per 15^{am} 8^i huius. Ducatur autem area huius circuli in altitudinem cubi et exibit chilindrus equalis cubo dato. Nam si duo equalia equaliter augeantur, equalia sunt producta.
5 Iste autem chilindrus est equalis spere per immediate [precedentem] in fine; ergo et cubus, quod est propositum. Nam ratiocinatio talis est dato cubo equum chilindrum statuere datoque chilindro equam speram fabricare, ergo et dato cubo equam speram contingit reperire; quod est propositum. Et hec est conversa 14^e huius.

17.ª DATO CIRCULO SPERAM AB EO CIRCUMDUCTO DESCRIPTAM REPERIRE.

Duc dyametrum circuli in se cubice, exibit cubus speram circuli circumscribens. A quo cubo speram inscriptam extrahe per ea que in 10ª
5 huius, et propositum notum erit.

Exemplum: Detur circulus cuius dyameter 7; erit eius cubus 343; a quo extractis 10^{mis}/21, remanet 179⅔ pro spera a motu circuli derelicta; quod est propositum.

69v /18.ª ROMBI SUPERFICIEM INDAGARE.

Rombus nunc ad superficiem nunc ad corpus equivoce sumitur. De rombo qui est superficies in precedentibus est ostensum. Nunc autem de corpore rombico hic agitur, quod ex duobus conis equicruriis super
5 basim unicam est confectum. Cuius superficies agnoscitur per mensuram utriusque superficiei cuiusque coni. Superficies autem cuiuslibet coni in 5ª huius extitit mensurata; quare propositum.

19.ª ROMBI MAGNITUDINEM CORPOREAM DECLARARE.

Sit rombus qui ex duobus equicruriis componitur *ABDG* [Fig. I.6.14], cuius basis communis utrique cono circulus qui circa dyametrum *BG*, altitudo autem *AD*. Exponaturque aliquis conus *HTK* habens basem
5 equalem superficiei coni *ABG* per ea que in 5ª huius, altitudinem autem equalem *DZ* perpendiculari super latus *AB* continue protractum. Erit ergo ille conus *HTK* equalis rombo supradicto per 18^{am} primi Archimenidis ubi sepe. Et quia iam coni equicrurii inventa est mensura per 6^{am} huius, igitur propositum. Aut sic: quia ille rombus ex duobus conis equicruriis com-
10 ponitur, utroque cono mensurato per 6^{am} huius concluditur propositum.

Prop. 16
     5 precedentem *Ua, om. PdPeXbXn*
  5–6 in fine *mg. Pd*
     9 Et . . . huius *om. Xb*

Prop. 17
    1–8 Dato. . . . propositum *inser. Pd post* date *in linea 12ª Prop. 14*
      8 *Post istam propositionem add. mg. Pd* Hic proprie finis 10^{mi} capituli. Resume
        (?) 8 propositiones; in papiro sunt.

20.ª CURTE PIRAMIDIS LATERATE MENSURAM EXPONERE.

Si aliqua piramis laterata plano equidistanti basi secta fuerit, quod a sectione in verticem continetur figuram retinet piramidis laterate. Quod autem a sectione in basim clauditur curta piramis dicitur laterata, cuius
5 quantitas nota erit per demptionem parve piramidis a piramide tota.

Exemplum: Sit ipsa piramis incurtata cuius basis plurilatera prout libuerit figuranti equilatera tamen et equiangula cuiusque caput CD equidistans basi, axis eius EF [Fig. I.6.15]. Perfice igitur piramidem eductis AC, BD usque ad concursum in G per 4um petitum. Erunt ergo
10 latera CG, DG per 41^{am} 2^e partis 5^i huius, et inde tota AG et BG nota; similiter AE nota quia est semidyameter circuli inscripti basi. Quare per penultimam primi erit EG nota, quod est ponere totam piramidem esse notam per 2^{am} huius. A qua dempta parva piramide nota CDG, nota per eandem, remanet nota tota piramis incurtata; quod est propositum. Et si
15 sit basis AB multilatera qualitercunque contingat ut trigona, tetragona, pentagona inequilatera aut inequiangula proutlibet ars inveniendi mensuram talis piramidis incurtate nullatenus a precedenti piramide mutanda est. Et nota quod omne solidum rectilineum cuius caput equidistans basi base minus existat curta piramis appellatur. Igitur hec conclusio ad omnia
20 talia dicitur generalis.

21.ª CURTE PIRAMIDIS ROTUNDE QUANTITATEM COMPREHENDERE.

Si aliqua piramis rotunda plano equidistanti basi secta fuerit, quod a sectione in verticem comprehenditur formam non amittit, quod autem a
5 sectione in basim relinquitur curta rotunda piramis nuncupatur. Cuius quantitas erit nota per ablationem parve piramidis que a sectione in verticem includitur note per 6^{am} huius a quantitate totius piramidis cognita per eandem.

Exemplum: Sit piramis antedicta AD [Fig. I.6.16] cuius basis circulus
10 qui circa dyametrum AB cuiusque caput equidistans basi circulus qui circa dyametrum CD, axis autem EF. Continuatis in directum lateribus AC, BD donec necessario concurrant in G per 4um petitum, erunt ergo latera CG, DG. Et inde totum latus AG, BG notum per 41^{am} 2^e partis 5^i huius. Et quia AE semidyameter basis etiam nota est, igitur et per penultimam
15 primi axis EG. Quare et tota magnitudo piramidis ABG nota erit per 6^{am} huius. A qua dempta quantitate parve piramidis que est CDG nota per

Prop. 20

      6 plurilatera *PdPeUa* plurilaterata *XbXn*
      8 equidistans *Ua* eqd̄' *PdPe* equidistanti *Xb* equidem *Xn*
      9 petitum *PdPe* petitionem *XbUaXn*
      10 partis *XbUaXn* ₽ *PdPe*
      11 semidyameter *PeUa* (*hic et alibi*) semidiameter *PdXbXn* (*hic et alibi*)
      12 erit *?Pd, PeUaXn, om. Xb*
      20 generalis: esse generalis *Xb*

Prop. 21

      16 CDG *mg. Pd, corr. ex* ABG

eandem, remanet curte piramidis quantitas tibi nota; quod fuit propositum. Et si huius piramidis superficiem vis metiri, perfecta piramide ab eius superficie nota per 5ᵃᵐ huius deme superficiem parve piramidis notam per
20 eandem et remanet superficies piramidis incurtate.

Ad idem per 16ᵃᵐ Archimenidis ubi supra: Sit conus cuius trigonum per axem *ABG*, sectus plano equidistanti basi per lineam *DE*, axis autem
70r coni *BH* [Fig. I.6.17]. / Et aliquis circulus exponatur cuius semidyameter sit media proportionalis inter *AD* latus curte piramidis et simul utramque
25 *DZ*, *AH* semidyametrum basium; erit ipse circulus equalis superficiei piramidis incurtate. Ergo mensurato circulo per primam 6ⁱ huius habebitur propositum.

22.ᵃ ARCUATI ROMBI SUPERFICIEM INTUERI.

Sit arcus circuli minor semicircumferentia super suam cordam fixam ut axis immobilis in giro revolvatur usquequo ad locum unde moveri inceperat revertatur. Corpus inde relictum speroidale Archimenides primitus
5 nominavit, et recte figuram dragine effigiat aut ovalem. Nos autem propter vicinitatem possimus rombum curvilineum nuncupare, cuius quidem superficies a nobis inquiritur mensuranda. Sit ergo dicta figura *ABGD*, maior dyameter *AG*, minor vero *BD* [Fig. I.6.18]. Et super maiorem dyametrum circulus describatur super centrum *T*. Demonstravit autem
10 Archimenides in libro de speroidalibus et conoidalibus theoreumate 5°, quod quam proportionem habet minor dyameter ad maiorem, eam habet spatium speroidale ad circulum qui circa dyametrum maiorem describitur. Proportionem autem illarum dyametrorum non est difficile reperire mensuratis *AT*, *TB*. Quare propositum notum constat.
15 Et nota quod huius corporis speroidalis tres sunt modi [Fig. I.6.19]: unus quando centrum unius arcus est in reliquo et econtra, voceturque perfectus; alius autem quando amborum arcus includunt centra sua, dicaturque diminutus; alius vero quando centra exeunt arcus suos sitque superhabundans; quorum trium mensura nullatenus variatur.

23.ᵃ ARCUATI ROMBI MAGNITUDINEM PERSCRUTARI.

Sit dictus rombus *ABDG*, cuius maior dyameter *BG*, minor vero *AD* [Fig. I.6.20]. Secetur igitur plano perpendiculari ad axem *BG* secundum minorem dyametrum *AD* per centrum *T*. Est autem illa sectio circulus
5 super quem ymaginetur conus elevari *ABD*. Nunc autem ex 28ᵃ Archimenidis in de speroidalibus dimidium speroidale duplum est ad conum

---

18–20 Et . . . incurtate *mg. Pd*
    21 Archimenidis: Euclidis *Pe*
    22 plano ?*Pd, XnUa* plana *PeXb* / equidistanti *corr. ex* equidis *Ua* eq̄d' *PdPeXb* equidem *Xn*

Prop. 22
        3 usquoque *Pd*
        5 dragine *PdPeXb* draginem *XnUa* alibi draconem *mg. Ua*
        6 rombum *PdPeXb* rumbum *UaXn*
        7 mensurandi *Pe*

ABD, cuius basis circulus qui circa dyametrum *AD*, altitudo vero *TB*. Ergo ipso cono duplato cuius notitia ex 6ª huius habita est, sequitur mensuram semirombi arcuati et per consequens totius rombi notam esse.

24.ª CHILINDRI CURVILINEI QUANTITATEM ATTINGERE.

Ad differentiam chilindri recti de quo scriptum est in 13ª Archimenidis in de spera hic signanter chilindrus curvilineus nominatur. Nam ille ex rectis, iste autem ex curvis lateribus figuratur. Et si corporis speroidalis,
5 i.e. rombi arcuati, ut precedens conclusio figuravit, plano recto ad axem due vertices amputentur, chilindrus curvilineus producetur. Sit ergo speroidale *ABGZ* [Fig. I.6.21], cuius medium plano secetur, ut dictum est, recto ad axem non per centrum. Sitque sectio *ADG*, que necessario circulus est. Mensurata ergo portione speroidali *ABG*, dimidii speroidalis
10 residuum notum erit, cum ipsum totum semisperoidale iam notum fuerit per precedentem. Intellige ergo conum *ABG* literis designatum, cuius basis circulus qui circa *AG*. Nunc autem ex 30ª Archimenidis in de speroidalibus conclusum est quod omnis figure speroidalis secte non per centrum plano recto ad axem minor portio ad conum habentem eandem
15 basem cum portione et altitudinem equalem hanc habet proportionem quam simul utraque, scilicet medietas axis speroidalis et axis maioris portionis, ad axem eiusdem maioris portionis. Igitur que est proportio *TZ* et *DZ* simul ad *DZ*, ea est portionis *ABG* ad conum eisdem literis interclusum. Sed proportionem dictarum linearum notam esse contingit. Ex
20 earum mensuratione, quare propositum.

Exemplum: Sit pro libito *BT* 14 et *DT* 7. Erit ergo et *TZ* 14, et pone *ZH* equalem, protracta in directum *TZ*. Erunt ergo *TZ*, *DZ* simul iuncte 35 et totidem est *DH*. Est ergo proportio *DH* ad *DZ* nota, scilicet sicut 35 ad 21. Sed illa est proportio portionis corporalis curvilinee *ABG* ad
25 conum eisdem literis figuratum. Igitur quia mensura coni habita est in 6ª huius, et mensura portionis sepedicte nota manet. Notum ergo est residuum semisperoidale; quo duplato chilindrus curvilineus notus exit; quod fuit propositum. Hoc autem corpus solet vocare dolium gens commune,
29 cuius mensuram hactenus nulliter demonstratam geometrice potui repe-
70v rire / quamvis quidam practicantes putaverunt dolium mensurare. Sed transeunt iuxta latera veritatis cum illa mensura non sit geometrica sed vulgaris. Doctrina autem excellentis Archimendis hanc conclusionem et multas alias diu sopitas ex elementorum gremio exterius enodavit.

25.ª A ROTUNDA PIRAMIDE EQUICRURIO ROMBO DEMPTO RELICTUM MENSURARE.

Sit *ABC* piramis rotunda [Fig. I.6.22] sive conus, in quo rombus equicrurius *CDFE*. Quo dempto circumacceptum, quod est *DABE*,

Prop. 23

    7 ABD *corr.* Pd *ex* ABG

Prop. 24

     8 recto ad axem *mg.* Pd
     29 nulliter *PdUa, lac.* Xb *nullibus* Pe *nulli cui* Xn

5   remanet mensurandum. Sic per 19^am Archimenidis in primo de spera et
    chilindro: Si conus equicrurius plano secetur equedistante basi, a facto
    autem circulo conus describatur, verticem habens centrum basis, fac-
    tusque rombus auferatur a toto cono, circumaccepto equalis erit conus
    habens basem equalem superficiei coni intermedie equidistantium pla-
10 norum, altitudinem autem equalem catheto a centro basis ducto ad unum
    latus coni.
        Exemplum [Fig. I.6.23]: Esto conus equicrurius *ABG* et secetur plano
    equidistante basi per lineam *DE*. Centrum autem basis *Z*. Et a circulo
    qui circa dyametrum *DE* conus describatur, verticem habens *Z*; erit itaque
15 rombus *BDZE* ex equicruriis conis compositus. Exponatur igitur aliquis
    conus *KTL* cuius basis sit equalis superficiei intermedie ipsarum *DE*, *AG*,
    scilicet quam superficiem claudunt linee *AD*, *EG*, altitudo autem
    ducto a puncto *Z* catheto ad latus *AB*, scilicet *ZH*, sit equalis [ipsi *ZH*].
    Demonstravit Archimenides quod si a cono *ABG* intelligatur ablatus
20 rombus *BDEZ* circumaccepto equalis est conus *TKL*. Sed eius coni
    mensuram ostendit 6^a huius; quare propositum.
        Item aliter: Si a toto cono equicrurio noto per 6^am huius rombus ille
    notus per 19^am huius auferatur, quod remanet necessario notum constat.
    Et in hoc 10^m capitulum huius operis restringatur.

Here Begins the Tenth Chapter

[Proemium]

In the beginning of his work, which he left to us unfinished or at least a
complete copy [of it] has not come into our hands, the author proposed
for the last two chapters to determine the measure of a spherical body
and of other bodies completely irregular. What he intended and by what
means he would have proceeded I am not able to know. But, following
the proposal of his general title, I intend, so far as I can, and by the will
of God, to discourse on the measures of spherical bodies and their segments, as well as on pyramids, cones, prisms, the cylinder, the rhomboidal
body[1] and diverse segments of these same bodies, on the capacity of vases
and their composition, on bodies, both those unusually shaped and those
that are curved, along with others which will appear in due course. And
with this, praise God, a proper end will be imposed on [this] work.
    For the demonstration of those things which follow, the *Elements* of
Euclid does not suffice, as it did in the preceding matters, for that book

---

Prop. 25

    6 equedistante *PdXb* equidistante *Xn Ua* equidem *?Pe*
    17 scilicet . . . EG *mg. Pd*
    18 ducto *corr. ex* ducti / catheto *corr. ex* catheti / [ipsi ZH] *sic in MSS, sed delendum?*

---

[1] See Commentary, Proemium, line 9.

does not arrive at such things, nor does any doctrine which I have seen excepting only [that contained] in the book of Archimedes *On the Sphere and the Cylinder*, which he penned[2] for his friend Dositheus after the lamentable death of Conon, and in the book *On Conoids and Spheroids* of the same author. For these three contemporary philosophers who corresponded with one another were firm lovers of geometric truth. But Archimedes excelled the others by far. None of the ancients in times past, excepting only Archimedes, was able to attain to [so] many serious and desirable conclusions. However, the very experienced intellect may investigate the higher things that remain, since in such matters no end to inquiry is imposed. Even though the range of things known appears to us as larger, surely a segment of things unknown remains.

Therefore, the propositions of Archimedes in the places cited above are those we postulate as having merit for us [i.e., by being true], for to solve them is no different than composing or recounting the book of Archimedes. Therefore, you ought to have [this] book and study it.

[Postulated Propositions from Archimedes'
On the Sphere and Cylinder]

I.13: The surface of every right cylinder, with the bases excepted, is equal to the circle whose radius is the mean proportional between the side of the cylinder and the diameter of the base of the cylinder.

I.14: The surface of every isosceles cone, with the base excepted, is equal to the circle whose radius is the mean proportional between the side of the cone and the radius of the circle which is the base of the cone.

I.18: To every [solid] rhombus composed of isosceles cones there is an equal cone which has a base equal to the surface of one of the cones composing the rhombus and an altitude equal to the perpendicular drawn from the apex of the second cone to one side of the first cone.

I.31 (=Gr. I.33): The surface of every sphere is four times the greatest circle in it.

I.32 (=Gr. I.34): Every sphere is four times the cone having a base equal to the greatest circle in the sphere and an altitude equal to the radius of the sphere.

I.33 (=Gr. I.34): Every cylinder having as its base the greatest circle in the sphere and its altitude equal to the diameter of the sphere is three halves of the sphere and its surface including the bases is three halves of the surface of the sphere.

I.40 (=Gr. I.42): The surface of every segment of a sphere that is less than the hemisphere is equal to a circle whose radius is equal to a straight line drawn from the apex of the segment to the circumference of the circle which is the base of the segment of the sphere.

---

[2] I am at a loss to render accurately the word *prostillavit*, which is absent from lexicons. It may have been a word coined from *stilus*. Another possibility is that it was coined from the root meaning of στέλλω in Greek.

I.42 (=Gr. I.44): To every sector of a sphere there is an equal cone having a base equal to the surface of the segment of the sphere and an altitude equal to the radius [of the sphere].

II.2: To every segment of a sphere there is an equal cone having the same base as the segment and an altitude equal to a straight line which has the same ratio to the altitude of the segment as the sum of the radius of the sphere and altitude of the complementary segment to the altitude of that complementary segment.

Archimedes has demonstrated all of these conclusions in the book *On the Sphere and the Cylinder*. This book begins as follows: "Archimedes to Dositheus greetings. On a former occasion I sent to you propositions which were to be explained by us etc." And the book *On Conoids and Spheroids* begins as follows: "Archimedes to Dositheus, prosperity, etc."

1. TO MEASURE THE VOLUME OF A PRISM.

A prism is a columnlike body with sides [that are rectilinear surfaces and] whose base is a polylateral, rectilinear surface, such as a triangle, a quadrangle, a pentagon, a hexagon. [The sides of the base can be] increased [in number] as much as one wishes and it can be either equilateral or of unequal sides. Let the prism be described. Its volume is had as follows: Multiply the area of the base (found by the ninth proposition of the first part of the fifth chapter of this work)[1] by its altitude. That which results is the number of the prism which you seek.

Example: Let there be a prism whose triangular base *ABC* is of unequal sides: 3, 4, and 5 [see Fig. I.6.1]. Hence, the area of the base is 6. Let its altitude *BD* be 10. Therefore, its volume is 60, from the definition of the body. For we say that a body is produced when the altitude is multiplied by the surface. A serratile body[2] is measured in the same way, for one species of prism is that whose two bases are triangular and whose three [other surfaces] are parallelograms. In fact, under this measure falls every rectilinear body whose opposite bases are equal, whether it be of parallel sides because they are equal or whether they are [merely] of parallel line elements, because if you wish to measure all of its surfaces you have the art of this in the preceding [chapters]. And you see that sometimes the number of the measure of the area of a body exceeds the number of the corporeal volume, so that if there is a cube whose base side is 2 feet, the volume of the cube will be 8 [cubic] feet but the magnitude of its surfaces will be 24 [square] feet, for each surface of it contains 4 [square] feet and there are six surfaces. Therefore, the proposition [holds]. Also, since in the same cube there are 8 [cubic] feet, each of which is a cube and in each [unit] cube there are six surfaces, it is clear that

---

Prop. 1

[1] See Commentary, Prop. 1, line 6.

[2] This is a triangular prism. See the Campanus version of the *Elementa* (Basel, 1546), p. 346. Cf. *Archimedes in the Middle Ages*, Vol. 1, p. 438.

there are in the [total] cube 48 square feet, and thus [it is] in the other [bodies] in their own way.

2. TO MAKE MANIFEST THE VOLUME OF A PYRAMID.

Since every pyramid is ⅓ its columnar [body],[1] by the third of the added [propositions] of the twelfth [book of the *Elements*],[2] and since by the immediately preceding [proposition] you had the volume of the column or prism, you have the proposition known to you. You wish an example of this [see Fig. I.6.2a]: Let there be a pyramid whose base is a scalene triangle *ABC*, as in the preceding, with sides 3, 4, 5, while its altitude or axis is 10. The volume of that prism will be 60, by the aforesaid [proposition], and its third part is 20, which is the magnitude which you seek.

It happens that sometimes the sides of the base are surds, and consequently also the base. Therefore, it is necessary to know the art of surds, their multiplication, their subtraction and the extraction of their roots, all of which we suppose you to be trained in from arithmetic. And this art I have set in order elsewhere in the *Quadripartitum numerorum*.[3]

Example: Let there be the pyramid whose basis is an equilateral triangle each side of which is 10 [see Fig. I.6.2b]. The surface will be a surd by the fifth [proposition][4] of the third part of the fifth [chapter] of this [work] and the root will be $5\sqrt{75}$. Let the altitude be any quantity you wish. Hence, let it be 10. Therefore, multiply $10 \times 5\sqrt{75}$. The result is $50\sqrt{75}$, which equals $\sqrt{187500}$, by the second [proposition] of the third part of the fifth [chapter] of this work.[5] The third part of this is $\sqrt{20833⅓}$, which is the volume of the aforesaid pyramid. And so, therefore, this pyramid will be a surd. And it would be loosely in numbers about 144 plus a small amount and it suffices for the mechanician to speak in this way. Hence, it is necessary that irrationality happens to lines, surfaces, and bodies.

3. TO MEASURE THE SURFACE MAGNITUDE OF A CYLINDER.

The cylinder is a round column whose bases are two circles that are parallel and equal. Let there be a cylinder whose base circle is *A* and the diameter of the circle is *GD* [see Fig. I.6.3]. Now the side or altitude of the cylinder is *EZ*. By VI.10 [of the *Elements*],[1] let the mean, *H*, between *GD* and *EZ* be found. And with *H* constructed as a diameter, describe on it a circle, which we let be *B*. But this circle *B* will be equal to the surface of the cylinder, with the bases excepted, by I.13 of the *On the*

Prop. 2

  [1] That is, the prism raised on the same base.

  [2] See Commentary, Prop. 2, lines 2–3.

  [3] For the significance of this reference to the *Quadripartitum numerorum*, see Chapter 2 above.

  [4] See Commentary, Prop. 2, lines 14–15.

  [5] *Ibid.*, line 17.

Prop. 3

  [1] See Commentary, Prop. 3, line 5.

Sphere and the Cylinder of Archimedes.[2] Therefore, since you know how to measure the circle, by the first [proposition] of the sixth [chapter] of this [work],[3] no longer can you be ignorant of the magnitude of the surface of the cylinder.

Example: Let there be a cylinder whose base circle has a diameter *GD* of 7, and let its side *EZ* be 28. The mean [proportional] will be 14. If a circle is described on this mean, its area will be 616, which is equal to the magnitude of the surface of the cylinder, with the bases excepted.

Another [example] for the same: Multiply the circumference of the base circle of the cylinder, which is 22 by hypothesis, into the height of the cylinder, which is 28 by supposition. The result is 616, the same quantity as before. If you add to this the magnitude of the two bases of the cylinder, which are two equal circles, the result will be 693, the whole surface magnitude of the cylinder, which is that proposed.

4. TO SEEK THE VOLUME OF A CYLINDER.

Multiply the area of one base, which is a circle, found by the first [proposition] of the sixth [chapter] of this [work], into the height of the cylinder and the result, by definition, is the quantity which was to be sought.

Let there be an example: Let the diameter of the base circle of a cylinder be 7 [see Fig. I.6.4]. Therefore, the area of the base will be 38½, by the first [proposition] of the sixth [chapter] of this [work]. Let its height be 10. Therefore, the area taken 10 times gives 385, obviously the volume of the cylinder. If you are faced with an irrationality of the lines, proceed as has been demonstrated in the preceding [examples].

5. TO FIND THE SURFACE OF AN ISOSCELES CONE.

An isosceles cone is a round pyramid whose base is a circle and whose apex is a point from which all lines drawn to the circumference of the circle are equal. The surface of such a figure is measured as follows. Let there be an isosceles cone whose base circle is *A* with a radius of *G*, while a side of the cone is *D* [see Fig. I.6.5]. Therefore, you may find the mean line *E* between *G* and *D*, by VI.10 [of the *Elements*].[1] With line *E* made the radius, describe a circle according to that radius, which circle we let be *B*. But that circle *B* will be equal to the conical surface, with the base excepted, by [I.]14 of Archimedes in the place mentioned above.[2] Therefore, with circle *B* measured by I.6 of this [work], the surface magnitude of the isosceles cone, the base excepted, will stand as known. If you add the base, for it is the circle, to the aforesaid quantity, the proposition will be known. And note that the ratio of the surface of the cone to its

---

[2] See Proemium above, lines 30–32.

[3] See Chap. 4 above, note 1.

Prop. 5

[1] See Commentary, Prop. 3, line 5.

[2] See Proemium, lines 33–35.

base is the same as that of the side of the cone to the radius of the base, by [I.]15 of Archimedes in the place mentioned above,[3] from which you could measure its surface.

6. TO INVESTIGATE THE VOLUME OF AN ISOSCELES CONE.

Since any isosceles cone [see Fig. I.6.6] is ⅓ of its cylinder, i.e., of its round column, by XII.9 [of the *Elements*][1] in which it was proved that every round column is 3 times its [round] pyramid, and since the volume of a cylinder is known by the fourth proposition of this [chapter], therefore its third part will also be known, which third part is the cone. But the height of this cone, or its axis, is known by a knowledge of the side of a cone and the radius of the circle which is the base, by the penultimate [proposition] of the first [book of the *Elements*].[2] For subtract the square of the radius from the square of the side and the square of the axis of the cone remains, which is that proposed. And in the same way one finds this axis of a pyramid, if there is any doubt of this.

7. TO BISECT A GIVEN SPHERE.

On the given sphere describe any circle with center B [see Fig. I.6.7] and bisect that circle, i.e., its circumference, in the same way as with a straight line by I.10 of the *Elements*,[1] for there is no difference, since from one point to another point is a straight line. Or with the compass unchanged, divide the circle (which has been described) into six equal parts, since the radius is equal to the side of an [inscribed] hexagon, by IV.15 [of the *Elements*][2] and II.2 of this [work]. And [so] necessarily the circle has been bisected. For if it [has been divided] into six parts, therefore [it has been divided] into two parts. And with the points of division marked as A, C then make a circle pass through the three points A, B and C and that circle is the greatest in the sphere and it is necessary that it [the sphere] be bisected since that circle is the common base of each hemisphere and the radii are equal. Hence the proposition.

8. TO MEASURE THE SPHERICAL SURFACE.

Since the surface of any sphere is four times the greatest circle of those in the sphere by I.31 (=Gr. I.33)[1] of Archimedes in the place [cited] above,

[3] The author neglected to give this proposition in the Proemium, but see the Moerbeke text Vol. 2, 26rK.

Prop. 6
   [1] See Commentary, Prop. 6, line 3.
   [2] See *Archimedes in the Middle Ages*, Vol. 1, p. 78, comment 25. Cf. the *Elementa* (Basel, 1546), p. 37.

Prop. 7
   [1] See *Archimedes in the Middle Ages*, Vol. 1, p. 164, comment 82. Cf. the *Elementa* (Basel, 1546), p. 14.
   [2] See Commentary, Prop. 7, lines 6–7.

Prop. 8
   [1] See Proemium, lines 40–41.

therefore by VI.1 of this [work]² you exert yourself to measure the greatest circle, i.e., the one bisecting the sphere, by the preceding [proposition]. And take its area four times. That which results is equal to the surface of the said sphere.

In another way: From I.33 (=Gr. I.34) of the same [Archimedes],³ the surface, including the bases, of the cylinder which has as its base the greatest circle which is in the sphere and as its height the diameter of the sphere is ³⁄₂ the surface of the sphere. But now you have already known the surface of the cylinder by the third proposition [of this chapter]. Therefore, with ⅓ part of this surface of the cylinder subtracted, the surface of our sphere remains.

9. TO CONCLUDE THE MAGNITUDE OF THE SURFACE OF A SEGMENT OF A SPHERE.

In the first place, let that surface segment be less than the surface of the hemisphere. From I.40 (=Gr. I.42) of Archimedes in the place often [cited],¹ the circle having a radius equal to the line drawn from the apex of the segment to the circumference of the circle which is the base of the segment is equal to the surface of the segment which you seek.

Example: Let that [surface] segment less than the surface of a hemisphere be in the sphere whose greatest circle is *ABG* [see Fig. I.6.8], and let the base of the segment be *AG* [and] at right angles to the greatest circle. Let the apex be *B*. Let *BA* be the straight line descending from the apex of the segment to the circumference of the circle which is the base [of the segment]. With *BA* made the radius and with the circle *D* drawn, this circle will be equal to the surface of the aforesaid segment. Therefore, with circle *D* measured by VI.1 of this [work],² so also will the [surface] segment be measured, which is that proposed.

But let that [surface] segment *ACG* be greater than a hemisphere, with its base circle about diameter *AG* being at right angles to the greatest circle. Let *CA* be the straight line drawn from the apex of the segment to the circumference of the base [of the segment]. With this straight line made the radius of circle *Z*, this circle will be equal to the surface of the segment exceeding the hemisphere, which is demonstrated in the place cited above.³ Thus the proposition is had.

10. TO DISCOVER THE VOLUME OF A SPHERICAL BODY.

Since (1) every sphere is four times the cone having a base equal to the greatest circle in the sphere and a height equal to the radius of the sphere

---

² See Chap. 4 above, note 1.

³ See Proemium, lines 45–47.

Prop. 9

¹ See Proemium, lines 48–50.

² See Chap. 4, note 1.

³ That is, I.41 (=Gr. I.43) of *On the Sphere and the Cylinder*. This is not actually quoted in the Proemium. Consult the Moerbeke text Vol. 2, 30vR–S.

by [I.]32 (=Gr. I.34) of Archimedes in the place [cited] above,[1] and since (2) you had the measure of this cone in the sixth [proposition] of this [chapter], therefore the measure of a sphere will no longer be concealed from you.

It is pleasing to adduce an example [see Fig. I.6.9]: Let there be a sphere whose diameter is 7. The volume of the cylinder of the hemisphere is 134¾, by the fourth [proposition] of this [chapter]. Its ⅓ part, 44¹¹/₁₂, is the volume of the cone by the sixth [proposition], of this [chapter]. This you take 4 times and the result is 179⅔, which is the volume of the whole sphere that you seek. This is that proposed.

In another way: From the [I.]33 (=Gr. I.34) of the same [work of Archimedes],[2] a cylinder having as a base the greatest circle in the sphere and as an altitude the diameter of the sphere is ³⁄₂ the sphere. Therefore, since the cylinder of the said sphere is 269½ by the fourth [proposition] of this [chapter], if a third part of it is subtracted, 179⅔ remains as the aforesaid volume of the sphere.

In another way: by means of a cube, for the cube circumscribing a sphere is to the cylinder of the same sphere in a ratio of 14 to 11 [by the second proposition of the *Measurement of the Circle* of Archimedes and the first and four propositions of this chapter].[3] Therefore from the volume of the cube, which is 343 on the basis of the hypothesis of the value of the diameter [of 7], take away ³⁄₁₄ of it, or 73½, and there remains 269½, which is the volume of the cylinder. If a third part is subtracted from it as before, the above said volume of the sphere remains. Or as follows: since the ratio of cube to cylinder about the same sphere is known and of cylinder to sphere, therefore, by VI.7 of this work,[4] the ratio of the cube to sphere is 21 to 11.[5] Therefore, from the cube, which is 343 by hypothesis, take ¹⁰⁄₂₁ of it, or 163½, and 179⅔ remains, which comprises the spherical magnitude. This is that proposed.

11. TO COMPREHEND THE VOLUME OF A SECTOR OF A SPHERE.

Let there be a sphere in which there is a greatest circle *ABG* drawn on center *D* [see Fig. I.6.10] and let there be a cone (1) having a base circle equal to the surface of the [sector of the] sphere which is represented by the arc *ABG* and determined by those things [given] in the ninth [proposition] of this [chapter], and (2) having a height equal to radius *BD*. The sector

---

Prop. 10

   [1] See Proemium, lines 42–44.

   [2] *Ibid.*, lines 45–47. In my text of Moerbeke, this appears not as I.33 but as a corollary to I.32. (Vol. 2, 29rT).

   [3] That is: (1) cube = $B_1 \cdot h$ (Prop. 1 of this chap.), and (2) cylinder = $B_2 \cdot h$ (Prop. 4), and (3) $\dfrac{B_1}{B_2} = \dfrac{14}{11}$ (Prop. 2 of *Meas. of Circle*); therefore, (4) $\dfrac{\text{cube}}{\text{cylinder}} = \dfrac{14}{11}$.

   [4] See Commentary, Prop. 10, line 21.

   [5] Cf. Johannes de Tinemue, *De curvis superficiebus*, Prop. X, ed. of M. Clagett in *Archimedes in the Middle Ages*, Vol. 1, p. 504.

of sphere *ABGD* will be equal to the said cone, by [I.]42 (=Gr. I.44) of Archimedes in the place [cited] before.[1] And since the measure of a cone is had by the sixth [proposition] of this [chapter], therefore so is that of the sector; which is that proposed.

12. TO DEMONSTRATE THE VOLUME OF A SPHERICAL SEGMENT.

Let there be a greatest circle in the sphere, with diameter *AG* and center *T* [see Fig. I.6.11]. And let the sphere be cut by plane *BZ* at right angles to *AG* in point *E*. And let $(TA + AE)/AE = DE/GE$, i.e., if $(TA + AE)$ is multiplied by *GE* and the product is divided by *AE*, it will result in *DE*. Again, let $(TG + GE)/GE = RE/EA$, which is produced as above [so that $RE = \{(TG + GE)/GE\} \cdot EA$] and let cones be described by the circle about diameter *BZ* and these cones have as apexes points *D* and *R*. I say that cone *BZD* is equal to the segment of the sphere in the direction of *G*, while cone *BZR* is equal to the segment in the direction of *A*, by II.2 of Archimedes in the place previously [cited].[1] And since the measure of any cone has been prescribed in the sixth [proposition] of this [chapter], therefore the measure of the said segments is known; which is that proposed.

Example: Let *TA*, the radius of the sphere, be 14, *TE* 7; *GE* will be 7. *DE* is sought. $(TA + AE)/AE = 35/21 = DE/GE$. [Hence] *DE* $= (35 \cdot 7)/21 = 11\frac{2}{3}$, which is placed as the height of the cone whose base is on diameter *BZ*. And that cone will be equal to the spherical segment *BGZ*; and thus for the other segment.

13. TO SQUARE A SPHERICAL SURFACE.

Since the surface of a sphere is 4 times the maximum circle of those in the sphere by [I.]31 (=Gr. I.33) of Archimedes in the place [cited] not long ago,[1] and since the quadrature of the circle is concluded in VIII.14 of this [work],[2] therefore the quadrature of the spherical surface is also concluded. Or as follows: Let the maximum circle of the same sphere be squared by VIII.14 of this [work], and let that square be quadrupled by VI.22 of this [work],[3] and that [quadruplicated] square will be equal to the surface of the sphere; which is that proposed.

14. TO CUBE A SPHERE.

This is nothing else but to describe a cube equal to the given sphere, which is as follows. Since a cube circumscribed about a sphere is in a

Prop. 11
   [1] See Proemium, lines 51–53.

Prop. 12
   [1] See Proemium, lines 54–57.

Prop. 13
   [1] See Proemium, lines 40–41.
   [2] See Chap. 5 above, Text, Prop. 14.
   [3] See Commentary, Prop. 13, line 6.

known ratio to the sphere, i.e., $^{21}/_{11}$, by those things [treated] in the tenth [proposition] of this [chapter], therefore if $^{10}/_{21}$ is taken from that cube a rectangular solid remains which is equal to the sphere, as will be proved. But that solid can be cubed by VII.22 of this [work],[1] therefore, also the sphere; which is that proposed.

The demonstration of that which is to be proved: The aforesaid cube is divided into 21 equal parts by the division of its base and side by IV.5 of this [work].[2] And with 10 of these parts removed, 11 such parts remain which will form a rectangular solid by XI.25 [of the *Elements* of Euclid].[3] Hence the proposition.

In another way as follows [see Fig. I.6.12]: Let the maximum circle A of the given sphere be equal to square B by VIII.14 of this [work].[4] Let the area of either be multiplied by the diameter of the sphere. A cylinder C equal to a rectangular solid will result by the [following] axiom: "if equals are equally increased the products are equal," or by VII.21 [of the *Elements*][5] and by definition of [such a solid]. But cylinder C is $^3/_2$ the given sphere by [I.]33 [=Cor. Gr. I.34] of Archimedes in the place recently [cited]. Therefore the solid D is also $^3/_2$ the same sphere. Therefore, with its $^1/_3$ part removed from the solid, the rectangular solid remaining, which is E, is equal to the given sphere. But this aforesaid solid E can be cubed into F by VII.22 of this [work].[6] Therefore, that the given sphere is equal to cube F has been necessarily concluded; which is that proposed.

15. TO CONSTRUCT A SPHERE EQUAL TO A CONE OR CYLINDER.

Let there be cone A to which we want to find an equal sphere [see Fig. I.6.13]. Let there be cylinder E, $^3/_2$ of this cone A, and let its base circle be about diameter GD and its axis EZ. By VII.16 of this [work],[1] let two mean proportionals HT and MN be assumed between these [lines] GD, EZ, so that $GD/HT = HT/MN = MN/EZ$. Also let a cylinder be conceived whose base circle is about diameter HT and whose axis is RL equal to HT. With [such] a diameter posited let sphere B be described. I say, therefore, that cone A is equal to sphere B. For it is clear that cylinder E is equal to cylinder R. Since $GD/HT = HT/MN = MN/EZ$, therefore permutatively GD/MN, et cetera. But HT is equal to RL by hypothesis. Therefore, $GD/MN = GD^2/HT^2 =$ circle E/circle R,[2] by XII.2 [of the

---

Prop. 14
   [1] See Commentary, Prop. 14, line 6.
   [2] *Ibid.*, line 9.
   [3] *Ibid.*, line 10.
   [4] See Chap. 5, Text, Prop. 14.
   [5] See Commentary, Prop. 14, line 15.
   [6] *Ibid.*, line 6.

Prop. 15
   [1] See Chap. 3 above, Text, Prop. 16.
   [2] That is: (1) $\dfrac{GD}{MN} = \dfrac{HT^2}{MN^2}$, and (2) $\dfrac{HT^2}{MN^2} = \dfrac{GD^2}{HT^2}$; therefore (3) $\dfrac{GD}{MN} = \dfrac{GD^2}{HT^2}$.

Elements].[3] Therefore, circle E/circle $R = RL/EZ$.[4] Therefore, the bases and altitudes of cylinders E and R are [reciprocally] proportional. Therefore, by XII.12 (=Gr. XII.15)[5] [of the *Elements*], the said cylinders are equal. But cylinder R is ³⁄₂ the sphere about diameter HT by XII.9 (=Gr. XII.10) [of the *Elements*].[6] Hence it is conceded that cylinder E is ³⁄₂ the same sphere. And because some time ago the same cylinder E was posited as ³⁄₂ cone A, therefore, the sphere whose diameter is HT and cone A are necessarily equal, by V.9 [of the *Elements*][7]; which is that proposed. With a cylinder posited in place of cone A, it ought to follow by the same deduction that it is equal to the sphere.

16. TO ERECT A SPHERE EQUAL TO A GIVEN CUBE.

Let there be a cube whose base is equal to circle A, by VIII.15 of this [work].[1] Then let the area of this circle be multiplied by the altitude of the cube and there will result a cylinder equal to the given cube. For if two equals are equally increased the products are equal. But this cylinder is equal to a sphere, by the end of the immediately preceding [proposition]; therefore, also is the cube [equal to a sphere]; which is that proposed. For the argument is as follows: It is possible to erect a cylinder equal to the given cube, and to construct a sphere equal to the given cylinder, therefore one can find a sphere equal to the given cube; which is that proposed. And this is the converse of the fourteenth [proposition] of this [chapter].

17. WITH A CIRCLE GIVEN, TO FIND THE SPHERE DESCRIBED BY THAT CIRCLE ROTATED.

Multiply the diameter of the circle by itself cubically, and there will result the cube circumscribing the sphere of the circle. From this cube extract the inscribed sphere by those things which are [discussed] in the tenth [proposition] of this [chapter], and the proposition will be known.

Example: Let a circle with diameter 7 be given. The cube of that diameter will be 343. From this subtract ¹⁰⁄₂₁ of it and 179²⁄₃ remains for the sphere produced by the motion of the circle; which is that proposed.

18. TO SEEK THE SURFACE OF A [SOLID] RHOMBUS.

"Rhombus" is equivocally taken, sometimes for a surface and sometimes for a solid. The surface rhombus was the subject of demonstration in the preceding material. But now we treat here the rhombic solid which

[3] See *Archimedes in the Middle Ages,* Vol. 1, p. 575, comment to 5, 11. Cf. the *Elementa* (Basel, 1546), p. 389.

[4] Since $\dfrac{GD}{MN} = \dfrac{RL}{EZ}$.

[5] See Commentary, Prop. 15, line 16.

[6] *Ibid.*, Prop. 6, line 3.

[7] *Ibid.*, Prop. 15, line 20.

Prop. 16

[1] That is, by Proposition 15 added to the quadrature tract inserted in Chap. 8 of the *De arte mensurandi* (for its text, see below, Part III, Chap. 1, Sect. I, n. 9).

is formed from two isosceles cones on a single base. The surface of the solid is known by means of the measure of the surface of each cone. But the surface of any cone stands as measured in the fifth [proposition] of this [chapter]. Hence the proposition.

19. TO SHOW THE VOLUME OF A RHOMBUS.

Let there be a rhombus *ABDG* which is composed of two isosceles cones [see Fig. I.6.14]. The common base of the cones is a circle about diameter *BG*. The [total] height [of the rhombus] is *AD*. Then let there be posited a cone *HTK* having a base equal to the surface of cone *ABG* (by those things which [are treated] in the fifth [proposition] of this [chapter]) and having an altitude equal to *DZ*, a perpendicular to side *AB* continually extended. Therefore that cone *HTK* will be equal to the above said rhombus by I.18 of Archimedes in the place often [cited].[1] And because the measure of an isosceles cone has already been found by the sixth [proposition] of this [chapter], hence the proposition [follows].

Or as follows: Since that rhombus is composed of two isosceles cones, with each one measured by the sixth [proposition] of this [chapter], the proposition is concluded.

20. TO EXPOUND THE VOLUME OF A TRUNCATED PYRAMID.

If a pyramid is cut by a plane parallel to the base, that which is contained between the section and the apex retains the figure of a pyramid. But that which is included between the section and the base is called a truncated pyramid, and its volume will be found by the subtraction of the small pyramid from the whole pyramid.

Example: Let there be a truncated pyramid whose base is a regular polygon of as many sides as you wish and whose upper surface *CD* is parallel to the base and whose axis is *EF* [See Fig. I.6.15]. Hence, complete the pyramid by extending *AC* and *BD* until they meet in *G*, by the fourth postulate [of Book I of the *Elements*].[1] Therefore, the sides *CG* and *DG* will be known by [proposition] 41 of the second part of the fifth [chapter] of this [work],[2] and so the full lines *AG* and *BG* will be known. Similarly, *AE* is known because it is the radius of the circle inscribed in the base. Therefore, by the penultimate [proposition] of Book I (=Gr. I.47 of the *Elements*),[3] *EG* will be known, which is to posit that the whole pyramid is known by the second [proposition] of this [chapter]. And so with the small pyramid *CDG* (known by the same proposition) taken away from it,

---

Prop. 19
  [1] See Proemium, lines 36–39.

Prop. 20
  [1] That is, the famous parallel postulate, numbered as the fourth one in the Campanus version of the *Elementa*. See Commentary, Prop. 20, line 9.
  [2] See Commentary, Prop. 20, line 10.
  [3] See *Archimedes in the Middle Ages*, Vol. 1, p. 78, comment 25. Cf. the *Elementa* (Basel, 1546), p. 37.

the whole truncated pyramid remains known, which is that proposed. And if the base *AB* is multilateral and the sides are equal or unequal in any fashion, as in a triangle, quadrangle, and pentagon, the art of finding the measure of such a truncated pyramid is in no way to be changed from the [method followed] for the preceding pyramid. And know that every rectilinear solid whose upper surface is parallel to and less than the base is called a truncated pyramid. Therefore this conclusion is said to be a general one for all such [truncated pyramids].

21. TO COMPREHEND THE VOLUME OF A TRUNCATED [ISOSCELES] CONE.

If an [isosceles] cone is cut by a plane parallel to the base, that which is included between the section and the apex does not lose its form. But that which is left from the section down to the base is called a truncated cone. Its volume will be known by taking away the small cone, which is included from the section to the apex (and is known by the sixth [proposition] of this [chapter]), from the quantity of the whole cone (known by the same [proposition]).

Example: Let the aforesaid [truncated] cone be *AD* [see Fig. I.6.16], with its base circle about diameter *AB* and its upper surface a circle parallel to the base and about diameter *CD*; while its axis is *EF*. With sides *AC* and *BD* continued directly until they necessarily meet in *G* (by the fourth postulate [of Book I of the *Elements*]),[1] hence there will be sides *CG* and *DG*. And hence whole side *AG* [and whole side] *BG* are known by the forty-first [proposition] of the second part of the fifth [chapter] of this [work].[2] And because the radius *AE* of the base is also known, therefore the axis *EG* is known by the penultimate [proposition] of [Bk.] I (=Gr. I.47 of the *Elements*).[3] Therefore, the whole volume of cone *ABG* will be known by the sixth [proposition] of this [work]. If from this whole cone is taken the volume of the small cone *CDG* (known by the same [proposition]), the volume of the truncated cone remains known to you; which was that proposed. And if you want to measure the surface of this [truncated] cone: With the cone completed, from its surface (known by the fifth [proposition] of this [chapter]) take the surface of the small cone (known by the same [proposition]) and the surface of the truncated cone remains.

[Argue] for the same [proposition] by [I.]16 of Archimedes in the place [cited] above:[4] Let there be a cone whose triangle through the axis is *ABG* and which is cut by a plane parallel to the base [passing] through line *DE* [see Fig. I.6.17]. Moreover, the axis of the cone is *BH*. And let a circle be posited whose radius is the mean proportional between (1) *AD*, the side

Prop. 21

[1] See Commentary, Prop. 20, line 9.

[2] *Ibid.*, line 10.

[3] See Prop. 20, note 3.

[4] Prop. I.16 of *On the Sphere and the Cylinder* is not given in the Proemium. See the Moerbeke text, Vol. 2, 26rO.

of the truncated cone, and (2) the sum of the radii of the bases, *DZ* and *AH*; this circle will be equal to the surface of the truncated cone. Therefore, with the circle measured by VI.1 of this [work], the proposition will be had.[5]

22. TO EXAMINE THE SURFACE OF AN ARCUATE RHOMBUS.

Let an arc of a circle less than a semicircle be rotated about its chord as a fixed axis until it returns to the place from which it began. The body thus described Archimedes first named a spheroid[1] and rightly represents the figure of a dragon or an oval. But we can call it a curvilinear rhombus because of [its] nearness [to a rhomboid]. [It is this] whose surface we seek to measure.[2] Therefore, let the said figure be *ABGD* with major diameter *AG* and minor *BD* [see Fig. I.6.18]. And on the major diameter let a circle be described about center *T*. But Archimedes has demonstrated in the book *On Spheroids and Conoids*, Prop. 5,[3] that the minor diameter has the same ratio to the major which the spheroidal space[4] has to the circle which is described about the major axis. But with *AT* and *TB* measured, it is not difficult to find the ratio of these diameters. Hence the proposition is clearly known.

And note that there are three kinds of such a spheroidal body [see Fig. I.6.19].[5] (1) when the center of one arc lies on the other arc and vice versa, and let that be called "perfect"; (2) when the arcs of both include their centers, and let that be called "diminished"; and (3) when the centers lie outside of their arcs, and let it be "superabundant." The measure of these three is not varied at all.

23. TO SEEK OUT THE MAGNITUDE OF AN ARCUATE RHOMBUS.

Let the said rhombus be *ABDG* with major diameter *BG* and minor *AD* [see Fig. I.6.20]. Hence let it be cut by a plane passing through minor

---

[5] See above, my Chap. 4, n. 1.

Prop. 22

[1] This is an error. The figure is rather that which Kepler called a "lemon" (*citrii mali figura*). See J. Kepler, *Supplementum ad Archimedem de stereometria figurarum* in the *Opera omnia*, ed. of C. Frisch, Vol. 4 (Frankfurt and Erlangen, 1863), pp. 576, 585–86.

[2] He seems to say here and in the enunciation that he wishes to find the measure of the surface area of the solid figure produced by the rotation of the circular segment about its chord. But all he actually seeks is the measurement of a plane section through the axes of that solid. And indeed the proposition he later quotes from *On Conoids and Spheroids* only permits the measurement of a plane section (that is, the ellipse) through the major and minor axes of an ellipsoid rather than the plane section of the "lemon" described in the first sentence. Hence, not only is his enunciation badly stated, but his demonstration is erroneous.

[3] For Prop. 5 (=Gr. 4), see the Moerbeke translation, Vol. 2, 46rK–L.

[4] That is, the ellipse (see note 2 above).

[5] Fig. I.6.19 shows all three figures as "lemons" and not Archimedean spheroids. For an explanation of the names "perfect," "diminished" and "superabundant," see Commentary, Prop. 22, lines 15–19.

diameter *AD* (and center *T*) and perpendicular to axis *BG*. That section is a circle on which it is imagined that cone *ABD* is elevated. Now from [Prop.] 28 (=Gr. Prop. 27) of *On Spheroids*[1] of Archimedes half the spheroid is double cone *ABD* whose base circle is about diameter *AD* and whose altitude is *TB*.[2] Therefore, if the cone, which is known by the sixth [proposition] of this [chapter], is doubled, it follows that the measure of half the arcuate rhombus is known and consequently that of the whole rhombus.

24. TO FIND THE VOLUME OF A CURVILINEAR CYLINDER.

Here the cylinder is named "curvilinear" to differentiate it from the straight cylinder which Archimedes wrote about in [I.]13 of the *On the Sphere*.[1] For that [straight cylinder] is constructed out of straight line [elements perpendicular to the circular base], while this [curvilinear cylinder] is constructed out of curved sides. And if two apexes of a spheroidal body, i.e., an arcuate rhomboid (as the preceding conclusion constructed), are cut off [each] by a plane at right [angles] to the axis, a curvilinear cylinder will be produced. Therefore, let there be a spheroid *ABGZ* [see Fig. I.6.21] whose middle is cut in the said manner by a plane that is at right [angles] to the axis but not [passing] through the center. And let the section be *ADG*, which section is necessarily a circle. Therefore, with the spheroidal segment *ABG* measured, the rest of the semispheroid will be known, since the whole semispheroid is already known by the preceding [proposition]. Therefore, imagine a cone designated by letters *ABG* whose base circle is about *AG*. Now from [Prop.] 30 (=Gr. 29)[2] of Archimedes' *On Spheroids* it has been concluded that the lesser segment of every spheroidal figure cut by a plane at right [angles] to the axis but not [passing] through the center has the same ratio to a cone (having the same base as the segment and equal in altitude) as the sum of half the spheroidal axis and the axis of the greater segment to the axis of that same greater segment. Therefore

$$(TZ + DZ)/DZ = \text{seg. } ABG/\text{cone } ABG.$$

But it happens that the ratio of the said lines is known. From mensuration of these lines, the proposition follows.

Prop. 23

[1] For Prop. 28 (=Gr. 27) of *On Conoids and Spheroids*, see the Moerbeke text, Vol. 2, 50vP–Q.

[2] This is, of course, only true if the "arcuate rhombus" of which the author speaks is actually a spheroid. In fact, the author is apparently misapplying it to a solid generated by the rotation of a circular segment about its chord, as in the preceding proposition.

Prop. 24

[1] See Proemium, lines 30–32.

[2] For Prop. 30 (=Gr. 29) of *On Conoids and Spheroids*, see the Moerbeke text, Vol. 2, 51rW. Again the author is misapplying this proposition to his arcuate rhombus, which does not appear to be an Archimedean spheroid.

Example: Let *BT* be 14 and *DT* 7, as you may wish. Hence, *TZ* will be 14. And place *ZH* equal to *TZ* and extended directly from *TZ*. Therefore *DH* = *TZ* + *DZ* = 35. Therefore *DH*/*DZ* = 35/21. But this is the ratio of the curvilinear, corporeal segment *ABG* to cone *ABG*. Therefore, since the measure of the cone is had in the sixth [proposition] of this [chapter], the measure of the oft-stated segment also remains known. Therefore the rest of the semispheroid is known. If this is doubled the curvilinear cylinder becomes known; which was that proposed. This body the common people are accustomed to call a cask whose measure I have found, up to now, demonstrated geometrically [only] in an invalid way, although certain artisans have thought they were measuring a cask. But they cross the bounds of truth, since their measure is not geometrical but is vulgar [i.e., numerically approximative].[3] But the doctrine of the excellent Archimedes has unlocked from the bosom of the *Elements* this conclusion and many others which have lain dormant for a long time.

25. TO MEASURE THAT WHICH REMAINS AFTER AN ISOSCELES RHOMBUS HAS BEEN SUBTRACTED FROM A CONE.

Let *ABC* be the round pyramid or cone, in which there is the isosceles rhombus *CDFE* [see Fig. I.6.22]. If the latter is subtracted, the surrounding body, which is *DABE*, remains to be measured. [One proceeds] thus by I.19 of Archimedes' *On the Sphere and the Cylinder*:[1] "If an isosceles cone is cut by a plane parallel to the base, and if on the circle so formed a cone having its apex at the center of the base is constructed, and if the rhombus so formed is subtracted from the whole cone, there will be equal to the surrounding body a cone having [its] base equal to the surface of the [truncated] cone lying between the parallel planes and [its] height equal to a perpendicular drawn from the center of the base to one side of the cone."

Example: Let there be an isosceles cone *ABG* [see Fig. I.6.23] and let it be cut by a plane parallel to the base [and passing] through line *DE*, while the center of the base is *Z*. And let a cone be constructed on the circle about diameter *DE* which has its apex *Z*. And the rhombus *BDZE* will be composed out of isosceles cones. Therefore let a cone *KTL* be posited whose base is equal to the surface lying between *DE* and *AG*, namely the surface included by lines *AD* and *EG*, and whose height is equal to the perpendicular drawn from point *Z* to side *AB*, namely equal to *ZH*. Archimedes has demonstrated that if rhombus *BDEZ* is considered as removed from cone *ABG*, cone *TKL* is equal to the surrounding body. But

---

[3] For a similar use of *vulgariter* in the context of a numerical approximation, see *Archimedes in the Middle Ages*, Vol. 1, p. 504, line 6.

Prop. 25

[1] Prop. I.19 was not given in the Proemium above but rather is stated in full here in the text (of course in the Latin translation of Moerbeke). This may be an indication that this was one of the propositions added to Chapter 10 of the *De arte mensurandi* at a later time. See the introduction to this chapter.

the sixth [proposition] of this [chapter] shows the measure of the cone. Hence the proposition.

Also, another way: If the rhombus known by the nineteenth [proposition] of this [chapter] is taken away from the whole cone (known by the sixth [proposition] of this [chapter]), that which remains is clearly and necessarily known.

And let the tenth chapter of this work be completed with this proposition.

Commentary

Proemium

9 "rombo" This probably refers to the solid rhombus of Propositions 18 and 19 as taken from the Moerbeke translation of *On the Sphere and the Cylinder*. But it may also include the so-called "arcuate rhombus" formed by the rotation of a circular segment about its chord (see Proposition 22). Needless to say, if the propositions concerning this latter figure (Propositions 22–24) were added later, as suggested in the introduction, then this reference to "rombo" can only be to the figure of Propositions 18 and 19.

Proposition 1

6 "9^{am} . . . 5^i" For V.9 of the *De arte mensurandi*, see MS Paris, BN lat. 7380, 21v (hereafter cited as *Pd*): "Cuiuslibet superficiei rectilinee aream invenire."

Proposition 2

2–3 "3^{am} . . . 12^{mi}" For this proposition, see the Campanus version of the *Elementa* (Basel, 1546), p. 400: "Omnis laterata columna tripla est ad unam pyramidem."

14–15 "per . . . huius" For Proposition 5 of the third part of Chapter 5 of the *De arte mensurandi*, see *Pd*, 34v: "Aream trianguli equilateri per numeros mensurare impossibile est."

17 "per . . . huius" For Prop. 2 of the third part of Chap. 5 of the *De arte mensurandi*, see *Pd*, 34v: "Si ab altero angulorum trianguli equilateri cuius latus rationale ad basim perpendicularis educatur, ipsa quidem necessario surda erit."

Proposition 3

5 "10^{am} 6^i" For VI.10, see the Campanus Version of the *Elementa* (Basel, 1546), p. 146: "Duabus lineis datis, tertiam eis in continua proportionalitate subiungere."

Proposition 6

3 "9^{am} 12^{mi}" For XII.9, see the Campanus version of the *Elementa* (Basel, 1546), p. 402: "Omnis columna rotunda pyramidi suae tripla esse comprobatur."

Proposition 7

6–7 "per . . . huius" For IV.15, see the Campanus version of the *Elementa* (Basel, 1546), p. 99: "Intra propositum circulum, hexagonum aequilaterum atque aequiangulum describere. Ex hoc itaque manifestum est, quod latus hexagoni aequum est dimidio diametri circuli cui inscribitur.'' For II.2 of the *De arte mensurandi*, see *Pd*, 5r: ''Latus exagoni circulo inscripti semidiametro eiusdem circuli equale est.''

Proposition 10

21 ''per . . . huius'' For VI.7 of the *De arte mensurandi*, see *Pd*, 42v: ''Si una quantitas duabus notis proportionetur, illarum duarum adinvicem proportio nota fiet.''

Proposition 13

6 ''in . . . 6^i'' For VI.22 of the *De arte mensurandi*, see *Pd*, 46r: ''Circuli dati duplum, triplum, quadruplum et sic deinceps figurare.''

Proposition 14

6 ''per . . . huis'' For VII.22 of the *De arte mensurandi*, see *Pd*, 54v: ''Datum solidum rectangulum cubicare.''

9 ''per . . . huius'' For IV.5 of the *De arte mensurandi*, see *Pd*, 18v: ''Datam lineam in quotlibet partes equales dividere.''

10 ''per . . . 11^m'' For XI.25, see the Campanus version of the *Elementa* (Basel, 1546), p. 368: ''Si superficies quaedam secet solidum parallelogrammum aequidistanter duabus ipsius solidi superficiebus oppositis, duo partialia corpora quae ad illam secantem superficiem velut ad communem terminum copulantur, suis basibus sunt proportionalia.''

15 ''si . . . 7^{mi}'' The axiom is perhaps a modification of the common Euclidian axiom of the addition of equals to equals. For VII.21, see the Campanus version of the *Elementa* (Basel, 1546), p. 185: ''Numeri secundum quamlibet proportionem minimi numerant quoslibet in eadem proportione, minor minorem et maior maiorem aequaliter.'' This proposition, of course, applies only to numbers and therefore does not give full authority for the argument. Hence, the axiom.

Proposition 15

16 ''per . . . 12^{mi}'' For XII.12 (=Gr. XII.15), see the Campanus version of the *Elementa* (Basel, 1546), p. 412: ''Si duae pyramides rotundae sive columnae fuerint aequales, suae bases et altitudines erunt mutuae. Si vero suae bases et altitudines mutuae fuerint, ipsas pyramides sive columnas aequales esse necesse est.''

20 ''per . . . 5^i'' For V.9, see the Campanus version of the *Elementa* (Basel, 1546), p. 121: ''Si fuerit aliquarum quantitatum ad unam quantitatem proportio una, ipsas esse aequales: si vero unius ad eas proportio una, ipsas aequales esse necesse est.''

Proposition 20

9 ''per . . . petitum'' For this postulate (numbered as the fourth), see the Campanus version of the *Elementa* (Basel,

1546), p. 3: "Si linea recta super duas lineas rectas ceciderit, duoque anguli ex una parte duobus rectis angulis minores fuerint, istas duas lineas in eandem partem protractas, proculdubio coniunctum iri."

10 "per . . . huius" For Prop. 41 of the second part of Chap. 5 of the *De arte mensurandi*, see *Pd*, 31v: "Dato capite, nota basi, unoquoque laterum numerato, quantum distat usquequo concurrant latera reperire."

Proposition 22

15–19 "Et . . . variatur." I believe that the names for these three varieties of the "lemon" come from the character of the arcs of the circular segments that are rotated to produce them. Thus the mean or middle arc with its center lying in the complementary arc is first designated as "perfect." Then the arc above it is an arc of a smaller or "diminished" circle, while that below it is the arc of a larger or "superabundant" circle.

CHAPTER 7

The Use of the Moerbeke Translations of Archimedes by Nicole Oresme and Henry of Hesse

Assuming that my arguments for Johannes de Muris' authorship of Chapters 6–12 of the *De arte mensurandi* are correct, one may be tempted at this point to conclude that the use of Moerbeke's translations of Archimedes at Paris was confined to the Parisian astronomer. But this is not so. There is indisputable evidence that at least two of Johannes' successors at Paris were also acquainted (either directly or indirectly) with the Moerbeke translations: Nicole Oresme and Henry of Hesse.

Nicole Oresme, one of the most original of medieval natural philosophers, appears to have taken his arts training at Paris in the middle 1340's. At least, when he entered the College of Navarre as a theology student in 1348, he was already a Master of Arts.[1] No doubt he was under some obligation to teach in arts, particularly in the early years of his theological training. Presumably it would have been in this early period (about 1348–52) that he prepared his various collections of *Questiones* on sundry works of Aristotle.[2] One could also suppose that at this time his attention was directed to the Moerbeke translations by Johannes or some other associate in the University arts circle. In whatever way he became acquainted with the Moerbeke translations of Archimedes, Oresme was able to para-

---

[1] The most accurate of the various biographical summaries of Oresme's activities is to be found in Nicole Oresme, *De proportionibus proportionum and Ad pauca respicientes*, ed. of E. Grant (Madison, Wisc., 1966), pp. 3–10. Reference is made there to other biographical accounts. The authority for my statement that Oresme was already a Master of Arts in 1348 is a document issued in 1349, on the basis of an earlier document of 1348, in which a list of Masters of Arts of the Norman Nation is given (see H. Denifle and A. Chatelain, *Chartularium Universitatis Parisiensis*, Vol. 2 [Paris, 1891], p. 638). Grant's biography obscures the essential fact by calling it a "list of students."

[2] For a list of Oresme's various works, see my *Nicole Oresme and the Medieval Geometry of Qualities and Motions* (Madison, Wisc., 1968), Bibliography, under "Oresme."

phrase copiously the text of the Flemish translator's version of Archimedes' *On Floating Bodies* in his *Questiones super de celo et mundo*,
which appears to date from about 1350. Oresme's direct use of *On Floating
Bodies* is of particular interest since it is the first such direct use of that
work in the Latin West. Oresme's dependence on the Archimedean work
appears in the course of the discussion of Book IV, Question 4: "Whether
anything heavy or light can rest naturally in the middle of another element
or species." The pertinent passage runs:[3]

[3] Nicole Oresme, *Questiones super de celo et mundo*, ed. and transl. of C. Kren (Dissertation, Univ. of Wisconsin, 1965), pp. 847–64: "secunda distinctio est quod respectu aque,
potest ymaginari solidum vel durum eque grave cum ipsa aqua aut magis gravis aut minus
et ita respectu alterius humidi sicud vini vel olei, et voco eque grave quando quantitas
aque et quantitas illius equales ad invicem, equaliter ponderarent in aere et in equilibra,
vel eque velociter descenderent per aerem ceteris paribus vel essent eque faciliter ad
portandum. Isto modo dicimus quod aurum est gravius quam argentum.
  "Tunc sit conclusio quod possible est esse aliquid equaliter grave cum aqua. Probatur quia
contingit dare aliquid gravius sicud ferrum vel plumbum, et aliquid levius sicud oleum vel
lignum, igitur possibile est dare aliquid eque grave sicud cera vel aliquid tale. Secundo
quia possibile est quod in aliquo mixto sit tantum de terra et de igne quod in aere sit
levius aqua et etiam quod sit gravius, igitur possibile est taliter proportionare quod equaliter
ita habet sicud aqua, nec ex hoc sequitur quod sit equaliter mixtum; et si non concederetur
de aqua tamen posset proportionari quod esset eque grave cum aliquo alio humido, sicud
oleo et vino. Dico tamen incidentabiliter quod hoc est difficile invenire quia in omnibus
diversarum rationum, difficile est invenire equalitatem precise vel similem proportionem,
tamen non est impossibile etiam quia in proposito aque sunt diversarum modorum et quedam
graviores aliis secundum diversitatem fontium et locorum et similiter salsa est gravior dulci,
ut patet secundo *Meteororum*. Habemus igitur tres modos corporum solidorum, scilicet
quoddam gravius aque, aliquod eque gravis et aliud minus.
  "Tunc de secundo dicendum est secundum hec tria et primo de eque gravi sit conclusio
quod omne tale, demissum in aqua, comprimeret aquam vel demergeretur quousque superficies superior esset eque alta cum superficie aque et non ultra. Probatur quia aqua sibi
equalis que occuparet illum locum hoc idem faceret quia sicud visum fuit non potest
supereminere nec etiam concavare naturaliter et hoc faceret secundum gravitatem, igitur
illud solidum sicud cera cum propositum sit equaliter grave illud idem faciet per suam
gravitatem. Confirmatur secundo quia non est levius aqua, igitur non supereminaret, nec
est gravius, igitur non descenderet sub ipsa. Tenet consequentia quia talis motus non potest
naturaliter nisi quando gravius est super minus grave, ut visum fuit prius. Et ista conclusio demonstratur aliter et magis mathematice ab Archimenide in libro *De incidentibus
in humido*, et est tertia conclusio primi libri.
  "Nunc sit secunda conclusio quod omne tale ubique est impelleretur in profunda aque
illud quiesceret ibidem. Probatur statim quia ex quo non est levius aqua non ascendit
sursum, nec ex quo est gravius amplius non descendit, si dimittatur. Ex quo sequitur correlative quod si moveatur per aquam, iste motus non est proprie naturalis nec violentus
sicud recte una gutta illiusmet aque ubique sit in suo toto scilicet in aqua ipsa quiescit
naturaliter, sed tamen in tali motu est quedam violentia propter divisionem et condensa-
tionem aque, et cetera.
  "Nunc sequitur videri de solido graviori sicud esset lapis, et sit prima conclusio quod
tale totaliter demergeretur et descenderet ad fundum. Statim patet quia ipsum est gravius
quam partes humidi subiacentes et ille sunt leviores et fluide, igitur fluerent superius et
illud descenderet. Et ista est septima conclusio libri predicti demonstrata mathematice ibidem.
  "Secunda conclusio sit quod illud tanta vi descendit quanta est gravius quam aqua sibi
equalis in magnitudine. Hoc patet statim quia per istum excessum gravitatis descendit et

A second distinction is that, in relation to water, one can imagine a solid or hard body equally heavy as the water itself, or one heavier, or less heavy, and similarly with respect to another fluid, like wine or oil. And I mean by equally heavy that a quantity of water and a quantity of that [other material] equal to each other [in volume] would weigh the same in air and in a balance or would descend equally quickly through the air, other things being equal, or would be equally easy to carry. In this way, we say that gold is heavier than silver.

Then, let it be a conclusion that it is possible to have something equally heavy as water. We can prove this, for it is possible to have something heavier, like

tantam virtutem habet quantam excedit gravitatem aque et hoc demonstrato mathematice in probatione predicte conclusionis, ubi supra. Per hoc patet correlative quod quacumque tarditate data adhuc aliquid potest tardius descendere in aqua qualibet propter diminutionem in infinitum huius excessus.

"Nunc restat videri de leviori, et est prima conclusio quod solidum levius quam humidum equale in magnitudine non totum mergeretur in humido. Probatur statim quia tale est levius quam aqua equalis, igitur non tantum descenderet sicud ipsa et ipsa descenderet usque ad equalitatem et ista est quarta conclusio libri predicti demonstrata aliter a mathematicis et patet ad sensum de ligno sicco quod non totum mergitur.

"Secunda conclusio est quod omne tale intantum demergeretur ut tanta moles humidi quanta est moles partis demerse habeant equalem gravitatem cum tota magnitudine. Verbi gratia, sit solidum seu lignum *AB* et pars demersa sit *B*, dico igitur quod aqua equalis ipsius *B* in magnitudine est precise ita gravis sicud totum *AB*, et hec est quinta libri predicti demonstrata mathematice. Sed pro nunc potest faciliter declarare quia per primam conclusionem si *AB* esset eque grave sicud aqua, tunc aqua quam occuparet esset eque gravis sicud *AB*. Nunc igitur si *AB* rarefiat vel per ymaginationem augeatur a parte superiori sine hoc quod fiat magis grave vel leve, non propter hoc ascendit magis vel descendit, igitur semper occupabit tantundem de aqua, igitur semper aqua equalis parti demerse esset eque gravis sicud totum *AB*.

"Tertia conclusio est quod si tale deprimatur infra aqua, tanta vi feretur sursum quanta est levior aqua vel quanta aqua est gravior, sicud sibi equalis in magnitudine et ita est sixta conclusio predicta et posset probari sicud una prius posita. Ex istis sequitur correlative quod si sit aliquod eque grave cum ipsa aqua in medio ipsius aque tunc quiescit. Si autem illud diminuitur vel condensetur, non mutata gravitate, tunc descenderet quod statim patet quia tunc erit gravius aqua, modo predicto quia aqua equalis non erit ita gravis. Iterum etiam si illud augeatur vel rarefiat, non mutata gravitate, tunc ascendit statim quia aqua equalis erit gravior.

"Ultima conclusio pro nunc sit ista; quod si solidum levius humido dimattatur in humido sicud lignum talis est proportio huius solidi in gravitate ad humidum sibi equalis in magnitudine, sicud partes demerse ad totum hoc solidum. Verbi gratia, sit lignum *AB* et pars demersa sit *B*, et aqua equalis toti *AB* sit *C*, dico igitur quod proportio gravitatis ipsius *AB* ad gravitatem ipsius *C* est sicud proportio partis *B* ad totum *AB* in magnitudine. Et ut magis pateat, ponatur in terminis (*!* numeris?): quod *B* sit quarta pars totius solidi, igitur erit sicud unum et *A* sicud 3, et totum *AB* sicud 4. Sit igitur gravitas totius *AB* una libra et quia proportio totius *AB* ad illam partem *B* est quadrupla, sequitur quod proportio aque equalis ad ipsum *AB* est quadrupla in gravitate. Et ista est prima conclusio secundi libri *De incidentibus in humido* et demonstratur ibidem sed potest nunc aliter declari quia aqua depulsa est equalis parti *B* et talis aqua equalis *B* in magnitudine est eque gravis sicud totum *AB*, ut patet per unam precendentem, igitur talis aqua est unius libre, igitur aqua quadrupla maior est 4 libre, sed aqua quadrupla maior est equalis toti *AB* per positum, igitur illa est 4 librarum et *AB* unius libre per positum, igitur est eadem proportio istarum gravitatum sicud *B* ad totum *AB* quod est compositum, et ista sunt intelligenda de humidibus uniformibus et similiter de solidis uniformibus et non concavatis vel diversimode figuratis."

I have altered Mrs. Kren's translation somewhat.

iron or lead, and something lighter, like oil or wood; therefore it is possible to find something equally heavy, like wax or some such thing. Second, because it is possible that in some mixture there may be just enough earth and fire so that the mixture may be lighter than water in air and also that there may be [just enough] that it may be heavier, therefore it is possible to assign a ratio [of elements in a mixture] so that it is equally [heavy] as water. Nor does it follow from this that the mixture is balanced [as to the elements]. Even if this might not be conceded in regard to water, still one could find a ratio which would be equally heavy as some other fluid, like oil or wine. However, I say incidentally, that this is difficult to find because in all things of diverse kinds it is difficult to find the exact equilibrium or a similar ratio, yet it is not impossible. Also, in our proposal, there are waters of diverse kinds and some are heavier than others owing to the diversity of sources and places; and similarly salt [water] is heavier than sweet, as is clear in the second [book] of the *Meteorology*. We have, therefore, three kinds of solid bodies: certain ones heavier than water, some equally heavy, and others less heavy.

Then for the second [point], one should consider [this problem] by referring to these three [kinds of body]: First as to the equally heavy, let it be a conclusion that every such [body], allowed to fall in water, would compress the water or would be forced down until its upper surface would be as equally high as the surface of the water and not further. The proof of this is that the water equal to [the body] which would occupy that place would act in the same way, for, as has been seen, it is not able to rise above nor even to form a hollow, naturally; and this it would do by its gravity; therefore that solid, such as wax, since it is proposed as equally heavy, will act in this same way by its own gravity. In the second place, we may confirm this because, as it is not lighter than water, it would accordingly not rise above it; nor is it heavier; therefore it would not descend under [the water] itself. The consequence holds because such motion can only [take place] naturally when the heavier is over the less heavy, as was seen previously. And this conclusion is demonstrated in another way, and more mathematically, by Archimedes in the book, *On Floating Bodies*, and it is the third conclusion of the first book.

Now let it be the second conclusion that every such thing, wherever it is pushed down in the depths of the water, would rest in that place. We can prove this immediately, for, since it is not lighter than water, it does not ascend upward; and since it is not heavier, neither does it descend further, if it is let drop. From this it follows, correlatively, that, if it is moved through the water, this motion is not, properly speaking, natural, nor is it violent, just as, correctly speaking, one drop of that water itself, anywhere it may be in its own totality, as in the water itself, rests naturally; but nonetheless in such motion there is a certain violence because of the division and condensation of the water, etc.

Now one must consider a solid heavier [than water], such as a stone; and let it be the first conclusion that such [a solid] would be totally submerged and would descend to the bottom. This is immediately evident since [the solid] itself is heavier than the parts of the liquid lying under it. These [latter] are lighter and are fluid; therefore they would flow over [the solid], and the solid would descend. And this is the seventh conclusion of the afore-mentioned book [of Archimedes] demonstrated mathematically in that place.

Let it be the second conclusion that [such a body] descends with as much force as it is heavier than the water equal to it in volume. This is immediately evident, for it descends as the result of this excess of gravity and it has as much power as its [gravity] exceeds the gravity of the water and this [is shown] by a mathematical demonstration in [Archimedes'] proof of the conclusion discussed above. By this it is evident, correlatively, that given any slowness whatsoever, [a body] can descend still more slowly in any water as by diminishing to infinity this excess [of force of a body over an equal volume of water].

Now it remains to consider [bodies] lighter [than water], and it is the first conclusion that a solid lighter than a liquid equal [to it] in volume is not totally submerged in the liquid. We prove this immediately, for such a [solid] is lighter than an equal [volume of] water, and hence it [the body] would not descend as much as it [the equal volume of water] and the latter would descend [only] to the level [of the water]. This is the fourth conclusion of the previously mentioned book [of Archimedes], demonstrated in another way by mathematics; and it is evident to the senses in the case of dry wood which is not totally submerged.

The second conclusion is that every such [solid] would be submerged to such a degree that a quantity of liquid equal [in volume] to the quantity of the immersed part [of the solid] would have a weight equal to that of the total quantity [of the solid]. For example, let there be a solid, let us say, wood, *AB* and let the immersed part be *B*, I say therefore that the water equal in volume to *B* itself is exactly as heavy as the total *AB*, and this is the fifth [conclusion] of the previously mentioned book [of Archimedes], demonstrated mathematically. But for the present one can easily explain this, for by the first conclusion, if *AB* were equally heavy as the water, then the water which occupies [that volume] would be equally heavy as *AB*. Now, therefore, if *AB* were rarefied or, by imagination, were increased at the upper part [which is not in the water] without being made heavier or lighter, it would not descend or ascend more on this account; therefore it will always occupy just as much water and so the water equal to the immersed part would always be equally heavy as the total *AB*.

The third conclusion is that, if such [a solid] is forced under the water, it will be borne upward by as much force as it is lighter than the water or as the water is heavier, [that is] as [an amount of water] equal to it in volume, and this is the sixth conclusion in the aforementioned [book of Archimedes]. It could be proved in the same way as the one previously stated. From these [conclusions] it follows correlatively that if there is a body which is equally heavy as the water itself, and if it is in the midst of the water, then it rests; if that [body] is either diminished or condensed, without changing its gravity, then it would descend. This is immediately evident since then it will be heavier than water in the aforementioned way, since the water equal [in volume] will not be as heavy. Further, if that [body] is increased or made less dense, without changing its gravity, then it immediately ascends because water equal to it [in volume] will be heavier.

For the present let the final conclusion be this: if a solid lighter than a liquid is allowed to fall in the liquid, as for example, wood, the ratio of this solid in weight to [the weight of] the liquid equal to it in volume is as the ratio of the immersed part [of the solid] to this whole solid. For example, let there be [a piece of] wood, *AB*, and let the immersed part be *B* and the water equal to the whole of *AB* be *C*, I say, therefore, that the ratio of the weight of *AB* itself to the weight of *C* itself is as the ratio of the part *B* to the whole *AB* in volume. To make it clearer, let it be presented in numbers. Let *B* be a fourth part of the entire solid, therefore [*B*] will be as one, and *A* as three, and the whole *AB* as four. Let, therefore, the weight of the whole *AB* be one pound; and since the ratio of the whole of *AB* to that part *B* is a quadruple one, it follows that the ratio of the water equal to *AB* itself is quadruple in weight. This is the first conclusion of the second book of the *On Floating Bodies* [of Archimedes] and is demonstrated there. But for now one can explain it in another way, because the water driven out is equal to part *B* and such a water equal to *B* in volume is equally heavy as the whole of *AB*, as is clear by one of the preceding [conclusions]; therefore such water weighs one pound; therefore water four times heavier is four pounds, but water four times heavier is equal to the whole of *AB* as posited; therefore that [water] weighs four pounds and *AB* one pound, as posited; consequently there is the same ratio of these weights as *B* is to the whole of *AB*, which has been agreed. And these [conclusions] are to be understood as applying to uniform liquids and similarly to uniform solids which are not hollow or shaped in diverse ways.

It will be evident to the reader who has his eye on the text of Archimedes that Oresme has quite faithfully (and sometimes in Moerbeke's very words) cited Propositions 3, 7, 4, 5 and 6 of Book I and Proposition 1 of Book II of the *On Floating Bodies*.[4] Before discussing these conclusions let us note one further reference to *On Floating Bodies*, this to Proposition 2 of Book I. It is made by Oresme earlier:[5]

Now, as to the second [point], let it be the first conclusion that wheresoever some portion of water or air may be, then at the surface and near another body the parts [of the water] try to maintain a [surface] equally [distant] relative to the center, so that that surface is a portion of the surface of a sphere whose center would be the [center of the] world. Aristotle proves that in the second [book] of this [work], and also Archimedes in the book, *On Weights*.

It will be noticed immediately that Oresme in this passage mistakenly gives the title as *On Weights*, while in the longer passage quoted above he gives the correct title, *On Floating Bodies*. This slip is easily explained since Oresme was equally familiar with a quite different and distinct Pseudo-Archimedean *On Floating Bodies* that also circulated with the alternate title of *De ponderibus Archimendis*[6] and whose Archimedean

---

[4] Note that I have followed Mrs. Kren in her translation of the title as *On Floating Bodies*, although Oresme apparently gave the title as *De incidentibus in humidum (On Bodies Falling into a Liquid)*. See note 6 below.

[5] *Questiones super de celo et mundo*, ed. cit., Bk. IV, Quest. 3, pp. 833–34: "Nunc ad secundum sit prima conclusio quod ubicumque sit aliqua portio aque vel aeris, tunc in superficie et prope aliud corpus partes nituntur equaliter stare respectu centri, ita quod illa superficies est portio superficiei sperice cuius centrum esset mundus. Illud probat Aristoteles secundo huius et etiam Archimenides in libro *De ponderibus*."

[6] Both titles of this work are found in its earliest manuscript: *De ponderibus Archimenidis et intitulatur de incidentibus in humidum* (see below, Appendix I, Section 4). The use of *incidentibus* ("bodies submerging or falling") instead of *insidentibus* (meaning "floating" when used with *in humido*) ought to be noted. As a matter of fact, Oresme used the erroneous *incidentibus* in referring to the title of the genuine *On Floating Bodies*, although the Moerbeke text has in the colophons of both books *De insidentibus in humido* (and in the title—possibly in a later hand—*De insidentibus aque*). It is easy to see how the form *incidentibus* might have appealed to him, since there are propositions in the work that

content I shall discuss below and publish once more in Appendix I, Section 4 below. This Pseudo-Archimedean tract is cited by Oresme (and always under the alternate title) in Book IV, Question 5 of his *Questiones super de celo et mundo*.[7] Hence, we can assume a trivial *lapsus mentis* on Oresme's part when he applied the title of the Pseudo-Archimedean text to a proposition drawn from the genuine *On Floating Bodies*. An alternate, and less probable, explanation of the mistake would be that Oresme had not studied the genuine work in any detailed way when he composed Question 3 and so supposed that it somehow was connected with the widely known Pseudo-Archimedean tract and that he therefore simply used the common title of that Pseudo-Archimedean work in making his citation. Perhaps some support may be given to that point of view by the fact that in Question 3 Oresme gives a fantastic and non-Archimedean explanation for the floating of ships[8] that seems strange in the face of the evident knowledge of the proper Archimedean propositions displayed later in Question 4.

On considering Oresme's use of the genuine *On Floating Bodies*, I should like (1) to review how much of the content of *On Floating Bodies* was already known from indirect sources before Oresme's period, and (2) to discuss the extent to which Oresme anticipated the union of hydrostatics and dynamics suggested by Alberti and Tartaglia and more fully developed by Benedetti. (These later authors will be treated below in their proper places.) As I showed some years ago in *The Science of Mechanics in the Middle Ages*, there were several short treatments of the Archimedean crown problem in Latin before the thirteenth century.[9] They reveal a knowledge of the concept of specific weight (without using the term "specific") and a practical understanding of the Principle of Archimedes in their use of the hydrostatic balance. Then in the thirteenth century a more formal treatise appeared, the so-called *De ponderibus Archimenidis* (or *De incidentibus in humidum*), to which we have referred above. This treatise is of great interest because of its geometrical form, its terminological distinction between "specific" weight and "numerical" (i.e., gross) weight, and its inclusion of the Principle of Archimedes (=the second half of Proposition 7 of the genuine *On Floating Bodies*) as its first proposition. This proposition is expressed as follows: "The weight of any body in air exceeds its weight in water by the weight of a volume of water equal to its own volume."[10]

---

do not concern "floating" bodies, but all the propositions concern bodies that are put into or fall into liquids. The change from *humido* to *humidum* is probably explained by the change from *insidentibus* to *incidentibus*, for the latter by indicating motion would govern the accusative.

[7] See Kren text, p. 869: "Patet per primam conclusionem *De ponderibus Archimenidis*." *Cf.* page 883, where the same citation is given. As I note below, this "first conclusion" was an expression of the Principle of Archimedes.

[8] *Ibid.*, pp. 833–37, pp. 1036–37.

[9] *The Science of Mechanics*, pp. 84–93.

[10] See below, Appendix I, Section 4, Proposition 1.

Further evidence of propositions that ultimately originated in the genuine *On Floating Bodies* is uniquely present in a Parisian codex of the *De ponderibus Archimenidis* (BN lat. 7377B, 89v–92v), which in this part is to be dated in the late thirteenth or early fourteenth century. After Proposition 1 there is an added proposition (without proof): "Every body floating in water displaces a volume of water whose weight is equal to its own weight."[11] This is equivalent to Proposition 5 of Book I of the genuine *On Floating Bodies*. Then at the end of the treatise the following statement is found:[12]

If water, by being rarefied, gradually becomes lighter, or if some body *e*, floating on the water, by condensing, gradually becomes heavier, then just as quickly as the body becomes heavier than the water equal to it in volume, it will immediately begin to descend and it will descend to the bottom of the water, as is evident [in the descent] from *h* to *i* [see Fig. I.7.1]. Or if both things happen, i.e. if the body becomes heavier and the water lighter, then that body will descend more quickly. An example of this exists when certain things seem to happen suddenly, although [in fact] their cause is successively seeking the end [i.e., aim] of its disposition, as in the case of falling stars and that of rain. This can be expressed by an example. Let *ab* be the surface of the water and *cd* its bottom. And let *e* be the body floating on the water, which body gradually increases its gravity. I say that it will gradually sink according to the ratio of its weight to the weight of the water equal to it in volume. For if its weight be one-half the weight of the water equal to it in volume, the part of the body which is in the water will be one-half of that body, as is evident in *f*. And if the weight of that body were equal to it in volume, the whole body will sink into the water but will not have the nature of tending to the bottom since it does not exceed in weight the water equal to it in volume, as is evident in *g*. But when it

---

[11] *Ibid.*, Var. to lines 58–76: "Omne corpus supernatans aque occupat in ea locum aque sui ponderis."

[12] Paris, BN lat. 7377B, 92v: "Si aquam subtiliatam paulatim contingat fieri leviorem vel aliquod corpus ut *e* supernatans aque paulatim condempsando gravius fieri, quantum cito corpus illud fiet gravius quam aqua sibi equalis in magnitudine, statim incipiet descendere et descendet usque ad fundum aque, ut patet ab *h* in *i*; vel si utrumque contingat, hoc est, corpus fieri gravius et aquam leviorem, tunc illud corpus velocius descendet. Hoc est exemplar quod quedam res videntur subito contingere, licet earum causa successive finem sue dispositionis expetet, sicut in stellis cadentibus et pluviis. Hoc potest opinari, verbi gratia, sit *ab* superficies aque, *cd* eius fundum. Et sit *e* corpus natans super aquam quod gravitatem paulatim et paulatim suscipiat. Dico quod mergetur paulatim secundum proportionem sui ponderis ad pondus aque sibi equalis in magnitudine (pars eius corporis existens in aqua *del. MS*). Nam si suum pondus sit subduplum ad pondus aque sibi equalis in magnitudine pars eius corporis existens in aqua erit subdupla ad ipsum corpus, ut patet in *f*. Et si pondus ipsius corporis fuerit equale ponderi aque ei equalis in magnitudine, totum corpus mergetur in aqua, nec habet rationem (?) tendendi ad fundum, cum non vincat in pondere aquam sibi equalem in magnitudine, ut patet in *g*. Sed quando vincet in pondere aquam (*corr. e* quam) sibi equalem in magnitudine, statim descendet ad fundum motu veloci, ut patet ab *h* in *i*, et hoc est quod proponebam demonstrare." I have made some corrections of my original text and have added the figure present in the manuscript. Heiberg's edition of the *Liber de ponderibus*, in *Mathematici graeci minores* (Copenhagen, 1927), pp. 93–107, uses BN lat. 7377B as one of its principal manuscripts but fails to include this interesting passage.

exceeds in weight the water equal to it in volume, it immediately descends to the bottom with a swift motion, as is evident [in the descent] from h to i. And this is what I was proposing to demonstrate.

This passage obviously reflects the three cases of a body specifically lighter than the water, specifically as heavy as the water, and specifically heavier than the water. It thus reflects, in a not too precise way, the conclusions of Propositions 3–5, and the first half of Proposition 7 of Book I of the genuine *On Floating Bodies*, and perhaps Proposition 1 of Book II. All such information the compositor of BN 7377B could have acquired from the genuine text of *On Floating Bodies* that was present in the later folios of William of Moerbeke's exemplar; or less likely it could have developed from the implications present in Seneca's *Natural Questions*.[13]

It is known that there are certain lakes which support people who do not know how to swim. There used to be a pond in Sicily, and there still is one in Syria, where bricks float and where it is impossible for objects thrown into it to sink even though they are heavy. The reason for this is clear. Weigh any object you like and compare [its weight] with any equal volume of water. If the water is heavier, it will support the object which is lighter and lift it just as high above the surface as it is lighter. If the bodies are heavier [than the water], they will sink. But if the weight of the water is equal to that of the object against which you are weighing it, the object will neither sink to the bottom nor be lifted up but will be in balance with the water and will float nearly submerged with no part of it sticking up [above the surface of the water].

But the passage attached to the *De ponderibus Archimenidis* in the Parisian codex also has some interesting implications for the question of the relation of velocity of fall through a fluid and the comparative specific weights of the body and the fluid, which question we shall shortly consider.

It seems likely that it was this Parisian codex of the *De ponderibus Archimenidis* which Johannes de Muris read when he took over a major part of the *De ponderibus* in his *Quadripartitum numerorum*.[14] For not only does Johannes use the first proposition of the *De ponderibus*—extant in all of the copies of that work—but he includes as well the substance of both additions to the Paris codex of the *De ponderibus*:[15]

---

[13] Seneca, *Naturales quaestiones*, with an English translation by T. H. Corcoran, Vol. 1 (Cambridge, Mass., 1971), Bk. III, 25.5, pp. 258–60: "Quosdam lacus esse qui nandi imperitos ferant notum est; erat in Sicilia, est adhuc in Syria stagnum in quo natant lateres et mergi proiecta non possunt, licet gravia sint. Huius rei palam causa est. Quamcumque vis rem expende et contra aquam statue, dummodo utriusque par sit modus; si aqua gravior est, leviorem rem quam ipsa est fert et tanto supra se extollet quanto erit levior; graviora descendent. At si aquae et eius rei quam contra pensabis par pondus erit, nec pessum ibit nec extabit, sed exaequabitur et natabit quidem sed paene mersa ac nulla eminens parte." The translation, however, is my own.

[14] Clagett, *The Science of Mechanics*, pp. 113–35.

[15] *Ibid.*, pp. 119 (English), 134 (Latin): "11ᵃ Omne corpus supernatans aque occupat in ea locum aque sui ponderis. Verbi gratia: Si fuerit medietas corporis supernatantis in aqua et medietas supra, erit aqua equalis in magnitudine medietati huius corporis equalis in

11. Every body floating in water displaces in the water a volume of water of its own weight.

For example: If half of the floating body were in the water and half outside of it, the water equal in volume to half of that body will be equal in weight to the whole body. Thus if ⅔ of the floating body is in the water and ⅓ of it outside of the water, the volume of water equal to ⅔ of that body will be equal in weight to the whole body. And if that body is equal in weight to water equal to it in volume, the whole body is submerged in the water; but it will not descend to the bottom, since it is not superior in weight to the water. Rather the [upper] surface [of the body] will be at the surface [of the water]. If, however, the body is superior in weight to the water which is equal to it in volume, it will descend immediately to the bottom.

The only major difference between Johannes' exposition and that of the Parisian additions lies in the dynamical considerations found in the Parisian codex, and absent in Johannes' treatment. As we shall see, Oresme, probably using the same Parisian codex, included the dynamical implications of the passage.

So now we are prepared to consider Oresme's contribution to the juncture of hydrostatics and dynamics. It seems probable that Oresme not only read the Parisian codex (BN lat. 7377B) of the *De ponderibus Archimenidis* and the *Quadripartitum numerorum* of his older contemporary Johannes de Muris, but that he was also acquainted with one other earlier work in which specific weight is tied in some fashion to velocity. This was the *Liber de ponderoso et levi*, translated from the Arabic in the twelfth or thirteenth century.[16] Let me quote its postulates and four of its five theorems (the latter without their proofs):[17]

pondere ipsi toti corpori, et sic de aliis partibus proportionaliter; ut si ⅔ corporis super-natantis sit infra aquam et ⅓ eius extra aquam, erit aqua equalis ⅔ eiusdem corporis equalis in pondere ipsi toti corpori. Et si fuerit pondus ipsius corporis equale in pondere aque equali et in magnitudine, totum corpus mergitur in aqua, sed non descendet ad fundum, cum non vincat aquam in pondere, sed superficies superficiei applicabitur. Si tamen corpus illud aquam vincat in pondere equalem ei in magnitudine statim descendet ad fundum.''

[16] Moody and Clagett, *The Medieval Science of Weights* (Madison, Wisc., 1952, 2nd printing, 1960), pp. 23–31. Cf. *The Science of Mechanics*, pp. 435–36.

[17] Moody and Clagett, *The Medieval Science of Weights*, pp. 26–31: "(Suppositiones) (1) Corpora equalia in magnitudine sunt que replent loca equalia. (2) Et que replent loca inequalia dicuntur diversa in magnitudine. (3) Et que dicuntur grandia in corporibus dicuntur ampla in locis. (4) Corpora equalia in virtute sunt quorum motus sunt in temporibus equalibus super loca equalia in eodem aere vel eadem aqua. (5) Et que pretereunt loca equalia diversis temporibus dicuntur diversa in fortitudine. (6) Et quod maius est virtute minus est tempore. (7) Corpora eiusdem generis sunt quorum equalium virtus est equalis. (8) Cum fuerint corpora equalia in magnitudine, diversa in virtute respectu eiusdem aeris vel aque, diversa sunt genere. (9) Et solidius est fortius. (Propositiones) I. CORPORUM QUE TEMPORIBUS EQUALIBUS LOCA PERTRANSEUNT INEQUALIA, QUOD MAIOREM PERTRANSIT LOCUM, MAIORIS ESSE VIRTUTIS. . . . II. SI DUORUM CORPORUM EIUSDEM GENERIS FUERIT UNUM MULTIPLEX ALTERIUS, ET VIRTUTEM ILLIUS VIRTUTIS ALTERIUS SIMILITER ESSE. . . . III. CORPORUM EIUSDEM GENERIS IN MAGNITUDINE ET POTENTIA PROPORTIO UNA. . . . V. CUM FUERIT CORPORUM IN MAGNITUDINE ET VIRTUTE PROPORTIO UNA, ERUNT EIUSDEM GENERIS. . . ."

(Postulates)

(1) Bodies equal in volume are those which fill equal places.

(2) And those which fill unequal places are said to be of different volume.

(3) And what are said to be large, among bodies, are said to be capacious, among places.

(4) Bodies are equal in force, whose motions through equal places, in the same air or the same water, are in equal times.

(5) And those which traverse equal places in different times, are said to be different in force.

(6) And that which is the greater in its force, is the lesser in its time.

(7) Bodies are of the same kind which, if of equal volume, are of equal force.

(8) When bodies which are equal in volume are different in force with respect to the same air or water, they are different in kind.

(9) And the denser body is the more powerful.

(Theorems)

I. Of bodies which traverse unequal places in equal times, that which traverses the greater place is of the greater force. . . .

II. If, of two bodies of the same kind, one is a multiple in size of the other, then its force will be similarly related to the force of the other. . . .

III. Of bodies of the same kind, the volumes and forces are proportional. . . .

V. When the volumes and the forces of several bodies are in the same proportion, the bodies are of the same kind. . . .

This author, in sum, holds that (1) the difference in speeds of bodies in the same medium defines difference in their force and (2) when bodies are equal in volume, their difference of speed in the same medium indicates a difference in kind reflected in a difference in specific weight. He does not state (although he perhaps believed) that bodies with the same specific weight (i.e. bodies of the same kind) but of differing volumes would all fall with the same speed in a given medium because the volumes of the resisting medium displaced would differ precisely as the volumes of the bodies. (In fact, no medieval author of whom I know makes this precise statement.) It is clear that he does not directly consider the resistance of the medium, as both the added fragment to the Parisian codex of *De ponderibus Archimenidis* and Oresme's discussion, quoted at length above, do.

In Oresme's passage we can see that he was the first author to be directly and specifically under the influence of the genuine *On Floating Bodies* and to cite its conclusions. But notice that, under the possible influence of the Parisian passage, he considers the resistance of the medium and pulls into his discussion dynamic considerations. (In this respect he anticipates Tartaglia's remarks in his Italian translation of Book I of *On Floating Bodies* [see below Part III, Chap. 4, Sect II]). Oresme specifically says that a body "descends with as much force as it is heavier than the water equal to it in volume." He also evidently believes that the greater the force the greater the velocity of fall, for in the same paragraph he says: "correlatively . . . given any slowness whatsoever [a body] can descend still more slowly in any water by diminishing

to infinity this excess [of force of a body over an equal volume of water]."
The reverse situation prevails in regard to bodies specifically lighter than
the water. If such a body is held down under the water and released,
it will ascend, Oresme holds, with a force that is dependent on how
much "it is lighter than the water" or how much "the water is heavier."
He cites Proposition 6 of the genuine *On Floating Bodies* as his authority.
In the course of discussing this conclusion, the influence of the added
passage of the Parisan codex of the *De ponderibus Archimenidis* is evident
when Oresme tells us that, if the body is condensed without changing its
gravity (i.e. its gross weight), then it will descend, for it will be heavier
than the water "since the water equal [in volume] will not be as heavy"
as it. "Further, if that [body] is increased or made less dense, without
changing its gravity, then it immediately ascends because water equal to
it [in volume] will be heavier" than it. Hence, it is quite clear in these
discussions that Oresme believes that the force and thus the speed of
fall depends on the excess of specific weight a body has over the water
in which it descends or conversely that the force or speed of ascent depends
on the excess of specific weight the water has over the body.

The implication of the Parisian additions and Oresme's discussion for
establishing a relationship between velocity of fall through a fluid medium
and specific weight are even more directly stated by Albert of Saxony,
Oresme's younger contemporary at Paris. Albert tells us:[18]

. . . it is to be supposed first that there are some things which are called
"equally heavy according to species" and some things which are "unequally
heavy." Accordingly, those things are called "equally heavy according to species"
which are so selected that equal portions of them in volume weigh the same.
On the other hand, those things are called "unequally heavy according to species"
which are so related that equal portions in volume do not weigh the same. Whence,
if two portions are taken—one of wood and the same amount of lead—the portion
of lead weighs more. Then let this be the first conclusion: With two solid bodies
given, it is possible without weighing [them] in a balance to find out [1] whether

---

[18] Clagett, *The Science of Mechanics*, pp. 136–37 (English), 142–43 (Latin): "[2]
Quantum ad secundum supponendum est primo, que dicantur equaliter gravia secundum
speciem et que inequaliter. Unde illa dicuntur equaliter gravia secundum speciem que sic
se habent quod equales portiones eorum in magnitudine equaliter ponderant. Illa vero
dicuntur inequaliter gravia secundum speciem que sic se habent quod portiones eorum
equales in magnitudine inequaliter ponderant. Unde si capiantur due portiones, una ligni
et tanta plumbi, portio plumbi plus ponderat.

"[3] Tunc sit prima conclusio: Datis duobus corporibus solidis, an sint eiusdem gravitatis
in specie vel diversarum, et quod eorum sit gravius, possibile est sine ponderatione in
equilibra invenire. Nam sint ille duo corpora *a* et *b* et capiantur de *a* et *b* portiones equales
in magnitudine, si *a* et *b* sint inequalia in magnitudine, et dimittuntur ille portiones
cadere in eandem aquam. Tunc si equevelociter descendunt in profundum aque vel tanta
pars de una quanta de alia [submergitur in aqua], dic quod dicta corpora sunt equalis
gravitatis in specie. Si autem ineque velociter descendunt usque ad profundum vel plus
de una illarum portionum submergitur in aqua et minus de alia, dic quod illud est
gravius secundum speciem cuius portio velocius descendit vel cuius portio submergitur plus
in aqua. . . ."

they are of the same or of different specific weights and [2] which of them is heavier. For let these two bodies be *a* and *b* and let equal volumes of *a* and *b* be taken—if *a* and *b* are unequal in volume [to start with]; and let these portions be released so that they fall in the same water. Then if they descend equally fast toward the bottom of the water, or if just as large a part of one as of the other [is submerged in the water], say that the said bodies are of equal specific weight. If, however, they descend to the bottom unequally fast, or more of one of these portions is submerged in the water and less of the other, say that the one is heavier according to species whose portion descends more quickly or whose portion is submerged further in the water.

It is clear that, although Albert abandons any reference to the genuine *On Floating Bodies*, he has given the most lucid statement of what we might call the dynamic definition of specific gravity for bodies that are specifically heavier than the fluid in which they are placed.

The one medieval author after Albert, who best pulled together most of the considerations found in the *De ponderibus Archimenidis* and in the treatments of Oresme and Albert of Saxony was Blasius of Parma in his *Tractatus de ponderibus* written in the last quarter of the fourteenth century:[19]

---

[19] Moody and Clagett, *The Medieval Science of Weights*, pp. 272–75: "(Suppositiones) I. NULLUM ELEMENTUM IN EIUS PROPRIA REGIONE PONDERAT. Hoc dicit Archimedes in tractatu *De insidentibus in liquido*. Cui magnus Aristoteles academicus contradicit in eius volumine *De universo* sub hoc tenore: Quodlibet elementum in regione propria preter ignem gravitatem habet. Que philosophia non multis placet nec dicendis confert. Et ideo relinquetur. II. QUODLIBET GRAVE APPETIT ESSE SUB LEVI ET LEVE SUPRA GRAVE QUIETARE. Patet hic sermo. Ea enim sic disposuit gloriosus Magister et sublimis, ut naturales scribunt in decorem universi et humane nature stabilitatem. III. TUNC SUNT CORPORA EQUALITER GRAVIA CUM SERVATA EADEM QUANTITATE ET FIGURA EQUALITER PONDERANT. Hoc patet sine alio processu. Unde in suppositione duo tanguntur. (1) Identitas figure. Unde identitas figure requiritur, quia alia et alia figura est causa accelerationis et tarditatis motus. Modo gravitas corporis maior vel minor non cognoscitur nisi per velociorem et tardiorem motum. (2) Et sic dicebatur servata eadem extensione, quoniam licet magnum lignum sit gravius plumbo, tamen [plumbum] ligno in eadem extensione gravius est. Nunc sequuntur conclusiones, quarum prima est hec: (Conclusiones sive Propositiones) I. PROPOSITIS DUOBUS PONDERIBUS NON FLUXIBILIBUS POSSIBILE EST SINE EQUILIBRI QUOD IPSORUM SIT GRAVIUS REPERIRE. Sciendum quod sunt quedam corpora fluxibilia, ut vinum, aqua, oleum; quedam solida et non fluxibilia, ut lignum, ferrum et cetera. Et quedam sunt corpora fluxibilia eiusdem rationis, ut due aque, et quedam diversarum rationum, ut aqua et oleum. Et dico idem de corporibus non fluxibilibus. Tunc probatur conclusio: Quia sit quod hec duo corpora non fluxibilia *a*, *b* eiusdem rationis vel diversarum rationum, et de hoc non sit cura. Que corpora ad aquam compellantur. Quo facto, vel utrumque eorum descendit per aquam vel utrumque supernatat et neutrum descendit, vel alterum descendit et alterum supernatat. Si utrumque descendit, videndum est quod horum velocius ad fundum procedit, quia illud altero est gravius. Si autem eque velociter ad fundum pertingerent, eque gravia dicerentur. Si vero neutrum descendet, tunc diligenter videatur cuius maior pars submergatur, quia illud erit altero gravius. Si vero unum supernataret et alterum deorsum moveretur, patet quod horum in hoc casu est gravius et quod levius. Si vero contingeret per huiusmodi aquam fundum intueri non posse propter multitudinem partium terrestrium, fiat versa vice ut quod huiusmodi corpora applicentur fundo cum hasta. Deinde removeatur

Part III

(Suppositions)

I. NO ELEMENT HAS WEIGHT IN ITS OWN REGION.

Archimedes says this in his treatise *On bodies floating in liquid*. But the great Aristotle in his work *On the Universe* contradicts this in the following way: "Any element at all, except fire, has weight in its own region." But this philosophy is not pleasing to many, nor is it produced with the necessary arguments. And therefore we set it aside.

II. EVERY HEAVY BODY SEEKS TO COME TO REST UNDER A LIGHT BODY AND EVERY LIGHT BODY ABOVE A HEAVY ONE.

This statement is obvious. For the Glorious and Sublime Master has arranged these things, as the natural philosophers say concerning the decor of the universe and the stability of the human soul.

III. BODIES ARE EQUALLY HEAVY [specifically] WHEN, WITH THE SAME VOLUME AND FIGURE TAKEN, THEY WEIGH THE SAME.

This is evident without any other procedure. Two things are touched upon in this supposition. (1) *Identity of figure*. Identity of figure is required because difference in figure is a cause of acceleration and retardation. Now the gravity of a body is not recognized as being more or less except by a faster or slower movement. (2) [*Equality of volume*]. It was stated that the same volume is taken, since although a large piece of wood is heavier than a piece of lead, yet the lead is heavier than the wood when they are of the same volume.

Now follow the conclusions, the first of which is this:

(Conclusions or Propositions)

I. IN THE CASE OF TWO NON-FLUID WEIGHTS IT IS POSSIBLE TO FIND OUT WHICH OF THEM IS HEAVIER WITHOUT A BALANCE.

It ought to be known that certain bodies are fluid, like wine, water, and oil; and certain are solid and non-fluid, like wood, iron, and so on. And some fluid bodies are of the same nature, such as two waters, and certain are different in nature, such as water and oil. I say the same thing for non-fluid bodies.

Proof of the conclusion: Let there be two non-fluid bodies, *a* and *b*, either of the same nature or different natures, it makes no difference. These bodies are forced into water. This having been done, either each of them descends in the water or each of them floats and neither descends, or one descends and the other floats. If each of them descends, it ought to be seen which of them proceeds more quickly to the bottom because this one is [specifically] heavier than the other. Moreover, if they arrive at the bottom equally quickly, they are said to be equally heavy. If neither of them descends, then it ought to be seen carefully which of them has the greater part submerged, for that one is heavier than the other. If in truth one of them were to float and the other to be moved downward, it is obvious in this case which of them would be heavier

aliqualiter ab utroque et videbitur ascensus istorum corporum vel alterius tantum et patebit conclusio, uno casu dumtaxat excepto, ut puta quod utrumque eorum haberet in fundo residentiam. Ideo pro illo casu sit talis operatio ut quod huiusmodi gravibus antequam compellantur ad fundum applicentur duo fila, quorum extremitates pertingant ad aridam tanquam ad speram aeris. Quibus extremitatibus appendantur duo gravia equalia quorum utrumque sit utroque ponderum residentium in fundo aque gravius. Hoc facto transeant ista fila per anulum aere fixum, et tunc videatur quod istorum ponderum tardius descendit versum superficiem terre. Illud est gravius. Et bene notetur ille casus et non contingat ipsum amplius in posterum repetere."

and which would be lighter. If it were to happen that the bottom of the water of this sort could not be seen because of the large number of earthy parts in the water, let the procedure be reversed, so these bodies are held on the bottom with pikes. Then let the pikes be removed from each body at the same time, and the speed of the ascent of each of the bodies will be seen, and the conclusion will be evident. But one case is excepted, namely, when both of them remain on the bottom. For this case proceed as follows. Before these weights are pushed to the bottom, two cords are attached, whose ends go out to some supports in the air. On these [exposed] ends are suspended two equal weights, each of which is heavier than each of the weights resting on the bottom [of the water]. With this done, the cords are passed through a ring fixed in the air. Then let it be observed which of the weights [outside] descends more slowly towards the surface of the earth, for that one is [fixed to] the heavier weight [to be tested]. And this case should be noted well so that it will not have to be repeated in the future.

The reference to Archimedes in the comment on the first supposition is not to the genuine *On Floating Bodies* but rather to the *De ponderibus Archimenidis* which has essentially the same first postulate as does Blasius.[20] There is no reference to the genuine *On Floating Bodies* anywhere in Blasius' treatise. At first glance it might seem that because Blasius does not specify in his comment to the first proposition that the bodies are of the same volume his account was closer to Benedetti's conclusion that bodies of the same specific weight but of unequal volumes would fall at the same speed. But his comment to the third supposition seems to imply that all his determinations concern bodies of the same figure and volume.

Having considered the place of Oresme in the medieval efforts to relate hydrostatics and dynamics, I should like to return to other aspects of his knowledge of Archimedes. For Oresme's knowledge of Archimedes was not limited to *On Floating Bodies*. He also had some understanding of *On Spiral Lines* as the following passage in his *De configurationibus qualitatum et motuum* (composed sometime in the 1350's) indicates:[21]

---

[20] Appendix I, Sect. 4, Postulate 1: "Nullum corpus in se ipso grave esse, ut aqua in aqua, oleum in oleo, aer in aere, non est alicuius gravitatis."

[21] See my *Nicole Oresme and the Medieval Geometry of Qualities,* p. 224:

"Verumptamen in huiusmodi curvitatis notitiam et uniformitatis ac diverse difformitatis eiusdem convenientius et facilius devenitur per ymaginationem motus localis quam figure, ita quod circa centrum *A* quiescens sit linea sive semidyameter *AB* et ymaginetur circumduci seu moveri. Si igitur punctus *C* continue maneat super *B* extremitatem semidyametric circumducte, ipsum *B* vel *C* describet curvitatem uniformem, videlicet circularem. Si autem punctus *C* continue descendat super semidyametrum appropinquando ad centrum velocitate uniformi et eadem semidyameter pro tunc uniformiter circumducatur, dico quod punctus *C* describet curvitatem uniformiter difformem, et eodem modo si ipsum *C* recederet uniformiter a centro, describeret curvitatem uniformiter difformem. Unde si in tempore in quo punctus *B* describit circumferentiam punctus *C* pertranseat totam semidyametrum precise uniformiter ascendendo motu qui esset rectus si semidyameter non circumvolveretur, in hoc casu punctus *C* describeret lineam curvitatis uniformiter difformis quam mathematici vocant helicen, forsan sic dictam a quadem specie hedere consimiliter tortuose, que secundum Plinium dicitur helix; et per talem lineam demonstrat Archimenides circuli quadraturam."

Be that as it may, we can arrive at a knowledge of curvature of this sort and of its uniformity and diverse difformity more fittingly and more easily by the imagery of local motion than by that of figures. For example, let line or radius *AB* be imagined as revolved or moved about center *A* which remains at rest. If, therefore, point *C* continually remains at point *B*, the extremity of the revolving radius, then *B* or *C* will describe uniform curvature, i.e., circular curvature. But if point *C* continually descends along the radius with uniform velocity towards the center, while the same radius is revolving uniformly, I say that point *C* will describe uniformly difform curvature. And in the same way, if *C* were to recede uniformly from the center, it would describe uniformly difform curvature. Whence if point *C*, moving uniformly in ascent [toward the center] with a motion which would be simply rectilinear if the radius were not revolving, traverses the whole radius in the same time as point *B* describes the circumference, in this case point *C* would describe a line of uniformly difform curvature which the mathematicians call the *helix* (spiral), perhaps so called from a certain species of ivy which is similarly curved and which according to Pliny is called *helix*. By such a line Archimedes demonstrates the quadrature of the circle.

The juxtaposition of the spiral with the problem of quadrature makes it seem probable that Oresme derived the substance of this passage either from the hybrid quadrature tract that was inserted in Chapter 8 of the *De arte mensurandi* (see Chapter 5 above) or from the brief treatment of the spiral in the *Quadripartitum numerorum* (see Chapter 1 above). In fact, it appears that Oresme knew both of these works.

In regard to his knowledge of the first of these works, let me initially point out that on the verso of the last folio of manuscript *Pd* of the *De arte mensurandi* appears the following:[22]

This book belongs to Henricus de Fontanis, who received it as a gift from [that] venerable man master Henricus Oresme Junior the late nephew of the most excellent doctor Master Nicolaus Oresme, once Bishop of Lisieux.

Since Oresme's nephew Henry is not known as a natural philosopher and since we know of another manuscript of one of Oresme's own works that might have been given to Henry by his uncle,[23] we are tempted to conclude that Henry received the manuscript of the *De arte mensurandi* from his uncle. If Oresme's knowledge of the spiral and its possible use in the problem of the quadrature of the circle arose from reading the hybrid tract in his own copy of the *De arte mensurandi*, the only point

---

[22] MS Paris, BN lat. 7380, 83v: "Iste liber est Henrici de Fontanis qui eum habuit ex dono venerabilis viri magistri Henrici Oresme junioris condam nepotis excellentissimi doctoris magistri Nicolai Oresme olim episcopi Lexoniensis."

[23] In MS Avranches, Bibl. Munic. 223 (which includes Oresme's *Le Livre de Politiques* and *Le Livre de yconomique*), 348v is found the following marginal note: "Liber iste Politi-corum est Henrici Oresme junioris canonici Baiocensis." It was Leopold Delisle who first suggested that this manuscript was the personal copy of Nicole Oresme and passed from him to Henry ("Observations sur plusieurs manuscrits de la Politique et l'Économique de Nicole Oresme," *Bibliothèque de l'École de Chartes*, 6me série, Vol. 5 [1869], pp. 608–09, whole article pp. 601–20).

that would need explaining is his association of Archimedes with such a solution of the problem, since the hybrid tract carries no indication of Archimedes' authorship. But this is an easily solved difficulty, since Oresme could have deduced that the source of the hybrid tract was Archimedes from the remarks made in the beginning of Chapter 6 of the *De arte mensurandi* (see Chapter 4 above).

Of course, it is possible, as I have suggested above, that the source of Oresme's remarks on the spiral was the brief treatment in the *Quadripartitum numerorum* which I have edited in Chapter 1 of this part, for all of the essential ingredients of Oresme's remarks are found therein. Furthermore, there is some other indication that Oresme knew of the *Quadripartitum numerorum*. He may have used certain propositions concerning the commensurability and incommensurability of celestial motions as a point of departure for his very original treatment of that subject.[24] Finally, on one occasion Oresme cites Johannes de Muris by name for the doctrine of finding any number of means that may be a reference to the discussion of continuous proportionality in the *Quadripartitum numerorum*.[25] Regardless of the source of Oresme's particular statement on the use of a spiral in the problem of quadrature, it seems likely that Oresme had at least a superficial knowledge of *On Spiral Lines* directly from the manuscript in which he found the translation of *On Floating Bodies*. For it seems probable that he either examined the Moerbeke autograph Vat. Ottob. lat. 1850 (assuming that it was brought to France and made its way to Paris) or a copy of it. All the evidence seems to point to the existence in Paris of the full corpus of the translations. For it is a noteworthy fact that *On Spiral Lines* is the first item in the Vatican manuscript and the *On Floating Bodies* is the last (item IX), while the other works of Archimedes cited at Paris are items IV–VII in the original codex.

I have focused attention in the immediately preceding paragraphs on Oresme's knowledge of the Archimedean spiral and its possible source or sources. I cannot leave this subject without reminding the reader that the passage on the spiral occurs in the context of a treatment of curvature. I have shown elsewhere how Oresme considered the spiral as an example of uniformly difform curvature and how he represented it by a right triangle after plotting the changing length of the radius against

---

[24] E. Grant, ed., *Nicole Oresme and the Kinematics of Circular Motion* (Madison, Wisc., 1971), pp. 97–102.

[25] The reference to Johannes de Muris occurs in the *De proportionibus proportionum*, ed. of E. Grant, p. 298: "Verumtamen supponitur quod tu scias inter duas lineas datas quotlibet (*see Variant*) medias in continua proportionalitate invenire. Et Euclides non docuit nisi tantum de una . . . sed reverendus Magister Johannes de Muris docebat invenire quotlibet sicut credo." This could be a rather imprecise reference, quoted from memory, to the discussion of continuous proportionality in Prop. 20 of Book I of the *Quadripartitum numerorum* (MS Vienna, Nationalbibl. 4770, 199v: "Quotvis proportiones continuas invenire").

the angular displacement of the radius.[26] Hence, the spiral was used by Oresme as an illustration in his effort to integrate variations of curvature into his basic configuration doctrine.

A word of caution must be expressed concerning Oresme's knowledge of Archimedes. We are not to think that because Oresme had some access to the Moerbeke translations he had any extensive knowledge of Archimedean mathematics (as, for example, of the basic techniques and content of *On Conoids and Spheroids*). If he had had such knowledge, his treatment of non-circular curves and their configurations in his *De configurationibus* would have been vastly different and indeed he would have come much closer to being the inventor of analytic geometry. As it was, his interesting configuration technique was but a pale foreshadowing of that powerful branch of mathematics.[27]

Before leaving the subject of Oresme's knowledge of Archimedes, I ought to mention that the French scholar gives in his *Questiones super de spera*, Question 4, two physical "solutions" of quadrature problems. The first runs:[28]

Some spherical body can be given which is equal to a plane body, such as a cube or a squared body. This conclusion is proved [as follows]. Let there be taken one body which is A [see Fig. I.7.2], of which one part, a hemisphere, is B, and the other part is CDF. Let it be imagined that this body descends to the center [of the world], that it is not impeded, and that it is absolutely heavy. Then by one conclusion in another question, the center of this body is identical with the center of the universe. Let the center of it therefore be E. Then a line [ab] is extended as a transversal. Then by the same proved conclusion so much of this body is on one side as on the other [side of the transversal]. Hence, $(B + C)$ [and] $(D + F)$ are equal. If therefore we subtract F, which [was made] equal to C itself, [and we subtract C], as is possible, it remains that [hemispherical body] B and [quadrangular body] D are equal bodies, which was to be proved.

The second, closely similar passage reads:[29]

[26] See my *Nicole Oresme and the Medieval Geometry of Qualities*, pp. 449–50.

[27] *Ibid.*, pp. 442–43.

[28] Edition of G. Droppers (Dissertation, University of Wisconsin, 1965), pp. 88–90: "3ª conclusio est quod est dare aliquod corpus spericum quod est equale alicui corpori plano sicut cubito vel quadrato. Ista conclusio probatur et capiatur unum corpus quod sit A cuius una pars sit medietas spere que sit B et alia que sit C D F. Ymaginetur istud corpus descendere ad centrum et non sit impedimentum et sit grave simpliciter. Tunc per unam conclusionem in alia questione centrum istius corporis erit idem cum centro mundi. Sit ergo centrum eius, E. Tunc protrahatur ex transverso una linea. Tunc per eandem conclusionem determinatam sequitur quod tantum est de corpore ab una parte istius linee sicut ab alia. Igitur B et C, D et F erunt equalia. Si ergo demamus ab F, equale ipsi C, sicut est possibile remanet quod B et D sunt corpora equalia quod erat probandum."

[29] *Ibid.*, pp. 92–94: "Iuxta 3 conclusionem de quiete adhuc probo quod aliqua superficies circularis sit equalis alicui quadrangulari. Et sit unum corpus $ABCD$ et sit ad modum unius fenestre ita quod sit planum de superficie ita quod sit eiusdem spisitudinis (!) in qualibet parte et dimittatur ire ad centrum ita quod punctus E sit in medio mundi. Tunc potest probari sicut prius quod tantum erit de gravitate ab una parte linee sicut ab alia. Ex quo sequitur quod A et B corpus et C et D sunt equalia in gravitate, quia etiam

In relation to the third conclusion on rest I now prove that some circular surface is equal to some quadrangular surface. And let there be a body *ABCD* [see Fig. I.7.3], and let it be in the shape of a window, so that it is a plane along its surface, [and] so that it is of the same thickness in any part. And let this body descend to the center, so that a point *E* [in it] will be in the center of the world. Then it can be proved as before that there is as much gravity on one side of a line as on the other. According to this it follows that the bodies (*A* + *B*) and (*C* + *D*) are equal in gravity, because they are uniformly equal in magnitude. But since they are of equal thickness by supposition, it follows that the ratio of the exterior surfaces is as the ratio of the bodies. By subtracting as before the result is that surface *A*, which is a semicircle, and surface *C* [which is quadrangular] are equal. Therefore by doubling *A* and by doubling *C*, the proposition is shown.

It is clear that both passages rest on the basic Aristotelian idea that the center of gravity of a body will be at rest in the center of the world. To this is added the further concept that equilibrium prevails because the force exerted by all of the matter in the body on one side of a transversal through the center just balances the force exerted by the matter on the other side of the transversal. I do not mean to imply that Oresme drew his understanding of the statics of balances that seems to underlie this treatment from Moerbeke's translation of Archimedes' *On the Equilibrium of Planes*. I would suppose rather that he was merely employing the commonly known balance idea which was present on all sides in the various treatises of the medieval corpus of statical works.[30] His physical treatment of quadrature should be compared with quite different physical arguments used in other treatments of the quadrature problem in the fourteenth century.[31]

Much less interesting and important than the evidences of Oresme's knowledge of the Moerbeke translations is the brief allusion to Proposition 2 of Book I of the genuine *On Floating Bodies* found in the *Questiones super communem perspectivam*, Question III, of Henry of Hesse. Henry was one of Oresme's associates (and philosophical heirs) at Paris

---

sunt uniforme equalia in magnitudine. Sed postquam sunt equalis spisitudinis per positum, sequitur quod proportio superficierum exteriorum est sicut proportio corporum. Et deducendo sicut prius habetur quod *A* superficies que est semicirculus et *C* superficies sunt equales. Igitur duplicato *A* et duplicato *C* habetur propositum.''

[30] See Moody and Clagett, *The Medieval Science of Weights*. Particularly important for Oresme's treatment would have been the treatise *De canonio* (pages 64–75) and the second book of the *De ratione ponderis* (pages 192–205). Both of these concern themselves with material beams.

[31] See *Archimedes in the Middle Ages*, Vol. 1, pp. 166, 562. It is of some interest that in Question 7 of the *Questiones super de spera* (ed. of Droppers, p. 146, lines 18–19) Oresme gives the following postulate: "et omnis linea recta brevior est quam linea curva de eodem puncto ad eundem punctum." At first glance one might suppose that it is drawn from the assumptions of the *On the Sphere and the Cylinder*. I believe however that Oresme probably took it from one of the several similar postulates attached to various versions of the *De mensura circuli* that circulated in the fourteenth century (see *Archimedes in the Middle Ages*, Vol. 1, pp. 167–68).

in the 1360's and 1370's.[32] Henry merely says,[33] almost in passing, that water is "most particularly constituted to reduce itself to a sphericity that is equidistant from the center of the world; this is evident in the second [book] of the *On the Heavens* [of Aristotle] and by Archimedes in the beginning of *On Floating Bodies*." It will immediately occur to the reader that Henry might have drawn this statement from the closely similar citation of Proposition 2 by Oresme given above. The only difference, aside from the context of discussion, is that Henry gives the title as *On Floating Bodies*[34] rather than Oresme's incorrect rendering of *On Weights*. But the similarity of citations is by no means a guarantee that Henry had his knowledge of this proposition from Oresme. He could easily have had access to the same manuscript of the Moerbeke translation as had Oresme.

The foregoing considerations of Oresme's and Henry of Hesse's use of the Moerbeke Archimedes bring to a close my examination of the first inroads made by the Moerbeke translation on the mathematics and science of the Parisian schoolmen of the fourteenth century. It is not impossible that, as more mathematical works and commentaries on the *De caelo* and other works of Aristotle are studied and published, further references to Archimedes will appear. But for the moment we can conclude that some use was made at Paris in the fourteenth century of six of the nine Archimedean translations of Moerbeke: *On Spiral Lines, On the Measurement of the Circle, On the Sphere and the Cylinder, On Conoids and Spheroids, On Floating Bodies* and Eutocius' *Commentary on the Sphere and the Cylinder*. No reference has yet been found to the three further works that are included in the Moerbeke corpus: *On the Equilibrium of Planes,*[35] *On the Quadrature of the Parabola* and Eutocius' *Commentary on the Equilibrium of Planes*. While the use of the Moerbeke translations which has been discussed in this part of my work can hardly be called extensive, it was, except in the case of *On Conoids and Spheroids*, accurate and substantially correct.

---

[32] See my *Nicole Oresme and the Medieval Geometry of Qualities*, pp. 114–21. (See in particular, L. Thorndike, *History of Magic*, Vol. 3, pp. 472–510.)

[33] MS Erfurt, Stadtbibl. Amplon. F.380, 30v, col. 1: "2° sequitur quod idem vas sine quacunque eius augmentatione fieret capacius. Patet quia aqua maxime esset nata sic se reducere ad spericitatem equedistantem centro mundi, sicut patet 2° celi et per Archimenidem in principio de incidentibus in humidum. Si ergo sic est, aqua plus tumet ultra vas in basso situ quam in altiori, quia terminatur per arcum minoris circuli contingentem latera vasis."

[34] That is to say, he gives the title as *De incidentibus in humidum* (see the preceding note), which, strictly speaking, ought not to be translated as *On Floating Bodies* (see note 6 above), although I have done so throughout for the sake of convenience and because in the case of both Oresme's and Henry of Hesse's usage the title does refer to the genuine Archimedean tract.

[35] While no reference to *On the Equilibrium of Planes* has been found, it is not impossible that the author of the statical proof given in the next chapter had read the Archimedean work.

CHAPTER 8

An Archimedean-Type Proof of the Law of the Lever

As I have indicated at the close of the preceding chapter, the first seven chapters of this part of my volume complete the investigation of the direct use of the Moerbeke translations of Archimedes at Paris in the fourteenth century. There now remains only to describe an anonymous proof of the law of the lever which appears as an appended part of the Pseudo-Archimedean *De ponderibus Archimenidis* in Parisian codex BN lat. 7377B, 93v–94r, and which was first mentioned by Pierre Duhem (see below, note 9). In fact, it appears shortly after the dynamic addition to the *De ponderibus Archimenidis* which I translated and discussed at length in the preceding chapter. This section of the manuscript was probably written in the late thirteenth or early fourteenth century at Paris. I would suppose that it dates before 1343, since, as we have seen, Johannes de Muris appears to have utilized it in the free version of *De ponderibus Archimenidis* included in his *Quadripartitum numerorum* of that date. The importance of the statical proof of the law of the lever to my investigations lies in the fact that the author of the proof seems deliberately to have substituted a statical-symmetrical proof of the Archimedean kind for the dynamical proof found in Jordanus' *Elementa de ponderibus*. I grant that there is no direct evidence that the author had read Archimedes' *On the Equilibrium of Planes*. But the fact that this unknown author seems to have employed the Moerbeke codex for his text of the *De ponderibus Archimenidis* (see Appendix I, Section 4) and that he included certain additions to the text that seem to reflect the genuine *On Floating bodies* of Archimedes which appeared at the end of the Archimedean translations in the Moerbeke codex make it likely that he had also read Moerbeke's translation of *On the Equilibrium of Planes* in the same codex. At any rate, the statical proof is an interesting one worth studying in the context of medieval statics.

It has been surmised that Jordanus' *Elementa*, written in the early thirteenth century, was composed to provide a theoretical background or justification for a brilliant little tract on the material balance of unequal arm lengths entitled *De canonio*.[1] The *De canonio*, containing four propositions, was translated from the Greek and appears to have had wide circulation in the thirteenth century.[2] Jordanus' *Elementa*, then, presents a series of propositions that lead up to a dynamic proof of the law of the lever (Proposition 8),[3] followed by a last theorem (Proposition 9) that forms a bridge between the analysis involving weightless beams and that of the *De canonio* involving material beams. It is this last proposition that appears to have stimulated our anonymous author to try a new way of introducing the *De canonio* and so I quote it in full:[4]

E.9 IF TWO OBLONG BODIES, WHOLLY SIMILAR AND EQUAL IN SIZE AND WEIGHT, ARE SUSPENDED ON A BALANCE BEAM IN SUCH MANNER THAT ONE IS FIXED HORIZONTALLY TO THE END OF ONE ARM, AND THE OTHER IS HUNG VERTICALLY, AND SO THAT THE DISTANCE FROM THE AXIS OF SUPPORT, TO THE POINT FROM WHICH THE VERTICALLY SUSPENDED BODY HANGS, IS THE SAME AS THE DISTANCE FROM THE AXIS OF SUPPORT TO THE MID-POINT OF THE OTHER BODY, THEN THE SUSPENDED WEIGHTS WILL BE OF EQUAL POSITIONAL GRAVITY.

Let A and B be the ends of the beam [see Fig. I.8.E.9], C the axis, and let the weight fixed horizontally to the beam be ADE, its mid point D; and let the other weight, which hangs, be BG. And let BC be equal to CAD. I say that the weights ADE and BG, in this position, will be of equal heaviness.

To make this evident, we say that if the beam, on the side of A, were as long as CE, and if there were suspended at A and E two equal weights z and y, and if a weight double each one of these, xl, were suspended from B, then in this position also xl would be equal in heaviness to z and y. For let its halves be x and l; then the weight x will be to the weight z, as EC is to CB; and the weight l will be to the weight y, in this position, as AC is to CB. Hence the ratio of xl to z plus y, in this position, will be the same as the ratio of EC plus AC to twice BC. But because twice BC is equal to EC plus AC, xl will likewise be equal in positional weight to z plus y. For this reason, therefore, since all the parts of GB are of equal weight, in this position, and since any two parts of ADE, equidistant from D, are equal in weight to two equal parts of BG, it follows that the whole of ADE is equal to the whole of BG (in positional weight). And this is what needed to be proved.

---

[1] For the general suggestion that the medieval *auctores de ponderibus* undertook to supply the missing theoretical underpinning for the *De canonio*, see E. A. Moody and M. Clagett, *The Medieval Science of Weights* (Madison, Wisc., 1952; 2nd printing, 1960), p. 61. For an excellent elaboration of this theme with special attention to Jordanus' *Elementa*, see J. Brown, "The *Scientia de ponderibus* in the Later Middle Ages" (Dissertation, University of Wisconsin, 1967).

[2] Brown in his above-mentioned dissertation (pages 10–11) lists 26 manuscripts of the *De canonio*, the largest number of manuscripts for any single work of the *corpus de ponderibus*.

[3] Moody and Clagett, *The Medieval Science of Weights*, pp. 128–40.

[4] *Ibid.*, p. 141. I shall not repeat the Latin text here. I have used Moody's translation except that I have restored the errors concerning proportions ("as EC is to CB" and "as AC is to CB") found in all of the manuscripts, errors which Moody had corrected in his translation without any comment. See the next note. I have substituted "ratio" as the translation of *proportio* for Moody's "proportion."

Now there is a multiple error of ratios in the proof ("as EC is to CB" and "as AC is to CB") in all of the manuscripts of the *Elementa* that may have caused later commentators to change the proof[5] and perhaps provided one of the reasons why our author decided to take a different tack. At any rate, from this proposition one passes to Proposition I of the *De canonio* (although in fact Proposition 9 of the *Elementa* concerns a balance between equal weights and *De canonio*, Proposition I, a balance between unequal weights):[6]

I. IF THERE IS A BEAM OF UNIFORM MAGNITUDE AND OF THE SAME SUBSTANCE, AND IF IT IS DIVIDED INTO TWO UNEQUAL PARTS, AND IF AT THE END OF THE SHORTER SEGMENT THERE IS SUSPENDED A WEIGHT WHICH HOLDS THE BEAM PARALLEL TO THE PLANE OF THE HORIZON, THEN THE RATIO OF THAT WEIGHT TO THE EXCESS OF THE WEIGHT OF THE LONGER SEGMENT OF THE BEAM OVER THE WEIGHT OF THE SHORTER SEGMENT IS AS THE RATIO OF THE LENGTH OF THE WHOLE BEAM TO TWICE THE LENGTH OF THE SHORTER SEGMENT.

Let the beam AB, then, be divided into two unequal segments at the point G [see Fig. I.8.Dc.1], and let the shorter segment be AG, and the longer one GB. And let z be the weight suspended from the point A. And let GD, equal in length to AG, be marked off. It is then evident that the remainder, DB, is the excess of the segment GB over the segment AG, both in length and in weight. I say therefore that the ratio of the weight z to the weight of the segment DB, is as the ratio of the length of AB to the length of AD.

The proof of this is as follows: A beam of the length AD, if understood to be suspended from the mid-point G, without any weight being attached at either of its ends, will undoubtedly be parallel to the plane of the horizon. And when, from the point A, the weight z is suspended, the beam DA will fall on the side of A, by reason of the gravity of the weight z. Consequently, that which holds the beam AD parallel to the horizon, is the weight of DB. And it has been demonstrated in the books which speak of these matters, that it makes no difference whether the weight of DB is equally distributed along the whole line DB, or whether it is suspended from the mid point of that segment. Let the weight db, then, be suspended from the point E. Since the line AE is divided into two unequal parts at the point G, and since the weight z is suspended from the point A and the weight db from the point E, and since the beam AE is then parallel to the horizon, the ratio of the segment EG to the segment GA will be as the ratio of the weight z to the weight db; as has been proved by Euclid, Archimedes, and others. And this is the foundation on which all [the propositions] depend. Now AB is twice EG, and AD is twice AG; therefore the ratio of the weight z to the weight of DB, is as the ratio of the line AB to the line AD.

It will be noticed that this proof depends on a series of specified assumptions: (1) a material beam without pendent weights but supported from its mid-point will be in equilibrium; (2) if a weight is suspended from one

---

[5] Brown has shown the significance of these errors in the preparation of later commentaries, *op. cit.*, pp. 7–8, 50, 78–79.

[6] Moody and Clagett, *The Medieval Science of Weights*, pp. 64–66.

end of such a beam it will decline at that end; (3) a material beam segment may be replaced by an equal pendent weight hung from the mid-point of the length of the beam segment without disturbing equilibrium; and (4) the law of the lever, i.e., unequal weights suspended at distances inversely proportional to the weights will be in equilibrium. It is only in connection with the last assumption, the general law of the lever, that the author specifies the previous mathematicians responsible for its proof: "Euclid, Archimedes, and others." Presumably the first three suppositions emerged from a consideration of symmetry and center of gravity in the manner of Archimedes' *On the Equilibrium of Planes*. Indeed, the third assumption is merely the inverse of the assumption that Archimedes makes in his lever proof (Proposition 6) when he distributes a weight along a weightless beam without altering the center of gravity.

Having examined Proposition I of the *De canonio* we can briefly note that Proposition II is the inverse of Proposition I (and thus constitutes a form of the lever law as applied to a material beam balance of unequal arm lengths). We give its enunciation without proof (which proof is an indirect one based on Proposition I):[7]

II. IF THE RATIO OF THE WEIGHT SUSPENDED AT THE END OF THE SHORTER SEGMENT, TO THE EXCESS OF THE WEIGHT OF THE LONGER SEGMENT OVER THE WEIGHT OF THE SHORTER ONE, IS AS THE RATIO OF THE LENGTH OF THE WHOLE BEAM TO TWICE THE LENGTH OF THE SHORTER ARM, THEN THE BEAM WILL HOLD PARALLEL TO THE PLANE OF THE HORIZON.

We are now prepared to consider the anonymous medieval proof from the Parisian manuscript. It was perhaps undertaken by someone disgruntled with the efficacy and soundness of Jordanus' *Elementa* as an introduction to the *De canonio*. Clearly, the author had read Proposition 9 of Jordanus' *Elementa*, for he uses the same term for a material beam segment: *oblongum*, a term not used in any of the other tracts on weights. He also uses the same expression for equilibrium: *equidistare orizonti* (although to be sure this expression was occasionally used in other tracts).[8] In considering Proposition 9, he perhaps was disturbed by the above noted errors in ratios that are found in Proposition 9 and possibly even more disturbed by the fact that one does not really need Proposition 9 at all in the passage to Proposition I of the *De canonio*. In fact, all that one really needs is Proposition 8. But presumably our author was also dissatisfied with the dynamic proof of Proposition 8. Hence, he seems to have decided to give an entirely new entrance into the problems of the *De canonio* by starting from the special assumption of the equilibrium of equal weights at equal distances and then proceeding by strictly symmetrical considerations to a modified form of the lever law where the

---

[7] *Ibid.*, p. 67.

[8] *Ibid.*, pp. 154, 174, 282. And see M. Clagett, *The Science of Mechanics in the Middle Ages* (Madison, Wisc., 1958; 2nd printing, 1961), p. 69, note 1.

basic beam is still weightless but where a material beam segment is balanced against a pendent weight. Hence, the whole of the *Elementa* is scrapped except a part of the actual wording of the lever law (*brachia libre fuerint proportionalia ponderibus ita ut breviori gravius appendatur*) which is straight out of Jordanus' eighth proposition.

Thus, if my interpretation of the proof is correct, it is Archimedean. But it is a direct proof, while that of Archimedes in Proposition 6 of *On the Equilibrium of Planes* is indirect since Archimedes reduces the situation involving unequal weights hung at inversely proportional distances to the special case of equal weights at equal distances. Before discussing the details of the anonymous proof itself it should be observed that the author specifies at the end of the proof four assumptions beyond his assumption in the body of the proof of the special case of the lever law. The numbers of these assumptions have been bracketed in the translation below. Assumption [2], which holds that a uniform material beam is in equilibrium when hung from its mid-point, is identical with assumption (1) of the proof of Proposition I of the *De canonio*. Both authors use it to authorize the elimination of the effects of equal beam segments about the center of movement, i.e., to make these equal material segments as if they were weightless. In addition the medieval author seems to use this assumption in the very beginning of his proof when he hangs his material beam segment from its mid-point and thus it affords a kind of substitute for a center of gravity concept. Assumption [3], which holds that if a material beam is not hung from the mid-point it declines on the side of the longer arm, is not directly used by the medieval author and probably is merely an effort on his part to complete assumption [2] by assuming that it is only in the mid-point that a uniform beam may be supported and preserve equilibrium. The author's assumption [4], which in effect establishes that the rules of addition and subtraction apply to quantities of weights, allows him to assume the direct proportionality of the lengths of uniform material beams and the weights of those lengths. Finally, assumption [1] is merely a geometric restatement of one of the basic steps in the proof. I have explained it in note 2 of the translation.

Turning from the assumptions to the proof itself, we note that the most interesting ploy of the author occurs when he moves the center of movement from point H in the weightless beam down to point C in the material beam segment. This is effectively the same as distributing the weight of the material segment along the weightless beam. In the fact that the material beam segment AE extends beyond the center of movement, we have a situation similar to that in Proposition 6 of Archimedes' *On the Equilibrium of Planes*, where in distributing the longer of two unequal weights along the weightless beam some of the distributed weight extends beyond the center of the whole weightless beam. Whether or not the author drew this technique from Archimedes I cannot say. All I can say is that if the author was composing this proof in Paris in the late thirteenth or early fourteenth century he could have had access to Moerbeke's translation of

On the Equilibrium of Planes in the same manuscript of the translations used by Johannes de Muris, Nicole Oresme, and perhaps others. I have already mentioned in the preceding chapter the anonymous author's possible use of such a manuscript in making other additions to the *De ponderibus Archimenidis*.

In order to understand better the intention of the author in his proof, I should like to add some further possible considerations that remain unspecified by the author. Let us suppose for a moment that not only is the initial material beam segment *AE* distributed over the weightless beam (as the author proposes) but also that weight *f*, its equal, is formed into a like beam and similarly distributed (this the author does not do). But lest the beams interpenetrate, let us have two abutting beams hanging as illustrated in Fig. I.8.1. Equilibrium remains even though the beams are not in line so long as they are affixed one to the other and the system is properly suspended. Now suppose, with the author, that we remove the equal segments *m* and *no* from the nearer beam and at the same time bring *l* and *A'E'* into line. The result is that we have a straight beam composed of *l* and *A'E'*, which is in equilibrium about *C*. Then, following the technique of *On the Equilibrium of Planes*, Proposition 6, we could say that this single beam is equivalent to having two weights, one *l* with its center at *Q* and the remaining segment *A'E'* with its center at *D*. And then if we leave *l* where it is and take the weight *f*, equal to the remaining segment *A'E'*, and hang it from *D*, we do not, in the Archimedean procedure, disturb the equilibrium and in fact we have the condition of equilibrium specified by the author of this anonymous proof. Then since it can be proved that $f/l = QC/CD$ and QC and CD are the distances at which *f* and *l* act and preserve equilibrium, we have thus shown that an equilibrium exists when the weights vary inversely as the distances.

One last observation concerning our anonymous proof is worth making. The form of the lever law that is here under consideration is but a step from that given in *De canonio*, Proposition II. In the latter the whole balance beam is material, while in the anonymous proposition the basic beam is still weightless with one of the weights being a material beam segment. Pierre Duhem, who first described the substance of this anonymous proof, noted its similarity with a proof of the lever law by Simon Stevin.[9]

In the text below, the figures are as given in the manuscript except that the proportion of the lines has been somewhat altered to agree with the ratios specified in the text. All the letters marking the quantities in the manuscript text and figures are lower-case letters. But following the practice of the *The Medieval Science of Weights*, I have used capital letters for line lengths and points, small letters for weights.

[9] Pierre Duhem, *Les Origines de la statique*, Vol. 1 (Paris, 1905), pp. 271–72, 287–89. For Stevin's proof, also see *The Principal Works of Simon Stevin*, Vol. 1: *General Introduction, Mechanics*, ed. of E. J. Dijksterhuis (Amsterdam, 1955), pp. 39–40, 116–23.

An Anonymous Lever-Law Proof

[Anonymi demonstratio]

/Pono pondus totius oblongi *ABCDE* esse equale ponderi *f* et sunt brachia libre *GH, HI* equalia [Fig. I.8.2]. Et pono dictum oblongum dependere ⟨a⟩ medio puncto sui, hoc est a puncto *B*, per perpendicularem *BG*, et pondus *f* dependere per perpendicularem *AK* (*! IK*). Et
5 quoniam puncta *G, I* equaliter distant a puncto *H*, quod est centrum motus, et ab ipsis dependent duo pondera equalia—scilicet oblongum predictum et pondus *f*—propter hoc equedistant *GH, HI*, que sunt brachia libre, orizonti. Tunc abscindam ex linea *AC* lineam *CP* equalem *CE*. Et faciam descendere *H*, quod est centrum motus, usque ad *C*. Deinde tollam
10 ab utroque lateri centri motus ex dicto oblongo duas partes equales, que sunt *m* et *no* (et tunc procedit ad secundam [figuram, Fig. I.8.3]). Et propter hoc remanebit *l* pars oblongi dependens a medio puncto sui, hoc est a puncto *Q*, equalis ponderis in illo situ ponderi *f*. Modo intendo probare quod proportio brachii *QC* ad brachium *CD* est tamquam pro-
15 portio ponderis *f* ad pondus *l*, que est pars oblongi. Dico in primis quod proportio linee *QC*, que est medietas totius linee *AE*, ad lineam *CD*, que est medietas linee *BD*, est tamquam proportio totius linee *AE* ad lineam *BD*. Sed proportio linee *AE* ad lineam *BD*, vel ad lineam *AP* sibi equalem, est tamquam proportio ponderis totius oblongi ad pondus *l* partis oblongi.
20 Sed pondus *f* est equale ponderi totius oblongi. Ergo a primo proportio linee *QC* ad lineam *CD* tamquam ponderis *f* ad ad (*!*) pondus *l*, que est pars oblongi totius. Et per hoc patet brachia libre fuerint proportionalia ponderibus suis ita ut breviori gravius appendatur [et] lingula examinis in neutram partem nutum faciet.

/Si linea in duo equalia duoque inequalia secetur, et a tota dematur
26 duplum illius quod a minori sectione et a dimidio linee interiacentis sectionibus aggregatur, id quod de tota linea remanet equale est ei quod utrique sectioni interiacet.

Quando aliquod oblongum equalis grossitiei et ponderis in omni parte
30 dependet a medio puncto sui, tunc equedistet orizonti.

Si vero non a medio puncto sui dependeat, tunc ex parte longiori declinat.

Omnis corporis pondus equale est omnibus ponderibus omnium partium suarum aggregatis.

[A Proof by an Anonymous Author][1]

I posit that the weight of the whole oblong *ABCDE* is equal to weight *f* and that the arms of the balance *GH* and *HI* are equal [see Fig. I.8.2].

[1] See Commentary, lines 1–24.

And I posit that the afore-mentioned oblong hangs from its mid-point, that is, from point B, by the perpendicular BG, and that the weight f hangs by the perpendicular IK. And since points G and I are equally distant from point H, which is the center of motion, and two equal weights hang from them—namely, the afore-mentioned oblong and weight f— for that reason GH and HI, which are the balance arms, are parallel to the horizon. Then from the line AC I shall mark off CP equal to CE. And I shall cause H, which is the center of movement, to descend to C. Then on either side of the center of movement I shall take from the afore-mentioned oblong two equal parts, which are m and no (and then [the demonstration] advances to the second [figure, Fig. I.8.3]). And for that reason part l of the oblong hung from its mid-point, that is from point Q, will remain of the same weight in that position as weight f [, that is, it will remain in equilibrium]. Now I intend to prove that the ratio of arm QC to arm CD is the same as the ratio of the weight of f to the weight of l which is part of the oblong. First of all, I say that the ratio of line QC, which is half of the whole line AE, to line CD, which is half of line BD, is as the ratio of the whole line AE to line BD. But the ratio of line AE to line BD, or to its equal, line AP, is as the ratio of the weight of the whole oblong to the weight of l, a part of the oblong. But the weight of f is equal to the weight of the whole oblong. Therefore, from above the ratio of QC to line CD is as that of weight f to the weight of l, which is part of the whole oblong. And by that reasoning it is evident that the arms of the balance are proportional to their weights in such a way that the heavier weight is hung from the shorter arm while the tongue of the balance makes no movement on either side.

---

[1] If a line is cut into equal halves and the two halves are cut unequally [in the same way], and there is subtracted from the whole line a magnitude double that of the combined length of the lesser segment and half of the length of the segment lying between [the two lesser segments], that which will remain of the whole line is equal to the segment lying between each of the cutoff segments.[2]

[2] This is more easily followed when expressed in specific quantities: (1) $AB = BE$; (2) $AB = (AP + PB)$ and $BE = (BD + DE)$; and (3) by subtraction, $AE - 2(PB + BC)$ $= BD = AP$. Note that this assumption was also included just before the statical proof, i.e. on folios 93r–v, accompanied by a short proof: "Sit itaque linea AE divisa per duo equalia in puncto B et per duo inequalia in puncto D. Et dividatur linea BD sectionibus interiacens (93v) per duo equalia in puncto C. Erit ergo linea CE constans ex minori sectione et dimidio linee sectionibus interiacentis, cuius dupla sit linea EP. Dico ergo quod linea AP est equalis linee BD divisionibus interiacenti, quod sic probatur. Nam quoniam linea EP est dupla linee CE, est propter hoc linea CE equalis linee PC. Si igitur ex lineis PC, CE equalibus lineas BC, CD equales auferas, remanebit linea PB equalis linee DE, quibus PB, DE equalibus de lineis AB, BE equalibus ablatis, remanebit linea AP equalis linee BD sectionibus interiacenti. Et sic patet propositum." The letters indicating magnitudes are those found on the beam in Fig. I.8.3.

[2] When some oblong body of equal denseness and weight in every part hangs from its mid-point then it is parallel to the horizon.

[3] If it does not hang from its mid-point then it declines on the side of the longer [segment].

[4] The weight of every heavy body is equal to the aggregate of the weights of all its parts.

Commentary

1–24 "Pono. . . . faciet." The proof can be represented succinctly as follows: (1) Since $ae = f$ and $GH = HI$, ae and f are in equilibrium. (Note: ae is the weight of segment AE.) (2) With the center of motion moved perpendicularly to C, the beam AE is effectively moved to the balance beam. Then remove from each side of C the equal material segments m and no (the weights respectively of segments CP and CE). Hence l remains in equilibrium with f (see the Introduction for a discussion of this point). (3) Now prove that $\dfrac{QC}{CD} = \dfrac{f}{l}$ as follows: 1) $\dfrac{QC}{CD} = \dfrac{AE}{BD}$ since $QC = \frac{1}{2}AE$ and $CD = \frac{1}{2}BD$; 2) $\dfrac{QC}{CD} = \dfrac{AE}{AP}$ since $AP = BD$ by assumption [1] appearing at end of text; 3) but $\dfrac{AE}{AP} = \dfrac{ae}{l} = \dfrac{f}{l}$ by assumption [4] at the end of the text; 4) therefore, $\dfrac{QC}{CD} = \dfrac{f}{l}$. (4) Hence l and f are in equilibrium when they are inversely proportional to the arm lengths.

PART II

The Arabo-Latin and Handbook Traditions of Archimedes in the Fourteenth and Early Fifteenth Centuries

CHAPTER 1

The Glasgow Collection of Quadrature Tracts

I have traced in the preceding part of this volume the influence of the Moerbeke translations of Archimedes at Paris in the fourteenth century. I now must return to the fate of the Arabo-Latin tradition in the same period. Much of this subject has already been treated in Volume One, for I presented there a series of versions derived from Gerard of Cremona's translation of Archimedes' *On the Measurement of the Circle* that in all likelihood should be assigned to the fourteenth century. Among these are the Pseudo-Bradwardine Version, the *Versio abbreviata*, the Corpus Christi Version, perhaps the Florence and Munich Versions, and certainly the *Questio de quadratura circuli* of Albert of Saxony. I also briefly mentioned in Volume One an interesting collection of quadrature tracts appearing in MS Glasgow, University Library Gen. 1115 (formerly BE 8.y.18), which came to my attention as Volume One was going to press. I have now made a more leisurely examination of this collection, which occupies folios 202r–14v, and am prepared to report the results of this examination. The manuscript is dated 4 December, 1480; it has been described in detail by N. Ker.[1] Notwithstanding that the manuscript was copied in 1480, it is evident that it includes only medieval tracts, though the fly leaves contain some later material. At any rate, the section on which I concentrate most likely originated in the fourteenth century. Let us first turn to the collection of quadrature tracts, which I shall now describe:

(1) 202r–03v. *Incipit Liber archimenidis de quadratura circuli*. This is the complete text of Gerard of Cremona's translation of Archimedes' *On the Measurement of the Circle*, which I have published in Volume One, pages 30–58. It includes not only the three propositions but the two corollaries to Proposition I. A collation of this copy with my text shows that it was taken from an exemplar of Tradition II. This is not surprising since

---

[1] N. Ker, *Medieval Manuscripts in British Libraries*, Vol. 2 (in preparation). Mr. Ker graciously supplied me with his forthcoming description of this manuscript. For the date, see folio 172v: "Et sic est finis geometrie euclidis perscripte manu die 4ᵃ decembris 1480. Explicit 15ᵘˢ et ultimus geometrie euclidis cum commento Magistri campani." Mr. Ker notes that the manuscript was written in France.

it bears the title used in the second tradition, namely, *Liber de quadratura circuli*, rather than that found in the first tradition (*De mensura circuli*).

(2) 203v–07v. No title. This is another distinct version of Archimedes' *On the Measurement of the Circle*. It appears to belong to the fourteenth century. I give a discussion of this tract below, followed by the text itself and an English translation.

(3) 208r–09r. *Incipit quadratura circuli secundum magistrum campanum cum commento eidem asscripto*. This item is the quadrature tract attributed to Campanus of Novara, which I have already published in Volume One, pages 581–609. Only a few observations need be made concerning this rather loose and inaccurate copy. A collation of it with my published text shows exclusive agreement in a large number of variant readings with manuscript *Er* (Erfurt, Stadtbibl. Amplon. Q.385, 51r–53r) of the fourteenth century. I conclude, therefore, that it was copied from that manuscript with a few changes. The colophon in *Er* ("Explicit quadratura circuli edita a magistro campano qui commentavit geometriam euclidis") has here been rendered as follows: "Explicit quadratura circuli edita a magistro campano cum commento eidem ascripto." It should be further remarked that the poem on quadrature, which appears in all but one manuscript of the text (see Volume One, pages 583 and 606, variant to line 121), is also present in the Glasgow manuscript (209r). On folio 209r there are two extraneous diagrams that are not related to the text of Campanus but rather to the supposed quadratures of Bryson and Antiphon. The first is entitled "quadratura brissonis sophistica" and the second "quadratura antiphontis erronea et mala" (cf. Volume One, pp. 426–29).

(4) 209v–10r. No title. This is Version III of the *Quadratura circuli per lunulas*, which I have published below in Appendix II, Text A. Though there is no certain evidence, I suppose this tract to date from the fourteenth century. It concludes (210r): "Explicit quadratura circuli secundum alium doctorem."

(5) 210r–11r. *Incipit quadratura circuli secundum alardum*. Despite its title, this was taken from Jordanus de Nemore's *De triangulis* (ed. of M. Curtze, Thorn, 1887), Book IV, Propositions 14–16. It concludes: "Explicit quadratura circuli secundum magistrum alardum in maiori commento." One supposes that the name *Alardus* is an abbreviatory form of *Adelardus*, i.e., Adelard of Bath. At least Adelard is so designated by Roger Bacon in quoting Version III of Adelard's translation of the *Elements*.[2] However, the name *Alardus* is given instead of Jordanus in one copy of Jordanus' *Elementa de ponderibus* (see MS Oxford, Corpus Christi College 251, 10r–12r). Presumably the confusion in the quadrature piece could have arisen from the presence of one of Adelard's versions of the *Elements* with Jordanus' *De triangulis* in the same manuscript, Adelard's name being attached to the *Elements* in the form *Alardus* and no name

---

[2] M. Clagett, "The Medieval Latin Translations from the Arabic of the *Elements* of Euclid," *Isis*, Vol. 44 (1953), p. 23, n. 18.

being placed on the *De triangulis*. Incidentally, I republished Proposition 16 from the *De triangulis* in Volume One, pages 572–74. The comment that appeared in the margin of MS *I* (*ibid.*, p. 572, variant to lines 18–21) is included in the text in the Glasgow manuscript. Further, the Glasgow manuscript includes an extra paragraph at the end of that proposition: "Si autem inter duas quantitates vis invenire terciam proporcionalem, quadra latus unius quantitatum, deinde quadra latus alterius, ut duo ista quadrata angulis se contingant. Postea ab angulis quadratorum produc lineas quas necesse est concurrere. Ex prima itaque 6^{ti} euclidis probabis istam superficiem esse inter duo quadrata medio loco proporcionalem."

(6) 211r–12v. *Sequuntur quedam extracta a commento eiusdem.* These are further propositions which are concerned with triangles and have nothing to do with quadrature. The first three appear in Jordanus' *De triangulis*, Book IV, Propositions 17–18, 21.

(7) 213r–14v. *Extractum a commento Jo. de muris capitulo octavo, ut facilius intelligantur que dicta sunt supra textum archimenidis.* This is Chapter 8 of Johannes de Muris' *De arte mensurandi*, which I have discussed and edited above, in Part I, Chapter 4. The only point worthy of notice is that the scribe formally attributes the piece to Johannes de Muris, although none of the manuscripts of the *De arte mensurandi* itself does so. This piece concludes the section on quadrature and the scribe adds at the end: "hec sufficiant pro quadratura circuli."

My concern in this chapter is with the second item of the collection, inasmuch as it is the only quadrature tract that has not been published before (except the fourth item which is the non-Archimedean quadrature by lunes printed below in Appendix II). The suppositions preceding Proposition I are similar to the suppositions found in the Cambridge Version of the *De mensura circuli* (see Volume One, p. 68) and the Corpus Christi Version (*ibid.*, pp. 170–72). Thus the first supposition ("Every chord is less than its arc") is equivalent to the second *petitio* of the Cambridge Version but is an inversion of the first *petitum* of the Corpus Christi Version ("An arc is greater than [its] chord"). The Glasgow Version's second supposition ("A curve is equal to a straight line") is equivalent to the second *petitum* of the Corpus Christi Version but is less precise and complete than the first *petitio* of the Cambridge Version ("There is some curved line equal to any straight line and some straight line equal to any curved line"). The third Glasgow supposition ("An arc terminated at the angles of one side of a rectilinear triangle is less than the other two sides") is quite distinct from both the third *petitio* of the Cambridge Version ("The perimeter of any including figure is greater than the perimeter of the included figure") and the third *petitum* of the Corpus Christi Version ("Any curved line sharing the two termini of a circumferential arc and including it in the direction of the convexity of the arc is greater than the arc"). However, it resembles one of the exemplifying statements of the Corpus Christi Version ("Similarly, if from the two termini of the circumferential arc *ABC* two straight lines are drawn in the direction of the convexity of the arc until they meet in one point, namely D, who could doubt that the bent line ADC composed of two straight lines is greater than arc ABC?''—see Volume One, p. 173 and the Figure 24c on p. 171). Everything considered, the Glasgow assumptions appear to resemble the Corpus Christi Version more closely than any other version. Hence it is not improbable that its author had read the Corpus Christi Version. Since, as I have reasoned in Volume One, page 167, the author of the Corpus Christi Version seems to have had knowledge of Archimedes' *On the Sphere and the Cylinder* and since the only version of that work available in the Middle Ages was the translation of William of Moerbeke executed in 1269, it is probable that that version postdated 1269 and consequently that the Glasgow Version was prepared even later, perhaps in the fourteenth century. My remarks below concerning the probable use of the Florence Version of Proposition III by the author of the Glasgow Version seem to confirm this later dating.

Turning to the propositions of the Glasgow Version, the reader of the first volume will immediately see that they resemble in content, structure, and terminology the various emended versions of Gerard of Cremona's translation of the *De mensura circuli* that I published in that volume. Thus the enunciation of Proposition I of the Glasgow Version (''Triangulum orthogonium cuius unum laterum continencium angulum rectum est equale circumferencie, reliquum vero semydyametro, circulo equum esse'') resembles the enunciations of three of the previously published emended versions: (1) that of Version F.IB (Volume One, p. 106): ''Circulum quadrare eo quod omnis triangulus orthogonius, cuius unum latus equatur circumferentie, reliquum latus semidyametro, equalis est ipsi circulo;'' (2) that of Gordanus (*ibid.*, p. 148): ''Sicut premissum est triangulus aliquis secundum Archimenidem alicui circulo est equalis; ille inquam triangulus ortogonius cuius duo latera rectum angulum ambientia sic se habent quod unum eorum est equale circumferentie, reliquum semidiametro circuli assignati;'' (3) and that of the Munich Version (*ibid.*, p. 198): ''Triangulus orthogonius, cuius unum latus est semidyameter circuli et reliquum angulum rectum cum semidyametro constituens equale circumferencie circuli fuerit, equalis est circulo.'' I have singled out these three versions of Proposition I for comparison with the Glasgow Version since they alone adopt the same order of statement as the Glasgow version, namely ''triangle equals circle.'' The remaining versions retain Gerard's order: ''circle equals triangle.''

The proof of Proposition I in the Glasgow Version reflects the tendencies exhibited in the various emended versions of the pristine text of Gerard: (1) a considerable elaboration of the argument beyond Gerard's (and Archimedes') lean proof; (2) a frequent citation of Euclid's *Elements* at appropriate places in the proof; (3) the specification by letter of the quantity by which the circle is supposed to exceed the triangle in the first part of the proof and the triangle the circle in the second (that letter is A in the Glasgow Version); and (4) the misapplication of the term *lunula* to a segment of a circle in the first half of the proof.[3] But one distinctive feature that separates the Glasgow Version from the others is the absence of geometric lettering. Except for the afore-mentioned, supposited excess of circle over triangle or triangle over circle, all other geometric quantities used in the proof of Proposition I remain unspecified by letter, the argument being entirely verbal. One might suppose that this characteristic reflects the absorption of this problem into the corpus of scholastic materials. However, not even the most scholastic of the various treatments of this problem already considered, namely that of Albert of Saxony, goes so far in removing literal designations of the geometrical magnitudes involved.

Proposition II of the Glasgow Version, though containing the substance of the proposition found in Gerard's text and the various emended versions, has more the character of a paraphrase. Still the lettering of the diagram is essentially that of the Gerard version. The circumscribing square *HG* of Gerard's diagram (Volume One, p. 47) has been moved by the author of the Glasgow Version so that it no longer circumscribes the circle but instead is erected on the diameter *AB* and thus becomes square *HB* (see Fig. II.1.1). This is somewhat surprising since in his enunciation the author has substituted "quadratum sibi circumscriptum" for Gerard's "quadratum diametri ipsius." However, the author is quite aware of what he has done, for he remarks in the proof that the circumscribed square is the same as the square of the diameter.

After giving a proof like that of the text of Gerard, the author presents an alternate proof that is merely a remanipulation of the geometrical magnitudes involved: (1) $2 \cdot$circum. square $= 4d \cdot r$, (2) $2 \cdot$circle $= d \cdot r \cdot 3\frac{1}{7}$, (3) circle/square $= d \cdot 3\frac{1}{7}/4d$, and (4), with d posited as 7, then circle/square $= (3\frac{1}{7} \cdot 7)/(4 \cdot 7) = 22/28 = 11/14$. Q.E.D.

The enunciation of Proposition III of the Glasgow Version is that found in the Gerard text (Volume One, p. 48) and in the Florence Version (*ibid.*, p. 112), the only difference being that *continens circulum* in the Gerard and Florence texts has become *circulum continens* in the Glasgow text. Now the proof of Proposition III in the Glasgow Version almost certainly had its origin in that of the Florence Version (*ibid.*, pp. 112–34) or in a source common to it and the Florence Version. Like the author of the Florence Version, the author of the Glasgow Version converts the mixed numbers that arise in the calculation of π to improper fractions. In his calculations he makes a few slips in presenting large numbers and some errors of calculation. These have all been flagged, with the correct numbers duly indicated.

In publishing the Glasgow text I have followed the procedures used in Volume One. The only significant departure from the manuscript as written

---

[3] See Volume 1, pp. 64–65, 80–81, 94, 144–145, 166, 168–69 and 194–95 for mention of the tendencies seen in the various elaborations of Proposition I that were prepared in the thirteenth and fourteenth centuries.

is in the punctuation adopted. I have punctuated and capitalized as I thought the meaning demanded. The enunciations of the propositions I have given in capital letters to reflect the fact that they appear in a larger hand in the manuscript than do the proofs. However, the suppositions preceding Proposition I, which are also given in a larger hand in the manuscript, I have printed in minuscules, following my earlier practice. Letters designating geometrical magnitudes are given here as majuscules though they appear in the manuscript as miniscules. This is the practice that I have everywhere followed in these volumes, at least for extensive texts. I have retained the scribe's inconsistent orthography: *paralellogramum* or *parallellogramum* (but never *parallelogrammum*); *dupplus*, *duplus*; *dyameter*, *diameter*; *semydyameter* or *semidiameter*. The scribe has always converted the "ti" before vowels to "ci." So we find *proporcio*, *eciam*, *peticio*, and so on. I have omitted the diagrams for Proposition I because they bear no letter designations (except for the above-noted excesses marked by *A* and assigned to a small square). They are merely the outline figures that are conventional for the versions published in Volume One (and the reader may easily consult such figures in that volume). However, I have included the figures for Propositions II and III where letter designations are found since they are needed to follow the text. The marginal folio numbers are, of course, those of the Glasgow manuscript. The reader will observe, finally, that I have added footnotes to the translation in order to clarify the author's errors and to relate his citations of the *Elements* to the text of Euclid. In view of the previous commentaries on the various versions of Volume One, I felt that no additional commentary was necessary.

The Glasgow Version of the *Liber Archimenidis de quadratura circuli*

[Liber Archimenidis de quadratura circuli]

[Peticiones]

203v   / [1] Omnis corda minor est arcu suo.

[2] Curva est equalis recte.

[3] Arcus terminatus ad angulos alicuius lateris trianguli rectilinei
5 reliquis duobus est minor.

Tit., Suppos. and Prop. I
  Tit. Liber . . . circuli *addidi*
    1 Peticiones *addidi*

[Proposiciones]

[I] TRIANGULUM ORTHOGONIUM CUIUS UNUM LATERUM CONTINENCIUM ANGULUM RECTUM EST EQUALE CIRCUM-FERENCIE, RELIQUUM VERO SEMYDYAMETRO, CIRCULO EQUUM ESSE.

Si non est equalis, ergo est maior vel minor. Quod si circulus maior est, ergo aliquanto. Sit illud A. A itaque cum triangulo est equalis circulo. Ergo A est minus circulo. Substrahe itaque per primam 10^{mi} plus medietate a circulo donec relinquatur minus A. Quod sic facies. Inscribe circulo quadratum per sextam 4^{ti}, quo substracto substraxeris plus medietate a circulo. Quod ut sic pateat. Seca quadratum ad medietates per lineam extensam in angulos oppositos. Cui ducta equidistante que contingat circulum complete paralellogramum. Quod cum triangulo qui est medietas quadrati inscripti circulo, (illud enim sectum in duos triangulos equales per lineam extensam inter angulos oppositos) stabit super eandem basim inter lineas equidistantes. Quare per 41^{m} primi paralellogramum trigono duplum est. Ille ergo triangulus medietas est illius paralellogrami. Ergo est maior duobus porcionibus circuli contentis duobus lateribus illius trianguli, que eciam sunt latera quadrati circulo inscripti, et arcubus eis conterminatis. Eodem modo constet reliquam medietatem quadrati esse maiorem duabus porcionibus. Ergo quadratum iis quatuor porcionibus maius est. Quare eo substracto relinquitur minus medietate circuli.

Illud autem relictum aut est minus A aut non. Si non, substrahe ab illo adhuc plus medietate secando latera quadrati per equalia per lineas exeuntes a circumferencia que eciam perpendiculariter ea secabunt et in centrum descendent per $3^{am}\ 3^{ii}$. Deinde ab uniuscuiusque termino qui est in circumferencia duc rectas in terminos laterum quadrati et apparebit quedam superficies 8 laterum equalium. Stabuntque super quodlibet laterum quadrati circulo inscripti duo / trianguli quos cum substraxero a porcionibus relictis post substraccionem quadrati et relinquetur minus medietate. Erunt enim singuli duo trianguli consistentes super latus quadrati plusquam medietas porcionis super idem latus consistentis, quod iterum probabis per paralellogramum descriptum super latus quadrati. Ita ergo substracto plus medietate residui relinquuntur octo lunule. Que si non sunt minores A substrahe adhuc plus medietate ducendo lineas que secent latera superficiei que continetur 8 lateribus et sic donec relinquatur minus A.

Dato iterum 8 lunulas minores esse A, infer superficiem illam multi-angulam esse maiorem dato triangulo. Quod sic improbatur. Duc lineam a centro in medium punctum alicuius lateris illius multiangule superficiei et stabit super eam perpendiculariter per $3^{am}\ 3^{ii}$ apparebitque triangulus

6 Proposiciones *addidi*
34 cum *corr. MS ex* circulo
35 et *del. MS?*
44 triangulo *corr. MS ex* circulo

stans super medietatem divisi lateris cuius unus angulus rectus est. Ergo
per 41 ⟨am⟩ primi id quod fit ex ductu linee a centro in illud latus in
medietatem illius lateris est dupplum ad illum triangulum. Eodem modo
50   quod fit ex ductu linee exeuntis a centro in reliquam medietatem dicti
divisi lateris est dupplum ad triangulum qui staret super illam medietatem
si duceretur ab illius medietatis termino linea in centrum. Ergo ea que
fiunt ex ductu linee procedentis a centro in medietates linee quam secat
sunt duppla ad duos triangulos stantes super illas medietates. Ergo sunt
55   duppla ad triangulum totalem. At eadem sunt equalia ei quod fit ex ductu
linee illius indivise eius, scilicet que exit a centro, in totalem divisam
super quam stat perpendiculariter per primam secundi. Ergo quod fit ex
ductu illius indivise in illam divisam est duplum ad illum totalem trigonum.
Eadem ratione singula illa que fiunt ex ductu illius linee indivise exeuntis
60   a centro in alia latera superficiei multiangule sunt duppla ad totales triangulos stantes in lateribus eiusdem multiangule superficiei. At illi trianguli
sufficienter constituunt illam superficiem. Ergo illa superficies multiangula
est subdupla ad ea que fiunt ex ductu dicte linee indivise in sua latera.
At illius superficiei latera simul sumpta minora sunt circumferencia per
65   primam peticionem. Ergo eciam sunt minora latere dicti trianguli quod est
per peticionem equale circumferencie. Item linea indivisa que exiens a
centro terminatur infra circumferenciam minor est semidyametro. Ergo
est eciam minor latere dicti trianguli quod datum est esse equale semidyametro. At illud quod fit ex ductu unius lateris dicti trianguli con-
70   tinentis angulum rectum in reliquum latus quod cum eo continet angulum
rectum est duplum ad datum triangulum, quod ex 41ª primi patet. Sed
producencia duplum superficiei multiangule sunt minora producentibus
duplum dati trianguli. Ergo productum producto minus est. Nam si minora
in minoribus sumerentur et compleretur paralellogramum, illud esset
75   minus contento sub lineis maioribus. Itaque dupplum ad triangulum est
maius duplo ad superficiem multiangulam. Quare sub/duplum maioris sub-
duplo minoris est maius, quod ex 15 ⟨a⟩ 5ⁱ colligi potest. Non igitur dici
potest circulum trigono maiorem esse.
   Sit igitur minor. Sitque A et circulus equalis trigono dato. Sive ergo A
80   sit equale circulo sive non. Circumscribe circulo quadratum per 7ᵃᵐ quarti.
Aut ergo quadratum erit equale vel maius vel minus A. Sive sit equale
sive minus, patebit deduccio ex sequentibus. Si autem sit maius A, substrahe ab eo plus medietate quod feceris substracto circulo, quod patebit
ducta dyametro equidistante alicui laterum quadrati figuratoque super eam
85   triangulo quod contingat latus quadrati. Erit enim ille triangulus medietas
parallellogrami stantis super dyametrum. Ergo erit maior duobus triangulis

47 medietatem *correxi ex* medietates
48 *post* centro *del. MS* ill. . . .
66 per peticionem *supra scr. MS*
74 minoribus *corr. MS ex* maioribus
75 triangulum: 3ˡᵘᵐ *MS et mg. scr.* triangulum
77 5ⁱ *correxi ex* 15ⁱ

quorum bases sunt curve relictis extra circulum. Ergo multo forcius semicirculus eisdem maior erit. Eodem modo proba reliquam medietatem aliis duobus triangulis relictis extra circulum maiorem esse. Relinquentur
90 itaque post substraccionem circuli quatuor trianguli stantes in curvis basibus. Qui si non sint minores A substrahe eciam ab eis plus medietate, ducendo ab angulis eorum rectas lineas in centrum quas secabis per contingentem terminatam ad latera quadrati. Eritque, hoc facto, parallellogramum (! octangulum?) poligonium circumscriptum circulo. Et ita
95 abstuleris plus medietate residui ablatis quatuor triangulis quorum quilibet habet unum angulum rectum quadrati prius descripti et stat super aliquod latus poligonii et erit quilibet divisus in duos triangulos.

Quod sic patebit. Ducantur a centro linee equidistantes lateribus quadrati in circulum. Deinde inter puncta duo singula illarum exeuncium a
100 centro—puncta dico que sunt in ipsa circumferencia—singulas lineas extendito et erunt ipse corde arcuum. Apparebunt itaque trianguli partim contenti in circumferencia partim extra. Et erit quilibet eque altus alicui parcialium triangulorum qui subtracti sunt. Et quemlibet illorum eque sibi alto maiorem esse per 17 ⟨am⟩ 3ii et 19 ⟨am⟩ primi et primam sexti convincito.
105 Itaque quilibet illorum parcialium triangulorum substractorum erit maior triangulo stante super circumferenciam sibi continuam. Ergo illis substractis substraxeris plus medietate a dato residuo. Si ergo residuum ultimo relictum non est minus, substrahe plus medietate ducendo lineas ab angulis poligonii in centrum et illas secando per contingentes terminatas
110 ad latera poligonii circumscripti circulo et ita deinceps.

Sit ergo iterum quod partes poligonii huius circumscripti circulo sint minores A, que scilicet sunt relicte extra circulum. Et ita sive A fuerit equale quadrato sive maius sive minus, erunt dicte particule minores A. Sed A et circulus sunt equales dato triangulo. Ergo poligonium circum-
115 scriptum circulo est minus dato triangulo. Quod sic destruas. Ex ductu semidiametri in latera poligonii producta rectangula sunt dupla ad poli-
205r gonium et ex ductu eiusdem semidyametri in latus / trianguli quod est equale circumferencie producitur duplum ad trigonum. Sed latera poligonii sunt maiora circumferencia per 3am peticionem, ergo et dicto latere trianguli.
120 Quare duplum poligonii duplo trianguli maius est. Ex hoc infer propositum.

Ex hac propositione et ultima secundi mediante prima communi sciencia quadraturam circuli demonstrare facile est.

[II] PROPORCIO AREE CIRCULI AD QUADRATUM SIBI CIRCUMSCRIPTUM EST SICUT PROPORCIO 11 AD 14.

Sit dati circuli dyameter AB et quadretur [Fig. II.1.1]. Sitque quadratum HB cuius medietas abscindatur per lineam GD contingentem circulum et
5 equidistantem linee AB. Tripletur itaque linea GD adiecta ei eius dupla, que sit DE. Et protrahatur ultra E donec EZ fiat 7a linee GD. Deinde duc AD et AE et AZ lineas et claude triangulos. Est ergo triangulus

88 eisdem corr. MS ex eiusdem
92 rectas correxi ex rectis

AGZ equalis dato circulo ex premissa, si tamen verum est quod dyameter triplatus (!) cum adieccione septime equat lineam continentem circulum.

10   Sit ergo *GD* linea quasi 7. Ergo *GZ* est quasi 22. Ergo ex prima sexti Euclidis proporcio trianguli *AGZ* ad triangulum *AGD* est quasi 22 ad 7. Sed proporcio trianguli *AGD* ad quadratum *HB* est quasi 7 ad 28. Quis enim hoc nescit? Ergo ex hoc patet proporcionem aree circuli ad quadratum sibi circumscriptum, quod est idem quadrato dyametri, esse in

15   proporcione 11 ad 14. Ad inscriptum autem in proporcione 11 ad 7, quia circumscriptum inscripto duplum est.

Aliter idem. Ex ductu quatuor dyametrorum in semidyametrum fit duplum quadrati circumscriptibilis circulo et ex ductu trium dyametrorum et septime unius in semidyametrum fit duplum ad circulum. Ergo que est

20   proporcio trium dyametrorum et septime ad quatuor dyametros eadem est circuli ad quadratum circumscriptum. Si ergo ponas dyametrum quasi 7, erunt tres dyametri et septima quasi 22; quatuor autem dyametri quasi 28, quorum numerorum proporciones sunt ut 11 ad 14. Et sic patet propositum.

[III] OMNIS LINEA CIRCULUM CONTINENS ADDIT SUPRA TRIPLUM DYAMETRI MINUS SEPTIMA ET PLUS 10 PARTIBUS 71 PARCIUM DYAMETRI.

Sit linea *AG* dyameter circuli quam contingat linea *ZD* in puncto *G*

5   [Fig. II.1.2]. Fiatque super *E* centrum circuli angulus *ZEG*, qui sit tercia unius recti. Ergo si angulo *ZEG* circumscriberetur, fieret eius dyameter linea *ZE* et latus exagoni in eo esset linea *ZG*. Quare oportet ut proporcio *EZ* ad *ZG* sit ut 306 ad 153.

Dividam autem angulum ZE⟨G⟩ in duo media per lineam *EH*. Ergo ex

10   3ª sexti Euclidis proporcio *EZ* ad *EG* est sicut proporcio *ZH* ad *HG*. Ergo coniunctim proporcio *ZE* et *EG* ad *EG* est sicut proporcio *ZG* ad *HG*. Ergo permutatim proporcio *ZE* et *EG* ad *ZG* est sicut proporcio

205v   / *EG* ad *HG*. Ponam *EZ* quasi 306, lineam vero *ZG* quasi 153. Erit ergo *EG* plus quam 265, quod ita probo. Quadratum linee *EZ* est equale qua-

15   dratis linearum *ZG* et *EG*. Sed quadratum *ZG* est quarta pars quadrati *EZ*. Ergo quadratum *EG* est triplum quadrati *ZG*. Invenires ergo quadratum *EG* esse quasi 70227 cuius radicem si queres in numeris erit ipsa quasi 265. Sed in operacione remanebunt 2. Ergo linea *EG* maior est quam 265. Ergo *ZE* et *EG* sunt plus quam 571. Sed proporcio *EG* ad *HG* est

20   sicut *ZE* et *EG* ad *ZG*. Ergo proporcio *EG* ad *HG* maior est proporcione 571 ad 153. Ergo coniunctim proporcio *EG* et *HG* ad *HG* maior est proporcione 571 et 153 ad 153. Ergo proporcio linearum *EG* et *HG* divisim (! coniunctim) in potencia ad *HG* in potencia maior est proporcione 571 et 153 in potencia ad 153 in potencia. Sed linea *EH* potest super *EG* et

25   *HG*. Quadrati autem numeri quorum 571 et 153 sunt radices valent, si

Prop. II
  8 tamen *delendum?*

congregentur in unum, 349450. Hec autem radix 153 producit 23409. Ergo maior est proporcio quadrati linee *EH* ad quadratum linee *HG* quam proporcio huius numeri, scilicet 349450, ad hunc numerum 23409. Ergo proporcio linee *EH* in longitudine ad lineam *HG* in longitudine maior est
30 proporcione 591 et octave unius ad 153.

Huiusmodi autem argumenti ratio hec est. Faciam quasi phisicas minucias cum denominacione ab 8va sumpta. Cum ergo reduxero 349450 ad minuta et deinde ad secunda multiplicando scilicet per 8, facta extraccione radicis ibi, hoc est in secundis, inveniam radicem 591 et unam
35 octavam nisi quod in operacione supersunt duo de summa cuius radix queritur fere 27 (*!* 22) integra.

Post hoc dividam angulum *HEG* per medium per lineam *TE*. Ergo iterum ex 3^a sexti Euclidis proporcio *HE* ad *EG* est sicut proporcio *HT* ad *TG*. Ergo coniunctim proporcio *HE* et *EG* ad *EG* est sicut proporcio *HG* ad
40 *TG*. Ergo permutatim proporcio *HE* et *EG* ad *HG* est sicut proporcio *EG* ad *TG*. Sed proporcio *HE* ad *HG* maior est proporcione 591 et unius octave ad 153. Proporcio quoque *EG* ad *HG* est maior proporcione 571 ad 153, ut preostensum est. Ergo proporcio *HE* et *EG* ad *HG* maior est proporcione 1162 et ⅛ ad 153. Ergo similiter proporcio *EG* ad *TG* maior
45 est proporcione 1162 et ⅛ ad 153. Ergo proporcio *TE* in potencia ad *TG* in potencia maior est proporcione 1162 et ⅛ in potencia et 153 in potencia ad 153 in potencia. Ergo proporcio *TE* in longitudine ad *TG* in longitudine maior est proporcione 1172 et ⅛ ad 153. Si enim quadrares 1162 et ⅛, quadrares eciam 153, et numeros quadratos componeres, et
50 deinde minucias quales dixi reduceres, invenires radicem tocius summe 1172 et unam octavam fere. Dico autem ''fere'' quia in operacione
206r [supersunt] de summa cuius radix / quereretur 79 si memini, ymo quia memini.

Angulum quoque *TEG* dividam per medium linea *KE*. Patebit quia
55 secundum processum in predictis quod proporcio *EG* ad *KG* maior est proporcione 2334 et quarte partis ad 153. Est enim proporcio *EG* ad *KG* sicut proporcio *TE* et *EG* ad *TG*. Sed proporcio *TE* ad *TG* maior est proporcione 1172 et ⅛ ad 153. Similiter proporcio *EG* ad *TG* maior est proporcione 1162 et ⅛ ad 153. Ex quo apparet proporcionem *EG* ad *KG*
60 maiorem esse proporcione 2334 et ¼ ad 153. Ergo proporcio *EG* et *KG* ad *KG* maior est proporcione 2334 et ¼ et 153 ad 153. Ergo proporcio *KE* in potencia ad *KG* in potencia est maior proporcione 2334 et ¼ et 153 in potencia ad 153 in potencia. Quadrentur ergo hec due summe, scilicet hec 2334 et ¼ et iterum hec summa 153. Et quadrata eorum reducantur

Prop. III
    35 duo *delendum?*
    39 coniunctim *supra scr. MS*
    44 similiter *supra scr. MS*
    45 *ante* TE *scr. et del. MS* EG ad TG
    52 supersunt *addidi*
    61 *ante* 153² *del. MS* 19

65 in minucias quasi phisicas denominatas a quaternario usque ad secunda et congregentur in unam summam et inveniatur radix 2339 et ¼ nisi quod in operacione superfluunt fere 291. Ergo proporcio *KE* ad *KG* maior est proporcione 2339 et unius 4e ad 153.

Cum ergo divisero angulum *KEG* in duo equalia per lineam *EL*, ap-
70 parebit consideranti quod proporcio *EG* ad *LG* maior est proporcione 4673 et medietatis ad 153. Et quia angulus *EZG* tercia [pars] est unius recti neccesse est angulum *LEG* esse 48ᵛᵃᵐ unius recti.

Faciam autem super *E* punctum angulum *GEM* equalem angulo *LEG*. Ergo angulus *LEM* est 24⁽ᵃ⁾ pars anguli recti. Ergo linea *LM* est latus
75 poligonii habentis 96 angulos equales et circumscripti circulo *AG*. Et quia ostensum est quod proporcio *EG* ad *GL* est maior proporcione 4673 et medietatis ad 153, oporet proporcionem *AG* dupli ad *EG* ad lineam *LM* duplam ad *GL*, similiter esse maiorem proporcione 4673 et medietatis ad 153. Ergo ex 15⁽ᵃ⁾ 5ⁱ Euclidis maior est proporcio *AG* dyametri ad lineam cir-
80 cumdantem poligonium, de quo dixi, proporcione 4673 et medietatis ad 14688. Vocetur autem linea claudens poligonium *LMS*. Ergo est maior proporcio 14688 ad 4673 et medietatem quam proporcio linee *LMS* ad lineam *AG*, ergo et quam proporcio circumferencie *AFG* ad dyametrum *AG*. Sed numerus 14688 addit super triplum huius numeri 4673 et medietatis hanc
85 summam que est 667 et unam secundam et ipsa est minor septima huius summe 4673 et medietatis vel una secunda. Ergo id quod addit linea continens poligonium—ymo circulum—super triplum dyametri *AG* est minus septima dyametri.

Quod autem linea circulum continens maior sit triplo dyametri sui non
90 dubitat qui videt quod exagonus circulo inscriptus continetur lineis que
206v / equant triplum dyametri et est (!) minor circumferencia.

Sit iterum circuli *ABG* dyameter *AB* (! *AG*). Consistatque super arcum angulus *GAB* et sit tercia recti [Fig. II.1.3]. Clauso ergo circulo erit *BG*
latus exagoni. Erit igitur *BG* ut 780. Erit ergo *AG* linea, que est duppla
95 linee *BG*, ut 1560. Sed quadratum *AG* est equale quadratis linearum *AB* et *BG*. Quadretur ergo linea *AG*, que sit ut 1560, et fiet eius quadratum 2433600. Quadratum autem linee *BG*, que est ut 780, erit ut 608400. Si ergo hanc minorem summam substrahas ab illa maiore, remanebunt 1825200. Huius ergo summe residue radix est linea *AB*. Sed summa cuius
100 radix est hec summa 1351 vacat unitate hanc summam 1825⟨2⟩00. Ergo linea *AB* est minus quam 1351. Ergo proporcio *AB* ad *BG* est minor proporcione 1351 ad 780, etc.

Dividam autem per medium *GAB* angulum linea *AH*, que secat *BG* lineam in puncto *Z* et continuabo puncta *HZG* (! *H* et *G*). Vides ergo duos
105 [triangulos] qui sunt *GAH* et *ZAB*, qui sunt similes. Et est proporcio *AH*

66 2339 *corr. MS ex* 2334
75 *post* quia *scr. MS et delevi* est
89 triplo *correxi ex* triangulo
105 *post* sunt² *scr. et del. MS* equales

ad *HG* sicut proporcio *AB* ad *BZ*. Item in triangulo *GAB* secatur angulus
GAB per medium linea ducta super *GB* basim. Ergo ex 3ª 6[i] Euclidis
proporcio *AG* ad *AB* est sicut proporcio *GZ* ad *ZB*. Et ex hoc habes quod
proporcio *AG* et *AB* coniunctarum ad *BG* est sicut proporcio *AB* ad *BZ*.
110 Ergo proporcio *AH* ad *HG* et proporcio *AG* et *AB* coniunctarum ad *GB*
est una. Sed proporcio *AG* ad *BG* est sicut proporcio 1560 ad 780. Et
proporcio *AB* ad *BG* est minor quam proporcio 1350 (*!* 1351) ad 780.
Ergo eciam proporcio *AH* ad *HG* est minor proporcione 2911 ad 780.
Ergo proporcio quadrati linee *AH* ad quadratum linee *HG* est minor
115 proporcione quadrati numeri qui quadrat numerum 2911 et numeri quadrantis numerum 780 ad quadratum numeri 780.

Sit autem numerus cuius numerus quadratus constans ex eis qui quadrant numeros qui sunt 2911 et 780. Ergo proporcio ⟨radicis⟩ quadrati
linee *AG*, quod valet quadrata linearum *AH* et *HG*, ⟨ad lineam *HG*⟩ est
120 minor proporcione radicis quadrati (*?*) numeri ad 780. Sed 3013 et unum
secundum et ¼ hec summa est maior radice numeri quadrati. Ergo maior
est proporcio *AG* linee ad lineam *HG* quam proporcio huius summe 3013
et ½ et ¼ ad 780. Non est autem dubium quin 3013 et ¾ sint plus vera
radice quadrati numeri, est enim quadratus numerus, scilicet 9082321.
125 Numerus autem 3013 cum ¾ est fere radix huius summe que est 9082688.
Supersunt enim in operacione una 16 ⟨a⟩ et ¾, si non erravi.

Item dividam angulum *GAH* per medium linea *AT* que in *C* puncto secet
lineam *HG*. Apparebunt igitur duo trianguli similes qui sunt *GAT* et *AHC*.
Unde oportet quod proporcio *AT* ad *TG* sit ut proporcio *AH* ad *HC*. Et
7r quia linea *AC*, secans / per medium angulum *GAH*, incidit *GH* basim, facile
131 est secundum premissa probare quod proporcio linearum *AG* et *AH* ad
lineam *HG* est sicut proporcio *AT* linee ad *TG*. Probatum est autem quod
proporcio *AG* ad *HG* est minor proporcione 3013 et trium 4[arum] ad 780.
Ostensum est quoque quod proporcio *AH* ad *HG* minor est proporcione
135 2911 ad 780. Ergo proporcio *AT* linee ad *TG* minor est proporcione 5924
et ¾ ad 780. Sed proporcio 5924 et ¾ ad 780 est sicut proporcio 1823 ad 240,
quia proporcio 5924 et ¾ ad 1823 est sicut et trium et ¼ ad unum. Similiter
proporcio 780 ad 240 est tripla sesquiquarta. Ergo permutatim proporcio
1823 ad 240 est sicut proporcio 5924 et trium 4[arum] ad 78⟨0⟩. Ergo pro-
140 porcio *AT* linee ad lineam *TG* est minor proporcione 1823 ad 240. Ergo
proporcio quadratorum *AT* linee et *TG* linee ad quadratum linee *TG* est
minor proporcione duorum numerorum, quorum unus quadrat 1823 numerum et alter numerum 240, ad quadratum numeri 240. Sed numerum
1823 quadrat numerus qui est 3323329 et numerum qui est 240 quadrat
145 numerus qui est 57600. Adde unum alteri et fiet numerus 3380929. Ergo
proporcio quadrati linee *AG* quod valet quadrata linearum *AT* et *TG* ad

117 quadratus *correxi ex* quasi
118 radicis *addidi*
119 ad . . . HG *addidi*
130 GAH *correxi ex* GAC
145 57600 *correxi ex* 15608

quadratum linee *TG* minor est proporcione huius numeri 3380929 ad 57600. Ergo minor est proporcio linee *AG* ad lineam *TG* proporcione radicis numeri huius 3380929 ad 240. Sed si multiplicaretur in se hec
150 summa 1838 et $^9/_{11}^{me}$ fieret plus hoc numero 3380929. Quod si vis videre, multiplica in se 1838 et deinde in se duc $^9/_{11}$. Postea duppla $^9/_{11}$ et in dupplum illud duc 1838. Et his omnibus compositis in unum habebis iuxta secundum Euclidis quadratum 1838 et $^9/_{11}$ eritque illud plus quam 3380929. Ergo radix huius numeri proximi minor est quam 1838 et $^9/_{11}$. Ergo eciam
155 minor est proporcio linee *AG* ad lineam *TG* proporcione numeri 1838 et $^9/_{11}$ ad 240.

Item diviso per medium angulo *GAT* per lineam *AK* secantem *GT* in puncto *D*, proba secundum modum premissum quod proporcio *AK* ad *KG* minor est proporcione 3661 et $^9/_{11}$ ad 240. Hec autem proporcio est sicut
160 proporcio 1007 ad 66, quia proporcio 3661 et $^9/_{11}$ ad 1007, itemque proporcio 240 ad 66, est sicut proporcio 40 ad 11. Ergo proporcio *AK* ad *KG* est minor proporcione scilicet 1007 ad 66. Secundum modum premissum proba deinde quod proporcio *AG* ad *KG* minor est proporcione 1009 et unius sexti ad 66. Si enim componeres quadratum numeri 1007 et quad-
165 ratum numeri 66, fieret 10⟨1⟩8405 qui numerus minor est summa quam producit 1009 et $^1/_6$ in se multiplicata, est enim hec summa 10⟨1⟩8417 et preterea aliquid plus quod reieci in operacione.

Item diviso *GAK* angulo per medium linea *AL* que lineam *KG* secet in puncto *F*, si ergo predicta vides, probare scis quod proporcio *AL* ad *LG*
170 minor est proporcione 2016 et unius sexte ad 66. Quare oportet secundum
207v premissum modum operandi quod proporcio *AG* ad *GL* minor sit / proporcione 2017 et unius 4te ad 66. Videre enim poteris si operari non pigritaveris quod 2017 et $^1/_4$ sunt plus radice summe constantis ex duabus summis quarum una quadrat 2016 et $^1/_4$ (! $^1/_6$), altera quadrat 66.

175 Considera ergo: angulus *GAB* tercia est unius recti. Ergo angulus *GAL* est 48 ⟨a⟩ unius recti anguli. Ergo si fieret angulus centralis cadens in arcum *GL* ipse esset 24 ⟨a⟩ pars anguli recti. Ergo esset 96 ⟨a⟩ pars 4^{or} rectorum. Ergo linea *LG* est latus poligonii inscripti circulo habentis 96 angulos equales. Ergo minor est proporcio linee *AG* ad totalem ambitum
180 huius poligonii quam proporcio 2017 et $^1/_4$ ad 66 nonagesies sexies sumpta. Sed tociens sumpta faciunt 6336. Ergo maior est proporcio poligonii in totali ambitu suo ad dyametrum *AG* quam sit proporcio 6336 ad 2017 et $^1/_4$. Sed 6336 addunt super triplum huius summe 2017 et $^1/_4$ plusquam decies 71 ⟨am⟩ partem huius summe 2017 et $^1/_4$. Ergo eciam totalis ambitus poligonii
185 addit super triplum *AG* dyametri plusquam decem partes de partibus 71. Ergo multo forcius linea continens circulum addit super triplum dyametri plus 10 partibus septuagintaunius parcium dyametri.

147 minor *correxi ex* minus
161 KG *del. MS et injuste add.* HG
165 108405 *MS*
166 108417 *MS*
172 2017 *correxi ex* 7017
187 septuagintaunius: 71u' *MS*

Cum ergo probavero quod 6336 addunt super triplum 2017 et unius 4ᵉ plusquam 10 partes septuagintaunius parcium eiusdem summe, habebo tandem quod diu intendi demonstrare. Dividam ergo 6336 per 2017 et ¼ et exibit ternarius et remanebunt 314 (! 284) integra et ¼. Reducam ergo integra ad quartas et adiciam unam quartam et fient 4ᵗᵉ quas numerabunt 1257 (! 1137). Quibus reductis ad minucias alterius denominacionis multiplicato tam numerante quam denominante numero per 71 fient 89247 (! 80727) ducentesime octogesime 4ᵉ. Item cum reduxero ad 4ᵃˢ 2017 et adiecero unam 4ᵃᵐ, fiet, si non erravi, 8069 4ᵗᵉ, quibus ad alias minucias reductis multiplicato utroque numero per 71. Si minucie sunt producte, accepero ¹⁰/₇₁ᵃˢ. Habebo 80690 ducentesimas octogesimas quartas, que summa minor est 89247 (! 80727) ducentesemis octogesimis 4ⁱˢ. Ex hoc propositum patet.

Caveas tamen, lector, ne forte in operando alicubi erraveris; nec tamen me errasse putes si minucias omisi quas, ubi non curam, deerant. "Non curam" cum quod querebatur non minus sine ipsis proveniret.

[Archimedes' *Book on the Quadrature of the Circle*]

[Suppositions]

[1] Every chord is less than its arc.

[2] A curve is equal to a straight line.

[3] An arc terminated at the angles of one side of a rectilinear triangle is less than the other two sides.

[Propositions]

[I] A RIGHT TRIANGLE ONE OF WHOSE SIDES CONTAINING THE RIGHT ANGLE IS EQUAL TO THE CIRCUMFERENCE [OF A CIRCLE] AND THE OTHER TO THE RADIUS IS EQUAL TO THE CIRCLE.

If it is not equal, hence it is greater or less. But if the circle is greater, it is so by some amount. Let that amount be A. And so A together with the triangle is equal to the circle. Hence A is less than the circle. So, by X.1 [of the *Elements* of Euclid][1] subtract more than half the circle [continuously] until there remains a quantity less than A. This you will do as follows. Inscribe a square in the circle by IV.6 [of the *Elements*].[2]

---

189 septuagintaunius: 71' *MS*

Prop. I

[1] Vol. 1, p. 60n. For the Campanus text, see the *Elementa* (Basel, 1546), p. 244.

[2] Vol. 1, p. 137, comment 9. Cf. *Elementa* (Basel, 1546), p. 91.

With this subtraction completed, you will have subtracted more than half the circle. Let this be evident as follows. Bisect the square by a line extending to opposite angles. Then, having drawn a tangent to the circle that is parallel to the [bisecting] line, complete the rectangle. This rectangle and the triangle which is half the square inscribed in the circle (for the square was divided into two equal triangles by the line extending between the opposite angles) stand on the same base and are included between parallel lines. Hence by I.41 [of the *Elements*][3] the rectangle is double the triangle. Therefore, the triangle is one-half the rectangle. Therefore it (the triangle) is greater than the two segments of the circle contained by (1) the two sides of the triangle, which are also the sides of the square inscribed in the circle, and (2) the arcs that are coterminal with the sides. It is apparent in the same way that the other half of the square is greater than the [other two] segments. Hence the square is greater than the four segments. Therefore, with the square subtracted, less than half of the circle remains.

Either this remainder is less than *A* or it is not. If not, subtract more than half from it by bisecting the sides of the square by means of lines proceeding from the circumference, intersecting the sides perpendicularly and descending to the center. [This is done] on the authority of III.3 [of the *Elements*].[4] Then from the terminus of each [such bisecting line] that lies in the circumference draw two straight lines to the termini of the sides of the square. Thus will arise a certain surface of eight equal sides. On each of the sides of the square inscribed in the circle will stand two triangles. If, after subtracting the square, I subtract these two triangles from [each of] the [four] remaining segments, a quantity less than half [of the segments] will remain. For each pair of triangles on a side of the square is greater than half of the segment lying on [that] same side. This you will again prove by constructing a rectangle on the side of the square. Therefore, with more than half of the remainder so subtracted, there will remain eight small segments. But if these segments [*in toto*] are not less *A*, once again subtract more than half by drawing lines which [bi]sect the sides of the octagon. This procedure is followed until a quantity less than *A* remains.

But again if it be given that the eight small segments are less than *A*, infer that this polygon is greater than the given triangle. [Now] this is refuted as follows. Draw a line from the center to the midpoint of one side of the polygon. This line will be perpendicular to the side by III.3 [of the *Elements*].[5] On half of the side [so] divided a right triangle will be formed. Hence by I.41 [of the *Elements*],[6] the product of the line drawn from the center to that side and one half of that side is double the triangle. In the same way, the product of the line drawn from the center and the

---

[3] Vol. 1, p. 78, comment 33. Cf. *Elementa* (Basel, 1546), p. 33.
[4] Vol. 1, p. 78, comment 40. Cf. *Elementa* (Basel, 1546), p. 56.
[5] See note 4.
[6] See note 3.

other half of the said divided side is double the triangle which would stand on that half [of the divided line] if a line were drawn from the terminus of the half to the center. Therefore, the products arising from the multiplication of the line proceeding from the center and [both] halves of the line which it divides are double the two triangles standing on the halves [of the divided line]. Therefore, they are double the whole triangle. But they are equal to the product of (1) that undivided line proceeding from the center and (2) the whole divided line on which it stands perpendicularly, by II.1 [of the *Elements*].[7] Therefore, the product of the undivided line and the divided line is double the whole triangle [on that divided line]. By the same reasoning the individual products of the undivided lines proceeding from the center and the other sides of the polygon are double the whole triangles standing on the sides of the same polygon. But those triangles make up the whole surface. Therefore, the polygon is one-half the product of the said undivided line and the polygon's sides. But the sides added together are less than the circumference, by the first supposition. Therefore, they are also less than the side of the said triangle which by supposition is equal to the circumference. Further the undivided line which proceeds from the center and is terminated inside of the circumference is less than the radius. Hence it is also less than the side of the said triangle which was given as equal to the radius. Now the product of one side of the said triangle containing the right angle and the other side which with the former contains the right angle is double the given triangle. This is evident from I.41 [of the *Elements*].[8] But the multipliers producing double the polygon are less than the multipliers producing double the given triangle. Therefore, the [one] product is less than the [other] product. For if the lesser lines were joined to lesser lines and a rectangle formed from them, that rectangle would be less than the rectangle contained by the greater lines. And so double the triangle is greater than double the polygon. Therefore, half the greater is more than half the less. This can be inferred from V.15 [of the *Elements*].[9] Therefore, the circle cannot be said to be greater than the triangle.

Therefore, let it be less than the triangle. And so *A* and the circle [together] are equal to the given triangle. Therefore *A* may be either equal to the circle or not equal to it. Circumscribe a square in the circle by IV.7 [of the *Elements*].[10] Therefore, the square will be equal to, greater than, or less than *A*. Whether it is equal or less than *A*, the deduction will be evident from what follows. But if it is greater than *A*, subtract more than half from it. This you will have done when the circle has been subtracted. This will be evident after a diameter parallel to one of the sides of the square has been drawn and a triangle touching the side of the square has been constructed on the diameter. For the triangle will

---

[7] Vol. 1, p. 191, comment 66–67. Cf. *Elementa* (Basel, 1546), p. 40.

[8] See note 3.

[9] Vol. 1, p. 79, comment 50. Cf. *Elementa* (Basel, 1546), p. 125.

[10] Vol. 1, p. 137, comment 33. Cf. *Elementa* (Basel, 1546), p. 91.

be half of the rectangle standing on the diameter. Therefore it will be greater than the two triangles that remain outside of the circle and whose bases are curved lines. Therefore, the semicircle will be greater than these same [mixed triangles] by even more. In the same way prove that the other half [of the circle] is greater than the other two [mixed] triangles that remain outside of the circle. And so after the subtraction of the circle there will remain four triangles standing on curved bases. If they are not less than A, subtract more than half from them by drawing straight lines to the center from their angles, straight lines which will intersect a tangent terminated at the sides of the squares. With this done, an octangular polygon will have been circumscribed about the circle. And so you will have subtracted more than half of the remainder when you have removed the four triangles, each of which has one right angle of the previously described square and each of which stands on a side of the polygon. And each triangle will be divided into two triangles.

This will be evident as follows. Let lines parallel to the sides of the square described about the circle be drawn from the center. Then between two individual points of these lines going out from the center (i.e. between the points which are in the circumference) draw single lines that will be chords of arcs. And so triangles will be formed that are partly contained inside of the circumference and partly outside. Each of these triangles will have the same altitude as the partial triangles that were subtracted. And conclude that each of the latter triangles is greater than the [corresponding triangle] equal to it in altitude, by III.17 (=Gr. III.18), I. 19 and VI.1 [of the *Elements*].[11] And so each of the partial triangles that have been subtracted will be greater than the [mixed] triangle standing on the circumference continuous with it. Therefore, with those [partial triangles] subtracted, you will have subtracted more than half of the given remainder. Hence, if the remainder that is left over at the end [of your subtraction] is not less [than A], subtract more than half by drawing lines from the angles of the polygon to the center and cutting these lines by tangents terminating at the sides of the polygon circumscribed about the circle, and so on continuously.

Therefore, again let it be that the parts of this polygon circumscribed about the circle which remain outside of the circle are less than A. And so, whether A is equal, greater than, or less than the square, the said small segments will be less than A. But A and the circle are equal to the given triangle. Therefore, the polygon circumscribed about the circle is less than the given triangle. This you will refute as follows. The rectangles produced by multiplying the radius by sides of the polygon are double the polygon and the product of the same radius and the side of the [initial] triangle equal to the circumference is double the triangle. But the sides of the polygon [together] are greater than the circumference by the third

[11] Vol. 1, pp. 90, comment 61; 192, comment 191; 79, comment 70. Cf. *Elementa* (Basel, 1546), pp. 69, 18, 138.

supposition; therefore, they are greater than the said side of the triangle. Therefore, double the polygon is greater than double the triangle. From this infer the proposition.

From this proposition and the last [proposition] of [Book] II [of the *Elements*][12] by means of the first axiom [of Book I of the *Elements*][13] it is easy to demonstrate the quadrature of the circle.

[II] THE RATIO OF THE AREA OF A CIRCLE TO A SQUARE CIRCUMSCRIBED ABOUT IT IS AS THE RATIO OF 11 TO 14.

Let *AB* be the diameter of the given circle, and let it be squared [see Fig. II.1.1]. Let the square be *HB* and let it be bisected by line *GD* tangent to the circle and parallel to line *AB*. Let line *GD* be tripled by the addition to it of its double, *DE*. Then let the resulting line be extended beyond *E* by the distance *EZ*, which is $\frac{1}{7}$ of line *GD*. Then draw *AD*, *AE* and *AZ*, thus completing the triangles. Therefore, $\triangle AGZ$ is equal to the given circle by the preceding [proposition], if it is true that $3\frac{1}{7}$ the diameter equals the circumference of the circle. Hence let line *GD* be 7. Therefore *GZ* is as 22. Hence by VI.1 [of the *Elements*][1] of Euclid, $\triangle AGZ/\triangle AGD = 22/7$. But $\triangle AGD/\square HB = 7/28$. For who is ignorant of this? Therefore, from this it is evident that the ratio of the area of a circle to a square circumscribed about it (which is identical to the square of the diameter) is as the ratio of 11 to 14. But to the inscribed square it has a ratio of 11 to 7 because the circumscribed square is double the inscribed square.

Another proof of the same proposition. From the product of 4 diameters and a radius arises a quantity double the square circumscribed about the circle; and from the product of $3\frac{1}{7}$ the diameter and a radius arises a quantity double the circle. Therefore, the ratio of $3\frac{1}{7}$ diameters to 4 diameters is the same as that of the circle to the circumscribed square. Hence, if you posit the diameter as 7, $3\frac{1}{7}$ the diameter will be 22. Now 4 diameters equal 28. Hence the ratio of these numbers is 11 to 14. And thus the proposition is evident.

[III] EVERY CIRCUMFERENCE OF A CIRCLE EXCEEDS THREE TIMES ITS DIAMETER BY AN AMOUNT LESS THAN ONE-SEVENTH AND MORE THAN $^{10}/_{71}$ OF THE DIAMETER.

Let the diameter of the circle be line *AG* [see Fig. II.1.2], which line *ZD* touches in point *G*. Let angle *ZEG* (which is $\frac{1}{3}$ of a right angle) be constructed at center *E*. Therefore, if a circle were circumscribed about angle *ZEG*, line *ZE* would be its diameter and line *ZG* would be the side of a hexagon [inscribed] in it. Therefore, $\dfrac{EZ}{ZG} = \dfrac{306}{153}$.

[12] Vol. 1, p. 79, comment 82–83. Cf. *Elementa* (Basel, 1546), p. 51.

[13] See the *Elementa* (Basel, 1546), p. 3: "Quae uni et eidem sunt aequalia, et sibi invicem sunt aequalia."

Prop. II

[1] Vol. 1, p. 79, comment 70. Cf. *Elementa* (Basel, 1546), p. 138.

Now I bisect $\angle ZEG$ by line EH. Therefore, by VI.3 [of the *Elements*] of Euclid,[1]

$$\frac{EZ}{EG} = \frac{ZH}{GH} .$$

Therefore, *compenendo*,

$$\frac{(ZE + EG)}{EG} = \frac{ZG}{HG} .$$

Therefore, alternately,

$$\frac{(ZE + EG)}{ZG} = \frac{EG}{HG} .$$

I posit EZ as 306 and line ZG as 153. Therefore, $EG > 265$, which I prove as follows. $EZ^2 = ZG^2 + EG^2$. But $ZG^2 = EZ^2/4$. Therefore, $EG^2 = 3 ZG^2$. You would find, therefore, that $EG^2 = 70227$, whose root, if you seek it in numbers, will be as 265, except that in the operation 2 will be left over. Therefore, line $EG > 265$. Therefore, $ZE + EG > 571$. But

$$\frac{EG}{HG} = \frac{(ZE + EG)}{ZG} .$$

Therefore,

$$\frac{EG}{HG} > \frac{571}{153} .$$

Therefore, *componendo*,

$$\frac{(EG + HG)}{HG} > \frac{(571 + 153)}{153} .$$

Therefore,

$$\frac{(EG^2 + HG^2)}{HG^2} > \frac{(571^2 + 153^2)}{153^2} .$$

But $EH^2 = EG^2 + HG^2$. Now the square numbers whose roots are 571 and 153 equal, when added together, 349450. But this root, 153, produces [when squared] 23409. Therefore, $\dfrac{EH^2}{HG^2} > \dfrac{349450}{23409}$. Therefore,

$$\frac{EH}{HG} > \frac{591\frac{1}{8}}{153} .$$

Prop. III

[1] Vol. 1, p. 139, comment 15. Cf. *Elementa* (Basel, 1546), p. 140.

The nature of this argument is as follows. I shall convert the numbers to common fractions, with the denomination assumed from an eighth. Hence when I convert 349450 to minutes (i.e., to eighths) and then to seconds (i.e. 64ths), evidently by multiplying it by 8 [each time], with the root extracted there—that is the root of the number expressed in seconds (i.e., 64ths), I find the root to be 591⅛, except that in the operation almost 27 (! 22) integers are left over from the number whose root is sought.

After this, I shall bisect $\angle HEG$ by line TE. Therefore, once more by VI.3 of Euclid (see note 1),

$$\frac{HE}{EG} = \frac{HT}{TG} .$$

Therefore, *componendo*,

$$\frac{(HE + EG)}{EG} = \frac{HG}{TG} .$$

Therefore, alternately,

$$\frac{(HE + EG)}{HG} = \frac{EG}{TG} .$$

But

$$\frac{HE}{HG} > \frac{591⅛}{153} .$$

Also,

$$\frac{EG}{HG} > \frac{571}{153} ,$$

as was demonstrated before. Therefore,

$$\frac{(HE + EG)}{HG} > \frac{1162⅛}{153} .$$

Therefore, similarly,

$$\frac{EG}{TG} > \frac{1162⅛}{153} .$$

Therefore

$$\frac{TE^2}{TG^2} > \frac{((1162⅛)^2 + 153^2)}{153^2} .$$

Therefore,

$$\frac{TE}{TG} > \frac{1172⅛}{153} .$$

For, if you square 1162⅛ and also square 153, and then add the square numbers, converting them to fractions of the sort I have said, you will find the root of the whole sum to be almost 1172⅛. I say "almost" because in the operation 79 (*! actually*, 66½) is left over from the sum whose root is sought—if I remember it; nay because I remember it.

I shall also bisect $\angle TEG$ by line KE. It will be evident, following the procedure used above, that

$$\frac{EG}{KG} > \frac{2334¼}{153} .$$

For

$$\frac{EG}{KG} = \frac{(TE + EG)}{TG} .$$

But

$$\frac{TE}{TG} > \frac{1172⅛}{153} .$$

Similarly,

$$\frac{EG}{TG} > \frac{1162⅛}{153} .$$

From this it is apparent that

$$\frac{EG}{KG} > \frac{2334¼}{153} .$$

Therefore,

$$\frac{(EG + KG)}{KG} > \frac{(2334¼ + 153)}{153} .$$

Therefore,

$$\frac{KE^2}{KG^2} > \frac{((2334¼)^2 + 153^2)}{153^2} .$$

Therefore, let these two numbers, namely 2334¼ and 153, be squared. Then let these squares be converted to minutes denominated by 4 and then to seconds (i.e. 16ths). Let these be brought together in one sum, whose root is found to be 2339¼, except that almost 291 (*! actually* 41½) is left over. Therefore, $\frac{KE}{KG} > \frac{2339¼}{153}$.

When I shall bisect $\angle KEG$ by line EL, it will be apparent to one who considers this that $\frac{EG}{LG} > \frac{4673½}{153}$. And because $\angle EZG$ is ⅓ of a right angle, it is necessary that $\angle LEG$ is ¹⁄₄₈ of a right angle.

Now I shall construct at point E $\angle GEM$ equal to $\angle LEG$. Therefore, $\angle LEM$ is ¹⁄₂₄ of a right angle. Therefore, line LM is the side of a polygon having 96 equal angles and circumscribed about circle AG. And because it has been demonstrated that $\frac{EG}{GL} > \frac{4673½}{153}$, it is necessary similarly that $\dfrac{AG}{LM} > \dfrac{4673\frac{1}{2}}{153}$, since $AG = 2\,EG$ and $LM = 2\,GL$. Therefore, by V.15 of Euclid,[2] the ratio of diameter AG to the perimeter of the polygon of which I have spoken is greater than the ratio of $4673\frac{1}{2}$ to 14688.

Let the perimeter of the polygon be designated as LMS. Therefore,

$$\frac{14688}{4673\frac{1}{2}} > \frac{\text{line } LMS}{\text{line } AG}\,.$$

Therefore,

$$\frac{14688}{4673\frac{1}{2}} > \frac{\text{circumference } AFG}{\text{diameter } AG}\,.$$

But

$$\frac{14688}{4673\frac{1}{2}} = 3 + \frac{667\frac{1}{2}}{4673\frac{1}{2}}\,,$$

which is less than $3\frac{1}{7}$. Therefore, the ratio of the perimeter of the polygon to the diameter AG is less than $3\frac{1}{7}$, as is also the ratio of the circumference to the diameter AG.

Moreover, that the circumference is greater than triple the diameter no one doubts who sees that the hexagon inscribed in a circle is contained by lines which [in sum] are equal to triple the diameter and are less than the circumference.

Again let the diameter of circle ABG be AG [see Fig. II.1.3]. Let angle GAB be constructed upon an arc and let it be $\frac{1}{3}$ of a right angle. With the circle completed, BG will be the side of a hexagon. Therefore $BG = 780$. Hence, since $AG = 2\,BG$, $AG = 1560$. But $AG^2 = AB^2 + BG^2$. Hence, if $AG = 1560$, $AG^2 = 2433600$; and if $BG = 780$, $BG^2 = 608400$. Thus $AB^2 = 2433600 - 608400 = 1825200$, or $AB = \sqrt{1825200}$. But the number whose square root is 1351 [i.e., 1825201] differs from 1825200 by 1. Therefore line AB is less than 1351. Hence, $\dfrac{AB}{BG} < \dfrac{1351}{780}$, etc.

Now I shall bisect $\angle GAB$ by line AH, which cuts line BG in point Z, and I shall connect points H and Z. You see, therefore, two similar triangles, namely GAH and ZAB. Therefore, $\dfrac{AH}{HG} = \dfrac{AB}{BZ}$. Also, in triangle GAB, angle GAB is bisected by the line intersecting base GB. Hence by VI.3 of Euclid,[3]

$$\frac{AG}{AB} = \frac{GZ}{ZB}\,.$$

Accordingly,

$$\frac{(AG + AB)}{BG} = \frac{AB}{BZ}\,.$$

[2] See Prop. I, n. 9.
[3] See above, n. 1.

Therefore,

$$\frac{AH}{HG} = \frac{(AG + AB)}{GB} .$$

But

$$\frac{AG}{BG} = \frac{1560}{780} ,$$

and

$$\frac{AB}{BG} < \frac{1351}{780} .$$

Hence,

$$\frac{AH}{HG} < \frac{2911}{780} .$$

Therefore,

$$\frac{AH^2}{HG^2} < \frac{(2911^2 + 780^2)}{780^2} .$$

Moreover, let there be a number whose square is equal to $2911^2 + 780^2$. Hence, with $AG^2 = AH^2 + HG^2$,

$$\frac{\sqrt{AG^2}}{HG} < \frac{\sqrt{2911^2 + 780^2}}{780} .$$

But $3013 + \frac{1}{2} + \frac{1}{4} > \sqrt{2911^2 + 780^2}$. Hence,

$$\frac{AG}{HG} < \frac{(3013 + \frac{1}{2} + \frac{1}{4})}{780} .$$

Further, there is no doubt that $3013\frac{3}{4}$ is greater than the true root of $(2911^2 + 780^2)$, for $2911^2 + 780^2 = 9082321$, while $3013\frac{3}{4}$ is almost equal to $\sqrt{9082689}$,[4] for $[(3013\frac{3}{4})^2$, i.e. $9082689\frac{1}{16}]$ exceeds $[9082689]$ by $\frac{1}{16}$, [and since 9082689 is greater than 9082321, then $3013]$ and $\frac{3}{4}$, [the root of $9082689\frac{1}{16}$, is greater than the true root of $2911^2 + 780^2$,] if I have not erred.[5]

I shall then bisect $\angle GAH$ by line AT, which intersects line HG in point C. Therefore, two similar triangles, GAT and AHC, will appear. Whence it is necessary that $\dfrac{AT}{TG} = \dfrac{AH}{HC}$. And because line AC bisects $\angle GAH$ and falls on base GH, it is easy to prove by what has been previously advanced that $\dfrac{(AG + AH)}{HG} = \dfrac{AT}{TG}$ .But it has been proved that

---

[4] Actually, $3013\frac{3}{4} = \sqrt{9082689\frac{1}{16}}$. Note I have changed the author's 9082688 to 9082689 because of my reconstruction of the succeeding clause.

[5] I have reconstructed this whole last clause on the basis of the Florence Version (Vol. 1, p. 126). The text as given in the Glasgow Version, if translated literally, says: "for they exceed in operation by $\frac{1}{16}$ and $\frac{3}{4}$, if I have not erred."

$$\frac{AG}{HG} < \frac{3013\frac{3}{4}}{780} \text{ . It has also been shown that } \frac{AH}{HG} < \frac{2911}{780} \text{ . Therefore,}$$

$$\frac{AT}{TG} < \frac{5924\frac{3}{4}}{780} \text{ .}$$

But

$$\frac{5924\frac{3}{4}}{780} = \frac{1823}{240}$$

because

$$\frac{5924\frac{3}{4}}{1823} = \frac{3\frac{1}{4}}{1} \text{ .}$$

Similarly,

$$\frac{780}{240} = \frac{3\frac{1}{4}}{1.}$$

Therefore, permutatively,

$$\frac{1823}{240} = \frac{5924\frac{3}{4}}{780} \text{ .}$$

Therefore,

$$\frac{AT}{TG} < \frac{1823}{240} \text{ .}$$

Therefore,

$$\frac{(AT^2 + TG^2)}{TG^2} < \frac{(1823^2 + 240^2)}{240^2} \text{ .}$$

But $1823^2 = 3323329$, and $240^2 = 57600$, and the sum of these squares is 3380929. Therefore, since $AG^2 = AT^2 + TG^2$, then

$$\frac{AG^2}{TG^2} < \frac{3380929}{57600} \text{ .}$$

Therefore, $\frac{AG}{TG} < \frac{\sqrt{3380929}}{240}$. But if we multiply the number $1838\frac{9}{11}$
by itself, the product will be greater than 3380929. (If you wish to check this, multiply 1838 by 1838, then $\frac{9}{11}$ by $\frac{9}{11}$, then 2 by $\frac{9}{11}$ by 1838. From the sum of these products, you will have, according to the second [book] of Euclid,[6] the square of $1838\frac{9}{11}$, and this will be greater than 3380929. Therefore, the root of the last number is less than $1838\frac{9}{11}$. Therefore,

$$\frac{AG}{TG} < \frac{1838\frac{9}{11}}{240} \text{ .}$$

Then with $\angle GAT$ bisected by line AK, which cuts GT in point D,

---

[6] The proposition intended is II.4. See the *Elementa* (Basel, 1546), p. 42: "Si fuerit linea in duas partes divisa, illud quod ex ductu totius in seipsam fit, aequum est iis quae ex ductu utriusque partis in seipsam et alterius in alteram bis."

prove by the method previously advanced that $\dfrac{AK}{KG} < \dfrac{3661\frac{9}{11}}{240}$. This last

ratio is equal to $\frac{1007}{66}$, because $\dfrac{3661\frac{9}{11}}{1007}$ and $\frac{240}{66}$ each equals $\frac{40}{11}$. There-

fore, $\dfrac{AK}{KG} < \dfrac{1007}{66}$. According to the method advanced before, prove

then that $\dfrac{AG}{KG} < \dfrac{1009\frac{1}{6}}{66}$. For $1007^2 + 66^2 = 1018405$, and 1018405

$< (1009\frac{1}{6})^2$, i.e., less than 1018417 plus something more which I have
rejected.[7]

Then with $\angle GAK$ bisected by line AL, which cuts line KG in point
F, by looking at the aforesaid procedures you will know how to prove

that $\dfrac{AL}{LG} < \dfrac{2016\frac{1}{6}}{66}$.

Hence it follows, according to the procedure advanced before, that

$\dfrac{AG}{GL} < \dfrac{2017\frac{1}{4}}{66}$. For you will be able to see, if you have not been slow

in proceeding, that $2017\frac{1}{4} > \sqrt{(2016\frac{1}{6})^2 + 66^2}$.

Consider, therefore, that $\angle GAB = \frac{1}{3}$ of a right angle. Hence $\angle GAL$
$= \frac{1}{48}$ of a right angle. Therefore, if a central angle were constructed
in arc GL, it would be $\frac{1}{24}$ of a right angle. Hence it would be $\frac{1}{96}$ of four
right angles. Therefore, LG is the side of a polygon inscribed in the
circle and having 96 equal angles. Therefore,

$$\frac{AG}{\text{perim. of polygon}} < \frac{2017\frac{1}{4}}{(66\cdot96)} \text{, i.e. } < \frac{2017\frac{1}{4}}{6336}.$$

Therefore, $\dfrac{\text{perim. of polygon}}{\text{diameter } AG} > \dfrac{6336}{2017\frac{1}{4}}$. But 6336 exceeds three times

$2017\frac{1}{4}$ by more than $\frac{10}{71}$ of $2017\frac{1}{4}$. Therefore, the total perimeter of the
polygon also exceeds three times the diameter by more than $\frac{10}{71}$ of the
diameter. Therefore even more does the circumference of the circle
exceed three times the diameter by more than $\frac{10}{71}$ of the diameter.

Therefore, when I shall have proved that 6336 exceeds three times
$2017\frac{1}{4}$ by more than $\frac{10}{71}$ of $2017\frac{1}{4}$, I shall finally have what I have
intended to demonstrate all the while. Therefore, I divide 6336 by
$2017\frac{1}{4}$, and the result is 3 plus a remainder of $284\frac{1}{4}$. Therefore, I convert
the integers to fourths and add one-fourth and the resulting remainder is
$\frac{1257}{4}$ (! $\frac{1137}{4}$). This remainder expressed in fourths I convert to a fraction
of another denomination by multiplying both numerator and denominator
by 71. The result is $\frac{89247}{284}$ (! $\frac{80727}{284}$). Also, when I convert 2017 to
fourths and add one-fourth, the result, if I have not erred, will be

---

[7] The exact figure is $1018417\frac{13}{36}$. See Vol. 1, p. 130. Notice that the scribe has miswritten
1018405 as 108405 and 1018417 as 108417.

$^{8069}/_4$. This will be converted to a fraction of another denomination by multiplying each number by 71 [thus producing $^{572899}/_{284}$].[8] Then I shall take $^{10}/_{71}$ of this [latter] fraction and I shall have $^{80690}/_{284}$. This figure is less than $^{89247}/_{284}$ (! $^{80727}/_{284}$) [to which the original remainder 284¼ was converted].[9] From this the proposition is evident.

But beware, reader, lest perhaps you will have erred somewhere in your calculations. But do not think that I have erred by omitting [some] fractions, for such fractions are missing where I have no concern [with them]. I say "I have no concern" since what was being sought would no less result without them.

---

[8] Compare Vol. 1, p. 132, line 340.

[9] Note that this error of 89247/284 appears here twice. The correct figure is 80727/284. The author would have had no help from the Florentine Version, for this figure was not given there.

CHAPTER 2

Philippus Elephantis' Knowledge
of Archimedes

Remnants of the Arabo-Latin tradition of Archimedes and of the *Liber de curvis superficiebus Archimenidis* associated in the manuscripts with that tradition are found in the *Mathematica* of Philippus Elephantis, an English physician who was at the University of Toulouse in 1356.[1] Philippus was also the author of glosses on the *Timaeus*, an *Ars naturalis* (i.e., *Physica*), an *Astronomia*, an *Ethica* and an *Alkimia*, the last two of which are still extant.[2] It is the *Mathematica*, preserved in MS Salamanca, Bibl. Univ. 2085, 1r–26r, that demands our attention, and particularly those propositions of the ninth part of the

[1] The best general account of Philippus Elephantis is that of G. Beaujouan, "La Science anglaise dans les bibliothèques de Salamanque au XVᵉ siècle," *Mediaeval and Renaissance Studies*, Vol. 5 (1961), pp. 263–69 (the whole article, pp. 249–69). See also *Las Leys d'amors*, ed. J. Anglade, Vol. 1 (Toulouse, 1919), pp. 36–37, 73 and Vol. 4 (1920), pp. 38–39, 147. (A provisional redaction of the *Leys d'amors* compiled by Guilhem Molinier was submitted in 1356 to a number of Toulousan professors including Philip Elephant.) Cf. E. Wickersheimer, *Dictionnaire biographique des médecins en France au moyen âge*, Vol. 2 (Paris, 1936), p. 601. P. Cattin, a student of Beaujouan's, has prepared a thesis on Elephantis. See the summary of Cattin's thesis *L'Oeuvre encyclopédique de Philippe Éléphant: mathématique, alchimie, éthique (milieu du XIVᵉ siècle)* in École Nationale des Chartes, *Positions des theses soutenues par les eleves de la promotion de 1969 pour obtenir le diplome d'archiviste paleographe* (Paris, 1969), pp. 9–15.

[2] The first four works were cited in the works of Henricus de Villena (1384–1434) in the early fifteenth century; see Beaujouan, "La Science anglaise," pp. 265–67. Cf. E. Cotarelo y Mori, *Don Enrique de Villena: su vida y obras* (Madrid, 1896), p. 162. The *Ethica* is included in MS Barcelona, Bibl. Univ. 591 and the *Alkimia* in MS Cambrai, Bibl. Munic. 919. On folio 66r of the latter Philip's name is given as *Philippus Elephantis Anglicus*. The similarity of the name with "Eliphat" (=Halifax) has been noted. The English form Oliphant (=Elephant) is well attested for the fourteenth century (see the *DNB*). Beaujouan (p. 268) calls attention to Henricus Elephantis and Jacobus Elephantis in the registers of the English Nation at the University of Paris at the beginning of the fifteenth century. Beaujouan (pp. 263–64) describes the basic similarity of the structures of the *Alkimia* and the *Mathematica*, each being divided into four *considerationes* of 12, 9, 9 and 7 parts. Beaujouan further believes that the *Mathematica*, *Alkimia* and *Ethica* constitute three books of a projected *Philosophia* in nine books (*Annuaire, 1966/1967*, p. 320). He indicates that Cattin has undertaken the transcription of the *Alkimia* (*Annuaire, 1967/1968*, p. 352).

185

section on geometry, i.e., Propositions 18, 21–25 and 28.[3] This part of the manuscript is on parchment and is written in a hand dated by Beaujouan as late fourteenth or early fifteenth century.[4] Elephantis' work was acquired by the library of the Colegio de San Bartolomé in 1440.[5]

Turning to the Archimedean propositions, we can initially observe that Proposition 21 is the first proposition of the *De mensura circuli*, and its enunciation certainly came from one or another of the versions elaborated from the translation of Gerard of Cremona. The use of the word *ambiencium* instead of *continentium* in the enunciation suggests the Version of Gordanus (see Volume One, page 148), though the full form of the enunciation having the order "circle equals triangle" rather than Gordanus' order of "triangle equals circle" raises the possibility that Philip's use of the same term as Gordanus' may be merely a coincidence, especially since Philip seems to have been fond of this term *ambiencium* in similar contexts (see, for example, the enunciations of Propositions 24–25 below).

The proof (or rather directions for proof) of Proposition 21 is quite sketchy and abandons the strict line of Archimedes' reasoning. It seems to reflect a procedure not unlike that found in the *Practica geometrie* of Leonardo Fibonacci (see Appendix I, Sect. 3[B], Distinctio III). Philip suggests that the stated right triangle with sides containing the right angle equal respectively to the circumference and the radius must equal the circle or otherwise be equal to a circumscribed or inscribed polygon. But the latter alternative is impossible since in the case of a circumscribed polygon the perimeter is greater than the circumference and so must enclose a greater space than the circle and in the case of the inscribed polygon the perimeter is less than the circumference and so must enclose less

---

[3] I must thank Cattin and Beaujouan for alerting me to the Archimedean propositions of the *Mathematica* and for sending me a preliminary transcription and photographs of the relevent section. I later obtained photographs of the whole treatise and so the responsibility for the text of the extract published below is strictly mine and must not rest on my kind correspondents. Beaujouan gives a good description of the whole manuscript in his *Manuscrits scientifiques médiévaux de l'Université de Salamanque et de ses "Colegios Mayores"* (Bordeaux, 1962), pp. 101–04; for the *Mathematica*, see pp. 101–03). The incipit gives a precise view of the organization of the *Mathematica*: "Mathematica est ars mensurandi. Mensura autem est duplex quia, vel est continuationis et dicitur geumetrica, vel est discretionis et dicitur arismetrica. Prima itaque consideratio est de 12^m principiis artis mathematice; 2^a de novem partibus arismeticis; 3^a de novem partibus geumetricis; quartaque de septem secundariis mathematice huic operi dabit finem." The third *consideratio* consists chiefly of propositions from the *Elements* of Euclid arranged in nine parts.

[4] Beaujouan, *Manuscrits scientifiques*, p. 104. Though the part of the manuscript containing the *Mathematica* does not ascribe it to Philip, we see the attribution to him on folio 68r in a hand of the end of the fifteenth or beginning of the sixteenth century (*ibid.*, p. 102). Furthermore in the inventory of the manuscripts acquired in 1440 by the Colegio de San Bartolomé it is designated *Mathematica Philipi Elephantis* (*ibid.*, p. 24). If any further evidence of Philip's authorship is needed, it can be sought in the style and organization, which, as I said above, duplicate those of the *Alkimia*.

[5] See the preceding note.

space. As it stands, the argument is grossly incomplete. The initial assumption that, if the stated triangle ($\frac{1}{2}$ $c \cdot r$) is not equal to the circle it is equal to a circumscribed or inscribed polygon, is not justified by Philip. Furthermore, the Archimedean convergence technique based on Proposition X.1 of the *Elements* is missing. Presumably Philip meant for Proposition 25 to apply here, so that in the first part of the proof, the measure of any such circumscribed regular polygon, $\frac{1}{2}$ $p \cdot r$, where p is greater than c, ensures that it will always be greater than $\frac{1}{2}$ $c \cdot r$, and so that in the second part of the proof where p is less than c, the measure of the regular polygon will always be less than $\frac{1}{2}$ $c \cdot r$. For an extensive treatment of the kind of proof implied by Philip's account, see my discussion of Pacioli's proof below in Part III, Chapter 2, Section IV, note 28.

In the second part of the proof the author undertakes to show that the circumference is equal to a straight line. As I have indicated in Volume One, this conclusion is a tacit or explicit assumption of all of the versions of the *De mensura circuli*. Philip no doubt realized this but believed that, having suggested a quadrature proof based on the idea that the circumference was a limit between the perimeter of all circumscribed and inscribed polygons, the actual equality of the circumference with a straight line could be extracted therefrom. Now Philip's proof is badly expressed but I believe its tenor to be the following. If on the basis of the first part of the enunciation we find a square equal to the circle, then the following proportion is true: $4\,s/c = r/(s/2)$, where s is the side of the square and c and r are respectively the radius and the circumference of the circle. This proportion is merely a restatement of the basic proposition $s^2 = \frac{1}{2}$ $c \cdot r$. This restatement then allows the author to hold that since r and $(s/2)$ are straight lines, as is $4\,s$, then there must exist some straight line occupying the position of c in the proportion. Thus this is an "existence" proof, i.e. it holds that such a straight line must exist whether or not it can be constructed geometrically. Presumably Philip's authority would have been the second added axiom in the Adelard and Campanus versions of Book I of the *Elements*. In the Campanus version the axiom reads: "However much one quantity is to a second quantity of the same kind [as the first], just that much will a third [given] quantity be to some fourth quantity of the same kind [as the third]."[6] One could say that the axiom "guarantees" the existence of some straight line occupying the position of c when we have straight lines r, $(s/2)$ and $4\,s$. But the proportion consisting of the four straight lines must be identical to the proportion involving the terms r, $(s/2)$, $4s$ and c, and the only

---

[6] *Elementa* (Basel, 1546), p. 3: "Quanta est aliqua quantitas ad quamlibet aliam eiusdem generis, tantam esse quamlibet tertiam ad aliquam quartam eiusdem generis. In quantitatibus continuis hoc universaliter verum est, sive antecedentes maiores fuerint consequentibus, sive minores: magnitudo enim decrescit in infinitum: in numeris autem non sic. Sed si fuerit primus submultiplex secundi, erit quilibet tertius aeque submultiplex alicuius quarti: quoniam numerus crescit in infinitum, sicut magnitudo in infinitum minuitur."

way that this could be so is for the straight line occupying the position of c in fact to be equal to c. This kind of reasoning was also used by one author of about this same period to justify the erroneous proof of quadrature by means of lunes (see below, Appendix II, n. 3). It also lurks behind the existence proof for quadrature found in Jordanus' *De triangulis* (see Volume One, page 572).

There is a difficulty in my interpretation of Philip's intention. It concerns my interpretation of the phrase "linea recta medie proportionis" as the "straight line which is the intermediate term in the proportion." For Philip goes on to give as the authority his Proposition VI.8 (=VI.9 of the Campanus Version, and VI.13 of the Greek version, of the *Elements*). This proposition is not concerned with terms that are in intermediate positions in a proportion but rather with finding a mean proportional between two given lines, i.e., a line in continuous proportion with the given lines. Thus Philip, by giving this authority, seems to be treating the phrase "linea recta medie proportionis" as "the line which is the mean proportional." But the perplexing problem here is that the line equal to c is not the mean proportional between $4s$ and r. The only way to render Philip's argument consistent with his clear statement of the proportion $4s/c = r/(s/2)$ is to assume that the wrong proposition has been cited as authority. A further, related, problem concerns the marginal reference of lines 14–17. If I have reconstructed it properly, it appears to hold that the circumference of the circle is a mean proportional between the perimeters of an inscribed and a circumscribed octagon. This is, of course, incorrect. Perhaps the author meant to convey only that the circumference is intermediate between the two in the sense that it lies between them (and is the ultimate limit if we were continuously to double the number of sides of the inscribed and circumscribed regular polygons). If such is the intent of the author, the reference becomes an oblique reference to the fact that the Archimedean proof, for the sake of convenience, stops its exhaustion procedure with the inscribed and circumscribed octagons.

Finally, in connection with Philip's treatment of Proposition 21, we should note that he designates the figure of the square superimposed upon the circle to which it is equal (see Fig. II.2.1.) as "pax et concordia," that is, "peace and harmony." The figure is so designated, I suppose, because it harmonizes or equates figures that might be thought to be hostile or incompatible, namely curvilinear and rectilinear figures.

Moving to the enunciation of Proposition 22, we are immediately impressed by the fact that, though the main proposition is in error in its formulation for the area of a hemisphere, the corollary is correct and is based on a proper formulation of the area of a sphere. We are told in the first part of the enunciation that the area of a hemisphere is equal to a right triangle whose sides about the right angle are equal respectively to the circumference of a great circle and to a quarter of the same circumference, needless to say, a completely erroneous statement. Also erroneous is the further statement that if we substitute "half a circle (!)" for "the quarter of the circumference" we shall have two triangles (or one rectangle) equal to the surface area of the whole sphere. Then follows a cryptic statement that the two triangles erected on the great circle are imagined to be terminated in a single point equidistant from that circle. If we accepted the statements so far described and did not have the corollary that follows, we would simply dismiss the whole as the exercise of a deeply confused author. But at the end of the enunciation, we are suddenly told that the surface of a sphere is equal to the lateral surface of a cylinder whose axis is equal to the diameter of the sphere and whose base diameter is that of a great circle of the sphere, a perfectly correct assertion from which we can conclude that the author knew that the surface area of a sphere is equal to the product of a circumference of its great circle and its diameter. How then can we explain the apparent contradiction between the first part of the enunciation and its concluding corollary? The explanation I offer is that Philip's original draft was difficult to read and the copyist, untutored in geometry, misread it. Pursuing this explanation, I would then say that the original enunciation read "diameter eiusdem circuli" in both places where we now read "quarta eiusdem circumferentie" and that it read "duplum diametri circuli" where we now have "medietas circuli." If I am right, the original enunciation would then have held that the surface of a hemisphere is equal to $\frac{1}{2} c \cdot d$, which is correct, and that the surface of the whole sphere is equal to two such triangles (joined right angle to right angle so that the base is $2 d$ and the altitude is c) or to the rectangle made up from them (by having their hypotenuses coincide). In either case the measure is $c \cdot d \ (=4\pi r^2)$. Now the measure $c \cdot d$ is the one given in Proposition VI of the *Liber de curvis superficiebus Archimenidis*, the terminology of which is quite similar to that used by Philip in asserting the measure of the hemisphere (Volume One, page 478): "Cuiuslibet *spere superficies est equalis* quadrangulo *rectangulo qui sub lineis equalibus* diametro spere et *circumferentie maximi circuli continetur.*" The words italicized are the same as those in Philip's enunciation. That "quadrangulo" does not appear in Philip's enunciation is explained by the fact that Philip's enunciation concerns the hemisphere and hence we find "triangulo rectangulo" instead of "quadrangulo rectangulo." The appearance of "quarta eiusdem circumferencie" instead of "diametro spere" would then be accounted for by my suggestion of scribal error. At any rate, the closeness of Philip's terminology to that of the author of the *Liber de curvis superficiebus* does suggest that Philip had read the enunciation in the earlier work. That Philip had consulted other parts of the *Liber de curvis superficiebus* cannot be denied when we compare the enunciations of his corollary to Proposition 22 and his Propositions 23 and 24 with the corresponding enunciations in the *Liber de curvis superficiebus*, as we shall see.

So, if we accept that Philip originally intended the measure $\frac{1}{2} c \cdot d$

for the surface of the hemisphere and $c \cdot d$ for that of the whole sphere, the rest of the enunciation and corollary fall into place. The above-noted statement concerning "the triangles erected on the greatest circle" can be easily interpreted in the manner that I have interpreted it in my English translation below. That is, Philip considers the two right triangles (each equal to a hemisphere) joined together so that their hypotenuses coincide, thus forming a rectangle. These joined triangles (or rectangle) are then conceived of as bent circumference-wise so that the base of the lower triangle, i.e., the base of the whole rectangle, coincides with the circumference of the great circle and the bent rectangle stands perpendicularly upon the plane of the great circle of the sphere. It is then evident that every point of the base of the upper triangle (or every point of the upper base of the rectangle) so bent is equidistant from the circumference of the great circle in as much as the base of the upper triangle (or the upper base of the rectangle) is parallel to the base of the lower triangle (or lower base of the rectangle). Now by bending the double triangle (or rectangle) circumference-wise on the circumference of a great circle and letting the bent rectangle be perpendicular to the plane of the great circle Philip has produced the lateral surface of a cylinder whose base circumference is the circumference of a great circle and whose axis is equal to the diameter of the sphere. And since the rectangle before bending had sides equal to c and d and hence the measure $c \cdot d$ equal to the surface area of a sphere, and since it is assumed that the rectangle will have the same measure whether bent or flat, it is evident that the surface area of the sphere is equal to the lateral surface of the cylinder produced by the bending of the rectangle. It is this conclusion that Philip has generalized in his corollary. Thus, with my interpretation, all parts of the enunciation and corollary hold together and we progress logically from the initial enunciation of the surface of a hemisphere to the lateral surface of a cylinder. The hidden assumption that I have posited for Philip's statement concerning the triangles erected on the circumference of a great circle, namely, that the measure of the rectangle bent circumference-wise is identical with its measure when flat, is reminiscent of the physical justification given by the author of the Corpus Christi Version of the *De mensura circuli* for the postulate that a curved line is equal to a straight line (Volume One, page 171): "For if a hair or a silk thread is bent around circumference-wise in a plane surface and then afterwards is extended in a straight line in the same plane, who will doubt—unless he is hare-brained—that the hair or thread is the same whether it is bent circumference-wise or extended in a straight line and is just as long the one time as the other."

Now I must return to the question of the similarity of Philip's enunciations with those of the *Liber de curvis superficiebus*. Though the similarity between Philip's corollary to Proposition 22 and the corollary to Proposition VI of the earlier work is more general than specific, it is certainly evident. The corollary in the earlier work read (*ibid.*, page 480);

"Ex hoc ergo manifestum . . . [quod] superficies spere est . . . equalis curve superficiei columpne cuius tam axis quam diameter basis equatur diametro spere." The terminological differences of the enunciation perhaps arise from the manner in which Philip has led up to the corollary from the initial enunciation about a hemispherical surface through the statement about the triangles (bent circumference-wise) on the circumference of a great circle.

Philip gives no proof for Proposition 22. He merely says that it is evident by a similar argument, no doubt meaning that its argument is like that of the proof of Proposition 21, that is, some form of the method of exhaustion. Assuming that Philip did not have access to the genuine *On the Sphere and Cylinder* of Archimedes but only to the *Liber de curvis superficiebus*, the presumption must be that his reference is to the form of exhaustion proof contained in the latter work, a method which Maurolico called "the easier way" (see below, Part III, Chapter 5, Section III and Text C, Commentary to Proposition X). In connection with his corollary to Proposition 22, Philip refers to his Proposition 18, whose text I have given below in my extract from the *Mathematica*. This cross reference can only be to Proposition 18 considered with its marginal additions. As first composed (without the marginal additions), this proposition represented Philip's effort to select and present the key propositions of Euclid's *Elements*, Proposition 18 of the ninth part being Proposition XII.9 of the *Elements* in the version of Campanus (the converse of Proposition XII.10 of the Greek *Elements*). It holds that a cylinder is triple a cone having the same base and altitude. Philip omits the Euclidian proof but notes its similarity with the proof of his Proposition 13 (=Proposition XII.2 of the *Elements*). Indeed the proof is similar, both employing a method of exhaustion that depends on the inscription of successively larger regular polygons within a circle.[7] In Proposition 18 the circle in question is the base circle of the cylinder and cone alike and the inscribed polygons are simultaneously the bases of prismatic columns and pyramids of the same altitude as the cylinder and cone.

Hence in its pristine form Philip's Proposition 18 was not a proper cross reference for his corollary to Proposition 22. But with the marginalia added, Proposition 18 became pertinent to that corollary. I have included the marginalia in my text below but have not included them in the translation. As added, the marginalia render this proposition false in so far as they make the proposition say that not only is a cylinder triple its cone but that a hemisphere (presumably one with base equal to the base of the cylinder and cone) is also triple that cone. In fact the first marginal reference should have been added in such a way that the proposition would hold that the cylinder is not only triple its cone but is also triple the hemisphere. This should be immediately evident to the reader: if the volume of the cylinder is $b \cdot h$ where $b = \frac{1}{2} c \cdot r$ and $h = 2r$, then the cylinder

---

[7] *Euclid the Elements*, tr. of T. L. Heath, Vol. 3 (Annapolis, Md., 1947), pp. 404–05.

is $c \cdot r^2$. But the sphere is $(2c/3) \cdot r^2 (= 4\pi r^3/3)$ and the hemisphere is $(c/3) \cdot r^2$. And so the cylinder is triple the hemisphere. It could be that in Philip's original draft this marginal reference was not clearly tied to the text and as a consequence the scribe inserted it incorrectly, perhaps after altering it from either "et semisspere sue," or less likely "et omni semisspere sue," to "et omnis semisspera." It should rather have been inserted after "sue" in line 2 so that the enunciation would read: "Omnis columpna rotunda piramidi sue et semisspere sue triplex esse probatur." The second marginal reference ("vel semisspere") presents a more difficult problem since there is no place for it in Philip's laconic remark that refers to the Euclidian proof of the pristine proposition not concerned with hemispheres. Needless to say, the vague reference to the exhaustion proof with its inscribed prismatic columns and pyramids would not apply at all to a proof establishing the asserted relationship between a cylinder and hemisphere. Hence there is no mathematical reason for its inclusion (whether by Philip or the scribe). One last point is worth making concerning the marginalia to Proposition 18. They constitute the only references to the volume of a sphere in the *Mathematica* and certainly there are no preliminary propositions leading up to the treatment of the sphere in Proposition 18. Hence the inclusion of the marginalia looks like a hasty and ill-conceived afterthought that came to Philip upon the completion of his Proposition 22.

Proposition 23 presents no problem. There can be no doubt that Philip took his enunciation from Proposition II of the *Liber de curvis super-ficiebus* (Volume One, page 460): "Cuiuslibet columpne rotunde curva superficies equalis est tetragono qui continetur sub lineis equalibus axi columpne et circumferentie basis." The only differences between this enunciation and Philip's are Philip's substitution of "cuiusque" for "cuiuslibet," his transposition of "curva superficies," his use of "equatur" instead of "equalis est" and his addition of "rectangulo" to "tetragono." It might be thought that it would have been better for Philip to have inserted this proposition in the text before Proposition 22 rather than after it since the lateral surface of a cylinder figures in the corollary to Proposition 22. However this criticism has no merit if I am right in my interpretation of the whole enunciation of Proposition 22, for there the surface of every sphere is seen to be transformable into an equivalent cylindrical lateral surface by the bending of the rec-tangle equal to the surface of the sphere on the circumference of the great circle. Proposition 23, on the other hand, concerns itself with the lateral surface of every right cylinder without reference to a sphere. Philip again offers no proof but remarks that it is evident *similiter*. The so-called "easier way" of the proof in the *Liber de curvis superficiebus* was no doubt in his mind.

As in the case of Proposition 23, Proposition 24 was drawn almost exactly from the enunciation of Proposition I of the *Liber de curvis super-ficiebus* (*ibid*., page 450): "Cuiuslibet rotunde piramidis curva super-ficies est equalis triangulo orthogonio, cuius unum laterum rectum angulum continentium equatur ypothenuse piramidis, reliquum circumferentie basis." In borrowing this enunciation Philip made only slight changes of the same kind as those made in Proposition 23, and I need not detail them again. Nor need I stress that once more Philip omits the proof but says that it is evident *similiter*, by which he presumably meant the proof of "the easier way" found in the *Liber de curvis superficiebus*.

I have to this point discussed all the Archimedean propositions of the *Mathematica*. But the reader will notice that I have included two further propositions in my extract below. The first of these, Proposition 25, I have included because of the part that it plays in many of the elaborated versions of the *De mensura circuli*. For example, it is similar to Propositions IIIA and IIIB in the Corpus Christi Version (*ibid*., page 174), to Proposition I of the Pseudo-Bradwardine Version (*ibid*., page 374), to Proposition I of the *Versio abbreviata* (*ibid*., page 390) and to Conclusion 5 of Albert of Saxony's *Questio de quadratura circuli* (*ibid*., page 414). Though no proof is given by Philip, he does cite Proposition 35 of the first part of his geometry (=Proposition I.38 of Euclid's *Elements*). Of the various versions of the *De mensura circuli* that include a proposition similar to Proposition 25 only the Pseudo-Bradwardine Version cites Euclid's Proposition I.38 in the course of the proof (*ibid*., page 376, line 48).

The second of the non-Archimedean propositions given below is Proposition 28. It comprises the first part of the *Quadratura per lunulas*, i.e., it asserts the equality of (1) the lune intercepted between a circumference on the diameter of a circle and the circumference on the side of a square inscribed in the first circle and (2) a quarter of that square. The source of this sound proposition could have been the *Quadratura per lunulas* that circulated in three versions (see below, Appendix II, Introduction) or possibly Proposition 26 of Chapter 6 of Johannes de Muris' *De arte mensurandi* (*ibid*., Text B). It is of some interest that Philip did not include the rest of the *Quadratura per lunulas*, which fallaciously argues for the quadrature of a circle on the basis of the supposed (but unproved) quadrature of a lune on the side of an inscribed hexagon.

In my text of the extracts from Philip's *Mathematica*, I have as usual capitalized the enunciations to suggest the fact that they appear in the manuscript in a larger hand than the proofs and comments. The marginal folio numbers refer to the Salamanca manuscript. In view of the rather complete discussion of the propositions here in this chapter, I have confined myself to giving footnotes to the English translation in which I identify Philip's citations.

An Extract from the *Mathematica* of Philippus Elephantis, Consideratio 3, Pars 9, Propositiones 18, 21–25, 28

[Mathematica Philippi Elephantis, Consideratio 3ª, Pars 9ª]

19v /18. OMNIS COLUMPNA ROTUNDA (*mg*. ET OMNIS SEMISSPERA) PIRAMIDI SUE TRIPLEX ESSE PROBATUR.

Hoc patet similiter sicut 13ª huius, quia omnis piramis laterata piramidis rotunde est pars tertia omnis columpne laterate columpne rotunde (*mg*.
5 vel semisspere). Et arguitur permutatim. . . .

21. OMNIS CIRCULUS EST EQUALIS TRIANGULO ORTOGONIO CUIUS UNUM LATUS AMBIENCIUM ANGULUM RECTUM EQUATUR CIRCUMFERENCIE ET ALIUD EQUATUR SEMI-DIAMETRO, OSTENDETURQUE EIUS CIRCUMFERENCIA ESSE
5 EQUALIS LINEE RECTE.

Hoc patet, quia alioquin ille triangulus erit equalis alicui figure poligonie inscripte circulo vel circumscripte. Sed ambitus omnis figure poligonie est maior circumferencia inscripti circuli; quapropter amplius continet. Et ambitus figure poligonie inscripte circulo est brevior circumferencia
10 quia eius latera sunt corde arcuum eiusdem; quapropter et minus continent.

Secundum patet, quia linea recta quadrans circulum est maior circum-ferencia circuli quanto perpendicularis sibi a centro circuli est minor semi-dyametro. (*mg*. et linea recta est equalis [circumferen]cie circuli, ita
15 scilicet quod est [media] proporcione inter ambitum [octogonii cir]-cumscripti circulo et [ambitum] octogonii circulo cir[cums]cripti, iuvante. . . .sexta eiusdem.) Quare necessario linea recta medie pro-porcionis inter lineam quadrantem circulum et semidyametrum est equalis circumferencie circuli, sicut docet ars 8ᵉ sexti huius qui perfecte intellegit.
20 Supponimus itaque quadratum circulo sibi equale et erigimus semi-dyametrum circuli ad circumferenciam per medium lateris quadrati distensum. Et hec figura dicitur "pax et concordia" [Fig. II.2.1].

20r /22. SIMILITER ARGUITUR QUOD MEDIETAS SUPERFICIEI SPERE EST EQUALIS TRIANGULO RECTANGULO QUI SUB LINEIS DUABUS EQUALIBUS HIIS QUARUM UNA EST CIRCUM-FERENCIA MAXIMI CIRCULI ET ALTERA QUARTA EIUSDEM
5 CIRCUMFERENCIE CONTINETUR. QUOD SI PRO QUARTA EIUSDEM CIRCUMFERENCIE PONATUR MEDIETAS CIRCULI, TUNC VEL FIENT DUO TRIANGULI EQUALES VEL FORTE, SI VOLUERIS, FIET QUADRILATERUM RECTANGULUM EQUALE SUPERFICIEI SPERE TOCIUS. OPORTET ITAQUE YMAGINARI
10 TRIANGULOS FUNDATOS IN CIRCULO MAXIMO TERMINARI IN

(*mg*. UNO PUNCTO EQUEDISTANTE CIRCULO ILLI. ET OMNIS SPERE AMBITUS EST EQUALIS AMBITUI COLUMPNE ROTUNDE CUIUS AXIS EQUATUR DYAMETRO SPERE ET DYAMETER DYAMETRO CIRCULI MAXIMI SPERE).

15   Hoc etiam patet similiter arguendo. Pro corollario nota 18 huius.

23. SIMILITER CUIUSQUE COLUMPNE ROTUNDE SUPER-FICIES CURVA EQUATUR TETRAGONO RECTANGULO QUI CONTINETUR SUB LINEIS EQUALIBUS AXI COLUMPNE ET CIRCUMFERENCIE BASIS.

5   Hoc satis patet similiter.

24. SIMILITER CUIUSQUE PIRAMIDIS ROTUNDE SUPERFICIES CURVA EQUATUR TRIANGULO ORTOGONIO CUIUS UNUM LATUS AMBIENCIUM ANGULUM RECTUM EQUATUR YPO-TENEUSE PIRAMIDIS ET RELIQUUM CIRCUMFERENCIE BASIS.

5   Hoc satis patet similiter.

25. OMNIS SUPERFICIES EQUILATERA INSCRIPTA CIRCULO VEL CIRCUMSCRIPTA EST EQUALIS TRIANGULO RECTAN-GULO CUIUS DUO LATERA AMBIENCIA ANGULUM RECTUM SUNT EQUALIA AMBITUI FIGURE ET LINEE PERPENDICULARI

5   A CENTRO CIRCULI DUCTE SUPER QUODCUMQUE LATUS FIGURE.

Hoc patet per 35 primi, quia super bases equalis distancie unus punctus, scilicet centrum, terminat triangulos omnes. . . .

28. SI SEMICIRCULO SUPER CORDAM QUE EST LATUS QUADRATI DESCRIBATUR SEMICIRCULUS BREVIOR, TUNC LUNULA CONTENTA INTER AMBAS CIRCUMFERENCIAS ERIT NECESSARIO EQUALIS TRIANGULO RECTILINEO CUIUS BASIS

5   EST CORDA PREDICTA ET VERTEX EST CENTRUM CIRCULI PRIMI.

Hoc patet sic. Sit, gracia exempli, corda predicta latus quadrati [Fig. II.2.2]. Tunc maior circulus est duplus breviori, quare (?) et (?) semicirculus semicirculo. Ergo dempta porcione circuli interioris erit

10   lunula equalis triangulo. Et arguitur per 13 et 12 precedentem.

[The *Mathematics* of Philip Elephant, Consideration 3, Part 9]

18. EVERY CYLINDER IS PROVED TO BE TRIPLE ITS CONE.

This is evident in the same way as [Proposition] 13 of this [part][1] be-

---

[1] Philip's Proposition IX.13 is Euclid's XII.2 (see Volume 1, p. 575, comment 5, 11). Philip's IX.18 (without the marginalia) is Campanus' XII.9 and is the converse of the Greek Euclid's XII.10. For a discussion of the relationship of the Euclidian proofs of these propositions, see the Introduction above note 7. Note further that I have not translated the marginalia here but have discussed them thoroughly in the Introduction.

cause every pyramid [whose regular polygonal base is inscribed in the base circle] of a cone is one third of every [corresponding prismatic] column [whose regular polygonal base is inscribed in the equal base circle] of a cylinder [the altitudes of all the figures being the same]. And it is argued permutatively. . . .

21. EVERY CIRCLE IS EQUAL TO A RIGHT TRIANGLE ONE OF WHOSE SIDES INCLUDING THE RIGHT ANGLE IS EQUAL TO THE CIRCUMFERENCE WHILE THE OTHER IS EQUAL TO THE RADIUS. AND ITS CIRCUMFERENCE WILL BE SHOWN TO BE EQUAL TO A STRAIGHT LINE.

This is evident, for otherwise that triangle will be equal to some polygonal figure inscribed in or circumscribed about the circle. But the perimeter of every polygonal figure is greater than the circumference of a circle inscribed in it; hence it contains more [space]. And the perimeter of every polygonal figure inscribed in a circle is less than the circumference because its sides are chords of the arcs of the same [circle]; and hence the sides [making up the perimeter] contain less [space].

The second [part] is evident because the straight line squaring the circle [i.e., the perimeter of the square equal to the circle] is greater than the circumference of the circle by the amount that the perpendicular drawn from the center of the circle to it [i.e., to the side of the square] is less than the radius.[2] Therefore, by necessity the straight line of the mean proportion [!, i.e., the straight line which is the intermediate term in the proportion] between the line squaring the circle and the radius is equal to the circumference of the circle, as the art of [Proposition] VI.8 of this [section][3] teaches [one] who understands it completely. And so we supposit a square equal to the circle and we erect a radius of the circle, extending it to the circumference through the middle of one side of the square. And this figure is called "peace and harmony" (see Fig. II.2.1).

22. IT IS SIMILARLY ARGUED THAT HALF OF THE SURFACE OF A SPHERE IS EQUAL TO A RIGHT TRIANGLE CONTAINED UNDER TWO LINES EQUAL TO THOSE OF WHICH ONE IS THE CIRCUMFERENCE OF THE LARGEST CIRCLE [IN THE SPHERE] AND THE OTHER IS A QUARTER (! THE DIAMETER?) OF THAT SAME CIRCUMFERENCE (! CIRCLE?). BUT IF A HALF (! DOUBLE THE DIAMETER?) OF THE CIRCLE IS SUBSTITUTED FOR THE QUARTER (! DIAMETER?) OF THAT SAME CIRCUMFERENCE (! CIRCLE?), THEN EITHER TWO EQUAL TRIANGLES ARISE, OR, IF YOU WISH, A RECTANGLE IS FORMED, EQUAL TO THE SURFACE OF THE WHOLE SPHERE. AND SO IT IS NECESSARY

---

[2] Again I have omitted translating the marginal comment but have discussed it in my introduction.

[3] Philip's Proposition VI.8 is Campanus' VI.9 and the Greek Euclid's VI.13. I have discussed Philip's apparent misuse of this porism in my Introduction.

TO IMAGINE THAT THE [TWO] TRIANGLES [JOINED SO THAT THEIR HYPOTENUSES COINCIDE AND PERPENDICULARLY] ERECTED [BY BENDING THEM CIRCUMFERENCE-WISE] ON THE GREATEST CIRCLE ARE TERMINATED [AT EACH POINT OF ALTITUDE] IN A POINT EQUIDISTANT TO THAT [GREATEST] CIRCLE. AND [CONSEQUENTLY] THE SURFACE OF EVERY SPHERE IS EQUAL TO THE SURFACE OF A CYLINDER WHOSE AXIS IS EQUAL TO THE DIAMETER OF THE SPHERE AND WHOSE [BASE] DIAMETER IS EQUAL TO THE DIAMETER OF THE GREATEST CIRCLE OF THE SPHERE.[4]

This is also evident by arguing in the same way. For the corollary, note the eighteenth [proposition] of this [part].[5]

23. SIMILARLY THE CURVED SURFACE OF ANY CYLINDER IS EQUAL TO THE RECTANGLE CONTAINED BY LINES EQUAL [RESPECTIVELY] TO THE AXIS OF THE CYLINDER AND THE CIRCUMFERENCE OF THE BASE.

This is evident enough in a similar way.

24. SIMILARLY THE CURVED SURFACE OF ANY CONE IS EQUAL TO A RIGHT TRIANGLE ONE OF WHOSE SIDES IN-CLUDING THE RIGHT ANGLE IS EQUAL TO THE HYPOTENUSE [I.E., SLANT HEIGHT] OF THE CONE WHILE THE OTHER IS EQUAL TO THE CIRCUMFERENCE OF THE BASE.

This is evident enough in a similar way.

25. EVERY EQUILATERAL SURFACE INSCRIBED IN OR CIRCUMSCRIBED ABOUT A CIRCLE IS EQUAL TO A RIGHT TRI-ANGLE WHOSE TWO SIDES INCLUDING THE RIGHT ANGLE ARE EQUAL [RESPECTIVELY] TO THE PERIMETER OF THE FIGURE AND TO THE LINE DRAWN PERPENDICULARLY FROM THE CENTER OF THE CIRCLE TO ANY SIDE OF THE FIGURE.

This is evident by [Proposition] I.35 [of this part],[6] because a single point, namely the center, terminates all the triangles on the bases at an equal distance.

28. IF ON A CHORD WHICH IS THE SIDE OF A SQUARE IN-SCRIBED IN A SEMICIRCLE THERE IS DESCRIBED A SMALLER SEMICIRCLE, THEN THE LUNE CONTAINED BETWEEN BOTH CIRCUMFERENCES [OF THE TWO SEMICIRCLES] WILL NECES-SARILY BE EQUAL TO THE RECTILINEAR TRIANGLE WHOSE

[4] I have discussed the difficulties of this enunciation in my Introduction, explaining the suggested corrections and additions.

[5] As I have explained in my Introduction, the cross reference to Philip's Proposition IX.18 is to the proposition with its marginalia added.

[6] Philip's Proposition I.35 is Euclid's I.38. See Volume 1, p. 221, comment 226.

BASE IS THE AFORESAID CHORD AND WHOSE VERTEX IS THE
CENTER OF THE FIRST CIRCLE.

This is evident as follows. For example, let the aforesaid chord be the
side of a square [see Fig. II.2.2]. Then the larger circle is double the
smaller circle; hence the [larger] semicircle [is double] the [smaller]
semicircle. Therefore, with the [common] segment of the interior circle
[and the exterior circle] removed, the lune will be equal to the triangle. And
this is argued by the thirteenth [proposition] and the twelfth before it.[7]

---

[7] Philip's Propositions IX.12 and IX.13 are respectively Euclid's XII.1 and XII.2. See
Volume 1, p. 511, comment 14; p. 575, comment 5, 11.

CHAPTER 3

The Handbook Tradition
of Archimedes

I. Archimedes and the Tradition of the *Agrimensores*

So far in these volumes I have not focused much attention on
medieval handbooks of practical geometry since they were primarily
transmitters of geometrical formulas expressed or implied, with sample
calculations, and did not (for the most part) include geometrical proofs.
Notable exceptions were Leonardo Fibonacci's *Practica geometrie* and
Johannes de Muris' *De arte mensurandi*. I often cited the first of these
works in Volume One, and have republished the Archimedean passages
here in Volume Three, Appendix I, Section 3[B]. The second work
has been studied in the first part of this volume.

It now becomes useful to mention at greater length the Archimedean
formulas that appear in the earlier handbooks since these earlier works
were often available to later students of geometry, who on occasion inserted comments that tied the handbook formulas to the Arabo-Latin
tradition of Archimedes represented primarily by the translations of
Gerard of Cremona of Archimedean tracts. Our account ought to begin
with the Archimedean formulas given in the section of the collection of
the *gromatici veteres* attributed to Epaphroditus and Vitruvius Rufus in
the celebrated Codex Arcerianus of Wolfenbüttel (a manuscript of the
sixth century written in Italy).[1] The problems given there illustrate the

---

[1] M. Cantor, *Die römischen Agrimensoren und ihre Stellung in der Geschichte der Feld-
messkunst* (Leipzig, 1875), pp. 213–14: "25. Sfera est, cuius diametrum ped. XIIII. quaero
huius sferae inauraturam. S. Q. semper diametrum duco bis, fit XXVIII. hoc multiplico in se.
fit DCCLXXXIIII. hoc duco XI, fit $\overline{VIII}$ DCXXIIII. sumptam partem XIIII. DCXG. tot ped.
erunt. 26. Si fuerit cyclus, cuius est diametrum ped. XIIII. quadrati huius cycly aream quaero.
S. Q. facio diametrum in se, fit CXCVI, et hoc duco XI.$\overline{II}$ CLVI. huius sumimus parte XIV, fit
CLIIII. tot ped. erunt huius cycli embadum, hoc est area. 27. Si fuerit circuitio ped. XLIIII,
diametrum ped. XIIII, quaero huius areae ped. S. Q. sumo circuitionem per partem dimidiam,
fit XXII, et diametrum per partem dimidiam, fit VII. hoc duco per XXII. fit CLIIII. tot erunt
huius areae ped. 28. Si fuerit emicyclus, cuius sit basis ped. XXVIII, curbatura ped. XIIII,
quaero huius emicicli area. S. Q. facio huius emicycli vasis per curbaturam, id est XXVIII
per XIIII, fit CCCXCII. hoc duco XI, fit $\overline{IIII}$ CCCXII. sumpta parte XIIII, fit CCCVIII. tot
ped. sunt huius emicycli area." (I have omitted the diagrams). For descriptions of the

199

following formulas for the area of a circle: $S = d^2 \cdot {}^{11}/_{14}$, $S = (d/2) \cdot (c/2)$, and $(S/2) = d \cdot r \cdot {}^{11}/_{14}$; and for the surface of a sphere: $S = 4 d^2 \cdot {}^{11}/_{14}$. (I give the formulas here and elsewhere in this chapter in a somewhat unconventional way in order to represent the step-by-step order followed by the authors in their determinations.) These same formulas and, in addition, one for the volume of a sphere, $V = d^3 \cdot {}^{11}/_{21}$, are found in Munich, Staatsbibl. 13084 (a manuscript of the ninth or tenth century) and I quote them in full from the edition of the Epaphroditus material of that manuscript by Mortet:[2]

[35] I seek the surface (*inauratam*) of a sphere whose diameter is 14 feet as follows: I multiply the diameter by 2, resulting in 28. This I multiply by itself, i.e. 28 by 28, and the result is 784. I multiply this by 11, and the result is 8624. With the fourteenth part of this taken, the result is 616. So many feet is the surface of this sphere.

[36] If there is a circle (*ciclus*) whose diameter is 14 feet, I seek the area of its square as follows: I multiply the diameter by itself, and the result is 196.

manuscript, Wolfenbüttel 2403, Aug. fol. 36, 23, see C. Thulin, "Die Handschriften des Corpus agrimensorum Romanorum," *Abhandlungen der Königlich Preussischen Akademie der Wissenschaften*, 1911, Philosophisch-historische Classe, Anhang II, pp. 10–39; N. Bubnov, ed., *Gerberti postea Silvestri II papae Opera mathematica* (Berlin, 1899), pp. 427–37; and E. A. Lowe, *Codici latini antiquiores*, Part IX (Oxford, 1959), p. 39.

² V. Mortet and P. Tannery, "Un nouveau texte des traités d'arpentage et de géométrie d'Epaphroditus et de Vitruvius Rufus," *Mémoires scientifiques de Paul Tannery*, Vol. 5 (Toulouse/Paris, 1922), pp. 70–74 (the whole text, pp. 29–78) reprinted from *Notices et extraits des manuscrits de la Bibliothèque Nationale et autres bibliothèques*, Vol. 35, 2ᵉ partie [1896], pp. 511–50): "[35] Spera est, cujus diametrum pedum XIIII fit, quęro hujus sperae inauratam [hoc est profunditatem sive spissitudinem]. Sequitur: duco diametrum bis, fit XXVIII; hoc multiplico in se, vicies octies XXVIII faciunt DCCLXXXIIII. Hoc duco per XI, fit V̄III DCXXIIII. Hujus summae sumpta parte XIIII, fiunt DCXVI. Tot pedum erit hujus sperae inaurata. [36] Si fuerit ciclus, cujus sit diametrum pedum XIIII, quadrati hujus aream quęro hoc modo: multiplico diametrum in se, fit CXCVI, et hoc duco undecies, fiunt ĪĪ CLVI; hujus summe sumo partem XIIIIᵃᵐ, fit CLIIII. Tot pedum erit hujus cicli embadum, hoc est area. Si fuerit circuitio pedum XLIIII, diametrum pedum XIIII, quęro hujus areae pedes per hunc modum: sumo circuitionis partem dimidiam, fit XXII, diametri partem dimidiam, quod est septem; hoc duco per XXII, fit CLIIII. Tot erunt hujus areae pedes. [37] Si fuerit emiciclus, cujus sit basis pedum XXVIII, curvatura pedum XIIII, quęro hujus emicicli aream. Sequitur: multiplico basem emicicli per curvaturam, id est XXVIII per XIIII, fit CCCXCII. Hoc duco per XI, fiunt ĪĪĪĪ CCCXII; sumpta parte quarta decima, fit CCCVIII. Tot pedum est hujus emicicli area. . . . [40] Si spera data fuerit, cujus diametrum sit pedum VII, ejus solidos pedes [quęro]. Sequitur: multiplico diametrum, id est VII, in cubo: primo in se, fit pedes XLVIIII: deinde hoc iterum per VII, fit pedes CCCXLIII. Hoc semper ducimus per XI, fit ĪĪĪ DCCLXXIII pedes; hujus sumemus partem XXI, fit pedes CLXXVIIII s. Tot erit □ pedum ejusdem inauratura. [41] Si datus fuerit circulus, cujus area habeat pedes sexcentos XVI, et scire volueris ejus diametrum, sic quęras: ducas quater decies areae pedum, fiunt pedes V̄III DCXXIIII; dehinc hanc summam partiaris per XI, fit undecima pars DCCLXXXIIII: hujus summę latus est XXVIII. Tot pedum erit diametrum." (I have omitted Mortet's and Tannery's editorial apparatus.) A less satisfactory version of this text is found in Munich, Staatsbibl. 14836, a manuscript of the eleventh century. See M. Curtze, "Die Handschrift No. 14836 der Königlich Hof- und Staatsbibliothek zu München," *Abhandlungen zur Geschichte der Mathematik*, 7. Heft (1895), pp. 115–18 for the Archimedean propositions (pp. 75–142 for the whole article).

This I multiply 11 times, resulting in 2156. I take a fourteenth part of this sum, and the result is 154. So many feet is the area of this circle. If there is a circumference of 44 feet and a diameter of 14 feet, I seek the area of this [circle] by this method: I take one-half part of the circumference, and the result is 22, [then] one-half part of the diameter, which is 7; I multiply the latter by 22, and the result is 154. So many will be the feet of this area.

[37] If there is a semicircle (*emiciclus*) whose base [i.e., diameter] is 28 feet and whose curvature [i.e., radius] is 14 feet, I seek the area of this semicircle as follows: I multiply the base of the semicircle by its curvature, i.e., 28 by 14, and the result is 392. I multiply this by 11, and the result is 4312. With a fourteenth part taken, the result is 308. So many feet is the area of this semicircle. . . .

[40] If a sphere with a diameter of 7 feet is given, I seek its solid feet [*solidos pedes*] as follows: I cube the diameter, i.e. 7, first by multiplying it by itself, resulting in 49 feet, and then again by 7, resulting in 343 feet. This number we always multiply by 11, and the result is 3773 feet. We take the twenty-first part, and the result is 179½ (! 179⅔) solid feet. So many feet will be the volume (*inauratura*) of this same sphere.

[41] If a circle is given whose area is 616 feet and you wish to know its diameter, seek [it] as follows: You multiply the area in feet by 14, resulting in 8624 feet. Then divide this sum by 11, and the eleventh part becomes 784. The root of this sum is 28. So many feet will be the diameter.

These formulas and their numerical examples are found on all sides in later treatises down into the Renaissance, as we shall see below. A passing word is called for concerning the curious terms *inaurata* and *inauratura*. They literally meant "gilded" and "gilding." But quite early *inauratura circuli* became the expression for the surface of a sphere, no doubt from the practice of covering a sphere with a golden surface.[3] Hence it seems properly applied to the surface of a sphere in section 35 but improperly implied to its volume in section 37. Later through the confusion of *inaurare* with *ornare*, we find that *inauratura circuli* has become *l'orneure du cercle* in a French *Pratike de géométrie* of the thirteenth century (see below, Section II, note 7). I should also point out that, though *circulus* is the word used for a circle in section 41, the word *ciclus* is so employed in section 36 and the word *emiciclus* for semicircle in section 37. Finally notice that in the case of a semicircle its diameter is called its *basis* and its radius its *curvatura*.

Though these extracts from Epaphroditus nowhere specifically include the formula $c = 3\frac{1}{7} \cdot d$, such a formula is assumed throughout: in the second part of section 36 where the circumference is designated as 44 and the diameter as 14, in sections 35, 36 and 37 where $4\,d^2$, d^2 and $r \cdot d$ are respectively multiplied by $^{11}/_{14}$, in section 40 where d^3 is multiplied by $^{11}/_{21}$, and in section 41 where the area of the circle is multiplied by $^{14}/_{11}$. The later tracts that are based on the collection of the *gromatici veteres* (such as the *Geometria incerti auctoris* and the *Epistola Adelboldi*) did include the formula $c = 3\frac{1}{7} \cdot d$, as we shall see below (notes 6 and 7). Hence Bubnov

---

[3] Mortet, "Une nouveau texte," pp. 70–72, n. [35]. Cf. Curtze, "Die Handschrift," pp. 141–42.

was convinced that the rule for finding the circumference from the diameter had been included in a fuller version of the Epaphroditus text now lost.[4]

Before leaving the text in Munich, Staatsbibl. 13084, I should consider three more passages that reveal in a somewhat corrupt manner formulas with further Archimedean implications, formulas that imply rules for the determination of the volumes of a truncated cone, a pair of such cones and a cylinder:[5]

[43] If there is an unequal column which is 13 feet wide at the bottom and 5 feet wide at the top and 30 feet high [and] if we wish to know how many solid feet it has, let us multiply its lower width by itself, i.e., 13 by 13, and the result is 169. Then let us multiply the upper width by itself, i.e. 5 by 5, and the result is 25. Then we multiply the upper width by the lower, for 5 times 13 becomes 65. Then we add the three products together and the result is 259. This we multiply by 11, and the result is 2849. Then we take one-fourteenth of this, and the result is 203½. Let us multiply this by 30, and the result is 6105. Let us take one eighth (! third?) of this sum and the result is 763 (! 2035?). So many cubic feet will be the solid feet of this column.

[46] If a cask (*cupa*), i.e., a *vuagina*, has for its diameter at the bottom 3 feet, at the top 2 feet and in the middle 5 feet, and is 12 feet high, [and] if you wish to know how many cubic feet (*amphoras*) it receives, you seek [it] as follows. Multiply the middle diameter by itself, and the result is 25. Then double that, and the result is 50. Then you multiply the [lower] diameter, i.e. 3, by itself, and the result is 9. Add this to 50, and the result is 59. Also multiply the third diameter, i.e., 2, by itself, and the result is 4. I add this to the above sum and the result is 63. Then I add together the lower and upper diameters and the result is 5. This I multiply by the middle diameter, i.e. 5, and the result is 25. This I add to the above sum and the result is 88.

[4] Bubnov, *Gerberti opera mathematica*, p. 356, n. 91.

[5] Mortet, "Une nouveau texte," pp. 75, 77–78: "[43] Si fuerit columna inaequalis, quae sit in imo lata pedum XIII, in summo lata pedum V, alta pedum XXX; si scire voluerimus quot pedes solidos haec habeat, multiplicemus latitudinem imam in se, hoc est: XIII fiunt CLXVIIII. Dehinc multiplicemus latitudin[e]m summam in se, hoc est: V fiunt XXV. Deinde ducamus summam per imam: quinquies enim XIII fiunt LXV. Post haec mittamus has tres summas in unum: fit CCLVIIII. Haec ducamus per XI: undecies CCLVIIII faciunt $\overline{\text{II}}$ DCCCXLVIIII. Hinc vero sumemus partem quartam decimam, quod sunt CCIII et semis, illudque ducemus per XXX: fiunt $\overline{\text{VI}}$ CV. Hujus summę sumamus octavam (!) partem: fiunt DCCLXIII (!); et tot pedes erunt solidi hujus columnę. . . . [46] Si cupa, id est vuagina, in imo per diametrum habet pedum III, in summo pedes II, in medio pedes V, alta pedum XII, si vis scire quot amphoras capiat, sic quęras: multiplica diametrum medium in se, hoc est V, fiunt XXV; id duplices, fiunt L. Post hęc, multiplices diametrum secundum in se, hoc est tres, fiunt VIIII, hoc est junge ad L; fiunt simul LVIIII. Item multiplica diametrum tertium in se, quod sunt II, fiunt IIII; jungo cum summa superiore, fiunt simul LXIII. Dehinc jungo in unum diametrum imum ac summum, fiunt V. Hoc multiplico per diametrum medium, hoc est V, fiunt XXV. Hoc jungo ad summam superiorem, fiunt in unum LXXXVIII. Illud duco per XI, fit DCCCCLXVIII. Hunc numerum divido per tertiam altitudinem, hoc est per diametrum tertium, quod est IIII, fiunt CCXLII. Tot erunt amphorae in cupa predicta. [47] Si fuerit puteus cujus diametrum sit pedum VII, altitudo pedum XL, et quęratur quot amphoras capiat. Sequitur: primum aream pedum inveniamus, cujus diametrum est pedum VII, hoc modo: ducas VII per se, fiunt XLVIIII. Hoc ducas per XI, fiunt DXXXVIIII. Hinc recide XVIII, remanent DXX. Hujus summę tolle XIII^{um} partem, quod est XL; hoc duc per altitudinem, fiunt mille sexcenti. Tot amphoras capiet predictus puteus." (Again I have omitted the editorial apparatus.)

I multiply that by 11, and the result is 968. I divide this number [by 28 and the result is 34½. I multiply this] by one third of the altitude, i.e. by the third diameter (! i.e., by the third of 12), which is 4, and the result is 242 (! 138?). So many feet will be the cubic feet in the cask.

[47] If there is a well whose diameter is 7 feet and whose depth is 40 feet, it is sought how many cubic feet it receives as follows: First let us find the area in feet [of the base] whose diameter is 7 in this way. You multiply 7 by itself, and the result is 49. You multiply this by 11 and the result is 539. Take away 19 and 520 remains (! *delete this?*). Of this sum take a thirteenth (! fourteenth?) part, which is 40 (! 38?). Multiply this by the depth, and the result is 1600 (! 1520?). So many cubic feet will the aforesaid well receive.

It is evident that the formula for a truncated cone in section 43 is slightly corrupt as given: $V = (d_1^2 + d_2^2 + d_1 \cdot d_2) \cdot \frac{11}{14} \cdot (h/8)$. Obviously the last multiplier should be $(h/3)$ rather than $(h/8)$. And indeed the correct formula was given in Book IV of the *Geometria incerti auctoris* that was also compiled from the *gromatici veteres* (see below, note 6). A similar corruption vitiates the text of section 46, where the problem involving two truncated cones with a common base is solved by this formula:

$$V = [2d_2^2 + d_1^2 + d_3^2 + d_2(d_1 + d_3)] \cdot 11 \cdot (3/h)$$

As I have suggested in my translation, in order for the formula to be correct the multipliers "11" and "(3/h)" should rather be "$\frac{11}{28}$" and "(h/3)." The same problem is given in Book IV of the *Geometria incerti auctoris* but in an even more corrupt fashion (see below, note 6). Finally, we should note the corrupt formula for the volume of a cylindrical well in section 47. As indicated in my translation, the original formula was, no doubt, $S = d^2 \cdot \frac{11}{14} \cdot h$. The formulas most conspicuous by their absence from this collection were those for the lateral surfaces of a cone and a cylinder and for the volume of the simple cone.

Let us turn to Book IV of the *Geometria incerti auctoris*. Bubnov believed it to have been compiled in the tenth century from a more complete codex of the *gromatici veteres*, his so-called *Codex vetustissimus* that appears to be lost.[6] For circumference and diameter problems

[6] Bubnov, *Gerberti opera mathematica*, pp. 346–47, 356–61: "18. Cujuscunque rotundi vel circuli si vis diametrum invenire et embadum, sic quaeras. Ex ipso ambitu XXII unitate ablata, reliqui, qui superfuerit, sumas tertiam, quae fiet diametrum. Embadum si vis invenire, vel tota circuitio per integrum diametrum ducenda est, et tunc quarta sumenda; vel dimidium circuitus per diametrum integrum et tunc medietas; vel quarta pars circuitus per diametrum et tunc totum. Quod idem esset, si per dimidium circuitus diametri duceretur dimidium. 19. In hemicyclo, cujus basis sit pedum XXVIII, diametrum XIIII, aream sic quaeras. Per diametrum ducas basim, fient pedes CCCXCII. His undecies ductis, fiunt pedes IIII CCCXII. Hujus sumpta decima quarta parte, fient CCCVIII; et tot pedum est hujus hemicycli area. 20. Sphaerae, cujus est pedum longitudo IIII, latitudo III, sic colligatur area. Longitudine et latitudine simul junctis, fient VII; dimidium horum III semis. Hi in se XII et quadrans. Hi undecies fient CXXXIIII dodrans. Horum sumpta parte decima quarta, fiunt pedes VIIII, unciae VII et semis unciae, id est septunx et semuncia. Sphaerae igitur haec erit area. Regula autem haec vera est in omni sphaera sive rotunda, sive oblonga. . . . 40. In circulo, cujus diametrum sit pedum XIV, embadum sic quaeras.

we find the following formulas: (cap. 18) $d = \dfrac{1}{3}\left(c - \dfrac{c}{22}\right)$, i.e., $d = (21c/22)/3$

$= 7c/22$; (cap. 40) $c = 22d/7$; and (cap. 43) $d = \sqrt{\dfrac{S \cdot 14}{11}}$. For the area of

the circle: (cap. 18), $S = c \cdot d \cdot \frac{1}{4}$, or $S = (c/2) \cdot d \cdot \frac{1}{2}$, or $S = (c/4) \cdot d$, or $S = (c/2) \cdot (d/2)$; (cap. 40) $S = d^2 \cdot {}^{11}\!/_{14}$; (cap. 19) $(S/2) = d \cdot r \cdot {}^{11}\!/_{14}$; (cap 42) $(S/2) = d^2 \cdot {}^{11}\!/_{28}$. For the surface of a sphere: (cap. 52) $S = d^2 \cdot {}^{22}\!/_{7}$. For the volume of a sphere: (cap. 47) $V = d^3 \cdot {}^{11}\!/_{21}$. For the surface of a *sphera*

Diametrum in se, fiunt CXCVI. Duc undecies, fiunt $\overline{\text{II}}$ CLVI, sume partem decimam quartam, fit CLIV; et tot pedum erit embadum. 41. Ex diametro circulum sic quaeras. Diametrum, exempli gratia XIV, ducas vigesies bis, fient CCCVIII; sumas partem septimam, fit XLIV, quod est circulus. 42. In hemicyclo, cujus sit basis pedum X, linea in centrum V, embadum sic quaeras. Duc in se diametrum, fit C. Hoc undecies multiplica, fit $\overline{\text{I}}$C. Hujus vigesimam octavam sume, erit in pedibus XXXIX et duabus septimis; et haec est area. Quod idem esset, si basim per lineam, quae ducitur in centrum, multiplicatam undecies duceres ac exinde decimam quartam acciperes. Quod verum est in omni integre dimidiata sphaera. 43. In circulo, cujus sit area pedum DCXVI, diametrum sic quaeras. Quaterdecies ducatur, fient area $\overline{\text{VIII}}$ DCXXIV. Hinc pars undecima fit DCCLXXXIV. Hujus numeri latus fit XXVIII; et hoc erit diametrum. . . . 47. Circulum incrassare si vis, diametrum ejus cubices, ipsam cubicationem ejus undecies ducas et ex ea summa vigesimam primam accipias, et haec erit sphaerae crassitudo. . . . 49. Puteus, cujus sit diametrum VII, altitudo XL pedum, tot amphoras capiet, quot processerint pedes ex hujusmodi diametri area altitudineque in invicem multiplicata, si pede uno longa [et lata] et alta fuerit amphora. 50. Cuppa, cujus latitudo ima pedum sit III, summa II, media V, altitudo vero XII, quot pedum sit solidorum ac per hoc quot amphoras capiat, sic quaeras. Latitudine media in se ducta, ac summa ab inde excreta triplicata, diametrisque summo et imo in se singulatim ductis, omne in unum, fit LXXXVIII. His undecies ductis, ac summae exinde natae quarta decima sumpta, fiunt LXIX et duae quartae decimae, id est una septima. His per tertiam altitudinis, id est per quaternarium, multiplicatis, venit numerus amphorarum CCLXXVI et VIII quartae decimae, id est IV septimae. Si fuerit cuppa, cujus ima latitudo sit pedum V, summa III, altitudo IX, quot amphoras capiat, sic quaeras. Ima in se fit XXV, summa quoque in se fit IX, utrisque in invicem fiunt XV. His tribus summis simul junctis fiunt XLIX. His undecies ductis, fiunt DXXXIX. Horum pars decima quarta fit XXXVIII semis. Haec per altitudinis tertiam ducta fiunt CXV semis. Tot erunt amphorae vel pedes solidi. His tribus regulis, de puteo scilicet et de duabus cuppis, diligenter inspectis, pene nullus erit puteus, vel cuppa, vel tonna aliqua, quin ejus possit indagari profunditas, nisi mira in eis fuerit diversitas. . . . 52. Circuli inauraturam sic quaeras. Diametrum circuli in se ductum vigesies bis multiplica. Effectae summae septimam accipias, et haec circuli erit inauratura; quod idem esset, si per diametrum circulum multiplicares. 53. Si fuerit columna inaequalis, cujus ima latitudo pedum sit XIII, summa V, altitudo XXX, ejus pedes sic quaeras. Ima latitudine in se multiplicata, ac summa in se, ac utraque invicem, hisque tribus summis simul compositis, fiunt pedes CCLIX. His undecies ductis, ac exinde effectae summae quarta decima detracta, venient CCIII semis, scilicet arearum summae et mediae ac infimae. His deinde per tertiam altitudinis multiplicatis, erunt solidi pedes $\overline{\text{II}}$ XXXV. . . . 56. Si datus fuerit puteus, cujus diametrum sit pedum V, et circa eum fuerit structura alta pedum XX, lata pedum II, ejus structurae pedes sic quaeras. Structurae latitudinem ducas in se, fient IV. His adjicias putei diametrum, erunt IX. Hi in se fient LXXXI. Ab his diametro putei in se dempto, remanent LVI. His undecies ductis et a summa, quae inde excreverit, quarta decima sumpta, erunt pedes areae XLIV. Hi per altitudinem, id est vigesies, ducti fiunt DCCCLXXX; tot erunt pedes structurae." (Here and in the succeeding note Bubnov's editorial apparatus has been omitted.) Bubnov (pp. 368–69) gives a chart showing the relationships of the various treatises in the gromatic tradition with a supposed *Codex vetustissimus*.

oblonga: (cap. 20), the erroneous formula $S = \left(\dfrac{d_1 + d_2}{2}\right)^2 \cdot {}^{11}/_{14}$. For the volume of a cylinder: (cap. 49) $V = (area\ of\ circle)\cdot h$. For the volume of a truncated cone: (caps. 50 and 53): $V = (d_1{}^2 + d_2{}^2 + d_1 \cdot d_2) \cdot {}^{11}/_{14} \cdot (h/3)$. Also derivative from the *gromatici veteres* are the formulas of the *Epistola Adelboldi ad Sylvestrum II papam*, written about 1000.[7] For the circle: $c = d \cdot 3^{1}/_7$ and $S = (d/2) \cdot (c/2)$; and for the sphere: $V = d^3 - (10d^3/21) = 11d^3/21$; and for the cylinder: $V = (area\ of\ circle)\cdot h$. Finally we should note that Book II of the so-called *Boethii quae dicitur geometria altera*, composed in Lorraine in the first half of the eleventh century, contained some Archimedean formulas drawn from the *gromatici veteres*[8] including: for a circle $(c/d) = {}^{44}/_{14}$, $S = d^2 \cdot {}^{11}/_{14}$ and $S = (c/2 \cdot d/2)$, $(S/2) = d \cdot r \cdot {}^{11}/_{14}$.

The foregoing material, if not a complete survey of the early medieval

---

[7] *Ibid.*, pp. 304–06: "3. Diametrum VII pedum mihi facio; ex hoc circulum sic quaero: triplico illud et ejus septimam triplicationi illi superaddo, et sic circulum in XXII pedes habeo. Medietate autem diametri, quod est III et semis, et medietate circuli, quod est XI, invicem multiplicatis, venit mihi area ejusdem circuli in XXXVIII pedes et semissem. Ecce diametrum, ecce circulum, ecce aream habeo. Sed ut crassitudinem inveniam, diametrum idem cubico, et cubum mihi ejusmodi facio, qui globositatem sphaerae lateribus contingat, angulis autem et lineis ab angulo in angulum procedentibus excedat. Ab hujusmodi cubo crassitudinem illam, quae a globositate usque ad angulos et lineas procedit, necesse est recidere, ut hac recisa solius sphaerae soliditas remaneat. Hanc recisionem hoc modo facio: summam totius cubi per vigesimas primas divido; ex his vigesimis primis decem excessionibus cubi deputo, undecim reliquas crassitudini sphaerae relinquo. Quod idem esset, si totius cubi summam XIes ducerem et ex illa concretione unam XXI subducerem. Haec enim una vigesima prima tanta esset, quantae illae XI, quae ex simplici cubo tollebantur. Ut lucidius fiat, quod dicimus, certis numeris crassitudines duas assignabimus, ut assignatas invicem comparare possimus, non ut haec aut veriora vos ignorare credamus, sed ut viis nostris vestrae diligentiae monstratis a vobis ducti deinceps errare nesciamus. 4. Circuli, cujus diametrum est VII pedum, crassitudinem sic quaero; cubico diametrum et dico: septies septem fiunt XLVIIII. Rursus septies XLVIIII fiunt CCCXLIII. Ecce cubus ejus quadrati, cujus unumquodque latus VII sit pedum, et hic cubus globositatem sphaerae ex toto concludit. Ut autem superexcedentia recidantur, sic facio: tollo vigesimam primam ex CCCXLIII, quae est XVI triens. Hanc si decies duco, habeo CLXIII triens, excessiones scilicet cubi. Si undecies, habeo CLXXVIIII bisse, sphaerae videlicet crassitudinem."

[8] M. Folkerts, ed., *"Boethius" Geometrie II* (Wiesbaden, 1970), pp. 166–67: "XXXII Sed quia de angularibus figuris studioso lectori sufficienter disputavimus, restat, ut breviter de circumductione sperae vel circuli explicemus. 2 Ponatur itaque circulus XLIIII pedibus in circumductione designatus. Diametrus autem XIIII pedum protensionibus describatur. 3 Cuius summa si per se excreverit, CXCVI nascentur. Hos per XI multiplicans ĪĪCL[X]VI efficies. Quorum XIIII. pars, id est CLIIII, aream huius cicli pandit, ut infra potest cerni. XXXIII Est et alia huius cicli inveniendi embadalis spatii ratio: 2 Sumatur etenim circumductivae quantitatis medietas, id est XXII, quae XLIIII est medietas, et per medietatem diametri, id est per VII, multiplicetur; et quod ex hac multiplicatione provenerit, embadum pandit. XXXIV His vero brevibus datis initiamentis de circularibus theorematibus dicendum esse censuimus de emiciclo protinus dicturi. 2 Conscribatur age emiciclus XXVIII in basi et in semidiametro XIIII pedes habens. 3 Cuius si areae podismus ignoretur, tali ratione adinvestigetur: 4 Multiplicetur ergo summa basis per semidiametri summam, et in CCCXCII pervenitur. Haec summa undecies aucta ĪĪĪĪCC[C]XI[I] producit. Quorum sumpta XIIII. parte, id est CCCVIII, arealis completur superficies, ut propter apparet." (Again I have omitted the editorial apparatus.)

sources of Archimedean formulas, does constitute a substantial representation of such formulas as were found in geometrical works before the translation of Archimedean tracts from the Arabic in the twelfth century. The most interesting point for our investigation concerning the formulas of the gromatic tradition is that they were not attributed to Archimedes. Indeed this lack of attribution of formulas (together with a complete detachment from demonstration) is rather characteristic of a great many practical manuals, even of those actually influenced by the new Archimedean tracts, as we shall see.

II. Archimedes in the Medieval Handbooks of Geometry in the Twelfth and Thirteenth Centuries

Geometrical handbooks from the twelfth through the early fifteenth century were influenced by at least three main traditions so far as their Archimedean content was concerned: (1) the gromatic tradition of the Roman *agrimensores* outlined in Section I; (2) an Arabic gromatic tradition not unlike that of the Roman tradition; and (3) the Archimedean tracts translated from the Arabic and the Greek, i.e., the *De mensura circuli* of Archimedes and the *Verba filiorum* of the Banū Mūsā translated by Gerard of Cremona from the Arabic in the twelfth century, the *Liber de curvis superficiebus* translated from or constructed on the basis of some Greek text in the late twelfth or early thirteenth century, and, less significantly, the rather complete translation of the works of Archimedes by William of Moerbeke from the Greek in 1269. The content of (1) has been described in Section I of this chapter, that of (3) in Volumes One and Two. A word is now in order concerning the content of (2).

The Arabic gromatic tradition is principally represented by two works translated into Latin in the twelfth century. The first of these is the *Liber embadorum* of Abraham bar Hiyya (Savasorda) written in Hebrew (but reflecting Arabic sources)[1] and translated into Latin by Plato of Tivoli in 1145. I have included the pertinent Archimedean passages below in Appendix I, Section 3[A]. Savasorda's work contains most of the same Archimedean formulas found in the collection of the Roman *gromatici veteres* and in the early medieval works based on that collection. For the circumferences of a circle: $c = d \cdot 3\frac{1}{7}$ (with the numerical example of a diameter of 14 and a circumference of 44). For the area of a circle: $S = (d/2) \cdot (c/2)$ and $S = d^2 - (\frac{1}{7} + \frac{1}{14}) \cdot d^2$, again exemplified by a circle with a diameter of 14. For the diameter of a circle when its area is known: $d = \sqrt{S + \frac{3}{11} \cdot S}$. For the diameter of a circle of which a segment is taken

---

[1] H. L. L. Busard, "L'Algèbre au moyen âge: Le 'Liber mensurationum' d'Abû Bekr," *Journal des savants* (Avril-Juin, 1968), pp. 67–69 (the whole article, pp. 65–124).

and you know the chord and the *sagitta*, i.e., the perpendicular from the middle of the chord to the arc of the segment:

$$d = \left[\left(\frac{chord}{2}\right)^2 \middle/ sagitta\right] + sagitta.$$

For the area of such a segment: $S = r \cdot (arc/2) - \frac{1}{2}\ chord \cdot (r - sagitta)$. For a so-called oblique circle (an ellipse?) the erroneous formula:

$$S = \left(\frac{d_1 + d_2}{2}\right)^2 \cdot \text{}^{11}/_{14} \text{ (see Appendix I, Section 3[A], n. 3)}.$$

For a cylinder (*rotunda columpna*): $V = (base\ circle) \cdot h$. For a cone (i.e., a *pyramis* with a *basis columpnaris*): $V = (base\ circle) \cdot (h/3)$, and for a truncated cone: $V = (d_1{}^2 + d_2{}^2 + d_1 \cdot d_2) \cdot (1 - \frac{1}{7} - \frac{1}{14}) \cdot (h/3)$. For a sphere: $S = d^2 \cdot 3\frac{1}{7}$ and $V = S \cdot (d/6)$, a numerical example with a diameter of 7 being given. For the segment of a sphere: $S = d \cdot h \cdot 3\frac{1}{7}$ and $V = S \cdot (d/6)$; the latter is incorrect, being the formula for a spherical sector rather than for a segment.

The second work to consider in the Arabic gromatic tradition is the *Liber mensurationum* of an unknown Abū Bakr, which has the full title in the Latin translation of Gerard of Cremona: *Liber in quo terrarum et corporum continentur mensurationes Ababuchri qui dicebatur Heus*.[2] Abū Bakr's

---

[2] *Ibid.*, pp. 67–68. For the Archimedean formulas see pp. 118–24: "Capitulum mensuracionis circuli. ⟨144.⟩ Verbi gracia: sit circulus cuius diametrus sit xiiii, quanta est ergo eius area? Regula autem sciendi eius aream est, ut multiplices diametrum in se et erit centum et 96, minue ergo septimam et septime eius medietatem et quod remanet, est eius area quod est centum et 54. Quod si vis, multiplica diametrum in tria et septimam et quod proveniet, erit 44 et hec est eius circulacio. Aream autem si vis, multiplica medietatem diametri in medietatem circulacionis et quod proveniet, erit area. ⟨145.⟩ Quod si tibi dixerit: area est centum et 54, quanta est diametrus? Erit eius investigacio, ut supra centum et 54 adiungas tres partes eius undecimas et quod proveniet, erit centum et 96, eius ergo assume radicem et erit diametrus. (p. 119) Modus vero inveniendi ipsum secundum aliabram est, ut ponas diametrum rem. Ipsam ergo in se multiplica et erit census, ex quo septimam eius et ipsius septime diminue medietatem et remanebunt 5 septime census et medietas septime census que equantur centum et 54, reintegra igitur censum tuum donec fit census quod erit per id quod est quantum sunt tres eius undecime partes. Adiunge ergo supra centum et 54 tres eius undecimas partes et erit census qui equatur centum et 96. Res igitur equatur 14 et ipsa est diametrus. Intellige et hec est eius forma. Capitulum mensuracionis semicirculi. ⟨146.⟩ Exempli causa: sit semicirculus cuius corda sit xiiii et eius sagitta sit septem, quanta est ergo eius area? Erit modus inveniendi eam, ut multiplices cordam eius qui est xiiii in se et quod proveniet, erit centum et 96, eius igitur septimam et medietatem septime minue et remanebunt centum et 54, quorum assume medietatem et erit area que est 77. Et similiter fac in omni semicirculo, multiplica scilicet cordam que est diametrus in se et minue septimam eius quod aggregatur et septime medietatem et residui assume medietatem et erit area et hec est eius forma. Capitulum mensuracionis ⟨porcionis⟩ semi-circulo maioris. ⟨147⟩. Verbi gracia: sit porcio maior semicirculo, cuius corda est sex et eius sagitta est novem et eius arcus est xx. Ad eius tamen arcus noticiam non pervenitur ex parte corde, licet iam sit perventum ad arcum. Regula vero sciendi illud est, ut scias ex quo circulo fit secta. Cum ergo illud volueris, multiplicabis medietatem corde in se et

formulas are almost exactly the same as those of Savasorda, except that the former specifies $S = [d^2 - (\frac{1}{7} + \frac{1}{14})d^2] \cdot 4$ for the surface of a sphere and adds an alternative formula for the volume of a sphere: $V = d^2 \cdot \frac{11}{14} \cdot \frac{2}{3} \cdot d$ and omits the formulas for the volume of a truncated cone and the volume of a segment of a sphere.

We are now in the position to examine a selected set of medieval geometrical manuals that repeat the various Archimedean formulas. Among the earliest general tracts that touch on geometry in the twelfth century is the compendium *Liber ysagogorum Alchorismi*, composed by a certain "Magister A," perhaps identical with Adelard of Bath. Geometry is mentioned only briefly in the fourth book "De musicis ac geometricis rationibus."[3] The principal influence on the geometrical section is clearly

erit novem. Ipsum ergo per sagittam divide et proveniet tibi unum. Deinde illud sagitte adde et erit decem et ipse est diametrus circuli ex quo ipsa fuit secta. Post hoc decem sume medietatem qui est 5 et ipsam in medietatem arcus que est decem multiplica et erit 50. Deinde scias (p. 120) quantum sagitta addit supra medietatem diametri et illud erit 4. Ipsum ergo in medietatem corde multiplica que est tria et erit xii. Illud itaque ad 50 iunge et erit sexaginta duo et ipsum est area. Intellige et hec est eius forma. Capitulum porcionis que est minor semicirculo. ⟨148.⟩ Verbi gracia: sit porcio cuius sagitta sit duo et eius corda sit 8 et sit arcus eius decem, quanta est ergo eius area? Regula vero sciendi eius aream est, ut scias ex quo circulo fuit secta. Cum ergo vis illud, multiplica medietatem corde in se et erit sedecim quam per sagittam divide et proveniet tibi octo. Ei ergo adiungas duo et erit decem qui est diametrus circuli ex quo secta fuit. Cuius assume medietatem que est quinque et multiplica ipsam in medietatem arcus et erit 25. Ipsum ergo serva, deinde scias quid est illud quod est inter medietatem diametri circuli, que est quinque, et sagittam. Illud autem est tria, ipsum ergo multiplica in medietatem corde et erit xii, quem si ex xxv minueris, remanebit tredecim et illud est area eius et hec est eius forma. . . . (p. 123). . . . Capitulum aree columpne. Et ipsa quidem est corpus in qua sunt duo circuli qui sunt duarum equalium extremitatum et grossitiei. (p. 124) ⟨156.⟩ Verbi gracia: est corpus cuius basis est circulus cuius diametrus est xiiii et eius superior extremitas similiter et eius altitudo que est secundum medium est 24. Regula vero sciendi aream eius est, ut multiplices diametrum in se et minuas septimam eius quod aggregatur et medietatem septime et quod remanet, in eius altitudinem multiplica et erit area et illud est tria milia et sexcenta et 96. Et hec est eius forma. Area corporee piramidis que est similis cumulo tritici. ⟨157.⟩ Verbi gracia: est piramis cuius basis est circulus, cuius diametrus est xiiii et perpendicularis est sex. Regula vero sciendi aream eius est, ut mensures circulum secundum quod ostendi tibi in mensuracione circuli et quod aggregatur, multiplices in terciam altitudinis et erit area. Et hec est eius forma. Capitulum mensuracionis spere. ⟨158.⟩ Verbi gracia: est spera cuius diametrus est quattuordecim, quanta est area superficiei eius? Regula vero sciendi ⟨illud⟩ est, ut multiplices diametrum in se et minuas septimam eius quod aggregatur et medietatem septime et quod remanet, multiplica semper in 4 [et erit area superficiei eius, et quod] aggregatur, multiplica in sextam diametri et erit area superficiei [*! del.*, mensura magnitudinis] eius. Iam autem predixi tibi in mensuracione spere, ut multiplices aream superficiei eius in sextam diametri ipsius, sed si vis, multiplica diametrum in se et minue septimam eius, quod aggregatur, et medietatem septime et quod remanet, in duas tercias diametri eius multiplica et erit mensura magnitudinis eius. Et hec est eius forma. Expletus est liber totus mensuracionis." I have omitted the editorial apparatus and figures. Though, as I have said, Abū Bakr did not include the formula for the volume of a truncated cone, he did include the similar formula for a truncated pyramid (Prop. 152), which I have here omitted.

[3] The first three books of this short work were published by M. Curtze, "Über eine Algorismus-Schrift des XII. Jahrhunderts," *Abhandlungen zur Geschichte der Mathematik*, 8. Heft (1898), pp. 3–27. The geometrical part in Book IV is described by Curtze, pp.

that of the Roman gromatic tradition and the gromatic formulas for a circle are given:

$$c = d \cdot 3^1/_7 \text{ or } c = d \cdot {}^{22}/_7; \ d = \frac{c - (c/22)}{3} \text{ or } d = c \cdot {}^7/_{22}.$$

But the author briefly reflects the Arabic tradition when he speaks of the formula

$$d = \sqrt{\frac{c^2}{10}} \text{ (which implies the value } \pi = \sqrt{10}).$$

This last approximation was often cited later and attributed to the Arabs or the Indians (see below, footnote 15 and Part III, Chap. 2, Sect. II, note 40). Finally, the *Liber ysagogorum* gives the gromatic formula for the volume of a sphere $V = d^3 \cdot {}^{11}/_{21}$. Perhaps the earliest of the formal geometrical handbooks of the twelfth century is the *Practica geometrie* of Hugh of St. Victor. But it is not very pertinent to our study of the Archimedean formulas, since it contains only one such formula, namely $c = 3^1/_7 \cdot d$, which the author has drawn from Macrobius.[4] Our account should rather begin with an anonymous *Practica geometrie*, with the incipit: "Artis cuiuslibet consummatio. . . ." It is from the late twelfth century (1193) and contains the conventional formulas for the ratio of the circumference to the diameter, the area of a circle, the surface and volume of a sphere, the volumes of a cylinder and a cone, and an incorrect but very old formula for the volume of a truncated cone.[5]

14–16, and there related to the tradition of the *gromatici veteres*. However, he does not give the text of this short book and so I here give the appropriate passage with the Archimedean formulas (Munich, Staatsbibl. 13021, 30r): "Omne diametrum ter ductum cum septime partis adiectione ambitum fere circinat, vel 20 (! 22) ductum et 7 divisum; et econverso omnis orbita sublata 22[a], [et eius] tertium pene pro diametro ponit, vel 7 ducta et 22 divisa. Latus autem decime multiplicationis ambitus in se eius diametrum verius indicat. Ad spericam vero quantitatem inveniendam diametrum eius cubicetur; oportet, ipsamque cubicationem 11[ies] ducas et eius 21[a] globositatem spere demonstrat." The same text exists in MS Paris, BN lat. 16208, 67r–71r (with a corrupt form of the above cited passage on 70r). Cf. *Mémoires scientifiques de Paul Tannery*, Vol. 5, pp. 343–45, and C. H. Haskins, *Studies in Mediaeval Science*, 2nd. ed. (Cambridge, Mass., 1927), p. 24.

[4] *Hugonis de Sancto Victore opera propaedeutica: Practica geometriae, De grammatica, Epitome Dindimi in philosophiam*, ed. of R. Baron (Notre Dame, Ind., 1966), p. 51: "Omne diametrum triplicatum et addita septima parte circulum facit. Igitur de omni circulo ablata XXII[a] parte et eius quod remanet sumpta tertia, quantitas diametri est." Cf. Macrobius, *In somnium Scipionis*, I, 20, ed. of J. Willis (Leipzig, 1963), p. 81.

[5] *Practica geometrie*, MS Dublin, Trinity College Libr. 403, 195r–97v (*sigl. D*). Cf. MS London, BM Harl. 1, 41v–42v (*sigl. H*). The latter manuscript is earlier but is considerably confused in its readings. Hence I have followed *D* with only an occasional reference to *H*. However, I have taken Fig. II.3.2.1 from *H* since it is missing in *D*. The text of the pertinent propositions follows: "20[a]. (*H*, 21 *D*) Circuli periferiam invenire. Hee linee curve quantitatem podisimatur (!), scilicet diametrum (!) triplicetur et addatur 7[a] eius pars et habebis periferiam circuli. Quod probatur per lineam rectam equalem curve, que si illi supponeretur ut recta curvaretur nec excederet nec excederetur. Hoc etiam ex peticione habeamus, et nota est quantitas recte per primam, ergo ei equalis ex ypotesi.

21ª. (*H, 22 D*) Circuli aream concludere. Medietas diametri ducatur in medietatem circumferencie. Productum dabit aream. Ut si diameter est 7 pedum, area erit 38 et dimidii pedis. Item aliter diametrum (*!*) in se, productum per 11 multiplicetur, summa per 14 dividatur. Denominacio dabit aream circuli. Probacio huius (*H*: 42r) propositionis habetur in archimenide, qui docet invenire ortogonium triangulum equale in (*!* equalem) circulo cuius area probata est. Ergo et area circuli. Quod sic probatur. Concesso quod linea curva sit equalis recte, fiat circulus et protrahatur semidiametrum (*!*) a circumferencia et vocetur *b* [Fig. II.3.2.1]. Protrahatur linea contingens a termino semidiametri, *c* equalis circumferencie *b*; a centro circuli, i.e., ex *e* (*! del.*) termino *a*, protrahatur linea *f* ad terminum *c*; illud ortogonium [triangulum] est equale circulo secundum archimenidem. Quod sic probatur. Protrahatur equedistans (*!*) a termino *c* et vocetur *e* et alia equidistans *c* et vocetur *d* a termino *e*, et habes quadrangulum duplum ad circulum. Quod sic probatur. Quadrangulum cuius (*D*: 195v) unum latus est *a* oppositum *e*, tercium *c*, quartum *d* fit ex ductu *a* in *c*, ut premissa docent, scilicet *a*, tria pedum et dimidii pedis, in (*H, om. D*) [*c*], 22 (*H, om. D*). Ergo quadrangulum continet 77 pedes, et area circuli fit ex ductu *a* in medietatem *c*, quia (*! quare?*) in medietatem *b*. Ergo area circuli est subdupla ad quadrangulum, continens 38 pedes et dimidium. Ergo medietas quadranguli est equalis circulo. Ergo orthogonium *acb* (*! a, c, f*) est equale circulo. Probo (*H, probatio D*) quod sit medietas eius quia paralellogramum (*!*) ortogonaliter (*! diagonaliter?*) dividitur. Ergo trianguli sunt equales per secundam. Et hoc erat propositum probare, scilicet aree (*corr. ex* are *in H et* area *in D*) que circuli est invenire quantitatem. . . . 23ª. (*H, 24 D*) Circuli inauraturam invenire. Meciatur diameter se, productum feriatur in 22, productum dividatur in 7; denominacio dabit circuli inauraturam, que semper quadrupla est ad aream eius. Eandem habebis si diameter mecietur periferiam, quod probatur ratione una ex proxima. Ut si diameter (*del. D, om. H*) 7 pedum est diameter, 154 erit inauratura. . . . 25ª. (*H, 26 D*) Circuli quadraturam reperire. Inveniatur area circuli per precedentem antepenultimam. Illius aree radix erit latus quadrati equalis circulo. Quod probatur, quia latus illud, scilicet radix, ductum in se facit aream quadrati equalem aree circuli. Ergo circulus quadratur. Ut si diameter circuli sit 7 pedum, radix aree, scilicet latus quadrati, 6 pedum et quinte pedis (*D*: 196r) et paulo plus, quod ductum in se reddet aream utriusque, hoc notato quod si numerus aree est surdus per minucias capias radicem, scilicet 6 pedes, 12 minuta, 16 secunda, 11 tercia in radice aree predicte, que ducte in se aream reddunt. Si autem insensibilis est excessus differre quasi neglectum poterit geometria. 26ª. (*H, 27 D*) Quadrati circulacionem invenire. Meciatur latus quadrati se (*H, om. D*). Productum multiplicetur per 14. Summa dividatur per 11. Denominacionis radix erit diameter circuli equalis predicto quadrato. Ut si latus quadrati 6 pedum et quinte pedis et paulo plus diameter circuli erit 7 pedum. Probatur per ipsam et per illam qua probatur area circuli. 27ª. (*H, 28 D*) Circuli quadrato inscripti excessum reperire. Per primas enim nota est area circuli; que si subtrahatur ab area quadrati inscribentis nota per precedentes, notus erit excessus. Ut si circuli diameter 7 pedum, excessus est quadrati 10 pedum et dimidii. . . . (*D*: 196v, *H* 42v). . . . (Bk. II) 1ª. Cubici corporis crassitudinem investigare. Sumatur quantitas lateris, que ducta in se faciat aream eius per primum librum. Illa area feriatur in ipsum latus. Productum dabit crassitudinem et pedes crassos. Hoc idem fit si cubicetur latus. Et hoc probatur ductis equidistantibus singulis seccionibus per equalitatem laterum et angulorum et arearum. Ut si 7 pedum latus cubici, 343 erit cubicus. 2ª. Columpne crassitudinem reperire. Sumatur area [basis] (*D*: 197r) ipsius per primum librum. Feriatur in longitudinem. Productum dabit propositum, quod probatur sicut et precedens per ductas equidistantes lineas [*et mg.*: Hoc opus conveniens est ad columpnam rotundam et lateratam]. 3ª. Circuli spericam crassitudinem perscrutari. Nota erit (*H, enim D*) circuli diametros per primum librum cuius crassitudinem volumus; illa cubicetur et habemus crassitudinem cubi qui spericam crassitudinem circuli lateribus contingit, et angulis et lineis ab angulo in angulis procedentibus per 20 (*! 10*) excedit, quem excessum oportet spere recindere (*!*) ut spere circuli quem prius habuimus remaneat soliditas. Quod sic facias: Summam cubi divide per 21; denominacionem ferias in 11 et habes globositatem spere quam queris. Ut si 7 pedum est diameter circuli, illam diametrum cubica, et surgunt 343 pedes, quos si dividas per 21 quasi pars horum 21ª est 16 pedes et tercia

Terminological similarities with the formulas of the *agrimensores* are evident, for example the expression *circuli inauratura* for the surface of a sphere and *circuli sperica crassitudo* for its volume. The most interesting part of the tract from my standpoint is a comment referring to Archimedes' proof of the proposition that the area of a circle is equal to a

pars pedis, scilicet denominacio que ducta in 10 facit 163 et terciam pedis, scilicet excessum cubi ad speram. Eadem ducta in 11 dat soliditatem spere, scilicet pedes 179 et duas 3as pedis, cui si denominacionem addas ductam in 10, que est excessus, redditur cubus, quod probatur per precedentes per equidistanciam laterum in singulis seccionibus. . . . (*D*: 197v). . . . 6^a. Corporis columpnaris piramidem invenire. Sumatur quantitas columpne per secundam huius libri. Illa erit tripla ad suam piramidem, ut probatur in 12$^{[o]}$ euclidis. 7^a. Modii capacitatem perscrutari. Sumatur diameter (*H, om. D*) fundi superioris et inferioris et equetur medietate excessus maioris addita minori. Inveniatur similiter area fundi [medii] ut de circulo docuimus per secundam, et videatur quot digitorum vel quot digitorum vel quot palmorum, ut docuimus. Illa area feriatur in altitudinem modii et habes quantitatem modii, quo palmorum erit. Eadem doctrina inveniatur quantitas cuiusvis vasis columpnaris parvi. . . ." (See also below, Section III, note 2.) The last formula for the volume of a *modius* with bases of differing diameters (i.e. in the form of a truncated cone) is erroneous. The author appears to be telling us to find a mean diameter between the diameters of the upper and lower bases, then to find the area of the mean circle and finally to multiply that area by the altitude. This would be equivalent to the formula $V = [(d_1 + d_2)/2]^2 \cdot {}^{11}/_{14} \cdot h$. The correct formula is $V = (d_1{}^2 + d_1 \cdot d_2 + d_2{}^2) \cdot {}^{11}/_{14} \cdot (h/3)$. The author's formula is identical to the approximation given by Hero in Book II of the *Stereometrica* and is perhaps of Egyptian origin (see D. E. Smith, *History of Mathematics*, Vol. 2 [Dover reprint, New York, 1958], p. 294 and particularly O. Neugebauer, "Die Geometrie der ägyptischen mathematischen Texte," *Quellen und Studien zur Geschichte der Mathematik, Astronomie und Physik*, Abt. B, Vol. 1 [1931], pp. 440–41) or more likely of Babylonian origin (see B. L. Van der Waerden, *Science Awakening* [Groningen, 1961], p. 75 and O. Neugebauer, "Mathematische Keilschrift-Texte," *Quellen und Studien etc.*, Abt. A, Vol. 3 [1935], p. 176). Cf. E. M. Bruins, *Codex Constantinopolitanus palatii veteris No. 1*, Vol. 3 (Leiden, 1964), p. 126, Problems 5 and 6. After completing this note, I had an opportunity to examine the excellent doctoral dissertation of Dr. Stephen K. Victor, "Practical Geometry in the High Middle Ages: An Edition with Translation and Commentary of the Artis cuiuslibet consummatio" (Dissertation, Harvard University, 1973). His text of the relevant Archimedean propositions does not differ substantially from mine, though based on many more manuscripts. One important difference concerns the reading of II.6 (=Victor's III.7) where according to Victor the reading of the original text is "Illa [i.e. quantitas columpne] erit *sexquialtera* ad suam pyramidem" rather than *H*'s (and *D*'s) ". . . . *tripla* ad suam pyramidem." It is difficult to see how this could be so (regardless of what the usually reliable tradition says), since all traditions add "ut probatur 12 Euclidis," and of course Euclid's XII.10 specifies that a cone is one third of its cylinder. We should also note that in the traditions followed by Victor in his text, propositions on altimetry follow as Book II, while in *H* and *D* the propositions on solids (Victor's Book III) comprise Book II. I have retained my own text simply because I wished to retain an important marginal note for the second proposition of Book II (=Victor's III. 3) not found in Victor's variant readings and some of my own corrections. There are also differences in the numbering of the propositions but the propositions can all be easily found in Victor's text. By perusing Victor's text one notes references to the latitude in "the Parisian region" (p. 255) and the zenith at Paris (p. 261) and a specific reference to the time in which the treatise is being written (p. 299): "Est autem hodierno die ipse altus locus solis 2 signa 27 gradus 40 minuta, scil. anno domini 1193. . . ." Victor notes a variant reading of 1188 for the date, which he rejects. It is a fairly safe conclusion that the tract was composed in Paris in about 1193.

right triangle whose sides about the right angle are equal respectively to the radius and the circumference (see note 5, Prop. I.21/22):

To conclude the area of a circle. Let half of the diameter be multiplied by half of the circumference. The product will give the area. So that if the diameter is 7 feet, the area will be 38½ feet. Again in another way: let the diameter be multiplied by itself, the product multiplied by 11, the sum divided by 14. The quotient will give the area of a circle. The proof of this proposition is had in Archimedes, who teaches how to find a right triangle equal to a circle whose area has been sought. Therefore, it is the area of the circle. This is proved as follows. It having been conceded that a curve is equal to a straight line, let a circle be drawn and its radius drawn from circumference b [see Fig. II.3.2.1]. Let a tangent c be drawn from the terminus of the radius, namely one equal to circumference b. From the center of the circle, that is from the terminus of a, let line f be drawn to the terminus of c. The right triangle [thus formed] is equal to the circle according to Archimedes. This is proved as follows. From the terminus of c let a line parallel [to the radius] be drawn and let it be designated e, and from the terminus of e [draw] another line parallel to c and let it be designated d. You will thus have a rectangle double the circle. This is proved as follows. The rectangle with one side a opposite to [side] e, the third side c and the fourth d arises from the product of a and c, as the premised data reveal, namely, a as 3½ feet and c as 22. Therefore, the rectangle contains 77 [square] feet and the area of the circle arises from the product of a and one-half c, and therefore [of a] and one-half b. There-fore, the area of the circle is one-half of the rectangle and [thus] contains 38½ feet. Therefore, half the rectangle is equal to the circle. Therefore, the right triangle a, c, f is equal to the circle. I prove that it is half because the rectangle is diagonally divided. Therefore, the [two] triangles are equal by the second [proposition]. And this is what was proposed for proof, namely to find the quantity of the area of the circle.

It is obvious that, despite the author's claims to construct a proof, there is no geometrical proof given for the basic proposition, which is of course Proposition I of the *De mensura circuli*. But even the pretense of proof is something of a novelty for early medieval metrical works. The reader will further note that there is a kind of geometrical ineptness ap-parent in the way that letters ambiguously stand for the termini of lines and the lines themselves, at least in the figure. The author is ob-viously not at home with formal Greek geometrical methods.

The use of the form *Archimenides* gives some (but hardly precise) evidence for one of the sources of the tract. Although the form *Archi-menides* does not appear in the pristine tradition of Gerard of Cremona's translation where the title and author are given as *Liber Arsamithis de mensura circuli*, it does appear in the second tradition (see Volume One, page 31). In fact, I suspect that the author took the form *Archimenides* from the Cambridge Version of the tract, which bears the title *Liber Archimenidis de quadratura circuli*. We do not know the exact date of the Cambridge Version. Before now I knew of no evidence that put it earlier than the thirteenth century. Its earliest manuscript is from the thirteenth century and its basic assumption that there is some straight line equal to any curved line (an assumption repeated by the author of the *Practica geometrie*) is not, so far as I know, expressed in any medieval geometrical work treating quadrature problems before the *Liber de curvis superficiebus*, a work that dates from the late twelfth or early thirteenth century (*ibid.*, pages 63, 440–41; 452, line 16).[6] Not only do the use of the form *Archimenides* and the repetition of the same basic assumption link the *Practica* with the Cambridge Version but also the metrical author's above-noted technique of designating linear magnitudes by single letters. Of all the various versions of the *De mensura circuli* only the Cambridge Version uses this technique. Incidentally, a later author, Gordanus, in his *Compilacio quorundam canonum in practicis astronomie et geometrie* borrows some of the exact phraseology of this passage of the *Practica geometrie* (*ibid.*, page 143, n. 4). If, then, my suspicion that the author of the *Practica geometrie* used the Cambridge Version of the *Liber de quadratura circuli* is correct, it is evident that the Cambridge Version must have been composed before 1193, the date of composition of the *Practica*.

At this point a word should be said about a French *Pratike de géométrie* of the thirteenth century, which is primarily a translation of the Latin *Practica*. Hence it contains the same Archimedean formulas (expressed in the same fashion) for the relation of the circumference to the diameter, the area of a circle, the surface and volume of a sphere and the volume of a cylinder.[7] Furthermore, like the Latin *Practica*, it omits formulas for

---

[6] I have said that I do not know of an explicit statement of the basic assumption of some straight line equal to any curved line before the *Liber de curvis superficiebus*, though it surely must have been in the minds of the early geometers who presented the Archimedean formulas. Alexander Neckam gives an interesting physical justification for solid quadratures in his *De naturis rerum*, Bk. II, cap. 173, ed. of T. Wright (London, 1863), p. 300: "Sed ad notiora descendamus, censentes illos esse geometriae ignaros qui putant ad assignationem aequalitatis formae similitudinem desiderari; unde non opinantur pilam rotundam et lanceam esse aequales. Sed eorum supina ignorantia convincenda est hoc modo. Fiat rotundum cereum corpus, ita ut quantitas ejus ex aequo se commetiatur quantitati pilae rotundae. Deinde dicta producatur extensa in parilitatem lanceae. Patet igitur quod haec cera est aequalis lanceae, sed quantacumque fuit haec cera, est haec cera, et e converso, prius igitur fuit aequalis lanceae."

[7] *Pratike de géométrie*, ed. of C. Henry, "Sur les deux plus anciens traités français d'algorisme et de géométrie," *Bullettino di bibliografia e di storia delle scienze matematiche e fisiche*, Vol. 15 (1882), pp. 58–59, 61–62 (whole article, pp. 49–70): "Apres che diron des figures circulers. [1] Se tu veus trover la circonference del compas, multeplie le dyametre du compas par .3. et si aiouste la septisme partie de soi, si auras la circonference. [2] Se tu veus trover laire del compas, multeplie la moitie de sen dyametre [par la moitie de la circonference;] la somme fera laire. Si comme se li dyametres est de .7., laire sera de .36. (! 38) et demi. Ce pues prover en autre maniere. [3] Se tu multeplies le dyametre par soi et tu multeplies cele somme par .13. (! 11) et tu devises cele somme par .14., la denominations fera laire de la circonference. Ce pues prover par le seconde. [4] Se tu veus trover lorneure du cercle, multeplie le dyametre par soi et cele somme multeplie par .22. et cele somme devise per .7. La denominations fera lorneure du cercle, car elle est quadruple a laire du cercle. En autre maniere le pues prover se tu multeplies la circonference par sen dyametre. Si com li dyametres est de .7., lorneure sera de .154. Ce pues prover par raison

the lateral surfaces of a cone and a cylinder. It does not, however, contain the passage concerning Archimedes nor the formula for the volume of a cone contained in the *Practica*. In view of its close relationship to the Latin *Practica*, it is not surprising that the *Pratike* contains terms that relate it to the Roman gromatic tradition. I have already mentioned the expression *l'orneure du cercle* for the surface of a sphere, which erroneously reflects the Latin *circuli inauratura*. Note also the use of *crasse mesure* for volume where the Latin text had *crassitudo*.

de nombre et par che pues tu trover ke .1. dyametres ki doubble a .1. autre fait laire quadruple a laire de celui, che pues prover par raison de nombre. [5] Se tu veus trover le quarre du cercle, la rachine de cele aire fera le coste du quarre ouni au cercle. Ce pues prover en tel maniere car cil costes mul(p. 59)teplies par soi fera laire du quarre ouni a laire du quarre du cercle. Si comme se li dyametres est de .7., li costes del quarre de .6. et une quinte; la quele se multeplie par soi, se fera laire de lun et de lautre; et note ke se li nombres de laire est seus et non entendables, tu prenderas la rachine par minuces. [6] Se tu veus trover la circonference (*!* dyametre) del quarre (*!* cercle), se tu multiplies le coste du quarre [ouni au cercle] par soi et tu multeplies cele somme par .14. et tu devises cele somme par .ii. (*!* 11), la rachine de la denomination fera la dyametre du cercle ouni au quarre. Se comme se li costes du quarre est de .6. et une quinte, li dyametres du cercle sera de .7. pies. Ce pues prover par le premiere et par le seconde. [7] Se tu veus trover le sorcrois du quarre au cercle escrit dedens le quarre, se tu proves laire du cercle par celes devant et tu proves laire du quarre par sen coste et tu soustrais lune somme del lautre, tu sarras le sorcrois de lune a lautre. Si comme se li dyametres du cercle est de .7., le sorcrois del quarre sera de .10. et demi. . . . (p. 61). . . . Or tavons enseignie le mesure des planeces, or te dirons des crasses mesures. [1] Se tu veus trover le mesure del combe (*i.e.*, coube) [du] quarre, keure li costes del quarre sor le combe (*!* costes?), la somme fera laire. Derechief keure li costes sor laire, la somme fera la combe (*i.e.*, coube) du quarre. Si comme se li costes est de .7., li coubles del quarre sera de .343., che pues prover par raison de nombre. [2] Se tu veus trover le coube dun piler reont tu troveras laire par le moitie de sen dyametre en sa [semi]circonference. Keure laire sor le lonc, la somme fera la coube du piler, che pues prover ausi ke devant. [3] Se tu veus trover la mesure del espere reonde, tu troveras le dyametre du cercle, par le premier livre, del quel tu quiers la crasse mesure. Tu cuberas (p. 62) che dyametre en son quarre et si note bien ke li coubes du quarre sorcroist le contenance del coube reont, le kel reont il te covient soustraire. Se tu veus trover le contenance del coube reont, che feras tu en tel maniere, tu deviseras le coube del quarre par .21. et multeplieras cele devision par .10.; la somme fera le sorcrois del coube quarre au coube reont. Derekief se tu multeplies cele misme devision par .2. (*!* 11), la somme fera la contenance del coube reont. Si comme se li dyametres du cercle est de .7. pies, se tu le cobes, la somme fera .343. Se tu devises cele somme par .21., la devision fera .16. pies et le tierce part dun piet. Se tu multeplies cele devision par .10., la somme fera .163. pies et le tierce part dun piet. Cest li sorcrois del coube quarre au coube reont. Derekief se tu multeplies cele misme devision par .2. (*!* 11), la somme fera .176. (*!* 179) pies et .2. [tierces] parties dun pie, che fera la contenance del coube reont ale quele tu assambleras le sorcrois saveras le coube del quare .343., ce pues prover par celes devant. [4] Se tu veus trover le contenanche du mui. Se tu mesures le dyametre du fons et la dyametre deseure ki atouche le .viii. et tu les devises par mi. Se tu troeves laire du fons [moien] par le dyametre et tu ses de quans pies li aire soit. Se tu multeplies cele aire par le haut dou mui, la somme te dira de quans pies li muis sera. . . ." Henry's text is inadequate and so I have suggested alternate readings, or explanations, repunctuated the text and substituted "v" for consonantal "u." Furthermore, I have added the proposition numbers in brackets. Stephen Victor is preparing a new edition of the *Pratike* based on the two extant manuscripts.

Clearly the most mature of the medieval geometrical manuals was the *Practica geometrie* of Leonardo Fibonacci, composed in 1220 or 1221. It contained the basic formulas from the gromatic traditions (at least in the forms found in the *Liber embadorum* of Savasorda). But more important it includes most of the conclusions and proofs found in the *Verba filiorum*, as the reader may see if he consults the text of Leonardo's Archimedean passages given below in Appendix I, Section 3[B]. I discuss Leonardo's understanding of Archimedean methods at considerable length below in Part III, Chapter 2, Section IV, where I evaluate Pacioli's use of Leonardo's *Practica*. Suffice to say here, in addition to containing the conventional formulas for the circle, the cylinder, the cone, the truncated cone, the sphere and segments of the sphere (all with numerical examples), it also contains some proofs. In this respect it far surpasses in geometrical maturity any of the preceding Latin manuals and most of those that follow, though, as I indicate in the Pacioli chapter below, Leonardo's understanding of Archimedean methods was somewhat defective.

Another popular *Practica geometrie* of the late twelfth or early thirteenth century deserves some notice, that which has the incipit: "Geometrie due sunt partes principales. . . ." While the substance of the Archimedean formulas is essentially that of both the Roman and Arabic gromatic traditions, the expression of the formulas is distinctive and differs from that found in all of the preceding texts.[8] This work contains

---

[8] *Practica geometrie*, MSS Paris, BN lat. 7377B, 87v–88v (*Sigl. P*); Vienna, National-bibl. 5184, 58r–v (*Sigl. V*): "[1] Et si planum fuerit circulare (*V*, circuale *P*), numerus secundum quem mensura tua (*V, om. P*) est in circumferencie (*P, del. juste V*) semidiametro illius circuli ducatur in numerum secundum quem mensura est in circumferencia; producti medietas erit area circuli. [2] Et si per dyametrum volueris scire circumferenciam vel econverso, numerus (*!*) secundum quem mensura tua est in dyametro, si dyameter est notus (*V et manu recent. P*; nota?), duc in (*P, om. V*) 22; productum divide per 7, et erit numerus secundum quem mensura tua est in circumferencia. [3] Quod si circumferencia est nota, duc numerum secundum quem mensura tua est in circumferencia (*P*: 88r) in 7; productum divide per 22, et exit numerus secundum quem mensura tua (*V, om. P*) est in dyametro. [4] Ex hoc etiam (*P, om. V*) patet qualiter area semicirculi practice inveniatur. [5] Et si proposita fuerit porcio (*V*, proportio *P*) minor semicirculo, numerus (*!*) secundum quem mensura tua est in (*P, om. V*) arcu porcionis duc in numerum secundum quem quadrata tua (*V, om. P*) mensura est in area circuli; productum divide per numerum secundum quem mensura tua est in tota circumferencia; et de eo quod exit in divisione, aufer aream trianguli que sub corda porcionis et duabus (*P*, duobus *V*) semidyametris continetur et relinquitur numerus secundum quem quadrata mensura tua est in data porcione. [6] Quod si fuerit porcio maior semicirculo, quere aream porcionis que deest ad perfeccionem circuli et subtrahe illam de area tocius circuli et relinquitur area date porcionis. [7] Et si volueris scire aream in (*P, om. V*) superficiei (*P et V*) date columpne, numerum secundum quem mensura tua est in latere date columpne duc in numerum secundum quem mensura tua est in circumferencia basis columpne, et numerus qui provenit est numerus secundum quem quadrata mensura tua (*V, suprascr. P*) in area superficiei columpne. [8] Et si totam superficiem columpne scire volueris, quere aream (*P*, areas *V*) duorum circulorum basium et adde predicte aree curve, et habes quod queris. [9] Et si fuerit area pyramidalis rotunda, duc numerum secundum quem mensura tua est in [*V et om. P*: yppotenusa piramidis

the following formulas. For a circle: $S = (r/2) \cdot c$, $c = d \cdot {}^{22}\!/_7$ and $d = c \cdot {}^7\!/_{22}$. For a circular segment less than a semicircle:

$$Sseg = [(arc/circum) \cdot Scirc] - triangle\ on\ chord\ with\ apex\ at\ center,$$

and for one greater than a semicircle: $Sseg = Scirc - Scomplementary\ seg$. For the surface of a sphere: $S = d \cdot c$. Further formulas not found in the earlier metrical tracts are included, for example, those for the lateral surface of a cylinder, $S = l \cdot c$ (where l is a vertical line element or side of the cylinder and c is the circumference of the base), the total surface of a cylinder: $S = Slat + two\ base\ circles$, the lateral surface of a cone: $S = \frac{1}{2} l \cdot c$ (where l is the slant height or, as it is called in the Middle Ages, the side or hypotenuse of the cone and c is the circumference of the base), the total surface of a cone: $S = Slat + base\ circle$, and the lateral surface of a truncated cone: $S = [(c_1 + c_2)/2] \cdot l$. The tract contains only a brief section on stereometry (at least in the two copies I have seen) which does not include the usual volumetric formulas but only a few observations on the proportions of solids that rest on Book XII of the *Elements* of Euclid. In all of this account, there is no mention of the name of Archimedes. The fact that the tract includes formulas for the lateral surface of a cylinder and the lateral surfaces of a cone and a truncated cone, formulas that are also present in the *Liber de curvis superficiebus* (see Volume One, pages 450–68), suggests some dependency on the latter work. The use by the author of the *Practica* of the term *ypotenusa* for a line element of the cone's surface and the single use of the expression *curva superficies* for lateral surface seem to confirm the relationship between the two treatises, in as much as both of these expressions apparently appeared for the first time in the *Liber de curvis superficiebus*.[9]

(*V*: 58v) in numerum secundum quem mensura tua est in] circumferencia basis; producti medietas erit area superficiei piramidis (*V, om. P*). [10] Cui si addideris quantitatem circuli basis ostendet (*P*, habes *V*) totam superficiem pyramidis. [11] Et si volueris scire aream superficiei date spere, duc numerum secundum quem mensura tua est in [*V et om. P*: dyametro spere in numerum secundum quem mensura tua est in] circumferencia maximi circuli in spera, et provenit numerus secundum quem quadrata mensura tua est in area superficiei spere. [12] Et si aream curve superficiei cupe date metiri volueris, numerum secundum quem mensura tua est in latere cupe duc in numerum (*P*: 88v) secundum quem mensura tua est (*P, om. V*) in medietate circumferencie oris (*P*, orbis *V*) cupe et iterum in medietatem (*V*, medietate *P*) circumferencie basis cupe et congrega (*P*, agrega *V*) producta, et provenit numerus secundum quem mensura tua quadrata est in area curve superficiei date cupe." I have generally followed *P*, noting the principal variant readings from *V*. I have, however, omitted mentioning several transpositions of terms in *V* and several deleted addenda in *V*. Nor have I noted some minor orthographic differences. The proposition numbers in brackets are mine. After completing this section, I discovered that the *Practica geometrie* has been recently edited by F. N. L. Britt, "A Critical Edition of Tractatus quadrantis," Dissertation, Emory University, 1972, pp. 208–55. The passage that I have given above is found on pages 247–51.

[9] One could imagine that these expressions might easily have developed out of the commonplace geometrical vocabulary of the early Middle Ages. Clearly the expression *curva superficies* could have arisen out of the application to *superficies* of the common distinction applied to *linea*. Just as there is a *curva linea* distinguishable from a *linea recta*

At any rate, it was this last treatise that made the expression popular. It is true that the formulas for the lateral surfaces of a cone and a segment of a cone were also given in the *Verba filiorum* (*ibid.*, pages 292 and 302) but the terms *ypotenusa* and *curva superficies* were not used therein.

Consideration of this *Practica geometrie* leads naturally to the investigation of the so-called *Quadrans vetus* written at Montpellier (probably in the 1270's) by an author sometimes called Johannes Anglicus and sometimes Robertus Anglicus, for the *Quadrans vetus* has an incipit that nearly duplicates that of the *Practica*: "Geometrie due sunt partes, theorica et practica. . . ." The section devoted to practical geometry toward the end of the treatise contains only the scantiest collection of Archimedean formulas.[10] These formulas show the terminological influence of the earlier *Practica* with incipit "Artis cuiuslibet consummatio. . . ." rather than of the *Practica* with incipit similar to that of the *Quadrans vetus*. We should note the inclusion of the formulas for the relationship of circumference to diameter, the area of the circle, the volume of a cylinder and the incorrect formula for a truncated cone, all virtually identical with those of the earlier *Practica*.

Somewhat more interesting for my study is the fact that several manuscripts of the *Quadrans vetus* contain a note that specifies, on the authority of Archimedes and Alfarabi, that the ratio of circumference to diameter is less than $3\frac{1}{7}$ and greater than $3\frac{10}{71}$.[11] This gloss is in fact an ab-

so there will be a *curva superficies* distinguishable from a *superficies plana*. As for the use of *ypotenusa* for an element of a cone's surface, this could have arisen from considering the definition of a cone given in Book XI of Euclid's *Elements* in one or another of the versions translated by Adelard of Bath (cf. the so-called Adelard II version in MS Oxford, Bodl. Libr. Auct. F.5.28, 35v): "Pyramis rotunda est figura solida, estque transitus trianguli rectanguli alterutro suorum laterum rectum angulum continentium fixo, donec ad locum suum unde incepit redeat, triangulo ipso circumducto." It would be evident to the reader of this definition that it is the hypotenuse of the right triangle whose rotation produces the cone that generates the lateral surface of the cone, and hence it would seem appropriate to speak of an element or side of the cone's surface as its hypotenuse.

[10] See the edition of P. Tannery in his "Le Traité du quadrant de maître Robert Anglès," *Mémoires scientifiques de Paul Tannery*, Vol. 5 (Toulouse/Paris, 1922), pp. 185, 188–89 (complete article, pp. 118–97, reprinted from *Notices et extraits des manuscrits de la Bibliothèque Nationale et autres bibliothèques*, Vol. 35, 2e partie (1897), pp. 561–640): "69. Si autem vis mensurare planum in longum et latum, tunc planum aut erit circulare, aut angulare. Si circulare, medietas dyametri ducatur in medietatem circumferencie, et productum dabit aream tocius circumferencie circuli. 70. Quantitas [vero] circumferencie habetur sic: tripletur dyameter et addatur ei septima pars, et productum dabit quantitatem circumferencie. . . . (p. 188). . . . 79. Si vero putei capacitatem vis habere, per aream putei, inventam ut supra dictum est, multiplicetur putei profunditas, et productum dat putei capacitatem. . . . 81. Si nunc alicuius modii rotundi vis habere capacitatem, sumatur dyameter fundi modii [rotundi] et dyameter superior, et equetur medietate excessus maioris addita minori. 82. Et inveniatur tunc area fundi [medii], ut dictum est de circulo, et videatur (p. 189) quod digitorum sit, vel palmorum; per aream illam multiplicetur altitudo modii ⟨et productum dabit quantitatem capacitatis modii⟩." Cf. the more recent edition of F. N. L. Britt, "A Critical Edition of Tractatus quadrantis," pp. 190–92, 201–03.

[11] The gloss is in the following manuscripts: London, BM Royal 12.C.IX, 27v; Darmstadt, Landesbibl. 2661, 142r; and Princeton Univ. Libr., Garrett 99, 167v. I have seen only the

breviatory copy of a longer and more precise note in an anonymous commentary or collection of glosses on the *Sphere* of Sacrobosco:[12]

Although there is no comparison or ratio between a curved line and a straight line, Archimedes and Alfarabi and other astronomers have said that the diameter tripled with a seventh part of it [added] constitutes the circumference. But not precisely, [for] as Archimedes has said, he who gives to the circumference [the value of] the diameter tripled with $^{10}/_{70}$ [of it added], gives more than he ought, while he who gives [the value as] the same diameter tripled with $^{10}/_{71}$ [added] gives less. Therefore, the ratio of it to the diameter lies between [3 and] $^{10}/_{70}$ and [3 and] $^{10}/_{71}$. However in a gross fashion it is supposed that the diameter tripled with its seventh added constitutes the circumference.

In a later gloss the same commentator makes specific reference to Archimedes' *Liber de quadratura circuli* as the source for the value $3\frac{1}{7}$.[13] The reference is presumably to Gerard of Cremona's translation in its second tradition or to one of the elaborations of that translation that bears the same title. At any rate, it is clear that the author of these glosses had access to Propositions II and III of the *De mensura circuli*.

Another work that included a section on practical geometry, in apparent imitation of the *Quadrans vetus*, was the *Quadrans novus* of Prophatius Judeus, written in Hebrew in about 1290, and first translated into Latin

---

last of these manuscripts, which reads: "Dicit archimenides et alfarabius: qui dat circumferentie dyametrum triplatam et eius 10 70as, dat plus quam debet habere; et que (*!* qui?) eandem dat c^{i} 4^{m} (*!* dyametrum) triplatam et eius 10 71as, dat minus quam debet habere. Ergo eius quantitas Ergo eius quantitas (*bis ! delendum?*) in (*!* inter?) 10 septuagesimas et 10 septuagesimasprimas consistit. In grosso tamen modo sup[p]onam (?) dyametrum triplatam cum suy septima continere." This is a gloss to statement no. 70 in the text given in the preceding footnote. Cf. the edition of F. N. L. Britt, p. 191, var. to line 4.

[12] L. Thorndike, *The Sphere of Sacrobosco and Its Commentators* (Chicago, 1949), p. 422: "De quantitate diametri terre et licet curve linee ad rectam nulla sit comparatio seu proportio, Archimedes et Alfarabius et alii cosmimetre dixerunt quod diameter triplata cum sua septima parte constituunt circumferentiam. Non tamen precise, ut dixit Archimedes: qui dat circumferentie diametrum triplatam et decem 70as, dat plus quam debet; qui vero dat eandem triplatam et decem 71as, dat minus. Ergo proportio eius ad circumferentiam est inter decem 70as et decem 71as. Grosso tamen modo supponitur quod diameter triplata cum sua septima constituunt circumferentiam. Verbi gratia, sit *ab* diameter 7 pedum. Triplentur septem et fiunt ter 7 21, ad quem addatur unus pes qui est septima pars de septem, et erit 22a pars circumferentie et exeunt 22 pedes circumferentia tota. Econverso ex circumferentia fiat diameter. Auferatur 22a pars circumferentie, scilicet unus pes et remanent 21 cuius tertia pars, scilicet 7 pedes, erit diameter."

[13] *Ibid.*, p. 423: "Notandum quod regula geometrie dicit quod diameter sive spissitudo, quod idem videlicet, alicuius rei triplata dabit longitudinem ipsius rei in circuitu. Et econverso tertia pars longitudinis in circuitu alicuius rei rotundi est diameter sive spissitudo illius rei, hoc tamen prenotato quod 22a pars longitudinis in circuitu prius subtrahatur. Dicit Macrobius, triplato diametro cum septima parte eius facit circulum. Verbi gratia, sit diameter alicuius rotundi 7 pedum. Triplatis 7 pedibus faciunt 21. Addam septimam partem diametri cum parte triplata et faciunt 22. Totus ergo circuitus illius rei erit 22 pedum. Nota quod idem est 22a pars circumferentie et una septima diametri. Archimedes *in libro de quadratura circuli* dicit quod sic se habet circumferentia ad diametrum quod continet ipsum ter et septimam eius unam fere."

in 1299.[14] It appeared in a version corrected and elaborated by Pierre de St. Omer (de Sancto Audemaro). My remarks concerning this tract are based on the last of these versions since it appears to contain the fullest geometrical section. Though the instrument invented by Prophatius is quite different from that described in the *Quadrans vetus*, the section on practical geometry contains the same basic Archimedean formulas but with further formulas and commentary added.[15] Again we note the influence

[14] G. Sarton, *Introduction to the History of Science*, Vol. 2 (Baltimore, 1931), p. 850.

[15] *Quadrans novus*, MS Dublin, Trinity College Libr. 403, 99r, 100v, 102v, 103v–04r: "Si autem vis mensurare planum in longum et latum, tunc planum aut erit circulare aut angulare. [1] Si circulare, tunc tripletur diameter circuli et addatur ei 7ᵃ pars eius et productum dabit quantitatem circumference. [2] Deinde per medietatem diametri multiplicetur medietas circumference et habetur area circuli. Verbi gracia. Sit circulus *abc*, cuius diameter *ac* sit 14 pedum; tripletur ergo diameter *ac*, et est 42, et addatur ei 7ᵃ pars, quod est 2, et resultat 44, que est quantitas circumference. Deinde per medietatem diametri, quod est 7, multiplicetur medietas circumference, quod est 22, et resultat 154 pedes, quod est area circuli dati. [3] Vel aliter: multiplica diametrum in seipsam, et hanc summam iterum multiplica per 11, et productum divide per 14, et numerus quociens denotabit aream. [4] Si autem econverso volueris scire, scilicet per circumferenciam, diametrum, subtrahe 22ᵃᵐ partem circumference ab ipsa circumferencia, et quod remanet divide per 3, et numerus quociens dabit tibi diametrum. [5] Vel aliter sic: multiplica circulum [i.e., circumferenciam] in semetipsum, et quod exierit divide per 10, et numeri inde provenientis quere radicem, que erit circuli diameter. [6] Vel sic: multiplica circulum in 20000 et divide quod colligitur per 62832, et quod tibi provenerit ex hac divisione erit diameter circuli. . . . (100v). . . . [7] Si adhuc volueris mensurare superficiem habentem arcum et cordam, per medietatem arcus multiplicetur medietas corde, et habetur area. . . . (102v). . . . [8] Si autem aream alicuius quadrati multiplicaveris per 14, et productum diviseris per 11, radix residui erit diameter alicuius circuli equalis illi quadrato. Unde si costa quadrati sit 6 pedum cum 5ᵃ parte unius, diameter circuli sibi equalis erit 7 pedum, et per hoc potes circulare quadratum. [9] Si vis scire excessum quadrati ad circulum scriptum infra illud quadratum ad maius quo scribi posset, subtrahe aream circuli ab area quadrati, et quod remanet erit excessus. Ut si diameter circuli sit 7 pedum, excessus erit 10 pedum cum dimidio. . . . (103v). . . . [10] Item cum volueris metiri corpus solidum habens circularem formam et longam densitatem, ut bussellus et huiusmodi, tripletur diameter illius vasis et addatur ei 7ᵃ pars, et habetur circumferencia. [Deinde per medietatem diametri multiplicetur medietas circumference, et habetur area circuli.] Deinde per aream multiplicetur profunditas, et habetur capacitas illius vasis. Verbi gracia, sit bussellus *abc*, diameter *ab*, sitque *ab* 14 pedum, vel 14 digitorum vel palmarum non est cura de qua vis ipsarum mensurarum. Sic gracia exempli: Tripletur ergo *ab* et addatur ei 7ᵃ pars, et habetur circumferencia, scilicet 44. Deinde per medietatem diametri multiplicetur medietas circumference, et habetur 154, que est area circuli. Deinde multiplicetur area per profunditatem vasis, que est *bc*, sitque *bc* 10, et habetur 1540, que est capacitas illius busselli. Ita penitus fac de omnibus talibus superficiebus (*!* corporibus?). . . . (104r). . . . [11] Cum volueris scire quantitatem corporis sperici sive capacitatem, cubes diametrum eius et habebis corpus quadratum maius ipso corpore sperico. Sed excessum eius ad corpus spericum sic invenies: quantitatem illius quadrati divide per 21, et numerum quociens (*!*) multiplica per 11, et productum erit quantitas spere. Verbi gracia: Sit spera *abc*, cuius diameter sit *ac*, et sit 7 pedum, et cubetur ipsa, ut sepcies 7 sepcies et proveniunt 343 pedes, et est quantitas corporis quadrati quod est maius corpore sperico. (104v) Et si hec quantitas, scilicet 343, dividatur per 21, provenient 16 pedes cum 3ᵃ parte unius pedis; quos 16 pedes cum 3ᵃ parte unius pedis si multiplicaveris per 11, provenient 179 pedes cum 2 terciis unius pedis, et hec erit quantitas dicte spere. Vel si illos 16 pedes cum una 3ᵃ multiplicaveris

of the early *Practica* with incipit "Artis cuiuslibet consummatio. . . ."
To the Archimedean treatment of the circle is added a brief passage
(No. 5 in note 14) from the *Canones sive regule super tabulas Toletanas*
of al-Zarqālī as translated by Gerard of Cremona that implies the Arabic
approximation of π as $\sqrt{10}$, to which also another non-Archimedean
approximation (No. 6) equivalent to $\pi = 20000/62832$ (or $\pi \approx 3.1416$)
is added. There is no mention of the name of Archimedes in the discussion
of the Archimedean formulas. The history of the tracts *Quadrans vetus*
and *Quadrans novus*, and a thorough study of their many manuscripts,
would probably reveal some elaborations and intermingling of the geometrical sections of both tracts. One example of such intermingling is
present in an anonymous geometrical tract found in Munich, Staatsbibl.
cod. 14908, 301v-06v, and dated 1456, which has the Archimedean propositions that appear in both quadrant tracts and depend on the tradition of
the *gromatici veteres* and which has the Arabic, non-Archimedean values
of π that appear in the *Quadrans novus*.[16]

III. Archimedes and the Handbook Tradition in the Fourteenth and Early Fifteenth Centuries

The popularity and influence of the early *Practica geometrie* with incipit
"Artis cuiuslibet consummatio. . . ." continued in the fourteenth
century. This is illustrated particularly by a pastiche *Liber theoreumancie
de arithmetica, geometria, musica*, whose earliest manuscript is from the
fourteenth century.[1] Its geometrical section, and especially its Archi-

---

per 10, provenient 163 pedes cum una 3ᵃ, et hoc erit excessus illius corporis quadrati ad
ipsam speram. Unde si istos 163 pedes cum una 3ᵃ pedis subtraxeris a quantitate corporis
quadrati, scilicet a 343 pedibus, habebis quantitatem corporis sperici dicti, scilicet 179
pedes cum duobus terciis unius pedis. Vel aliter invenies quantitatem illius corporis sperici.
Ut si multiplicaveris per 11 illum numerum quociens (*!*) qui provenit ex divisione quantitatis
corporis quadrati predicti per 21. Nam ille numerus qui proveniat erit quantitas corporis
sperici predicti. [12] Adhuc si vis scire superficiem corporis sperici, duc diametrum eius
in seipsam et illam summam multiplica per 22, et productum divide per 7, et numerus
quociens dabit superficiem spere. Ut si diameter sit 7 pedum, circumferencia erit 22, et
superficies spere erit 154." I have added the passage numbers in brackets. For the two
non-Archimedean values of π implied in passages [5] and [6], see above, note 3, and below,
Part III, Chapter 2, Sect. II, note 40. Passage [7] gives an erroneous formula for the area of a
circular segment, which is true only for a semicircle.

[16] The text of this tract has been edited by M. Curtze, "Miscellen zur Geschichte der
Mathematik im 14. und 15. Jahrhundert," *Bibliotheca mathematica*, Neue Folge, Vol. 8
(1894), pp. 107-15. For an up-to-date description of the manuscript, see K. Vogel, *Die
Practica des Algorismus Ratisbonensis* (Munich, 1954), pp. 12-19.

[1] Attention was called to this manuscript, Munich, Staatsbibl. 14684 by M. Curtze, "Die
Handschrift No. 14836 der Königl. Hof- und Staatsbibliothek zu München," *Abhandlungen
zur Geschichte der Mathematik*, 7. Heft (1895), p. 137, n. 1.

medean formulas, was drawn almost verbatim from the earlier *Practica*.[2]
To be sure, its propositions are somewhat rearranged and some commentary has been added. The proposition on the area of the circle with its reference to Archimedes' proof is given with little change, and furthermore

[2] I have used the excellent copy found in Munich, Staatsbibl. 56, where the sundry propositions taken from the *Practica geometrie* and quoted above in Section II, note 5 are found on folios 134v–36v. Here I shall give those propositions that mention the name "Archimenides" and in addition the proposition concerning the surface of a sphere: "(134v) Sequitur secunde partis huius libri theoreuma quintumdecimum . . . Circuli pariferiam (*!*) investigare. Hec linee curve quantitatem podismatur sic. Dyametrum triplicetur et ei addatur septima pars eius et habebitur periferia circuli, quod probatur per tractam lineam equalem curve, que si illi supponeretur ut recta curvaretur nec excederet nec excederetur. Sed nota erit quantitas recte, ergo et curve ei equalis quia dicit archimenides quod circumferencia est ad dyametrum suum fere tripla sexquiseptima. Est nota quod linea que circulum ambit grece dicitur periferia, latine circumferencia; dyameter vero linea que per centrum huic inde usque ad circumferenciam pertingit. Spacium vero quod includit circumferencia aream latine, embadum dicimus grece. . . .(135r). . . . Sedecimum theoreuma: Circuli dyametrum invenire. Hec sic probatur secundum archimenidem. De omni circumferencia, quantacumque sit, partem 22ᵃᵐ auferes, et remanentis numeri terciam partem dyametro attribues. Vel aliter: in circulo cuius embadum est 616 dyametrum sic queras; ducatur area [in] 14 et fiunt 8624. Summatur huic pars 11ᵃ, que est 784. Summatur radix huius, 28. Hoc erit dyametrum; ad similitudinem in aliis procedas. Sequitur decimumseptimum theoreuma: Circuli aream concludere. Hec sic probatur. Medietas dyametri ducatur in medietatem circumferencie, productum dabit aream. Ut si dyameter est 7 pedum, circumferencia 22ᵒʳᵘᵐ, area erit 38 et dimidii. Item aliter: dyameter ducatur in se, productum multiplicetur per 11, summa dividatur per 14; denominacio dabit aream circuli. Probacio huius proposicionis habetur ex archimenide qui docet invenire triangulum orthogonium equalem circulo cuius area probata est, ergo et area circuli. Quod sic probatur. Concesso quod linea curva equalis sit recte, fiat circulus et protrahatur semidyameter a circumferencia *b*; protrahaturque linea recta contingens a termino semidyametri et vocetur *c*, equalis circumferencie *b*; a centro circuli, scilicet termino *a*, protrahatur linea recta *f* ad terminum *c*. Illud orthogonium est equale circulo secundum archimenidem. Quod sic probatur. Protrahatur linea equedistans a termino *c* et vocetur *e* et alia equedistans *c* et vocetur *d* a termino *e* et a habes quadrangulum duplum ad circulum. Quod sic probatur. Quadrangulum cuius unum latus est *a*, oppositum *e*, tercium *c*, quartum *d*, fit ex ductu *a* in *c*, ut premissa docent. Sed *a* est trium pedum et dimidii, *c* 22ᵒʳᵘᵐ; ergo quadrangulum continet 77 pedes. Sed area circuli fit ex ductu *a* in medietatem *c*, quia in medietatem *b*. Ergo area circuli est subdupla, (135v) continens scilicet 38 pedes et dimidium, ad 77 pedes continentem. Ergo medietas quadranguli est equalis circulo, ergo orthogonium *a d f* est equale circulo. Probacio, quod sit medietas eius, quia parallelographum (*!*) orthogonaliter dividitur. Igitur trianguli sunt equales per huius libri 3ᵃᵐ, et hoc erat propositum probare, scilicet aream circuli invenire. Sequitur decimumoctavum theoreuma: Circuli spericam crassitudinem invenire. Archimenides dicit circulum incrassare si vis, diametrum eius cubices, et ipsam cubicacionem 11ᵉˢ ducas, ex eaque summa 20 (*del. MS*) 21ᵃᵐ partem minuas, et illa erit spere crassitudo. Item aliter secundum alium capias dyametrum circuli cuius crassitudinem volumus, per antepenultimam ille cubicetur et habemus crassitudinem cubi que spericam crassitudinem lateribus angulis et lineis ab angulo in angulum precedentibus (*!*) excedere contingit, quem excessum necesse est recidere ut spere circuli quam querimus remaneat soliditas, quod sic facias. Summam cubi divide per 21, denominacionem feriat (*! ferias*) in 10, productum dabit excessum cubi ad speram circuli, scilicet recisiones; eandem denominacionem ferias in 11, et habebis globositatem spere quam queris. Ut si 7 pedum est dyameter circuli, illum (*!*) dyametrum cubica et surgent 343; 21ᵐᵃ pars horum, scilicet 16 pedes et tercia pars pedis, denominacio, scilicet que ducta in

three other references to *Archimenides* (not present in the original work) are added (see note 2, Propositions 15–18), reflecting, I suppose, the rising influence of the Archimedean tracts.

The most interesting and important geometrical handbook of the fourteenth century is the *De arte mensurandi* of Johannes de Muris. I have examined the Archimedean sections of this work at considerable length in Part I of this volume. That investigation revealed a quite extensive influence of Archimedes' works on the presentation of the traditional Archimedean formulas. Furthermore, it showed that, for the first time, William of Moerbeke's translations were being used in a geometrical manual. But I believe that the *De arte mensurandi* also submitted to the influence of one or another version of Gerard of Cremona's translation of the *De mensura circuli* from the Arabic, as I have suggested in Part I, Chapter 4. Furthermore, the quotation I have given in footnote one of that chapter contains the conventional formulas for a circle of the earlier handbook tradition: $c = d \cdot 3\frac{1}{7}$, $d = c \cdot \frac{1}{3} \cdot \frac{21}{22}$, $S = r \cdot (c/2)$, $S = (d/2) \cdot (c/2)$, $S = [d \cdot (c/2)]/2$, $S = (c \cdot r)/2$, $S = (d \cdot c)/4$, $S = d^2 \cdot \frac{11}{14}$, $S = d^2 - (d^2/7)$ $- (d^2/14)$. In the same passage, Johannes noted that the reader ought to be content at that point (i.e., before examining the propositions from *On Spiral Lines* given later) with the approximate concord of a straight line and a curve. He adds that the reader will perhaps be satisfied with the justification provided by rolling the circumference of a circle on a surface until it completes a revolution. The straight line described on the plane will be equal to the curved line. This is identical to the justification given in the Corpus Christi Version of the *De mensura circuli* (see Volume One, page 170, lines 14–19). The rolling technique of this justification was to play a central role in the discussions of Charles de Bouelles later (see below, Part III, Chapter 6, Section IV).

Finally, in assaying the relationship between Johannes de Muris' work and the handbook traditions, I should reiterate a conclusion that I have already advanced in Part I, Chapter 6. Though Johannes gave numerous references to demonstrations in Archimedes' *On the Sphere and the Cylinder* and *On Conoids and Spheroids* in Chapter 10 of his *De arte*

---

10 facit 163 [et] 3^{am} pedis, scilicet excessum cubi ad speram. Eadem ducta in 11^{am} dabit soliditatem spere, scilicet 179 et duas tercias pedis, quam querebamus, cui si addatur excessus redditur cubus. Et hoc erat propositum. . . . Vicesimum theoreuma: Circuli inauraturam rimari. Est enim inauratura spacium inter (*!* intra?) duos circulos inclusum, quorum secundi dyameter est duplus (*!* equalis) ad primum (*!* primam), quod sic fit. Meciatur dyameter se, productum meciatur in 22, productum (136r) dividatur per 7, denominacio dabit circuli inauraturam, que semper quadrupla est ad aream eius. Eandem habebis si dyameter periferiam meciatur, quod probatur ratione numeri. Ut si 7 pedum est dyameter, 154 erit inauratura." The origin of the references to "Archimenides" I suppose to be as follows: those in propositions 15 and 16 from some version of Gerard of Cremona's translation of *De mensura circuli*, that in Proposition 17 from the original *Practica geometrie*, that in Proposition 18 from the *Liber de curvis superficiebus*, Proposition X (see Volume 1, p. 504). I hardly need point out that there is some confusion in the definition of the *circuli inauratura* given here in the *Liber theoreumantie*.

mensurandi, his main purpose remained that of the early manuals, namely to give metrical formulas with numerical examples. Such formulas included those for the lateral surface and volume of a cylinder, the lateral surface and volume of a cone and a truncated cone, the surface and volume of a sphere and its segments and sectors. It will also be recalled that, in addition to these various correct formulas, he offered some incorrect ones concerning his "arcuate rhombus." Still, whatever his overall objective was in Chapter 10 of the *De arte mensurandi*, the fact that he included formal demonstrations in other parts of the work and that he has often told us where demonstrations may be found (though he has not given them) shows that he was very much under the influence of the formal geometry available to him.

Far less interesting from the standpoint of the intrusion of the conclusions of the Archimedean tracts into the metrical tradition is the *Practica geometrie* of Johannes de Muris' contemporary at Paris, Dominicus de Clavasio (or Clivaxo). Dominicus' work was composed in 1346.[3] The Archimedean formulas found in the earlier manuals were repeated by Dominicus without any formal proofs, though other non-Archimedean metrical formulas were often proved by the Parisian master. In presenting the rules for determining the circumference, he asserts, under the probable influence of Proposition III of the *De mensura circuli*, that there is no certain, demonstrated ratio between the circumference and the diameter:[4]

Because there is not a certain demonstrated ratio between the circumference and the diameter, hence when I speak of the mensuration of a circle by a square, I

---

[3] H. L. L. Busard, "The Practica Geometriae of Dominicus de Clavasio," *Archive for History of Exact Sciences*, Vol. 2, No. 6 (1965), pp. 520–75. For the date of composition, see p. 520.

[4] *Ibid.*, p. 556: "Sequitur quartum quid nominis: Circumferencie circuli cuiuslibet ad suam dyametrum est proporcio tripla sesquiseptima vel ea circa. Unde manifestum est quod si dyameter est nota, circumferencia erit nota. Et si circumferencia nota, dyameter erit nota. Quia circumferencie ad dyametrum non est aliqua certa proporcio demonstrata, ideo quando loquor de mensuracione circuli cum quadrato, non intendo demonstrative loqui, sed solum docere invenire aream ita, quod error sensibilis non relinquatur. Supposita prima parte supposicionis correlaria satis patent quia, si dyameter est nota, tripla eius et producto adde septimam partem eiusdem dyametri et habebis circumferenciam, ut si dyameter esset 7, circumferencia esset 22; et si dyameter esset 2, circumferencia esset 6 cum duabus septimis unius; et si circumferencia esset nota, ab ea subtrahe 22^{am} partem et residui 3^{a} pars erit dyameter, ut si circumferencia est 22, subtrahe 22^{am} partem, que est unum, et remanet 21, cuius tercia pars est 7 et illa est dyameter vel sic: si per dyametrum vis habere circumferenciam, multiplica numerum dyametri per 22 et productum divide per 7 et exibit circumferencia, ut si dyameter sit 5, multiplica 5 per 22 et habebis 110, que divide per 7 et exibit 15 cum $^{5}/_{7}$, sed si per circumferenciam vis habere dyametrum, multiplica numerum circumferencie per numerum 7 et productum divide per 22 et exibit dyameter, ut si circumferencia sit 8, multiplica 8 per 7 et habebis 56 que divide per 22 et habebis duo integra et 12/22as et ista est dyameter." I have omitted Busard's apparatus and the diagrams here and in the following citations.

do not intend to speak demonstratively but only to teach how to find the area of a circle such that no sensible error remains.

This statement is followed by the standard formulas $c = d \cdot 3\frac{1}{7}$ and $d = [c - (c/22)]/3$. The remark that there is no demonstrated ratio between circumference and diameter is essentially the same as that found in the anonymous commentary on the *Sphere* of Sacrobosco that I quoted in Section II of this chapter (see that section, note 12). Dominicus expresses the same conclusion later when he remarks on the finding of the area of a circle in terms of a square:[5]

To find the area of a circle in terms of a given square measure without any sensible area remaining. In these [problems] in which a circle is compared to a square or vice versa, I cannot speak demonstratively since there is no demonstrated ratio between a circle and a square.

The fact that Dominicus did not believe that an exact numerical value for π can be demonstrated does not, I suppose, mean that he rejected the geometrical proof of Archimedes found in Proposition I of the *De mensura circuli*, which shows that, if we assume that there is some straight line equal to the circumference of a circle, the circle is equal to a right triangle with sides about the right angle equal respectively to the radius and the circumference. At least we know that Dominicus accepted and stated the Archimedean formula for the area of a circle, namely, $S = (d/2) \cdot (c/2)$.[6] I thus suppose that he would have agreed with Gordanus' *Compilacio quorundam canonum in practicis astronomie et geometrie*, where the author says that he will speak "demonstratively" when he gives the Archimedean proof for the quadrature of the circle (see Volume One, page 144n). But, if I am right in these suppositions, it is still somewhat puzzling that Dominicus did not include any formal demonstrations for the Archimedean formulas. For the fact that the altitude of an equilateral triangle is incommensurable to a side of the triangle did not prevent him from determining such an altitude on the basis of a general procedure which he had demonstrated by reference to Euclid's *Elements*. Could it

---

[5] *Ibid.*, p. 565: "Constructio 19ª: Circuli secundum datam mensuram quadratam non relinquendo errorem sensibilem aream invenire. In istis in quibus comparatur circulus ad quadratum vel e contra, non possum loqui demonstrative quia circuli et quadrati nulla est proporcio demonstrata. Sit circulus d et mensura quadrata data g, scias istius circuli dyametrum et circumferenciam, ut docetur in supposicione scilicet 4ª istius 2ⁱ et in 17ª constructione huius, cuius dyametri accipe medietatem et eciam medietatem circumferencie et duc medietatem dyametri in medietatem circumferencie et productum est area circuli. Sicut si dyameter est 7 pedum et circumferencia 22, duc 3 cum dimidio in 11 et sunt 38 cum dimidio. Et si g esset superficies pedalis, circulus eam contineret 38 vicibus cum medietate. Constructio 20ª: Semicirculi aream invenire. Scias aream tocius circuli et eius aree medietas est area semicirculi. Constructio 21ª: Nota dyametro alicuius circuli vel semicirculi aream invenire. Si dyameter est nota, circumferencia erit nota ut dicitur in supposicione huius 2ⁱ, quibus notis ducas medietatem dyametri in medietatem circumferencie et habebis aream circuli. Et istius aree medietas est area semicirculi. Eodem modo si circumferencia esset nota, area potest inveniri tam circuli quam semicirculi quia si circumferencia est nota, dyameter erit nota."

[6] This formula is given in the preceding footnote.

be that, like his contemporary Nicole Oresme, he believed that there were some irrational magnitudes more irrational than others (as for example, a ratio whose terms are not only immediately incommensurable but are also incommensurable in their squares is conceived as being more irrational than a ratio whose terms are immediately incommensurable but are commensurable in their squares) and that π represented such a magnitude of greater irrationality?[7] And thus could it be that the excessively irrational nature of such a magnitude made not only its exact numerical mensuration impossible but its geometrical demonstration highly suspect and unworthy of pursuing? Or was it simply that proofs involving quadrature were more difficult and lengthy and thus beyond the scope of Dominicus' work or perhaps even beyond his competence?

Be that as it may, his paramount concern with mensuration (and possibly his basic assumption that π itself already involves approximation) led him to present an approximative method of determining the area of a circular segment greater than a semicircle (and thus perhaps to reject the correct formula that he may have seen in the earlier manuals).[8] First he tells us to find the area of the semicircle (following the Archimedean rule he has just given—see note 6). Then we are to bisect the two arcs of the segment extending beyond the semicircle and draw a chord through the bisecting points. Then through these bisecting points we are to erect two lines perpendicular to the diameter of the circle of which this segment is a part and extending to the base of the segment which has itself been extended in both directions. Thus we have constructed a rectangle nearly equal to the excess of the segment beyond its semicircle. Finally we are to add the area of this rectangle to the previously determined area of the semicircle.

Shortly thereafter Dominicus gives the conventional formula for the surface of a sphere: $S = d \cdot c$, adding, as had many others, that the surface of the sphere was four times its greatest circle.[9] He introduces in

---

[7] M. Clagett, *Nicole Oresme and the Medieval Geometry of Qualities and Motions* (Madison, Wisc., 1968), pp. 473–76.

[8] Busard, "The Practica Geometriae," pp. 565–66: "Constructio 22ª: Porcionis circuli aream invenire. Si sit porcio maior, scias aream semicirculi, postea arcum residui in duobus locis divide per equalia sicut in puncto *c* et in puncto *d* et a punctis *c* et *d* divisionum supra dyametrum protrahe perpendiculares et unam illarum ducas in lineam que est inter duo puncta supra que cadunt perpendiculares que est linea *ab* et productum est area illius residui vel prope, quia in istis porcionibus difficile est habere areas. Si vero fuerit porcio minor, quere aream semicirculi et aream residui quod continetur inter dyametrum et cordam illius porcionis, quam subtrahe ab area semicirculi et relinquitur area porcionis minoris."

[9] *Ibid.*, p. 567: "Constructio 24ª: Aream convexi date spere invenire. Istius spere scias dyametrum et eciam circumferenciam maximi circuli. Postea ducas dyametrum in illam circumferenciam et productum est area. Unde constat quod superficies spere est quadrupla ad superficiem maximi circuli in ea contenti etc. Constructio 25ª: Aream concavi date spere invenire. Scias dyametrum et circumferenciam istius spere et dyametrum ducas in circumferenciam et productum est area quia tanta est area concavi spere continentis, quanta est convexi spere contente. Ex istis potes habere aream semispere concavi vel convexi quia, si tocius spere capias medietatem, eius medietas est quod queris."

connection with this problem the notion of the convex and concave surfaces of a sphere and indicates their identity. Dominicus then presents formulas for the lateral and total surfaces of a cylinder and a cone.[10] But in connection with the lateral surface of a cone, he errs by telling us to take one-half the product of the circumference of the base and the altitude (rather than the slant height) of the cone. This error is not merely a slip, for he gives us instructions as to how to find the altitude from the slant height and the radius of the base. In the formulas for the cylinder and the cone, the lateral surface in each case is designated as a *curva superficies*, an expression, we have seen, made popular by the *Liber de curvis superficiebus*. But if he had read the latter work, it is difficult to see how he could have ignored the correct formulation given there for the lateral surface of a cone, particularly since it was so cogently demonstrated in that tract.

Turning to Dominicus' volumetric formulas, we find that he has given the correct formula for the volume of a hemisphere, $V = (1 - \frac{1}{3})$ $\cdot(area\ of\ base\ circle\cdot radius)$, obviously equivalent to $V = 2\pi r^3/3$, which volume is of course doubled when one seeks the volume of the whole sphere.[11] In this problem, he notes that just as there is no certain, demonstrated ratio between a square and a circle, so there is no such ratio between a sphere and a "rectilinear" (i.e. rectiplanar) body, but that in these

---

[10] *Ibid.*, pp. 567–68: "Constructio 26ª: Columpne rotunde aream invenire. Columpna rotunda, ut dicitur 11 Euclidis, est transitus parallelogrammi rectanguli latere rectum angulum continente fixo, ipsaque superficie donec ad suum locum redeat circumducta. Illius columpne scias circumferenciam basis quam ducas in eius altitudinem et productum est area curve superficiei tue; si addas areas duorum circulorum habebis totam aream columpne, ut si columpne *abcd* circumferencia circuli *g* esset 6 pedum et altitudo columpne, que est linea *gh*, esset 8; ducas 6 in 8 et sunt 48 et illa est area. Et ymaginaveris quod circuli *g* et *h* stent plani et quod eorum circumferencie sint equidistantes et equales. Constructio 27ª: Rotunde piramidis aream invenire. Piramis rotunda est transitus trianguli rectanguli alterutro suorum laterum angulum rectum continencium fixo donec usque ad locum, unde moveri cepit, redeat triangulo ipso circumducto. Date piramidis queras altitudinem hoc est lineam rectam que cadit a cono piramidis super centrum circuli basis eius, quam altitudinem sic invenies: scias medietatem dyametri circuli basis, quam duc in se quadrate et eciam scias lineam rectam ⟨a⟩ circumferencia circuli ad summitatem coni piramidis quam lineam similiter ducas in se quadrate et ab eius quadrato subtrahe quadratum medietatis dyametri et residuum est quadratum altitudinis, cuius quere radicem quadratam quia ipsa est altitudo quia triangulus causatus ex medietate dyametri et altitudine piramidis et linea recta, que protenditur a circumferencie circuli basis ad conum piramidis, est rectangulus, igitur quadratum altitudinis cum quadrato semidyametri valent quadratum alterius linee, qua altitudine scita ducas eam in circumferenciam circuli basis et producti medietas est area curve superficiei tue; si addideris aream circuli basis, habebitur area tocius piramidis."

[11] *Ibid.*, p. 571: "Constructio 7ª: Semispere secundum datam mensuram cubicam capacitatem satis prope invenire. Sicut quadrati ad circulum nondum est aliqua certa proporcio demonstrata, sic nec eciam spere ad corpus rectilineum, sed in istis sufficit habere ita prope, quod non relinquitur error sensibilis. Si vero semispere vis habere capacitatem, scias aream oris illius semispere, quam ducas in semidyametrum et a producto subtrahe 3ᵃᵐ partem et residuum est capacitas semispere. Et si vis habere capacitatem tocius spere dupla capacitatem semispere et provenit capacitas tocius spere."

matters it suffices to have an approximation without any sensible error remaining. Dominicus also includes correct formulas for the volume of a cylinder and a cone.[12] In presenting the problem of finding the capacity of a well in terms of how many *situlae* it contains (the *situla* being of the shape of a truncated cone), he gives the erroneous, approximative formula for a *situla* of this shape that is found in the *Practica geometrie* with incipit: "Artis cuiuslibet consummatio. . . ."[13] This formula embraces the procedure of finding the mean circle and then multiplying it by the altitude; that is, it reflects the erroneous formula expressed by Hero (see Section II, note 5).

Toward the end of the fourteenth century a so-called *Geometria culmensis* was composed and dedicated to Conrad von Jungingen, Master General of the Teutonic Knights (1393–1407). I mention it as this point because it depends primarily on Dominicus de Clavasio's *Practica* for its geometric rules. The only Archimedean rules included therein are those for the circle, since the tract is concerned only with flat surfaces, there being no section on stereometry.[14] Quite distinct from Dominicus' *Practica*

[12] *Ibid.*, p. 572–73: "Conclusio (*!* constructio?) nona: Rotunde columpne secundum datam mensuram cubicam capacitatem invenire. Dico non relinquendo sensibilem defectum. Sit *a* columpna mensuranda, scias quociens area unius superficiei corporis cubici continetur in area circuli basis dicte columpne per 19[am] precedentis. Postea scias quociens altitudo corporis cubici continetur in altitudine columpne. Deinde duc unum numerum quociens in alium et productum est capacitas. . . . (p. 573). . . . Constructio 11[a]: Rotunde piramidis secundum datam mensuram cubicam capacitatem invenire. Quere aream circuli basis et eciam altitudinem. Et scias capacitatem columpne rotunde constitute super illam basim secundum altitudinem piramidis, ut docet 8[a] huius et illius capacitatis tercia pars est capacitas piramidis, quia omnis columpna rotunda: piramidi sue tripla esse comprobatur, ut dicitur in 9[a] 12[i]."

[13] *Ibid.*, p. 574: "Constructio 13[a]: Putei secundum datam situlam capacitatem habere. Quia situla communiter habet unum fundum maius alio, ideo equa maius minori, ut si unius fundi dyameter esset 6 et alterius 4, adde 6 ad 4 et habebis 10, cuius accipe medietatem et tunc habes fundum communem. Quo habito vide quociens continetur in area oris putei per 18[am] 2[i] huius. Postea scias putei profunditatem per terciam primi huius et scias quociens altitudo situle continetur in profunditate putei, postea numerum secundum quem area fundi communis situle continetur in area oris putei ducas in numerum secundum quem altitudo situle continetur in profunditate putei et productum est numerus denotans quot situlas continet puteus, ut si area communis fundi situle continetur in area oris putei 20 vicibus et altitudo situle continetur 100 vicibus in putei profunditate, ducas 20 in 100 et sunt 2000. Dico quod puteus tenet 2000 sitularum aque. Et si velles scire quot pintas, vide eodem modo quot pintas tenet situla et illum numerum multiplica per numerum, qui denotat quot situlas tenet puteus et productum est numerus denotans, quot pintas tenet puteus, ut si situla de quibus puteus continet 2000, contineret 30 pintas, multiplica 30 in 2000 et sunt 60,000 et tot pintas tenet puteus. Eodem modo si velles scire quot vitra vel quot mensuras rotundas quantumcumque parvas."

[14] *Geometria culmensis: Ein agronomischer Tractat aus der Zeit des Hochmeisters Conrad von Jungingen (1393–1407)*, ed. of H. Mendthal (Leipzig, 1886), pp. 65–72, where we find the formulas for a diameter in terms of its circumference, a circumference in terms of its diameter, the area of a circle and the area of segments of a circle—all with a considerable amount of direct or almost direct quotation from the text of Dominicus de

and its derivative *Geometria culmensis* (so far as revealing the influence of Archimedean tracts on the handbook tradition) is the *Liber de inquisicione capacitatis figurarum*.[15] This work must at least postdate the *Canones tabularum primi mobilis* of Johannes de Lineriis, which it cites.[16] The *Canones* was composed at Paris in 1322.[17] Like Dominicus' *Practica*, the *Liber de inquisicione* does not give formal demonstrations for the Archimedean formulas. On the other hand, unlike the Parisian's work, it does cite Archimedean tracts in which demonstrations may be found, those tracts being the *Liber trium fratrum* (i.e., the *Verba filiorum* of the Banū Mūsā) and the *Liber de curvis superficiebus*, which latter work the author attributed to *Archimenides*, as we shall see. After distinguishing *capacitas* used for surface or area from *capacitas* used for volume (i.e., for the *tota moles solidi*), the author begins with problems involving a circle.[18] These embrace numerical examples that reveal the

Clavasio. The Latin text is accompanied by a German translation of about the same period. I do not think the publication of the text of all of these propositions is needed but I can give a short passage that may be compared with the text in note 5: "(p. 69) Campi circularis aream invenire. 'In hiis, in quibus circulus ad quadratum conparatur seu tetragonum vel econverso, non possum loqui vere demonstrative et precise, quia circuli et quadrati adinvicem nulla est certa proporcio et precise demonstrata, sed in tantum est, quod non relinquitur error sensibilis.' " For the relationship between the *Geometria culmensis* and Dominicus' tract, see M. Curtze, "Mathematisch-historische Miscellen," *Bibliotheca mathematica*, Neue Folge, Vol. 9 (1895), pp. 107–10.

[15] Published by M. Curtze, "De inquisicione capacitatis figurarum: anonyme Abhandlung aus dem fünfzehnten Jahrhundert," *Abhandlungen zur Geschichte der Mathematik*, 8. Heft (1898), pp. 29–68.

[16] *Ibid.*, p. 46: "Posito igitur *ap* synu verso, quaeram arcum eius per quartam primi Magistri de Lineriis, et habetur sic." The procedure referred to can be found in Curtze's partial edition of the *Canones* of Johannes de Lineriis, "Urkunden zur Geschichte der Trigonometrie im christlichen Mittelalter," *Bibliotheca mathematica*, 3. Folge, Vol. 1 (1900), p. 393: "4. Sinus versi propositi arcum invenire."

[17] E. Poulle, "John of Lignères," *Dictionary of Scientific Biography*, Vol. 7 (New York, 1973), p. 123. Cf. Curtze, "Urkunden," p. 390.

[18] Curtze, "De inquisicione capacitatis," pp. 36–40, 43–44, 49–51 (with occasional corrections and additions from Munich, Staatsbibl. 56, 207r–09r, 211r, 214r–15r: sigl. *M* and Vienna, Nationalbibl. 5277, 101r–02v, 104r–v, 106v–07v: sigl. *V*): "Aliquid de inquisicione capacitatis figurarum et quibusdam arismetricis orsurus dico, quod figurae capacitas dupliciter [*add. MV*: quantum] ad presens. Sumitur uno modo pro superficie tantum, et sic est planicies, area, podismus, campus, spacium, pedatura, fundus, embadum, seu superficies figurae absoluta vel linea seu lineis interclusa. Alio modo est tota moles solidi in relacione alicuius mensurae eam mensurantis considerata etc. Et quia circulus est figura omnium figurarum simplicissima . . . ab illa igitur hic principium facere non indigne complacuit. . . . (p. 37). . . . 2. Datae dyametri circumferenciam circuli invenire. Esto, ut sit circulus *ab*, et dyametrus eius data, verbi gracia 14, sit *ab*. Quam dyametrum tripla, et proveniunt 42. Producto si ⅟₇ dyametri praedictae, scilicet 2, addideris, 44, quae sunt circuli circumferencia, producuntur. Patet per 7ᵃᵐ geometriae trium fratrum. 3. Datae circumferenciae circuli dyametrum indagare. Sit circumferencia circuli data, ut supra, verbi gracia 44. Ab ipsa igitur aufer 22ᵃᵐ partem, scilicet 2, et residui tercia pars, scilicet 14, fit dyameter circumferenciae circuli praedictae. Patet per dictam 7ᵃᵐ geometriae trium fratrum. 4. Dati circuli embadum invenire. Datum autem dico circulum, cuius dyameter est data. Esto igitur circulus *ab*, cuius centrum *d*, et dyameter *adb* verbi gracia 14, et circumferencia 44. Ducta

igitur medietate dyametri, scilicet *ad*, ut septem, in medietatem circumferenciae, ut in 22, provenit 154, quae sic dati embadum circuli producunt. Patet per quartam trium fratrum. Arcus dati sectoris aream invenire. Circuli sector, ut vult Euclides diffinicione 10ª tercii libri, est figura, quae sub duabus a centro ductis lineis et sub arcu, qui ab eis comprehenditur, continetur. Esto sector *adc* in dato circulo *acb*, cuius centrum *d*, dyameter *adb* ut 14, et circumferencia *acb* tota 44, arcus autem, scilicet *ac*, ut 11, (p. 38) embadum circuli per praecedentem 154. Sicut igitur se habet tota circumferencia *acb* ad arcum sectionis *ac*, sic se habet totum embadum circuli *acb* ad embadum sectoris *adc*. Patet per Ptolemaeum in almagesti dictione sexta capitulo 7°, ubi dicit: "Et quia proportio orbium ad arcus erit aequalis proporcioni superficierum ipsorum ad superficies sectorum." Idem patet per corrolarium quartae trium fratrum. Duc igitur arcum sectoris, ut numeri secundi, in circuli embadum, ut tercium, et divide per primum, scilicet per circumferenciam circuli, et 38 et ½ unius, quod est embadum sectoris, producitur. 6. Sphaerae, cuius maximus fuerit datus circulus, planiciem indagare. Esto sphaera, cuius maximus datus circulus sit *ab*, et dyameter tota verbi gracia 14. Ergo per quartam huius embadum circuli erit 154, quod si quadrupletur, exurgit embadum sphaerae praedictae, scilicet 616. Patet per 15ᵃᵐ(*! 14ᵃᵐ*) trium fratrum. Quod idem est, ac si dicatur: dyametrum in circumferenciam circuli multiplica. Idem enim producitur. 7. Datum circulum incrassare. Circulum incrassare voco sphaerae molem seu magnitudinem, cuius maior circulus fuerit datus, invenire. (p. 39). Esto circulus datus, cuius volo crassitudinem, *ab*, cuius dyameter *ab* ut 14, quam cubabo, et proveniunt 2744, quae sunt cubus dyametri circuli dati. Qui cubus per 10ᵃᵐ Archimenidis de curvis superficiebus habet se ad sphaeram dati circuli, sicut 21 ad 11. Ducatur igitur 11 in cubum, scilicet in 2744, et dividatur per 21, et 1437 et ⅓ unius, quae sunt moles seu crassitudo circuli dati, producuntur. [[*Add. M (208r) et V (102r); om. Curtze:* [8a] Date figure rectilinee cuiuscunque latus tetragonicum invenire. Latus tetragonicum dicitur illud quod si in se ducatur constituit quadratum equale figure date. Si igitur data figura rectilinea fuerit multiangula, ipsam ut facit Campanus in commento 32⁽ᵒ⁾ primi Euclidis aut secundum quod tibi (*M, ubi V*) figura occurrit (*?*) in triangulos ductis hinc inde ab angulis eius lineis resolve, et cuiuslibet (*M, cuiuscunque V*) trianguli per ultimam secundi Euclidis quadrate equale singillatim quere, quia quodlibet latus quadrati huiusmodi est latus tetragonicum trianguli illius cui (*M, cuius V*) quadratum equale invenisti. Dum igitur omnium triangulorum in quos data figura fuit resoluta sic ut prediciter, scilicet cuiuslibet singillatim latus tetragonicum inveneris ea in unum latus tetragonicum omnia sic converteris. Sit verbi gracia latus primi *ab*, secundi (*V: 102v*) *bc*, tercii *cd*, et cetera (*M, om. V*). Igitur (*M, ergo V*) applicabo *bc* orthogonaliter cum *ab* et protraham lineam *ac*. Ergo per penultimam primi Euclidis latus *ac* est latus tetragonicum primi et secundi triangulorum. Deinde iterum cum linea *ac* coniunge (*M, coniungam V*) orthogonaliter lineam *cd* et protraham lineam *ad* et per eandem eiusdem erit linea *ad* latus trium triangulorum et cetera. Si plures habueris et latus ultimo repertum [*add. V, om. M:* est latus] tetragonicum figure quod latus si quadraveris habebis quadratum figure date equale.]] 8. Dati circuli orthoparallelogrammum quadruplum invenire. Unde manifestum est, quod latus tetragonicum quartae orthoparallelogrammi praedicti est latus quadrati dato circulo aequalis. Esto datus circulus *ab*, cuius dyameter *ab*. A terminis igitur dyametri *ab* ducam duas lineas rectas perpendiculares ad lineam *ab*, et ut quaelibet illarum sit aequalis circumferenciae circuli dati *ab*, quae sint *ac* et *db*, et complebo orthoparallelogrammum ducta linea *cd*: ergo per sextam Archimenidis de curvis superficiebus ipsum orthoparallelogrammum *acdb* est aequale embado sphaereae circuli dati, ergo per 15ᵐ(*! 14ᵐ*) geometriae trium fratrum ipsum orthoparallelogrammum est quadruplum ad circulum datum *ab*, quod erat assumptum. Rursus ex ultimo (*! neccesitate MV*) praedicti orthoparallelogrammi quarta est aequalis circulo dato. Cuius quartae si per 40ᵃᵐ primi et ultimam secundi (p. 40) Euclidis latus tetragonicum quaesieris, ipsum erit latus quadrati circulo dato aequalis. [*Curtze, om. MV:* Radix quadrata areae circuli, scilicet 154, 14 ⁴¹/₁₀₀ (*! 12⁴¹/₁₀₀*) fere, vel in phisicis 12 integra 24 Mª. 36 2ª]. . . . (p. 43). . . . 16. Porcionis circuli dati arcus aream scrutari. Portio circuli est superficies inter datum arcum et cordam eius consistens. Sit circulus *ab*, cuius centrum *c*, et arcus datus porcionis circuli, (p. 44) quae quaeritur, *ab*, cuius corda *ab*. Quia igitur arcus *ab* est notus, erit corda eius *ab* nota, et lineae *ac* et *cb*, quia semidyametri dati circuli, notae. Ergo per 5ᵃᵐ huius sector *acb* erit notus, et per 11ᵃᵐ huius

formulas $c = d \cdot 3\frac{1}{7}$, the given diameter being 14 (see note 18, Prop. 2); $d = c/3\frac{1}{7}$, with the circumference given as 44 (*ibid.*, Prop. 3). The authority for these formulations is designated as Proposition 7 of the *Geometria trium fratrum*, though in fact the authority should rather be Proposition 6 of that work (see Volume One, page 278, lines 178–82). He then reveals the formula for the area of a circle by an example with the diameter given as 14: $S = (d/2) \cdot (c/2)$ (see note 18, Prop. 4). The authority for this last formula is designated as Proposition 4 of the *Geometria trium fratrum* (see Volume One, page 256). Then follows the formula for the area of a sector of a circle whose arc is 11 and whose diameter is 14: $S = [(arc/circum) \cdot area\ of\ circle]$ (see note 18, Prop. 5).

trigonus *acb* erit notus. Subtrahatur igitur trigonus de sectore, et residuum est porcio circuli inter arcum et cordam *ab* contenta. . . . (p. 49). . . . 24. Columpnae rotundae datorum basis et altitudinis aream invenire. Columpna rotunda, ut vult Euclides 11ma diffinicione (*!* circa principium *MV*) undecimi, est transitus parallelogrammi rectanguli latere rectum angulum continente fixo ipsaque superficie, donec ad suum locum redeat, circumducta. Columpnae datae basis circumferenciam, verbi gracia ut 44, duc in (p. 50) axem seu altitudinem columpnae, ut in 12, et per secundam Archimenidis provenit tota curva superficies columpnae, scilicet 528. Cui si areas duorum circulorum columpnae per quartam huius scitas adiunxeris, totalis superficies columpnae exurgit, [scilicet 836 *Curtze, om. MV*]. 25. Columpnae rotundae datorum basis et altitudinis capacitatem seu crassitudinem invenire. Sit columpna ut prius, cuius basis *fge* verbi gracia 154, et altitudo *ba* ut 12. Duc igitur basim in eius altitudinem, et proveniunt 1848, quae sunt crassitudo columpnae praedictae. Et de hiis columpnis rotundis et doleis et vasibus et eorum capacitatibus satis prius dictum est in tractatu collacionum de virga visoria, ideo hic non repetam illud. 26. Piramidis rotundae basis circulo et eius ypotenusa datis aream invenire. Piramis rotunda est transitus triangulis rectanguli alterutro suorum laterum rectum angulum continencium fixo, donec ad locum, unde cepit, redeat, triangulo ipso circumducto. Haec Euclides sui 11°. Quid autem sit ypotenusa patet in hiis versibus: Protracta linea basis est, erecta cathetus; Tenditur ad fines ypotenusa duos. Sit rotunda piramis *abc*, cuius sit basis nota, scilicet circulus *bec*, et similiter nota ypotenusa *ac*; et sit eius axis sive altitudo *ad*. Duc igitur circumferenciam circuli *bce* (*!* bec *MV*) in altitudinem *ad*, et producti medietatem accipe, quia ipsa est id, quod quaeritur, addita ei area circuli basis per 4^{am} huius nota. Si vero nescieris quantitatem altitudinis *ad*, duc medietatem dyametri circuli *bec* (p. 51) in se, et similiter unam ypotenusarum in se, et subtrahe unum quadratum ab alio, et residui radix quadrata est ipsa altitudo. . . . . 28. Piramidis rotundae aut lateratae regularis datae basis et altitudinis crassitudinem invenire. Duc superficiem basis eius in suam altitudinem, et provenit crassitudo columpnae basis praedictae. Cuius si ⅓ acceperis, ipsa eadem ⅓ erit crassitudo piramidis praedictae. Patet per 9^{am} duodecimi Euclidis et per 12^{am} addicionis Campani ibidem." I have omitted Curtze's apparatus and his diagrams. Notice that I have given the text of an added proposition that Curtze had omitted. Though not an Archimedean proposition, it is nevertheless interesting for introducing the concept of *latus tetragonicum* used in the next proposition (Proposition 8 in Curtze's text). The added proposition, which I have called 8a, is not numbered in the Vienna manuscript where the propositions are numbered nor in the Munich manuscript where no propositions are numbered. Hence, I have left the proposition numbers of the succeeding propositions as they are in the Curtze text. L. R. Shelby, "The Geometrical Knowledge of Mediaeval Master Masons," *Speculum*, Vol. 47 (1972), pp. 412–16 (whole article, pp. 395–421) has suggested that the well-known *Geometria deutsch* published by Matthias Roriczer in about 1487–88 made use of the *Liber de inquisicione*. The argument is interesting but not conclusive in view of the great difference in approach between the two treatises and the availability of the same basic geometrical formulas in so many practical manuals.

Ptolemy's *Almagest* and a corollary to Proposition 4 of the *Geometria trium fratrum* are cited (see Volume One, page 260, lines 39–45).

From the circle the author passes on to the surface of a sphere, where it is noted that the surface of the sphere is quadruple its greatest circle or is equal to the product of its diameter and the circumference of its great circle (see note 18, Prop. 6). The authority cited is Proposition 14 of the *Geometria trium fratrum* (see Volume One, page 330, lines 36–38).[19] Naturally enough the problem of finding the volume of a sphere follows, where the formula $V = d^3 \cdot {}^{11}\!/_{21}$ is implied (see note 18, Prop. 7) and the authority cited is Proposition 10 of the *Liber de curvis superficiebus* of Archimedes (see Volume One, page 504). The author thus has shifted from the *Geometria trium fratrum* to the *Liber de curvis superficiebus* for this problem because the form of the enunciation in this latter work ("The ratio of any sphere to the cube of its diameter is as the ratio of XI to XXI") fits better with the conventional gromatic formula than does the enunciation of the *Verba filiorum* ("The multiplication of the radius of every sphere by one-third of its surface area is the volume of the sphere."—*ibid.*, p. 333). The terms used for the volume are *moles* and *crassitudo*, the latter being the term that goes back to the Roman gromatic tradition.

The author's Proposition 8 (see note 18) returns to the surface of a sphere; it shows how to construct a rectangle equal to the surface of a sphere and it returns to Proposition 14 of the *Geometria trium fratrum* as its authority. Proposition 16 (see note 18) of the *Liber de inquisicione* illustrates the formula for the area of a segment of a circle and is the same as that given in the Arabic gromatic tradition that I have quoted in Section II above, i.e., the area of the sector is first determined and then the triangle with its base on the chord and its apex on the center of the circle is subtracted from the sector. Proposition 24 (see note 18) illustrates the correct formula for the lateral surface of a cylinder: $S = c \cdot h$, with Proposition 2 of the *Liber de curvis superficiebus* cited as its authority (see Volume One, page 460), while the next proposition illustrates the determination of the volume of a cylinder by multiplying the base circle by the altitude. The authority cited for this proposition is the author's own *Tractatus collacionum de virgo visoria*, in which he had treated of such cylinders, casks, and vases.

When in Proposition 26, the author turns to the lateral surface of a cone, he repeats the error found in the *Practica geometrie* of Dominicus de Clavasio, for the formula illustrated is $S = \frac{1}{2} c \cdot h$, where c is the cir-

---

[19] The Curtze text and the two manuscripts I have used all designate the authority as the 15th proposition of the *Geometria trium fratrum*. It is however the 14th, since the 15th considers the volume of a sphere, while the 14th considers its surface, and it is the surface of a sphere that is being treated in Proposition 6 of the *Liber de inquisicione*. The same error is made in Proposition 8 of the *Liber de inquisicione*. Hence it might be that the author had some version of the *Verba filiorum* that contained an additional theorem. However, I found no such version when I prepared the edition of this text for Volume One.

cumference of its base and h is its altitude rather than its slant height. This error is strange in view of the fact that the author has repeatedly cited both the *Verba filiorum* and the *Liber de curvis superficiebus* where the formula was correctly given and demonstrated. The last of the Archimedean formulas illustrated is the correct formula for the volume of a cone in Proposition 28 (see note 18).

Another manual of the late Middle Ages worthy of passing reference is an anonymous *Practica geometrie* with incipit: "Geometria est noticia omnium rerum in pondere et mensura per virtutem numerorum demonstrata. . . ." Bradwardine is the latest authority cited by name in the tract and hence the tract must date from some time after the Englishman's *Geometria speculativa*, whose date of composition is not precisely known but must fall before his death in 1349.[20] Our anonymous *Practica* may, however, have been composed considerably later, since the only manuscript of it which I know is Vat. Ottob. lat. 1576, in which it occupies folios 47r–50v following a *Practica* composed by a certain Christophorus in the period 1492–96.[21] The anonymous *Practica*, in the section on planimetry, contains the conventional formulas for the relationship of circumference and diameter and for the area of the circle.[22]

[20] See John Murdoch's article on Thomas Bradwardine in the *Dictionary of Scientific Biography*, Vol. 2 (New York, 1970), pp. 390–97 (and p. 395 for the *Geometria speculativa*).

[21] Christophorus' *Practica geometrie* occupies folios 1r–46v and is followed by the anonymous *Practica* that I am considering here. The colophon of the tract of Christophorus with its information on the date of composition has been given by J. F. Daly, "Mathematics in the Codices Ottoboniani Latini," *Manuscripta*, Vol. 8 (1964), p. 17. The tract contains the conventional Archimedean formulas. I have not treated it in this chapter because it lies far outside of its chronological limits. But it does illustrate the continuation of the *Practica* traditions deep into the Renaissance, noted at the end of this chapter.

[22] Vat. Ottob. lat. 1576, 48r–50v: "Sequitur iam de mensuracione circulorum. Ad circuli aream habendam necesse est circumferenciam eius esse notam (48v) aut eius diametrum, per alterutrum enim notificatur (*corr. ex* notificantur). Scita enim circumferencia, dividatur per tria cum ⅐, et quociens est diameter. Diametro nota, multiplica ipsam per 3 cum ⅐ parte et productum est circumferencia. Diametro igitur et circumferencia notis, si circuli aream habere volueris, duc diametrum in circumferenciam, de quibus cape unam quartam partem; aut medietatem diametri in circumferenciam, de quibus cape medium; vel medietatem circumferencie in diametrum, de quibus etiam capiatur medium; vel medietas (*!*) diametri in medietatem circumferencie, et semper patet (*?*) area circuli eadem. Est tum alius communis modus inveniendi per diametrum aream circuli, puta quod ducatur diameter in se et productum multiplicatur per 11, indeque proveniens dividatur per 14, et quociens erit area. Et sic per aream invenitur diameter opposito modo, ducendo aream per 14 et productum dividendo per 11. De quociente vero querere radicem et illa erit diameter talis circuli. Istis visis facile est videre aream alicuius figure infra circulum descripte, quia primo querenda est area circuli, postea area figure inscripte circulo iuxta denominacionem eius et illam ab area circuli subtrahere et restat area porcionum circuli. Hic restaret aliquid dicere de quadratura circuli. Ideo breviter dimissis omnibus opinionibus teneo cum Euclide, boetio, archimenide, bravardino atque aliis expertis quod circulus est quadrabilis. Presuppositis igitur tribus suppositionibus liquido patebit possibilitas proposui. Prima igitur suppositio est quod circulum quadrare non est circumferenciam eius in modum quadrati, ut aliqui putarent (*?*), disponere, sed est quadratum eiusdem continencie cum circulo invenire, non laborando in cassum an latera illius quadrati

After saying that he holds with Euclid, Boethius, Archimedes, and Bradwardine that the circle is squarable, he gives a long and trivial discussion
of finding a square equal to a circle where the area of the circle is
known to be 154. Before giving the procedure, the author advances three
suppositions. The first tells us that to square a circle is not to dispose the
circumference in the form of a square, as some would think, but is to find

simul iuncta sint maiora circuli periferia. 2^a supposicio est si quod ab uno trianguli
latere in seipsum ducto producitur equum fuerit duobus rectis quadratis que (49r) a duobus
reliquis lateribus describuntur, rectus est angulus cui latus illud opponitur. Et hanc asserit
euclides libro 1, propositione 47. . . . 3^a suppositio est: in omni triangulo rectanguli
(!) quadratum quod e[st] a latere recto angulo opposito in semetipso ducto describitur
equum est duobus quadratis que ex duobus reliquis lateribus circumscribuntur. Hec est
conversa prioris et 46 propositio euclidis eiusdem libri. . . . (49v). . . . Ex hiis infero
aliquod quadratum equale ad circulum. Sit enim circulus cuius diameter da divisa fuerit
in 14 partes equales [Fig. II.3.3.1]. Talis circulus secundum omnes 154 tales partes pro
area sua continebit. Postea protrahatur linea ec ortogonaliter resecens diametrum in
puncto c, quod est tercium [punctum] diametri da. Deinde protrahatur linea semi-
diametralis a centro b ad punctum e et sit linea illa be. Tunc sic arguitur: linea be latus
oppositum recto angulo c trianguli cbe continens et illius ergo quadratum erit 49. Con-
tinebitque quadratum linee be duo quadrata duorum laterum cb et ce prescise per 3^{am}
suppositionem. Dempto ergo quadrato linee cb a quadrato linee be restat quadratum
linee ce per 2^{am} suppositionem. Sed quadratum lateris cb est 16 cum linea cb sit 4.
Removeanturque 16 ab 49 quadrato lateris be, restant 33 quadratum lateris ce cuius ce
est radix, ut patet per 3^{am} supposicionem. Istis sic actis protrahatur linea ae. Et hanc
secundum intencionem euclidis et aliorum dico esse costam quadrati equalis continencie
cum circulo assignato 154 continente in sua area, quod patet sic. Ex hiis enim tribus
lineis ae, ec et ca constituitur triangulus rectangulus in puncto c. Ergo quadratum lateris
oppositi c angulo recto, puta linea (! linee) ae, continebit duo quadrata aliorum duorum
laterum simul additorum (! addita), ut patet per 2^{am} suppositionem. Sed ambo quadrata
illorum simul additorum (! addita) prescise continent 154 continenciam (-m *injuste del.*
MS) circuli assignata[m]. Ergo et quadratum illius linee opposite, puta ae cuius ipsa est
radix, eandem continenciam reddet, et sic circulus, ut manifeste deducitur, est quadratus.
Minor quod quia quadratum lateris ce est 33, ut statim probatum est. Item linea ea cum
contineat 4 (*correxi ex* ii14) ab c ad d (! b) et 7 ab b usque a quare erit radix de 121,
quia ducendo 11 in se proveniunt 121. Addantur igitur 121 cum 33; proveniunt prescise
(50r) 154, continencia circuli assignata. Et per consequens latus oppositum illis radix erit
quadrati 154 continentis, ut patet per premissa. Et hec de quadratura circulorum. Si quis
tamen alios modos quadrandi circulum habere voluerit, videat bravardinum et alios. Et
hec de planimetria. Sequitur de solidimetria. Primo quia iam dictum est de circulis dicamus
de corporibus spericis. Si eius aream (! crassitudinem) habere volueris, scias primo eius
diametrum per eius circumferenciam, quam duc in se cubice et productum ducatur in 11,
proveniensque dividatur per 21, et quociens reddit aream (! crassitudinem) spere. Si
autem quecunque alia corpora cuiuscunque denominacionis fuerint mensurare velis, vide
an ambo extremitates sint equales. Igitur (?) si sic, quere aream unius extremitatis per
regulas planimetrie et hanc duc in longitudinem et patet quesitum. Si vero extremitates
fuerint inequales, quere areas cuiuslibet, et ipsis additis de producto capiatur medium quod
ducatur in longitudinem et patet area. Sed quia piramidalia corpora in una parte nullius
sunt spissitudinis, ideo ad eorum areas habendas quere aream extremitatis et illam duc in
longitudinem productumque divide per tria et quociens erit area illius piramidis cuiuscunque
fuerit denominacionis. . . . Si vero tecta turrium circularium vel quadrilaterarum scire
velis, duc circumferenciam aut latitudinem quatuor laterum in longitudinem et de producto
cape medium et patet area superficialis illius turris circula(50v)ris vel quadrilatre (!).''

a square with the same content as the circle. The purpose of this supposition was to set aside the kind of quadrature outlined in the quadrature tract attributed to Campanus (see Volume One, pages 581–609). The other two suppositions are respectively the converse of the Pythagorean theorem and the Pythagorean theorem itself. Then the quadrature procedure outlined in the *Practica* is simply this. With a diameter of 14 and an area of 154, a perpendicular *ce* is erected on point *c* at three units from point *d* at the end of the diameter (see Fig. II.3.3.1). By the Pythagorean theorem *ce* is shown to be $\sqrt{33}$. Then since *ca* is 11, i.e. $\sqrt{121}$, the line drawn from *e* to *a* must be $\sqrt{154}$ and thus is the side of the square equal to the circle. From planimetry the author passes to the mensuration of solids which he designates as *solidimetria*. He then gives the gromatic formula for the volume of a sphere, $V = d^3 \cdot {}^{11}\!/_{21}$, calling the volume its *area*, as Leonardo Fibonacci and other authors occasionally did. He also gives the correct formula for the volumes of bodies of uniform width (such as cylinders and prismatic columns), but in the case of bodies of "unequal width" he appears to resort to the old formula which was included in the *Practica geometrie* with incipit: "Artis cuiuslibet consummatio . . . ," i.e. find the area of the mean cross section and multiply it by the length. He does, however, give the correct formula for pyramidal bodies, namely one-third of the product of the base and the altitude. Finally, our author seems to give an incorrect formula for the lateral surface of a circular or quadrilateral tower. For after multiplying the circumference (or perimeter) by the length, he takes half the product. It could be that the passage has been corrupted by the erroneous formula for the lateral surface of a cone that was transmitted by Dominicus de Clavasio and the author of the *Liber de inquisicione capacitatis figurarum*.

While there are several other manuals of the late medieval and early Renaissance period that could also be presented for their Archimedean content,[23] I shall content myself with mentioning only one more, the *Artis metrice practice compilatio* of Leonardo de Antoniis of Cremona, which represents a rather accurate summary of the handbook formulas. Contrary to the early identification of the author with Leonardo Mainardi, who flourished in about 1488, Antonio Favaro has demonstrated that the author was rather a Franciscan, who was writing on geometrical matters in Bologna as early as 1405–06, and who appears to have been still writing

[23] Some of the manuals are listed in L. Thorndike and P. Kibre, *A Catalogue of Incipits of Mediaeval Scientific Writings in Latin*, 2nd ed. (Cambridge, Mass., 1963), cc. 584–86. For example, see Book II of Leonardo da Pistoia's *Mathematica* (*ibid.*, c. 586). Mention should also be made of the anonymous geometrical manual dated 1456 and cited above in Sect. II, n. 16. See also Wigandus Durnheimer's *Geometria*, Vienna, Nationalbibl. cod. 5257, 1r–89v, completed in about 1390 at Paris (see Vol. I, p. 143, n. 3). This last tract, so far as its Archimedean parts are concerned, depended on Gordanus' *Compilacio* (*ibid.*). The reader should also consider Christophorus' *Practica geometrie* mentioned in note 21.

until at least 1438.[24] His work stimulated some correspondence in 1506 and 1507 between Paolo da Frezo of Pavia and Giorgio Fondulo of Cremona, correspondence which, among other matters, refers to Leonardo's approximation of the ratio of circumference to diameter as 318057 to 101250.[25] This approximation appeared in Leonardo's *Practica minutiarum*.[26] The *Artis metrice practice compilatio* was translated into Italian and some further practical rules were appended to it.[27] As we shall see later, Leonardo da Vinci was acquainted with it.

When we turn to the Archimedean formulas that appear in the second part of the second tract of the *Compilatio*, we discover all of the correct formulas for the circle and its segments that we have examined in the handbook traditions.[28] And in the third tract we find correct formulas for

---

[24] A. Favaro, "Intorno al presunto autore della *Artis metrice practice compilatio*," *Atti del Reale Istituto Veneto di Scienze, Lettere ed Arti*, Vol. 63 (1903–04), Parte secunda, pp. 377–95, and, especially, by the same author, "Nuove ricerche sul matematico Leonardo Cremonese," *Bibliotheca mathematica*, 3. Folge, Vol. 5 (1904), pp. 326–41 (particularly pp. 337–40).

[25] Favaro, "Nuove ricerche," p. 335.

[26] *Ibid.* Favaro quotes this approximation of π from MS Paris, BN lat. 7192, 20r: "Qua proportio circumferentie ad diametrum non est sicut 22 ad 7 sed magis prope veritatem est sicut 318057 ad 101250." Favaro says that this value appears to have been deduced from the sexigesimal value: 3; 8, 28, 41, 36. Ptolemy gives the value: 3; 8, 30 (see below Part III, Chap. 2, Sect. II, n. 39).

[27] M. Curtze, "Urkunden zur Geschichte der Mathematik im Mittelalter und der Renaissance," *Abhandlungen zur Geschichte der mathematischen Wissenschaften*, 13. Heft (1902), pp. 339–434: III. Die "Practica geometriae" des Leonardo Mainardi aus Cremona. It was in the introduction to this text that Curtze misidentified the author with Leonardo Mainardi, who flourished in the next half-century. For the anonymous formulas appended to the Italian translation of Leonardo's work, see pp. 416–33.

[28] I have examined three manuscripts of the Latin text of Leonardo's work: Paris, BN lat. 7192, 29r–53v (sigl. *P*); Milan, Bibl. Ambros. I.253 Inf., 11v–30v, new pag. (sigl. *M*); Parma, Bibl. Palat. Fond. Parm. 305, 7r–65v, new pag. (sigl. *Pa*). Boncompagni possessed two other manuscripts of this text (see Favaro, "Intorno al presunto autore," pp. 378–80). I include here and in the next footnote the pertinent Archimedean propositions from Paris, BN lat. 7192 (with only occasional references to manuscripts *M* and *Pa*). In doing so, I have omitted the traditional numerical examples: "(*P*: 45r, *M*: 23r, *Pa*: 33r) Secunda pars Secundi Tractatus. Nunc restat dicere de circulo ubi ponuntur quatuor conclusiones. Prima [*mg. P*: pᵃ conclusio:] Cum ex diametro volueris circumferentiam, multiplica diametrum per 3 et septimam partem (*Pa*: 33v) diametri. . . . [*mg. P*: 2ᵃ conclusio:] Cum volueris capacitatem circuli sive spatium infra circumferentiam, quod dicitur area, multiplica medietatem diametri in medietatem circumferentie. . . . (*P*: 45v, *Pa*: 34r). . . . vel sic levius invenies aream circuli. Multiplica quadratum medietatis diametri per 3 cum ¹/₇. [Tertia conclusio: (*M, om. PPa*)] Cum volueris scire quantitatem portionis minoris semicirculo, multiplica arcum portionis per ọ (*del. P*) quantitatem aree totius circuli et productum ị (*del. P*) divide per quantitatem totius circumferentie; et a numero exiente (*PM*, exeunti *Pa*) per divisionem remove (*Pa*: 34v) quantitatem trianguli facti ex duabus semidiametris dicti circuli et corda portionis. . . . (*P*: 46r, *M*: 23v, *Pa*: 35v). . . . Cum autem quantitatem minoris portionis iam inventam demeris de tota (*P*: 46v) area circuli, remanebit quantitas maioris portionis. Ex hoc cogno(*M*: 24r)scitur in quantum quadrangulum factum ex sagitta portionis circuli et diametro superat dictam portionem. Idem autem est sagitta quod (*del.?*) et sinus versus. . . ."

the lateral surface and volume of a cylinder, the lateral surface and volume of the cone and truncated cone, and for the surface and volume of a sphere (with some incorrect considerations of its segments).[29] In his discussion of the lateral surface of a cone, he proposes its equality with

[29] *Ibid.*: "(*P*: 46v, *M*: 24v, *Pa*: 36r) Tertius tractatus. Nunc vero (*del. P*) tertio divina favente gratia dicendum est de mensura corporum. Sed quia quedam sunt regularia quedam irregularia, non dicam aliquid de secundis. . . . (*P*: 48r, *M*: 25v). . . . De columnis [*mg. P*: 3ª conclusio:] (*Pa*: 39r) Columne igitur uniformis sive laterate sive rotunde (*Pa*, retonde *M*, rotonde *P hic et alibi*) quantitatem habebis multiplicando quantitatem basis per longitudinem columne. Ut in columna rotunda *ab*, multiplica aream circuli *a* per lineam *ab*. In laterata vero columna, multiplica superficiem *hefg* per lineam *ed*. [*mg. P*: 4ª conclusio:] Cum vero scire volueris superficiem columne rotunde, multiplica circumferentiam circuli per longitudinem columne. In laterata vero multiplica summam omnium laterum basis per longitudinem (*Pa*: 39v) columne. . . . (*P*: 48v, *M*: 26r) [*mg. P*: 5ª conclusio:] Si vero volueris quantitatem pyramidum eque altarum sicut columne, accipe 3[am] partem columne. . . . (*Pa*: 40r). . . . [*mg. P*: 6ª conclusio:]. Sed cum vis superficiem pyramidis, scias quod secundum opinionem aliquorum ipsa est medietas superficiei columne. Sed hoc non est verum. Necesse est enim superficie[m] pyramidis maiorem fore medietate superficie columne cum hypotemissa (*! hypotenusa*) sit maior axe. . . . (*Pa*: 40v). . . . (*M*: 26v) Cum vero columna est rotunda describe circulum cuius semidiameter sit prefata (*P*: 49r) hypotemissa (*! hypotenusa*) facto centro *e*. Deinde de (*MPa, om. P*) circumferentia eius accipiendo tot partes quot sunt in (*MPa, om. P*) circumferentia (*Pa*: 41r) circuli basis columne, duc a centro *e* duas ǫ (*del. P*) rectas lineas includentes arcum acceptum et habebis sectorem circuli quem queris, cuius quantitatem scies per 3[am] conclusionem secunde partis. . . . (*Pa*: 41v). . . . (*M*: 27r) [*mg. P*: 7ª conclusio:] Ex quinta conclusione sequitur quod scies portionem pyramidis dummodo scias locum sectionis axis vel lateris pyramidis. . . . (*P*: 49v, *Pa*: 42r). . . . [*mg. P*: 8ª conclusio:] Cum autem proponitur pyramis truncata, perfice eam et tunc scies primo ipsam per 4[am] conclusionem (*Pa*: 42v) et eius ambas portiones per 7[am] conclusionem. . . . Ex hoc sequitur quod pratica (*!*) multorum est falax et demonstrationum ignara que dicit quod pyramis sic truncata mensuratur isto modo, videlicet in pyramide *agdb* [Fig. II.3.3.2], cum latus *gd* superet latus *ab*, debes medietatem excessus addere ipsi *al* ut fiat linea *cabh* et tunc columna facta (*P*: 50r) secundum *ch* et secundum longitudinem que est *an* (*Pa*: 43r) equatur proposite pyramidi. Dico esse falsum. . . . (*P*: 52r, *M*: 29r). . . . [*mg. P*: 13ª conclusio:] (*Pa*: 47v) Portionem columne ostendere. Aream partis basis eius multiplica per longitudinem eius et habebis intentum. Aream vero partis basis scies per ea que dicta sunt in secunda parte huius operis sive sit pars superficiei angularis sive circularis. . . . (*P*: 52v). . . . (*M*: 29v) De spheris. [*mg. P*: 17ª conclusio:] Cum vis quantitatem sphere, multiplica quantitatem (*del. P*) aream maioris circuli eius per duas 3[as] diametri eius et habebis intentum. . . . (*P*: 53r). . . . [*mg. P*: 18ª conclusio:] Cum vis superficiem sphere, multiplica circumferentiam circuli maioris per diametrum eius et habebis quesitum. . . . (*In Pa conclusions 17 and 18 are transposed, 17 on [49v], 18 on [48v]*) [*mg. P*: 18ª conclusio:] (*Pa*: 50r) Cumque portionem sphere minorem vel maiorem medietate volueris, quere primo portionem circuli maioris secundum quod dictum est in 2ª parte huius operis. Sicut igitur portio circuli ad circulum ita portio sphere ad spheram. Nota quod si fiat tabula sinuum secundum proportionem (*M*, portionem *PPa*) 22 ad 7 sicut facta est secundum proportionem 360 ad 120 sicut eam feci, tunc cum arcus ab orizonte est gradus (*MPa, om. P*) 23, minuta 49, secunda 55, habetur quarta pars aree circuli, et sic 4ª pars sphere, sicut fit per arcum *ae* (*Pa*: 50v) cuius sinus rectus *fh* debet multiplicari per sinum rectum arcus *ce* [Fig. II.3.3.3], videlicet per *ef*, et productum debet demi de sectore circuli *ehgc* habito ex multiplicatione totius aree per arcum *ecg* et provenientis divisione per totam circumferentiam. Sunt (*MPa*, Sun *P*) autem illi sinus, videlicet *fh*: gradus 23, minuta 8, secunda 29, *ef*: gradus 52, minuta 23, secunda 20, quibus respondent 1; 24, 51 pro primo sinu, pro secundo vero

the sector of a circle whose arc is equal to the slant height of the cone, a formulation that appears to have influenced Leonardo da Vinci's consideration of the formation of a cone by the removal of a sector of a circle and the joining of the terminal radii of the sector remaining (see below, Part III, Chapter 3, note 26). It is worth noticing further that the author specifically challenges the principal errors that plagued the earlier manuals, such as the incorrect formulas for the volume of a truncated cone that were presented in the *Practica geometrie* with incipit: "Artis cuiuslibet consummatio . . ." and the false formula for the lateral surface of a cone that appeared in the *Practica geometrie* of Dominicus de Clavasio and in the *Liber de inquisicione capacitatis figurarum*. The author's constant appeal to trigonometric methods is particularly noteworthy. Finally, it is worth pointing out that this rather complete account of the handbook formulas nowhere mentions the name of Archimedes, returning in a sense to the earliest form of the *Practica*.

Of course geometric manuals that parroted the old handbook traditions did not suddenly stop with the expanded activity of the Renaissance. As we shall see, manuals continued to be prepared during the next century and a half and the Archimedean formulas were repeated on all sides by such authors as Nicholas of Cusa, Regiomontanus, Piero della Francesca, Nicolas Chuquet,[30] Luca Pacioli, Leonardo da Vinci, and many others.

3; 12, 5, cum diameter est 7. Ex hoc cognoscitur in quantum portio cubi facta ex sagitta et diametro circuli superat portionem sphere. Cum enim quadratum diametri sit 49, sagitta vero *cf* sit [gradus] 2, minuta 5, secunda 9. Multiplicatisque 49 per (*P*: 53v) 2 et minuta 5, secunda 9 fiant 102, minuta 12, secunda 21, quarta vero pars sphere est 44, minuta 55, que cum subtracta fuerit a 102, minuta 12, secunda 21, remanent 57, minuta 17, secunda 21. Et in tantum prefata portio cubi superat portionem sphere prefatam. Item si prefatam portionem cubi demeris de medietate cubi, scies in quantum huius residuum superat (*M*: 30r) 4ᵃᵐ partem sphere. (*Pa*: 51r) Cum enim cubus ǫ (*del. P*) circumscriptus sphere prout diameter est 7 sit 343, cuius medietas est 171, minuta 30, a qua cum portio cubi prefata, videlicet 104; 32, dempta fuerit, residuum erit 69; 17, 39, quod quidem residuum comparatum quarte parti sphere, videlicet ipsis 44, minuta 55, superat eam, ut patet, in 24, minuta 22, secunda 39. Horum quivis lector fueris cognosce multa ab aliis dicta me posuisse et aliqua aliorum correcta. Et aliqua deo donante posita, advertendo in sententia circuli quod proportio circumferentie circuli ad diametrum non est sicut 22 ad 7, quamquam tum propter facilitatem tum quia non est huius (*Pa*: 51v) operis id reprobare hanc proportionem dixerim, presertim etiam cum id non multum distet a vero. Que vero sit proportio alibi dixi demonstrativa conclusione fere. Finis." The statement at the end is an obvious reference to the value given in Leonardo's *Practica minutiarum* (see above, n. 26). The preceding treatment of the segment of a sphere rests on the erroneous belief that the segment of a sphere is related to the whole sphere as the corresponding segment of its great circle is related to the whole great circle. Notice finally that at the end of the second conclusion of the second tract Leonardo gives the rarely used formula $S = r^2 \cdot 3\frac{1}{7}$ for the area of a circle, perhaps taking it from the *Verba filiorum* (see Vol. 1, pp. 224, 324).

[30] The *Géométrie* of Nicolas Chuquet (MS Paris, BN fr. 1346, 211r–268v and BN n. a. fr. 1052, 39r–67v [the latter incomplete]) came to my attention too late for me to include in this volume a study of this important work. However, it has been treated in detail in a thesis of H. l'Huiller, *La Géométrie de Nicolas Chuquet et le renouveau des mathématiques au XVᵉ siècle*, described in École Nationale des Chartes, *Positions des thèses soutenues par*

les élèves de la promotion de 1976 pour obtenir le diplôme d'archiviste paléographe (Paris, 1976), pp. 95–104. I must be satisfied here with quotations from this summary: (p. 96): "A la fin de son *Triparty*, Nicolas Chuquet indique qu'il est parisien, bachelier en médecine, et qu'il écrit à Lyon en 1484 ce manuscrit qui contient en outre l'Arithmétique commerciale et la Géométrie. Ces maigres données furent longtemps les seuls éléments connus de son existence. Le dépouillement de relevés de taxes de la ville de Lyon nous a permis de fixer à 1489 son arrivée dans la rue de la Grenette (près de Saint-Nizier). Il y est connu comme 'escripvain' pendant quatre ans, puis comme 'maître d'algorisme'. Il meurt entre l'automne 1487 et le printemps 1489. Près de lui, dans la rue Neuve située à quelque deux cents pas de la Grenette, habitait Estienne de La Roche; maître d'algorisme, celui-ci a possédé le manuscrit définitif de Nicolas Chuquet et l'a pillé, sans bien le comprendre, pour publier sous son nom une Arithmétique en 1520 et la rééditer en 1538. Les deux hommes se sont vraisemblablement connus et Nicolas Chuquet a sans doute été le précepteur d'Estienne de La Roche." (p. 97) "Le ms. Paris fr. 1346 a toujours été considéré comme étant le seul à conserver l'oeuvre de Nicolas Chuquet. De fait, il en est le manuscrit définitif, et comporte tous ses ouvrages connus. De plus, l'ensemble, texte et figures, est entièrement de sa main. La Géométrie occupe 52 feuillets (fol. 211r°–263v°) d'un volume qui en comporte 324, d'un papier de mediocre qualité, originaire du sud-est de la France actuelle, sans filigrane. On trouve également une partie de la geometrie dans le ms Paris n. a. fr. 1052, fol. 39r°–67v°. C'est un ouvrage antérieur au texte définitif, d'une quinzaine d'annees au plus, et qui se révèle être également de la main de Nicolas Chuquet. . . . Nicolas Chuquet définit lui-même son oeuvre comme une 'pratique de géométrie'; et effectivement elle est en partie tributaire d'une traditon d'ouvrages ainsi intitulés qui remontent à la *Practica Geometrie* d'Hugues de Saint-Victor." (p. 101) "*L'influence italienne sur la Géométrie de Chuquet.*—Toute une partie de la Géométrie de Chuquet témoigne d'une forte influence italienne. Celle-ci se fait sentir aussi bien sur les exercices les plus simples que sur les problèmes plus complexes. Elle vient de sources qui lui sont tout à fait contemporaines, comme le ms. Siena L. IV. 18, le *Trattato d'abaco* de Piero della Francesca, le *Tractatus Geometriae* de Luca Pacioli. Cependant, même si la langue de Chuquet comporte des italianismes, son traité de Géométrie n'est pas une traduction." (p. 102) "NICOLAS CHUQUET ET LA QUADRATURE DU CERCLE. Comme un certain nombre de géomètres du Moyen Âge, Nicolas Chuquet a tenté de 'quadriffier le cercle'. Il présente trois tentatives tributaires de trois traditions différentes. *La quadrature par les lunules.*—C'est un procédé remontant à Simplicius, qui procède d'une erreur d'appréciation des diverses quadratures de lunules obtenues par Hippocrate de Chio. On construit une lunule sur le côté du carré inscrit, puis trois lunules sur les côtés du demi-hexagone inscrit auxquelles on ajoute le demi-cercle construit sur un des côtés; on obtient deux figures courbes faciles à 'quadriffier'. A partir de là, certains géomètres ont pensé parvenir à la quadrature du cercle. Chuquet se contente d'exposer les deux constructions sans tirer de conclusion. *La 'triangulature du cercle'*—Nicolas Chuquet présente ensuite un procédé original, celui de la recherche d'un triangle *isocèle* égal au cercle; sa base est égale à la circonference, sa hauteur au rayon. Il s'est vraisemblablement inspiré de la Première Proposition du traité d'Archimède *De la mesure du cercle. La quadrature par les polygones médians, méthode des périmetres.*—Chuquet expose ensuite le procédé qui est resté longtemps un des plus utilisés pour le calcul de π, celui des polygones réguliers médians. Il cite comme source d'inspiration le *Grand Art Général* de Raimond Lulle. Dans cet ouvrage, en effet, le philosophe majorquin presente une quadrature par le carré moyen, mais par les surfaces et non par les périmètres. Dans un ouvrage antérieur, *De la triangulature et quadrature du cercle*, il a tenté de résoudre le problème par les périmètres, et pour les premiers polygones réguliers. Quelle que soit l'influence de ce procédé sur celui de Nicolas Chuquet, il est une démarche qui a totalement échappé à celui-ci: Raimond Lulle fait allusion à la manière dont la scolastique a abordé le problème, distinguant entre *quadrature ad sensum* et *quadrature ad intellectum*, et se réfère expressément à la première. Dans ces conditions, sa quadrature n'a pas de véritable valeur scientifique."

CHAPTER 4

Giovanni Fontana and the
Medieval Archimedes

I. Fontana's Life and Works

So far in this part of the volume I have primarily discussed the knowledge of the Arabo-Latin Archimedes in the fourteenth and early fifteenth centuries, contrasting it with the influence of the translations of William of Moerbeke. Both traditions unite rather fleetingly in the writings of a Venetian physician Giovanni Fontana. In respect to his knowledge of Archimedes, Fontana still belongs to the medieval sections of my work, since the books he read were those of the medieval traditions of Archimedes; and thus, unlike most of his successors, whose works will be examined in the rest of this volume, Fontana apparently did not know the new translations of Jacobus Cremonensis, completed about 1450. I hasten to add, however, that though Fontana's reading was perforce almost exclusively medieval, his paramount interest lay in the construction and description of machines and instruments. This interest was expressed in notebooks with pictorial illustrations and in detailed descriptive works. In fact, his preparation of notebooks seems to represent an early stage in the progressive development of such notebooks that culminates in the copious notebooks of Leonardo da Vinci.

Giovanni Fontana was born in Venice (he is invariably referred to as "Venetus" or "de Venetiis") sometime during the 1390's.[1] His father's name was Michael, as is evident from the University documents cited below. The form of name always used by Giovanni himself is Johannes Fontana. On the basis of a rather ambiguous statement in one of his notebooks it has recently been claimed that he received the apellation

---

[1] No extensive account of Fontana's life has been prepared. But see L. Thorndike, *A History of Magic and Experimental Science*, Vol. 4 (New York, 1934), pp. 150–82, and the various authors mentioned by Thorndike. I have given further references in the footnotes below. The date of birth as "sometime during the 1390's" is an inference from the fact that Fontana received his licentiate and doctorate of arts at the University of Padua in 1418, as I note below.

"Fontana" from a fountain which he invented.[2] This has some plausibility since he displays great interest in fountains in his main notebook. On the other hand, the passage on which the claim is based is not clear and the Paduan University records most often refer to him as Iohannes de Fontana (as we shall see), thus suggesting a place name that has become a family name. Nothing is known of Giovanni's early years. One assumes they were spent in the neighborhood of Venice since he recalls a generation later a terrible storm that hit Venice, which was almost certainly the great wind of 1410.[3] University records place him at Padua as early as 26 May, 1417, when he appears as a witness to a multiple examination and where he is designated as "master John, son of Michael de la Fontana of Venice."[4] The examination for his licentiate in arts and the public conferral of his doctorate of arts are dated respectively 18 June, 1418 (at the episcopal palace), and 19 June, 1418 (at the cathedral church).[5] He was listed in the records of these ceremonies as "Iohannes de Fontana de Venetiis" and "Iohannes Fontana quondam circumspecti viri domini Michaelis de Venetiis." His promotors were Antonius Cermisonus, Galeacius de Sancta Sophia, Stephanus de Doctoribus and (for the doctorate only) the well-known Augustinian Paul of Venice. Fontana also

[2] F. D. Prager, "Fontana on Fountains: Venetian Hydraulics of 1418," *Physis*, Anno XIII (1971), pp. 341–60, at p. 343. The passage on which Prager makes his claim is contained in Fontana's *Bellicorum instrumentorum liber*, Munich, Staatsbibl. Icon. 242, 62v, which is partly in normal writing and partly in cipher and which Prager transcribes as follows (p. 360): "De fortibus (*so misprinted, but actually* fontibus) forsitan non est inventus artificialior durabiliorque. Est quoque proprie *fantaxium quo ego Johanes 'Fontana'. Semper eum in viis studere placuit . . .*" (the italicized Latin is written in cipher). In fact the statement in cipher is a good deal more ambiguous than Prager's transcription reveals. I would transcribe the crucial part as follows: "fantaxiu[!] quo- (or i)a i (!) ego Iohx(or v)anes e fonto(! a)na i (!) semper e[um] in viis studere placuit." Obviously there are errors and/or superfluous letters. But I can suggest a reading alternative to that of Prager that eliminates fewer of the supposed superfluities: "Est quoque proprie fantaxiu[m]. Quia 'ego Iohan[n]es e Fontana', [mihi] semper e[um] in viis studere placuit." The meaning then might be that because his family originally derived from Fontana (which became part of his name), he always had a keen interest in studying the fountain.

[3] See Fontana's *Liber de omnibus rebus naturalibus* (Venice, 1544), 71r–v (III, 6): "Et ipse memor sum anno ab incarnatione domini nostri M.CCCC.[X] decima die mensis Augusti qua celebratur festum beatissimi Laurentii martiris christi venetiarum in urbe vidisse mirabiles in aere, aqua et terra conquassationes post meridiem a consimili vento factas: ita ut innumerabiles naviculae cum hominibus ab inundationibus aquarum absortae fuerint. Arbores immensae exhumatae, tecta fere omnium edifitiorum civitatis a suis tegulis discoperta sumaria domorum omnia obrupta, multarum turrium pyramides ceciderunt murique plures corruerunt, lapides per aerem et trabes vehebantur. Nec ullus tutus homo videbatur. Inde maximi terrores omnibus aderant ea videntibus, qualia ab ipsa urbe condita unquam non (71v) fuerant. Tandem (ut existimatur) eadem die orationibus hominum, dei ira: quae ad desolandam et disrumpendam civitatem credebatur placata fuit, et diaboli: qui sub specie corvorum et vocibus raucis per sonantibus inter nubes cernebantur (ut quidam referunt) fugati sunt. Ego quidem ipsa die qui inter pericula fueram in terra et in medio aquarum a divina clementia conservatus fui." Cf. Thorndike, *A History of Magic*, Vol. 4, p. 153.

[4] C. Zonta and G. Brotto, eds., *Acta graduum academicorum gymnasii Patavini ab anno 1406 ad annum 1450*, Vol. 1, 2nd ed. (Padua, 1970), p. 168 (Doc. no. 418).

[5] *Ibid.*, pp. 185–86 (Docs. ns. 471–72).

appears as rector of arts at the University in documents dating from 7 July, 1418, to 6 April, 1419.[6] Since, as I have said, there is some dispute concerning the proper form of his name, we should note that in ten of the latter documents he appears as Iohannes de Fontana, in one as Iohannes de la Fontana, and in three he is misdesignated as Antonius de Fontana. Finally, the examination for his medical degree on 17 May, 1421, is recorded, at which time he was referred to as "magister Iohannes Fontana de Venetiis artium doctor."[7] Among his promotors were the same three as for his licentiate in arts plus Bartholomeus de Montagnana. Later in his *Liber de omnibus rebus naturalibus* he implies that he studied under or knew Blasius of Parma (d. 1416), Paul of Venice (d. 1429), and Prosdocimus de Beldomandis (d. 1428).[8]

The names of other, more obscure friends of Giovanni are occasionally mentioned: a Ludovicus Venetus, to whom he addressed his *Nova compositio horologii* (see work No. 1 below); a Polixcus (i.e., Poliscus), the object of address of his *Horologium aqueum* (see work No. 2); and a certain Octavian whom he addresses in his *Liber de omnibus rebus naturalibus*.[9] He also mentions "a certain man of subtle genius and invention who constructed an instrument in 1416 called The Mirror of the Planets."[10] He further records that he was sent by the Doge of Venice to Brescia to visit the condottiere Francesco Carmagnola, then captain general of the Milanese army.[11] This visit must have been before 23 Feb-

---

[6] *Ibid.*, p. 186 (Doc. no. 474 of 7 July, 1418) appears as Iohannes de Fontana de Venetiis; p. 187 (Doc. no. 478 of 10 July, 1418) as Antonius de Fontana de Venetiis; p. 189 (Doc. no. 481 of 6 Aug., 1418 as Antonius de Venetiis; (Doc. no. 482 of 7 Aug., 1418) as Antonius de Fontana de Venetiis; (Doc. no. 483 of 16 Aug., 1418) as Iohannes de Fontana de Venetiis; p. 190 (Doc. no. 486 of 14 Sept., 1418) as Iohannes de Fontana de Venetiis; p. 192 (Doc. no. 490 of 19 Oct., 1418) as Iohannes de la Fontana de Venetiis; (Doc. no. 492 of 10 Nov., 1418) as Iohannes de Fontana; p. 196 (Doc. no. 501 of 24 Dec., 1418) as Iohannes de Fontana de Venetiis; p. 197 (Doc. no. 503 of 31 Dec., 1418) as Iohannes de Fontana de Venetiis; p. 198 (Doc. no. 506 of 3 Febr., 1419) as Iohannes de Fontana de Venetiis; p. 199 (Doc. no. 507 of 5 Febr., 1419) as Iohannes de Fontana; p. 201 (Doc. no. 513 of 6 April, 1419) as Iohannes de Fontana; (Doc. no. 514 of 6 April, 1419) as Iohannes de Fontana.

[7] *Ibid.*, p. 207 (Doc. no. 554).

[8] Ed. of 1544, 2v, 35v, 41v, 75r; cf. Thorndike, *A History of Magic*, Vol. 4, pp. 152–53. Paul is also mentioned on folio 105r: "In primis itaque de proportione elementorum adinvicem inquit Paulus hermitarum, ut refert ex auctoribus librorum naturalium collegisse. . . ." This last reference was not noted by Thorndike.

[9] Ed. of 1544, 22v, 26v, 41r; cf. Thorndike, *A History of Magic*, Vol. 4, p. 153. The references to Octavian on folios 22v and 26v were not mentioned by Thorndike. Incidentally, Fontana mentions still another friend on folio 119r: "Constantinus Venetus michi fidelis amicus qui plurimis annis per regna magni kan peragravit multa similia se vidisse retulit."

[10] Ed. of 1544, II, 16, 45v (misprinted as 46); cf. Thorndike, *A History of Magic*, Vol. 4, p. 153.

[11] Ed. of 1544, 130v; cf. Thorndike, *A History of Magic*, Vol. 4, pp. 153–54 and F. Fossati, "Carmagnola, Francesco," *Enciclopedia italiana*, Vol. 9 (1931), pp. 81–82. My colleague Professor Felix Gilbert has suggested 1421 as the probable date of the visit, since Carmagnola had recently conquered Brescia and after that time was occupied with military actions in other parts of Northern Italy.

ruary, 1425, when Carmagnola changed to the Venetian side, and was most likely in 1421. Fontana also appears to have visited Crete and Rome at some unspecified times.[12] We know that he dedicated a work *De arte pictoria* to Jacopo Bellini before 1440 (see below, work No. 13). Furthermore, sometime in the 1430's he appears to have gone to Udine as its municipal physician. While there he composed his detailed work on mensuration *De trigono balistario*, which he dedicated to Domenico Bragadino, who succeeded Paolo da Pergola as the public reader in logic and philosophy and who was Luca Pacioli's teacher (see below, Part III, Chap. 2, Sect. IV, n. 3). The colophon of the latter work tells us that it was "edited and completed . . . at Udine on the last day of February, 1440, by Giovanni Fontana, the Venetian, salaried as the medical physician in this same place [i.e., Udine]" (see work No. 7 below). Incidentally, Birkenmajer believed that Thorndike had misunderstood "in this same place" (*eodem in loco*) when identifying it with Udine, believing rather that Venice was meant.[13] But Birkenmajer cannot have been correct since the word "Venetian" (*Venetus*) in the colophon is an adjectival form and the expression "in this same place" must refer to the only noun of place given, namely, Udine. Furthermore, as neither Birkenmajer nor Thorndike mentioned, the adjectival "Venetus" was a marginal addition to the autograph manuscript made by Fontana and so was not in the original statement. Hence "Utino" was the only possible referent when the sentence was first written. Further, when we read the last chapter or epilogue of the work, we see that Fontana had been practicing medicine for some time in this city.[14] This epilogue is of considerable interest.

---

[12] Ed. of 1544, 130v; cf. A. Birkenmajer, "Zur Lebensgeschichte und wissenschaftlichen Tätigkeit von Giovanni Fontana (1395?–1455?)," *Isis*, Vol. 17 (1932), pp. 34–53, at p. 48. See also folio 96v: "Clima quartum . . . et capit in se insulam Cipri et insulam Rhodi et insulam Cretae (in qua iam sumus). . . ." This passage, not noted by Birkenmajer, seems to imply that Fontana was in Crete when composing this part of the work. A visit to Rome can be inferred from a reference on folio 133v: "Et est hodie Romae pyramis altissima lapidea in cuius facie scriptum est, cinis Cesaris, in sumitate (*!*) ipsius Romani pomum aureum formaverunt intus continens Cesaris cineres. Quam pyramidem ipse vidi extra ecclesiam sancti Petri, quam admiratus magnitudinem et artem suam nescivi apprehendere an ex uno lapide precisa an ex pluribus integrata lapidibus. . . ."

[13] Birkenmajer, "Zur Lebensgeschichte," p. 36, n. 10. Cf. Thorndike, *A History of Magic*, Vol. 4, p. 155, n. 20.

[14] *De trigono balistario*, Bk. II, Cap. 25, MS Oxford, Bodl. Libr. Canon. Misc. 47, 219v (220v): "Iterum, preclare atque percare dominice, trigoni balistarii nostri post longam eius edictionem aliam fabricam deinde hanc perutilem et facilem explanationem in quibis duobis libris perpendere certissime et experiri potes quantum ad omnium genera mensurarum instrumentum hoc conferat et architeto (*!*) atque phylosopho quam gratum esse debeat.

"Comoditates equidem eius quasdam excerptas ex antiquorum dictis et instrumentis invenies multasque novissime ex me habitas et in usum redactas; pluras quoque adinvenissem experientias si librorum mathematicorum copia ac temporis spatium hoc in loco mihi non defuisset, quibus nimium egere videbar pro huius editionis integritate.

"Si vero quedam neglecta sint vel superflue dicta videantur tibi aut minus sapide minusque graviter quam tua expectet intelligentia, indulge, queso, mihi pro tua summa humanitate.

Like the work as a whole it was addressed to Domenico Bragadino. Fontana stresses that he would have been able to add more "experiences" from earlier works had he not been lacking "copies of mathematical works and sufficient leisure in this place," that is, Udine. His time was taken up in his medical practice. He describes in a very humane way how, while waking, or studying or eating, he hears the sighs and cries of those languishing in illness. Even at night he dreams of them. Hence he spent much time in reading and seeking ways to cure them, leaving only inter- mittent intervals in which to write. We certainly get the impression that he is residing and practicing in a city without great library resources, which obviously fits Udine rather than Venice. I should add that he must have had a fairly good collection of manuscripts in his own library in view of his not inconsiderable citation of earlier authors. Two of his manuscripts survive: Paris, BN lat. 9335, the important collection of translations by Gerard of Cremona (see work No. 6 below) and Oxford, Bodl. Libr. Digby 47, a collection of astrological texts.[15]

The last activity that we can definitely associate with Giovanni Fontana is the composition of the large and rambling *Liber de omnibus rebus naturalibus*, which can be definitely placed after 1440 (since it cites the

Scis me huius loci salario deditum et ut ita dixerim quodammodo famulatui infirmorum assiduo, quibus tam solicitum me oportuit et continuum esse, ut vigilans et studens et comedens videar audire semper subspiria ipsorum languentium et per vias cotidie et ubique clamantibus illis occurrere, dormiens quoque in sompnis concipere ymagines eorum deformes et obscuras. Adde quod non parum existimandum censeo semper examinare cogi[tare?] aut legere quod pro eorum salute sit offerendum illis vel prohibendum ne malo ipso pereant.

"Noscis profato quantam esse debeat ipsa cura infirmantium que mentis et corporis omnem valitudinem at denique omnes medici vires cons[tanter?] requirit. Multis itaque cum intervallis temporum studiorumque diversionibus et adversantibus multis huic intentioni et librum prolixum et hunc abreviatum quos de trigono balistario concepi ad finem duxi.

"Tu quidem, vir electissime, dulci mente ipsa suscipias que licet tarde libenter tamen ofer[entur]. Et ubi quid superfluum invenies reseca. Quod vero tibi placitum fuerit amore mei conserva. In hiis tamen libris multa comperies capitula et in singulo plures comoditates instrumenti. Placuit certe mihi formas frequenter mutare trigonicas, situs quoque et vias applicationis eius atque mensurandi diversificare figuras cum unus pluribus suficisset modus aut plures modi uni convenissent.

"Hoc fecisse volui ut multorum generum mensurationis experientie et usus instrumenti ballistarii (!) multiplices haberentur.

"Potuissem unumquodque capitulum longius extendere et plurificare capitula, sed hec satis fuisse iudicavi, ex quibus veluti radicibus sufitientibus quisque valebit adinvenire experientias consequentes et innumeras et tu potissime qui ad omne quantumcunque dificile ingenium bene habes et ad subtilia studia semper intendis.

"Vale feliciter et virtutes tuas egregias, que multe sunt, in alios etiam conferas amicos. Iterum vale et utinam numerum annorum mathusalem [*corr. mg. ex* melchisadech] et sapientiam salomonis bene transcendere possis."

[15] A. A. Björnbo, "Hermannus Dalmata als Übersetzer astronomischer Arbeiten," *Bibliotheca mathematica*, 3. Folge, Vol. 4 (1903), pp. 130–33, at p. 131, n. 1, indicates that the last page of Digby 47 contains the statement: "Iste liber est Johannis Fontana physici Veneti." Cf. Birkenmajer, "Zur Lebensgeschichte," p. 47.

De trigono balistario). It mentions the Jubilee year of 1450 and may indeed have been written as late as 1454 (see work No. 8 below) and perhaps partially in Crete (see above, note 12).

Before describing Fontana's limited knowledge and use of Archimedes, I think it useful to present an up-to-date list of his works compiled by the examination of all of his extant works.

The Extant Works of Giovanni Fontana

1. *Nova compositio horologii*, addressed to his friend Ludovicus Venetus. MS: Bologna, Bibl. Univ. 2705, 1r–51v, 15c.

Inc.: "Nova composicio horalegi (*!*) quod ex pulverum casu consistit feliciter incipit, n (*del. ?*) [in]cepta et completa per famosissimum artium et medicine doctorem peritissimum dominum Iohannem fontanam de Venetiis ad ludovicum venetum suum. Prohemium. Tole, carissime et peramande adolescens, quod longediu tantis affectibus et desiderio postulasti primo opus manibus meis constructum integrum et completum et hunc parvum tractatum quo mediante et conservare et construere idem possis." (Note: the author's name has been written in an erasure.)

Colophon: "Explicit nova horalogii (*!*) compositio quod ex pulverum casu fit acta et composita per peritissimum artium ac medicine doctorem dominum Iohannem Fontana (*!*) venetum padue 1418 cum studuit in artibus et medicina. Deo gratias Amen." (Again note that the author's name as well as place and date of composition is written in an erasure.)

Comments: This tract was completed at Padua in 1418. I believe it was his first work, for whenever he mentions there his other works it is always in terms of something he intends to write, as for example a *Liber de ponderibus* (see work No. 10),[16] a work on military and other machines (perhaps work No. 4 below),[17] and perhaps one on the aesthetic aspects of machines.[18] In this work on sand-clocks he quotes earlier authors, including Euclid (15v, 19r), Aristotle (19v), the *Libri de ponderibus* (13r, 19v, 27r) or the *Libri de ponderositate* (18r), and Jordanus (19r). We can also note his suggestion of the possibility of a perpetual motion machine.[19] Finally, I believe that this manuscript is not written in Fontana's hand. It would be hard to explain the wild variability in spelling technical terms, e.g., the forms *horalegum, horalogum, horalogium,*

---

[16] *Nova compositio, ms. cit.*, 13v: "Et ego de ponderibus quisquam favente deo alibi practicum dicturus sum."

[17] *Ibid.*, 38r: "Ex quibus eciam infero consequenter ascensus aquarum perpetuum et motus animalium artificialium, specula et instrumenta bellica et multos difficillimos effectus fieri posse que domino prestante vitam et sapienciam michi alias describam."

[18] *Ibid.*, 51r: "[A]ccipe igitur, amice carissime, hec que tibi cupienti scripsi et operatus sum. Et cum intellexeris omnia que in hoc libello scribuntur alia tibi ingernata aperiam et exponam que non ad propriam temporis horalegorum (*!*) certitudinem fiunt sed ad spectaculum et pulcritudinem eorum formantur ut admirentur homines. Qualia iam in presenti opere dicere non intendo, nam nimis in longum sermonem extenderem et metam huius operis transgrederer."

[19] *Ibid.*, 38r, the passage immediately preceding that of note 17: "Ex istis ulterius infero facili ingenio construi posse rotam que perpetuo circularem motum haberet ad quam habendam plurimi valentes phylosophi et architectores longo tempori et vigiliis insudarunt."

that appear along side the correct form *horologium*, except as the work of a scribe who was himself unfamiliar with the technical vocabulary. In contrast, in the *De trigono balistario*, written in Fontana's hand, this and other technical terms are quite accurately rendered.

2. *Horologium aqueum*, addressed to a certain Polixcus (i.e. Poliscus).
MS: same as in 1, 53r–75v.

Inc.: "Horalegum (*!*) aqueum quod celeberrimus artium et medicine doctor magister Iacobus (*!*) fontana de venetiis edidit ad polixcum (*?*) suum. Prohemium. Atende, precor, mi Polixce dulcissime, si ceteris mundi rebus optimus amor preponi debeat, isque pretio diligencia pariter et omni studio custodiri. Nescio vel non intelligo verbis tuis aut precibus sine iniuria non complacere posse. Quibus meum tam dulciter animum et ingenium moves quod iam de horalogio (*!*) aqueo formam quodam sub compendio in scriptis agam. Eamdemque componendi et figurandi canones utiles et neccessarios modos describam. Animadvertas igitur ut opus ipsum facile quod nuper ostendam tibi concipere deo favente integre possis." (Once more note that "Iacobus fontana de" is written in an erasure, as is the ". . . xcum (*?*)" in "Polixcum.")

Colophon: "Explicit quedam horalegi (*!*) per motum aquarum compositio edita per clarissimum artium et medicine doctorem magistrum Iacobum (*!*) fontana[m] venetum perfecta. M.CCCC.X . . . die ultima octobris." (The name of the author is again written in an erasure, and the rest of the date has been erased.)

Comments: Because of the above-noted erasure of the rest of the date, we cannot date the work exactly. It must however postdate the *Nova compositio* of 1418, which it cites,[20] and antedate the *De trigono balistario* of 1440, in which it is cited (see note 56 below). In fact, I believe that the work was composed about the same time as the first and third works, that is, close to 1418 when he was studying at the University, for it is cited in the *Tractatus de pisce* described as written in Giovanni's adolescence (see below, work No. 3, note 25). In this work on the water clock, he again promises a *De ponderibus*,[21] some *Tractatus diversorum modorum horologii mixti* (see note 20) and a *De motibus aquarum* (see work No. 11 below).[22] His mention of a *Tractatus de*

[20] *Horologium aqueum*, *ms. cit.*, 63v: "Similiter cum componerem horalegum (*!*) ex proprietate elementi terre, quia ex casu pulverum cuius tractatus etsi ante istum compilaverim hunc tamen sequi debet intelligi servando elementorum ordinem rectum lucide exposui horis omnibus precise portiones equales materiarum vel pulverum respondere sic et deo favente cum componam tractatus diversorum modorum horalegi (*!*) mixti quia ex metallis, ex lignis et huiusmodi sic et ibi diversas narrabo mensuras rerum in comparatione ad horas suas." Note that he speaks here not only of the *Nova compositio* which he had already composed but also of *Tractatus diversorum modorum horalegi (!) mixti*, which he hoped to compose but apparently did not (see work No. 18 below).

[21] *Ibid.*,66r: "Et ut finem meis imponam verbis de his modis gravitandi et ponderandi materiam relinquo. Nam in tractatibus de ponderibus amplissime et alias causas plures cognosces et deo favente ut promisi alias tractatum in pratica (*!*) super his constituam."

[22] *Ibid.*, 66r: "Dabo tibi tamen alias modum utilem magis quo mediante eadem aqua ad superiorem piscidem veniens tandem ad infimam revertetur. Et forte de proximo ostendam tibi experienciam eius favente deo et tempore succedente, tu vero si fueris

rotalegis omnium generum[23] may be a reference to some work on the use of geared wheels in horologues or to a more general work on wheels and continuous or perpetual motion.

3. *Tractatus* (or *Metrologum*) *de pisce, cane et volucre*.

MS: same as in works 1 and 2, 85r–105v.

Inc.: "In nomine domini nostri Yesu Christi. Incipit tractatus de pisce, cane et volucre quem doctissimus artium et medicine doctor magister Iohannes fontana venetus in adolescencia sua edidit. Incipit prohemium. Solent ab artificibus et ingeniosis viris dimensiones linearum, superficierum et corporum, situs et differencie multifarie mensurari." ·

Colophon: "Explicit metrologum de pisce, cane et volucre, quod celeberimus (*!*) artium ac medicine doctor magister Iohannes fontana venetus cum adhuc adolescens esset edidit et notavit."

Comments: This is a treatise on the measurement of depths under water, distances on the earth's surface and heights in the air and the instruments to be used for such measures.[24] Presumably it was written shortly after the first two works in the codex since it is noted in both the incipit and the colophon that it was completed during his adolescence. Some of the instruments and machines described here are depicted in his main notebook (see note 37 below). The earlier tracts on horologues are mentioned.[25] He also mentions his decision to compose a tract on machines and military engines (see work No. 4 below), promising somewhat more than he delivered.[26] He again describes a work on wheels (i.e., his *De*

expers ingernatorum de artificialibus fontibus diversis in ascensu aque fere perpetues, quos in quodam libro de motibus aquarum, ascensu, evacuatione, tumore, velocitate et aliis earumdem passionibus et actibus habendis construxi, facile huic operi concedere potes cautelam qua mediante revertetur aqua in infimam piscidem." Cf. 68v: "Ad hec tamen facile componenda maxime tibi prodesse potest liber de aquarum passionibus et motibus aliquibus de quibus ymaginor et opto plurima scribere cum de ductibus aquarum librum annotabo si deus voluerit ibidem varia et diversorum opera consideranda sunt que in hunc nostrum presentem finem evenirent. . . ."

[23] *Ibid.*, 71v: ". . . dico quemadmodum sermone prolixo in tractatu de rotalegis omnium generum explicavi quod in operibus artificialibus in quibus aliquid motum continuum habet fieri sepe contingit opus est ut aliquid motum interpolatum habeat, scilicet quod aliquando moveri debeat et aliquando quiescere propter finem aliquem ordinatum."

[24] Thorndike briefly describes this work in *A History of Magic*, Vol. 4, pp. 172–75.

[25] *Tractatus de pisce, ms. cit.*, 85v–86r: "De primo tamen horalogio (*!*) dictum fuit sufficienter in aliis tractatibus." Cf. 86r–v: "Quod dictum est de horalego (*!*) pulverum idem intelligamus de horologio aqueo facto per descensum aque vel ascensum. Similiter intelligere debemus de horologio quod ex aeris motu vel exspiratione factum fuerit ex vesica vel utre fol[l]e vel tympano vel aliter. Pariformiter eciam de horologio igneo quod aut ex fumo vel ex candela subtili vel ex consumptione olei aut similis in lampade formatur, que in quibusdam tractatibus meis difuse satis explanata sunt."

[26] *Ibid.*, 90v: "Quomodo vero possit homo sub aqua stare sine mortis periculo multipliciter declarabitur cum de machinis et artis bellice fabricis deo favente dicturum librum componam quem dudum describere optavi. Nam ibidem invenietur quomodo sub alveo fluminis fieri possunt cave et meatus per quos armati exercitus incedere valebunt absque periculo, qualiter adhuc sub aqua cum vegetibus vel saccis de corio similes aditus esse poterunt. Et quod mirabilius erit ostendetur virum indutum totum corio sub aqua pedibus ambulare vel natare posse tempore notabili valde et fere incredibili, in quibus artingeniis habet homo semper aerem respirationi convenientem." Though the reference appears to

rotalegis) in a context similar to that in which he mentioned it in his *Horologium aqueum.*[27] Students of medieval mechanics will note with interest his use of the medieval impetus theory (92r–95v). A chapter on kinematics (Chap. 8) and how speeds are to be measured by horologues anticipates parts of Chapter 24 of *De trigono balistario* edited below (see the Commentary to the text below, Proposition 1, lines 22–30; see also the Commentary, Proposition 3, line 31, where the texts of Chapters 2 and 3 of the *Tractatus de pisce* are given).

4. *Bellicorum instrumentorum liber cum figuris et fictitiis literis conscriptus*
   MS: Munich, Staatsbibl. Icon. 242, 1r–70r.
   Inc. (1v): "Alphasaf antiquissimum ingenium est ad bellica opera adinventum. . . ."
   Colophon: There is no colophon but the last item on 70r runs "Apparentia nocturna ad terrorem videntium. *Habes modum cum lanterna quam propriis oculis vid[i]sti ex mea mima fabricatam et proprio i[n]genio.*" (The italicized sentence is written in cipher.)
   Comments: This is apparently the work projected by Fontana under the title *De machinis et artis bellice fabricis liber* (see note 26 above; cf. note 17). This and the succeeding work are written in a simple cipher but punctuated by rubrics or introductory statements in normal writing.[28] The work is a notebook embracing a wide variety of instruments and machines with brief descriptions and drawings that goes beyond the title given above and added by a later owner. Of all the works of Fontana this has received the most scholarly attention.[29] Though it bears no contemporary indication of title and authorship at the beginning or end, Fontana gives his name several times in the course of his comments in

be a work like the *Bellicorum instrumentorum liber* (see work No. 4), no such explanations or machines appear to be given in that work. It could be that he meant to write a more detailed work but failed to do so.

[27] *Ibid.*, 94v–95r; "Verum quartum modum intelligeret qui sciret perpetuam rotam mobilem componere. . . . Sed de hac rota tractatum feci in quo plurimorum fantastice mobilitatis rote scribuntur opiniones et fallaces multum tamen sensibus apparentes pro quibus veluti alkimiste in arte sua multi phy[losophi] vel architecti laborantes tempus et expensas amiserunt. Describuntur eciam ipsius rote quidam modi prolongissimo tempore satis possibiles." The remark linking the investigators of perpetual motion machines with the alchemists is not unlike a scornful remark of Leonardo da Vinci (*Forster II*, 92v): "O speculators on continuous motion, how many designs of a similar nature have you created. Go and accompany the seekers after gold."

[28] The cipher is described in H. Omont, "Un traité de physique et d'alchimie du XVe siècle en écriture cryptographique," *Bibliothèque de l'École des Chartes*, Vol. 58 (1897), pp. 253–58, an article devoted to work No. 5 below. The cipher employed in both works is the same.

[29] In addition to Prager's "Fontana on Fountains" cited in note 2 above, I should mention S. J. von Romocki, *Geschichte der Explosivstoffe*, Vol. 1 (Berlin, 1895), pp. 231–40; M. Jähns, *Geschichte der Kriegswissenschaften vornehmlich in Deutschland*, Part I (Munich/Leipzig, 1889), pp. 276–77; C. Huelsen, "Der 'Liber instrumentorum' des Giovanni Fontana," *Festgabe Hugo Blümner überreicht zum 9. August 1914 von Freunden und Schülern* (Zurich, 1914), pp. 507–15; F. M. Feldhaus, *Die Technik der Antike und des Mittelalters* (Potsdam, 1931), pp. 347–48, and L. White, *Medieval Technology and Social Change* (Oxford, 1962), p. 98. P. L. Rose has indicated his intention to edit this text.

cipher: folios 10r,[30] 22v,[31] 48r,[32] and 62v.[33] Among his own works Fontana cites his *De pulveribus* (i.e. the *Nova compositio*),[34] *De laberintis*,[35] *De aque ductibus*,[36] and *De pisce*.[37] Citation of the first work assures that the notebook must have been composed after 1418. All of these works were apparently germinating about the same time during his early days at the University of Padua and hence the conventionally assigned date of about 1420 cannot be far off the mark.[38] It should be noticed that gen-

[30] *Bellicorum instrumentorum liber, ms. cit.*, 10r: ". . . . Se[d] ego Iohan[n]es Fontana multiplices pinsi in libello de laberintis. . . ." For fuller text, see note 35 below.

[31] *Ibid.*, 22v: "*Ego Iohan[n]es Fontana novos adinveni fontes, partim ex antiquorum fundamentis collectos, partim ex proprio ingenio.*"

[32] *Ibid.*, 48r: "*Si rota cum argento vivo et capsulis intra pe[r]foratis superponatur, suc[c]essive descendit per illam, quod pulcer[r]imum est. Unde ego Iohan[n]es Fontana cepi nova multa perficere ex hoc p[ro]vedimento sicud postquam perfecero, tibi notum faciam.*"

[33] The passage is transcribed in note 2 above.

[34] Prager, "Fontana on Fountains," p. 344, n. 20, cites 7r as the location for the reference to the *De pulveribus*. In fact it occurs on 6v: "Reliqua pars instrumentorum artingenii bellici intrinseca que dirigit ea que apparent extrinsecus hic subscribitur . . . (*then after a brief description in cipher, he writes still in cipher:*) Hec tamen prolixe tibi in libell[o] de pulveribus et similia descri[p]s[i]; quare hec tibi unita (?) relinqui."

[35] *Ibid.*, 10r: "*de lab[er]intis non datur ordo, sed quamvis laberintus iste sit q[u]adrus, potest in omnem modum angulorum fieri. Se[d] ego Iohan[n]es Fontana multiplices pinsi in libello de laberintis secundum quemque (!) genera figurarum ex propria fanta[xia] invicem dif[f]erentes, ubi sunt viarum perditiones, vie prolixe, ob [s]curitates, amfra[c]tus inordinationes timores, revolutiones et devia loca, reditiones atque conversiones, quibus intrantes decipiuntur.*" This was carelessly deciphered by Huelsen, "Der 'Liber instrumentorum'," p. 511. He wrongly deciphered *secundum* as *secundo* and thus left the erroneous impression that the work *De laberintis* was comprised of two books.

[36] Both references are somewhat ambiguous, the first as to whether it is a title (14v): "de aquarum ductibus hoc ingenium est et proprie deservit fontibus, fluviis et cadentibus aquis," the second as to whether the title is of Giovanni's work (48r): "Serpentina turris tot habet utilitates quot et linea girativa que ad colu[m]nam aplicatur, ut in libello de aque ductibus intitulato ostenditur." But in view of references by Fontana to a work of similar title which he intended to compose or did compose, the second passage is most likely a reference to his own work (see work No. 11 below).

[37] *Ibid.*, 37r: "de pisce, ave et lepore habes tractatum meum sufitientem." Written in normal writing, this accompanies sketches of a mechanical bird, hare and fish similar to the mechanical animals for measurement described in the *De pisce* (100r–03v). Notice the substitution here of "ave et lepore" for "cane et volucre" in the title of the work as given in the Bologna manuscript (see work No. 3 above). Notice also that opposite the title on 36v Fontana describes in normal writing a proposal for a self-moving cart of the sort mentioned in the *De pisce*. The statements in the two manuscripts are so similar that they deserve textual comparison. In the Munich manuscript the passage runs (36v): "feriunt quidam hunc carrum in plano ex se moveri posse quia posteriores rotte (!) facte maiores una cum pondere supper (!) trabem obliquam sic a po[n]derato gravitat et ponderat aut premit in rotas minores anteriores." The comparable passage in *Tractatus de pisce* states (93r): "Propter quod ymaginatus fuit quidam pauce experientie quod si quadriga fieret duas habens rotas posteriores magnas et anteriores parvas honore super-posito de se moveretur quoniam pondus super partem anteriorem declinando provocaret ad motum." Compare also the ambulatory chair described and pictured on folios 17v and 18r of the Munich manuscript with that described on 94r of the Bologna manuscript. They are identical machines.

[38] See Jähns, *Geschichte der Kriegswissenschaften*, p. 276, and von Romocki, *Geschichte der Explosivstoffe*, Vol. 1, p. 232, both of whom date the work about 1420. Birkenmajer,

erally Fontana does not here cite literary sources (other than his own works), although to be sure he mentions the name of Alkindi in association with fountains (28v, 46v, 61v), that of an unknown Bionius (14v) and also that of Archimedes, as I shall mention below. It is evident throughout that Fontana was familiar with the *Liber Philonis de ingeniis specialibus ducendi aquam*,[39] though that work is not specifically cited.

5. *Secretum de thesauro experimentorum ymaginationis hominum*.

MS: Paris, BN Nouv. acquis. lat. 635, 140 numbered leaves plus four preliminary leaves (A–D), with folios D and 111 unnumbered, 15c.

Inc.: An introductory table of contents commences as follows (1r): "Tabula divisionis omnium partium huius libri in dictiones et capitula. Tres sunt partes totius libri. Prima pars est theorica et in sermone universali. 2ª pars est practica et in speciali narratione. 3ª pars est operativa in actu particulari. . . ." The text itself begins (5r): "Incipit secretum de thesauro experimentorum ymaginationis hominum, quod. . . . (*erasure*: Iohannes fontana venetus?) taliter opinatus est et sub compendio conscripsit. Prohemium." And then in cipher: "Iustum est primum (*or* primo) Deo gracias agere pro omnibus bonis operibus nostris. . . ."

Colophon: "Et sic sit finis huius operis cum benedictione Dei. Amen." This is followed by four lines in a hand of the eighteenth century: "Ioannes Carolus Lisca f. p. c. Flaminii omnia accurate perlegit, colsideravit (!) et laudavit, et gratias egit Deo O. M. omnipotenti." Cf. folio 128r for another note of Lisca's: "A Carolo Lisca comite non parum in mathematicis erudito hec artifixiosa memoria non fuit laudata. 1721." Both notes are in cipher except for "Lisca" (in each instance) and the expression "Deo O.M.", which are written normally.

Comments: This mixture of occult rules, natural philosophy, and experimental material, accompanied by many drawings, is very schematic in form without full discussion. It is written entirely in the same cipher as the preceding work save for the table of contents, the various titles and the colophon.[40] In view of the identity of the cipher and the similarity of drawings in the two notebooks, we can safely conclude the identity

---

"Zur Lebensgeschichte," p. 41 suggests a date later in Fontana's career because of the fact he cites so many other works in the *Bellicorum instrumentorum liber*. But since I have already suggested that at least three of the works cited in the Munich notebook were composed in 1418 and the immediately following years, I see no reason to believe that this work was composed much later than 1420.

[39] See Prager, "Fontana on Fountains," pp. 349, 351, 353–54, 357–58. Prager suggests in one place (p. 346) that Fontana's knowledge of the devices of Philo, Hero and Ctesibius might have been indirectly acquired from Arabic sources. But see notes 63 and 64 below. Incidentally, Prager three times (pp. 346, 358 and 360) gives an incorrect citation of the last of three citations of Alkindi. He gives 60v instead of the correct citation of 61v.

[40] The work is described, the table of contents given and the cipher explained by H. Omont, "Un traité de physique," pp. 253–58. In a succeeding article, "Nouvelles acquisitions du Départment des Manuscrits de la Bibliothèque Nationale pendant les années 1896–97," *Bibliothèque de l'École des Chartes*, Vol. 59 (1898), p. 92, Omont suggests a possible attribution to Fontana but without specifying the reason for this attribution.

of the authors.[41] This work shows the constant substitution of "x" for "s" found in other works of Fontana. Lisca has touched up the faded writing in cipher on many pages.

6. Notes on the *Liber de speculis comburentibus* of Alhazen.

MS: Paris, BN lat. 9335, 134r.

Inc.: "Dicta atque notata per me Johannem Fontana[m] physicum Venetum et probata pro declaratione speculi ardentis quedam sunt principia declaranda."

Colophon: "Et hec sunt que declarare voluimus; reliqua habentur in tractatu."

Comments: These notes were added in Fontana's hand and thus indicate his ownership of this important manuscript of Gerard of Cremona's translations, including, as we shall see, two important Archimedean works. Fontana has alerted the reader of Alhazen's tract to his notes by the following statement on folio 88r: "In hoc libro in carta 134 ego iohannes fontana posui 3 formas extractas ex eadem pyramide ex sectione mukefi secundum artem predictam." The passage in the *De speculis comburentibus* on which Fontana is commenting is the following (88r): "Hec est summa sermonis in opere speculi concavi, quod est secundum figuram corporis (*or* compositionis) mukefi. Qualiter autem faciam speculum concavum comburentem. . . . Et imaginabimur longitudinem quesitam sicut *.dz.* et protrahemus in lamina sectionem ex sectione mukefi. . . ."[42] The notes thus concern a *sectio mukefi*, i.e. a parabolic section, *mukefi* being a transcription of the Arabic term. There is some similarity in terminology and content between the notes and a treatise called *Speculi almukefi compositio*, attributed in two manuscripts to Roger Bacon.[43] And interestingly enough a work with a closely similar

---

[41] For example, compare the following drawings: lettered cylinder locks (Paris 32r, Munich 49r), circular labyrinths (Paris 47r, Munich 9v), towers and arrows (Paris 69r, Munich 15v), keys (Paris 72r and 104r, Munich 36r), clepsydras (Paris 76v, Munich 11v), details of bellows (Paris 94r, Munich 26v), swords (Paris 98v, Munich 50r), lettered pyramid locks with keys (Paris 128v, Munich 42v–43r). This last comparison clinches the identity of authorship of the two works, since in each manuscript the drawing is accompanied by the same conundrum: "frifac.bononie.bona.cuf.anitidit (*Munich*: anitidiḅ.).eseb. Si dubitas versum frustra (*om. Munich*), agis (*Munich*: temptabis) per universum." No doubt a trained art historian would find many points of stylistic similarity in these and other drawings in the two manuscripts. A complete transcription of the Paris manuscript, which I have not attempted because of the often faded ink, would be of interest in the effort to correlate this work with Fontana's other works and perhaps would even reveal references to Fontana's works that have escaped me.

[42] Compare the printed text of the *De speculis*: J. L. Heiberg and E. Wiedemann, "Ibn al Haitams Schrift über parabolische Hohlspiegel," *Bibliotheca mathematica*, 3. Folge, Vol. 10 (1909–10), pp. 201–37, at pp. 229–30.

[43] The two manuscripts in which the work is assigned to Roger Bacon are Oxford, Bodl. Libr. Canon. Misc. 480, 47r–54r, 15c, and Florence, Bibl. Med. Laur. Ashburn. 957, 95r–110v, 15–16c. Other manuscripts are Vienna, Nationalbibl. 5258, 27r–38v, 15c (in Regiomontanus' hand), Verona, Bibl. Capitolare 206, 1r–8v, 16c, and London, BM Cotton Tiberius B.IX, 231r–35r, 14c. A. G. Watson, "A Merton College Manuscript Reconstructed; Harley 625; Digby 178, fols. 1–14, 88–115; Cotton Tiberius B. IX, fols. 1–4,

title is assigned to Giovanni Fontana in MS Vat. Barb. lat. 350, 61r: "Libellus de speculo mikesi (=mukefi) magistri Iohannis fontana (!) venetus (!)." This title appears in the upper margin of the folio in a hand later than that of the treatise which begins on that folio. Whether the marginal title refers to an actual work of Fontana or not, it is certainly misapplied to the work in the Barberini codex, the latter being Henry of Hesse's *De reprobatione eccentricorum et epiciculorum*.[44] It has been thought possible that the floating title of Fontana's work does apply to the above-noted work of similar title attributed to Roger Bacon.[45] But this is unlikely since one manuscript of the latter work appears to date from the fourteenth century (see note 43). The fact that it cites Witelo is no guarantee that it is later than Roger since Witelo's great optical work was composed around the year 1270 or shortly thereafter and Bacon lived until at least 1292.[46] Nor is the citation of Campanus' version of the *Elements* by the author of the tract on the parabola sufficient reason to rule out Bacon as its author since that work too could have been available to Bacon.[47] However, I must say that, like the sixteenth-century editor Gogava, I too doubt Bacon's authorship of the tract, for Bacon's works appear to me, as they did to Gogava, to lack the interest in formal mathematical proofs displayed in the tract on the parabola.[48] The ascription of the tract to Bacon can easily be explained by the fact that in the earlier of the two manuscripts bearing that ascription it follows immedi-

225–35," *Bodleian Library Record*, Vol. 9 (1976), pp. 207–16, has argued persuasively that this part of the last manuscript was a part of a John Dee manuscript that had once been owned by Simon Bredon and left by him to Merton College in 1372. A reworked edition of this work was published by A. Gogava in his *Cl. Ptolemaei . . . operis quadripartiti in Latinam sermonem traductio . . . Item de sectione conica orthogona quae parabola dicitur: Deque speculo ustorio, libelli duo, hactenus desiderati* (Louvain, 1548), sign. P 4r–S 2r, i.e., 60v–70r. It is essentially Regiomontanus' shortened version. I have edited both the original version and that of Regiomontanus in my forthcoming *A History of Conic Sections in the Middle Ages 1150–1550*, Chaps. 4 and 5.

[44] Cf. C. Kren, "A Medieval Objection to 'Ptolemy,' " *The British Journal for the History of Science*, Vol. 4 (1969), pp. 378–93, and particularly p. 378, n. 1. Thorndike, *A History of Magic*, Vol. 4, p. 176, n. 106, gave the correct incipit but did not realize that the work was by Henry of Hesse. Subsequently, this incipit was correctly identified in L. Thorndike and P. Kibre, *A Catalogue of Incipits of Mediaeval Scientific Writings in Latin*, 2nd ed. (Cambridge, Mass., 1963), c. 309.

[45] Thorndike, *A History of Magic*, Vol. 4, pp. 177–78 noted the similarity of the title ascribed to Fontana in the Barberini manuscript with that of the work attributed to Bacon.

[46] Thorndike, *ibid.*, claims, however, that Witelo is never cited by Bacon. Nor do Crombie and North mention Witelo among the main optical sources of Bacon's works (see the article "Bacon, Roger" in *Dictionary of Scientific Biography*, Vol. 1, pp. 377–85, at p. 379).

[47] Though he does not rigorously follow Campanus' proofs, Bacon did praise Campanus of Novara by name (Crombie and North, *ibid.*, p. 381).

[48] Gogava in the preface to his above-cited edition of the tract (sign. P 4r, i.e., 60r) among his arguments against Bacon's authorship of this and the succeeding tract *De speculo ustorio* states: "Adde quod in omnibus Rogerii libris ne vestigium quidem apparet eruditi istius Geometrarum pulveribus et Mathematici acuminis, quorum aliquid in his libellis agnoscere licet." Crombie and North are even firmer in their expression of a similar opinion concerning Bacon's knowledge of mathematics (*ibid.*, p. 381): "Apart from mathematically trivial results in such practical contexts as engineering, optics, astronomy and the like, his works apparently contain not a single proof, nor a single theorem. . . ."

ately after Bacon's *De compositione medicinarum* and the scribe, perhaps faced with an exemplar that assigned Bacon's name to *De compositione medicinarum* but left the succeeding treatise unassigned, might well have decided on Bacon's authorship for both treatises.[49]

7. *Tractatus de trigono balistario*, dedicated to Dominicus Bragadinus.
MS: Oxford, Bodl. Libr. Canon. Misc. 47, *in toto*.

Inc.: "In nomine domini nostri yhesu christi incipit tractatus de trigono balistario abreviatus ex libro maiore quem de eodem trigono cum demonstrationibus geometricis Iohannes fontana venetus physicus medicus scripsit ad nobilem et preclarum virum compatrem suum dominicum bragadino (!). Capitulum primum de fabrica trigoni et primo est prohemium. Postquam domino deo nostro vero sublimi glorioso et eterno placitum est ut librum de spera mundi complerem, supper (!) multa phylosophorum instrumenta diu per orbem iam delata atque famosa mensuris proprie dedita formas et experientias studio diligenti pernotavi. . . ."

Colophon: "Editus et explectus (!) est tractatus iste de trigono balistario anno gratie M°CCCC°XL° in utino die ultimo februarii per Iohannem fontanam venetum (*mg.*) physicum medicum eodem in loco salariatum ad laudem omnipotentis dei qui trinus et unus est per omnia secula. Deo gratias."

Comments: This is an extraordinarily detailed handbook of mensuration by the use of Fontana's "triangle," compiled in two books concerned respectively with the measurement of terrestrial distances and objects and with astronomical measurements.[50] Notice that we are told in the title that this work is an abrégé of a longer work on the same subject that was provided with geometrical demonstrations. This longer work is twice referred to under the curious title of *De scimetria*.[51] While the main contents of this important work are not germane to the subject of my investigation, I have published and discussed the section on spiral lines below. I here merely remind the reader that it was dedicated to the Venetian mathematician Domenico Bragadino and completed in 1440 at Udine. The work is useful in establishing the list of Fontana's works. Aside from

---

[49] The *De compositione medicinarum* concludes and the *Speculi almukefi compositio* begins on folio 47r of Bodl. Libr. Canon. Misc. 480.

[50] This important handbook has never been adequately described. For a brief description, see Thorndike in the Queries and Answers section of *Isis*, Vol. 14 (1930), pp. 221–22 and his similar observations in *History of Magic*, Vol. 4, p. 155.

[51] *De trigono balistario, ms. cit.*, 1r: "Reliqua vero ipsius magni voluminis [*mg.*: qui de scimetria nuncupatur] in plures scidi tractatus, quorum maximus est de geometricis supplementis ubi theoreumata multa fulcita sunt mathematicis regulis et demonstrationibus approbata, ut illis (*mg.*) qui subtilius hoc artifitium intelligere volunt illis (*del.*) non videatur ipsum opus sine ratione factum. Ibidem namque de lineis et angulis et superfitiebus et corporibus rectis, scilicet et curvis, amplissime monstravi, quibusque modis fieri et dividi et valeant metiri." Cf. 185v(186v): "Quod autem dyameter sit cxx graduum ita intelligas quoniam non est verum quod si voluerimus dividere dyametrum in partes equales gradibus circumferentie sui circuli et proprie si circumferentia in rectum extendi intelligatur inveniemus dyametrum non esse cxx graduum sed centum et xv fere cum probaverimus in libro nostro de scimetria." Usually the longer work is referred to as the *Tractatus maior de trigono* (see the next note).

citing the longer *De trigono balistario* many times,[52] it mentions Fontana's *De arte pictoria*,[53] his *De spera solida*,[54] his *De speculo medicinali*,[55] and his *Horologium aqueum*.[56]

8. *Liber de omnibus rebus naturalibus quae continentur in mundo, videlicet coelestibus et terrestribus necnon mathematicis et de angelis motoribus quae (!) coelorum* (Venice, 1544), published falsely under the name of Pompilius Azalus of Piacenza, who dedicated the work to Charles V.

Comments: No manuscript of this work is known but Thorndike has conclusively demonstrated that it was composed by Giovanni Fontana.[57]

[52] For example, see *De trigono balistario, ms. cit.*, 71r–v(80r–v): "Demostravimus in tractatu nostro maiori de trigono, unde liber iste extractus est, quod non quecunque duo puncta equidistant a superfitie orizontis unius equidistant a centro mundi, neque quecunque equidistant a centro predicto equidistant a superfitie orizontis . . ."; 82r(91r): "hec conclusio in tractatu maiore de trigono demonstratur geometrice. In vero si non credideris, potes etiam per experiencias certificari . . ."; 191r(192r): "Aliqua subcidente replicabo scripta in tractatu maiore de trigono et que amplius in tractatu de spera legere poteris." See also the citations of the preceding note.

[53] *Ibid.*, 75v(84v): "Sunt etiam varie figure umbrarum, ut in perspectiva notatur in extensione ipsarum, qualis est umbra pyramidalis et umbra rombitoydes (?) et umbra columnaris, et iterum variantur frequenter ad formam oppaci, ut quedam sint oblonge, quedam triangulares vel plurium angulorum, quedam rotunde, et alie secundum diversitatem corporum umbras fatientium et situs eorum et aspectus corporis luminosi ad illa et dispositionem suscipientium, de quibus alibi prolixius naratur (!), et ego in libro de arte pictoria multa de hiis pertractavi." Cf. 50v(59v): "Similia tantum particularius depingenda in libro de arte pictoria magis explanata per me reperies."

[54] *Ibid.*, 1r (see the incipit above). Cf. 163r(164r): "Et ego similes scripsi bene ordinatas in tractatu meo de spera solida ubi insequutus tabulam stellarum habitam a Ptolomeo (!) in libro almagest[i] distinctionem ad[d]idi super gradus et minuta longitudinis cuiuscunque stelle, gradus et minuta (*del in mg.*) ut haberem verum locum eius ad tempus meum, quia ad annum 1440 in quo ipsum tractatum scripsi." For the reference to the *De spera* on folio 191r(192r), see note 52 above. See also folio 193r(194r): "Gradus circuli ecliptice noscere describentes equales arcus artifitialium dierum solarium et equales arcus noctium in eadem regione atque de (*del.*) diebus artifitialibus et noctibus stellarum fixarum equalibus gradus convenientes reperire. Hec conclusio famosa est et facilis quoniam in tractatibus de speris communibus ut etiam in tractatu nostro de spera demonstratur." See also 200r(201r): "Ut alias diximus, sicut etiam patebit distincte in tractatu nostro de spera, non est verum quod si stella citius oriatur in loco uno quam in alio quod citius mediat celum vel occidat in eodem neque econverso ubi percipitur quod longitudo locorum non solum facit diversitatem in ortu et occasu sed etiam latitudo." Finally see folio 213v(214v): "et tu exempla in libro de spera habes manifesta."

[55] *Ibid.*, 160v(161v): "Et si festum est solempne scribam ex rubeo, reliqua vero ex nigro, uti in kalendario propter quod habebo bonum kalendarium secundum martilogium equatum, quale est illud quod in speculo meo notavi et in eius tractatu." Above all see folio 161r(162r): "Et ego pulcerrime in speculo meo medicinali quod ad medicos ordinavi plurima utiliter signavi, cuius tractatus incipit 'Tale tibi medice speculum componere potes'." This last statement occurs in a section that Fontana has crossed out.

[56] *Ibid.*, 172v(173v): "Tertio si non haberem horologium verificatum, tale mihi statuam horologium quod in libro de horologio aquarum explanavi."

[57] This work was first identified by Thorndike in his "An Unidentified Work by Giovanni da' Fontana: *Liber de omnibus rebus naturalibus*," *Isis*, Vol. 15 (1931), pp. 31–46. Much of this article was repeated with some revision in his *History of Magic*, Vol. 4, pp. 150–82. Birkenmajer, "Zur Lebensgeschichte," pp. 42–43, 47–49, 51–53 gives additional information on this work.

It mentions the Jubilee year of 1450.[58] A mention of 1536 is a rare instance of an insertion by Azalus.[59] Birkenmajer has convincingly argued for a composition date of 1454.[60] Fontana may have written part of it in Crete (see above, note 12). The treatise is long and rambling and has many passages indicating Fontana's wide scientific interests,[61] including, as we shall see, some references to Archimedes. Thorndike and Birkenmajer have mentioned the many medieval authors cited by Fontana.[62] We should note Fontana's great fondness for Ovid, whom he quotes again and again. A reference to Chyron (!), *De ductibus aquarum* has been taken by Birkenmajer as one to Hero's *Pneumatica*.[63] But Grant believes that

[58] Ed. of 1544, 38v. Cf. Thorndike, *A History of Magic*, Vol. 4, p. 154.

[59] Ed. of 1544, 6v. Cf. Thorndike, *A History of Magic*, Vol. 4, p. 154, and Birkenmajer, "Zur Lebensgeschichte," pp. 51–52. See the next note.

[60] The passage which allows Birkenmajer to fix the date of composition is that cited in the preceding footnote (ed. of 1544, 6v): "Nec illis credendum est . . . qui fatentur quod mundus factus sit ante adventum Salvatoris per annos quinque milia et ducentos vel circa; et hodie sumus in annum (!) gratiae milesimo quingentesimo XXXVI post Christi nativitatem. Quare a principio mundi usque ad praesens transacti sunt anni sex milia setticenti et quinquaginta et quatuor vel circa; et forsitan erit mundi finis usque ad annos duodecim vel saltem apparitio antichristi." The year 1536 is undoubtedly Azalus' insertion of his own date. Birkenmajer, "Zur Lebensgeschichte," p. 52, proposes that the number of years since the creation here specified as 6754 ought rather have been given as 6654. Birkenmajer makes his change to 6654 because of the fact that the author states it will be 12 years to the end of the world. An accepted apocalyptic year was 6666. If we subtract 12 from that number, it would make the time of composition the year 6654 from the creation; and since the author specifies that the creation was 5200 years before the birth of Christ, the latter number is subtracted from 6654 to produce the Christian year of 1454 as the time at which the work was composed.

[61] Thorndike in the article and chapter cited in note 57 describes some of Fontana's scientific opinions, emphasizing his geographical knowledge. Birkenmajer in the parts of his "Zur Lebensgeschichte" cited in that same footnote supplements Thorndike's account.

[62] Thorndike, *A History of Magic*, Vol. 4, pp. 162–63, 168–69, singles out the following authors mentioned by Fontana: Marco Polo, Odoric, Johannes Anglicus, Nicholas of Venice, Giovanni de' Dondi, Johannes de Lineriis, Peter of Abano, al-Zarqālī, the Alfonsine Tables, Sacrobosco, Michael Scot, and Albertus Magnus. Thorndike had already mentioned Fontana's knowledge of Paul of Venice, Blasius of Parma, and Prosdocimus de Beldomandis. Birkenmajer, "Zur Lebensgeschichte," p. 52, adds the names of Chyron (! see the next note), Archimedes, and Ptolemy. In fact, Fontana cites a great many authors—ancient and medieval—not mentioned by Thorndike or Birkenmajer: Albategni, Albumasar, Alcabitius, Alfraganus, Algazel, Aquinas, Aristotle, Arnald (of Villanova?), Augustine, Averroes, Avicenna, Bede, the Bible, Boethius, Campanus, Euclid, Franciscus in suo tractatu de sphera (80r), Galen, Gerard of Cremona, Hali, Hermes Trismegistus, Isidore, Jordanus de Nemore, Lincolniensis (Grosseteste), Lucan, Marinus, Mileus (i.e. Menelaus), Ovid, Plato, Pliny, Auctor de perspectiva, Magister sententiarum (i.e. Peter Lombard), Rogerius (Bacon), Thābit ibn Qurra, Valerius, and Vitruvius. I have no doubt missed others.

[63] "Zur Lebensgeschichte," p. 52. The reference in the ed. of 1544, 22r, runs: "Hac experientia cognita ab architectis artificibus inventus et conditus fuit fons ex tribus cannis iucunditate et iucositate (!) participans. Atque multa ingeniosa quae Chyron de ductibus aquarum commemorat, eodem praeternaturali aeris praessione (!) pulchrum effectum habent atque mirandum."

"on the basis of the Philo manuscripts with similar titles. . . . , it seems more reasonable to construe 'Chyron' as a corruption of 'Philo'."[64] Fontana also cites four of his own works: *De arte pictoria,*[65] *De aque ductibus,*[66] *De spera solida*[67] and *De trigono balistario.*[68] Finally we should note that he mentions his residence in Udine.[69]

9. A medical recipe of "Magister Johannes Font. de Veneciis" was found in the foresheet of MS No. 101 (147) of Baldassarre Boncompagni's library at Rome.[70] I do not know its present location. I suppose that it may be a part of Fontana's *De speculo medicinali* (see work No. 16 below).

[64] E. Grant, "Henricus Aristippus, William of Moerbeke and Two Alleged Mediaeval Translations of Hero's *Pneumatica*," *Speculum*, Vol. 46 (1971), pp. 668–69, n. 52 (the whole article, pp. 656–69).

[65] Ed. of 1544, II, Chap. 13 [misprinted as Chap. 14], 74v: "Hiatus tamen maior apparet quam vorago. Nam secundum magis et minus differunt. In praedicta namque scientia veritas ostenditur, quod eorum quae videntur a longe, quae albedine aut lumine plus participant propinquiora apparent quam ipsa sint, et quae nigredinae videntur esse remotiora quam sint. Ab hac naturali experientia ars pictoria optimos canones accepit, ut in libello ad iacobum bellinum Venetum pictorem insignem certe descripsi, quibusque modis colores obscuros et claros apponere sciret, tali cum ratione, quod non solum unius imaginis partes relevatae viderentur in plano depictae, verum extra manum vel pedem porrigere crederentur inspectae, et eorum quae in eadem superficie hominum, animalium vel montium equantur quaedam per miliaria distare apparerent atque eiusmodi. Ars quidem pingendi docet propinqua claris, remota obscuris mediaque permixtis sub coloribus tingi deberi."

[66] *Ibid.*, 83v: "Unde, fili mi, scias quod non parum etiam in artificialibus scientiam habere multum in hoc confert; unde scire debes quod naturaliter aqua tantum potest ascendere quantum a loco descendit, et iterum naturaliter ultra communes sibi terminos scandere ad locum aliquem, ut vacuum prohibeat aut corporum plurium unionem et iterum violenter impulsam vel attractam ad altiora loca posse pervenire. Quorum omnium varia ac multa exempla et rationes in libello de artificialibus fontibus et aquarum ductibus patefecimus, de quibus pauca ad propositum intelligenda rememorabimus. Nam si vas aquam continens statueris in altitudine et aliud non continens aquam in alia altitudine equali, struxerisque a fundo primi in fundum secundi fistulam solidam diligenti artifitio utrisque coniunctam, aqua prioris vasis per cannam descendens iterum psalliet in vas alterum. Quo motu aqua in secundo vase sursum scaturire et ascendere videbitur, donec cum ea quae in primo vase descendit equalis reddatur in superficie. Pariformiter imaginandum est, quod aqua, quae naturaliter scaturit ex fonte in plano alicuius montis, per venas et meatus solidos a natura factos subterraneos veniat ex loco eque alto vel altiore alterius montis proximi vel distantis. . . ."

[67] *Ibid.*, 36r: "Ego similiter, cum quendam tractatum de sphaera solida componerem et alium de Trigono Balistario instrumento novissimo in similes errores incidi sequens Alfonsi canones et aliorum vestigia."

[68] See the preceding note.

[69] Ed. of 1544, 127r: "Sed ipse in Utino vidi quandam foeminam locantem ova gallinarum aellecta (! electa) sparsim super stratum unum fimi equi, deinde superponere fimum similem et desuper alium ordinem ovorum et iterum cum fimo cooperire, et sic gradatim, et ad dies paucos pullos habere secundum numerum ovorum."

[70] E. Narducci, *Catalogo di manoscritti ora posseduti da D. Baldassarre Boncompagni*, 2nd ed. (Rome, 1892), p. 64. Birkenmajer, "Zur Lebensgeschichte," p. 43, n. 41, says that in the auction catalogue of the library of 1898 the manuscript bore the number 78.

Works Mentioned by Fontana but not yet Discovered

10. *Liber de ponderibus*.

Fontana twice expressed his intention of writing such a work: in the *Nova compositio* (see note 16 above) and in the *Horologium aqueum* (see note 21 above). There is no further mention of it in any of his later treatises. Hence it is possible that he never completed the *De ponderibus*.

11. *Libellus de aque ductibus*.

He mentions such a projected work twice in his *Horologium aqueum* (see note 22 above). The citation of a work with this title in his *Bellicorum instrumentorum liber*, without naming himself as author, is probably a reference to it (see note 36 above). Finally he categorically states that he has composed such a work in his *De omnibus rebus naturalibus* (see note 66 above). This is not surprising in view of his great interest in hydraulic machines of all kinds.

12. *De laberintis libellus*.

This work is mentioned in the *Bellicorum instrumentorum liber* (see note 35 above). I have already remarked that Fontana included diagrams of labyrinths in both of his notebooks (see note 41 above).

13. *Libellus de arte pictoria ad Iacobum Bellinum*.

This work predates 1440 since it was twice mentioned in the *De trigono balistario* of that date (see note 53 above). The work and its dedication to Jacopo Bellini are mentioned in the *Liber de omnibus rebus naturalibus* (see note 65 above).

14. *De spera solida*.

Like the preceding work this one must have been composed by 1440 since it was many times cited in the *De trigono balistario* (see note 54 above). One of those citations seems to affirm that it too was composed in 1440. It also received mention in the *Liber de rebus omnibus naturalibus* (see note 67 above).

15. *Tractatus maior de trigono balistario*.

This tract was also known under the title *De scimetria* (see note 51 above). It was many times mentioned in its extant abridgment (see note 52 above). As I have already indicated, its chief distinction from the abridgment was the inclusion of geometrical demonstrations. Hence from the point of view of my investigation this is the most desired of the missing works.

16. *De speculo medicinali*.

This work was also prepared by 1440 since it was cited twice in the *De trigono balistario*, once with its incipit (see note 55 above). I would suppose that it was a product of his reading and medical practice at Udine.

17. *De rotalegis omnium generum*.

Mentioned in Fontana's *Horologium aqueum* and in his *Tractatus de pisce* (see notes 23 and 27 above). It was perhaps composed after the *Nova compositio* and before the *Horologium aqueum*, since in the former work Fontana mentions a perpetual motion machine without mentioning that he had composed a work discussing the problem (see note 19 above) and in the latter he mentions such a work, as I have said.

18. *Tractatus diversorum modorum horologii mixti*.

Fontana expresses his intention of writing such a work or works in his *Horologium aqueum* (see note 20 above). No further mention of such a work is found in his writings. Perhaps he only partially achieved his intention by writing a section on horologues and their use in physical measurements in the *Tractatus de pisce* (Chapters 2–3, 8), written, I believe, shortly after the *Horologium aqueum*.

Works doubtfully attributed to Fontana

19. *De speculo mukefi*.

I have discussed this work in detail in my discussion of Fontana's notes on Alhazen's *De speculis comburentibus* (see work No. 6 above). I concluded there that conclusive evidence of such a tract by Fontana is lacking. For the sake of completeness I give the incipit, desinit and colophon of the work bearing a similar title attributed to Roger Bacon.

Inc.: "Speculi almukefi compositio secundum Rugerium Bacon ordinis minorum. Quia universorum (*or* diversorum) quos de speculis ad datam distantiam comburentibus tractare perpendi seu quorum vidi tractatus in scriptis omnes et singuli duas supposuerunt conclusiones ab Apollonio Perseo (*!*) allegatas. . . ."

Desinit and Colophon: ". . . in conclusiones quas Appolonius (*!*) magnus in libro suo de cognitis figuris inseruit cum nunquam viderim eius librum quamquam exactissimam diligenciam appensuerim (*or* apposuerim) eum vidisse. Ideo presenti opusculo cum laude dei predicta (*or* dicta) sufficiant etc. Explicit."

MSS and edition: see note 43 above. The incipit and desinit noted above are transcribed from MS Oxford, Bodl. Libr. Canon. Misc. 480, 47r–54r, 15c, with variant readings given in parentheses from MS Florence, Bibl. Med. Laur. Ashburn. 957, 95r–110v, late 15c or early 16c.

20. *Protheus*.

MS. Florence, Bibl. Med. Laur. Ashburn. 957, 71r–94v, late 15c or early 16c.

Inc.: "Incipit Protheus. Studiosum ut video me putatis, optime gerra, dum mihi rem tanta vetustate collapsam et a nemine resumptam in lucem quodam quasi post liminio iniungitis revocandam. Faciam quidem quod potero. . . ."

Desinit (no colophon): "Si autem cimbala seu tintinnabula minus recte sonent, adlimatedente (?) vel lapide corrigatur."

Comments: Thorndike has assigned this work to Fontana tentatively, but only on the slimmest evidence.[71] It shares with Fontana's work an interest in hydraulic subjects and is much preoccupied with siphons. Its constant citation of Virgil and its generally humanistic tone so uncharacteristic of Fontana's writings cast doubt on the suggested authorship of Fontana, though to be sure Fontana's last work, the *Liber de omnibus rebus naturalibus*, is somewhat humanistic in character and often quotes Ovid. Among the antique or medieval works cited in *Protheus* are Michael Scot's *Introductorium*,[72] Hero's *Pneumatica*,[73] Philo's *Pneumatica*,[74] Ctesibius' *Pneumatica* (via Vitruvius),[75] Vitruvius' *De architectura*,[76] a medieval fragment on the determination of the com-

---

[71] Thorndike, *A History of Magic*, Vol. 4, pp. 179–80.

[72] *Protheus, ms. cit.*, 73r–v: ". . . cum secundum philosophos nonnullos decios (!) maioritate aquam superare terras et decies aere[m] superasse aquas abinde aera (!) decies superasse ignes extiterat divulgatum; in qua sententia michaelem scothum introductorio sue astrologie declinasse vel assentiendo procubuisse certum est cum quo et ceteri multi." Cf. 72v: "Refert michael scotus quod omnis homo parvus vel magnus resolvitur in solam unciam limositatis terre in qua fuit solus creatus adam."

[73] *Ibid.*, 75v–76r: "Urinantes etiam sub aquis multas metretas in profundo mari gerunt super terga respirantes ut pati violentiam aque possint respirantes primo aere modico in naribus assumpto sicut scribitur in libro beronis (! Heronis) de vacuo et inani." Cf. Grant, "Henricus Aristippus," p. 661, n. 21.

[74] *Ibid.*, 88r: "Multe etiam vasorum forme invente sunt per philosophos ad hoc opus, quorum rationes sunt in occulto vel male recepte. Nam in philone sic habetur."

[75] *Ibid.*, 86r: "Fiunt etiam idraule que trahunt aquas et intrahendo per suos cannonios mirabiles voces et sonitus edunt secundum doctrinam echesibi (! Ctesibii) beronis (! Heronis), victruvii et aliorum de quorum doctrina multa ab antiquis inventa per desidiam nostri temporis pro parte perierunt et cotidie ad nihilum rediguntur." Cf. 89v: "Nec tamen sola hec ratio Echesebi fertur exquisita, sed etiam plures . . ."; 90v: "Primumque ab esbio alexandrino qui etiam spiritus naturales articasque (!) doctrinas adinvenit"; 91r: "Ergo cum idem clesbius animadvertisset ex celi tactu et pressionibus spiritus voces nasci hiis principiis usus ydraulicas machinas primus instituit. Item et aquarum expressiones, antoma, topicasque macchinas, multaque deliciarum (!) genera horlogiorum (!) ex aquarum cooperationibus posteris explicavit." All of these citations appear to be in line with the sundry references to Ctesibius in Vitruvius' *On Architecture*.

[76] There are two notable passages in *Protheus* taken from Vitruvius. The first of these is found on folios 91v–92r: "Sunt etiam aliqua ingenia a philosofis inventa ad onera levanda que habent diversos intra se motus et tamen optime concordant ad invicem pariuntque miros effectus ut sunt euteia et cicleteia, i.e., rotundi potentia et porrecti. Nam sine rotundi rotatione motus porrecti nihil agunt et sine porrecto motu rota com[m]unis potentia mutabilis est ad faciendas elevationes oneris magni. Patet hoc in rotis que girant cordas et habent vectes ferreos vel ligneos quibus circumaguntur, est enim maxima potentia vectis. Videmus enim quomodo cum vectium pressione levamus soli onus lapidis tam grandis quem non levarent multi et multi simul. Habet itaque vectis suum centrum circa lingulam in suo capite conformatam et quo longius a suo centro pressio fiet citius levabit onus; et si nimis plus debito subintrabit lingula ut non queat pressari in imum sed ex latere vectis, supra se lapidem ponere fulcitum habebit. Idem etiam accidit de velo navis. Nam si iuxta navim elevatur modicum vel circa quasi medium mali, non potest navis habere celerem motum sed tardum. Si autem elevatur in summitate mali, tunc elongatis velis a centro quod est in proximo pedis mali recipient vela motum celerem sine mora, nec gravabunt navim seu

ponents of silver and gold in an alloy,[77] and the Pseudo-Archimedean *De ponderibus* (see the discussion below).

II. Fontana and Archimedes

With Fontana's bibliography firmly established we are now in a position to examine the influence exerted by the medieval Archimedean traditions on Fontana's works. No trace of direct Archimedean influence is found on the first three works: the *Nova compositio*, the *Horologium aqueum*, and the *Tractatus de pisce*. But in the last of the three works there is a statement concerning the varying concavity of the surface of the water in a water clock at different heights that may reflect Proposition 2 of Archimedes' *On Floating Bodies* (Vol. 2, 55vD), though it more likely represents the more ancient views of Aristotle (287b 1):[1]

malum, posito simili vento ut prius erat et non maiori.'' The source of this passage was the *De architectura*, X.3, ed. of F. Krohn (Leipzig, 1912), pp. 232–34. Vitruvius had based his account on Chapter six of the Pseudo-Aristotelian *Mechanica* (851a–b) and repeats its false analysis of the supposed mechanical advantage of a sail raised higher on a mast. The other significant passage drawn from Vitruvius is Protheus' description of the crown problem, as I shall show below. It might be thought that Protheus' extensive use of Vitruvius is an indication that the author was later than Fontana, but this is a dubious argument since Fontana cites Vitruvius in the Venetian's *Liber de omnibus rebus naturalibus*, ed. of 1544, 117r.

[77] *Ibid.*, 93v–94r contains in its entirety the fragment "omne aurum purum," which goes back to the tenth century and which I have published below in Appendix I, Sect. 4, Fragment 1.

[1] *Tractatus de pisce*, MS Bologna, Bibl. Univ. 2705, 87v–88r: "Sed diceres quod aqua in superiori parte vasis minus curvatur quam [in] inferiori, propter hoc quod cum circumferencia ipsius semper sit mundo concentrica, illa que superius est plus a centro mundi distat et debet esse portio circuli maioris quam que proprior est centro mundi. Sed maioris circuli minus curvatur arcus quam minoris. Igitur et in aqua non erit dicendum quod in omnibus partibus signationum vasis servet equalitatem nec planiciem. Item sophysta diceret hoc fundamento supposito quod horologium in plano formatum in summitate montis non valeret nec econverso, eo quod eadem aqua in vase eodem in vale plus curvabitur quam in monte. Ad hec dicitur quod, licet hec vera sint et concedenda, quia tamen insensibiliter est hec curvatio maior et minor cum hec distancia altitudinis parva sit in comparatione ad dyametrum mundi, non curat architectus quantum curaret geometra differencias demonstrans. De hoc tamen alibi sermo amplior erit." Fontana says the same thing later in his *Liber de omnibus rebus naturalibus*, ed. of 1544, 79v–80r: "Capitulum xx in quo demonstratur quod aqua naturaliter sit ad sphaericitatem tendens atque rotunda. Conveniens est demonstrare quod elementum aquae sit rotundum, hoc est, quod eius superficies (80r) ad sphaericitatem tendat. . . . Est opinio quorundam subtilium (sed forsan veritate im[m]utatorum) quod aqua quanto est a centro mundi remotior, eius superficies curvatur curvatione maioris circuli seu maioris sphaer[a]e quam si sit centro mundi propinquior. Et videtur ratione dictum atque verum. Nam duorum circulorum inequalium concentricorum, indubie centrum commune plus distat a circunferentia maioris circuli quam minoris, sed quia Geometrice est demonstrandum quod circulus maius minus curvatur quam circumferentia minoris, ut patet in exemplo signato in quo eadem corda adcordat arcum *abc* circuli minoris et arcum *afd* circuli maioris ex eadem parte revolutorum, inferunt ex his quod Tina vel vas, lati et plani orificii aqua plenum usque ad summum plus continebit in valle quam in alto monte. Siquidem superficies aquae plana

You might answer that the water [level] in the upper part of the vase is less curved than in the lower part. For since the circumference of it is always concentric with the earth, that which is higher is more distant from the center of the earth and ought to be a segment of a larger circle [i.e., circumference] than that which is closer to the center of the earth. But the arc of a larger circle is less curved than that of a smaller circle. Therefore it ought not to be said in regard to the water that in all the marked parts of the vase it (the water level) retains evenness or flatness. . . . To these objections it is replied that, though they are true and to be conceded, still, because the curvedness [of the surface of the water] is [only] insensibly larger or smaller (the distance of the altitude being small in comparison with the diameter of the earth), the engineer is not concerned [with the curvature] in the way that a geometer is who demonstrates these differences. But on this matter there is more ample discussion elsewhere.

I would scarcely have brought up a possible Archimedean influence for this passage were there not another passage elsewhere that shows at least indirect influence of *On Floating Bodies* on Fontana. This occurs in Fontana's *Bellicorum instrumentorum liber*, where beneath a drawing showing the length of the hull divided into three distinct parts and above one showing a cross-sectional framework of each of the three parts we find the following statement:[2]

foret utrobique in alto et basso loco in quo minus distat a centro mundi se reducit ad sphaericitatem minoris circuli, et in alto ad sphaericitatem maioris, gibbabit plus aqua super rectitudinem labiorum Tinae in loco basso constitutae quam in alto et plus ibidem continebit.'' But Fontana does not go on to give the practical answer he developed in the earlier work. Incidentally, this same kind of argument plays a role in statics when it is argued that the weights on the end of a balance tend to press toward the center of the world and therefore the force-lines are not parallel lines at right angles to the beam of the balance but are rather lines converging at the center of the world. This argument was refuted by a medieval commentator in much the same way that Fontana answered the argument on the varying curvature of water surface, namely by saying that the suspension chords vary only insensibly from parallelity to the vertical through the center of the earth. See the *Aliud commentum* on the *Liber de ponderibus* as edited by J. Brown, *The "Scientia de ponderibus" in the Later Middle Ages* (Dissertation, University of Wisconsin, 1967), pp. 237–39 (cf. *Liber Iordani viri clarissimi de ponderibus propositiones XIII* [Nuremberg, 1533], sign. B iii verso): ''Notandum quod hec conclusio fundatur in hoc, quod appendicula equidistent linee directionis, quod tamen est falsum, eo quod concurrunt cum ea in centro terre si in infinitum protraherentur. Verum est quod, propter brevitatem appendiculorum et longam distantiam eorum a centro terre, ista appendicula insensibiliter in inferioribus distant a lineis equidistantibus linee directionis.'' This answer is a refutation in advance of the same kinds of criticism of Jordanus made by Benedetti and Ubaldi. The answer also anticipates the similar answer given by Galileo in his *Discorsi e dimostrazioni matematiche intorno a due nuove scienze* (*Le Opere di Galileo*, Vol. 8 [Florence, 1898], pp. 274–75) to Simplicius who asserts that the assumption of the horizontal plane as a straight line is false since the horizon must be curved.

[2] *Bellicorum instrumentorum liber*, MS Munich, Staatsbibl. Icon. 242, 10v: ''Navis occisionis quia periclitantur in ea homines incauti, prudentes vero salvantur. *Credunt plures tuti accedere et est navis in partes divix*[a] *artifitio, que in tranquilitate maris secura videtur sed eius tempestatem non substinet. Et modus compositionis totus hic non ostenditur nec describitur. Sed recur*[r]*e ad Archimenidem, experimento ultimo libri secundi.''* (The italicized part of this citation is in cipher; then follows in a later hand using normal writing: ''Modus non exponitur, recurre ad Archimedem.'')

It is called a ship of slaughter because incautious men are in danger in it while prudent men are saved. Several people accept it as safe. It is a ship divided into parts, which seems secure in a quiet sea but does not weather the sea's roughness. The whole method of composition is not demonstrated or described here, but have recourse to Archimenides, the last experiment of Book II.

The whole statement is by no means clear and the reference to Archimedes is particularly puzzling. If the latter refers to a genuine work of Archimedes, then certainly it must be to *On Floating Bodies*, the only work of Archimedes that considers floating bodies and their stability (see below, Part III, Chapter 4, Section III). However, it is not clear why Fontana should refer to the last proposition of Book II as an *experimentum*, since that complex proposition with its five cases considering the stability or instability of right-paraboloids under certain conditions is a highly abstract geometrical exercise that could hardly be described by the word *experimentum*. Furthermore, it takes a great stretch of the imagination to see how this proposition could be fruitfully applied to the construction of the hull depicted here. Finally the use of the medieval form of the name "Archimenides" does not reflect Moerbeke's translation where the less popular "Greek" form, "Archimedes," usually appears. Thus, all in all, it is quite unlikely that Fontana's citation is to a genuine work of Archimedes.

But if the reference is not to a genuine work of Archimedes, it must be to some Pseudo-Archimedean work. The only possible candidate among the known Pseudo-Archimedean works is the *Liber de ponderibus Archimenidis*, which I have re-edited below in Appendix I, Section 4. Still there are certain difficulties in concluding that this is the work intended by Fontana: (1) The reference seems to imply that the cited work of Archimedes concerns ship construction or the theory necessary for ship construction, but the *Liber de ponderibus Archimenidis* in its early version primarily concerns rather the problem of determining the components of alloys and mixtures (see particularly the last proposition which considers such an alloy or mixture). (2) The reference specifically designates the appropriate conclusion (or rather "experiment") as the "last of the second book," but the *De ponderibus Archimenidis* in its earliest version consists of a single book. We can, I believe, solve these difficulties if we do not confine ourselves to the early version of *De ponderibus Archimenidis* but consult the reworked text of it that appears in Book IV of Johannes de Muris' *Quadripartitum numerorum*. In this reworked version of *De ponderibus Archimenidis* the last two propositions are appropriate in a general way to the problem of ship construction since they deal with the basic principle of floating bodies and with the determination of whether a vessel made of material specifically heavier than water floats:[3]

---

[3] M. Clagett, *The Science of Mechanics in the Middle Ages* (Madison, Wisc., 1959; 2nd print., 1961), pp. 119–20. See the Latin text on pp. 134–35.

11. Every body floating in water displaces in the water a volume of water of its own weight.

For example: If half of the floating body were in the water and half outside of it, the water equal in volume to half of that body will be equal in weight to the whole body. And it is proportionally the same in regard to other fractions. Thus if ⅔ of the floating body is in the water and ⅓ of it outside of the water, the volume of water equal to ⅔ of that body will be equal in weight to the whole body. And if that body is equal in weight to water equal to it in volume, the whole body is submerged in the water; but it will not descend to the bottom, since it is not superior in weight to the water. Rather the [upper] surface [of the body] will be at the surface [of the water]. If, however, the body is superior in weight to the water which is equal to it in volume, it will descend immediately to the bottom.

12. If there is a vessel made of submergible material (i.e. specifically heavier than water), to find out whether or not it will float in water.

Let there be an iron vessel. I wish to know whether it will float in water. I take a quantity of iron which weighs the same as the said vessel. I also take as much water as fills up the said vessel. I further take water equal in volume to the said iron, and I join together these two quantities of water. These two waters denote the weight of the said vessel if the whole vessel is [just] submerged in the water. Leaving it in air, I shall consider whether the said iron body weighs more than the said waters joined together, or less. For if more, the vessel will be submerged; if not, it will float; which is that which was proposed.

An example in numbers: Let the vessel be iron—and cubical if you wish. Its capacity is 64 feet and the weight in air is 8 pounds. The ratio of iron to water in specific weight would be 8 to 1. So the iron weighs more than the water in an eightfold proportion. Thus let there be taken a quantity of iron equal in weight to the said vessel, namely, of 8 pounds. And let a quantity of water be taken which fills up the said vessel, and it will contain 64 feet, and its weight will be known by a balance; let that weight be 15 pounds. Take another quantity of water equal in volume to the said quantity of iron; and so it will weigh—by hypothesis—1 pound. Join these quantities of water together; they make 16 [pounds]. And since the quantity of iron weighs 8 and the waters joined together 16, it is clear that the vessel will float; since the weight of a quantity of iron equal in weight to the said vessel is not superior to that of the waters but is inferior to it, hence the whole vessel will not enter the water but will float. And say that half of it is in the water with the other half floating when the weight of the waters joined together is double the weight of the quantity of iron. If they were equal in weight, the whole vessel would enter the water up to the surface, but it would not be immersed [further]. If, however, the waters joined together weighed 16 and the quantity of iron 12, ¾ of the vessel would be in the water and ¼ would float, and so in other cases proportionally; this it was proposed to explain.

It is clear that the last or twelfth proposition does have an experimental form and thus would justify Fontana's reference to it as an *experimentum*. It is true that the numerical example given there describes a vessel or vase that has a capacity of only "64 feet" and a weight in air of "8 pounds." But presumably Fontana was supposing that a similar procedure would have to be used in ship construction if that ship at least in part contained material specifically heavier than water. The second difficulty, namely the appearance in Fontana's citation of the phrase "the second book," can be explained in one of two ways. Either it is an imprecise reflection of the fact that Johannes de Muris' version is designated as the "Secundus tractatus." Or perhaps the manuscript used by Fontana contained both the early version of *De ponderibus Archimenidis* and the modified version of Johannes, the latter being designated as Book II. The second explanation is attractive, for it would also explain why the medieval form Archimenides was used by Fontana since presumably the first book or early version would have been accompanied by the title *De ponderibus Archimenidis*. But whatever the explanation of the second difficulty, it seems to me quite reasonable to conclude that Fontana's reference is to the modified version of *De ponderibus Archimenidis*. I should add that perhaps light would be shed on the source intended by Fontana in this citation, and indeed possibly also on the source of Fontana's passage on the curvature of water surfaces, if Fontana's lost *De ponderibus* could be located.

Moving to Fontana's Parisian notebook, the *Secretum de thesauro* (MS Paris, BN Nouv. acquis. lat. 635), we find no mention of Archimedes. However, Fontana presents on folio 68r a drawing of a kind of hydrostatic balance (see Fig. II.4.1), which I suspect that he devised for assaying the soundness of gold coins or other specimens of gold. The cipher between the two cylinders I read as follows: "Ista est duples (! -x) equilibris, quia in parte dextra aqua as[c]endit et in sinistra des[c]endit aer, ambo violenter." I would render this in English as follows: "This is a 'double balance' because on the right side the water ascends and on the left the air descends, and both by violent motion." I am not sure how this balance was supposed to work but I can suggest the following. Equal weights of the specimen to be tested and gold were put respectively in the suspended and graduated containers on the left and the right. Meanwhile the left cylindrical chamber was filled with water and the right was left with air alone. Then I suppose the cylinders to be connected at the base by a channel with some kind of valve in the middle of the channel. Then the valve was to be opened and the water in the left cylinder allowed to flow into the right chamber, seeking its level. If the specimen to be tested was gold, its container would then be submerged to exactly the same mark on its outside as would submerge the container on the right side with gold. But if the gold in the specimen had been debased, the left-hand container with the specimen would be less submerged. In view of the possible connection of such a balance with the crown problem, it is an interesting curiosity that the decorative design in the middle of the balance support looks somewhat like an exotic crown. I need hardly add that Fontana's interest in the hydrostatic balance probably did not come from perusing Archimedes' genuine *On Floating Bodies*, but more likely from his having read one or more of the various medieval texts that implied its use, such as the *Carmen de ponderibus*, the medieval fragment beginning "Omne aurum purum"[4] or the above-noted *De ponderibus Archimenidis*. Before leaving the *Secretum de thesauro*, I should note in passing Fontana's interest in spiral forms as exhibited in the drawings on folios 28r, 31r and 50r, the last illustrating a curious spiral balance. I do not mean to suggest, however, that these drawings indicate a knowledge at this time of Archimedes' *On Spiral Lines*, since not a whisper of formal geometrical considerations accompanies them. However, in view of Fontana's later interest in the geometry of spirals in his *De trigono balistario* (which I shall discuss below), his earlier concern with the spiral form is not completely without interest.

The content of Fontana's notes on Alhazen's *De speculis comburentibus* (work No. 6 described in Section I above) has no special interest for our Archimedean studies, though we can remark that in at least one manuscript Alhazen's tract is ascribed to Archimedes.[5] But the fact that is of great importance to us is that these notes reveal Fontana's ownership of manuscript Paris, BN lat. 9335, the most important manuscript to contain collected translations of Gerard of Cremona. Among the various translations appearing in the manuscript are those of Archimedes' *De mensura circuli* and the *Verba filiorum* of the Banū Mūsā, both of which I have edited in Volume One. Thus Fontana had in his possession the best copy of each of the two most important works of the Arabo-Latin tradition of Archimedes. The further significance of this ownership will be evident in my analysis below of Fontana's references to Archimedes in his *Liber de omnibus rebus naturalibus*.

The most significant piece of Archimedean material found in Fontana's works is his treatment of spiral lines in Book II, Chapter 24 of the *Tractatus de trigono balistario*. I have edited the whole chapter below in order to indicate the context of the discussion of spiral lines. Like Chapter 31 of the first tractate of Book IV of Johannes de Muris' *Quadripartitum numerorum* (see above, Part I, Chapter 1), Fontana's Chapter 24 is a discussion of kinematics, only much expanded. That is, Fontana first treats of the measurement of rectilinear and curvilinear motions (Propositions 1–4), then of the distinction between curvilinear and angular velocities

---

[4] *Ibid.*, pp. 84–93, and see below Appendix I, Sect. 4.

[5] See below, Part III, Chap. 5, Sect. II, n. 6 where the assignment of the work to Archimedes is discussed. In the *Liber de omnibus rebus naturalibus*, ed. of 1544, lllv, Fontana indicates his knowledge of Alhazen's tract when he mentions the parabolic burning mirror and indicates "Archimedes or Apollo or someone else" as its possible discoverer: "Hoies(*!*) item ex speculo miram experientiam ut radii solis oppositum proprie concavum existens ignem generat, et fortem gignisse ignem, quo oppidum incensum est vel fugatus hostilis exercitus. Illud calybeum est speculum quod secundum sectionem Muchefi diligenter structum reperiritur (*!*), O mirabilis industria, sive Archimenides sive Apollo sive alter prius invenerit."

(Proposition 5), then of the measurement of angular velocity (Propositions 6–9) and finally of spiral motion (Propositions 10–13). The kinematics expressed in the first nine propositions was commonplace by the first half of the fourteenth century.[6] One quite distinctive feature of Fontana's account, however, is the way in which time is to be measured in Proposition 3. This is not surprising in view of his great concern with horologues in the first three of his works.

Turning to the propositions on spiral motion themselves, we should first note that the ultimate source of these propositions is unquestionably Archimedes' *On Spiral Lines* in the translation of William of Moerbeke. Fontana's Proposition 10 is a restatement in kinematic fashion of Proposition 12 of *On Spiral Lines* (see Vol. 2, 13rW–X), while Fontana's Proposition 11 is an inference from that same Archimedean proposition. Similarly Fontana's Proposition 12 has its ultimate origin in Archimedes' Proposition 15 (*ibid.*, 13vJ) and Fontana's Proposition 13 is a further inference from that proposition. In short, Archimedes' Propositions 12 and 15 lie behind Fontana's set of four propositions on spiral lines. Now Fontana could have read these propositions either in the full text of *On Spiral Lines* (two manuscripts of which might have been available: the Moerbeke autograph, manuscript *O*, and the fourteenth-century copy, manuscript *R*) or in the hybrid *Circuli quadratura* added to the eighth chapter of Johannes de Muris' *De arte mensurandi* where the Archimedean Propositions 12 and 15 reappear as Propositions 8 and 11 (see my text of the hybrid tract above, Part I, Chapter 5). We cannot decide on the basis of Fontana's discussion alone which of these two possible sources Fontana used. There is, however, independent evidence that Fontana was acquainted with Johannes de Muris' *De arte mensurandi*, as I shall now show in my analysis of the Archimedean references in Fontana's *Liber de omnibus rebus naturalibus*. The probability then is that the hybrid tract provided Fontana with his knowledge of the Archimedean propositions on spirals. In appending to this section my text of Chapter 24 of Book II of the *Tractatus de trigono balistario*, MS Oxford, Bodl. Libr. Canon. Misc. 47, 216v(217v)–219v(220v), I have followed my usual procedures, punctuating and capitalizing as seems required by good sense. I have also provided an English translation and commentary. In the footnotes I have given the folio numbers of the earlier propositions of the *De trigono balistario* cited by Fontana.

In the last of Fontana's extant works, the *Liber de omnibus rebus naturalibus*, we find specific citations of Archimedes, albeit in a curious fashion:[7]

[6] Clagett, *The Science of Mechanics*, Chapters 3 and 4.

[7] Ed. of 1544, 106v–07r: "[Bk. V] Cap. iiii. de mensuris elementorum et de semidiametris eorum. . . . Memento regulae Archimenidis et Arsamith[is] optimorum computistarum, quod scilicet proportio circumferentiae circuli ad suam diametrum est tripla et plusquam septima partes (*!* parte) diametri et minus octava parte eiusdem, sed quia talis proportio est fere tripla sexquiseptima, ita in presenti nos accipiemus, ut communiter accipitur, ne

Remember the rule of Archimenides and Arsamith, the best computists, namely that the ratio of the circumference of a circle to its diameter is more (*!*) than $3\frac{1}{7}$ and less (*!*) than $3\frac{1}{8}$. But because such a ratio is almost $3\frac{1}{7}$, so in this present matter we shall accept it, as it is commonly accepted, to save the labor [of calculating] with fractions. . . . The volume of any of the spherical elements we know how to calculate correctly by geometric rule as follows: (1) In the first place we shall find the area of its maximum circle, which shall be known easily, [for,] if we multiply the radius by the semicircumference, the product will give the area of the circle by the common rule. (2) Then if we multiply this area by the diameter of this circle, the product will give the volume of a cylinder or round column circumscribing the sphere. (3) And since such a cylinder is in $\frac{3}{2}$ ratio to the sphere by the eighth of Archimenides, [and] in *On Conoids and Spheroids*, if a third part [of the cylinder] is subtracted, the volume of the sphere will remain.

We should first note the inadvertent error by which "more" and "less" have been incorrectly interchanged. Obviously π is less than $3\frac{1}{7}$ and more than $3\frac{1}{8}$. Much more interesting is the curious statement that the rule for π is that of both Archimenides and Arsamith, thus making two different people out of two different transcriptions of the Arabic form of Archimedes' name. But this can be easily explained if we remember that Fontana owned the Parisian manuscript BN lat. 9335. For in that manuscript, Gerard's translation of *De mensura circuli*, which of course includes the determination of the bounds of π as its third proposition, is attributed to *Arsamith* in its title: *Liber Arsamithis de mensura circuli* (see Vol. 1, p. 31). But also contained in the same manuscript is the *Verba filiorum* of the Banū Mūsā, which includes as Proposition VI a determination of the bounds of π that the authors attributed to *Archimenides* (*ibid.*, page 264). And though the results of the two determinations are the same, the texts differ markedly. Hence Fontana's conclusion that two different authors composed them, namely Arsamith and Archimenides.

One further remark concerning Fontana's statement regarding the bounds of π. Notice that the lower bound has been altered by Fontana to $3\frac{1}{8}$ from $3\frac{10}{71}$ as appearing in the two texts in BN lat. 9335. The only author before Fontana to have made the same alteration was Johannes de Muris in his *De arte mensurandi*, where in Chapter 8 of his text Johannes has kept the Archimedean bounds intact in his proof but altered the lower bound to $3\frac{1}{8}$ in his enunciation (see above, Part I, Chap. 4).

labor sit in fractionibus. . . . Corpulentia vero uniuscuiusque spherarum elementorum per regulam geometricam sic scire valebimus, quoniam primo inveniemus aream sui maximi circuli, que facilis nota erit: si duxerimus semidiametrum in semicircunferentiam, productum dabit aream per regulam communem; deinde si multiplicaverimus hanc aream per diametrum ipsius circuli, productum dabit capacitatem chilindri sive columnae rotundae circumscribentis sphaeram. Et quoniam talis chilindrus est in propositione (*!* proportione) sexquialtera ad ipsam sphaeram per octavam archimenidis, inde (*!* in de) cononydalibus (*!* conoydalibus) et spoydalibus (*!* speroydalibus) demta tertia parte remanebit quantitas corpulentiae sphaerae.''

It seems probable therefore that Fontana made his similar change of the lower bound under the influence of Johannes de Muris. This would gain further support if my subsequent argument for the influence of the *De arte mensurandi* on the rest of the passage is correct.

Now let us turn to the second part of the passage I have given above from Fontana's *Liber de omnibus rebus naturalibus*. It will be noticed that Fontana designates as "the common rule" the assertion that the area of a circle is equal to the product of its radius and semicircumference. This, of course, is Proposition I of *On the Measurement of the Circle* and would have been available to Fontana in both of the above-mentioned texts in Paris, BN lat. 9335 (see Vol. 1, pp. 40 and 256), in Johannes de Muris' *De arte mensurandi* (see above, Part I, Chap. 4) and in many of the geometrical manuals. By calling it the common rule, he no doubt implies that it is so well-known that no source for it need be cited. He is, however, more specific in specifying the sources for his assertion that a cylinder is ³⁄₂ its inscribed sphere. Fontana's first authority for this statement is "the eighth of Archimenides." This can be readily identified as Proposition VIII of the *Liber de curvis superficiebus Archimenidis* (see Vol. 1, p. 496), one of the most popular of the medieval Archimedean texts. But Fontana also specifies *On Conoids and Spheroids* as a further authority for the proposition. Needless to say this assertion is in error, for the work of Archimedes in which the proposition is maintained is, of course, *On the Sphere and the Cylinder*. The error seems peculiar since there is no evidence that Fontana read either of the Archimedean texts. But I think it can be explained if we assume that Fontana had consulted Johannes de Muris' *De arte mensurandi*. For recall that in the Proemium to Chapter Ten of his *De arte mensurandi* Johannes de Muris gave as if they were suppositions a series of propositions drawn from Moerbeke's translation of *On the Sphere and the Cylinder* (see above, Part I, Chapter 6). Among these was Proposition I.33 (=Gr I.34) stating the proposed relationship between a cylinder and its inscribed sphere. Now this list of propositions was preceded by a statement that both *On the Sphere and the Cylinder* and *On Conoids and Spheroids* are needed for the demonstration of what follows. And so if one hastily referred to this introductory statement he might well have concluded that the postulated propositions were from both works; and if he were even more hasty, he might conclude that the second title, namely *On Conoids and Spheroids*, being the last title mentioned before the propositions, was the source for the propositions. It was in such a way, I believe, that Fontana's error arose. I readily admit, however, that if Fontana had looked at the passage following the list of propositions he would have seen the explicit statement that they were demonstrated in *On the Sphere and the Cylinder*. But this, I suggest, he did not do and so fell into his error.

Though the foregoing represent the only direct citations of Archimedes

in the *Liber de omnibus rebus naturalibus*, there are other passages that
have Archimedean implications. Some remarks on the varying density of
water at least indirectly reflect *On Floating Bodies*, perhaps through the
medieval *Liber de ponderibus Archimenidis* or the Pseudo-Euclidian
De ponderoso et levi.[8] We can also note Fontana's inclusion of definitions
of a straight line and a plane that ultimately derive from Archimedes' *On
the Sphere and the Cylinder*, perhaps through one or another version of
Euclid's *Elements*.[9] Finally, Fontana's distinction of center of gravity from
center of magnitude is traditionally medieval and does not reveal any
direct knowledge of *On the Equilibrium of Planes*.[10] It was perhaps one
of the sources of Leonardo da Vinci's similar distinctions (see below,
Part III, Chapter 3, note 38).

Though the *Protheus* is probably not by Fontana, I ought perhaps to
indicate briefly its Archimedean references since I did discuss it among
Fontana's works. The first reference is clearly to Postulate 1 of Pseudo-
Archimedes' *Liber de ponderibus Archimenidis*. The passage purports to
explain why a swimmer under water is not crushed by the weight of water
above him. The answer according to *Protheus* is that water has no weight

---

[8] *Ibid.*, 81v–82r: "Hac de causa cognoverunt navem oneratam, quam mare substinuit
ad flumen perventam, aut totaliter submergit aut profundari plus quam in ipso mari, et ita
incauti mercatores, barchas nimis replentes per mare, ad flumen portus venientes, ad
pericula accesserunt, atque merces submersas ibidem perdiderunt et se difficulter salvarunt.
Est etiam asserendum ubi plus est de aquae profundo dorsum (*!*) aquae valentius esse
ad sub referendum, hoc idem confirmantes qui de ponderibus libros condiderunt, hac
ratione, quoniam ubi plus de forma reperitur ibi plus de virtute sit, et quoniam experientia
certiores nos reddit, quae rationem persaepe clarificat, ubi ratio obfusca habeatur et dubia.
Ideo cavendum est ne nave nimis gravata ex pellago ad portum applicans periculum
submersionis incurrat. . . Iam non est hesitandum quod aqua quanto fuerit grassior et
spissior magis substinet, ideo homo natans melius et diutius postest in tranquillo mari sub-
stineri quam in flumine et in medio maris quam propre littora."

[9] *Ibid.*, 8v: "Si finita intelligatur, linea recta est brevissima extensio ab uno extremo ad
aliud; linea non recta est quae inter extrema curvatur. . . superficies plana est quae tam
secundum longitudinem quam secundum latitudinem brevissime extenditur, superficies non
plana est quae concavitatem vel convexam habet." Cf. Volume 1, p. 627.

[10] Ed. of 1544, 11v: "Ea propter diligentius est intelligendum duplex esse centrum in
aliquo elemento, unum magnitudinis, alterum gravitatis; illud dicendum est centrum
gravitatis quod est vere medium inter partes aquae (*!* aeque) graves, quale constat centrum motus librae, eius brachia a rectitudine non discendunt. Sed illud est dicendum centrum magnitudinis quod est vere medium inter extrema, ut punctus medius in ligno bipedali,
qui per pedale tantum ab utroque distat extremorum, ut centrum circuli vel sphaere. Et
quamvis dicta centra sint ratione differentia, sunt quandoque realiter idem quod accidit in
sphaera motus (*!*), ut et in libra aequalium brachiorum atque equapotentium (*!*). Aliquando
sunt a se invicem remota, qualia inveniuntur ut libra cuius unum brachium est curtum
et grossum, alterum vero longum et grossum (*! subtile?*), erit tunc centrum gravitatis punctus
ad quem partes coniunguntur sed centrum magnitudinis situm in brachio longiore in puncto
eque ab extremis librae distaverit. Item in sphaerico magnae gravitatis in quo sit una
medietatum altera gravior, centrum gravitatis erit in ea differens a centro figurae sphaere,
tantum enim de medietate ponderosiori addere oportet medietati leviori pro habendo centro
gravitatis, quod existant ex lateribus partes aequidistantes licet in magnitudine impares,
omnia huiuscemodi rationibus ut cernis ingeniose de ponderibus plane demonstrant."

in water.[11] The second reference is a description of the crown problem based on the account in Vitruvius' *De architectura*.[12]

I have now reached the end of my account of Fontana's knowledge of Archimedes. We have seen that in all probability he had read the *Liber de ponderibus Archimenidis* with its brief traces of the genuine *On Floating Bodies*. I have suggested that he was familiar with the modified version of the Pseudo-Archimedean text that appeared in Johannes de Muris' *Quadripartitum numerorum*. He also read Gerard of Cremona's translation of *De mensura circuli* from the Arabic as well as the famous translator's version of the *Verba filiorum* of the Banū Mūsā. Fontana was also familiar with the *Liber de curvis superficiebus Archimenidis* and Johannes de Muris' *De arte mensurandi*. And so it is apparent that Fontana had some knowledge of the principal medieval Archimedean texts, though it is doubtful that he had direct access to the full corpus of Moerbeke's translations. It seems that his limited knowledge of those translations as exhibited in the *Tractatus de trigono balistario* and in his *Liber de omnibus rebus naturalibus* came rather from a reading of Johannes de Muris' *De arte mensurandi*.

With the consideration of the works of Giovanni Fontana we come to the end of those investigations that reveal an exclusive preoccupation with the medieval Archimedean traditions. From this time forward the new translations of Jacobus Cremonensis completed about 1450 and other Renaissance treatments of Archimedes produced in conjunction with the medieval traditions a complex pattern of Archimedean knowledge. It is this pattern that is the object of Part III of this volume.

[11] MS Florence, Bibl. Med. Laur. Ashburn. 957, 76v: "Hec est potissima causa quare hos qui in profundo maris natant non conprimi certum est a multa aque ponderositate, initente (?) super eorum terga. Demonstratum enim, extat archimenidi questio, liquido in liquido posito: cum eque sunt ponderositatis corpora: nec si habbundant liquida superficiei: nec premunt subiacentia, ablatis enim prius prementibus desursum remaneret in eodem loco corpus."

[12] *Ibid.*, 93r–v: "De syracusano. Yero siracusanus cum aurum coronam diis manibus votivam constituisset locandam pretio: cuidam redemptori constituit esse faciendam. Is redemptor illam fecit et exinde auro detracto certum pondus argenti miscuit: adeo argute ut non quisque perpendere posset nisi funderetur, et sui ponderis id debiti respondi-disseṭ (*del*. t) visus est. Ad tempus vero cum examine fraus pateret redemptoris, sed de quota quantitate titubaret et a nemine veritatem scire posset. Indignatus se deceptum adiit ad archimenidem, rogitans ut de hoc meditaretur. Is diu cogitans casu venit in balneum et dum intraret consideravit quantum in aquam se mersisset quantum aque foras effluxisset. Itaque cum rationes omnes invicem conperasset et explicationes videret et patentes subito foris nudus et cum gaudio exultans demum tendens alta voce clamitans se nodosissimam questionem absolvisse. (93v) Tunc fertur duas massas equalis ponderis confecisse: argenteam unam et alteram ex auro, vas quoddam aqua replens, in quo demissa argentea, cuius quanta magnitudo in vase depressa est tantum defluxit aque. Itaque invenit ex eo quod ad certum pondus argenti certa aque mensura responderet. Simili modo fecit ex auro et subtili investigatione invenit furṭum respectu habito ad parvitatem auri masse et maioritatem argenti, seu corpulentie ipsius computato scrupulatim aque fluxu. Hiis premissis ad maiorem intelligentiam talis datur regula." For the text of Vitruvius, see below, Part III, Chap. 6, Sect. II, ns. 1–2.

The *Tractatus Johannis Fontane de trigono balistario*
Book II, Chapter 24

Tractatus Johannis Fontane de trigono balistario
Lib. II
/ Capitulum 24

1. QUOD DUORUM MOBILIUM IN DISTANTIA MEDIA VEL
MINORE MOTORUM MOTU RECTO VEL CIRCULARI CONTINUO
ET REGULARI VELOTIUS AUT TARDIUS MOVEATUR CON-
5   CLUDERE SI VESTIGIA SUORUM PERCIPIANTUR MOTUUM.
    Sint duo mobilia *a* et *b* mota ut proponitur que moveri videantur. Et
sive moveantur per circulos vel arcus circulorum sive per rectas lineas,
notabo duas lineas curvas vel rectas ab illis mobilibus descriptas in eodem
tempore vel in temporibus equalibus, sive ille linee sint descripte a prin-
10   cipio usque ad finem motus sive in partibus illorum motuum, quia non
est cura in proposito dummodo quelibet sint notabilis quantitatis et in
determinato et noto tempore descripta.
    Tempus vero illud haberi potest per aliquod horologium artifitiale vel
per horas aut dies naturales, sicut in precedente.
15   Quod si moveantur per arcus circulorum, cognoscam per 8^{am} capituli
31 partis precedentis huius tractatus quantitatem propriam cuiuslibet
illorum arcuum.
    Sed si ipsa mobilia per rectas lineas moveantur, inveniam quantitatem
cuiuslibet illarum linearum per aliquam capitulorum de mensuris longi-
20   tudinis vel latitudinis vel altitudinis vel profunditatis secundum quod
linea illa visui obicitur, que capitula in precedente parte habita sunt.
    Et tunc subito ap[p]arebit si ipsa mobilia equevelociter moventur vel
mota sint aut non presup[p]ositis regulis de velocitate motus, quoniam illa
mobilia dicuntur equevelociter moveri que in temporibus equalibus vel
25   eodem [tempore] describunt equales lineas, et non equevelociter que
inequales describunt in eodem tempore vel temporibus equalibus, et illud
altero velotius movetur quod in minori tempore describit lineam equalem
aut in equali vel eodem tempore maiorem, et illud tardius consequenter

Prop. 1
    2–3 in . . . minore *mg.*
    11 quelibet *mg.*
    14 sicut . . . precedente *mg.*
    15 *ante* arcus *del. Fon.* circulos vel
    16 *post* 31 *del. Fon.* huius vel per aliquam capituli / *post* tractatus *del. Fon.* vel
        per aliquam capituli xv huius partis
    17 *post* arcuum *del. Fon.* et iterum quantitatem continuam per capitulum

movetur quod in equali vel in eodem tempore describit minorem
30 lineam vel in maiore equalem. Unde Autolicus in principio libri sui de
spera mota inquit "punctus equali motu dicitur moveri cum quantitates
equales et similes in equalibus pertransit temporibus" et inequales in
inequalibus.

7r (218r)   Siquidem / note sint quantitates proprie ipsorum arcuum vel linearum in
35 eodem vel equalibus temporibus descriptorum ab illis mobilibus, ex dictis
regulis facile concluditur si equevelociter moventur aut quod illorum
velotius moveatur.

2. IN QUA PROPORTIONE UNUM DUORUM MOBILIUM QUE
IN DISTANTIA MEDIA VEL MINORE SIMILIBUS ET CONTINUIS
MOTIBUS REGULARIBUS RECTIS VEL CIRCULARIBUS MOVERI
VIDEANTUR NON EQUALITER MOTORUM VELOTIUS VEL
5 TARDIUS ALTERO MOVEATUR IUDICARE.

Considerabo, ut in commento precedentis, quantitates proprias
linearum descriptarum ab ipsis duobus mobilibus in temporibus equalibus
per precedentem, sive sint arcus sive recte linee. Et nota erit per 7
suppositionem capituli 7 precedentis partis proportio inter dictas lineas.
10   Et in qua proportione linea maior se habet ad minorem in eadem
proportione mobile qui illam maiorem describit velotius movetur illo qui
minorem describit.

Secundo ad idem cognoscam per precedentem quantitates duorum temporum inequalium in quibus illa mobilia describunt equales arcus vel
15 lineas rectas. Et nota erit per al[1]egantam (!) proportio maioris temporis
ad tempus minus, et in ea proportione mobile qui in minori tempore
describit lineam rectam vel arcum equalem movetur altero velotius.

3. QUANTITATEM TEMPORIS NOTARE IN QUO ALIQUOD
VISIBILE VIDETUR MOVERI A CERTO LOCO IN CERTUM
LOCUM MOTU RECTO VEL CIRCULARI VEL ALIO.

Si fuerit tale mobile sol vel stella quod ad motum primi mobilis moveatur,
5 tempus ipsius motus ab aliquo termino in alium notum erit per 4 vel xi vel
aliam capituli 18 huius postquam per aliquam capituli 15 huius et proprie
per 4 vel 5 eius[dem] notus fuerit arcus circuli paral[1]eli in eo tempore
descripti.

Si vero sit aliud mobile vel in celo vel infra celum quod moveri videatur
10 ab aliquo loco in alium locum certum, tunc cum fuerit in primo termino
quia in termino a quo notabo horam presentem per aliquam capituli 18
et similiter cum fuerit in termino ad quem cognoscam horas preteritas
post illam horam quoniam ipse sunt tempus motus illius.

Sed quia fortas[s]e in perquirendo presentem horam per modum dictum

Prop. 2
    8 per precedentem *mg.*
    13 per precedentem *mg.*
    17 *post* lineam *del. Fon.* vel

15 si fuisset ignota in principio motus illius mobilis aliquod tempus ulterius
habitur etiam sensibile in quo ipsum mobile aliquod spatium describit.
Cum operatio per instrumentum non sit in instanti, ad maiorem cautellam
et precisionem bonum est tunc ac[c]ipere altitudinem solis (si sit de die)
vel altitudinem alicuius stelle fixe note (si sit nox), per primam capituli
20 14 huius, cum fuerit mobile in principio motus et similiter cum fuerit in
fine.

Et postea com[m]ode sciri poterit illa vel alia quantitas gradualis illius
arcus paral[l]eli descripti ab ipso sole vel stella inter duas altitudines per
4^{am} vel 5 capituli 18 huius et illum arcum per 4^{am} capituli 19 tandem
25 convertere in horas naturales, quoniam illud erit tempus illius motus.

Item ad idem et facile convenit horologium bene equatum artifitiale.
Quando in eo duo puncta notantur, unum in principio motus illius
mobilis a determinato loco et aliud cum ipsum mobile pervenerit ad
alium locum, quoniam ipsum horologium declarabit tempus in quo illud
30 mobile motum fuerit ab ipso termino a quo ad ipsum terminum ad quem.

Et ut scriberem in commento 3 capituli xii huius, conveniens erit habere
duo vasa et in superiore aquam simplicem imponere, que cum mobile
a determinato loco incipere moveri videatur per foramen quod est in fundo
vasis superioris incipiat exstilare et exeat donec mobile pervenerit ad
35 terminum ad quem limitatum, et tunc vas inferius quod efusam aquam
suscepit subito est inde removendum ne plus aque recipiat.

Hec enim aqua in inferiore vase recepta erit mensura pro noscendo
tempore mobilis in quo inter duos predictos terminos motum fecit.

Quare cum placuerit post residuum aque quod in primo vase erat fuerit
217v (218v) efusum in terra vel abiectum, / aqua secundi vasis erit in eo ponenda. Cum
41 fuerit certum principium alicuius hore diei solaris, aqua (?) egredi
permittatur per foramen fundi in vas secundum. Et cum finiverit exitus
eius illico notanda est hora presens, et tempus istud in quo tota hec
aqua egreditur est tempus equale illi in quo mobile motum fuit a prefacto
45 termino in dictum terminum, ut intelligenti liquere potest.

4. COMPRENDERE SI IDEM MOBILE IN DISTANTIA MEDIA VEL MINORE VISUM PER RECTAM LINEAM VEL ARCUM MOVEATUR VELOCITATE EQUALI ET UNIFORMI.

Cognoscam per primam huius tempora in quibus describit equales
5 lineas ad idem punctum medium coniunctas quia unam immediate post
aliam et similiter unam distantem ab alia et similiter unam cum altera
communicantem. Et si tempora ipsa sint equalia, in illis temporibus
equevelociter ac uniformiter movetur. Sed si predicta tempora non sint
equalia, non movetur equevelociter.

Prop. 3
     32 *post* simplicem *del. Fon.* mundi (?)

Prop. 4
     3 et uniformi *mg.*
     8 movetur *mg.*

10   Secundo cognoscam duas lineas distinctas quas ipsum mobile in temporibus equalibus pertransit, que si sint equales in eisdem temporibus equevelociter movetur, et si inequales non equevelociter.

5. NON QUECUNQUE EQUALITER CIRCUUNT EQUALITER MOVENTUR.

    Alias diximus in alio libro quod ad hoc quod aliqua dicantur equaliter circuire requiritur quod equales angulos super centrum suorum
5   motuum describant in temporibus equalibus aut quod pertranseant similes arcus circuli vel circulorum quia arcus gradualiter equales, et in commento 2 huius diximus quod ad hoc quod aliqua dicantur equaliter moveri motu circulari requiritur quod describant in temporibus equalibus arcus equales in quantitate propria.

10   Et ideo eorum que circulariter moventur quedam equaliter circuunt et equaliter moventur, ut sunt gradus vel stelle eiusdem circuli equinotialis vel paral[l]eli ad motum primi mobilis.

    Aliqua sunt que neque equaliter circuunt nec equaliter moventur motu circulari, ut sunt saturnus et luna super polos zodiaci propriis motibus
15   revoluti.

    Alia sunt que equaliter circuunt sed non equaliter moventur, ut sunt due stelle quarum una est in equinotiali et altera prope polum.

6. PERCEPTIS ARCUBUS QUOS DUO MOBILIA DESCRIBUNT, FACILE EST NOSCERE SI IPSA MOBILIA EQUEVELOCITER CIRCUUNT VEL NON, ET QUOD EORUM VELOTIUS AUT TARDIUS CIRCUAT.

5   Sint ergo *a* et *b* duo visibilia visa circulariter moveri et cognoscam graduales quantitates arcuum descriptorum ab illis in temporibus equalibus per 4^am capituli 31 partis precedentis vel per aliquam capituli 15 huius.

    Et si fuerint arcus in illis temporibus equales gradualiter descripti, tunc *a* et *b* equaliter circuunt per precedentem, tempora vero equalia
10   habere possum per primam huius. Sed si invenio quod in temporibus equalibus describant arcus inequales gradualiter aut arcus gradualiter equales in temporibus inequalibus, ipsa mobilia non equevelociter circuunt.

    Et illud mobile quod in tempore equali describit arcum plurium
15   graduum aut in tempore minore equalem arcum gradualiter velotius circuit quam alterum.

7. CUM PERCIPITUR VESTIGIUM MOTUS MOBILIS CIRCULARITER MOTI MANIFESTE APPARENS NOSCERE SI IN ILLO TEMPORE EQUALI VELOCITATE CIRCUAT AN NON.

    Hec conclusio ex precedenti posset liquere quoniam si invenio quod
5   in temporibus equalibus ipsum mobile semper equales arcus gradualiter

---

Prop. 6
    15 *post* graduum *del. Fon.* velotius circuit quam alterum cum etiam

describat, ipsum equevelociter circuit per 5 huius. Si vero aliter sit
ut in temporibus equalibus describat arcus inequales vel arcus equales in
temporibus inequalibus, certum erit ex dictis in eadem quod non equaliter
circuit.

8. RECTE IUDICARE IN QUA PROPORTIONE UNUM DUORUM MOBILIUM QUE NON EQUALI VELOCITATE CIRCUIRE VIDENTUR ALTERO VELOTIUS CIRCUAT AUT TARDIUS.

218r (219r)   /Considerabo quantitates angulorum ab illis duobus mobilibus de-
5   scriptorum in temporibus equalibus super centra circulorum suorum
motuum, que note erunt ex notitia graduali suorum arcuum habita
ex 4ª capituli xxxi precedentis partis vel aliqua capituli 15 huius.

Et nota erit per 7 suppositionem 7 capituli precedentis partis proportio
anguli vel arcus maioris ad minorem et in ea proportione mobile illum
10   arcum describens velotius circuit quam mobile describens angulum vel
arcum minorem predictum in eodem tempore vel equali.

Vel aliter, cognoscam quantitatem temporum per primam huius in
quibus ipsa mobilia describunt equales arcus gradualiter sive equales
angulos super centra suorum motuum, et in qua proportione se habet
15   tempus maius ad minus in eadem proportione mobile quod describit
arcum suum in tempore minore velotius circuit quam aliud.

9. CUM ALIQUOD MOBILE CIRCULARITER MOVERI VIDEATUR IN EQUALI VELOCITATE, PERQUIRERE IN QUA HORA VELOTIUS VEL TARDIUS VOLVATUR.

Ista conclusio sequitur ex precedenti quia si consideravero duo tempora
5   equalia sui motus, in eo tempore velotius circuit in quo maiorem
arcum gradualiter vel angulum describit in centro et ille tardius in quo
minorem.

Et similiter si consideravero duo tempora in quibus equales describit
arcus gradualiter, in illo tempore velotius circuit quod fuerit altero tempore
10   minus et in illo tempore tardius quod fuerit altero tempore maius.

Et in qua proportione se habet arcus maior gradualiter ad arcum
minorem vel tempus maius ad tempus minus in eadem proportione illud
volvitur velotius, quod perquirendum fuerat.

10. SI QUOD MOBILE AB EXTREMO LINEE FIXO PER SUPERFITIEM PLANAM EQUEVELOCITER CIRCUMDUCTE PARIFERIAM (!) DESCRIBENTIS INTERIM PER IPSAM RECTAM

Prop. 8
    10 circuit *supra scr. Fon. et del.* moveat (?)
    16 circuit *mg., et del. Fon.* movetur

Prop. 9
    3 volvatur: circuat *mg.*
    9 *post* circuit *del. Fon.* in
    10 *post* tardius *del. Fon.* in
    13 volvitur *mg., in textu del. Fon.* movetur

LINEAM EQUALI VELOCITATE MOVEATUR, CONTINUO PER
5 DISTANTIAS EQUALITER SE EXCEDENTES A CENTRO DISTAT
IN TEMPORIBUS EQUALIBUS.

Imaginemur [Fig. II.4.2] rectam lineam *ab* super planum que super
extremum eius *a* circumferatur equaliter circuendo donec circulum describat. Et iterum ymaginemur unum mobile quod incipiciat (!) moveri a
10 centro *a* semper per ipsam rectam lineam *ab* equali velocitate, ita quod
simul incipiat linea *ab* circumduci et mobile illud moveri a loco *a*; et
describet mobile ad motum suum per rectam et ad motum raptus per
lineam circumductam lineam girantem vel involutam vel elicem a pluribus
dictam.

15 Quibus habitis dico quod in temporibus equalibus mobile circumductum
inequaliter distat a centro *a*, ut patet cum continuo ab eo elongetur, et
quod ille distantie equaliter se excedunt. Et licet non deberem hoc
demonstrare sed aquiescere, volo tamen in proposito.

Quare ponamus quod mobile sit in aliquo puncto intrinseco linee *ab*
20 qui dicam *c*. Deinde continuetur motus donec pervenerit ad alium punctum eius qui dicatur *d* et iterum continuetur motus donec veniat
ad punctum *e* linee *ab* et ulterius perveniat ad punctum *f* linee *ab*. Et
ymaginemur lineas distantiarum a centro que sunt linee recte *ac* et *ad* et
ae et *af* et *ag* et huiusmodi. Dico quod per quantum excessum linea *ag*
25 excedit lineam *af* per tantum linea *af* excedit lineam *ae* et linea *ae*
excedit lineam *ad* et linea *ad* excedit lineam *ac* dummodo tempora in
quibus describuntur ab ipso mobili partes *cd* et *de* et *ef* et *fg* et similes
arcus *aeg* elicis sint equalia, et ita de reliquis notare et intelligere debes.

/11. DUARUM RECTARUM LINEARUM DATARUM IN PLANO A
CENTRO AD ARCUM ELICIS IN PRIMA REVOLUTIONE DE-
SCRIPTE AB ALIQUO MOBILI EQUA VELOCITATE MOTO PER
RECTAM LINEAM EQUEVELOCITER CIRCUENTE UTI PONE-
5 BATUR IN PRECEDENTE UNIUS AD ALTERAM PROPORTIONEM
EXTRAHERE.

Sit dispositio figure ut in commento precedentis in plano aliquo signata
accomodato [Fig. II.4.3]. Volo scire que proportio est linee *fa* ad lineam
da. Et primo sit linea *ab* principium revolutionis elicis quia semidiameter
10 circuli contingentis elicem in puncto *a* nullo modo secans elicem. Et
extendam lineam *ac* donec at[t]ingat circumferentiam circuli qui a linea *ab*
circumducta describi intelligitur. Sitque punctus in circumferentia
vocatus *k*.

Et iterum extendam lineam *ad* usque ad circumferentiam ipsius
15 circuli que sit *adl*. Et iterum extendam lineam *af* usque ad eandem

Prop. 10
    24 *post* ag *del. Fon.* et ah

Prop. 11
    1 11 *correxi ex* xi

circumferentiam que sit *afm*; quas extensiones faciam per 5 (*!* 9) capituli x precedentis partis. Postea cognoscam gradualem quantitatem arcus *bkl* et similiter gradualem quantitatem arcus *bklm* per 9 capituli xi predicte partis. Et nota erit proportio arcus *bklm* ad arcum *bkl* per 7 suppositionem

20 capituli 7 eiusdem partis.

Et dico quod in eadem proportione se habet linea *af* ducta a centro ad arcum elicis ad lineam *ad* ductam similiter ab eodem centro ad ipsum arcum in qua proportione se habet arcus *bklm* ad arcum *bkl*, quia in quo tempore punctus *b* extremum linee *ab* circumducte super punctum *a* fixum

25 describit arcum *bkl* circuli in eodem tempore mobile per lineam *ab* movetur a loco *a* ad locum *d*.

Et iterum in quo tempore *b* describit arcum *bklm* in eodem tempore mobile movetur a puncto *a* ad punctum *f* ex posito in proposito.

Et similiter sciri potest proportio linee *af* ad lineam *ac* et ad quamlibet

30 aliam incidente[m] in arcum elicis a centro *a* productam etc.

12. DUARUM RECTARUM LINEARUM DATARUM A CENTRO AD ARCUM ELICIS IN SECUNDA VEL TERTIA VEL ALIA ULTERIORE REVOLUTIONE DESCRIPTE AB ALIQUO MOBILI EQUEVELOCITER MOTO PER RECTAM LINEAM EQUALITER

5 CIRCUENTEM UT IN PRECEDENTIBUS DUABUS UNIUS AD ALTERAM PROPORTIONEM INDAGARI.

Replicabo figuram in plano descriptam in commentis duarum precedentium ubi ponitur quod linea *ab* est principium revolutionis elicis super centrum *a* revoluta describens circumferentiam *bklm* [Fig. II.4.4]. Sed

10 prima revolutio elicis sit *acdfg* et secunda revolutio sit *gpqrs* et tertia sit *stuxy* et relique consequenter maiores. Et sit una linea *agsyb* et similiter alia linea *acptk* et iterum linea una *adqul* et rursus alia linea *afrxm*.

Volo scire proportionem linee recte *ar* ducte ad revolutionem secundam elicis ad lineam *aq* similiter ad ipsam secundam revolutionem incidentem.

15 Et primo cognoscam gradualem quantitatem arcus *bklm* per 9 capituli xi precedentis partis, quam coniungam toti quantitati circumferentie circuli quia gradibus 360, et vocabo hoc aggregatum primum.

Similiter cognoscam quantitatem arcus *bkl*, cui ad[d]am gradus totius periferie quia gradus 360, et vocabo [hoc] aggregatum secundum. Et nota

20 erit per 7 suppositionem capituli 7 partis predicte proportio aggregati primi ad aggregatum secundum et tantam dico esse proportionem linee *ar* ad lineam *aq*, nam in equali tempore mobile motum per lineam *ab* describit lineam *ar* in quo tempore *b* describit totam circumferentiam circuli et arcum eiusdem circuli *bklm*; et iterum in eodem tempore

25 mobile [motum] per rectam lineam describit lineam *aq* in quo punctus *b* describit totam circumferentiam circuli et arcum *bkl*, ex posito.

Et per similem modum haberi potest proportio linee *ar* ad lineam *ap*, est enim tanta quanta est proportio graduum totius circumferentie et arcus *bklm* ad gradus totius circumferentie et arcus *bk*.

28 *post* proposito *del. Fon.* quare cum eadem sit proportio

30   Sed si volam scire proportionem linee *ax* ad lineam *au* tertie revolutionis, operabor sicut dictum est, hoc variato quod ubi in modo ad[d]ebam immediate / precedente ad[d]ebam arcui *bklm* et similiter arcui *bkl* gradus 360, qui sunt gradus unius revolutionis complete, in isto casu ad[d]am bis illos gradus quia gradus duarum revolutionum completarum. Et postea

35   qualis erit proportio illorum aggregatorum ex gradibus talis erit proportio linearum *ax* et *au*.

Et ita si habeo lineas incidentes super arcum tertie elicis ut *am* (! *au*) et *al* (! *at*) vel super arcum quarte vel quinte vel ulterioris elicis totiens addam gradus 360 quot sunt revolutiones elicis dempta una revolutione et

40   procedam deinde sicut exemplificatum est.

13. CUM SEMIDYAMETER CIRCULI SECUERIT PLURES REVOLUTIONES ELICIS DESCRIPTE SUPER CENTRUM EIUSDEM CIRCULI UT IN PRECEDENTI DICTUM EST, PROPORTIONEM PARTIUM DYAMETRI VEL DYAMETRORUM SEPARATARUM

5   PER ELICES PATEFACERE.

Stante figura [Fig. II.4.4] precedentis commenti intelligamus lineam *afrxm* semidyametrum circuli a linea *ab* revoluti et consideremus quod ipsa semidyameter secat plures revolutiones elicis super centrum *a* revolute, quoniam secat revolutionem primam in puncto *f* et secundam in

10   puncto *r* et tertiam in puncto *x*.

Similiter semidyameter *adqul* plures revolutiones elicis secat, primam in puncto *d* et secundam in puncto *q* et tertiam in puncto *u*, pariformiter semidiameter *acptk* et relique.

Volo primo scire proportionem partis *ar* linee *am* semidyametri ad

15   partem *fa* eiusdem.

Cognoscam ergo gradualem quantitatem arcus periferie *bklm* per 9 capituli xi precedentis partis, qui arcus finitur ad ipsam semidyametrum *am*. Et similiter cognoscam gradualem quantitatem *bklm* et totius periferie simul iunctarum. Et qualis est proportio graduum huius aggregati ad gradus

20   similiter notos arcus *bkl*[*m*] talis est proportio linee *ar* ad lineam *af*, nam in quo tempore describitur a linea *ab* tota periferia circuli semel et ulterius arcus *bklm* in eodem tempore describit mobile a centro *a* per rectam lineam motum lineam *ar*; et in quo tempore linea *ab* describit arcum *bkl*[*m*] in eodem tempore ipsum mobile describit lineam *af*.

25   Sed per 7 suppositionem capituli 7 partis precedentis nota est proportio graduum totius periferie et arcus *bklm* simul iunctorum ad gradus arcus *bkl*[*m*]. Ergo et nota est proportio linee *ar* ad lineam *fa*.

Et per similem modum cognosci potest proportio linee *ax* ad lineam *af* nisi quod arcui *bklm* addendi sunt gradus duarum revolutionum

30   quoniam linea *ax* incidit super tertiam revolutionem elicis; et si incideret

Prop. 12
        31 *post* hoc *del. Fon.* adito
Prop. 13
        19 *post* proportio *del. Fon.* h
        29 *post* revolutionum *del. Fon.* ut dicebam in precedentis commento

super quartam revolutionem elicis, adderem ter gradus totius periferie circuli, nam semper tot periferie complecte (!) sunt addende arcui in quem linea ipsa terminatur quot sunt revolutiones elicis in quas incidit dempta una, uti dicebatur in commento precedentis conclusionis.

35   Et per istum modum vel similem sciri potest qualis est proportio linee *aq* ad lineam *ad* vel linee *au* ad lineam *aq* et huiusmodi.

Et si scire volam proportionem linee *rx* ad lineam *fr*, quia linea *rx* non describitur nisi in tempore quo revolvitur tota periferia semel, et similiter linea *fr* pertransitur in tempore quo tota periferia semel de-
40   scribitur, tunc linea *rx* erit equalis linee *fr* et similiter linea *fr* equalis linee *fa*. Et pariformiter concludere possumus quod linee *ad* et *dq* et *qu* sunt equales.

Et ita consequenter si volam scire proportionem partium eiusdem dyametri vel diversarum dyametrorum eiusdem circuli simul cum elice uni-
45   formiter revoluti, ut predictum est, quarum quelibet pars terminetur ad concavum unius revolutionis et ad convexum alterius revolutionis eiusdem elicis, semper considerabo tempora, data vel cognita per primam huius, in quibus ille / recte linee partiales a mobili per dyametrum equevelociter lato designantur, et qualis est proportio temporum talis est proportio
50   linearum, ex fundamento prescripto in hoc capitulo.

Quia tamen non multum videntur ad propositum instrumenti nostri, non amplius de similibus motibus dicendum; hoc in loco decrevi presenti libro finem imponere.

219v(220v)

The Treatise of Giovanni Fontana on the Triangle Shaped like a Crossbow
BK II
Chapter 24

1. IN THE CASE OF TWO MOBILES AT A MODERATE DIS-TANCE OR CLOSE AT HAND MOVING WITH A CONTINUOUS AND REGULAR RECTILINEAR OR CIRCULAR [I.E. CURVI-LINEAR] MOTION, TO CONCLUDE WHICH OF THEM IS MOVED THE MORE QUICKLY OR THE MORE SLOWLY IF THE PATHS OF THEIR MOTIONS ARE PERCEIVED.

Let there be two mobiles *a* and *b*, moved as proposed, and whose motions may be seen. And whether they are moved through circles or arcs of circles, or through straight lines, I shall note the two curved or straight lines described by these mobiles in the same time or in equal times (whether these lines are described from the beginning up to the end of the motion or in parts of those motions, because it is of no concern

52 *post* loco *del. Fon.* censeo

which in our proposition so long as they [the lines] are of determinable magnitude and in a determined and known time).[1]

Now that time can be had by some man-made horologue or by means of natural hours or days, as in the preceding.

If they are moved through arcs of circles, I shall know by the eighth [proposition] of Chapter 31 of the preceding part of this tract the proper quantity [i.e. length] of each of these arcs.[2]

But if these mobiles are moved through straight lines, I shall find the quantity of each of those lines by some [proposition] in the chapters on the measures of length, width, altitude, or depth, according as that line is presented to the sight. These chapters are had in the preceding part [of this tract].[3]

And then it will be immediately apparent whether or not these mobiles are moved equally fast by means of the presupposed rules concerning the velocity of motion, since those mobiles are defined as "equally swiftly moved" which in equal times or in the same [time] describe equal lines, and as "not equally swiftly moved" which describe unequal lines in the same time or in equal times, and that one is moved more swiftly than the other which describes an equal line in less time or a greater line in an equal or the same time, and consequently that one is moved more slowly which describes a lesser line in an equal or the same time or an equal line in greater time.[4] Whence Autolycus in the beginning of his book *On the Moved Sphere* says "a point is said to be moved with equal [i.e., uniform] motion when it traverses equal and similar magnitudes in equal times" and unequal magnitudes in unequal times.[5]

If indeed the proper quantities of these arcs or lines described by those mobiles in the same or in equal times are known it is easily concluded from the said rules whether they are moved equally fast or which of them is moved the more swiftly.

2. IN THE CASE OF TWO MOBILES (SEEN TO BE MOVED AT A MODERATE DISTANCE OR CLOSE AT HAND WITH SIMILAR AND CONTINUOUS BUT UNEQUAL REGULAR MOTIONS—EITHER RECTILINEAR OR CIRCULAR), TO JUDGE THE RATIO BY WHICH ONE IS MOVED MORE SWIFTLY OR MORE SLOWLY THAN THE OTHER.

As in the comment on the preceding [proposition] and following its conclusion, I shall consider the proper quantities of the lines described by these two mobiles in equal times—whether these lines be arcs or

Prop. 1

   [1] See the Commentary, Prop. 1, lines 9–12.

   [2] See MS Canon. Misc. 47, 122v (130v).

   [3] *Ibid.*, *passim*, but see particularly Part I, Chapters 24–30, 83r(92r)–121r(129r).

   [4] See Com., Prop. 1, lines 22–30.

   [5] For the kinematics of Autolycus, see M. Clagett, *The Science of Mechanics in the Middle Ages* (Madison, Wisc., 1959; 2nd. print., 1961), pp. 164–66.

straight lines. And the ratio between the said lines will be known by the seventh supposition of Chapter 7 of the preceding part.[1]

And the ratio the greater line has to the lesser is the same ratio as that by which the mobile describing the greater line moves more swiftly than the mobile describing the lesser line.

Secondly, for the same determination I shall know by the preceding [proposition] the quantities of the two unequal times in which those mobiles describe the equal arcs or straight lines. And the ratio of the greater time to the lesser will be known by what has been asserted, and it is by this ratio that the mobile describing the equal straight line or arc in less time is moved more swiftly than the other.

3. TO NOTE THE QUANTITY OF TIME IN WHICH SOME VISIBLE [BODY] IS SEEN TO BE MOVED FROM ONE CERTAIN PLACE TO ANOTHER CERTAIN PLACE WITH A RECTILINEAR OR CIRCULAR OR SOME OTHER MOTION.

If the sun or a star is such a mobile which is moved at the motion of the *primum mobile*, the time of its motion from one terminus to another will be known by the fourth, eleventh, or another [proposition] of Chapter 18 of this [part],[1] since by one [proposition] of Chapter 15 of this part, and properly by the fourth or the fifth of the same, will be known the arc of the parallel circle described in this time.[2]

Now if there is some mobile, either in the heavens or below the heavens, which may be seen to be moved from one place to another certain place, then when it is in the first terminus (for it will be in the *terminus a quo*) I shall note the present hour by one [proposition] of Chapter 18,[3] and similarly when it is in the *terminus ad quem* I shall recognize the hours elapsed since the [initial] hour, because these hours constitute the time of that motion.

But if the hour at the beginning of that motion was unknown as we sought the present hour by the said method, perhaps some later time in which this mobile describes some space will be observable. Since an operation with an instrument is not instantaneous, for greater caution and precision it is good then to take the altitude of the sun (if it is day time) or the altitude of a known fixed star (if it is night time), [proceeding] by the first [proposition] of Chapter 14 of this [part],[4] both at the beginning of the motion and likewise at its end.

Then afterwards one can conveniently determine that or some other quantity in degrees of the arc of the parallel described by the sun or

Prop. 2
[1] See MS Canon. Misc. 47, 18v.

Prop. 3
[1] For Part II, Chap. 18, see MS Canon. Misc. 47, 193v(194v)–200v(201v).
[2] For Part II, Chap. 15, see *ibid.*, 183r(184r)–185r(186r).
[3] See note 1.
[4] MS Canon. Misc. 47, 176v(177v).

star between the two altitudes. [This can be known] by the fourth or the fifth [proposition] of Chapter 18 of this [part][5] and the arc can in the end be converted into natural hours by [using] the fourth proposition of Chapter 19 of this [part] since that will be the time of the motion.[6]

Also, for the same [determination] a man-made horologe that has been properly graduated is useful. When two points are noted by it, one at the beginning of the motion of that mobile where it is at a determined place and the other when that mobile arrives at another place, since the horologe will reveal the time during which that mobile is moved from the *terminus a quo* to the *terminus ad quem*.

For this it will be useful, as I wrote in the comment on the third [proposition] of Chapter 12 of this [part], to have two vases and to fill the upper one with plain water.[7] When the mobile is seen to begin its motion from a determined place, let the water begin to flow through a hole which is in the bottom of the upper vase and let it continue to flow out until the mobile arrives at the *terminus ad quem*. At this point the lower vase, which has received the water that flowed out [from the upper], is to be removed immediately so that it does not receive any more water. For the water received in the lower vase will be the measure by which we know the time during which the mobile has produced its motion between the aforesaid two termini.

Therefore, when one pleases, after the rest of the water which was in the first vase has been poured out on to the ground or thrown away, the water of the second vase is to be placed in it. Then when the beginning of some hour of the solar day is surely determined, let the water be permitted to flow out through the hole in the bottom into the second vase. When it is finished flowing, at that moment the present hour is to be noted, and the time during which all of the water flowed out is equal to the time during which the mobile produced its motion from the one pre-determined terminus to the other, as is clear to someone with understanding.

4. TO COMPREHEND WHETHER A SINGLE MOBILE (SEEN AT A MODERATE DISTANCE OR CLOSE AT HAND) IS MOVED ALONG A STRAIGHT LINE OR AN ARC WITH AN EQUAL AND UNIFORM VELOCITY.

By the first [proposition] of this [chapter] I shall know the times in which it describes equal lines joined at the same intermediary point, for [it described] one immediately after another. In the same way [I shall learn the time in which it describes] one line that is distant from another [equal line] and similarly one line that shares a common part with another [equal line]. And if these times are equal, the mobile is moved equally and uniformly fast in those times. But if the aforesaid times are not equal, it is not moved equally fast.

[5] See note 1.
[6] MS Canon. Misc. 47, 202v(203v).
[7] See Com., Prop. 3, line 31.

Secondly, I shall know two distinct lines which the mobile traverses in equal times. If these lines are equal, it is moved equally fast in these same times. If they are not equal, it is not moved equally fast.

5. NOT ALL THINGS THAT REVOLVE EQUALLY [FAST] ARE ALSO MOVED EQUALLY [FAST].

In this regard, we have said elsewhere, in another book, that for things to be defined as "equally revolving," it is required that they describe at the center of their motions equal angles in equal times, or that they traverse similar arcs of a circle or circles because such arcs are equal in degrees.[1] And in the comment to the second [proposition] of this [chapter] we have said in this matter that for things to be defined as "equally moved in circular [i.e. curvilinear] motion," it is required that they describe in equal times arcs that are equal in proper quantity [i.e., in length].

And therefore, of those things which are moved circularly, some revolve equally [fast] and as well are moved equally [fast]. Such are the degrees [i.e. points] or stars on the same equinoctial circle or parallel [that move] at the motion of the *primum mobile*.

There are some which neither revolve equally [fast] nor are moved equally [fast] in circular [i.e. curvilinear] motion. An example is Saturn and the Moon, which revolve on the poles of the zodiac with their proper [and distinct] motions.

[Finally] there are others which revolve equally [fast] but which do not move equally [fast in curvilinear motion]. An example is two [fixed] stars one of which is in the equinoctial circle and the other is near the pole.

6. WITH THE ARCS WHICH TWO MOBILES DESCRIBE PERCEIVED, IT IS EASY TO KNOW WHETHER THESE MOBILES REVOLVE EQUALLY FAST OR NOT, AND [IF NOT] WHICH OF THEM REVOLVES THE MORE SWIFTLY OR THE MORE SLOWLY.

Therefore, let *a* and *b* be two visible [mobiles] seen to be moved circularly and I shall know the quantities in degree of the arcs described by them in equal times by the fourth [proposition] of Chapter 31 of the preceding [part][1] or by some [proposition] of Chapter 15 of this [part].[2]

If the arcs described in those times are equal in degrees, then *a* and *b* revolve equally [fast] according to the preceding [proposition], and I can find their equal times by [using] the first [proposition] of this [chapter]. But if I find that they describe, in equal times, arcs that are unequal in degrees or that they describe arcs equal in degrees in unequal times, these mobiles do not revolve equally fast.

Prop. 5
  [1] See Com., Prop. 5, line 3.

Prop. 6
  [1] MS Canon. Misc. 47, 122r(130r).
  [2] See above, Prop. 3, note 2.

And the mobile revolves more swiftly than the other that describes an arc of more degrees in equal time or an arc of equal degrees in less time.

7. GIVEN THAT THE APPARENT PATH OF THE MOTION OF A MOBILE MOVED CIRCULARLY IS CLEARLY PERCEIVED, TO KNOW WHETHER OR NOT THE MOBILE REVOLVES IN THAT TIME WITH EQUAL [I.E. UNIFORM] VELOCITY.

This conclusion is clear from the preceding one, since, if I find that this mobile always describes arcs equal in degrees in equal times, it revolves equally [i.e. uniformly] fast, according to the fifth [proposition] of this [chapter]. But if in equal times it describes unequal arcs or equal arcs in unequal times, it will be certain from the statements in the same [proposition] that the mobile does not revolve equally [i.e. uniformly fast].

8. TO JUDGE CORRECTLY THE RATIO BY WHICH ONE OF TWO BODIES THAT ARE SEEN TO BE REVOLVING UNEQUALLY FAST IS REVOLVING MORE SWIFTLY OR MORE SLOWLY THAN THE OTHER.

I shall consider the quantities of the angles described by those two mobiles in equal times on the centers of the circles of their motions. These will be known from the knowledge of the degrees of their arcs that is had by [using] the fourth [proposition] of Chapter 31 of the preceding part or a proposition of Chapter 15 of this [part].[1]

And by the seventh supposition of Chapter 7 of the preceding part,[2] the ratio of the larger angle or arc to the smaller will be known. And it is by this ratio that the mobile describing that [larger] arc revolves more swiftly than the mobile describing the aforesaid smaller angle or arc in the same or equal time.

Or [proceeding] in another way, I shall know, by the first [proposition] of this [chapter], the quantities of the times in which these mobiles describe arcs equal in degrees or equal angles on the centers of their motions. And the ratio the longer time has to the shorter is the same ratio by which the mobile describing its arc in less time revolves more swiftly than the other [mobile].

9. GIVEN THAT SOME MOBILE IS [INITIALLY] SEEN TO RE-VOLVE WITH EQUAL [I.E. UNIFORM] VELOCITY, TO FIND OUT AT WHAT HOUR IT REVOLVES MORE SWIFTLY OR MORE SLOWLY.

This conclusion follows from the preceding one. For, if I consider two equal time periods of its motion, in the period in which it describes an arc greater in degrees or a greater angle at the center it revolves more swiftly; and it revolves more slowly in the period in which it describes a smaller [arc or angle].

Prop. 8
   [1] See above, Prop. 6, notes 1–2.
   [2] See above, Prop. 2, note 1.

And similarly if I consider two time periods in which it describes arcs equal in degrees, it revolves more swiftly in the period which is less than the other period and more slowly in the period which is longer than the other period.

And the ratio that the arc greater in degrees has to the lesser arc or the ratio that the longer time has to the shorter is the same as the ratio by which the mobile revolves more swiftly, which was to be sought.

10. IF A MOBILE IS MOVED WITH EQUAL VELOCITY [I.E. UNIFORMLY] ALONG A STRAIGHT LINE, STARTING FROM THE FIXED EXTREME OF THAT LINE, WHILE THE LINE ROTATES WITH EQUAL VELOCITY [I.E. UNIFORMLY] IN A PLANE SURFACE TO DESCRIBE A CIRCLE, THE MOBILE IS CONTINUALLY DISTANT FROM THE CENTER BY DISTANCES THAT EQUALLY EXCEED EACH OTHER IN EQUAL TIMES.[1]

Let us imagine a straight line ab which is equally [i.e. uniformly] rotated in a plane around its extreme a until it describes a circle [see Fig. II.4.2]. Again let us imagine a mobile which begins to be moved from the center a along straight line ab with equal [i.e. uniform] velocity, so that line ab begins to be rotated at the same time that the mobile begins to be moved from position a. And the mobile will, by its rectilinear motion and the motion of the rotating line, describe a gyrating or involuted line, called by many a spiral.

With these things assumed, I say that in equal times the revolving mobile is unequally distant from the center a, as is evident since it is continually farther away from it, but that these distances [from the center] exceed one another equally. And although I ought not demonstrate this but simply acquiesce in it, still I wish it to be a proposition.

Therefore, let us posit that the mobile is at some intrinsic point of line ab, which I shall say is c. Then let the motion continue until it arrives at another point of it, which we let be called d, and again let the motion be continued until it comes to point e of line ab and finally until it comes to point f of line ab. And let us imagine the lines of the distances from the center to be ac, ad, ae, af and ag, and [other lines] of this sort. I say that

$$\text{line } ag - \text{line } af = \text{line } af - \text{line } ae, \text{ and}$$

$$\text{line } ae - \text{line } ad = \text{line } ad - \text{line } ac,$$

while the times in which the mobile describes the segments cd, de, ef and fg and the corresponding arcs of spiral aeg are equal. And you ought to understand and note the rest [of the lines and times] in the same way.

11. TO FIND THE RATIO, ONE TO THE OTHER, OF TWO STRAIGHT LINES GIVEN IN A PLANE [AND EXTENDING] FROM THE CENTER TO THE ARC OF A SPIRAL DESCRIBED

Prop. 10
[1] See Volume 2, 13rW–X, and the discussion in Section II of this chapter.

IN THE FIRST REVOLUTION BY SOME MOBILE MOVED WITH
EQUAL [I.E. UNIFORM] VELOCITY ALONG A STRAIGHT LINE
WHICH IS ROTATING EQUALLY FAST [I.E. UNIFORMLY] (AS
WAS POSED IN THE PRECEDING [PROPOSITION]).

Let the disposition of the figure be designated in some plane, as in the
comment on the preceding [proposition]. I wish to know the ratio of line
fa to line *da* [see Fig. II.4.3]. First let line *ab* be the origin of the revolution
of a spiral [i.e. its initial line], for the radius of the circle touching the
spiral in point *a* cuts the spiral in no way. And I shall extend line *ac*
until it touches the circumference of the circle which is understood to be
described by line *ab* in rotation. And let the point on the circumference
be called *k*.

And again I shall extend line *ad* to the circumference of the circle,
making line *adl*. And once more I shall extend line *af* to the same circumference, producing line *afm*. I shall accomplish these prolongations
by the ninth [proposition] of Chapter 10 of the preceding part.[1] Afterwards I shall know the quantity in degrees of arc *bkl* and similarly the
quantity in degrees of arc *bklm*, by the ninth [proposition] of Chapter 11
of the aforesaid part.[2] And the ratio of arc *bklm* to arc *bkl* will be known
by the seventh supposition of Chapter 7 of the same part.[3]

And I say that the ratio of line *af* (drawn from the center to the arc of
the spiral) to line *ad* (similarly drawn from the same center to this arc)
is the same as the ratio of arc *bklm* to arc *bkl*, because in the same time
that point *b* (the end of line *ab* rotating about the fixed point *a*) describes arc *bkl* of the circle the mobile is moved along line *ab* from point
a to point *d*. And, further, in the same time that *b* describes arc *bklm*
the mobile is moved from point *a* to point *f*, from that which was posited.

And similarly we can know the ratio of line *af* to line *ac* and to any other
line falling on the arc of the spiral from center *a*, etc.

12. TO FIND THE RATIO, ONE TO THE OTHER, OF TWO GIVEN
STRAIGHT LINES [DRAWN] FROM THE CENTER TO THE ARC OF
A SPIRAL DESCRIBED IN THE SECOND, THIRD OR ANY OTHER
FURTHER REVOLUTION BY SOME MOBILE MOVED EQUALLY
FAST [I.E. UNIFORMLY] ALONG A STRAIGHT LINE ROTATING
EQUALLY [I.E. UNIFORMLY], AS IN THE PRECEDING TWO
[PROPOSITIONS].[1]

I shall reproduce the plane figure described in the comments on the two
preceding [propositions], where it is posited that line *ab* is the origin of

Prop. 11

[1] MS Canon. Misc. 47, 29r.

[2] *Ibid.*, 35v.

[3] See above, Prop. 2, note 1.

Prop. 12

[1] See Volume 2, 13vJ, and the discussion in Section II above. Notice that Fontana has
added to the statement of the problem spirals of the third and further revolutions, but
such additional spirals are embraced by the proof of Archimedes (see 13vN).

revolution of the spiral on center *a* and [*ab* is] rotated [with terminus *b*] describing circumference *bklm* [see Fig. II.4.4]. But let the first revolution of the spiral be *acdfg*, the second revolution be *gpqrs*, the third be *stuxy* and the remaining larger ones following [in the same way]. And let one line be *agsyb* and similarly another line *acptk*, and, further, a line *adqul*, and, once more, another line *afrxm*.

I wish to know the ratio of line *ar* (drawn to the second revolution of the spiral) to line *aq* (similarly proceeding to this second revolution).

In the first place, I shall know the quantity in degrees of arc *bklm*, by the ninth [proposition] of Chapter 11 of the preceding part.[2] This I add to the total quantity of the circumference of the circle, namely to 360°, and I shall call this the first sum.

Similarly, I shall know the quantity of arc *bkl*, to which I add the degrees of the whole circumference, namely 360°; and I shall call this the second sum. The ratio of the first sum to the second sum will be known by the seventh supposition of Chapter 7 of the aforesaid part.[3] I say that this ratio is the same as that of line *ar* to line *aq*, for in the same time that the mobile moving along line *ab* describes line *ar*, point *b* describes the whole circumference plus arc *bklm* of the same circle. Again, in the same time that the mobile [moving] along the straight line describes line *aq*, point *b* describes the whole circumference of the circle plus arc *bkl*, from that which was proposed.

And by a similar method we can find the ratio of line *ar* to line *ap*, for it is the same as the ratio of the degrees of the whole circumference plus arc *bklm* to the degrees of the whole circumference plus arc *bk*.

But if I wish to know the ratio of line *ax* to line *au* of the third revolution, I shall proceed as has been said, except that where in the immediately preceding case I was adding 360° (i.e. the degrees of one complete revolution) to arc *bklm* and similarly to arc *bkl*, in this case I shall add [to these arcs] twice these degrees [i.e., 720°], i.e. the degrees of two complete revolutions. And then whatever will be the ratio of those sums of degrees, that also will be the ratio of lines *ax* and *au*.

And so if I have lines falling on the arc of the third spiral like *am* (*! au?*) and *al* (*! at?*) or on the arc of the fourth spiral or that of the fifth or [some other] further spiral, I add 360° as many times as there are revolutions but with one revolution subtracted, and then I shall proceed as has been shown in the examples.[4]

13. GIVEN THAT THE RADIUS OF A CIRCLE CUTS SEVERAL REVOLUTIONS OF A SPIRAL DESCRIBED ON THE CENTER OF THE SAME CIRCLE AS STATED IN THE PRECEDING [PROPOSITION], TO FIND THE RATIO OF THE SEGMENTS OF THE DIAM-

---

[2] See Prop. 11, note 2.

[3] See Prop. 2, note 1.

[4] See Volume 2, 13vN.

ETER OR DIAMETERS THAT HAVE BEEN INTERCEPTED BY THE SPIRALS.

Using the figure given in the comment on the preceding [Proposition, i.e. Fig. II.4.4], let us understand line *afrxm* to be the radius of the circle described by line *ab* in rotation. And we should consider that this radius cuts several revolutions of the spiral generated on center *a*, since it cuts the first revolution in point *f*, the second in point *r*, and the third in point *x*.

Similarly radius *adqul* cuts several revolutions of the spiral, the first in point *d*, the second in point *q*, and the third in point *u*. The same is true for radius *acptk* and the remaining [radii].

I wish to know first the ratio of line segment *ar* of radius *am* to segment *fa* of the same [radius].

Therefore, I shall [first] know the quantity in degrees of arc *bklm* of the circumference, by the ninth [proposition] of Chapter 11 of the preceding part.[1] This arc is terminated at the radius *am*. And similarly I shall know the quantity in degrees of *bklm* plus the whole circumference. And whatever is the ratio of this sum in degrees to the similarly known degrees of arc *bklm*, this is also the ratio of line *ar* to line *af*, for in the same time that line *ab* describes the whole circumference once plus arc *bklm*, the mobile moving from center *a* along the straight line describes line *ar*. And in the same time that line *ab* describes arc *bklm*, the mobile describes line *af*.

But by the seventh supposition of Chapter 7 of the preceding part[2] we know the ratio of the sum of the circumference plus arc *bklm* to the degrees of arc *bklm*. Therefore, the ratio of line *ar* to line *fa* is known.

By a similar method we can learn the ratio of line *ax* to line *af*, except that the [720] degrees of two revolutions are to be added to arc *bklm* since line *ax* falls on the third revolution of the spiral. And if it would fall on the fourth revolution of the spiral, I would add the degrees of the whole circumference of the circle three times, for always as many complete circumferences are to be added to the arc in which this line is terminated as there are revolutions of the spiral on which it falls but with one revolution subtracted, as was said in the comment on the preceding conclusion.

And by this same or a similar method can be known the ratio of line *aq* to line *ad*, or that of line *au* to line *aq*, and others of this sort.

And if I wish to know the ratio of line *rx* to line *fr*, for line *rx* is only described in the time in which one revolution of the whole circumference is accomplished, and similarly line *fr* is traversed in the time in which one whole circumference is described, then line *rx* will be equal to line *fr*, and similarly line *fr* will be equal to line *fa*. And in the same way we can conclude that *ad* and *dq* and *qu* are [mutually] equal.

And so consequently if I wish to know the ratio of the segments of the same diameter or different diameters of the same circle revolving uni-

Prop. 13
  [1] See Prop. 11, note 2.
  [2] See Prop. 2, note 1.

formly and simultaneously with the spiral, as has been said before (and each segment of which is terminated on the concave side of one revolution and the convex side of another revolution of the same spiral), I shall always consider the times in which these line segments are described by the mobile moving equally fast [i.e. with uniform velocity] along the diameter—these times having been given or known by the first [proposition] of this [chapter]. And whatever is the ratio of the times, such is the ratio of the lines, on the basis of what has been prescribed in this chapter.

However, since these considerations do not seem to be very apropos of our instrument, no more ought to be said concerning similar motions. At this point I have decided to put an end to this present work.

Commentary to the *Tractatus de trigono balistario*

Proposition 1

9–12 "sive . . . descripta" Cf. the *Nova compositio horologii*, MS Bologna, Bibl. Univ. 2705, 18v–19r: "Hoc est quod ex regulis sciencie arismetrice in pluribus locis colligere potes, quoniam unifformi (!) motu existente in toto tempore qualis est proportio partis temporis ad integrum tempus talis est partis motus ad totum motum, ut liquet ex multis proposicionibus quas Jordanus et Euclides faciunt."

22–30 "Et . . . equalem." Fontana here gives the substance of the basic Aristotelian kinematic definitions. Cf. M. Clagett, *The Science of Mechanics in the Middle Ages* (Madison, Wisc., 1959; 2nd. print., 1961), pp. 175–82. The rules are stated at some length and related to horologues in Fontana's *Tractatus de pisce*, Chap. 8 (MS Bologna, Bibl. Univ. 2705, 97v–98r): "Capitulum octavum de inventione proportionum et quantitatum temporum, motuum et spatiorum. Volo consequenter docere qualiter cum predictis horologiis habere possimus proportionem duorum temporum vel duorum motuum vel duorum spatiorum cum tempus, motum et spatium mensurare contingat. Sint *a* et *b* duo tempora quibus horologium discurrat de numero predictorum quorum notabilis differencia semper apparet in quocunque parvo tempore. Et notetur quantum de horologio correspondet tempori *a* et similiter quantum correspondet tempori *b*. Quod si fuerit horologium illud compositum per designationes partium aliquotarum temporis, ut per dies, horas et fractiones horarum, patebit de se proportio, cum iam descripta sit utrobique temporis quantitas et inter notas quantitates nota sit proportio apud intelligentem species proportionum. Si vero fuerit horologium per designationes partium suarum vel alias differencias sive fuerint partes ille vel differencie arcus rotarum vel revolutiones ipsarum vel designationes vasorum vel partes candelarum combustarum vel pulveres vel aque particule cadentes vel alia similia hiis que predicta sunt, cum hec se habeant inter se proportionabiliter qualiter et tempora quibus correspondent, erit eadem proportio inter tempora que est inter ista reperta fuerit. Sed inter hec (*mg.*) proportio est nota ex noticia terminorum, igitur et temporum predictorum proportio nota similiter reddetur. De motibus vero ac spatiis sic erit declaratio, quoniam si motus sciantur esse (*mg.*) eque veloces, erit proportio spatii ad spatium qualis est temporis ad tempus correlative conveniens; quare si tempora equalia sint, fuerint equalia, sint (*mg.*) spatia sint (*del.*) similiter equalia. Si vero inequalia fuerint, sicut se habebit maius tempus ad minus, sic spatium maius descriptum ad (98r) minus. Si vero motus ponantur non eque veloces sed tempora equalia cognita sint, talis erit proportio motus ad motum qualis erit spatii ad spatium, cum maius spatium velociori motui et minus tardiori concedatur et esse oporteat. Quod si tempora fuerint inequalia sed spatia equalia cum inequali velocitate motuum, talis erit proportio motus qui in minori perficitur tempore ad alium qualis est maioris temporis ad minus. Sed cum proportio eorundem temporum sit nota, erit ipsorum similiter proportio cognita. Quod si cum inequalitate velocitatis motuum et inequalitate temporum et inequalitate spatiorum volueris hoc investigare diligenter. Ex predicta radice habere poteris, quoniam accipias equales spatiorum partes pertransitas et qualis erit proportio temporis maioris ad minus eorum in quibus ipse partes sunt pertransite, talis erit proportio velocioris motus ad minus velocem, vel accipe partes equales temporum et in qua proportione se habebunt spatiorum partes illis temporibus pertransite in eadem se habebunt ipsi motus, dummodo quilibet predictorum motuum sit uniformis in velocitate sua a principio usque ad finem. Has tamen regulas colligere potes in libris physicorum in quibus ponuntur canones de proportionibus et reliqua que deficiunt in hoc loco ex hoc fundamento comprehendere.'' The scribe here oscillates between ''proportio'' and ''proporcio'' and between ''spatium'' and ''spacium''. I have in all cases adopted ''ti'' before a vowel instead of ''ci'' where the scribe is inconsistent. I have followed him however in ''differencia'' which he consistently uses.

Proposition 3

31 ''in commento 3 capituli xii huius'' See MS Canon. Misc. 47, 172v(173v)–173r(174r): ''Si non haberem horologium verificatum, tale mihi statuam horologium quod in libro de horologio aquarum explanavi. Et est: preparabo duo vasa unum sub alio

vitreata vel de vitro confecta atque nitidissima. Et superius vas habeat in fundo parvum foramen quod reta (*del.*) vel (*del.*) spina obturari possit ex parte exteriori et (*del.*) ad placitum et deobturari ut libet, et obturato foramine et (*del.*) impleatur vas superius aqua p (*del.*) mundissima, vas vero inferius nil in se preter aerem contineat. Et statim cum ipsa stella fixa (*mg.*) de qua parum ante dicebam supra (*del.*) incipit oriri, removebo spinam ut aqua exstilare possit ex superiore vase in vas in(173r[174r])ferius constitutum et ita effluere permittam continuo donec ipsa stella sit iuncta orizonti occidentali et statim obturabo foramen fundi superioris vasis, vel inferius vas inde removebo ne plus aque in ipsum fluat. Nam ipsa aqua fluxa in receptaculo inferiore contenta erit correspondens tempori arcus quem ipsa stella fixa describit in emisperio nostro ab oriente usque ad occidentem. Propter quod oportet in hac et similibus operationibus stellam elligere que in eadem nocte oriatur et occidat tempore existente sereno et a vaporibus depurato iuxta orizontem. . . .'' (The remainder of this passage tells us nothing more about the nature of the horologue.) Now as I have noted in Section I, Fontana was much concerned with horologues in his first three works, and, though the accounts in the first two works are far too detailed for even summarizing here, the account given in Chapters 2 and 3 of the third work *De pisce*, which concentrates on time pieces for measuring motions of short duration, can be usefully quoted (MS Bologna, Bibl. Univ. 2705, 85v–87v): "Capitulum secundum de formatione horologii inter particulas temporis et motus distinguentis. Utile primo videtur michi preponere horologicum instrumentum motus et temporis et spatii consequenter discretivum. Nam tempus mensurat motum, ut probant physici, motus vero spatium, ut dicatur maior motus qui fit longiori tempore. Similiterque spatium maius est quod longiori motu describitur, intellecta semper paritate sophysticationeque neglecta. Tale m (*del.* m) quidem horologium erit in proposito conveniens cum fuerit velocis motus et perceptibilis differencie in omnibus partibus suis.

"Pro quo videtur advertendum esse quod quedam sunt horologia motus tardi valde que ad mensuras temporum motus celi proprius acta sunt (*del.*) et constructa sunt. Eaque perfectiora tantum exstimantur ab aliquibus quantum eorum motus plus tarditate participant. Sunt et alia que ad operationes et motus parvi temporis sunt ordinata, nec non composita que plurimum indigent celeritate ut in qualibet temporis parte differencie motuum percipiantur et comprehendantur, prima quidem horum tempus, secunda vero motum videntur magis distinguere.

"De primo tamen (86r) horalogio (*!*) dictum fuit sufficienter in aliis tractatibus. Nunc vero de secundo quo magis egemus in presenti spetialius dicentur cum alibi non dictum fuerit quantum (*mg.*). Idem enim horologium tantum elegantius, utilius et certius consistit quantum maiorem habet sensibilitatem et differenciam in omnibus partibus suis, licet secundum opinionem meam talis conditio conveniens sit omnibus horalegis (*!*) etiam pro distinctione partium temporis omnium (*? actus?*) vel motus.

"Si tamen construere voluerimus ipsum, faciamus ex pulveribus copiosum. Componamus igitur vasa pulverum longa valde sed multum angusta, sicque modica pulveris quantitas de profunditate corporis vasis notabilem partem oc[c]upabit in omni temporis parte ponens in ictibus oculi et parvis hanelitibus ne dum in magnis temporibus differencias. Et proprie si fuerit foramen per quod pulvis descendit debite quantificatum et taliter ut operi convenire videtur, quoniam si nimis flueret de pulvere propter quod ultra sufficientem quantitatem oporteret vasa facere minoretur illud. Similiter quando tam parvum esset quod in parvo tempore portio nimis modica pulverum descenderet magnificetur adlibitum ut partes pulverum et vasorum que parvis temporibus proportionantur distinguantur. Sint quoque vasa signata exterius in partibus que temporibus equalibus casus pulverum correspondeant. Non dico de hora in horam tantum sed de centesima parte et minori in tantumdem partem ipsius hore et quanto partes fuerint breviores tanto redetur perfectius opus, quoniam motus mensurandus vel spatium modice quantitatis esse contingit et in parva temporis parte mensurari dividantur igitur vasa in horas et hore in minuta et minuta in secunda et secunda in tertia et tertia in quarta etc. Quod dictum est de horalego (*!*) pulverum idem intelligamus de horologio aqueo facto per descensum aque vel ascensum. Similiter intelligere debemus de horologio quod ex aeris motu vel exspiratione factum fuerit ex vesica vel utre fol[l]e vel (86v) tympano vel aliter. Pariformiter etiam de horologio igneo quod aut ex fumo vel ex candela subtili vel ex consumptione olei aut similis in lampade formatur, que in quibusdam tractatibus meis difuse satis explanata sunt. In quibus omnibus licet signare tempora et horas distinguere in partes minimas quod facere congruit si velocis motus fuerit horologium compositum ut particulis hore pars sensibilis in horologio correspondeat. Similiter si veles hoc ex horologio rotalego regulam prefatam observa. Modum tamen tibi super rotalegum

dare volo quem non audivi nec alibi scripsi mirabiliter dis-
tinguentem inter temporum particulas non minus quam in aliis
predictis horologiis.

"Cohordinentur plures rote dentice adinvicem in una politen-
cula (?) cum ventilario posite, que (mg.) ab uno pondere
circumducuntur. In ea quidem rota pigriori que in horis multis
completis unicam perficiat circulationem signetur numerus
illarum horarum. In altera vero velociori rota signa minuta
horarum sint, in alia vero (del.) similiter que velocius ducitur
signa secunda horarum, et in sequenti velocius mota tertia
horarum distinguantur et sic consequenter fiat.

"Exemplum tamen describam clarissimum. Sit prima rota, que
in die naturali moveri debeat, habens dentes 144, divisa in 24
horas, et sunt pro qualibet hora sex dentes. Aplicabo sibi
roticulum dentium sex existentem in alio polifluo, in quo
similiter firmabitur rota secunda quam ponam habere dentes
240 et dividam illam in 60 particulas, quarum quelibet erit
minutum hore, dentibus quatuor attributum. Huic rote similiter
adaptabo roticulum quatuor dentium in alio polifluo cum rota
tertia firmatum, quam rotam distinguam in 60 particulas ut
rota secunda, quarum quelibet valebit tertium unum hore unius
et aliquibus dentibus accomodata pariformiter. Faciam de aliis
rotis si plures voluero quamlibet distinguendo in particulas
equales 60. Et tandem addam aervolum ultime illarum ut in
motu continuo sequatur uniformitas. Quibus sic dispositis cum
pondus descendet movebuntur rote: (87r) prima quidem in die
naturali semel, secunda vero semel in hora, tertia vero semel in
minuto hore, quarta vero semel in tertio eiusdem, et sic de
aliis, ut patere potest intelligenti. Quod dixi de numero dentium,
de partibus etiam horarum, possem per alios numeros dentium
et horarum partium adlibitum disponere atque componere.

"Capitulum tertium de quodam alio temporaneo et mensura-
torio instrumento. Si tamen expeditius habere voluerimus men-
suratorium temporale faciliorisque dispositionis et ad propositum
satis validum, cum uno vaso oblongo et stricto tale perficiemus.
Vas illud plenum sit aqua vel pulveribus siccisque caducis,
habens in fundo foramen notabile, totumque sit exterius
signatum in particulas valde parvas. Cumque descendent
exterius aque vel pulveres valde celeriter continuo particule
altitudinis vasis remanebunt vacue. Et est simile hiis aliqualiter
que diximus horologiis de casu pulveris vel aque sed differens
ab illis in hoc quod hic aqua vel pulvis cadens non recipitur
in vase consimiliter facto eidem ex quo cadit sed in terram vel
in alio vase spargitur et cum fuerit opus reiterare in priori vase
predicto pulveres vel aqua debent iterum poni in equali vel in

inequali mensura in qua prius ponebantur secundum exigenciam temporis mensurationis.

"Preterea signa facta in vasis superficie secundum eius longitudinem non sunt hore et quandoque non valent horam sed partes sunt temporis innominate satis. Sed advertendum quod licet hic et alibi ut in horologiis signationes in vasis [que] formentur ex casu pulverum aut ex casu aquarum certior erit significatio per cadentem aquam quam per cadentes pulveres ex eo quod superficies aque propter suam fluxibilitatem et liquiditatem semper in vase (87v) reditur equalis et fere plana, reservans significationes suas equaliter in omni replicatione in singulis signis vasis sive fuerint signa in vase superiori sive in inferiori temporum significativa. Pulveres vero cum cadunt de vase superiori in vas inferius non habent in aliquo predictorum superficiem superiorem equalem. Nam in superiori cavus conus eversus causatur eo quod pulveres de medio cadunt et latera ipsius sunt adherencia vasi et quandoque tardius quandoque velocius ruunt. Similiter in inferiori cumulus efficitur in medio qui non eque precipitatur vel spargitur ad latera vasis in equis temporibus. Quare nec in superiori nec in inferiori signationes equas semper observant temporibus correlativas. Et hinc error tanto maior est quanto foraminis angustia minor et quanto sunt vasa maioris circuli vel maioris latitudinis, ut te docere potest experientia.

"Propter quod intelligendum quod omne grave non impeditum semper magis inclinatur descendere per breviorem lineam vel dyametrum mundi cum fuerit extra locum naturalem positum quam per lineam obliquatam. Verum tamen liquida per obliquum facilius moventur quam que sunt pulverulenta. Sic aqua que de vase descendit non sensibiliter format in superiori vase cavam pyramidem, nec in inferiori cumulum, quoniam subito partes aque superiores replent ex motu transversali locum de-pressiorem, pulveres vero quia non ita motui laterali habiliter moventur priusquam repleant illa depressiora loca que in periferia cumuli vel in fundo fovee comprehenduntur tempus requirunt donec pulveres alte constituti per lineam minus obliquam et per consequens linee recte descensus propiorem agilius descendere possint." (Then follows the passage quoted above in Section II, note 1.)

Proposition 5

3 "in alio libro" I have not been able to find the explicit definition in the earlier works of Fontana but it is given in the *Liber de omnibus rebus naturalibus*, ed. of 1544, 38r: "Pari-formiter quando describit equales angulos super centrum in temporibus equalibus, id dicitur equaliter circuire." Earlier in

this same work (23r), Fontana makes the same distinction between equal angular motions and equal curvilinear motions that is made here in his comment to Proposition 5: "Sed advertendum quod in motibus circularibus aliud est equaliter moveri et equaliter [circuire], nam illa equaliter moventur quae in temporibus equalibus equalia spatia vel equales describunt arcus, sed illa aequaliter [circuunt] quae super caelum (! centrum) circuli aequales angulos signant vel similes arcus describunt, et illa describere dicuntur similes arcus quando unum eorum totidem gradus pertransit de circunferentia sui circuli quotidem alterum de circunferentia sui circuli in eodem tempore vel aequali." This distinction is common among the fourteenth century authors (see Clagett, *The Science of Mechanics*, pp. 217, 229, 376).